Introduction to

Early Medieval Western Europe, 300–900

The sword, the plough and the book

Matthew Innes

Routledge
Taylor & Francis Group
LONDON AND NEW YORK

First published 2007 by Routledge
2 Park Square, Milton Park, Abingdon, Oxon OX14 4RN

Simultaneously published in the USA and Canada by Routledge
711 Third Avenue, New York, NY 10017

Routledge is an imprint of the Taylor & Francis Group, an informa business

Typeset in Great Britain by Saxon Graphics Ltd, Derby
Printed and bound in Great Britain by CPI Antony Rowe, Chippenham, Wiltshire

British Library Cataloguing in Publication Data
A catalogue record for this book is available from the British Library

Library of Congress Cataloging in Publication Data
A catalog record for this book has been requested

ISBN 10: 0-415-21506-4 (hbk)
ISBN 10: 0-415-21507-2 (pbk)
ISBN 10: 0-203-64491-3 (ebk)

ISBN 13: 978-0-415-21506-0 (hbk)
ISBN 13: 978-0-415-21507-7 (pbk)
ISBN 13: 978-0-203-64491-1 (ebk)

Contents

List of figures ix
List of maps xii
Preface and acknowledgements xiii

Introduction: Rome, the barbarians, and the fate of western Europe 1

PART I THE TRANSFORMATION OF THE ROMAN WEST

1 **A new Roman order: state, church and society in the late empire** 17
Summary 18
Chronology 19
The rise of the provinces 20
The emergence of a new Roman order 23
List of emperors 25
Soldiers and civilians: the late Roman army 26
Essay: The image of the emperor 27
Cities, tax and office: elites and the late Roman state 31
Christianity and empire 39
Essay: Christianity and Roman culture 43
The peculiarity of the late Roman west 50
Bibliographical essay 54

2 **Barbarians, the Roman frontier and the crisis of the western empire** 63
Summary 64
Chronology 65
List of emperors 66
Invasions, migrations and identities: the problems of barbarian history 66
Kings and farmers: barbarian social and political organisation 71
Roman frontiers and barbarian society 74
Essay: Roman goods beyond the frontier: Gudme-Lundeborg 75
Adrianople and its aftermath: Goths and Romans in the late fourth century 80
Emperors, usurpers and barbarians: the crisis of the western empire 82
Bibliographical essay 89

3 **The fifth-century west and the 'fall of Rome'** 95
Summary 96
Chronology 97
List of emperors 98
Reinventing the western empire: barbarian federates and Roman warlords 98
The age of Aetius and the Huns 106
Going it alone: Gallic elites and empire after 454 110
The Vandal problem: Africa and the western Mediterranean 115
Essay: Vandals, *villas* and poets 119
The end of the western empire: Italian generals and the imperial title 120
How did the western empire end? 124
Bibliographical essay 130

PART II THE END OF THE ANCIENT MEDITERRANEAN

4 **The western Mediterranean in the age of 'reconquest'** 139
Summary 140
Chronology 141
Italy under Gothic management 142
Gothic identities and Italian allegiances 145
Essay: Gothic identity and material culture 153
The Christian empire and the 'reconquest' of the western Mediterranean 156
The paradox of 'reconquest': the Gothic wars and the transformation of Italian society 163
The new social order: Italy as a frontier province 168
Bibliographical essay 172

5 **Arabs, Avars and amphoras: causes and consequences of imperial collapse** 179
Summary 180
Chronology 181
List of emperors 182
Imperial collapse and the rise of Islam 182
Mediterranean exchange: the economics of decline 188
Collapsing frontiers: the Balkans 194
Fracturing allegiances: Constantinople, Rome and Ravenna 199
Bibliographical essay 207

PART III KINGDOMS AND COMMUNITIES IN THE POST-ROMAN WEST

6 **Hispania and Italy: contrasting communities** 213
Summary 214
Chronology: Visigothic kingdom and Umayyad al-Andalus 215
Chronology: Lombard Italy 216
Visigothic kings and Hispanic landlords 217
Court and regions: the seventh-century Visigothic kingdom 222
The making of al-Andalus 230

The Lombard alternative 238
Italy as a warrior society 248
Bibliographical essay 255

7 **Gaul and Germany: the Merovingian world** 265
Summary 266
Chronology 267
Franks and frontiers 268
Essay: The burial of Childeric 270
Conquest and conversion: the Merovingian unification of Gaul 271
Sixth-century society: cities, bishops and counts 277
The remaking of the kingdom 285
Bishops, monasteries and aristocrats: social change in the seventh century 290
Courts and kingdoms in the seventh century 297
Bibliographical essay 303

8 **Britain and Ireland: kings and peoples** 315
Summary 316
Chronology 317
The end of the Roman province 318
Post-Roman consolidation: the 'Celtic revival' 324
Essay: Dunadd and Dalriada 328
Post-Roman crisis: the Anglo-Saxon settlement 331
Celtic kingships and Celtic churches 337
Anglo-Saxon kingship and conversion 346
Essay: Sutton Hoo and Anglo-Saxon kingship 351
Essay: Culture and identity in the age of Bede 357
Vikings and kings: Britain and Ireland in the ninth century 365
Essay: Repton: Viking warbands and Anglo-Saxon kings 372
Bibliographical essay 381

PART IV: THE CAROLINGIAN MOMENT: WESTERN EUROPE IN THE EIGHT AND NINTH CENTURIES

9 **'The invincible race of the Franks': conquest, Christianisation and Carolingian kingship** 397
Summary 399
Chronology 399
Carolingian claims and Merovingian legitimacy 400
The expansion of the Frankish realm: Aquitaine and Italy 407
The expansion of the Frankish realm: east of the Rhine 410
Beyond plunder and tribute 417
Bibliographical essay 419

10 **'Peace unity and concord among the Christian people': Carolingian order and its architects** 427
Summary 428
Assemblies, capitularies and counts 429
Essay: Carolingian palaces 430

Kinship, lordship and aristocratic society 439
Peasants and polyptychs 446
Towns and trade 450
Bishops, councils and correction 456
Essay: The Carolingian court and the diffusion of culture 458
Bibliographical essay 480

11 Paradoxes of empire: western Europe in the ninth century 491
Summary 492
Chronology 493
Interpreting the ninth century 494
The imperial title and the problem of political unity 498
Carolingian kingship at its zenith 506
Neighbours, raiders and traders: the frontiers of the Christian empire 515
The end of the Carolingian Empire 531
Bibliographical essay 534

Epilogue: the sword, the plough and the book 541

Index 547

Figures

1.1	A coin of Diocletian. Copyright Art Archive. Ref. AA346842	27
1.2	An official bust of Constantine. Copyright Art Archive. Ref. AA355987	27
1.3	The Arch of Constantine, erected by the Senate of Rome in 314 to commemorate his tenth year on the throne. Copyright Art Archive. Ref: AA385446	28
1.4	From the Codex Calendar of 354. Museum of Wurzburg, Ref: 00229492. Copyright Interfoto/Alinari Archives, Florence	43
1.5	The Sevso treasure. Source: Institute of Archaeology, University of Oxford. Copyright Xlander Limited, Trustee of the Marquess of Northampton, 1987 Settlement	44
2.1	The Great Hall at Gudme. Copyright National Museum of Denmark	75
2.2	The Broholm Treasure. Copyright National Museum of Denmark	76
3.1	Carthage personified in a fifth-century mosaic from the city. Copyright Art Archive. Ref. AA 375758	119
4.1	Mausoleum of Theodoric in Ravenna. Copyright Foto archivio comune di Ravenna	153
4.2	Mosaic from San Apollinaire Nuovo, originally Theodoric's Arian foundation in Ravenna, showing Theodoric's palace	154
4.3	Mosaic showing Justinian at San Vitale, Ravenna. Copyright Art Archive. Ref. AA347301	155
4.4	Mosaic showing Theodora at San Vitale, Ravenna. Copyright Art Archive. Ref. AA348600	155
8.1	Ogham inscription and carved footmark from the summit of the hill fort at Dunadd, possibly originally serving a ceremonial function 1963. Ref. AG/382. Copyright Royal Commission on the Ancient and Historical Monuments of Scotland (National Monuments Record of Scotland)	328

8.2 Dunadd hill fort, seen from the southeast, 1988. Copyright Royal Commission on the Ancient and Historical Monuments of Scotland (National Monuments Record of Scotland) 329
8.3 Initial excavation of the boat burial in mound 1, 1938. Copyright British Museum 351
8.4 Helmet found in the boat burial in mound 1. Copyright British Museum 352
8.5 Staff and stag, possibly serving as royal insignia, found in the boat burial in mound 1. Copyright British Museum 352
8.6 An evangelist page showing St Mark from the Lindisfarne Gospels. Copyright The British Library. Ref. 02B03421P 357
8.7 Secular patronage: the metalwork and treasure of an unknown Pictish potentate found on St Ninian's Isle. Ref. 18132. Copyright Trustees of the National Museums of Scotland 358
8.8 Stone cross (south face) from Ruthwell in Dumfriesshire, modern Scotland, but in our period part of Anglo-Saxon Northumbria. Photo 1999. Ref. D/46788. Copyright Royal Commission on the Ancient and Historical Monuments of Scotland, National Monuments Record of Scotland 359
8.9 The emulation of Rome as a statement of royal power: the central panel of St Andrew's sarcophagus. Photo 1996, St Andrew's Cathedral Museum. Copyright Trustees of the National Museums of Scotland 360
8.10 Repton as a royal mausoleum: Crypt of St Wystan's Church, Repton, Derbyshire, showing ninth-century columns and probable site of Mercian royal graves. Copyright Mick Sharp Photography 372
8.11 Grave goods found in Viking burials at Repton and Ingelby Wood (a) Thor's hammer from Repton, ref. C814A; (b) Silver band (part of a ring), Ingleby Wood, ref. C813B; (c) Iron buckles, Ingleby Wood, ref. C813A. (d) Repton sword. Photos: Eric Mathews. Copyright Derby Museum and Art Gallery 373
8.12 The 'Repton Stone', probably depicting an eighth-century king on horseback. Photo: Eric Mathews. Copyright Derby Museum and Art Gallery 373
10.1 Charlemagne's Palace Chapel at Aachen. Copyright Domkapitel, Aachen. Photo: Ann Munchow 430
10.2 Internal view of the Palace Chapel at Aachen. Copyright Domkapitel, Aachen 431
10.3 Charlemagne's sarcophagus showing the rape of Proserpina, from the Aachen Domkapitel. Copyright Domkapitel, Aachen. Photo: Pit Siebigs 432
10.4 'Moore Bede' folio. A note in this manuscript of Bede's *Ecclesiastical History*, produced by the monks of the author's own abbey of Wearmouth-Jarrow, records its acquisition for the collection at Charlemagne's court. Manuscript KK5.16. Copyright University Library, University of Cambridge 459

10.5 Lorsch Gospels cover. The magnificent ivory cover which adorned one of a series of magnificent illuminated Gospel Books produced at Charlemagne's court; this one was acquired by the abbey of Lorsch, whose abbot was one of the signatories of Charlemagne's will, after the emperor's death. Ref. JX856. Copyright Board of Trustees of the Victoria and Albert Museum, London 460
10.6 Plan of St-Gallen. This plan of the model monastery, strongly influenced by the 'corrected' monastic rule and observance agreed at the Council of Aachen in 817, was sent by the Bishop of Constance to the abbot at St-Gallen; it demonstrates the continuing involvement of abbots and bishops in court-centred debates over 'correction'. Copyright Stiftsbibliothek, St-Gallen, Switzerland 461
10.7 Capitulary *de Villis*. Charlemagne's careful regulation of royal estates, evidenced in the capitulary *de Villis*, was to serve as a template for the efforts of ninth-century abbots and bishops to manage their estates. Ref: Codex Guelf. 254 Helmst (fols 9–16). Copyright Herzog August Bibliothek, Wolfenbüttel 462

Maps

Map 1 The later Roman Empire and its neighbours 21
Map 2 Barbarian settlements in the fifth-century empire 100
Map 3 The Mediterranean world in the sixth and seventh centuries 183
Map 4 The Iberian Peninsula in the early Middle Ages 218
Map 5 Italy in the early Middle Ages 239
Map 6 Merovingian Gaul 286
Map 7 Britain and Ireland in the early Middle Ages 319
Map 8 The Frankish world in the eighth century 401
Map 9 The Carolingian world in the ninth century 495

Preface and acknowledgements

Finishing a book always involves reflecting on the character of the time passed whilst writing it. Just over five years ago when I began seriously working on this project, I little imagined how many changes I would be experiencing, personally and professionally, in the near future. I hope the exhilaration this has involved has coloured my presentation of what ought to be perhaps the most exhilarating period in our history. First and foremost, I would like to thank my family – Jayne from the beginning of this project and Joseph and Gregory for the second half – for making it such an enjoyable and exciting time. Second, the unquenchable camaraderie and goodwill of my friends and colleagues at Birkbeck have enabled eventful times to be both full of intellectual stimulation and tremendous fun. Last but far from least, it is a pleasure to acknowledge manifold academic debts. My engagement with and understanding of the subjects covered here is itself a huge debt to my teachers, not only Rosamond McKitterick, whose undergraduate teaching inspired me to undertake research under her supervision, but also that remarkable generation of scholars who have collectively transformed the status of the early medieval period in the UK, and placed a distinctive strand of Anglophone scholarship at the centre of an increasingly international debate: without their achievements this book would not have been possible. It is to be hoped that the example they have set for collegial, constructive and courteous debate continues to inform what is in many ways a new field. Certainly that spirit has informed the many discussions of specific issues and problems with very many friends and colleagues that have shaped almost every page of what follows. A list of names could not do justice to these very many conversations, but very particular and special thanks are due to Caroline Humfress, whose critical inquisition on the later Roman Empire immeasurably enlivened and sharpened my discussion, and to Sean Brady whose acuity as a reader and questioner immeasurably speeded the completion of this book.

Writing this book has been a doubly enjoyable process because it has enabled me to read and reflect on the major primary sources for the period, and reflect critically on the shape of the historiography, and in particular on those issues where the contours of academic debate are shaped by concerns other than the potential of the testimony of the available sources. Throughout, I have tried both to indicate the patterns of consensus or controversy within current scholarship, the nature and problems of the source material, and where appropriate the manner in which the two might be helpfully realigned. In other words, this is, as the title indicates, a work of introduction, but by 'introduction' I understand not the unquestioning transmission of some weak distillation meant to represent the collective wisdom of specialists, but a more dynamic process of interrogation, outlining what questions historians are asking, how they are attempting to answer them, and why they matter. I would therefore underline that the bibliographical essays are an integral part of what is designed to be an argued interpretation. Although in many ways it can feel like a tremendous intellectual privilege to force oneself to address specialist work from the outside, searching for wider patterns and meanings in the past, it is also a humbling experience that brings with it a heavy responsibility. Throughout, I have tried to eschew that form of argument which attempts to reduce a conflicting school of interpretation to absurdity by arguing that it was simply an inevitable historiographical child of its time and place: historical scholarship is a difficult and iterative dialectic where constructive engagement with our sources takes place within a critical but respectful dialogue with our predecessors. I understand this book as the result of a concerted dialogue of this type, conditioned by my efforts to compare, relate and synthesise the diverse regions, sources and problems involved in the study of western Europe between the fourth and ninth centuries. I would therefore see it as just as much a work of research as a monograph of more familiar form.

It follows from what I have said that I see this as a work with an argument, one that I hope is clearly articulated at both beginning and end. This seems to me both necessary and timely. Necessary, because any work that presents itself as a neutral presentation of 'what really happened' is simply obscuring the processes of argument and interpretation on which its own view of the past rests. Better to directly admit what questions are being posed, and how they are to be addressed, and acknowledge that this inevitably conditions choices about how to structure the infinite variety of the past so as to create the illusion of a linear story. Timely, because the huge achievement of early medievalists in the late twentieth century has been the establishment of a subdiscipline with all its associated conventions, institutions and networks. As a result, the old lazy generalisations are no longer tenable, but until recently new stories with which to replace them had been relatively slow to emerge, and whooping barbarians could continue to wreak havoc in the resulting vacuum. Of course, there are real dangers in any attempt at synthesis, and the last thing the field needs is the erection of a new canonical 'grand narrative' with all the pitfalls and problems that involves. What I have attempted is to ask, then address, a series of questions about what happened in post-Roman western Europe and how it differed from what happened elsewhere in the post-classical world, then to follow through the story of the working out of these distinctive developments. In other words, by explicitly raising a series of questions, then structuring my history as a response, I hope to both give a sense of patterned change whilst maintaining a critical engagement with inherited paradigms. It follows that this is far from the only possible way of structuring understanding: my only claim is that I, at least, have found it useful. I should add that it is an argument, and a story, about western

Europe: but one which, I hope, far from being informed by Eurocentricism actually attempts to explain western European history as a deviation from patterns observable elsewhere in post-classical Eurasia.

One final point. The shape of this book follows directly from the issues it addresses in terms of both chronology and geography. In essaying the history of western Europe from the fourth to the ninth centuries, it differs from normal chronologies, which would see the 'early medieval west' stretching from the fifth to the tenth centuries. The prime implication of recent work on the 'barbarian kingdoms', however, is that they cannot be understood other than in the context of the shifting late Roman and Christian heritage, hence it is necessary to begin with an analysis of the fourth-century Roman world. Ending in the ninth century is likewise justified by the agenda I set about the trajectories of post-Roman transformation. As the structure of this book makes clear, one process of transformation in the west ran from the fourth through to the seventh centuries, by which time we can clearly see a fundamental change in the morphology of western societies, and in the degree and mechanisms of their interaction with the successor states of the eastern Mediterranean: Parts I and II analyse the process, and Part III the societies it produced. The decision to press on beyond the seventh century to the ninth rests on my profound conviction that the Carolingian period needs to be understood as a separate dynamic, but one which is best seen as capping these post-Roman developments and can be seen as marking the definitive emergence of a distinctive western European cultural and social pattern. I am, of course, hugely aware of the dangers of what one anonymous reader of my initial proposal called the 'Frankish metanarrative'. Although in Part IV the Franks under Carolingian leadership do indeed come 'romping home' (in the words of the ninth-century *Ludwigslied*), that is because the limitations and paradoxes of the Carolingian achievement are central to the problems I am addressing. In other words, I attempt to acknowledge the centrality of the Carolingian period in defining the unique trajectory of the west's post-Roman trajectory, without taking the Carolingian self-representation at face value. My discussion privileges the regional constellations pulled together in the eighth century, which emerged, redefined, as the central political actors of the ninth; Scandinavia, central Europe, and the Mediterranean all play an important role in this story. This is not, then, an effort to reduce western European history to a normalising Carolingian template, which might be seen as the precursor of the European experiment of the late twentieth century, so much as an attempt to explain the longer-term significance of Carolingian developments. A history of the 'early medieval' encompassing the tenth century – and peering down the well-trodden pathways seeing the end of the first millennium as marking the fundamental break in early European history – would have been an even bigger and more complex book. It would also have been profoundly unsatisfying, to my mind at least, for the sweeping models of millennial change have always failed to engage properly with the rich evidence of the Carolingian period, which is as a result caricatured either as a hangover of the ancient state, or as a shortlived but essentially personal and superficial venture based on the wartrail. Neither view will do, and this book will hopefully demonstrate why not. Whilst the tenth and eleventh centuries need retelling in terms of diverse regional responses to changes and models inaugurated in the Carolingian period, this diversity worked within the parameters of a broader Carolingian template. Before we attempt to understand its legacy, we must understand the historical processes generating that template, and its distinctive features. That is the story of the pages that follow.

Introduction: Rome, the barbarians, and the fate of western Europe

On January 1st 414 the Gothic king Ataulf married Gallia Placidia, daughter of the Roman Emperor Theodosius, at Narbonne in southern Gaul. A contemporary historian, Orosius, tells us that, at the reception, Ataulf spoke to his guests – Roman nobles as well as Goths – on the future of the empire:

> His most earnest prayer, he told the company, had been to wipe out the name Roman, to convert the entire territory of Rome into a Gothic Empire, to make a *Gothia* of *Romania*, to become a Caesar Augustus. But – he had learned from experience – the Goths did not obey laws, because of their uncheckable barbarism; and one must not banish laws from a state, for without them a state is not a state. At any rate, he had chosen to win glory by restoring the state in its integrity by means of Gothic power, and to extend the Roman name; to be remembered by posterity for having restored Rome, since he had not been able to transform it. So he was abstaining from warfare and aspiring to peace.[1]

Four years earlier these Goths, under the leadership of Ataulf's brother-in-law and predecessor Alaric, had famously sacked the city of Rome, an unprecedented happening that sent shockwaves through the Roman world. Gallia Placidia had been taken hostage in the course of these events, giving the Goths a potent hand in their negotiations with the imperial court. The marriage of this Roman princess to her Gothic 'host' was likewise unprecedented, giving as it did a barbarian ruler ties of kinship to the imperial house; it took place at the culmination of negotiations confirming the settlement of Ataulf and his Goths in southern Gaul as military 'protectors' of Roman society.

As we will see, although called 'barbarians' by Roman writers like Orosius, Ataulf and his ilk were not bloodthirsty outsiders intent on the simple destruction of the Roman Empire, but insiders, familiar with the Roman system. Ataulf and Alaric's Goths were a conglomerate group that had coalesced within the empire, in the Balkans in the last decades of the fourth century, as the allies and armies of Roman emperors. The sack of Rome in 410 followed the final breakdown of increasingly strained negotiations between the Roman Senate, the imperial court, and the leaders of the Roman military, over the continued service of these Goths. As barbarian warbands like these Goths had replaced regular army units as the military arm of the Roman state, so barbarian warlords like Ataulf were becoming the effective power-brokers in the empire's western provinces.

Any discussion of Orosius' account of Ataulf's speech at his wedding banquet is a reminder of how carefully historians need to read their sources: the first lesson that any student of this period must learn. Orosius wrote history, that is a story aiming to order and understand actual events. Hence his pains to identify a trustworthy friend who was present at the banquet as an eyewitness. But a history like Orosius' was not a straightforward report: it was a carefully crafted attempt to retell the past in a compelling pattern that supported a particular argument at a moment of controversy. Ancient historical writing allowed the embellishment or even invention of set-piece speeches by major characters if they helped reveal the deeper truths of history and aided the flow of the narrative. So this is what Ataulf ought to have said at this point in the particular story Orosius sought to tell. For modern readers to use a text like Ataulf's speech to gain historical understanding, they need to understand the aims and objective of Orosius as author. In the process of engaging with the text in this way, they also engage with the opinions and values of those in the past whose texts preserved one version of that past for us.

Orosius' account of Ataulf's speech voices a series of hopes and fears about the future of the provinces of western Europe. The beliefs and practices which defined 'being Roman' were undergoing profound and often traumatic change. The story of Ataulf and Gallia's wedding culminates in a monumental work, *Histories against the Pagans*, in which Orosius aimed to refute the arguments of some Romans, that the misfortunes befalling the empire – and above all the sack of Rome in 410 – were a direct result of the abandoning of the old gods, who had guaranteed victory for centuries, in favour of a new Christian God who jealously acknowledged no others. And the wedding of the daughter of the emperor to a Gothic king, like the negotiations leading to Gothic settlement in Gaul, pointed to the pressures transforming Roman society. Orosius voiced through Ataulf's mouth hopes of rapprochement, turning on the possibility that barbarians, stereotypically wild and lawless in Roman eyes, could aspire to learn the benefits of Roman civilisation, and work in service of the Roman state. But Orosius completed his work in 418, two years after Ataulf's death: if some of Orosius' readers would have seen the wedding feast at Narbonne as symbolising a new era, others would have seen Ataulf's grandiose plans as ridiculous boasts, knowing with hindsight that Gallia was soon to remarry a Roman general and work to restore traditional Roman order in the west.

Today's historians, working from complex and fascinating raw materials like Orosius' text, are only beginning to understand the hopes and fears entertained by Orosius' contemporaries. Our changing views of Orosius' world are the result of insistent questioning of the orthodoxies that have been dominant for centuries. Until very recently, historians' perceptions have been governed by the deep-rooted stereotypes that conditioned Roman writers' depictions of barbarians. In the early modern Europe of the Renaissance, as scholars sought to understand the classical Roman past on its own terms, as a model to be recreated in the present, perceptions of the essential destructiveness of barbarians and their fatal impact upon Roman society hardened. As a result, European history increasingly came to be seen as divided into three quite distinct slices: the ancient world, above all the 'golden age' of classical Rome, and the modern world separated by a vast and unfortunate gulf, the 'middle ages' in between. A negative and didactic view of the transition from ancient to medieval almost inevitably followed. Most influential – indeed, still shaping perceptions of the period – was the moralising of the late eighteenth century English writer Edward Gibbon, who cast it as a story of 'decline and fall', a title echoing the Biblical book of Genesis and the fall of mankind into sin. Gibbon, rehearsing the conventional view that Rome's first-century golden age was 'the period in history during which the condition of the human race was most happy and prosperous', saw the succeeding millennium as marking 'the triumph of barbarism and religion'.[2]

Yet, simultaneously, these same 'barbarians' have been seen since the Middle Ages as the lineal ancestors of contemporary societies. From the eighth and ninth centuries on, writers of histories explained the emergence of their societies in terms of the lock, stock and barrel migration and replacement of the population of Roman provinces by barbarian incomers. Solidarities in the present were thus projected back into, and legitimated by, shared pasts. The nineteenth century saw these histories firmly established in school and university curricula with the 'age of migrations' marking the first chapter of the histories of the peoples and nations of modern Europe. Such histories forged national identities that underpinned the claims of modern nation-states and were embedded in school curricula as those states sponsored universal education. Whilst this kind of identification between modern present and medieval past might seem to sit uneasily with the sense of rupture and calamity underpinning the threefold division between ancient, medieval and modern, in fact tensions between these two impulses could be resolved in a number of ways. The primitive and barbaric nature of medieval ancestors made, after all, for a national story focused on the gradual development of modern society with all its benefits out of medieval chaos, as institutions were perfected and manners civilised. These were 'young peoples' in need of education, but full of growth and vigour, to be compared to Gibbon's vivid sketch of the decadence and decay of ancient civilisation.

The immediately post-Roman period has thus been characterised as witnessing, in the words of so many textbooks, the 'birth' of Europe. Organic metaphors – in which Europe's history follows the life-cycle of a human being, born with the end of Roman domination in the west – proliferate. Yet these metaphors bring with them two important assumptions: a wholesale break between ancient Roman civilisation and the medieval west, and the wholesale identification of the peoples and nations of modern Europe with the 'barbarians' of late Roman writers. These long-embedded views, which presented the history of the post-Roman west as essentially a tale of destruction as barbarians carved out wholly new societies from the smouldering ashes of what had gone before, have deterred serious scholarship from the actual transformations taking place. Outside the works of a few isolated authors, for most of the nineteenth and twentieth centuries the history of the post-Roman west was described in terms of ancestral cultures imported wholesale with biologically distinct barbarian 'peoples'. This was a story of origins, where conflict and division were straightforward reflections of inherited cultural traits and clear ethnic divisions, and in which the only extraneous influence was that of the Christian church.

Attempts to study the emergence of medieval western European societies in fuller terms than these cultural genealogies were further hindered by the belief that these were the 'dark ages'. This label, popular because of its evocation of received ideas of destruction and decline, drew on the idea that this period was also 'dark' because the absence of source material meant that little historical light could be shed on it: hence tracing the movements of peoples and cultures was the best that could be attempted. In actual fact, the overall volume of surviving material from the early medieval west far surpasses that available from the eastern Mediterranean, where the Roman Empire survived, in mutated form, in Byzantium, or indeed that available from the Roman Empire of antiquity.[3] By the time we reach the formation of a new, western, empire under Charlemagne and his successors, the volume of surviving source material is unprecedented, and not reached again until the decades around 1100. Social historians have tens of thousands of legal documents, preserved in the archives of the church, which allow us to build up a picture of society in action for the very first time in western European history. Cultural historians can delight in an explosion of manuscripts copied – over seven thousand survive from the ninth century alone – and new works composed making this the formative period for Latin Christendom. Political historians are able to interrogate a babble of comment in the forms of histories, biographies, poems, dreams and visions, and a stream of legislation, with over a hundred royal edicts, or capitularies, from Charlemagne's reign alone, plus several hundred royal grants of privileges. Of course, the overall pattern of survival is patchy: the ninth century is far better documented than preceding periods, where we tend to have clusters of sources illuminating particularly controversial events, alongside long periods of near silence. In part, the higher profile of the Carolingian period is a result of institutional continuities, particularly in the major churches of western Europe. There are clear indications that preceding periods produced huge volumes of written material that did not survive precisely because of institutional discontinuity. Those factors which mean that some sources survive whilst others are lost – normally as much tied up with the active agency of those institutions that preserved them as much as brute luck – should never be forgotten, as they effectively chose whose perspectives remain.

Even given this unevenness of survival, and the difficulty of using much of this material, paucity of sources should never in and of itself be taken as a reason for writing off the post-Roman period in the west. The genuine gaps in the evidence exist for good reasons, and part of the historian's job is to understand the factors that made some events and issues produce pamphlet wars or clusters of documents that can be used by today's historians, whereas others produce no such ripples in our surviving record. When invoked by historians, paucity of evidence can easily be an excuse or a sign of ignorance. In fact, the real lesson of the explosion of recent scholarship on the early medieval west is that historians who take the period seriously, and are prepared to think hard about what questions they ask or read carefully sources hitherto ignored, can reach new understandings which complicate and eventually discredit traditional pictures of catastrophic decline leading to social and cultural meltdown.

The lead in taking the post-Roman period seriously came from cultural historians, above all historians of Christianity. Given that the fourth century had seen the adoption of Christianity as the official religion of the Roman Empire, and thereafter the conversion of western Europe not only within, but also beyond, the former Roman frontier, this had always been a crucial period in the history of the church. Traditionally, though, reactions to early medieval Christianity had been ambivalent: this was a 'heroic age' of conversion, but the substance of much religious belief was written off by many as not reaching the standards of 'true' Christianity of later centuries. In part, this was a shadow cast by the Reformation, the Protestant reformers' sense of a break with the medieval, Catholic, past and the Catholic church's subsequent reaction. In part it reflected the force of received ideas about post-Roman collapse. But as twentieth-century historians became more interested in past religious practice as something that had to be understood on its own terms, rather than judged from modern standpoints, new histories drawing on the most abundant seams of early medieval sources became possible. Just as art historians began to take the visual culture of the early Christian church seriously, and to understand it in terms of the religious experiences and programmes of its consumers and producers, so a new generation of historians focusing on religious belief and practice, rather than the institutional history of the church, came to the fore. Here, a new sense of the essential continuity and underlying unity of religious history from the fourth to the seventh centuries led to the coining of a new label for this period, 'late antiquity'. Popularised through the work of Peter Brown, with its vivid evocations of past individuals and their mental worlds, the notion that this period could be studied in exactly those terms used from more familiar, later, eras with stunning results inspired a generation of scholarship, particularly in the English-speaking world.[4]

Religious histories of 'late antiquity', for all their sudden and dramatic impact, were not working in a vacuum: they proved so influential partly because they could draw on older, often isolated but still powerful voices from political, social and economic history. One key text, endlessly tested in university exam questions, was the masterpiece of the early twentieth-century Belgian economic historian, Henri Pirenne, *Mohammed and Charlemagne*.[5] A student of medieval cities by training, Pirenne believed changing patterns of long-distance trade were fundamental to the collapse of the Roman world. Here, he argued, the break had come not with the barbarian invasions, which had left luxury trade around the Mediterranean relatively undisturbed, but with the Arab conquests of the seventh and eighth centuries, which had left western Europe a closed, landlocked economy. Pirenne's work, of course, betrays much about modern European unease about Islam, and the perception of the Orient as the Other in opposition to which the Christian west could be defined. But the expertise and material needed to investigate Christian–Islamic relations in this period was sparse (alas, it still is), and his thesis had its greatest impact in effectively questioning traditional divisions between the Roman and barbarian periods in the west. In fact, the difficulty of assembling data to discuss economic history meant that, right up until the end of the twentieth century, research was conducted in a direct dialogue with Pirenne. It is only very recently that advances in both the volume of available archaeological material, and our sophistication in its interpretation, have moved debate on.

Pirenne's work, influential though it was, long stood isolated in attempting to bridge the gap between Rome and the barbarian west. But slowly, previously dominant views of a distinct Germanic cultural heritage from which early medieval societies could be directly derived, began to be questioned as a post-war generation came to academic maturity. This questioning was due, in part at least, to the malevolent abuse of the Germanic past in Nazi Europe. But it also drew on a venerable tradition of scholarship regarding the laws and institutions of the Roman Empire, which made possible the kind of detailed institutional history exemplified by A. H. M. Jones' monumental three-volume work on the later Roman Empire.[6] Research like Jones', for all his pessimism on the political fate of the west, pointed to the necessity of taking the structures of the later empire seriously. It added credibility to the views of a vociferous but often ignored minority, who had contended that a full understanding of Roman institutions might help us understand the post-Roman west more fully. As empirical work on landed estates and legal custom began to illuminate the structures of medieval societies as contorted transformations of Roman administrative practice, so in the political sphere research into the formation of ruling elites and the practices of government in the post-Roman west came to emphasise symbiosis between Romans and barbarians.[7] Inspired by the brilliant success of the new religious histories of 'late antiquity', by the last decades of the twentieth century a new generation of social and political historians was searching for continuity rather than expecting collapse. Some French historians, inspired by research tracing the emergence of a distinctively medieval or 'feudal' social order of knights and serfs in the tenth and eleventh centuries, went so far as to describe the entire half millennium from the end of Roman rule to the empire of Charlemagne in terms of ancient continuity; others identified the categories of Roman taxation as conditioning social structure into the ninth century. Such claims – excessive in that they came close to denying change – inevitably provoked a backlash, but gradual transformation was now the order of the day.[8]

Most daring of all, one strand of scholarship slowly began to question whether the most durable units of historical discussion – the barbarian 'peoples' whose migrations and invasions had for centuries been seen as shaping the early medieval west – were quite as solid as they seemed. Drawing on archaeological and ethnological scholarship, some German and Austrian historians from the 1960s onwards stressed that ethnic identity was not a genetically fixed constant, but a matter of culture. Ethnicity came from belonging to a group, sharing in its myths and histories, following its laws and customs, and early medieval 'peoples' could be seen not as stable groups marching into the empire, but as temporary coalitions thrown together by circumstance, and able to create new shared identities through their common experiences. These ideas, when they were seized on by Anglo-American scholars from the 1990s onwards, began to dissolve a whole range of certainties. Was this really an 'age of migrations'? Was the end of the Roman Empire in the west anything more than a 'crisis of identity', a matter of 'shifting frontiers'? And was it best understood in terms of the different traditions and histories of the peoples of Europe? For some, particularly in North America, these challenges questioned a whole tradition of how Europeans understood their past, in categories that legitimated the nation-states of the present.[9]

One vital, but often overlooked, point about the changing interpretations of the post-Roman west remains to be made. New views have come about in part because more research is now done than would once have been thought possible, let alone advisable. Late antique and early medieval history have become specialist areas with their own academic journals, conferences and networks. The increased volume of research has been possible largely because rather than repeating the sweeping judgements that for so long sufficed, more scholars are now looking more seriously at the original sources, in their own right. The old generalisations have been replaced by a new attention to proper source criticism, which involves working out why our sources were written and preserved, who they were written for, whose views they articulate – in short, by a stress on the need to place each source in its proper context if it is to be understood. Source-criticism of this kind may sound traditional, old-fashioned even, but much has been pioneering too in developing new approaches and new questions.[10]

The return to the sources, and the insistent attempts to understand the cultural, social and political worlds of those who wrote them, has been vitally important. But it has also left scholarship in a relatively fragmented state. Much of the best new work takes us into a dialogue with an early medieval author or community, leaving us enlightened. But at the same time, the bigger picture – the overall patterns of continuity and change, the social and cultural dynamics – remains elusive. The major research initiatives that powered forward the discipline at the end of the twentieth century still tended to characterise the period in relatively unspecific terms, as witnessing 'the transformation of the Roman world'.[11] It is no accident that it is only very very recently, at the beginning of the twenty-first century, that the first attempts to synthesise so much new research have been made.[12] Given this lack of synthesis, it is not surprising that items as basic as the period divisions and descriptions we use to organise our knowledge remain fuzzy. 'Late antiquity' is perhaps the most popular shorthand used to refer to the 'post-classical world', but no-one has attempted a succinct definition of what characterises the 'late antique'. Notions of 'late antiquity' had their origins in an insistence that the Christian and Islamic cultures, polities and societies of the Roman Empire and its Mediterranean successor states, the Byzantine Empire and Islamic Caliphate, were essentially outgrowths from ancient, classical civilisation. It is difficult to see a 'late antiquity' encompassing the differently structured societies and cultures of the former Roman provinces of western Europe, particularly after the seventh century, and to pose the question takes us back to the central debate. Did the end of the Roman Empire in the west mark a fundamental break? Specialists on western European history have, indeed, tended to bypass the question by using a different label, 'early medieval', referring to the period from the fifth century onwards. But there has been even less discussion of what might characterise the 'early medieval'. It identifies the period in terms of what it is not, pointing to societies that are definitely not ancient, but also not yet fully medieval. Worse, it potentially invokes the metaphor of organic growth, pointing to an early, and thus presumably immature and infant, form of the medieval.

Let us end by returning to Orosius' account of Ataulf and Gallia's wedding banquet. Orosius, as we saw, acknowledges the deep-rooted stereotypes that presented barbarians as violent outsiders bent on the destruction of Roman civilisation, but has Ataulf confront these expectations. The hopes he expresses – that Gothic arms could be used to restore the Roman state – point to a future of Roman and barbarian symbiosis and co-operation, in which barbarian warbands are integrated into the fabric of Roman society, and barbarian leaders forge a new political elite seeking to preserve the Roman state. But, in the long run, this possible future did not come to pass. In the sixth-century west, we do not find a renewed and transformed empire, able to weld barbarian leaders into a new elite and so preserve the framework of imperial government and reanimate the social, economic and cultural systems it sustained. By the seventh century, we find a series of barbarian kings, legitimating their position with claims to 'ethnic' leadership of their 'people', ruling societies in which the characteristic institutions of the late Roman state – its complex and overlapping administrative hierarchies, its systems of tax assessment and collection – were in wholesale atrophy. This was a world in which ethnicity became the language of politics, as ideas of freedom were uncoupled from notions of citizenship and those obligations towards the state which in the Roman world had been seen as guaranteeing civilisation, and free status instead became tied up with the carrying of weapons in the service of the king and the ownership of land. The result was a society of militarised landlords, tied to royal courts by systems of patronage and reward, whose position was slowly legitimated by their complex relationships to the Christian churches they founded and funded; churches whose liberties themselves rested in immunity from the demands of the state, and who provided through the Old Testament a powerful ideological template for seeing earthly society as encapsulated in the struggles of a people united before God under their king. By the eighth century, the elites which had coalesced around the Frankish kings in Gaul were able to acquire the political and military momentum to absorb many of these societies, integrating regional leaders into the relatively open and loose structures of Frankish rule. Eventually the scale of this new western European polity almost inevitably led to Charlemagne's imperial claims.

Older views, seeing a clash of civilisations as Roman encountered barbarian, have been rightly abandoned. But we should not see western Europe's post-Roman development as the result of a somehow inevitable process of transformation. After all, empires elsewhere did undergo transformations but succeeded in maintaining the infrastructure of the state, and their bureaucracies and taxation systems continued to underwrite society and culture. In the Roman Empire's other successor states, Byzantium and the Islamic Caliphate, indeed right across the Eurasian world as far as China, rough outsiders and warlords were moulded into new elites within the surviving infrastructure of the state, or on occasion remoulded the state apparatus for their own designs. Charlemagne's realm was different. In this sense, it was not a true successor state to the Roman Empire at all. As a result, western Europe in the post-Roman period stands oddly apart.

It is the working out of these changes, over the half millennium following Ataulf and Gallia Placidia's wedding, that is the subject of this book. It is my contention that we can only fully understand these changes if we place them in sharp relief, not as the inevitable result of seamless post-Roman transformation but, in comparative perspective, as a surprising trajectory unique to western Europe. This book aims to bring together the results of the exciting and important new research into the early medieval west that has already been discussed in an accessible form requiring no prior knowledge of the period. By doing so, it will also offer a new historical synthesis. It focuses on the three aspects of society highlighted in the title. Historical sociologists have characterised all agrarian societies as structured by the mutual relationship of the plough, the sword and the book. That is, by the ways in which military and cultural elites extracted surplus from the land on which the majority of the population worked, creating a thin veneer of cultural and political life and holding together disparate local worlds of agrarian exploitation.[13] The story we will follow – and it is a story, presented in narrative form and recounting the transformations of the societies of western Europe – is the story of how, unusually, in the early medieval west, these relationships ceased to be structured through the institutions of the state; of how, instead of being negotiated through the administrative and fiscal practices, social power came to rest directly on control over land and labour, on the ability to exercise military force, and on access to the supernatural through the Christian church. We begin with Orosius' world, where the very identity of Roman order was a matter of sweeping change and sharp debate. If we are to understand the transformation of Rome's western provinces into barbarian kingdoms, we need to trace the transformations within the Roman Empire of which Orosius attempted to make sense. The first chapter will explore these, as a backdrop to the encounter between the provincial societies of western Europe and their barbarian neighbours that are the focus of the succeeding two chapters. Subsequently, we will follow the fates of the constituent regions of western Europe through the attempt of Charlemagne and his successors to create a very different order, five hundred years later.

Bibliographical essay

The best ways for readers new to the field to find their way around the early medieval west is through a number of exciting surveys of thematic development, particularly on religious history. The work of Peter Brown deserves particular mention here, covering religious and cultural history through a series of vivid evocations of particular individuals. His *The World of Late Antiquity* (London, 1971) remains a classic, but most recently see his brilliant update *The Rise of Western Christendom, 300–1000* (2nd edn, London, 2003) – and note that, the title notwithstanding, there is brilliant material here on the near east to the eighth century, but relatively little on the ninth and tenth-century west. For a different but complementary perspective to Brown's, see the magisterial R. Markus, *The End of Ancient Christianity* (Cambridge, 1990). For a rattling narrative of mission, see R. Fletcher, *The Conversion of Europe* (London, 1997). Also important is the comparative study of cultural transformations in Byzantium and the west offered by J. Herrin, *The Formation of Christendom* (London, 1987); for a wider still perspective, seeing the west as a primitive outlier of a cultural universe centred in the near and middle east, see G. Fowden, *Empire to Commonwealth: Consequences of Monotheism in Late Antiquity* (London, 1993). Most recently, Julia Smith has offered a cultural history properly grounded in social context: *Europe after Rome: A New Cultural History* (Oxford, 2005). Chris Wickham's *Mapping the Early Middle Ages* (Oxford, 2005) is the first proper modern synthesis of early medieval social history, with important insights on economics and politics, whilst M. McCormick, *Origins of the European Economy: Communications and Commerce 300–900* (Cambridge, 2001), uses new methodologies to present a new model of long-distance trade. Synthesis of a different kind, based on the archaeology and looking at long-term changes in the interaction between human society and the physical environment, is offered by K. Randsborg, *The First Millennium AD in Europe and the Mediterranean* (London, 1991); see also R. Hodges and D. Whitehouse, *Mohammed, Charlemagne and the Origins of Europe: Archaeology and the Pirenne Thesis* (London, 1983).

In contrast to these exciting syntheses focusing on particular themes, up-to-date surveys offering exhaustive coverage are difficult to come by; most general books are to be avoided, as they rehearse older and now discredited ideas about social collapse and ethnic traditions. Among works used as student textbooks, R. Collins' *Early Medieval Europe 300–1000* (3rd edn, London, 2005) is conversant with new research and offers a 'kings and battles' narrative approach; compare J. Moorhead's *The Roman Empire Divided, 400–700* (London, 2001) is preferable. But the genre of 'textbook accounts', with the idea that an agreed backbone narrative, based on high politics, is possible, is itself looking dated. Most of those involved in teaching the period prefer to use more focused and three-dimensional studies, often focusing on a particular region or period: these are best available from the individual chapter bibliographies below, but special mention must be made of two new politically focused studies of the end of the western Roman Empire: P. Heather, *The Fall of Rome: A New History* (London, 2005) and B. Ward-Perkins, *The Fall of Rome and the End of Civilisation* (Oxford, 2005).

Better still, there are also a number of up-to-date multi-authored handbooks, offering stimulating and research-based coverage of a wide variety of themes. For the late Roman and Byzantine world, P. Brown, G. Bowersock and O. Grabar, eds, *Late Antiquity: A Guide to the Postclassical World* (Princeton, 1999) is indispensable; for the early medieval west, R. McKitterick, ed., *The Early Middle Ages* (Oxford, 2001) offers short surveys of politics, economics, society, religion and culture, whilst L. Webster, ed., *The Transformation of the Roman World* (London, 1997) is a lavishly illustrated introduction. Exhaustive coverage, region by region and theme by theme, with excellent bibliographies, is offered by the relevant volumes of the new *Cambridge Ancient History* (vol. 13, 337–425, ed. Av. Cameron and P. Garnsey, 1998; vol. 14, 425–600, ed. Av. Cameron, B. Ward-Perkins and M. Whitby, 2000) and the *New Cambridge*

Medieval History (vol. 1, 400–700, ed. P. Fouracre, 2006; vol. 2, 700–900, ed. R. McKitterick, 1997). There are also some useful essays collected in the relevant sections of B. Rosenwein and L. Little, eds, *Debating the Middle Ages* (London, 1998) and, with less unity of purpose, in J. L. Nelson and P. Linehan, eds, *The Medieval World* (London, 2001) for the history and K. Randsborg, ed., *The Birth of Europe* (Rome, 1989) for the archaeology.

Perhaps the best way into the most exciting work on the period, though, is through the collections of papers arising from the European Science Foundation (ESF) project on 'The Transformation of the Roman World' which ran from 1994–9, and its various spin-offs: relevant volumes are published in a dedicated series by Brill (Leiden, Boston and Cologne). The ESF project recruited dedicated teams to research thematic strands, and the outputs were inevitably not uniform; and attempts at providing a new synthesis based on all the various strands were limited – see the important comments of P. Delogu and T. Noble in the plenary conference, E. Chrysos, ed., *East and West: Modes of Communication* (1999). But the best of the resulting books offer stimulating and exhaustive coverage of specific themes right through the period. Highlights here include the volumes on economics which place our understanding on a new footing: see R. Hodges and W. Bowden, eds, *The Sixth Century: Production, Distribution and Demand* (1998) and I. Hansen and C. Wickham, eds, *The Long Eighth Century* (2000). Of the political volumes, those concentrated on identities and frontiers shifted understandings: see W. Pohl, ed., *Kingdoms of the Empire* (1997), Pohl and H. Reimitz, eds, *Strategies of Distinction: The Creation of Ethnic Communities* (1998), Pohl, Reimitz and I. Wood, eds, *The Transformation of Frontiers from Late Antiquity to the Carolingians* (2001), and Pohl, H.-W. Goetz and J. Jarnut, eds, *Regna and Gentes* (2003), with spin-offs such as Pohl and Reimitz, eds, *Grenze und Differenz im frühen Mittelalter* (Vienna, 2000), and Pohl and M. Diesenberger, eds, *Integration und Herrschaft* (Vienna, 2001). The absence of any dedicated treatment of gender in the ESF project is rectified by L. Brubacker and J. Smith, eds, *Gender in the Early Medieval World: East and West, 300–900* (Cambridge, 2004) and a rich synthesis by J. Smith, 'Did women have a transformation of the Roman world?', *Gender & History* 12 (2000): a special issue devoted to gender in the middle ages, also published as A. Mulder-Bakker and P. Stafford, eds, *Gendering the Middle Ages* (Oxford, 2001). Finally, the two ESF volumes on towns and urbanism provide excellent syntheses of perhaps the most thriving area of archaeological and historical research: see G. P. Brogiolo and B. Ward-Perkins, eds, *The Idea and Ideology of the Town from Late Antiquity to the Early Middle Ages* (1999) and G. P. Brogiolo, N. Christie and N. Gauthier, eds, *Towns and their Territories from Late Antiquity to the Early Middle Ages* (2000). Collections on towns, indeed, have become a recognisable genre of publication: see e.g. N. Christie and S. Loseby, eds, *Towns in Transition* (Leicester, 1995), and G. Ripoll and J. Gurt, *Sedes Regiae, 400–800* (Barcelona, 2000) on capitals. Rural settlement – the area of the most exciting and interesting new work – is sadly lacking in accessible syntheses, but the essays in N. Christie, ed., *Landscapes of Change: Rural Evolutions in Late Antiquity* (Aldershot, 2004) offer excellent coverage. Finally, outside the remit of the ESF but invaluable on the archaeological material is a new series, again published by Brill, on Late Antique Archaeology; one particularly valuable feature is the bibliographical essay in each volume: see in particular the invaluable methodological and historiographical discussions in vol. 1, L. Lavan and W. Bowden, eds, *Theory and Practice in Late Antique Archaeology* (Leiden, 2001). A similar initiative on early medieval archaeology would be timely.

A wider comparative perspective is almost wholly absent, with the notable exception of Wickham's articles cited n. 13. My subtitle drew on E. Gellner, *Plough, Sword and Book: The Structure of Human History* (London, 1988); for other perspectives on the structure of agrarian empires see e.g. P. Crone, *Pre-Industrial Societies* (Oxford, 1989), M. Mann, *The Sources of Social Power* Vol. 1 (Cambridge, 1986). The fact that the early medieval west sits uneasily in syntheses of 'agrarian empires' is itself instructive.

Historiography is also less well served than it should be: early medievalists have tended to be doers rather than theorisers, and many of the best comments have come in the course of older works rather than as self-standing discussions. There are useful surveys of particular topics in the medieval sections of M. Bentley, ed., *Companion to Historiography* (London, 1997). There are also discussions of a handful of major figures. On Gibbon see e.g. R. McKitterick and R. Quinault, eds, *Edward Gibbon and Empire* (Cambridge, 1997), D. Womersley, ed., *Edward Gibbon: Bicentenary Essays* (Oxford, 1997). On Pirenne, there is a biography by B. Lyon, *Henri Pirenne: A Biographical and Intellectual Study* (Ghent, 1974); most of the many conferences and volumes devoted to him discuss the fate of his thesis in the light of then current research: start with P. Delogu's chapter in W. Bowden and R. Hodges, eds, *The Sixth Century: Production, Distribution and Demand* (Leiden, 1998). On Peter Brown, see the essays on the impact of his *World of Late Antiquity* published in *Symbolae Osloenses* 72 (1997), and note also M. de Jong, 'Rethinking early medieval Christianity', *Early Medieval Europe* 7 (1998), a stimulating survey of religious history. On ethnicity and its uses there is an excellent bibliography: start with P. Geary, *The Ethnic Origins of Europe: The Peoples of Europe in the Early Middle Ages* (Princeton, 2001), which is in many ways the best way into the political history of the early medieval west. The way into recent controversy is via A. Gillett, ed., *On Barbarian Identity* (Turnhout, 2002), particularly Walter Pohl's rejoinder pointing to the long tradition of German-language scholarship, especially the work of Reinhard Wenskus and Herwig Wolfram. It is worth noting that this German scholarship had a delayed reception in the Anglophone world, via Geary's early works in the mid-1980s. The use of a model of 'Germanic culture' is criticised, in very different ways rooted in very different traditions, by W. Goffart, 'Two notes on Germanic antiquity today', *Traditio* 50 (1995) and J. Jarnut, 'Germanisch. Plädoyer für die Abschaffung eines obsolten Zentralbegriffes der Frühmittelalterforschung', in W. Pohl, ed., *Die Suche nach den Ursprüngen* (Vienna, 2004). Aside from Geary's comments, the social, cultural and political functions of European historical consciousness of the early medieval period remain understudied. R. Morrissey, *Charlemagne and France* (Notre Dame, 2003) offers a model study of one figure in a particular national culture.

On methodology the text which started the ball rolling was Goffart's *The Narrators of Barbarian History AD550–800* (Princeton, 1988), which argued that four of the major narrative histories which provide the foundations of our understanding of the period needed to be analysed as literary works constructing a particular argument for a particular audience. Goffart's work has inspired an explosion of studies aiming to understand a particular text as a conscious authorial product in a particular context. W. Pohl, 'History in fragments: Montecassino's politics of memory', *Early Medieval Europe* 10 (2001) is the best way into debate. This reading of historical narratives has in part drawn on strategies developed earlier to deal with what is apparently the most unwielding source genre of all, saints' lives or hagiography: see here P. Geary, 'Saints, scholars and society: the elusive goal', in his *Living with the Dead in the Middle Ages* (Ithaca, 1993), and for an illuminating case-study in a wider context, P. Fouracre, 'Merovingian hagiography and Merovingian history', *Past & Present* 127 (1990). Pohl, McKitterick and others have stressed the importance of individual manuscripts – which often edited, combined or altered texts – as witnesses to understandings of the past: see e.g. R. McKitterick, *History and Memory in the Carolingian World* (Cambridge, 2004) and H. Reimitz, 'Social networks and identities in Frankish historiography', in R. Corrandini, M. Diesenberger and H. Reimitz, eds, *The Construction of Communities in the Early Middle Ages* (Leiden, 2004).

Work on documentary sources has been slower to move away from older traditions which saw them as uncomplicated reflections of 'what really happened', but has drawn on a variety of techniques to use dry-as-dust records of court hearings and conveyancing to illuminate social, economic and political history. The distribution of evidence makes this a particularly important approach from *c.* 700, although similar work is possible on the earlier period. One important strand has been work on dispute-resolution: the classic here is W. Davies and P. Fouracre, eds, *The Settlement of Disputes in Early Medieval Europe* (Cambridge, 1986), and see now the excellent introductory essay, with exhaustive bibliography, in W. Brown and P. Gorecki, eds, *Conflict in Medieval Europe* (London, 2004), and, for comparison, T. Gagos and P. van Minnen, *Settling a Dispute: Toward a Legal Anthropology of Late Antique Egypt* (Ann Arbor, 1994). Another is the study of the networks and connections revealed by documents: the crucial texts here are W. Davies, *Small Worlds: The Village Community in Early Medieval Brittany* (London, 1989) and B. Rosenwein, *To Be the Neighbor of St Peter: The Social Meaning of Cluny's Property, 909–1049* (Ithaca, 1989). Both these latter works rested on the collation of information in databases. Other work, similarly trying to correlate connections between individuals, was able to draw on older traditions of scholarship which attempted to use this material to reconstruct landowning families – some by local historians attempting to reconstruct genealogy, but in the second half of the twentieth century also using the results to illuminate the structures of kinship and politics: T. Reuter's contribution to M. Bentley, ed., *Companion to Historiography* (London, 1990) is particularly useful here, and see a major new research project devoted to the study of elites, which has helpfully published historiographical surveys on the web: lamop.univ-paris1.fr/lamop/LAMOP/elite. Methodologically innovative, but building on these traditions of utilising data of association and movement as well as archaeology, is McCormick's *Origins of the European Economy*.

One central contention of this research is the need to study the original texts in their own right. This focus – on the centrality of source-criticism and interpretation – has made late antiquity and the early Middle Ages one of the most exciting periods of history to teach and study, precisely because understanding it necessitates a close engagement with the original sources with all their problems, not the imbibing of a narrative created by modern historians. It is thus no surprise that one major area of important publications remains the translation of primary sources. References to primary sources in the individual chapter bibliographies that follow will be as exhaustive as possible, but will inevitably miss the many useful collections of translated sources covering the period as a whole. Here, Christian texts are particularly well served by collections such as J. Hillgarth, *Christianity and Paganism* (Ann Arbor, 1975), T. Head and T. Noble, *Soldiers of Christ* (London, 1998) and T. Head, *Medieval Hagiography* (London, 2001). All the major narrative sources for our period are available in easily available and affordable translations, a number in the Penguin Classics series, whilst a vast amount of material on late antiquity and early Christianity is becoming accessible through series such as Liverpool University Press' Translated Texts for Historians; for the later part of our period, the excellent volumes in Manchester University Press' Manchester Medieval Sources are beginning to perform a similar service. Early Christian sources are particularly well-served, thanks to their continuing importance to modern Christians: particularly useful for the earlier part of our period here are the *Select Library of Nicene and Post-Nicene Fathers*, ed. P. Schaff (London, 1890–1900), and the Catholic University of America's Fathers of the Church series. In making translated material easily and widely available, the internet has the potential to transform the study of the period: indeed, given the inevitable issues about quality control on the world wide web, it is perhaps best used by the student as a way of reading primary source material, rather than secondary opinion and interpretation, through sites such as www.ccel.org/fathers, an online library of early Christian texts, or the internet medieval sourcebook (www.fordham.edu/halsall/sbook.html), which offers a basic outline course in medieval history. Documentary sources, perhaps even better suited than narratives to the possibilities inherent in electronic presentation, are sadly harder to find.

Notes

1. Orosius, *Histories against the Pagans*, 7.43.5, tr. I. Raymond (New York, 1936).
2. E. Gibbon, *The History of the Decline and Fall of the Roman Empire*, 6 vols. (1776–88). Chapter 3, p. 70; Concluding Remarks; there are many subsequent editions and abridgements.
3. See the welcome comments of M. McCormick, *Origins of the European Economy: Communications and Commerce 300–900* (Cambridge, 2001), pp. 781–2.
4. The crucial work was P. R. L. Brown, *The World of Late Antiquity* (London, 1971).

5. H. Pirenne, *Mohammed and Charlemagne* (London, 1939); this was first published posthumously in 1937.
6. A. H. M. Jones, *The Later Roman Empire, 284–602: A Social, Economic and Administrative Survey*, 3 vols (Oxford, 1964).
7. E.g. W. Goffart, *Rome's Fall and After* (London, 1986), chapters 7–9 (estate management) and 1 & 5 (politics); also W. Goffart, *Barbarians and Romans AD418–584: The Techniques of Accommodation* (Princeton, 1980).
8. See C. Wickham, 'The fall of Rome will not take place', in L. Little and B. Rosenwein, eds, *Debating the Middle Ages* (London, 1998), for the backlash against the school exemplified by J. Durliat, *Les finances publiques de Diocletian aux Carolingiens, 284–888* (Sigmaringen, 1990).
9. For a good introduction, see P. Geary, *The Ethnic Origins of Europe: The Peoples of Europe in the Early Middle Ages* (Princeton, 2001).
10. For a survey followed by a case study, see W. Pohl, 'History in fragments: Montecassino's politics of memory', *Early Medieval Europe* 10 (2001); critical thinking of a parallel manner on the methodology of using documentary sources is urgently needed.
11. See I. Wood, 'The European Science Foundation's research project on the transformation of the Roman world and the emergence of early medieval Europe', *Early Medieval Europe* 6 (1997).
12. For new synthesis see J. Smith, *Europe after Rome: A New Cultural History* (Oxford, 2005) and C. Wickham, *Mapping the Early Middle Ages* (Oxford, 2005).
13. Fundamental on western difference here are C. Wickham, 'The other transition: from antiquity to feudalism', *Past & Present* 103 (1984) and 'The uniqueness of the east', *Journal of Peasant Studies* 12 (1985), both reprinted in his *Land and Power: Studies in Italian and European Social History, 300–1100* (London, 1994).

Part I

The Transformation of the Roman West

1

A new Roman order: state, church and society in the late empire

Contents

Summary

Chronology

The rise of the provinces

Map 1: the later Roman Empire

The emergence of a new Roman order

List of emperors

Essay: The image of the emperor

Soldiers and civilians: the late Roman army

Cities, tax and office: elites and the late Roman state

Christianity and empire

Essay: Christianity and Roman culture

The peculiarity of the late Roman west

Bibliographical essay

Summary

After political and financial instability in the third century, a 'new empire' emerged, piecemeal, in the reigns of the Emperor Diocletian and his contemporaries, and his successor Constantine. A reformed land tax tapped around ten per cent of the agrarian surplus, and funded a bulked up administration and army. The complex and overlapping hierarchies of military and civilian office, with the emperor at their apex, offered the opportunity of fame and fortune for ambitious provincials, and created a web of patronage which bound the empire together.

The wealthy aristocrats who dominated the Roman Senate had become increasingly divorced from military leadership in the third century, and so unable to make viable claims for the imperial office. Fourth-century emperors were overwhelmingly military and provincial in their backgrounds, and Gaul, northern Italy, the Balkans and the Near East became the sites of favoured imperial residence, with Rome merely a place for ceremonial visits. Diocletian had acknowledged that the size of the empire necessitated multiple emperors if provinces were to be kept happy and prevented from backing usurpers, and in the course of the fourth century the presence of separate emperors based in east and west became the norm. Family ties and the continuing political relationships between the different provinces within the empire meant that political division did not inevitably lead to fragmentation, but it did highlight important differences between east and west. Above all, Italy and large areas of the west remained dominated by the traditional elite of senators, who, although highly influential, enjoyed an uneasy relationship with the imperial establishment and those responsible for the day-to-day running of government. In the east, on the other hand, the interface between provincial elites and the court at Constantine's new capital, Constantinople, was less problematical.

After Constantine, emperors embraced Christianity, with the brief but famous exception of Julian's attempt to promote a reinvented paganism in 360–3. 'Paganism' was not outlawed or actively suppressed until the reign of Theodosius I, but for most of the fourth century lived in a sometimes uneasy co-existence with the Christian church and its imperial patrons. By the last decades of the fourth century, however, the actions of bishops and monks in leading local campaigns against pagan temples and worship demanded imperial action to outlaw traditional cults. Imperial backing also changed the nature of the Christian community. It was no longer a persecuted sect but a state-backed church, integrated into the empire. Tensions occasioned by the shift from sect to church explain the prevalence of disputes about doctrine and the recurrent problem of heresy, as well as the recurrent appeal of ascetic movements which allowed groups of Christians to attempt to mark themselves off as spiritual elites.

Chronology

284	Diocletian acclaimed emperor
303–11	'Great persecution' of Christians
305	Resignation of senior emperors, Maximian and Diocletian
306	Constantine proclaimed emperor at York on father's death
306–24	Conflict between various imperial candidates marks end of Tetrarchy
312	Constantine victorious at Milvian Bridge
313	Constantine and Licinius at Milan extend toleration to all religions
314	Council of Arles
324	Constantine defeats Licinius and unites east with west; foundation of Constantinople
325	Council of Nicaea
337	Death of Constantine
357	Julian junior emperor in Gaul, defeats Alemans at Strasbourg
359	Julian raised on shield and proclaimed Augustus by soldiers at Paris
361–3	Reign of Julian, restoration of paganism
362–3	Julian campaigns in Persia, defeated and killed
364	Jovian, Julian's successor, murdered, succeeded by Valentinian I (west) and Valens (east)
371	Execution of pagan mystic Maximus, Julian's spiritual advisor
372–97	Ambrose bishop of Milan
379–95	Reign of Theodosius I
382	Gratian legislates against paganism, removes Altar of Victory from senate
384	Execution of Priscillian
385	Theodosius forced to perform penance by Ambrose, bishop of Milan
c. 390	Ammianus Marcellinus publishes his *Histories*
391–2	Culmination of anti-pagan legislation; destruction of temple of Alexandria
392–4	Eugenius' rebellion
395–430	Augustine bishop of Carthage
418	Orosius' *Histories against the Pagans*
425	Augustine's *City of God*
438	Publication of Theodosian Code, collecting imperial legislation since Constantine

The rise of the provinces

We began with Orosius, reflecting on the history of the Roman Empire from the perspective of now dominant Christian church at the beginning of the fifth century. Orosius' career reflects the ties that bound together the Roman Empire. Born in Bracara in modern Portugal, facing the Atlantic, after being ordained a priest he travelled to Hippo in modern Tunisia in North Africa, where he studied with the local bishop, Augustine. His career also encompassed a spell in the Near East, in and around Jerusalem, before a failed attempt to return to the Iberian peninsula. As Orosius could testify, the Roman Empire in the fourth century was vast, complex and often contradictory. Stretching from the Middle East to Britain, it encompassed an almost bewildering regional diversity. The Mediterranean remained the heart of the empire, and the key to communication, contact and exchange within it, as Orosius' journeys suggest. But Rome's frontiers lay well beyond the immediate hinterland of the Mediterranean: along the coastlines of Britain and Gaul, down the Rhine and along the Danube and the southern shore of the Black Sea, embracing the Near East and Egypt and then including the coastal fringe of northern Africa to Hispania. Orosius' horizons reflect this geography. The later Roman Empire was thus far more than the political articulation of an organic Mediterranean cultural unity. In the fourth century, regions such as Gaul and the Balkans enjoyed their political heydays in the west, whilst the Near East and Egypt were emerging as the basis for the stability of the new imperial city of Constantinople and the eastern part of the empire.

Rome itself, the 'eternal city' so long synonymous with imperial success, played little role in Orosius' itinerary. In part, this was because of the new prominence of the Biblical landscape of the Near East as a source of identity. But it also reflected change in the imperial system. The empire could no longer be understood in terms of the dominance of Rome over the provinces, or of the Mediterranean core over European, Near Eastern and African hinterlands. Regionalism, particularly in matters cultural, becomes ever more evident in the sources.

Orosius was thus born into a society where what it was to be Roman was changing, most dramatically in the religious sphere, with the adoption of Christianity as the official religion of the empire, but more subtly and pervasively in a myriad other ways. In the earlier centuries of the Empire, provincial societies had been slowly integrated into the Roman cultural, political and social universe: 'Romanisation' had never involved the imposition of a fixed blueprint, but rather the selective adoption of Roman ways by regional elites within their own cultural traditions. In the early empire, these regional elites might strive to be granted Roman citizenship with all its privileges. To be Roman was, in a sense, to aspire to be part of a thin and wide caste, visible in the cities, fortresses and sculpture of the provinces. In the course of the third century, that had changed, most notably with the formal grant of Roman citizenship to all free subjects of the empire by Caracalla in 212, thus making the right to be judged by Roman law, but also the obligation to pay taxes to the Roman state, universal. Moreover, as Orosius' text shows, the adoption of Christianity as the state religion in the fourth century further complicated

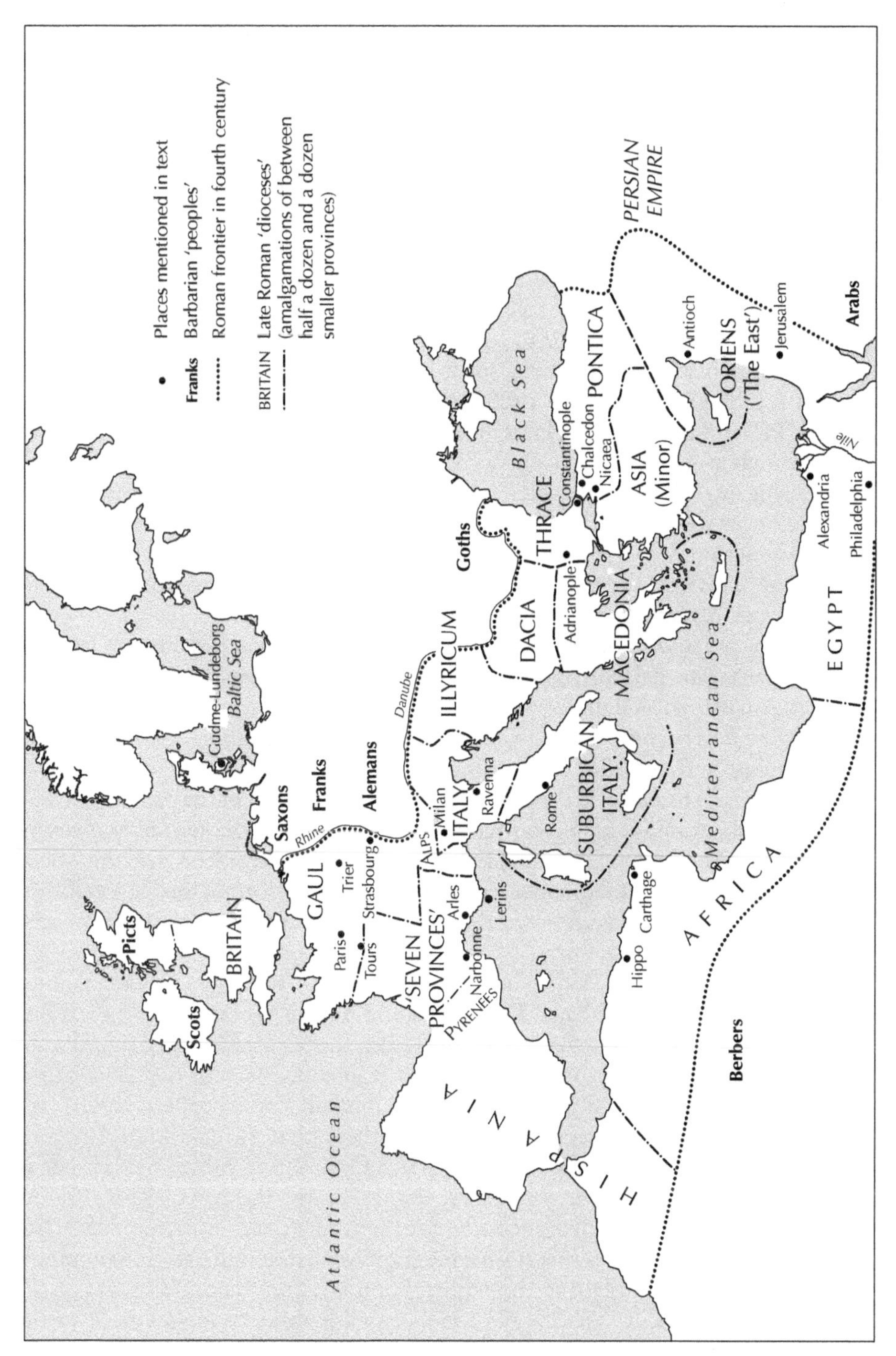

Map 1 The later Roman Empire and its neighbours

matters. Precisely how these changes worked through on the ground remains unclear, but the period between the last decades of the third century and the first decades of the fifth – labelled by historians the 'later Roman Empire' – is characterised by a new relationship between provincial elites and the imperial centre. Rather than seeing provincials competing for a place in an order defined and regulated at the city of Rome itself, in the regions we meet a variety of local 'takes' on Roman order. These worked within the framework provided by a governmental machine no longer firmly identified with the city of Rome, but located in imperial courts which were increasingly located in the provinces and populated by provincials and soldiers.

The late empire thus saw regionalisation without fragmentation. Orosius, a provincial by birth and education, spent his time in Jerusalem debating the theological teachings of Pelagius, a Christian teacher originally from Britain. But despite Pelagius' provincial origins, he made his name teaching in Rome itself, and his teachings were discussed right across the Roman world, in a debate in which the ancient seat of empire played a central role. In a world where the Roman state was no longer wholly identified with the city of Rome, the frameworks of Roman government and law still structured and sustained the careers of the able and ambitious. This was the period in which the Roman administration reached its greatest size, its ambitions articulated in the imperial decrees which were eventually collected and published in 438 in the classic statement of Roman law, the Theodosian Code. Pelagius, condemned as a heretic in a campaign led by Orosius' teacher, Augustine, well understood the expanding ambitions of the Roman state, which were nowhere more obvious than in the Code's recitation of imperial legislation against 'wrong belief' and 'wrong believers'.[1]

In a sense, the fourth century was shaped by the triumph of the provinces – and of provincials of middling background who rose through the administrative and military service – within the imperial system. It is no accident that this social milieu produced the major historian of the period, Ammianus Marcellinus. Ammianus was a military officer originally from Antioch, one of the provincial capitals increasingly favoured by fourth-century emperors; attached to the imperial staff, he was a participant in the politics of the reigns of Constantius, Julian, Valentinian and Valens. Writing in Latin during his retirement in a Rome enlivened by controversy over the removal from the Senate House of the Altar of Victory, which had traditionally guaranteed Roman success, in the name of the new official state religion of Christianity, Ammianus was concerned with the questions regarding changing Roman identities that so exercised Orosius. Ammianus eschewed issues of religion, instead presenting Julian, the last pagan emperor, as a model of civic patriotism, and celebrated the city of Rome and its history. In keeping with this veneration for the Roman past, he ignored the taste for gossipy and sometimes sensational biographies that dominated contemporary historical writing, works like the wildly popular anonymous *Histories of the Augustuses* or Aurelius Victor's *On the Caesars*. Instead he looked back to the great narrative histories of the eternal city and its rulers from the 'golden age' of the first century, seeking to continue Tacitus' *Histories* into the present.[2]

The emergence of a new Roman order

Historians of the later Roman Empire are hampered by the lack of a continuous contemporary historical narrative. The surviving text of Ammianus covers the years 354 to 378 in the vivid detail of a participant, and allows real insight into the workings of late Roman state and society. The first 13 of Ammianus' 31 books, which would have offered a whistle-stop account of the 250 years since the end of Tacitus' work, do not survive, and Ammianus elected to avoid the reign of the current Emperor Theodosius, where political sensitivities would have tempered the frank opinions which colour his treatment of previous regimes. Not that there is a dearth of source material for the fourth and fifth centuries. Far from it: evidence is plentiful in the imperial rulings collected in the Theodosian code, panegyrics, poetry, letters and the voluminous literature of the increasingly powerful Christian church. But without an interlocutor like Ammianus, piecing together the course of events becomes a more complex and necessarily fragmentary exercise, and the process whereby Ammianus' world was created inevitably becomes shadowy and poorly understood.

Historians have traditionally seen the late Roman Empire as emerging from a 'third-century crisis' that marked a real watershed. In fact, recent research has shown that very term 'crisis' is problematical: we have next to no extended contemporary sources for the period, and modern perceptions have been led by the political and monetary instability evident from the rapid turnover of emperors, and the debasement of the coinage, and barbarian invasion. From a regional perspective, social and economic structures look far more durable. Indeed, in Egypt, admittedly not prone to the worst depredations of civil war and incursion, even the well-documented price inflation in this period seems to be a result of a greatly expanded demand for official coinage which the government could not meet, rather than economic collapse. It was the political architecture of imperial government that needed reshaping, not the fabric of provincial society, and the later Roman system that emerged in the decades around the year 300 reflected this.

The merry-go-round of emperors, many reigning only a few months, was made possible by a system in which the imperial succession was open to all bidders. Succession depended on the ability of a candidate to win acceptance and defeat his rivals, which made the support of the army the trump card. Under late second and early third-century emperors, such as Marcus Aurelius (161–80) and Septimus Severus (193–211), the army had been expanded, soldiers' pay doubled, and the political power of military commanders dramatically increased. In the third century, the political power of the Roman Senate was gradually eclipsed as effective power came to lie in the hands of army leaders in the provinces. And, given that in the course of the second century members of the Roman Senate had ceased to enjoy a monopoly on military command, this led to men of lowly, provincial social background making a bid for the empire. What made the third century almost a continuous succession crisis was the recurrent inability of candidates to win lasting support over any extensive area. Indeed, perhaps the most striking element of the convoluted political narrative is the frequency with which provincial elites in the west advanced one of their own, often a leading local military commander, as a would-be emperor, bypassing the traditional leaders of Roman society in the senate.

Would-be emperors often did not aim to exert power over the empire as a whole. From 258–74, for example, much of the west was happy to maintain its own, effectively independent, 'Gallic Empire', under Postumus and his successors, whilst there were similar attempts to create an independent state at Palmyra in the east. In a way, these patterns are striking testimony to the Romanisation of provincial society: what inhabitants of Britain, Gaul and Hispania wanted was an accessible and active emperor in the provinces, an energetic patron and protector with a presence in their province. But they also point to the growing political power of the army, and the ties between military leaders and the elites of the provinces in which they were stationed. And regionalised military power, particularly in the western provinces, was also a result of the activities of the empire's neighbours along the Rhine and Danube frontiers, who took advantage of the political and financial problems of the Roman government, and the constant involvement of the army in internal conflicts. The third century saw large-scale infiltrations into Gaul and the Balkans in particular, whilst Alemans raided Italy, Herules laid siege to Athens and Gothic pirates menaced the coasts of the Aegean. These barbarian invasions are remarkably little studied compared to the barbarian incursions of the late fourth and fifth centuries. They were clearly caused by the political crisis of the imperial centre, which meant that the traditional practices of diplomatic patronage which maintained peaceful relations along the frontiers collapsed.

The problems of the coinage similarly point to difficulties in holding together the provinces. Roman coinage was essentially fiscal – that is, it was a medium in which revenue was raised and with which the state discharged its duties, above all paying the army. The army had traditionally been paid in silver coinage raised through taxation, so as to keep it divorced from the society of the areas in which it was stationed; similarly, units were wherever possible stationed away from their home area. Third-century emperors had real problems raising sufficient tax revenue to maintain these cash payments. Growth in the size of the army, and in soldiers' pay – the former a result of endemic conflict, the latter politically necessary because of the power of the military – increased the strain. The imperial response was to mint more coins, which inevitably led to debasement and a decrease in the value of the coin, to the extent that by the 260s, the coinage had virtually no silver content. Inevitably, this caused difficulties in supplying the army, which was forced to begin requisitioning in kind and taking ad hoc levies. Both practices effectively cut out the government as the middleman, collecting tax revenue and then redistributing it to the army; instead, direct transfers of resources from civilian to soldier created local relationships between the two.

The coming to power of Diocletian in 284, and his long reign which ended with resignation in 305, is normally seen as crucial in re-establishing political stability. Many of the measures introduced by Diocletian had been anticipated by earlier third-century emperors, and the reigns of Aurelian (270–5) and Probus (276–82) had seen military successes against barbarian raiders and separatist regimes within the empire. It would be a mistake to see any programme, but the series of practical solutions affected by Diocletian and Constantine (reigned 306–37) created a new governmental system. Diocletian acknowledged the needs of the provinces for an active emperor, offering protection and distributing patronage, by instituting a system of multiple emperors, the Tetrarchy. Indeed, research is now stressing the important role played by Diocletian's imperial colleagues, particularly Licinius and Maximian. There were to be two senior emperors, each styled Augustus, one based in western Europe, one in the Balkans and the east. A junior emperor, or Caesar, assisted each. Although Constantine, who sought to found a dynasty, abandoned it, the Tetrarchy did avoid the kind of succession crises that had proved so debilitating for so much of the third century. In fact, the idea of associating more than one emperor to ensure the succession and enable the regime to be present in more than one region was frequently used by later fourth-century emperors. Both the Tetrarchy system and these later uses of multiple associated rulers provided outlying provinces and the legions stationed within them with accessible imperial leaders, and thereby avoided the danger of provincial elites proclaiming usurpers. Moreover, the cornerstone of the administrative system of Diocletian and Constantine – the rigid separation of military and civilian offices with only the emperor enjoying rights of command in both spheres – likewise minimised the danger of recurrent attempts on the imperial office that had plagued the third century.

These pressures may also explain a tentative move towards dynasticism. Constantine had been acclaimed emperor on his father's death by his father's troops in a distant province, like so many of his predecessors, but the question of the succession posed by his overthrow of the Tetrarchy was answered by kinship. On Constantine's death, the army murdered his half-brothers and ensured the succession of his sons. The House of Constantine enjoyed such a hold on legitimacy

List of emperors (simplified)

Diocletian, 284–305, with Maximian 286–305
After 305 Constantius (305–6), Galerius (305–11), Severus (306–7), Licinius (308–24)
Constantine I 306–37
Constantine's sons: Constantine II 337–40, Constans 337–50, Constantius II 337–61
Usurpers: Magnentius 350–3, Vetranio 350, Nepotianus 350
Julian 361–3 (nephew of Constantine I)
Jovian 363–4
Valentinian I 364–75, with brother Valens in east, 364–78
Gratian, son of Valentinian 367–83, in west
Valentinian II, son of Gratian 388–92, in west
Theodosius I 379–95
Usurpers in west: Magnus Maximus, 383–7, Eugenius 392–4
Theodosius' sons: Arcadius in east 395–408, and Honorius, in west 395–423

that, by the end of the reign of the longest-lived of his sons, Constantius II, in the absence of any direct heirs attention came to focus on the surviving descendents of Constantine's half-brother, Jovian and Julian. It was only Julian's childless death that led to the end of the dynasty, although even then another distant relative, Procopius, was to stage a bid, and later usurpers attempted to link themselves to Constantine's memory. Julian's ultimate successor, Valentinian, also attempted to found a dynasty, and whilst his line failed, by the end of the fourth century the house of Theodosius succeeded in creating a new dynastic legitimacy.

In spite of this nascent dynasticism, the imperial office remained rooted in military leadership, and the prerequisite for any viable bid for the imperial purple was significant army backing. Indeed, from Diocletian to Theodosius, the social origin of emperors was remarkably uniform. They were men of humble provincial background who had made their reputation on the battlefield. Even those who owed their position to dynastic ties had to demonstrate their mettle as military commanders: the young Julian, for example, was stationed as Caesar in Gaul by his uncle Constantius II, probably in the hope that the inexperienced youth would ruin himself through haplessness in the field. When Julian proved to be a successful general he was proclaimed Augustus by his troops. Change is apparent not only in the sociology of the new ruling elite, but also in the geography of power within the empire. Emperors, who no longer ruled through the Roman Senate, by and large avoided Rome, apart from the occasional ceremonial visit. Rather than control of Rome, it was military success in the provinces that was the key to secure power. New imperial residences in the provinces, close to the frontiers, emerged: Trier in Gaul, Milan in northern Italy, Constantine's foundation at Constantinople at the junction of the Balkans and Asia Minor, and Ammianus' home town Antioch in the Near East.

Soldiers and civilians: the late Roman army

To penetrate beneath the rhetoric surrounding the person of the emperor and his court, it is necessary to turn to the sands of Egypt. Thanks to the peculiar climatic and social conditions that have allowed the preservation of rich deposits of papyrus documents at a number of Egyptian sites, we can glimpse the more mundane world of landowners, tax collectors and army officers at work. One such figure was Flavius Abinnaeus, a military commander of the rank of *praefectus alae*, based at Dionysias, one of Diocletian's new system of fortified garrisons, from 341–51, after which he retired to an estate in nearby Philadelphia, where a collection of over 80 papyrus documents was discovered in the 1890s.[5]

Men like Abinnaeus were the real winners in the new political settlement: the ruling class of the late empire was profoundly military and provincial. In the conflicts of the third century the army had grown in size, and under Diocletian in particular it underwent further dramatic expansion, with the creation of new legions. The army topped 400,000 men, perhaps reaching 600,000, and some contemporary critics saw its size as evidence of tyranny. Obviously, this led to increased demands being placed on an already strained infrastructure. The local

Essay

The image of the emperor

This period also witnessed a dramatic shift in how emperors chose to present themselves to their subjects. The roots of the imperial office as first citizen were forgotten as a monarchical style established itself. Formal demeanour on state occasions had always co-existed with more informal interaction, but in the fourth and fifth centuries the balance shifted decisively in favour of the former. Diocletian had inaugurated a more formalised court ritual, modelled on that of the Persians, which emphasised the divine qualities of the emperor. The sacralisation of the imperial office accelerated after the adoption of Christianity. Ammianus Marcellinus gives a wonderfully vivid account of how ceremonial created a sacred aura for the emperor in his description of Constantius II's visit to Rome, to celebrate 20 years on the throne, in 357. Pointing out the debts to Persian court ceremonial, and the cost of the new style of magnificence, Ammianus used his account to critique Constantius' style: 'his object was simply to display his gold-inlaid standards and his retinue in a procession of inordinate length'. At the heart of Ammianus' opposition is the belief that ceremonial on this scale departed from Roman precedent; he thus presents the citizenly behaviour of his hero, Julian, mixing freely with his peers at his court in Gaul, as a counterpoint. Constantius' procession, on the other hand 'might have been designed as a show of strength to overawe the Rhine or Euphrates', but showed a lack of respect for Rome with its ancient monuments and traditions. Religious politics played a part here: Ammianus wholly ignores the fact that on his visit the Christian Constantius removed the Altar of Victory from the Senate House, thereby rejecting those aspects of the imperial cult which were intimately linked with traditional Roman religion, and beginning a controversy which continued as Ammianus himself wrote. For Ammianus, Constantius' demeanour, designed to emphasise the emperor's unique standing, ultimately smacked of a pride which failed to acknowledge Rome's special status: 'The

Figure 1.1 A coin of Diocletian

Figure 1.2 An official bust of Constantine

Emperor was greeted with welcoming cheers, but in spite of the din he exhibited no emotion, but kept the same impassive air he commonly wore before his subjects in the provinces.'[3] However vocal the misgivings of Ammianus and his like, by the time of the Theodosian dynasty ceremonial in carefully created closed settings had become central to the exercise of the imperial office. This created a visage of legitimacy and stability and emphasised the sacred aura of the emperor as mediator between God and man, a fixed point of order. The conventions of official art and panegyric were likewise altered to stress the vertical distance between emperor and subject. It was through such media as the official images that were publicly displayed in the cities, and portraits on coins, that the emperor's sacred persona was made visible to the population. But we should hesitate before assuming that imperial pretensions were always and everywhere accepted uncritically, as a law of 394 dealing with the defacing or ridiculing of imperial images reminds us.[4]

Figure 1.3 The Arch of Constantine, erected by the Senate of Rome in 314 to commemorate his tenth year on the throne

requisitioning which had emerged in the third century was institutionalised, with the creation of grain and fodder rations that fell more predictably and regularly on local communities. The reformed tax system, perhaps Diocletian's most important achievement, must often have also functioned as a mechanism for effecting local 'in kind' transfers to support military units, although the restoration of the imperial finances allowed necessary cash payments to be resumed. Abinnaeus' letters show us that the work of requisitioning supplies, as defined by fiscal law, was the central occupation of a military commander, and one which required recurrent negotiation and occasional conflict with provincial authorities and rural communities.[6]

The logistical problems of maintaining this larger army were met by changes in patterns of deployment. In general, units in the fourth-century army were smaller, more dispersed, and stationed in smaller garrisons than their predecessors; increasing numbers of soldiers came to be stationed in cities, where the logistics of provisioning were more easily overcome. The archaeology certainly suggests that the long-distance transfers of goods and resources that had been necessary to maintain earlier imperial armies were a thing of the past. Regional economic networks were now dominant, and military needs were met through them, as we see graphically in Abinnaeus' Egypt. This changed the nature of the links between military units and the provinces in which they were stationed. Whilst in theory there had always been rigid separation of soldiers from civilians, in practice the lines were always prone to blurring. Fourth-century legislation dealing with soldiers who abandoned their posts, or disappeared into their host communities, had many precedents. Abinnaeus' papyri show soldiers spending their time hunting, networking with the local gentry, and making good as local landowners, often taking lucrative advantage of their rights to billeting, supplies and transport. For many, then, military service may have been a motor of geographical and social mobility. Abinnaeus himself was a Syrian by origin, who married into a family of property-owners in Alexandria, before retiring to estates acquired at Philadelphia. Soldiers – or veterans – also enjoyed the right to appeal to the separate military jurisdiction of their commander, and therefore privileged access to networks of patronage and protection, as vividly illustrated in Abinnaeus' archive.[7]

Nonetheless, a military career was not appealing to all. Recruitment was another recurrent concern of the laws. To see this as evidence of a 'manpower crisis' which can be identified as the underlying cause of Roman decline is mistaken: the evidence for overall population trends is difficult, but it suggests gradual, not calamitous decline. Rather, problems of recruitment are best seen as a result of the army's increased size, and its changed relationship to its 'host' societies. Regionalisation may again explain much. In the early empire, entry into the army was a powerful conduit for non-Romans from the provinces to enter into the heart of the Roman world. By the fourth century, for those in the ranks at least, this seems to have been a less attractive option than previously, and enforced conscription began to play a more important role.

Obviously, maintaining an army of the size established by the end of the third century necessitated continuous and heavy recruitment, especially given that most soldiers were notionally required to serve for a 20 or 24-year term. Emperors required the sons of soldiers to enlist themselves. By the beginning of the fifth century, emperors used this requirement as a way to raise cash from the sons of veterans, doubtlessly a sensible measure given that paternity is no guarantee of military competence or, indeed, training. There were also periodic efforts at conscription, with quotas based on landholding used to determine how many recruits were required from a given area. Again, the powerful were expert at avoiding such campaigns, which often proved fruitful in raising cash from those wishing to buy exemption.[8]

Internal conflict was a recurrent feature of the late Roman Empire, and frantic recruitment in an attempt to outnumber internal opponents was a recurrent feature of civil war right through the period from Constantine to Theodosius. Indeed, it was these internal needs that were, in all probability, the driving force for change in the size and personnel of the army. Obviously changes in the makeup, deployment and size of the army had strategic ramifications, although to see them as manifestations of a fundamental change in the empire's 'grand strategy', rather than practical responses to the changing social realities and military necessities, is probably mistaken. The emergence of a field army or *comitatus*, which underwent a marked enlargement under Constantine, was central: these forces were the backbone of the army, stationed within the empire and ready to respond to threats whenever and wherever they arose. Smaller frontier forces were stationed to keep a watchful eye on barbarian neighbours, and slow any incursions that did take place. Concern about internal challenges – which, after all, tended to originate in the northern provinces of Gaul and Britain – was arguably more important than any new policy of 'defence in depth' against external foes in this new pattern of deployment. This had the additional advantage of making the logistics of supply much easier, as was the case with Abinnaeus' cavalry unit based in the fertile Fayum.

In any case, the increased demand for troops coupled with the problems of internal recruitment led, inevitably, to the recurrent recruitment of barbarians from beyond the frontier, particularly in western Europe, as we will examine more fully below. It is vital to distinguish between the form of recruitment favoured by fourth-century emperors, in which barbarian warriors were thoroughly assimilated into regular Roman units, often in the aftermath of military defeat; and the hiring of barbarian groupings wholesale as 'federates' that emerged by the fifth century. Ultimately, it is striking just how many fourth-century Roman victories were won by barbarian recruits defeating other barbarians: a telling testimony to the efficiency of Roman organisation and the lack of any sense of common identity amongst Rome's neighbours.

These changes altered the character of society not just along the frontiers, but also in the provinces immediately within them. Across the empire as a whole, the need for defence took on a new prominence. Before the third century, cities had not been walled. By the fourth century, walls were synonymous with the status of a city, and on official calendars characteristic defensive walls were central to their depiction. New defensive fortification was not only a prerogative of cities: in Britain and Gaul, for example, a whole range of defensive structures, such as fortified posthouses along key routes of communication, emerged well within the empire. Already in the fourth century we see the emergence of a series of increasingly militarised regional communities in the empire's northwestern provinces, behind which the inhabitants of the shores of the Mediterranean were able to shelter and maintain a division between civilian and military power. We have no archive comparable to Abinnaeus' from Gaul, only Ammianus' vivid accounts of the careers of military staff attached to the young Julian, men like Dagaleif and Nevitta. Had we a Gallic Abinnaeus we would be more fully aware of the regional differences between the intricate interplay between administrative hierarchies and military coercion which defined Abinnaeus' position, and the rough world evoked by Ammianus, where barbarian recruits jostled with provincials in fortified garrisons.

Cities, tax and office: elites and the late Roman state

Abinnaeus' letters show us not only soldiers at work and play: they also underline the absolute centrality of the taxation system to late Roman society. It is striking that the recurrent negotiations, disputes and complaints they document centre not on title to land, but on fiscally-based entitlements to demand cash, goods, transport, hospitality or labour. Under Diocletian, the taxation system had undergone a thorough revision, with new valuations of landed property made, and subject to review every five years from 287 on. These assessments, along with a head-tax for which the evidence is difficult, were the basis of tax liabilities. The actual workings of the system remain obscure, although documents of practice like Abinnaeus' letters can shed light. But it succeeded in tapping into ten per cent of the fruits of what was, more than ever, a predominantly agrarian economy. In a ruralised society, this was a huge proportion of wealth. Tax assessments and tax revenues were the primary means by which wealth was redistributed. Like modern governments, late Roman emperors were under intense pressure to justify their taking of tax, often resented by tax-payers. There is a steady undercurrent of criticism of spending on the army in particular in fourth-century political debate. In part, such criticism was structural, for in a huge agrarian empire, local government agents with the rights to collect tax enjoyed tremendous freedom of action. Thus in Abinnaeus' letters, we meet repeated complaints to local authorities about unjust or unjustified exactions.[9]

It is clear that there were effectively two levels of tax extraction: that of the tax demands and tax law of the imperial government; and that of the complex relationships between local authorities, the agencies of tax collection, and rural communities, at which the requests and rules of the government were worked out on the ground. At the upper level, that of the imperial government, tax revenue was accounted in cash terms, allowing emperors and their servants to allocate resources according to a notional 'budget' for the empire as a whole. However, quite unlike a modern state, there was no facility to borrow against future revenue: accounting was hand to mouth.

At a local level, actual transfers might easily take place in kind as well as in cash, and there was considerable flexibility. City councils, made up of local landowners, were responsible for the 'take' from their city and its hinterland: an onerous and sometimes expensive duty. The problems of keeping accurate records of tax assessment – the census detailing who owned what and what it was worth – were manifold and provoked recurrent legislation, and although on occasion imperial agents might inspect local tax registers, by and large they were left to city councils.

Much local level taxation was probably levied in kind, and when tax revenue was allotted to a local beneficiary, for example a local military unit, it is unlikely that it was ever converted into cash: Constantine was even moved to complain about military renders of foodstuffs going rotten before they could be collected by the beneficiaries.[10] Here, the allocation of tax revenues was effectively the state granting rights to extract a fixed percentage of the agrarian surplus to particular parties, as Abinnaeus' documents vividly illustrate, and the rhythm of fiscal obligation and collection allowed the raising of loans against liabilities and obligations.[11] Of course, not all taxation was passed on locally and in kind. But even when revenue was to be passed on to provincial and central government, it may most often have been local elites who transformed the agrarian surplus they collected into cash.

At a grass roots level, 'tax' may have been all but indistinguishable from rent to those who paid it. The tax system probably played an important role in cementing the dominance of local elites, who were simultaneously tax collectors and landlords for their tenants, and who could pressurise impoverished neighbours through practices such as money-lending to enable the poor to meet their dues, or taking on the tax liability of an estate as a means of establishing a title to it. Through such practices, the role of local elites in levying taxation helped widen social divisions. Indeed, the state played a vital role in enforcing an increasing rigidity in rural society, for the need to establish tax liability led to legislation tying peasants to the land, and thus encouraging the legal dependence of the cultivating class on their landlords: this was the origin of the *coloni* who are so evident in late Roman legislation.

The Roman Empire is sometimes described as a 'slave society'. Slavery – the legal possession of one human being by another – certainly was a basic social institution, and ideas of freedom and identity were shaped by the everyday existence of the unfree as an unchallenged fact, accepted as unthinkingly by late Roman Christians as it had been by their pagan ancestors. But slavery as an economic force – the large-scale estates worked by gangs of slaves which had been a significant source of wealth for the Italian elite prior to the third century – was all but gone by the late empire. North of the Alps, it had never been common in any case, and in the context of demographic decline and watchful frontier defence it was difficult to sustain. Slaves were still numerically an important social group, playing a fundamental role in aristocratic households and family life. Aristocratic estates, however, were farmed by peasant households who eked out a living from their harvests whilst passing on rent to their landlord; where these peasants were unfree, they were doubtless subject to greater landlord control than their free neighbours, but they were still in economic terms rent-paying peasants, not gang slaves. In fact, as we saw, the most marked feature of the late Roman countryside was the manifold ways in which the changed structure of the state increased both formal and informal landlord power over the peasantry. That the state encouraged a growing chasm between landowners – the *possessores* who appear in legislation as the crucial class in rural society – and the peasantry who farmed the land may appear regressive, but in terms of strict economic analysis it encouraged growth through increased pressure from landlords and tax-collectors.

The mechanisms of redistribution associated with the tax system also determined the basic structures of the later Roman economy. The movement of resources to meet the demands of the state, rather than the calculations of profit we associate with a modern market economy, probably accounts for most of the long-distance exchange that can be traced through the archaeological record, for example the export of grain and olive oil from Africa to Italy and Gaul. We can even see the system at work thanks to the remarkable find, on an island just off the modern seafront at Carthage, of a document recording an annual shipment of olive oil to Rome, written up by the harbour official.[12] Late Roman 'traders' were often agents charged with provisioning an elite household or military unit, that is effectively franchise-holders, and much 'trade' was underpinned by the state infrastructure of requisitioned transport and supplies. Even what 'commercial' transactions there were may have predominantly ridden 'piggyback' on such exchanges, only viable thanks to the journeys made to effect 'official' transfers. Whilst such a system might appear irrational and ultimately unworkable to our eyes, the Roman Empire was not part of a fluid global market, and in that context such strategies made sense and could serve to stimulate local economies, as in the case of African exports across the Mediterranean. The cost and difficulties of long-distance transport, particularly by land, were such that local or regional exchanges were always the most rational economic strategy, and the collapse of the silver coinage and the payment of soldiers in cash had led to the ending of the long range exchanges associated with provisioning the army in the early empire. The dominance of local and regional networks in the late Roman economy was thus intimately linked to the changing demands of the state's fiscal system. Indeed, the decrease in the range and volume of long-distance exchange in the late Roman west, clear in the archaeological record, is intimately linked to the rise of regional networks to supply the armies of the Rhine frontier and the northwestern provinces. By the fourth century, the brisk exchanges which saw large-scale imports of Hispanic fish sauce into early imperial Rome were a thing of the past in the western Mediterranean. Long-distance exchange in the west was increasingly bound up with the annual transfers by which North Africa fed Rome, reflected in the archaeological dominance of the African Red Slip pottery in which foodstuffs were carried. In the east, by comparison, inter-regional exchange was stimulated by the rapid growth of Constantinople and the movements of Egyptian grain to feed the city's inhabitants; here, although these fiscal structures determined the rhythms of the economy, a greater volume of regional and inter-regional exchange in a context of growing prosperity may have meant that economic life was less dominated by the state than in the west.

The exact scale of the increase in tax liability resulting from Diocletian's reforms is unclear. Recurrent complaints of over-taxation and rapacious tax-collectors need to be taken with a pinch of salt, and the Egyptian documentary evidence suggests that the actual ability of the state to tap the agrarian surplus, viewed from a long perspective, remained at a broadly similar level. On the other hand, expansion of the army on the scale undertaken between Marcus Aurelius and Constantine must have necessitated an increase in revenue, and it may be that late antiquity saw the regularisation of previously ad hoc or notionally voluntary liabilities. Certainly a vastly enlarged apparatus of administration points to the increased impact of the state on the localities and a more effective enforcement of assessments, as well as itself necessitating a greater 'take'. Again, Diocletian and Constantine's reigns saw the crucial changes. Diocletian's division of provinces into a greater number of smaller units, and Constantine's formal separation of civil from military power – both designed to increase imperial control and prevent the dangers of over-powerful local figures seeking to go it alone or launch an imperial bid – led to a corresponding multiplication of the personnel of government, with a civil governor and military commander for each province. The two parallel hierarchies, civil and military, each had their own administrative machines, with governors, commanders, prefects and masters all having their own households and officers. Judging from the *Notitia Dignitatum*, an early fifth-century listing of the various offices and their staff, around 30,000 people enjoyed a position within this arcane and complex structure. Under Constantine and his successor Constantius II, a small number of praetorian prefects emerged as the key imperial agents in the provinces. Originally leaders of the imperial bodyguards (the praetorians) attached to the emperor's court, their role was gradually territorialised as that of a civilian governor. This created a small number of dioceses, practically ruled by a praetorian prefect, in theoretical co-operation but often actual conflict with his military counterpart, the master of the soldiers. The areas thus ruled were huge: in the west, one praetorian prefecture based in Gaul also included Britain and Hispania, whilst Africa and Italy were likewise ruled by a single praetorian prefect, as were the Balkan provinces. The imperial administration should thus not be seen as a homogenous entity, but as a series of parallel but overlapping hierarchies, serving the military, the civil administration, and the imperial court, with administrative posts tied to the personal offices of generals, governors and of course the emperor.

Office holders were not salaried bureaucrats: for many, office within the imperial system was not a full-time job, but a matter of taking a particular role and responsibility, which normally was reinforced by, and in turn reinforced, one's social position. This was most clearly the case at the very lowest level of 'government', that of the city and its hinterland – the *civitas*. Here, 'office' by and large involved taking an honorary position which gave a certain social niche in return for undertaking and underwriting specific official duties. In Africa, Hispania and Italy, for example, local landowners demonstrated their standing by overseeing their city's observance of the imperial cult, a practice which continued, in a secularised form, into the fifth century. The key position, however, was membership of the city council, or *curia*. In theory, office brought local landowners into a symbiotic relationship with the state, giving them the opportunities to assert their status and underwrite their dominance within the community, whilst ensuring that they organised public services locally, on occasion digging into their own pockets to do so. In practice, however, there seems to have been a growing problem of the evasion of curial office. The scale of imperial legislation on the obligations of the curial classes dwarfs almost any other topic: the compilers of the Theodosian Code found no fewer than 192 laws or rulings on this topic from the reign of Constantine to their own times. Although the evasion of obligations was in part a systemic problem with a long history, the reluctance by fourth-century landowners to take on curial office probably reflects the increasingly onerous demands of the expanded state. It certainly relates to changes in the imperial system. In the early empire, cities were islands of Roman culture in the provinces, and pre-eminence there opened up the possibilities of Roman citizenship and entry into imperial society. By the fourth century, ambitious and able provincials sought to make their fortune through entry into the office of a provincial governor, or onto the military staff. By doing so, and gaining a place in the vastly-expanded imperial administration, they gained status without needing to demonstrate civic munificence; and that status brought with it immunity from curial service. After Constantine, those who followed a career in the parallel structure of the Christian church and entered the priesthood were likewise brought immunities from duties on city councils – immunities which imperial legislation repeatedly tried to clarify and limit.[13]

So in a world of increasing imperial demands, the incentives for serving one's city were decreasing, and the new avenues for advancement allowed the able and ambitious to bypass their obligations. It is thus no surprise that inscriptions recording elite patronage of the community through public building or patronage of cities drop dramatically in the third and fourth centuries, with the emperor and the church coming to dominate what had previously been the arena where local landowners had competed. In fact, when and where the well-to-do wished to demonstrate their care for their city and their community, they now did so through patronage of the church – after all, the building and elaboration of the church needed funding – rather than through the old arena of public building and municipal patronage. In a way, then, the church, and through it the spiritual community, came to replace the old structures of civic life. Where, in the early empire, local elites had competed for pre-eminence through their care for their city, underpinning an administrative system that had been remarkably light and effective, in the later empire, the centre came to play an increasingly direct role in ensuring that government on the most local of levels was carried out.

These changes in social structures help us understand the dramatic changes in the fabric of city life which archaeology has begun to uncover. There are inevitable problems in generalising about the fate of cities en masse. Each site needs to be analysed in its strictly local context, for there were real regional differences between the economics and politics of the provinces, and cities did not exist in a vacuum, but as part of a hierarchy of settlements within which each site must be placed. For example, the dramatic development of fourth-century Trier was a direct result of the city's new status as a favoured imperial residence, and stands out from the patchier evidence elsewhere in northern Gaul. As a general picture, in the west in particular there are clear suggestions of declining urban populations, with evidence for late Roman occupation generally thinner than that for the early empire. It would be going too far to see this as evidence for a crisis in urban life, even in the frontier provinces of Gaul and Britain where the evidence is patchiest. Here, the third and fourth centuries did see incursions from beyond the frontier that caused genuine disruption to provincial life. It is no accident that late Roman cities were defined by often new defensive walls which marked the boundaries of urban space. But there is no need to invoke barbarian violence – which in any case ought to have encouraged the population to seek solace behind garrisoned walls – as a prime cause of changes in city life. The general context of demographic decline allied to changes in social and political structures is the key to understanding the archaeological record. Here, what is striking are changes in topography, even in the east, or in Africa, where there is stronger evidence for continuing, and in some cases prospering, urban life. The monumental public spaces and official buildings that had lain at the centre of early imperial cities, in forms and plans recognisable across the entire empire, remained, but the focus of new patronage was now the Christian church. Christian buildings did not obey the established rules of public monumentality and topographical centrality, but followed the geography of private patronage by devout and wealthy Christians. Moreover, many churches, founded to commemorate the Christian dead, and especially Christian heroes who had died as martyrs under earlier persecution, were founded on the edges of urban space, because cemeteries were placed beyond the boundaries of the community of the living, who were anxious to avoid pollution from the dead.

These changes to the shape of urban life did not mean that cities ceased to function as administrative or indeed social and economic centres for the surrounding areas. Indeed, as the residence of the bishop, and embodiment of the Christian community, that centrality arguably took on new forms. But the balance between cities and the countryside was shifting. Just as in the empire as a whole, the relationship between Rome and the provinces was altered, so on the level of the individual *civitas*, the walled city found its supremacy over its hinterland challenged. Contrast the patchiness of visible investment in city living with the vitality of the country residences or *villas* across the countryside. In many provinces, this was the golden age of the *villa*. Even in northern Gaul and Britain, where in the first half of the fifth century *villa* sites were abandoned as the frontier collapsed, in the middle decades of the fourth century confident elites were building high-status rural residences. What we are dealing with, then, is a shift in elite investment from competition for public pre-eminence in the city to a life of rural luxury. This did not divorce elites from the network of cities, but it shifted the balance between city and country; after all, with the new opportunities for gaining favour and patronage through the administration, it was no longer necessary to gain entry to the imperial system through civic pre-eminence.

The inhabitants of the lavish *villas* that dotted the countryside thus sought positions in the imperial administration. Normally only tenable for a fixed, temporary period, they brought with them privileges, such as free travel on public business. The rank they conferred, and the contacts they created, were permanent. Even emperors were men from relatively humble, provincial, backgrounds, and the military hierarchy, and the administrative offices of prefects, commanders and governors, were more or less entirely made up of provincials. Indeed, regional ties are clearly apparent even at the highest political level, with emperors tending to promote gaggles of their provincial contacts to the key political offices when they assumed power: thus the teacher and poet Ausonius of Bordeaux rose to become Gratian's chief minister, whilst Theodosius I promoted a number of his Hispanic neighbours and friends. Office within the imperial administration thus became the most important engine of upward social mobility, allowing local landowners to become members of an empire-wide elite. Given the importance of imperial patronage in this new system, and the increasing social mobility it opened up, it is no surprise that factions frequently accused their rivals of using intrigue, and even illicit magic, to shape imperial policy. The overlapping of parallel hierarchies of office actually encouraged such conflict, which in a way secured the emperor's position in that it enabled him to adjudicate between rival groupings. Ammianus' vivid vignettes of a world of accusation and anxiety, jealousy and rumour, underlines the extent to which political conflict centred on influence at court and access to the emperor.[14]

The dramatic expansion of the administration, following the reforms of Diocletian and Constantine, thus provided a new arena in which the state engaged with local elites, tying them firmly into the imperial system. In a way, direct patronage from the emperor replaced the earlier system of local competition for pre-eminence. This interaction between the formal structures of the state and the vast informal influence of local elites indicates a deeper symbiosis within the late Roman political system: that between the official, public administrative chain of command, and the unofficial, private bonds of patronage which held the system together and made it work. The overlapping and often mutually reinforcing presence of two parallel systems was not a sign of political failure. Modern historians stress that no pre-modern polity works like a 'state' in our terms, with power delegated according to rules enforced from above, because without a modern communications infrastructure, power must necessarily be shared with those with muscle on the ground. For this reason, we must pause before we condemn the late Roman system for inefficiency and unwieldiness. Inevitably, the interplay between position and patronage allowed officials to enrich themselves and help their friends and clients (and Ammianus liked nothing more than to retell a good scandal), but it would be a mistake to see 'corruption' as a root cause of the problems of the late empire. Recurrent laws against corruption should be seen as evidence for imperial concern that the patronage system should not subvert good government, not for a failure on the part of the emperor to control local office-holders. After all, the Theodosian Code was a collection of specific edicts, not an abstract rulebook; the material it contains demonstrates imperial determination to stay in control, not an increase in 'corruption'. Within the newly expanded administration, it was increasingly possible for emperors to use sometimes competing and overlapping hierarchies of officials to serve as checks and balances on one another, and so 'corruption' is probably more visible precisely because emperors had better information about it and were more able to move against it than previously. In any case, given that effective government on the ground required the use of personal influence, the boundary between 'private' and 'official' interests was always somewhat blurred, and legislation could even be seen as an attempt to clarify matters by defining and policing that boundary.

More than that, the expanded administration offered a mechanism through which the local power of landowners could be integrated into the infrastructure of the state. Before the third-century crisis, competition between landowners for pre-eminence within the localities through public service, which had brought contact with Rome and integration into the Roman elite, allowed a vast empire to be governed on the cheap. But the increasing regionalism, the new military necessities, and the entrenchment of the private interests of landowners that emerged in the third century made a return to such a system impossible. The late Roman solution, using an expanded state that was a new institutionalised mechanism to integrate local landowners into the imperial infrastructure, made sense: it is absolutely typical of ancient agrarian empires.

The magnetic pull of imperial service was a vital cohesive force, culturally and socially as well as politically. Culturally, the centrality of imperial service helped maintain traditional Roman values, in spite of the rise of what was effectively a new ruling class of parvenu provincials. Holding office involved behaving in the appropriate manner, and respecting long-established cultural values, centred on a classical education. Correct language, sharpened through the study of grammar and correct argument, and honed through the study of rhetoric, were the key to persuasion. Law was central to the Roman self-image. As law was seen as ensuring civilisation, so the possession of law marked the civilised Romans off from the barbarians around them. Law infused public life, and the powerful were expected to show virtuosity in rhetoric, acquired through a thorough classical education in their youth. There was no single fixed legal corpus or text. Rather, law was interpreted and transmitted through the writings of approved jurists. The activities of late Roman government itself added to the complexity of law, thanks to the constitutive force of imperial rulings and judgements, often the ad hoc result of petitions regarding specific cases and so inevitably subject to conflicts and shifts. The *quaestor*, the official responsible for the drafting of imperial proclamations, thus played a central role in the shaping of the law. The scale of imperial legal activity is reflected in the complexity of the codification of imperial law made under Theodosius II and acclaimed by the senate in 438: although imperial rulings were preserved in municipal and official archives, and promulgated through public display and recitation, the Theodosian Code took a panel of experts nine years of detailed research across the empire to put together. The constant flow of petitions from the provinces to the imperial court and the issuing of commands and rulings in response lay at the heart of the operation of government. The Theodosian Code was effectively a collection of these rulings, vitally important as they established law by precedent and through legal argument and action; it should not be read as a monolithic or unchanging rulebook, a description of a fixed state structure.

Socially, imperial service was a defining force because rank was intimately tied to position in the administration. Late Roman society was profoundly hierarchical, and status was not only something ascribed by peers, but formally defined by the state. There existed a highly formalised ladder of titles, and progress up the ladder was dependent on office-holding and political favour. Indeed, some positions – such as the role of consul, normally awarded to an individual at the peak of their political influence – shade modern distinctions between rank and office. The minute gradations of rank that entitled one to the title 'most excellent', 'most distinguished' or 'most illustrious' were not empty words, but marked out a place in society, determining matters of precedence and etiquette at gatherings. It is no accident that fourth-century emperors expanded this *cursus honorum*, adding new subgrades and introducing whole new groups of people into it, for example through the new rank of *comes* or companion. The importance of these intricacies, and their role in keeping the person of the emperor at the apex of the governmental hierarchy, is aptly demonstrated in Abinnaeus' career. After 33 years commanding a frontier detachment of Parthian archers at Diospolis, Abinnaeus' big break came with a mission escorting ambassadors to Constantinople, where following an audience with the emperor, and the ceremonial 'adoration of the purple', he was granted the honorific rank of *protector* and the commandership of the cavalry fortress of Dionysias. On presenting the imperial mandate placing him in his new post to the governor of Egypt, however, Abinnaeus was told that Dionysias already had a commander who could produce similar documents; further visits to Constantinople, and further imperial mandates, were needed to gain him his post in 342, and overcome an attempt to dismiss him in 344–5. Visits to the capital were expensive and fraught with difficulties, as Abinnaeus' frantic attempts to generate funds and mobilise patrons show, and provincial governors could obstruct and delay the carrying out of imperial orders by querying their validity. But ultimately it was contact with the person of the emperor, either in person through the 'adoration of the purple' and the honour it generated, or through official documents that transmitted the transformative qualities of the imperial will into the provinces. Imperial charisma thus defined the over-arching hierarchy which held late Roman society together.[15]

Christianity and empire

We began this chapter with Orosius, defending Christianity against the accusation that it had brought calamity to the empire, whereas the traditional Roman gods had guaranteed victory. Perhaps even more dramatic than the social and political changes of the fourth century was the cultural revolution which saw Christianity adopted as the official religion of the Roman state.

The scale of cultural change is far from immediately apparent to the reader of the sources. Classical culture remained intensely conservative even as new social groups adopted it as they rose to positions of political and cultural power. Thus the likes of the pagan Ammianus and the Christian Ausonius both looked back to a first-century golden age and judged literary attainment with reference to traditional models. But beneath the formal continuity, a profound cultural change was taking place, and one centred on man's relationship with the gods. Some have even seen late antiquity as a period of increased religiosity, an 'age of anxiety' in which men turned to the supernatural and the divine in reaction to earthly insecurity, marked by the rise of 'popular religion'. Such a thesis, resting on a series of highly subjective judgements, and attempting to generalise about the mental world of entire populations from a handful of highly rhetorical literary sources, cannot be proven. It is also in danger of privileging traditional Roman culture as being somehow 'like us' and following Gibbon in seeing the rise of 'superstition'; both are views that do not stand up to sustained investigation.

If we are to understand the religious changes of late antiquity, we need to do so against their actual background, not by judging them against some misplaced template of secularism and toleration. The legal and philosophical rationalism of classical high culture did not exist in isolation: it was an agreed way of arguing about public affairs, and one which combined with a variety of religious practices and beliefs, and allowed elite men and women to pursue mysteries and cults in private. Ancient religion was incredibly heterogeneous. It can be characterised as syncretism in the positive sense that it encompassed a multiplicity of different ideas and rites from originally distinct belief systems. It was also remarkably localised. Most cities honoured their own gods and maintained their own cults, the most popular of which might enjoy a wider following. Even 'official' Roman religion was in origin the religion of the city of Rome, in which, on certain high festivals, subjects and allies were expected to participate to show their political allegiance. Combined with this was the imperial cult, developed with the emergence of a monarchy in the place of the earlier Republican system, and spread by emperors in the first centuries AD. To the extent that there was any religious common ground across the empire, it was provided by these practices, but even the reception and observance of the imperial cult differed greatly from province to province. Our shorthand term, 'paganism', gives a misleading unity and coherence to the traditional mixture of polytheisms within the empire. Indeed, it was itself defined by triumphant Christians such as Orosius who saw their religious opponents as representatives of a single phenomenon, and denigrated them as crude country dwellers (the literal meaning of *paganus*).

Against this background, the third and fourth centuries saw the growth of a new religious sensibility, seeking to identify a unifying principle in the universe. Ancient philosophical traditions, for example, were reworked to produce a variety of brands of neo-Platonism, which interpreted the teachings of Plato in terms of a search for a spiritual unity behind the world; and neo-Platonic philosophers and teachers practised asceticism in a manner parallel to that of contemporary Christian Holy Men, performing magical acts to such an extent that they were derided by their critics as conjurers. A whole variety of mystery cults, most originating in the east and promising revealed truth to the initiate, gained popularity in the third century. Emperors themselves dabbled in some of these new cults, and so long as they did not make any claim to the exclusive loyalty of their followers they posed no problem to the imperial government. Indeed, in the third century we see emperors attempting to mobilise new cults in giving their position a new religious legitimation, with coins and styles linking the imperial office with divinities such as Hercules and Sol Invictus.

Christianity – like Judaism, another monotheistic cult from the Near East which underwent dramatic expansion in this period – enjoyed an unusual level of organisation and self-consciousness. They hence endured the intermittent hostility of the imperial government, normally as a scapegoat in times of crisis since the first century. Certainly the 'great persecution' of 303–11 was a result of a perception that loyalty to the Christian faith was undermining obedience to the state. Diocletian launched the policy after sacrifices made in association with the imperial cult had produced misleading omens, allegedly because Christians were present. But the perception of conflicting loyalties may have owed much to increasing imperial ambitions, as Diocletian attempted to increase the religious aura of his office. Even then, we should pause before we take the highly-charged accounts that survive at face value: Lactantius' *On the Deaths of the Persecutors* is a highly rhetorical attack on Diocletian, written under his successor, Constantine, after he had converted to Christianity. Although we do know of prominent Christian leaders who were martyred, imprisoned and tortured, there seems to have been little popular support for persecution, and the implementation was patchy. But persecution clearly caused a profound shock to the increasingly confident Christian communities of the empire, forcing them to chose between compromise – the handover of scriptures and buildings to the local authorities and participation in official sacrifices – and martyrdom.

Against this background of an increased imperial interest in legitimation through tapping new religious currents, the decision of Constantine to adopt Christianity is less dramatic than it sounds. Whilst reversing Diocletian's policy towards the Christians, the underlying logic of Constantine's strategy – using religious allegiance as a means to accentuate the emperor's position in the eyes of his subjects – was identical. Not that we should see Constantine's conversion as a cynical ploy for political support. Such an argument is difficult to sustain in light of what we know about the social origins and numerical strength of Christians at the beginning of the fourth century: the Christians were a sizeable, but in no area dominant, community, drawn from the middling ranks of Roman society. The cynical interpretation implies that Constantine was somehow immune from the spiritual movements that affected his contemporaries. In fact, Constantine's turning to the Christian God may have been the logical conclusion to a search for a single supernatural patron, which would explain his earlier allegiances to the cults of Sol Invictus and Apollo.

The actual events behind Constantine's conversion are more or less impossible to penetrate through the myth-making of the Christian authors who recorded it. The Christian legend of the conversion, as it was to be reiterated through the centuries, claimed that Constantine turned to the Christian God before the crucial victory against his rivals at the Battle of the Milvian Bridge, just outside Rome, in 312, and was rewarded with victory. This claim can be traced back to Lactantius, writing *circa* 319, who claimed that Constantine had always been sympathetic to Christianity, and was told in a dream to place the Christian chi-rho sign on the shields of his soldiers. This legend was developed in the course of the reign: Constantine's official biographer, Eusebius, bishop of Caesarea, claimed that the emperor's troops had seen a cross in the sky with the words 'by this sign you shall be victorious'.[16] But the temptation of Christian authors – particularly when, like Eusebius, they were presenting an authorised version of the past – to see conversion as a dramatic moment of revelation may be misleading. Eusebius' *Ecclesiastical History*, written closer to the events, makes no mention of any special prodigies, and strictly contemporary sources – panegyrics praising Constantine, coins and inscriptions reflecting his official image – do not suggest a dramatic change in religious policy in 312. Given that Rome, which Constantine won at the Milvian Bridge, was a pagan city central to traditional Roman religion, this is hardly surprising. Sol Invictus was not removed from Constantine's coins until the 320s, whilst the official titulature of the emperor as *pontifex maximus* (literally 'chief priest' of the imperial cult) was not dropped until the reign of Gratian in the 380s.

Constantine's decisive political victory was the key event in the transformation of Christianity from a persecuted cult to a state religion. An agreement with Licinius – who had a reputation for relative lenience towards Christians – was concluded at Milan in 313 guaranteeing freedom of worship for Christians. In 314 Constantine was able to preside at a meeting of bishops at Arles in southern Gaul and grant them important privileges. By the end of the reign, Eusebius was able to celebrate Constantine as an avowedly Christian ruler, God's representative on earth, who aimed to recreate the city of God on earth. The emperor's mausoleum at Constantinople presented him as the thirteenth Apostle, responsible for bringing Christianity to those outside the church. His sarcophagus was ringed by pillars representing the twelve Apostles, and surrounded by the relics of martyrs, translated here in defiance of long-standing Roman taboos against interference with the remains of the dead.[17] But Constantine's conversion did not lead to positive moves against traditional Roman religion, other than some limitations on the practice of cult motivated primarily by a distaste for animal sacrifices. Even this legislation against sacrifices was enforced only patchily, and was aimed primarily at public sacrifice. There was no purge of non-Christians, nor any massed conversion of the emperor's followers; it was common practice to appoint provincial governors whose religious outlook reflected the views of their province, and through the century the office of prefect of Rome tended to alternate between pagan and Christian. Those fourth-century pagans, such as Julian's 'guru' Maximus who was executed in 371, who attracted positive action and eventually elimination from the imperial government did so because they were found guilty of sorcery – that is, illicit magic normally connected with the person of the emperor or succession to the imperial office. This charge was not exclusively made against pagans – indeed, the first Christian heretic to be executed by the secular authorities, the charismatic Priscillian of Avila (in modern Spain), was likewise executed on allegations of sorcery. Religious co-existence – toleration would probably be too positive a term – was to continue throughout the fourth century. But the active support of the emperor gave Christianity a dominant position within the complex religious map of the fourth-century empire.

Christian dominance rested on the positive support and official status that imperial backing gave the church. For one thing, as the official imperial religion, Christianity proved attractive to those rising socially through the administrative structures of the new empire (even though right through the fourth century it remained quite possible for pagans to enjoy high office). Constantine, moreover, had vastly increased the wealth of the church through land endowments and fiscal privileges. He also funded an extensive programme of church building, notably in Rome through the building of St Peter's on the site of the martyr's grave and the granting of an imperial palace, the Lateran, to the bishop, and in the 'new Rome' he founded on the site of the Greek city of Byzantium, Constantinople, immediately on his defeat of Licinius. As a new foundation, Constantinople was free of the cultural and historical baggage of Rome, and so could be created as a Christian city dominated by an imperial establishment following the new imperial religion.

Essay

Christianity and Roman culture

Christianity, for all its imperial backing, had to co-exist with traditional Roman culture in order to penetrate late Roman society. Christian authors had shared the basic schooling of all educated Romans in the classics of the pagan past, and to engage with a contemporary audience they had to draw on these inherited cultural models. Hence the famous worries of the Christian teacher Jerome, that he was in reality a follower of the classic poet Virgil, not Christ.[18] So too the art and artefacts commissioned by wealthy Christian patrons demonstrated impeccable good taste in a highly traditional milieu of public display. In a world where the heroes of Roman history and classical mythology were the central figures in the cultural landscape, the dividing lines between Christian and pagan culture inevitably blurred. Traditional Roman religion was rooted in the common acknowledgement of the heroes of classical culture and the great events of the Roman past, celebrated and commemorated through the ceremonies and festivals which determined the rhythms of urban life: it was more a matter of participation in a shared public culture than a phenomenon that fits our category of religion, although individuals were free to express personal beliefs in a variety of private cults. After

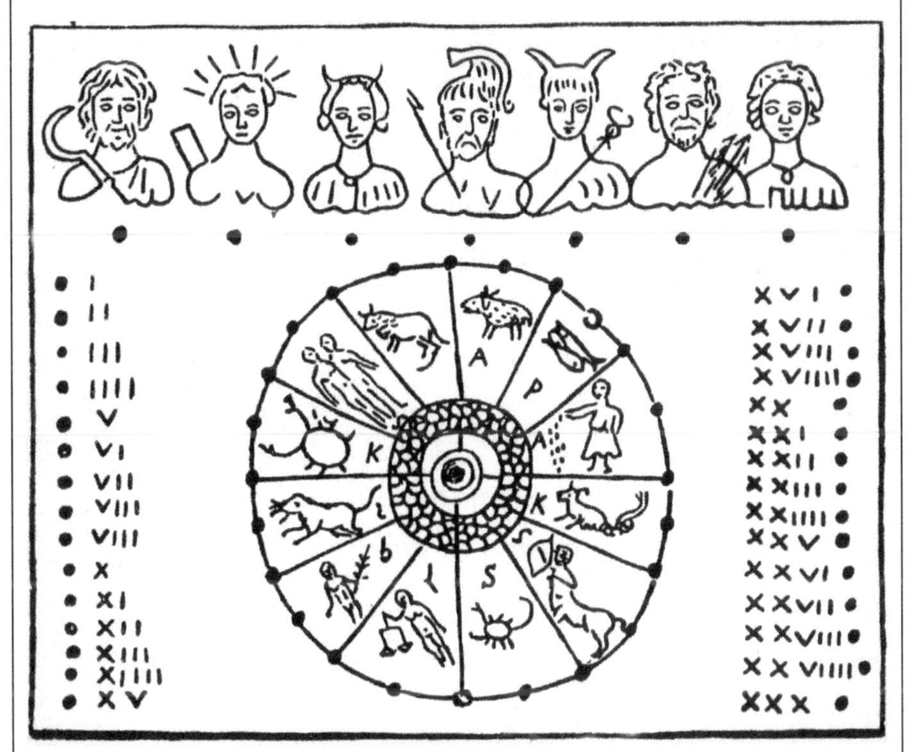

Figure 1.4 From the Codex Calendar of 354

Constantine, whilst the public sacrifices and rites associated with the imperial cult slowly passed away, the veneration of classical myth and Roman history remained, even if the divine status of its central figures was questioned. This world of uneasy co-existence and blurred cultural boundaries is vividly illustrated by the 'Codex Calendar of 354', with its magnificent illustrations of the anniversaries and festivals which marked the annual calendar of the city of Rome.[19]

Away from the symbolic centre of empire comes the Sevso treasure, a collection of fourteen silver pieces that would have graced the country *villa* of any high status Roman. Legal actions over the fabulously valuable hoard make any judgement on its original owner and their abode hazardous, but the vivid depictions of hunting and feasting from classical myth which adorn the plates must have animated and articulated the aristocratic lifestyle of a wealthy provincial.[20]

Figure 1.5 The Sevso treasure

And just as the church came to enjoy an effective monopoly on the imperial patronage traditionally granted to local cults and other good causes, bishops and priests were granted the liberties and privileges traditionally given to those working for the public good. Their immunity from most state obligations gave them equivalent status to high-ranking officials within the imperial government; and, like those on the emperor's business, they were allowed to make use of the state post in their travel. In other words, promotion of Christianity was seen as a part of the state's duties, performed for the good of its subjects.

In the long term, this integration of the church's hierarchy, and above all of bishops, into the official infrastructure of the state was to be of paramount significance. In the course of the fourth century bishops were able to establish themselves as effective leaders of their city communities, thanks to the wealth and privileges they gained through imperial backing. 'Good works', particularly protection for widows, and charitable patronage offered to the urban poor through doles and pious foundations, allowed bishops to build up a ready-made power base within their cities. Julian, in his short-lived removal of imperial backing for Christianity, targeted these elements of episcopal activity in particular as central to the growing institutional power of the church. Ecclesiastical building presented bishops as patrons of their cities in a manner reminiscent of the civic munificence of local elites in earlier centuries. Episcopal influence meant that their backing was worth pursuing, if necessary by throwing oneself on episcopal charity; hence rights of asylum within great churches developed, and were eventually recognised in imperial law by the beginning of the fifth century. And the involvement of the imperial government meant that episcopal patronage was not just informal, but came to include some jurisdiction. Imperial backing for the church meant that bishops enjoyed a proximity to the emperor and an ability to affect the operations of the imperial government on behalf of their city, one of the multitude of patrons necessary if one was to make the late Roman system work. It is thus no surprise that cities increasingly turned to men trained to exercise this kind of patronage since youth when it came to choosing bishops. By the last decades of the fourth century well-connected and upwardly mobile men of an identical type with those who manned the imperial government dominated the episcopate. Through young men like Ambrose, the first senator to become a bishop following his election by the people of Milan in 372, or Augustine, a well-educated and well-connected provincial aristocrat who became bishop of Hippo in North Africa in 395, the social and cultural traditions of the late Roman ruling elite were translated into the church. The roots of Christian success in the fourth century lay in the establishment of episcopal power as the pre-eminent force on a local level.

The system of bishops in their cities mirrored the basic structures of Roman government and society precisely because bishops were integrated into those structures. On a provincial level the church's own hierarchies likewise mirrored those of empire, with metropolitans (archbishops) exercising jurisdiction over their neighbours on account of the pre-eminence of their cities. The bishops of a handful of major cities developed claims to exercise jurisdictions comparable to those of the praetorian prefects, in some cases reflected in the adoption of the title of Patriarch. This was clearest in the east, with the bishops of Alexandria, Antioch and Constantinople establishing formal privileges of this kind, and in Africa where the bishop of Carthage was *de facto* leader of the local church. In the west, although Arles aspired to a similar status at the beginning of the fifth century when it was the effective 'capital' of the remaining Roman possessions in Gaul, political fragmentation meant that this was a matter of controversy and constant debate and hence the city was unable to develop into a patriarchate comparable to those of the east. In Italy, the position of the bishop of Rome was different again, for his authority was rooted in the unique status of his city. Drawing on claims that St Peter, who held the keys to Heaven, had been first bishop of Rome and so the current bishop was his lineal successor, the Roman church claimed a pre-eminence in the universal church, claims which were elaborated particularly by Leo I (440–61), and confirmed by the universal council held at Chalcedon in 451. These claims to spiritual pre-eminence did not bring with them any pretensions to govern the church in the manner of later popes: that was a development of the eleventh and twelfth centuries. The somewhat intangible authority accorded the bishop of Rome paralleled the role of the eternal city itself within the empire, as a symbolic centre with a limited role in actual government. The pope's regular, practical, jurisdiction did not extend beyond those areas of central and southern Italy where he was a 'super-metropolitan', but as a final arbiter on matters of controversy he enjoyed a special status. In fact, the ambivalence of Rome's political position may have helped bolster this spiritual authority. Distant from the centres of imperial power, the bishop of Rome made a useful figure for final appeal in difficult disputes within the church, particularly within the churches of the east, because he was relatively independent of the emperor, unlike say the patriarchs of Constantinople, who were effectively courtiers.

Just as in the secular world bishops became the mediating links between their cities and the imperial government, so episcopal leadership of the local Christian community was founded on the ability to mediate with the Christian community as a whole, and ultimately with God. Late-fourth-century bishops like Ambrose in Milan and Damasus in Rome expended much time and effort establishing episcopal control over the relics of the saints which were rapidly becoming the focal points of religious observance, physically moving them into the public space of the great basilicas of the city. Relics were appealing objects of piety for bishops, because this was a society that looked to the charismatic and exceptional figure as a means of gaining direct access to God, just as a powerful secular patron offered the possibility of direct access to the emperor. The holy men and women, performing feats of extraordinary piety that defied the normal rules of mortal life thus enjoyed a particular appeal. But for bishops and those exercising 'official' power, living repositories of charismatic appeal were potentially threatening; relics, on the other hand, could not answer back. Thus bishops were happy to encourage their congregations to pray at the tombs of long-dead heroes of the age of Christian persecution, even to venerate the bones of the martyrs: such figures must be now with God, so physical contact with their earthly remnants offered contact and the hope of intercession. Whilst the theological implications of such observances aroused debate and some criticism, relic-cults were pliable conduits for popular piety. When subjected to episcopal supervision, they were far safer than informal, household-based religious groupings, led by laymen and women, which stood outside the public sphere of ecclesiastical power. What we might term *villa* piety was particularly suspect. Priscillian, a lay religious teacher with a significant following among female aristocrats, was denounced as a heretic because of such distrust. Even a figure like Jerome, the author of what was to become the standard Latin translation of the Bible, was subject to some suspicion due to his working as a private teacher in aristocratic households in Rome, where he attracted a particular following among pious noblewomen.

These suspicions are indicative of the tensions wrought upon the Christian community as a result of the transition from oppressed cult to state church. Internal dissent, and particularly doctrinal strife in which accusations of heresy flew with vigour, were perhaps the most marked feature of the late Roman church. As the loose agglomeration of local Christian groupings that made up the pre-Constantinian church was integrated into the infrastructure of the empire, internal differences inevitably became increasingly apparent. The church council called by Constantine at Nicaea in 325, immediately after his final conquest of the east, was attended by bishops from right across the empire and seen by later generations as the first ecumenical or universal council; it was a result of the emperor's concern to iron out these divisions. The council's decisions were based on the collective voice of the bishops, meeting under imperial guidance and enforced by imperial decree, and Constantine's leading role in the council shows the pretensions of the emperor to religious leadership. The central issue dealt with at Nicaea was the need to create some sense of Christian unity from the diverse regional practices in matters such as the date of Easter or the manner of prayer (the Council found in favour of kneeling, not standing). This inevitably spilled over into issues of doctrine, and here Constantine aimed at creating a broad-based consensus. The statement of correct doctrine, focusing on the proper relations between Christ and God, approved by the council, came to be styled the Nicene Creed, and was set against the teaching of Arius, a theologian teaching in Alexandria whose views on the relationship between God and Christ attracted a significant amount of attention and support.

After Nicaea, Constantine was anxious to allow Arius' followers to redefine their position so as to allow them to re-enter the church, and was frustrated when a hard-line party led by Athanasius, deacon and then bishop of Alexandria, attempted to prevent this. Athanasius' long and turbulent career caused much controversy and stretched into the 370s, leading to the elevation of the Nicene Creed as a key touchstone of orthodox doctrine in matters Christological, and the exclusion of a whole body of non-Nicene Christians on the grounds that they were Arian heretics. Heresy here was not a question of a wilful attempt to break away from any universally accepted or clearly defined orthodoxy, but defined the process through which what was ultimately to be regarded as orthodoxy emerged; the dividing lines were far from clear-cut or static until the final decades of the fourth century. Indeed, the elimination of what had now become a rival, Arian, church became a live issue for many late-fourth-century bishops. Ambrose in Milan had to force an unwilling Valentinian II to grant imperial support against the rival Arian bishop in the city, 'discovering' the relics of two long-dead martyrs to strengthen his hand. His contemporary Damasus, bishop of Rome from 366–84, mounted a violent war against a kaleidoscope of rival factions, ignoring the authorities who urged restraint, and establishing control over the focal points of popular devotion through his lavish patronage of the graves of the martyrs.[21]

The kind of internal tensions that gave rise to the dispute over Arianism were more explosive still in North Africa. Here, as elsewhere, some Christian groups had refused to co-operate with the imperial government and hand over books and buildings in the persecutions of Diocletian, and had survived as an alternative church into the reign of Constantine. Regarding themselves as a true church united in being oppressed, these 'Donatists' refused to recognise the more mainstream 'official' church, which had been more pliable to pressure in the 'great persecution' and now, of course, enjoyed imperial backing. Again, Constantine's conversion led to imperial involvement in this local dispute within the Christian community, and Constantine's actions followed the traditional pattern of imperial handling of secular appeals in local quarrels, in an attempt to restore a broad-based consensus acceptable to both groups. As with Arianism, though, imperial intervention could offer no real solution to the differences between varied Christian sects. A century later, Augustine, as bishop of Hippo, spent much of his time dealing with his local Donatist opponents, and attempting to mobilise the agencies of the imperial government to do so; but Donatism enjoyed such local support that provincial governors were always wary of moving against it. As Donatism was a religious movement whose strength rested on its local hold, it makes sense to see a tension between regionalism and uniformity underlying heresy, just as regional idioms affected local churches elsewhere in the empire, for example with the Coptic church dominant in Egypt. But this does not make Donatism in any sense an anti-Roman movement of regional or popular revolt: concerns about salvation, and the nature of the church, were the motive forces.

The internal problems of the African church illustrate quite graphically the fundamental cause of Christian dissension in the fourth century. The Donatists continued the sect mentality that had sustained the early church, fuelled by a sense of belonging to a small, elect, group whose purity guaranteed its members a safe passage to Heaven. Augustine, on the other hand, was probably the most eloquent and persuasive proponent of the universality of the Christian church, a community that united all groups, embracing the lukewarm and lazy as well as the pious. For, Augustine claimed, sin was all around in the secular world, and God's mercy, which was necessary to purge the soul of sin, was mysterious and inscrutable in its working. Christians needed to be aware of their own sinfulness, and in their participation in the universal church seek the divine blessing which would cleanse them. Augustine's condemnation of the followers of Pelagius rested on similar concerns. Pelagius, a Briton who found fortune as a religious teacher in Rome in the 380s, practised a severe asceticism, and preached that it was possible to avoid sin. Augustine argued that this undermined the need for divine grace, making salvation something that could be gained automatically, claims which Pelagius and his followers denied. For the church to work as a community encompassing the entire Roman world, and offering salvation to all its members, universalism was necessary. But becoming universal involved a profound transformation of the church itself, and the abandonment of the old certainties of days in which Christians were a clearly defined and holy minority. Indeed, the conflict between Augustine and Pelagius continued to reverberate through much of the west as it slipped from Roman control in the fifth century, so fundamental were the issues it raised about the role of the church in the Christian community and the relationship between man and God. And these issues in a way paralleled the political choices now facing western elites.

The appeal of belonging to a small select sect was powerful. One response, followed by many and admired by all, was asceticism. Self-denial, feats of endurance and self-control, were established as praiseworthy acts in classical culture, and late antique Christians believed that through such actions they could become closer to God. Ascetic practices also marked their practitioners to become members of a spiritual elite *within* the church, and were often particularly appealing to traditional elites used to exercising a leadership rooted in self-control. Moreover, asceticism was not necessarily incompatible with membership of a group. In the fourth century some groups of ascetics seeking God in the Egyptian desert came to organise themselves in religious communities of monks, their collective feats heightening their closeness to God, and this model quickly spread to the west through figures such as John Cassian, who set up a community on the isle of Lerins off the southern coast of Gaul. Not all went to such lengths. It was quite possible to follow asceticism in a domestic setting and, in doing so, to create a holy household. Such practices seem to have been particularly appealing to aristocratic women from those of the Theodosian imperial dynasty down, as it allowed them a rare freedom of agency, and the transformation of their domestic power into something determinative of their whole family's position.

For many asceticism was a potential mechanism for combining the universality of the church with a sense of belonging to a spiritual elite. But the implicit claims of some ascetics to form a spiritual elite whose relationship to the official structures of the church was unclear gave rise to recurrent suspicion. Hence the ambivalence of many western bishops towards Cassian and his followers. And in a world in which theological debate was rife, it was a short step from episcopal jealousy of local ascetic leaders to an accusation of heresy, as in the case of both Pelagius and Priscillian. By the early fifth century, accusations of Priscillianism or Pelagianism seem to have been little more than a convenient label for religious groups whose spiritual claims made them a threat to local bishops, or whose geographical location placed them on or beyond the fringes of Roman control.

By the last decades of the fourth century, the rising tide of asceticism, allied to the growing influence of the episcopate, began to bring the uneasy co-existence of Christianity and traditional religious practices which had typified the post-Constantinian period into doubt. In the 380s and 390s the regimes of Gratian and Theodosius produced a steady stream of legislation that mobilised the strong arm of the state against traditional religious practices by placing strict limits on those aspects of traditional religious cults deemed offensive to Christian tastes. This reached its apogee with two edicts of 391 and 392 which banned all pagan cults, whether private or public. These edicts were an articulation of the strident orthodoxy that defined the regime of Theodosius, and it was praetorian prefects and other officials in the provinces who took the lead in its generation. In Alexandria in 391 it was a mob of monks, egged on by the local bishop, which led the destruction of the temple of Sarapis, the local god who had traditionally ensured the Nile's life-giving annual flood. The local governor wrote to the emperor complaining of this illegal disorder, and feared that if the Nile's flood did fail, a mass apostasy would result. But a stridently orthodox emperor such as Theodosius, when faced with the bevy of complaint and petition that such activities inevitably generated, had little choice but to back the Christian party. Such backing could be reluctant: after the destruction of the Jewish synagogue at Callinicum in 388, Theodosius ordered the Christians responsible to be punished, but was himself trumped by Ambrose, bishop of Milan, seat of the imperial court, who refused to allow Theodosius into church until he reversed his judgement. Two years later, Ambrose was even able to impose penance on the emperor over his massacre of civilians at Thessalonica in retaliation for local disorder. These shifts of imperial policy effectively gave the green light to hard-line Christians throughout the empire to turn on their opponents, provided they had sufficient local support.[22]

In such a situation, matters of religious affiliation inevitably spilled over into the political arena: hence the usurper Magnus Maximus had the Hispanic charismatic Priscillian executed at Trier in 384 to emphasise his backing for religious orthodoxy against heresy, albeit to a horrified reaction from a large section of Christian opinion. Matters of religious observance similarly spilled over into the revolt of Eugenius in 392–4, who courted a section of the Roman Senate still attached to the traditional gods. Theodosius' partisans were thus able to portray the Christian Eugenius as an apostate and his defeat as a replay of Constantine's victory at the Milvian Bridge. In the provinces, Christian violence on the ground, increasingly tolerated and indeed legitimated by imperial legislation in the last quarter of the fourth century, was the key to the Christianisation of the countryside, as temples like that of Sarapis at Alexandria were destroyed by the monastic shock-troops of now dominant Christianity, whilst in Gaul the bishop of Tours, a Pannonian soldier turned monk named Martin, devoted himself to the destruction of the traditional cult-sites that dotted the countryside.[23] With the destruction of these traditional foci of local devotion and loyalty by Christian Holy Men offering a wholly different type of communion with the divine, the religious landscape of the Roman world had undergone a dramatic transformation.

The peculiarity of the late Roman west

The all-encompassing nature and breakneck pace of the changes in cultural and religious life which took place between Diocletian and Theodosius provide a signal warning against the tendency to discuss the later Roman Empire as static or homogenous. Change, rather than restoration or stability, should be seen as the keynote of the fourth century. Think of the rise of Constantinople. Effectively Constantine's new city, albeit one built on the site of a small urban centre, within half a century of its foundation it had emerged as the location of the dominant court within the empire as a whole. What had previously been an obscure backwater in an eastern province was now pre-eminent over the empire's old Roman heartland. In Constantinople's success we see reflected the key dynamics of the fourth century – growing regionalism, the rise of the provinces, and an increasingly entrenched division between east and west; the power of imperial patronage, the increased size of the imperial government, and the growth of a new military and administrative establishment around the emperor; and the centrality of Christianity to the self-identity of the new regime, with the creation of an aggressively and self-consciously Christian city without the baggage of traditional gods and historical cults.

Change of this scale and at this speed could not fail to cause tension. Indeed, understanding the different fates that were to befall the eastern and western empires is dependent on understanding the different ways in which the tensions engendered by change were processed in east and west. The key to these differences was the presence, in the west, of the empire's traditional ruling class, the senators of Rome.

Historically, the Roman Senate, the forum through which this group expressed itself, had played a central political role in the empire as a whole, and indeed in the Republican period it had been the ultimate ruling body. In the early empire, the apogee of a successful career was to be granted membership of the senate, which normally meant taking up residence in Rome itself. Hence, before the third-century crisis, Rome remained in a very real sense the capital of the empire. Members of the senate played the crucial role in ruling the empire as provincial governors and generals, and thereby forged the links with provincial elites and military units which enabled the most successful to advance to the imperial office. The rise of provincial, military emperors in the course of the third century effectively ended the political centrality of Rome and the senate, and by the time of Diocletian its direct political influence was at a nadir. Above all, the fact that members of the senate no longer led armies cut them off from the chance of gaining the imperial office itself. And the actual constitutional power of the senate was by now all but negligible. Confirmations of imperial elections and celebrations of imperial triumph became ceremonial occasions, whilst the day-to-day matters of government were firmly lodged in the imperial court and its administrative apparatus.

In the 'new empire' the road to political power now lay through imperial service in courts now distant from Rome, dominated by military men and upwardly-mobile provincials. It was long believed that senatorial political power continued to be negligible in the fourth century, as emperors favoured new groups directly dependant on imperial patronage. However, careful research has shown that in the course of the fourth century the entrenched influence and vast wealth of the members of the senate, particularly in Italy and the western Mediterranean, underpinned a reassertion of senatorial power within the new political system. Not only could senators wield considerable informal influence, but they also received high offices, notably as provincial governors and praetorian prefects, in roles that were well suited to wealthy aristocrats willing to play the bountiful patron. Indeed, they needed to take up office to have their membership of the senate formally granted. The traditional leaders of Roman society were able to succeed in maintaining an entrenched and strictly limited definition of senatorial status. The proliferation of new offices in the imperial service, which brought with them formal titles and so, technically, membership of the senate, vastly expanded the number of potential senators. In the east, where a new senate was created at the 'new Rome', Constantinople, imperial patronage was able to create a new ruling elite. In the west, however, the long-established dominance of the great Roman families, the distance between the imperial court and central Italy, and the historical tradition of the senate of Rome, prevented such a development. Constantius II restricted membership of the senate to those with hereditary claims, whilst traditional obligations on senators, for example concerning residence at Rome and the holding of circuses by office-holders for the population of the city, were similarly reinforced. Thus a small number of the western super-rich continued to dominate the senate, and to exercise relatively traditional forms of patronage which enabled their continued domination of Rome and, through their estates and contacts, much of the western Mediterranean from Africa up through Sicily and Italy to southern Gaul and Hispania. Periods holding prestigious offices, perhaps serving as a praetor in one's youth, holding a provincial governorship later in life, and ending one's public career as prefect of Rome, were almost rites of passage that served to underline a family's standing in society. Thus was senatorial power integrated into the structure of the late Roman state, as the civilian power of the senate was allowed to dominate Italy and the shores of the western Mediterranean, sheltered by the imperial military establishment in the frontier provinces.

Senatorial dominance of the city of Rome and its immediate hinterland, and the physical distance of the imperial court, helped foster a strong, and highly elitist, group identity, and one which was informed by Rome's long and glorious past. Ammianus gives a memorable denunciation of the snobbery and pique meted out to a lowborn newcomer, a provincial and a soldier to boot, in his retirement at Rome.[24] This elitism took the form of a strong attachment to traditional culture and the Roman past. It is thus scarcely surprising that Rome remained probably the last stronghold of paganism in the west. The self-consciousness of the senatorial aristocracy was tied up with the Roman past and the Roman state as celebrated in the traditional rites of Roman religion. Hence the controversy over the removal of the Altar of Victory, the veneration of which had long been held to ensure the continued success of the Roman state, from the Senate House, first by Constantius II in 357, then again, after its restoration under Julian, by Gratian in 382. Symmachus, prefect of Rome, led an intense lobbying campaign for its restoration, but was trumped by Ambrose, bishop of Milan, the main imperial residence in Italy. Pagans even claimed that in 408, as Rome was besieged by the Goths, the traditional rites which had before guaranteed success had been resuscitated.[25]

This political culture, centred on Rome and its glorious heritage, was ultimately based on the vast private wealth of senators, which allowed them to win political support through the demonstration of public-spirited patronage. Symmachus, for example, was able to spend 2000 pounds of gold holding games to mark his son's gaining of the office of praetor. The annual income of the richest senators was alleged to be 4000 pounds of gold, over six times that of their first-century predecessors. Individuals enjoyed large, scattered estates, miniature states in their own right, not just in Italy but also across the western Mediterranean provinces. Jerome's patron, Melania the Younger, was able to free 8000 unfree dependants as an act of piety, and distribute over 30,000 coins in charity with impunity; the sale of her Gallic and Hispanic estates still left her with holdings dotted across Italy, the Mediterranean islands and Africa.[26] The senatorial aristocracy was able to use its dominance of the imperial administration to entrench these economic interests. Not only were attempts to tax senatorial wealth under Diocletian and Constantine successfully resisted, and immunities for senatorial land from many state imposts maintained, but senatorial political power also meant that the collection of taxation or the recruitment of soldiers from senatorial estates was difficult. In this way, even when emperors from Constantine onwards ensured the reintegration of the senatorial aristocracy into the state, this privileged group was able to maintain private resources on a scale second only to the state, and shape itself into an articulate, coherent and powerful voice, independent of the imperial court.

This was essentially a western phenomenon, rooted in Roman history. In the east, great estates and provincial elites certainly existed, conducting their business affairs from the cities; the Egyptian papyri show them dominant in many areas, but also document a class of small-scale landowners which was nowhere absent. But even in the fourth and fifth centuries when imperial patronage and the pull of the court at Constantinople enabled a handful of powerful families to consolidate their position, eastern senators never constituted a supra-provincial elite whose position was independent of the imperial court. In contrast, the economic and social dominance of the senatorial aristocracy in the western Mediterranean does seem to be unique in scale. It was not based on domination of a single province, nor on access to the imperial court and thus imperial patronage. Rather, the western senatorial aristocracy's dominance of a huge area – stretching out from central Italy to southern Italy, Sicily, and North Africa, and to southern Gaul and Hispania – was ultimately independent of imperial patronage, if exercised in harmony with the structures of imperial government. The estates of this group determined the rhythms of economic life and inter-regional exchange in this core area of the western empire. Moreover, Rome and the institution of the senate gave this group its own focus and a self-consciousness independent of the imperial court, and a cultural identity quite distinct from that of the imperial government. Whilst the imperial establishment focused its activities in the provinces and along the frontiers, its military might sheltering the senatorial aristocracy's dominance of the empire's historical heartland in the western Mediterranean, a political symbiosis was possible. Indeed, for much of the fourth century such a symbiosis was conspicuously successful as a careful use of the patronage afforded by appointments to governorships and prefectures allowed emperors to cultivate amiable relations with the senate. But the relationships between the imperial court and the local power of landlords were always potentially far more complex in the west than in the east. The implications of this complexity were to become clear in the differing fates of eastern and western empires in the fifth century.

Bibliographical essay

New work on the later Roman Empire and late antiquity emerges at a startling pace, most of it in English thanks above all to the inspiring example of Peter Brown. As a result, the following bibliography is more Anglophone than any of the others, and more an introductory guide, with no claims at comprehensiveness; it also focuses particularly on the structure of the late empire, at the expense of much excellent work on the culture of the later Roman world.

General works

G. Bowersock, P. Brown and O. Grabar, *Late Antiquity* (Cambridge, MA and London, 1999), covers the main themes. Averil Cameron, *The Later Roman Empire, 284–430* (London, 1993), is an excellent, concise overview of the 'long fourth century', whilst P. Garnsey and C. Humfress, *The Evolution of Late Antiquity* (London, 2001), offers incisive introductions to key topics, and Av. Cameron and P. Garnsey, eds, *Cambridge Ancient History* 13 (Cambridge, 1998) gives up-to-date and comprehensive coverage. A. H. M. Jones, *The Later Roman Empire: A Social, Administrative and Economic Survey*, 2 vols (Oxford, 1964) remains the point of reference for anyone interested in the structures of the later empire, above all as revealed in legal evidence. Two books by F. Millar cover the Roman Empire in its entirety, but are useful introductions to the late empire: *The Roman Empire and its Neighbours* (London, 1981) and *The Emperor in the Roman World* (London, 1977). Probably the most stimulating avenues into the late empire are provided by two books by J. Matthews which combine research and synthesis: *Western Aristocracies and the Imperial Court, 364–425* (Oxford, 1975), which is the best treatment of politics in action, and *The Roman Empire of Ammianus* (London, 1989), which interrogates our main source for his insights into key areas of late Roman life. Much of the best recent work in a general vein focuses on the conversion of the empire and its consequences both for late Roman society and the Christian church: see the separate section on religion below.

Translated sources

The later Roman Empire is not the prime focus of this book, so the following is far from comprehensive: a good listing of the plentiful fourth-century sources and translations is available in Cameron's *Later Roman Empire.* There are several good collections of translated excerpts, which are perhaps the best way into the period: M. Maas, *Readings in Late Antiquity: A Sourcebook* (London, 2000) and A. D. Lee, *Pagans and Christians in Late Antiquity: A Sourcebook* (London, 2000).

Ammianus Marcellinus' *Res Gestae*, the main and most readable narrative history, is available in a facing translation by J. C. Rolfe in the Loeb Classical Library (London, 1935–9); an excellent translation, by A. Wallace-Hadrill, of a fairly full selection of excerpts is available in the *Penguin Classics* series (London, 1986). Matthews' work (above) is the indispensable guide to Ammianus, see also, amongst a large bibliography, J. W. Drivjers and D. Hunt, eds, *The Late Roman World and its Historian: Interpreting Ammianus Marcellinus* (London & New York, 1999).

Most of the other 'classics' of the late Roman period are religious in orientation. For a highly moralised version of Diocletian's reign see Lactantius, *On the Deaths of the Persecutors*, tr. J. Creed (Oxford, 1984). Eusebius' *Ecclesiastical History* is available in the Penguin Classics series, tr. G. Williamson (London, 1966); see also his oration celebrating the 30th year of Constantine's reign, H. Drake, tr., *In Praise of Constantine* (Berkeley, 1976) and his *Life of Constantine*, tr. A. Cameron and S. Hall (Oxford, 2000). Augustine's most important work, *The City of God*, is available in many translations including Penguin Classics, as is his autobiographical *Confessions*. Useful not only for Augustine, but also for early Christian texts in general, including Ambrose, Jerome and Cassian, are the online translations available at www.ccel.org/fathers2. On issues of doctrine and church government, see the collected sources in J. Stevenson, *A New Eusebius* (London, 1957) and *Creeds, Councils and Controversies* (London, 1966).

The key legal text, the Theodosian Code, is translated by C. Pharr (New York, 1969). For administrative structures see also the *Notitia Dignitatum*, tr. W. Fairley (Philadephia, 1899); on it R. Goodburn and R. Bartholomew, *Aspects of the Notitia Dignitatum* (Oxford, 1976) and J. C. Mann, 'The Notitia Dignitatum – dating and survival', *Britannia* 22 (1991).

Regional studies

Regional studies are relatively scarce, and predominantly archaeological, perhaps owing to the nature of the evidence: our written sources lend themselves best to political narrative and cultural analysis, but more could be done. This gap is particularly evident in relation to Italy, although T. Potter, *Roman Italy* (London, 1987) is good on the archaeology, and Matthews' *Western Aristocracies* has a wealth of detail on the senatorial elite. For what is possible in an area of rich documentation, see the survey by R. Bagnall, *Egypt in Late Antiquity* (Princeton, 1993) and the rewarding case study by D. Rathbone, *Economic Rationalism and Rural Society in Third Century Egypt* (Cambridge, 1991). For an imperial residence in the east, see J. H. W. G. Liebeschuetz, *Antioch: City and Imperial Administration in the Late Roman Empire* (Oxford, 1974). On North Africa the best starting point is the two volumes of collected essays by B. Shaw, *Environment and Society in Roman North Africa* and *Nomads and Christians in Roman North Africa* (both London, 1995), and the classic C. Lepelley, *Les cités de l'Afrique romaine au bas-Empire* 2 vols (Paris, 1979–81), and in English his contribution to J. Rich, ed., *The City in Late Antiquity* (London, 1992). On Spain, see now M. Kulikowski, *Late Roman Spain and its Cities* (Baltimore, 2004), and the essays in K. Bowes and M. Kulikowski, eds, *Hispania in Late Antiquity* (Leiden, 2005). On Gaul, the fundamental studies are E. Wightman, *Gallia Belgica* (London, 1985) and R. van Dam, *Leadership and Community in Late Antique Gaul* (Berkeley, 1988); see also H. Sivan, *Ausonius of Bordeaux: The Genesis of a Gallic Aristocracy* (London, 1993). The standard survey of Britain is P. Salway, *Roman Britain* (Oxford, 1984).

The late Roman state

On the third-century crisis, R. Macmullen, *Roman Government's Response to Crisis, AD 235–337* (New Haven, 1984) and G. Alfoldy, 'The third century crisis as seen by contemporaries', *Greek, Roman and Byzantine Studies* 15 (1974); also chapter 6 of his *Social History of Rome* (London, 1985). Also G. de Ste Croix, 'Why were the early Christians persecuted?', *Past & Present* 26 (1963), with reply by A. Sherwin-White, *Past & Present* 27 (1964). But regional studies, notably Rathbone's book on Egypt, challenge traditional views of crisis; for the west, see J. Drinkwater, *The Gallic Empire* (Stuttgart, 1987). S. Corcoran, *The Empire of the Tetrarchs: Imperial Pronouncements and Government AD 284–324* (Oxford, 1996) provides fundamental rethinking of the crucial period in the Roman recovery; a more traditional and accessible narrative is S. Williams, *Diocletian and the Roman Recovery* (New York, 1985). On Constantine's reign there is now N. Lenski, ed., *Cambridge Companion to the Age of Constantine* (Cambridge, 2006) to add to T. D. Barnes, *Constantine and Eusebius* (Harvard, 1986); also H. Drake, *Constantine and the Bishops: The Politics of Intolerance* (Berkeley, 2000). Useful biographical treatments of later fourth-century emperors include R. Browning, *The Emperor Julian* (Berkeley, 1976); G. Bowersock, *Julian the Apostate* (Cambridge, MA, 1978); Julian's own writings are translated by S. Lieu (Liverpool, 1989); N. Lenski, *Valens and the Fourth-Century Empire* (California, 2002); S. Williams and G. Friel, *Theodosius: The Empire at Bay* (London, 1994) for a conventional narrative.

On imperial ideology, S. MacCormack, *Art and Ceremony in Late Antiquity* (Berkeley, 1981) is difficult but important; see also 'Change and continuity in late antiquity: the ceremony of Adventus', *Historia* 21 (1972) and M. McCormick, *Eternal Victory: Triumphal Rulership in Late Antiquity, Byzantium and the Early Middle Ages* (Cambridge, 1986).

Jones' work remains the fundamental guide to the government; the best introduction is now C. Kelly, *Ruling the Later Roman Empire* (Cambridge, MA, 2004); compare the negative evaluation of R. Macmullen, *Corruption and the Decline of Rome* (New Haven, 1988). On changing relationships between cities and the imperial government see F. Millar, 'Empire and city, Augustus to Julian: obligations, excuses and status', *Journal of Roman Studies* 73 (1983), and see literature on cities, below. There is useful material on government, in a much longer perspective of Roman history as a whole, in J. Lendon, *Empire of Honour: The Art of Government in the Roman World* (Oxford, 1997), and in the perspective of late Roman Christianisation in P. Brown, *Power and Persuasion in Late Antiquity* (London, 1992); see also J. Ando, *Provincial Loyalty and Imperial Ideology in the Roman Empire* (Berkeley, 1999).

On law, see J. Harries, *Law and Empire in Late Antiquity* (Cambridge, 1999); J. Matthews, *Laying Down the Law: A Study of the Theodosian Code* (New Haven, 2000); J. Harries and I. Wood, eds, *The Theodosian Code: Studies in the Imperial Law of Late Antiquity* (London, 1993); T. Honore, *Law in the Crisis of Empire: The Theodosian Dynasty and its Quaestors AD 379–455* (Oxford, 1998). For law in practice see J. Harries, 'Resolving disputes: the frontiers of law in late antiquity', in R. Mathisen, ed., *Law, Society and Authority in Late Antiquity* (Oxford, 2001).

For the world of the senate and the workings of politics, see T. D. Barnes, *The New Empire of Diocletian and Constantine* (Cambridge, MA, 1982); for the late third and early fourth century, and for the later fourth and early fifth century, Matthews' *Western Aristocracies*; for a taster see J. Matthews, 'The Letters of Symmachus', in J. W. Binns, ed., *Latin Literature in the Fourth Century* (London, 1974). M. Arnheim, *The Senatorial Aristocracy in the Later Roman Empire* (Oxford, 1972) is the standard work, but for western elites see now R. Salzmann, *The Making of a Christian Aristocracy: Social and Religious Change in the Western Roman Empire* (London, 2002). On changing definitions of social status, P. Garnsey, *Social Status and Legal Privilege in the Roman Empire* (Oxford, 1970) remains a classic. The data in R. Mathisen, 'Imperial honorifics and senatorial status in late Roman legal documents', in Mathisen, *Law, Society and Authority in Late Antiquity* (Oxford, 2001) is important for the significance of service and status. By way of comparison on the east Roman ruling elite see P. Heather, 'New men for new Constantines: creating a ruling elite in the eastern Mediterranean', in P. Magdalino, ed., *New Constantines* (London, 1994).

For the bureaucracy and social mobility see K. Hopkins, 'Social mobility in the late Roman Empire: the case of Ausonius', *Classical Quarterly* 11 (1961); 'Elite mobility in the later Roman empire', *Past & Present* 32 (1965); J. Matthews, 'Gallic supporters of Theodosius', *Latomus* 30 (1971).

Society

See for senatorial family power J. Harries, 'Treasures in Heaven: property and inheritance among the senators of late Rome', in E. Craik, ed., *Marriage and Property* (Aberdeen, 1984), J. Hillner, 'Domus, family and inheritance: the senatorial family house in late antique Rome', *Journal of Roman Studies* 93 (2003). On the family more generally see J. Evans Grubbs, *Law and the Family in Late Antiquity: The Emperor Constantine's Marriage Legislation* (Oxford, 1995); G. Nathan, *The Family in Late Antiquity: The Rise of Christianity and the Endurance of Tradition* (London, 1999); on gender roles and women, G. Clark, *Women in Late Antiquity: Pagan and Christian Lifestyles* (Oxford, 1994), A. Arjava, *Women and the Law in Late Antiquity* (Oxford, 1996).

On rural society see A. Wallace-Hadrill, ed., *Patronage in Ancient Society* (London, 1989), esp. P. Garnsey and G. Woolf, 'Patronage of the rural poor in the Roman world', and J. F. Drinkwater, 'Patronage in Roman Gaul and the problem of the Bacaudae'. For aristocratic *villas*, J. Perceval, *The Roman Villa* (London, 1976). On the peasantry and the colonate, see A. H. M. Jones, *The Roman Economy* (Oxford, 1974), chapters 14 and 21; E. Wightman, 'Peasants and potentates', *American Journal of Ancient History* 3 (1978); A. Sirks, 'The farmer, the landlord and the law in the fifth century', in R. Mathisen, ed., *Law, Society and Authority in Late Antiquity* (Oxford, 2001); for slaves C. R. Whittaker, 'Circe's pigs: from slavery to serfdom in the late Roman world', *Slavery and Abolition* 8 (1987); R. Macmullen, 'Late Roman slavery', *Historia* 36 (1987), with reply by R. Samson, *Historia* 38 (1989); also P. Garnsey, *Ideas of Slavery from Aristotle to Augustine* (Cambridge, 1996).

K. Greene, *The Archaeology of the Roman Economy* (London, 1991) is a good introduction to the archaeological evidence. For the economics of the countryside see now the controversial J. Banaji, *Agrarian Change in Late Antiquity* (Oxford, 2001); P. Sarris, 'The origins of the manorial economy: new evidence from late antiquity', *English Historical Review* 119 (2004). Good syntheses, using archaeology, in W. Bowden, L. Lavan and C. Machado, eds, *Recent Research on the Late Antique Countryside* (Leiden, 2004), and T. Burns and J. Eadie, *Urban Centers and Rural Contexts in Late Antiquity* (Michigan, 2001). There is important new work being undertaken on the northern Gallic countryside in the fourth and fifth centuries, stressing the abandonment of the *villas* and the emergence of new settlement forms in the decades after *c.* 350: P. van Ossel and P. Ouzoulias, 'Rural settlement economy in northern Gaul in the late Empire', *Journal of Roman Archaeology* 13 (2000), with full references to earlier work in French.

On commerce, and the role of the state therein, see C. R. Whittaker, 'Late Roman trade and traders', in P. Garnsey, ed., *Trade in the Ancient Economy* (Berkeley, 1983); K. Hopkins, 'Taxes and trade in the Roman Empire, 200 BC to AD 400', *Journal of Roman Studies* 70 (1980); C. Wickham, 'Marx, Sherlock Holmes and Late Roman Commerce', *Journal of Roman Studies* 78 (1988), reprinted in his *Land and Power* (London, 1994).

On cities see J. H. W. G. Liebeschuetz, *The Decline and Fall of the Roman City* (Oxford, 2001), L. Lavan, ed., *Recent Research on Late Antique Urbanism*, Journal of Roman Archaeology Supplement 21 (Portsmouth, RI, 2001); J. W. Rich, ed., *The City in Late Antiquity* (London, 1992); S. Barnish, 'The transformation of classical cities and the Pirenne debate', *Journal of Roman Archaeology* 2 (1989); M. Whittow, 'Ruling the late Roman and early Byzantine city: a continuous history', *Past & Present* 129 (1990). For the changing shape of the city of Rome in particular, see now J. Curran, *Pagan City and Christian Capital: Rome in Late Antiquity* (Oxford, 2000); B. Lancon, *Rome in Late Antiquity* (Edinburgh, 2000) and W. Harris, ed., *The Transformations of the Urbs Romana in Late Antiquity*, Journal of Roman Archaeology Supplement 33 (Portsmouth, RI, 1999).

The army

E. Luttwak, *The Grand Strategy of the Roman Empire* (London, 1976) launched the idea of a shift in strategy after the third century, to 'defence in depth'; but see the critiques of J. C. Mann, 'Power, force and the frontiers of the Empire', *Journal of Roman Studies* 69 (1979) and F. Miller, 'Emperors, frontiers and foreign relations, 31 BC – AD 378', *Britannia* 13 (1982), and the bibliographical essay on frontiers and barbarian policy, chapter 2 below.

H. Elton, *Warfare in Roman Europe, 350–425* (Oxford, 1996) is a robust and revisionist study of the later Roman army, and P. Southern and K. Dixon, *The Late Roman Army* (London, 1996) provides a sound survey. See also R. Macmullen, *Soldier and Civilian in the Later Roman Empire* (Cambridge, MA, 1963). On the size of the army, R. Macmullen, 'How big was the Roman imperial army?', *Klio* 62

(1981), 'The Roman Emperor's army costs', *Latomus* 43 (1984) and R. Duncan-Jones, 'Pay and numbers in Diocletian's army', *Chiron* 8 (1978), reprinted in *Structure and Scale in the Roman Economy* (Cambridge, 1990), pp. 105–17.

The most important discussion of military organisation, local society and the state are J.-M. Carrie, 'L'esercito, trasformazioni funzionali ed economie locali', in A. Giardina, ed., *Societa romana e impero tradoantico* I (Rome and Bari, 1986), and his 'L'état de la recherche de nouveaux modes de financement des armies, IVe–VIIIe siècles', in A. Cameron, ed., *The Byzantine and Islamic Near East III: States, Resources and Armies* (Princeton, 1992).

Christianity

There is no shortage of excellent work here, much of it well written and accessible; this has been the real area of growth in recent scholarship. Among the best introductions are R. Fox, *Pagans and Christians* (London, 1986), R. Markus, *Christianity in the Roman World* (London, 1974) and *The End of Ancient Christianity* (Cambridge, 1991).

The best account of the Christianisation of the Roman world is now P. Brown, *Authority and the Sacred* (Cambridge, 1996). On the rise of Christianity in the fourth century, there are critical discussions in A. Momigliano, ed., *The Conflict between Christianity and Paganism in the Fourth Century AD* (Oxford, 1963), especially Jones on the social background to the rise of Christianity and Momigliano on the relationship between Christian and pagan culture. P. Brown, 'Aspects of the Christianisation of the Roman aristocracy', *Journal of Roman Studies* 51 (1961), reprinted in his *Religion and Society in the Age of Augustine* (London, 1972), is another crucial discussion. See also R. Macmullen, *Christianising the Roman Empire* (New Haven, 1984); and his 'What difference did Christianity make?', *Historia* 35 (1986). For a socio-geographical approach to the spread of Christianity, see M. Humphries, *Communities of the Blessed: Social Environment and Religious Change in Northern Italy, AD 200–400* (Oxford, 1999); on the public face of the now dominant church, R. Lim, *Public Disputation, Power and the Social Order in Late Antiquity* (Berkeley, 1995). For Christianisation and the texture of urban culture, M. R. Salzmann, *On Roman Time* (Berkeley, 1992).

On divisions within the fourth-century church and the tensions leading to them, the articles by P. Brown collected in *Religion and Society in the Age of Augustine* (London, 1972) are crucial, focusing particularly on Donatism and Pelagianism; several are directed at the interpretative framework underpinning W. H. C. Frend, *The Donatist Church* (Oxford, 1971), and already critiqued by A. H. M. Jones, 'Were the ancient heresies national or social movements in disguise?', *Journal of Theological Studies* 10 (1959). See also R. Williams, *Arius, Heresy and Tradition* (London, 1987); M. Barnes and D. Williams, eds, *Arianism after Arius* (London 1987); R. Williams, ed., *The Making of Orthodoxy* (Cambridge, 1989). On Priscillian see H. Chadwick, *Priscillian of Avila* (Oxford, 1976) and V. Burrus, *The Making of a Heretic* (Berkeley, 1998).

On Christian attacks on paganism, see G. Fowden, 'Bishops and temples in the eastern Roman empire 320–425', *Journal of Hellenic Studies* 29 (1978), which is important on the 'turning of the tide' against paganism in the decades around 400; on pagan reaction in the west see J. O'Donnell, 'The demise of paganism', *Traditio* 35 (1979) and generally on late Roman paganism see P. Chuvin, *A Chronicle of the Last Pagans* (Cambridge, MA, 1990), and Fowden's important study on 'The pagan holy man in late antiquity', *Journal of Hellenic Studies* 102 (1982). For the 'pagan revival' of the late fourth century see Alan Cameron, 'The Latin revival of the fourth century', in W. Treadgold, ed., *Renaissances before the Renaissance* (Stanford, 1984).

On bishops, see, in addition to studies of Augustine and Ambrose below, P. Brown, *Politics and Persuasion in Late Antiquity* (Madison, 1992) and *Poverty and Leadership in Late Antiquity* (Hanover, 2002); H. Chadwick, 'The role of the Christian bishop in ancient society', no. III in his *Heresy and Orthodoxy in the Early Church* (London, 1991); G. Bowersock, 'From Emperor to Bishop: the self-conscious transformation of political power in the fourth century AD', *Classical Philology* 81 (1986). See now the excellent treatment of bishops as an elite by C. Rapp, *Holy Bishops in Late Antiquity* (Berkeley, 2004).

On asceticism and early monasticism see E. A. Clark, *Ascetic Piety and Women's Faith* (Lewiston, 1986); P. Brown, *The Body and Society* (New York, 1988); P. Rousseau, *Pachomius: the Making of a Community in Fourth-Century Egypt* (Berkeley, 1985) and *Ascetics, Authority and the Church in the Age of Jerome and Cassian* (Oxford, 1978); D. Chitty, *The Desert a City* (London, 1966). P. Brown, *Society and the Holy in Late Antiquity* (Berkeley, 1982) reprints his classic work on holy men, notably 'The rise and function of the holy man in late antiquity', *Journal of Roman Studies* 61 (1971), which is fundamental; see now Brown's 'The rise and function of the holy man in late antiquity, 1971–97', *Journal of Early Christian Studies* 6 (1998) and C. Rapp, '"For next to God you are my salvation": reflections on the rise of the holy man in late antiquity', in J. Howard-Johnston and P. Haywood, eds, *The Cults of the Saints in Late Antiquity and the Early Middle Ages* (Oxford, 2001); this whole volume is devoted to discussing Brown's work.

Relic cults are the subject of Brown's inspiring and influential *The Cult of the Saints: Its Rise and Function in Late Antiquity* (Chicago, 1981). For a critic of relic-cults, see G. Clark, 'Translating relics: Victricius of Rouen and fourth-century debate', *Early Medieval Europe* 10 (2001). On the closely related issues of changing attitudes to death and burial see J. Harries, 'Death and the dead in the late Roman west', in S. Bassett, ed., *Death in Towns* (Leicester, 1992) and G. Wataghin Catino, 'The ideology of urban burial', in G. P. Brogiolo and B. Ward-Perkins, eds, *The Idea and Ideal of the Town between Late Antiquity and the Early Middle Ages* (Leiden, 1999).

P. Brown, *Augustine of Hippo* (London, 1967) is the classic biography of a key figure; see also R. Markus, *Saeculum: History and Society in the Theology of Augustine* (London, 1970) on Augustine's thought. On other major figures see N. McLynn, *Ambrose of Milan: Church and Court in a Christian Capital* (Berkeley, 1994), J. N. D. Kelly, *Jerome: His Life, Writings and Controversies* (London, 1975), O. Chadwick, *John Cassian* (Oxford, 1968), C. Stancliffe, *St Martin and his Hagiographer* (Oxford, 1983).

Notes

1. Theodosian Code, tr. C. Pharr (Berkeley, 1956), book 16, esp. chapter 5.
2. See Ammianus' attacks on the levity of contemporary culture, *Res Gestae*, trans. W. Hamilton and A. Wallace-Hadrill as *The Later Roman Empire 354–378* (London, 1986), 14.6 and 28.4; Aurelius Victor, tr. H. W. Bird (Liverpool, 1994) and the *Scriptores Historae Augustae*, tr. A. Birley, *The Lives of the Later Caesars: The Augustan History* (London, 1976).
3. Ammianus Marcellinus, 16: 10; for Julian see 22: 7.
4. Theodosian Code, 15.7.12; my thanks to Caroline Humfress for this reference.
5. H. Bell *et al.*, ed. & trans., *The Abinnaeus Archive: Papers of a Roman Officer in the Reign of Constantius II* (Oxford, 1962); on Abinnaeus, T. D. Barnes, 'The career of Abinnaeus', *Phoenix* 39 (1985), and the useful material at http://www.trismegistos.org/arch.php.
6. Abinnaeus archive nos 3, 13, 26 and 29 for the mechanisms of tax-collection; 66–70, 72–4 are registers, and 80 an account of *annona* collected.
7. Abinnaeus' background: note esp. nos 22, 62–4, for his wife's property. Appeals: Abinnaeus archive nos 44–57; nos 18, 28 and 32 concern accusations of illegal behaviour and forced exactions against soldiers.
8. Legislation on the army is collected in book 7 of the Theodosian Code, see esp. 7.1.
9. See esp. Abinnaeus archive nos 18, 28, 32, in the context of the material n. 6 above.
10. Theodosian Code, 7.4.1, with thanks to Caroline Humfress.
11. Note Abinnaeus archive nos 58–9, borrowing to fund a crucial visit to Constantinople; for more on loans e.g. no. 43.
12. J. T. Peña, 'The mobilization of state olive oil in Roman Africa: the evidence of late fourth century ostraca from Carthage', in Peña, ed., *Carthage Papers*, Journal of Roman Archaeology Supplement 28 (Portsmouth, RI, 1998).
13. Theodosian Code 12.1, 'On decurions', reproduces 192 legislative acts; there is also plentiful material in other sections: e.g. concerning Christian priests limitations begin with 16.2.3 (329) and are further developed thereafter.
14. Amongst many possible examples, see e.g. Count Paul's accusations about sorcery and treason (Ammianus, 19.12), the purges of Maximian at Rome (Ammianus, 28.1), and the treason trials under Valens at Antioch (Ammianus, 29.1).
15. See Abinnaeus archive nos 1–2 (the only two documents in Latin, the offical language of administration), also 58–9.
16. Lactantius, *On the Deaths of the Persecutors*, tr. J. Creed (Oxford, 1989), 44: 5–6; Eusebius, *Life of Constantine*, tr. Av. Cameron and H. Drake (Oxford, 1999), 1: 28–29.
17. Eusebius, *Life of Constantine*, 4: 64.
18. Jerome, Letter 22, to Eustochium, tr. F. A. Wright, *Letters of Jerome* (London, 1933) (many other trans.).
19. M. R. Salzmann, *On Roman Time: The Codex Calendar of 354* (Berkeley, 1992).

20. M. Mungo and A. Bennett, *The Sevso Treasure* I, Journal of Roman Archaeology Supplement 12 (Portsmouth, RI, 1994).
21. Ambrose, *Letters*, tr. M. Beyenka (Washington, 1954), no. 20; N. McLynn, *Ambrose of Milan: Church and Court in a Christian Capital* (Berkeley, 1994), pp. 158–219; M. Saghy, '*Scinditur in partes populus*: Pope Damasus and the Martyrs of Rome', *Early Medieval Europe* 9 (2000).
22. Legislation against 'paganism' is collected in 16.10 of the Theodosian Code, see esp. 16.10.11–12 for the edicts of 391 and 392. Alexandria: Sozomen, *Ecclesiastical History*, 7: 15; Callincum and Thessalonica: Ambrose, *Letters*, nos. 40, 41, 51.
23. Alexandria n. 22 above; religious conflict under Theodosius n. 25 below; for Gaul, Sulpicius Severus, *Life of St Martin*, tr. T. Head and T. Noble, *Soldiers of Christ* (London, 1998).
24. Ammianus, 14.6, 28.4.
25. See R. H. Barrow, *Prefect and Emperor: the Relationes of Symmachus* (Oxford, 1982), for discussion and text of *Relatio* 3; also Ambrose, *Letters* 17–18, and for pagan claims about 408 Zosimus, *New History*, tr. R. Ridley (Canberra, 1982), 5.7.2.
26. For senatorial wealth see Symmachus, *Letters*, ed. J.-P. Callu (4 vols, Paris, 1972–2002); Olympiodorus, fragment 44, tr. R. C. Blockley, *The Fragmentary Classicising Historians of the Later Roman Empire* 2 (Liverpool, 1982); E. A. Clark, ed., *The Life of Melania the Younger* (Toronto, 1984).

2

Barbarians, the Roman frontier and the crisis of the western empire

Contents

Summary

Chronology

List of emperors

Invasions, migrations and identities: the problems of barbarian history

Kings and farmers: barbarian social and political organisation

Essay: Roman goods beyond the frontier: Gudme-Lundeborg

Roman frontiers and barbarian society

Adrianople and its aftermath: Goths and Romans in the late fourth century

Emperors, usurpers and barbarians: the crisis of the western empire

Bibliographical essay

Summary

Along its eastern frontier, the Roman Empire stood in a long-term stalemate with a similar, civilised and highly organised rival, the Persian Empire. In the west, beyond the Rhine and Danube was a kaleidoscope of small, fragmented, barbarian polities. There was a long history of contact and interaction between these barbarians and the Romans. In the third and fourth centuries, the emergence of new groups of barbarians – the Franks, the Alemans and the Goths – went hand-in-hand with the emergence of an increasingly powerful warrior elite. This elite was increasingly tied into the Roman world, both because of the profound cultural, diplomatic and economic influence in the immediate hinterland of the frontier, and because communities beyond the frontier were becoming the most fertile recruitment ground for the Roman army.

In the last quarter of the fourth century, the patterns of interaction between the empire and its barbarian neighbours began to change. The immigration and assimilation of barbarians was a time-honoured Roman practice, but mishandling of groups of Goths crossing the Danube frontier led, in 378, to the defeat of the eastern Roman army and the death of the eastern Emperor Valens at Adrianople. Although Roman control in the Balkans was rapidly re-established, and the Goths were settled in the region, this was a severe defeat leaving Roman military manpower depleted, and allowing the Gothic settlers in the Balkans to become an important military force for the Romans.

The political dominance of the east allowed Constantinople to command the lion's share of remaining Roman military resources, a fact compounded by the recurrent problem of usurpers in Britain, Gaul and Hispania and the losses occasioned by the resulting civil wars in the west. As a result western military strategy in particular became increasingly reliant on barbarian allies and recruits. The western court was removed to Ravenna in Italy, and the western provinces left denuded of troops, as internal conflict between Ravenna and Constantinople enjoyed first call on Roman resources. In 407–13, the west descended into outright crisis. Emperor and senate lurched into an anti-barbarian reaction, refusing to pay for the services of the Goths led by Alaric and overthrowing the military leader Stilicho and his barbarian troops, whilst Britain, Gaul and Hispania were lost as barbarians took advantage of the military vacuum, and provincial elites backed a new rash of usurpers.

Chronology

368–75	Major Roman campaigns in Britain, along the Rhine and Danube
376–86	Goths seek admission to empire along Danube frontier
378	Goths in Balkans rebel, defeat and kill Valens at Adrianople
382	Theodosius I makes treaty with Goths in Balkans
383–8	Usurper Magnus Maximus in west
392–4	Usurper Eugenius in west
395–407	Master of soldiers Stilicho politically dominant in west
402	Alaric's Goths mount failed invasion of Italy
402	Western imperial court removed to Ravenna
404–6	Failed invasion of Italy by Radagaisus' Goths
406–7	Vandals, Sueves and Alans cross Rhine
407–11	Usurper Constantine III ruler of Britain, Gaul and Hispania
408	Stilicho overthrown and his barbarian troops purged
408–12	Alaric's Goths in Italy seeking supplies from imperial government
410	Alaric's Goths plunder Rome for three days
411–13	Usurper Jovinus in Gaul

List of emperors (simplified)

West	East
Valentinian I, 364–75	Valens, 364–78
Gratian, 367–83	Theodosius I, 379–95
Valentinian II, 388–92	
Western usurpers:	
Magnus Maximus, 383–8,	
Eugenius, 392–4	
Honorius, son of Theodosius, 395–423	Arcadius, son of Theodosius, 395–408
Western usurpers including:	
Constantine III, 407–11	
Maximus, 409–11	
Priscus Attalus, 409–10, 413–15	
Jovinus, 411–13	

Invasions, migrations and identities: the problems of barbarian history

Barbarian invasions and the fall of the Roman Empire are two phenomena that are inextricably linked. Given that the western Roman Empire was eventually replaced by a series of barbarian kingdoms, it is natural to see the relationship between barbarian invasions and the fall of Rome as straightforward, self-evident even: barbarians smashed the western empire to pieces and created their own states in its place. The sources describing events in the critical period, the half-century centred on 400 AD, make it clear that this was not the case. Even the most summary skim of the political and military narrative of the fourth and fifth centuries reveals how few head-on clashes there were between Romans and barbarians. Most of the barbarian groupings whose doings dominate the period were engaged in far more complex long-term relationships with the empire. Most barbarians who settled within the empire did so as allies or clients of the Roman government – or, rather, a Roman government, for internal conflicts between east and west, and within the western regime, were a key feature of this period, and these internal struggles for power took primacy in Roman eyes.

If it is impossible to present the fall of Rome as the outcome of a straightforward clash of civilisations, then explanation must focus on internal developments within the empire, and the changing patterns of interaction between the empire and its barbarian neighbours. The significance of internal factors is underlined by the differing fates of the eastern and western parts of the Roman Empire. It was only in the west that the Roman government lost control in the course of the fifth century. The eastern provinces, ruled from Constantinople, survived as the political entity that we know as the Byzantine Empire, seen by contemporaries as simply the Roman Empire continuing undisturbed. The contrast between east and west is significant, because in many ways the potential dangers facing the east were greater, with the Danube frontier and the Balkans – the gateway to Constantinople – under pressure from the Goths through the fourth century, and bearing the brunt of the most powerful barbarian enemy faced by the empire, the Huns, in the fifth. Along its eastern frontiers in Asia Minor, however, Constantinople was faced with a different threat entirely: the Persian Empire of the Sassanids, a complex ancient state and long-term military opponent, with whom there was a long land frontier dotted with garrisons and fortifications. Although the Persian Empire indubitably constituted a larger and more highly organised opponent than the barbarians in the west, paradoxically its very scale and stability also made it a more predictable neighbour. In the problem periods of the fourth and fifth centuries negotiated peaces were the order of the day – not least as the Persians also needed to divert attention and resources to the threat posed by the Huns through the Caucasus.

In the west, widespread barbarian incursions had been one element of the third-century 'crisis', and the empire had been forced to abandon some of its most advanced positions, notably provinces beyond the Rhine and Danube. Whilst energetic imperial campaigning through the fourth century enabled the new frontier along the Rhine and Danube to be maintained, by the fifth century barbarian tribes were admitted into the empire on more or less 'official' terms, in a radical development of policy which is central to the fate of the western empire. To understand the history of the fourth- and fifth-century west it is vital to understand changing Roman policy towards the barbarians.

As the complexity and variety of Roman–barbarian relationships becomes more fully understood it is becoming increasingly clear that the barbarians were as much catalysts, interacting with internal problems within the Roman army and ruling elite, as straightforward causes of decline. Indeed, the very term 'barbarian invasions', so often coupled with 'the fall of Rome', is highly misleading. We need to avoid seeing all conflicts between Romans and barbarians as manifestations of a single phenomenon. There were significant differences between the efforts of barbarian rulers on the frontier to expand their local power over the artificial boundaries created by Rome, and the systematic attempts of the Huns to live as plundering parasites off the Roman state.

The difficulty of assessing the aims and motivations of barbarian activity are augmented by the nature of the sources. The written evidence, by its very nature, inevitably reflects the Roman viewpoint. For Roman writers, the label 'barbarian' carried with it a whole set of pejorative implications. Barbarians were lacking in all restraint, above all lacking in law and the self-control that allowed civilisation. The presentation of barbarians in late Roman sources, then, is highly stereotypical. It is also often highly conventional, drawing on older ideas and famed descriptions, just as tribal names from the distant past were frequently recycled and applied to current barbarians. These conventions together made up an ethnographic ideology, which made barbarians the mirror image of Romans. For Roman writers talking about uncivilised barbarians was thus ultimately a way of talking about Roman civilisation. This is clearest in probably the most famous Roman work on the barbarians, the account of *Germania* written by Tacitus at the end of the first century AD. For generations, this work was mined as a crucial source for studying early barbarian politics and society, but Tacitus had little contact with the peoples he described, and instead was voicing his criticisms of the Rome of his time by presenting its neighbours as noble savages – uncivilised certainly, but not lacking in virtues. The major historian of the fourth-century empire and its dealings with the barbarians, Ammianus Marcellinus, similarly drew on these long-standing ethnographic traditions, recycling stereotypical descriptions going back to Herodotus in his account of contemporary adversaries. His account of the Huns and Alans, for example, is very similar to that of the Arabs, stressing their savagery which makes them closer to beasts than men, living in extremes of climate and terrain and so lacking the characteristics of civilisation: 'like unreasoning beasts they are at the mercy of their maddest impulses'. By the end of the fourth century, Christianity had complicated the ideology of the barbarian: Jerome, for example, writing to Roman friends from the Holy Land about the events of 410, drew on standard stereotypes which made barbarians more animal than human on account of their savagery and lack of self-control, but also equated barbarian incursions with Biblical prophecies about the coming of the Antichrist.[1]

The problem with approaching barbarian societies from the written sources is, therefore, a huge one. It is sobering to remember that even our convenient labels, 'barbarian' and 'Germanic', do not rest on contemporary self-consciousness, but are Roman terms adopted by modern historians. It is unlikely that those groups which we label the 'barbarians' or the 'Germanic peoples' had any sense of common identity, let alone purpose. There is certainly no evidence of co-operation or shared goals between them, and the idea that they shared a common culture is first explicitly stated four hundred years later at the court of Charlemagne; the case for these ideas having earlier roots rests on complex arguments over the interpretation of the iconography of certain objects in the archaeological record, and the deeply problematic evidence of legendary traditions first committed to writing in the ninth century or, more often, later still. Our modern classification of these groups as 'Germanic' rests on the work of philologists who have underlined the common origin of their languages, but in the fourth and fifth centuries not all 'Germanic' languages were mutually comprehensible; no perception of a shared linguistic heritage was voiced by contemporaries, who used the label 'German', derived from the Roman term for their opponents on the Rhine, intermittently and inconsistently. Modern historians who have seen the 'Germanic' peoples as sharing a common culture similarly can point to no contemporary commentator who argues thus; the evident similarities of social organisation amongst the Roman Empire's western neighbours are best explained by their common experience and geographical proximity.

In fact, even the ethnic labels given to specific barbarian groupings by Roman writers need to be used with care. Using such labels was, in itself, a classic strategy of distinguishing 'us' from 'them': people within the Roman Empire simply existed, needing no such identification, whilst those beyond had to be given an ethnic identifier. This practice of labelling has encouraged modern historians to use ethnic identities – Frank, Goth and so on – as the basic categories when describing barbarian society, and for many (perhaps most) writers, the history of the late Roman and post-Roman period has been seen as the parallel histories of the various tribes which succeeded the Roman Empire. Yet such ethnonyms were not fixed or immutable. Barbarian populations were heterogeneous, and subject to continual remixing, to such an extent that we cannot see Franks, Goths and the like as distinct biological groups: these were not tribes, in the sense of political organisations built on kinship. The roots of these identities lay in a sense of belonging to a group, and perhaps sharing in its common core of legends and traditions (which were likely themselves to alter over time). There remains much disagreement over how such identities were created and recreated over time, but the fact that they were created, not simply given, is fundamental. And identity was not monolithic or exclusive. The Franks and Goths were made up of smaller groupings, such as Bructeri or Greuthingi, and so an individual presumably could have several overlapping senses of identity. This explains how politically successful groupings could 'swallow up' smaller or less successful neighbours who might then disappear from the written sources, and sometimes from the pages of history altogether.

The fact that barbarian identity was fluid explains why it has tended to prove impossible to detect ethnic boundaries. Sharp dividing lines in the material culture evident in archaeological excavations, which we would expect if different barbarian peoples were biologically and culturally distinct, are simply not there: the boundaries between peoples which we can deduce from the written sources are invisible in the archaeology. Rather, the material culture of the barbarians consists of interleaving and overlapping regional cultures, and it is impossible to relate types of burial, or dress, or settlement, to ethnic or political units. It is quite possible that some high-status goods, particularly those deposited intentionally (in burials, for example) carried a symbolic meaning, but the problem for us is decoding that meaning. Political or ethnic allegiances were not passively reflected by participation in a culture sharply distinguished from that of neighbouring peoples, but some high-status artefacts – brooches, buckles, jewellery or weapons – may have been actively used as badges of ethnic or political allegiance. The symbolism of dress and adornment was, indeed, carefully regulated by law within the Roman world. But beyond the frontier we have no written sources to reconstruct such rules, and can only rely on careful hypotheses based on the remaining finds, which come overwhelmingly from graves and reflect not the use of such badges in life but their conscious manipulation in death ritual.

So why all the fuss about ethnic identities in the first place? Most nineteenth- and twentieth-century historians saw the 'nations' of the present as direct descendents of a homogenous tribal forbear in an essentially continuous history. Whilst some theories, in which ethnic descent was linked to ideas about innate racial characteristics, are now thoroughly discredited, the sense of continuity between the barbarian peoples of the late Roman period and the nations of modern Europe is not only the preserve of extremists. Even today, textbooks and popular histories trace the Anglo-Saxons or Franks as 'our' ancestors. For the historian of the later Roman and post-Roman world, however, the realisation that barbarian 'peoples' were not tribal communities bound together by blood, but political constellations held together by human leaders who, if they were successful for long enough, might develop some rudimentary cultural homogeneity, is of paramount importance. It means that one of the most deeply embedded ways of looking at the fourth- and fifth-century barbarian world – as consisting of fixed groupings, each of whose movements affected its neighbours, producing a kind of domino effect which eventually pushed some groups into the Roman world – is mistaken. If being a Frank, or a Goth, was not a simple matter of biology, but a social identity nurtured by participation in a common culture, then changes in the ethnic or political map could occur without wholesale replacements of population through lock, stock and barrel migration. Rather, the changing ethnic geography of late antique Europe relates in the first instance to mutating configurations of power, as elites contracted and expanded their spheres of influence. This did not necessarily involve large-scale movements of population amongst those who worked the land, as opposed to the constant cycle of exile and alliance among the fluid warrior elites who exercised military and political power.

The problems of explaining the ethnic changes suggested by changing Roman terminology for the populations beyond their frontier, and of reconciling these written sources with the archaeological evidence, have been explored in particular depth by historians of the Goths. Goths first emerge as raiders of the Roman Empire in the third century, wreaking havoc from the Black Sea down to Greece, and moving both by ship and by land. From the third century onwards, Roman writers describe the populations of the area from the northern shores of the Black Sea to the lower Danube in central Europe as 'Goths'. Jordanes, the author of a history of the Goths, probably working in Constantinople in 551, traced Gothic origins back to the semi-mythical 'isle of Scandza', and then delineated a series of migrations across the Baltic, to the Black Sea and then into central Europe. Was Jordanes – who may have been drawing on an earlier sixth-century Gothic history written by Cassiodorus, a Roman advisor of the Gothic king Theodoric – repeating a Gothic oral tradition based on a dim memory of an actual migration from the islands of the Baltic or Scandinavian coast centuries earlier? Roman ethnography tended to trace barbarian origins to the frozen north, and others in Jordanes' time traced the Goths' origins to 'furthest Thule' in the northern ocean. His work needs to be read in the context of Roman ethnography, and his story of the Goths' migrations placed them firmly in the pantheon of ancient legend and myth – hence encounters with the Amazons, summarily dismissed by modern historians – and may have served to give his sixth-century Goths a pedigree as impressive as that of the Romans. This origin legend helped explain who the Goths were, and how they came to be where they were, in Jordanes' own time; it has been shown that his account distorted the political history of the Goths, overcoming the discontinuities of conquest by the Huns and migration into the empire to claim legitimating links between Theodoric's dynasty and the semi-legendary leaders of the fourth century. So it must be read first of all in its immediate context. But is it legitimate for historians to attempt to move beyond this context, by filtering out elements that they feel are improbable?[2]

Can the archaeology help? The emergence of the Goths north of the lower Danube in the fourth century is roughly contemporary with the appearance of artefact, building and burial types referred to as constituting the Chernagov culture. As the Chernagov culture grew out of, and replaced, an earlier archaeological culture, the Wielbark culture, which originated on the southern Baltic coast; this pattern of cultural change has been seen as confirming Jordanes, and providing an itinerary of Gothic migrations. There is no need, however, to see culture change as evidence for large-scale population replacement, particularly given the fact that the emergence of the Chernagov culture was slow and gradual, and that it developed out of indigenous traditions and remained interleaved and enmeshed with other idioms. There were natural nodes of contact between the Baltic and central Europe: the archaeology shows that it was along rivers such as the Vistula that objects and cultural idioms were transmitted, and that cultural influence along such channels was two-way, suggesting mechanisms such as trade, exchange and emulation as much as migration. This is not to suggest that the transmission of cultural idioms was merely a matter of fashion. The spread of cultural idioms associated with the Goths probably indicates the desire of indigenous populations to align themselves with Gothic elites. That is, behind these patterns of cultural diffusion probably lies the expanding power of an elite that identified itself as Gothic, originating on the Baltic and slowly establishing its sway across the region from the Black Sea to the lower Danube. This Gothic expansion must have involved some migration, but there is little to suggest a wholesale replacement of population. The myths reworked, for his own contemporary purposes, by Jordanes rest on an origin legend that simplified the complex processes behind the growth of Gothic power.[3]

In fact, the case of the Goths north of the Danube is typical of developments in the third and fourth centuries, with the gradual emergence of new barbarian peoples in the Roman sources, first as raiders in the third century, then as neighbours, sometimes allies and sometimes enemies, in the fourth. Along the Rhine frontier, two new peoples, the Franks to the north and the Alemans to the south, emerge; in Scotland, another new people, the Picts. Still more than with the Goths, the archaeological evidence is difficult to reconcile with wholesale tribal migrations and the physical movement of peoples, with little evidence for dramatic change, political or social. The new names used by Roman writers for their barbarian neighbours – all of which seem to reflect large-scale, inclusive confederations of smaller groups – the Franks being 'the fierce people', the Alemans 'all the people', the Picts 'the painted people' – suggest the gradual emergence of new forms of political organisation among the empire's neighbours, not a world of constant migration and movement.

Kings and farmers: barbarian social and political organisation

For all the academic debate on ethnic allegiances as political identities, developments in the social and economic organisation of the barbarian world were arguably more important in shaping late antique Europe. It is here that archaeology comes into its own, allowing a fuller understanding of barbarian society than is possible from the ethnographic stereotypes of Roman authors. Most importantly of all, archaeology gives the lie to the idea, still repeated by some modern historians, that beyond the Roman frontier laid a restless ferment of peoples on the move.

Barbarian society beyond the Roman frontier was settled and overwhelmingly sedentary. This was a world of hamlets and small villages of farmers engaged in agriculture. Settlement was characteristically reasonably scattered and small-scale – even where ecology or the concentration of power determined the concentration of human habitation, as at the elite site of Feddersen Wierde on the North Sea coast of the modern Netherlands, settlements consisted of no more than a dozen households. Archaeology and written sources for social organisation in the region under Gothic domination, in central Europe beyond the Danube, likewise suggests a world of farmer-households coming together in settlement-communities. The household was the basic unit of society, with each of the longhouses – structures typically 20m long and 5m wide – found at sites such as Feddersen Wierde, Vallhager on the north German coast, or Vorbasse in Denmark, having its own dependent structures and areas within the settlement. Such boundaries within settlements clearly indicate a property-based society, and households were large, perhaps 20 humans bound together in a patriarchal structure based on the rights of one over another. Households consisted not only of an immediate kin-group, but also more distant, dependent relatives and free and unfree labourers.[4]

Within settlements there was often a considerable fluidity of location, largely because wooden buildings tended to need to be periodically rebuilt (coastal areas where settlement was built on terps, man-made mounds, as at Feddersen Wierde, are an exception). Such settlement shift should not be confused with population migration or nomadism: it was a mechanism by which small, scattered but settled communities adapted to their environment, relocating their dwellings but cultivating and exploiting essentially the same land. And the environment played a central role in determining economic strategies. Hence the only real exceptions to the general picture of settled agriculture came in areas better suited to alternatives, a mixed economy of pastoralism alongside agricultural cultivation, as in some areas of central Europe beyond the Danube. Even the Huns, when they attempted to base their empire on the Hungarian plain, the endpoint of the Eurasian steppe, were forced to adapt their traditional nomadic economy, which was simply not viable here; contrary to nomadic traditions, Attila even set up a sedentary court.[5]

There is little backing in the archaeology for an increasing barbarian population pressing hard on Rome's frontiers. Demographic trends are more or less impossible to extract with any certainty from archaeological evidence that is inevitably fragmentary, but whilst there is clear evidence for increased complexity and wealth in barbarian society, there is no indication of large-scale demographic pressure leading to dramatic growth in the number or size of settlements. Periodic relocation was a time-honoured practice as settlements developed and evolved: it cannot be seen as evidence for lock, stock and barrel migration. There are some exceptions to this rule: coastal settlements in some areas of the North Sea coast, most famously Feddersen Wierde, were abandoned because of rising sea levels, which destroyed the delicate ecological balance on which increasingly complex and populous settlements relied. On close inspection, the idea of a dramatic population boom amongst peoples beyond the frontier derives from the pseudo-scientific ethnographical theories of classical writers, who believed that those who lived in the north showed a greater propensity to procreate on account of the cold climate.[6] The archaeological record is thus important here in rectifying received ideas based on Roman stereotypes about barbarians.

The archaeology can help us understand political organisation too, although here we inevitably are forced to rely more on Roman written sources. Certainly the archaeological record suggests that the distribution of wealth and power within barbarian society became increasingly concentrated between the third to the fifth centuries. This is evident both in the development of clearer internal hierarchies within agrarian settlements, but also in the emergence of separate, high-status, sites, suggesting the political dominance of a warrior elite. Along the upper Rhine and Danube frontiers in central and southern Germany, for example, Roman fortifications were faced by a series of hillforts, most famously the Runde Burg at Urach in modern Switzerland, many with evidence of metalworking and conspicuous consumption by resident elites. At Gennep on the upper Rhine there is evidence of a fifth-century elite residence with attached ironworking complex, again indicating the concentration of power, evident in control over labour and resources, similarly reflected in the increasing economic specialisation, and architectural scale, evident at Feddersen Wierde, where in its last phase the biggest longhouses grow in size and complexity, reaching over 40m in length.[7]

Relating these processes evident from the archaeology to the rulers and units described in the written sources is problematic. On closer investigation, the large united peoples that Roman nomenclature suggests dissolve into a welter of smaller groups and petty rulers. Thus amongst the Franks we find groups with their own, distinct, names, such as Bructeri and Hattuari, and it is quite clear that in the normal run of things there was no single ruler of the Franks, Alemans or Goths. The Aleman army whose defeat by Julian at Strasbourg in 357 is described in detail by Ammianus Marcellinus was led by a two supreme kings, Chnodomar and Serapio, and also included five lesser kings and ten princes. Whilst the relationship between Roman labels and barbarian reality is problematic, the image of a series of local rulers with effectively independent status is supported by other written sources, and is thus probably an accurate picture of barbarian politics; presumably the units ruled over by these more local leaders sustained their own identities beneath the Aleman umbrella. It was only periodically and temporarily that a particularly successful ruler might succeed in establishing some kind of personal overlordship over his neighbours – Ammianus mentions treaties and promises of booty here.[8]

A class of 'kings' was emerging at the head of an increasingly secure and powerful elite, but 'royal' power was only imperfectly institutionalised, and was thus often dependent on the support of lesser 'kings' and warrior retinues. Hence the rulers of Quadi, negotiating a treaty with Valentinian I on the Danube in 375, were forced to admit that they could not guarantee that their people would follow the terms of the treaty they, as rulers, had agreed, whilst the Gothic king Athanaric was abandoned when his rule was unsuccessful and felt to be against the public good.[9]

The basis of barbarian kingship must remain cloudy. The archaeology strongly suggests the emergence of an increasingly defined social elite, and local leaders must have had to maintain their position through winning the loyalty of this elite through gift-giving and military success. At the end of the first century, Tacitus had attempted to distinguish kings (Latin: *rex*, plural *reges*), who ruled on account of their nobility (probably implying descent), from warleaders (Latin: *dux*, plural *duces*), whose power rested on strength (Tacitus uses the highly loaded term *virtus*, literally 'virtue').[10] This passage has spawned a huge bibliography, and it has become common to see two distinct forms of political leadership, constitutionally separate, one permanent, based on birth, and with ceremonial and quasi-religious roots, the other temporary, based on military command. Such a hard and fast distinction is probably too schematic a reading of Tacitus' brief comments, which are commonplaces. But ceremonial, judicial and religious functions on one hand, and military command on the other, were doubtless the keys to political power in barbarian society. There are hints that rulers enjoyed religious or ceremonial legitimation, which underwrote their position in peacetime, notably in Ammianus' comparison of a Burgundian leader with Egyptian priest-kings.[11] But in the third, fourth and fifth centuries barbarian society was undergoing fundamental transformations which were making military leadership ever more central. In late antiquity, successful barbarian rulers, whatever their origins, were those who won in battle, and rewarded their followers in victory.

Roman frontiers and barbarian society

It was contact with Rome in peace and in war that was the central dynamic in these transformations in barbarian politics. In ideology, the Roman Empire had no boundaries, but was coterminous with the civilisation: the world has thus divided between regions conquered and civilised, and those yet to be brought within Rome's civilising yoke. But in reality, the empire had clear frontiers, and it was interaction across these frontiers that both enabled the emergence of militarised barbarian elites, and bound those elites into the Roman world, in the course of the third and fourth centuries. Whilst the Rhine and Danube were the limits of normal military presence, they were not negotiated frontiers like those of a modern state. Emperors and generals felt no qualms about passing beyond as and when military needs dictated, and there was no sense that this move involved moving from Roman soil into the sovereign territory of another regime.

In terms of military strategy, the maintenance of these limits along the Rhine and Danube were crucial. The frontier was marked by a series of fortifications and garrisons, whose maintenance was one of the emperor's most visible roles: every emperor between Diocletian and Valentinian received praise for building or repair here. The role of these emplacements was to watch, gather intelligence, and ensure Roman control of a series of strategic points and the infrastructure of roads and fortifications that joined them together. With the dispersal of field armies (*comitatus*, plural *comitatenses*) into cities in the interior, garrisons on the frontier – the *limitanei*, or frontier troops – were seldom large enough to defeat anything other than low-level raiding, head on; but they could hold out behind their fortifications

Essay

Roman goods beyond the frontier: Gudme-Lundeborg

The impact of Rome on the emergence of barbarian elites is dramatically demonstrated by a series of finds on the eastern coast of the Danish island of Funen, in the vicinity of Gudme. The discovery, in 1833, of the Broholm treasure, a gold hoard of 49 objects weighing over 4kg, first drew attention to the area. The excavation in the 1860s of a cemetery at Møllegårdsmarken confirmed that Gudme was a centre of power in the late Roman period: with around 2,300 graves from the first century BC to the fifth century AD, this is the largest as well as the wealthiest cemetery in Danish prehistory. Renewed excavation at Gudme in the 1980s has uncovered settlement sites from the second century AD through to the eighth century: as well as a wealth of small finds and hoards, bowed halls, the largest 40m long, suggest the concentration of resources.

Roman objects – notably coins (607), glass, and metal artefacts – are common at Gudme. Excavations at Lundeborg, on the coast around 4km east of Gudme, indicate how these goods were obtained. Here, a thin coastal strip 900m long has yielded a rich series of deposits, notably Roman glass products and Roman coins, beginning at the start of the third century, peaking in the fourth, contracting in the fifth but continuing into the early medieval period. Lundeborg was a beach

Figure 2.1 The Great Hall at Gudme

Figure 2.2 The Broholm Treasure

market, as more than 8,000 iron ship's rivets indicate. It was also a centre of production in metal, wood and other materials. Indeed, the large number of bracteates – gold medallions loosely inspired by Roman coins with their imperial portraits – in the Gudme area indicates their manufacture at, and distribution from, Lundeborg.

At Lundeborg, unlike Gudme, there is no evidence of permanent settlement. This was a seasonal fair, important for both the import of Roman goods and for craft production. This was presumably controlled by the inhabitants of Gudme, who were thus able to exercise a monopoly over the circulation of high-status goods across much of southern Scandinavia. This monopoly may have rested on religious as well as political power. Gudme itself means 'home of the gods', and the surrounding hills are named Gudbjerg, 'hill of the gods', Galdbjerg, 'hill of sacrifice', and Albjerg, 'hill of the shrine'. The rich hoard evidence probably indicates the ritual deposition of wealth in this religious context. The bracteates have been seen as depicting scenes from religious myths, with the insignia of Roman imperial portraiture – notably the diadem – influencing the depiction of mythological figures.

whilst a full-scale response was organised. In the mid-350s, for example, when an Aleman force was able to establish control over a huge swathe of territory from the Rhine west into central Gaul, Roman frontier forces were able to hold out in their fortifications, some for several years, until Julian was able to mount an effective campaign to drive the Alemans back over the Rhine.[12]

Maintaining the frontier was not just a matter of military might and defensive strategy: political management of the barbarian rulers beyond the frontier was just as important, and of course immeasurably cheaper. There was a carefully managed flow of 'gifts' to barbarian rulers beyond the frontier. This strategy was followed just as much in times of Roman strength as in moments where Roman attention was diverted elsewhere, its beauty being that the line between the buying of continued peace and the reward of friendly clients was always blurred. Where possible, the empire required the handing over of the children of barbarian rulers into Roman hands; not only did the children act as hostages guaranteeing the future good behaviour of their parents, but they also received an education in Roman ways which they would not forget when they returned home. The Aleman king Mederic, for example, 'was initiated into certain Greek mysteries [the religious cult of Mithras, popular among soldiers] during a long period as a hostage in Gaul'.[13] Where these more subtle forms of persuasion proved unsuccessful, more interventionist forms of political management were necessary: potentially dangerous or hostile barbarian rulers might find themselves the objects of Roman military expeditions designed to ravage their homeland and force their submission. However Roman diplomacy also stretched to more underhand stratagems, such as paying friendly clients to attack dangerous neighbours, or even political assassination.

Even in political terms, then, the frontier was as much a zone of interaction as a line of demarcation. Exchange was particularly intense in cultural and economic terms. The penetration of Roman goods amongst indigenous elites, and the creation of political, cultural and social ties between these elites and the empire had preceded the original Roman conquest of many of the empire's western provinces. The end of Roman expansion had not ended the propensity of elites beyond the imperial frontier to look to Rome in such a way. The quantity of Roman goods in the archaeological record follows a gradually declining gradient the further we move beyond the frontier. In the immediate hinterland of the frontier, in those regions congruent with the empire, the penetration of Roman goods (and so presumably Roman contacts and ideas) was widespread. Deeper into the barbarian world, beyond the immediate hinterland of the frontier, Roman goods were more scarce, and their circulation was easier for the elite to control: they served as symbols of power, pure and simple. For example, bracteates – coin-shaped medallions bearing depictions of Roman emperors – served as badges of status in northern Germany and southern Scandinavia. This economically 'irrational' use of Roman goods should serve as a reminder that not all exchange across the frontier took the form of trade made for profit. Even close to the frontier, it may be that many Roman status symbols were originally gifts made in return for political support. And whilst trade with the empire clearly was socially and economically an important force in the barbarian communities close to the frontier, it was not something which necessarily operated independently of political factors. Favoured leaders were able to monopolise economic, as well as political and social, contact with the empire, in order to entrench their own position and in return for supporting their Roman allies.

In other words, we can detect a whole series of symbiotic relationships between the empire and barbarian leaders beyond the frontier. The taking of plunder and tribute, when placed in the context of recurrent Roman alliances and subsidies, looks less like a statement of conquering intent, than an attempt to acquire Roman goods through force by those refused peaceable access. After all, Roman friendship was not bestowed disinterestedly. The moral economy of obligation was carefully manipulated to ensure that a pliable balance of power was maintained beyond the frontier. The emergence of a paramount barbarian leader, such as Chnodomar of the Alemans, was a sign of the failure of Roman policy: competition between smaller barbarian rulers, each wanting Roman backing to enhance their prestige, was the goal.

Interaction across the frontier had the effect of producing a fairly homogenous cultural zone that straddled the political boundary, including the peripheral provinces of the empire and those barbarian communities immediately congruent with the frontier. The Rhine and Danube, whilst excellent linear boundaries, instantly identifiable and easily defensible, did not mark fundamental geographical, social or topographical divides. They were places of contact with an organic hinterland on both banks. It is thus scarcely surprising that the frontier needed constant military maintenance. Throughout the third and fourth centuries, whenever imperial attention was elsewhere or troops were withdrawn, rulers from the barbarian bank of the Rhine began, almost invisibly, to make their sway felt within the empire, in a natural political extension of cultural, economic and social ties. By the fifth century, the military maintenance of the Rhine frontier by Roman troops was effectively abandoned and the process allowed to continue uninterrupted. It could, indeed, be argued that it was the constant intervention of emperors and Roman field armies which made the politics of the frontier so unstable and conflict-ridden, as Roman military and diplomatic activity had the effect of keeping the barbarian side of the frontier divided and politically unstable. Certainly it was the Roman government's determination to maintain its frontiers that led to the militarisation of both provincial society and barbarian elites.

The emergence in northern Gaul, southern Germany and along the Danube, of cultural and social units that straddled the frontier is one of the most striking examples of the rise of regionalism within the late empire. Links across the frontier, between barbarian societies and Roman provinces, were strong. Hence when Julian was despatched to Gaul as Constantius II's Caesar, one problem he faced was the sheer difficulty of tracking down the troops of the Frankish and Aleman kings who extended their kingdoms over the Rhine. Such were their links with the provincial society over which they ruled that they could simply disappear into it. It took two years of concerted military action, the ravaging of Frankish and Aleman centres immediately beyond the Rhine, and significant refortification, to reassert a linear political boundary. Whether those dwelling in Roman frontier provinces would have seen such events as restoration of Roman 'order' against a barbarian 'threat' must be doubted, not least given the barbarian origin of Julian's crack troops.

Significantly, one part of this settlement was the recognition that some barbarians at least were a part of Roman provincial society. The Frankish leader Charietto, for example, was allowed to settle around Trier, and became a Roman general guaranteeing the security of the province in which he now had a stake.[14]

This mixed barbarian-provincial frontier culture should not be seen solely in terms of 'barbarisation' within the empire. The potent and ultimately inseparable intermingling of barbarian and provincial drew on the attractions of Roman culture for barbarian elites. Such interaction did not only occur because of the exchange of goods and ideas across the frontier. As the third century had seen Roman withdrawal from positions beyond the Rhine in central Germany, and beyond the Danube and along the western coast of the Black Sea, many barbarian neighbours lived in former Roman provinces. Beyond the Rhine barbarians lived in houses 'carefully built in Roman fashion', whilst Christianity was exported beyond the Danube thanks to the imperial sponsored mission of Ulfilas, a priest whose parents had been Roman provincials in the area now settled by the Goths.[15]

The most crucial factor in the interaction between barbarian and Roman along the empire's frontiers was, however, the Roman use of barbarian soldiers. In the fourth century, barbarians were by far the best source of recruits for the Roman military. The enlisting of barbarian warriors into the Roman army was not a new practice: defeated enemies had often been forcibly recruited in the past, and campaigning along and beyond the frontier often proved the quickest and easiest way for fourth-century emperors to recruit battle-hardened troops for immediate use. Other barbarians voluntarily entered the imperial army, recognising the opportunities for enrichment and status it opened up. There were well-established processes for the reception and processing of such groups of recruits. Like all Roman soldiers, their weapons and equipment were state property, and they were carefully deployed and absorbed into Roman units. It is possible to overstate the degree of 'barbarisation' within the regular Roman army – the most recent attempt to quantify it, concentrating on named individuals in the officer classes, has suggested that perhaps a quarter of fourth-century Roman soldiers were of 'barbarian' origin. What these origins meant is less clear. They were not easily forgotten: Julian could insist that 'hardship was not inflicted on men who had left their homes across the Rhine on express condition that they should never be sent beyond the Alps', and acknowledged that his crack troops were recruited from 'sons of barbarians born on this side of the Rhine or of parents who came over to our side'. This did not make barbarian soldiers potential fifth columnists, especially given the lack of unity amongst the empire's barbarian neighbours and the opportunities opened up by imperial service. Even when there were accusations that three high-ranking Roman officers of barbarian origin had sent a 'secret warning' about an imminent campaign to their compatriots, the result was not an ambush of Roman forces but a series of barbarian ambassadors begging for peace. Similarly, when another officer of barbarian origin found himself facing execution as a result of false charges brought by his rivals, he decided that to return to his homeland was too dangerous as 'his fellow-countrymen the Franks would either kill him or take a bribe to hand him back'.[16]

The army was a real melting pot of influences, which were moulded in a barbarised military culture. In the fourth century, Roman army units adopted mock, or occasionally real, 'tribal' names, and war cries reminiscent of those favoured by barbarian warriors across the Rhine. Armies which had backed losers in civil wars were often said to have gone 'barbarian' in dress and attitudes. When, following victories over the Franks and Alemans, the Caesar Julian was proclaimed Augustus by his troops at Paris, he was raised on a shield in what is normally seen as a classic 'barbarian' ritual, here emerging in the context of a Roman army itself consisting overwhelmingly of provincial and barbarian troops. Julian, of course, was a Roman emperor leading an official Roman army, but the political culture within which he found himself in fourth-century Gaul had more in common with that of his barbarian opponents across the Rhine than he would have happily admitted.[17]

Adrianople and its aftermath: Goths and Romans in the late fourth century

After the barbarian invasions of the third century, the military, provincial emperors of the fourth century successfully maintained the Rhine–Danube frontier. Barbarian inroads typically came about when internal politics diverted imperial attention and Roman armies elsewhere. The last quarter of the fourth century, however, is normally seen as marking a new departure in Roman policy towards the barbarians, with one group of Goths admitted into the empire to supplement Roman military forces, and becoming an increasingly important ingredient in the complex politics of the time. The immediate context for these events was the destruction of the carefully maintained political balance beyond the Danube frontier. The growing power of the Huns was disrupting the Gothic polities that had maintained a status quo beyond the Danube and along the shores of the Black Sea for over a century. The Huns, drawing on the manpower of the recently defeated Alans, forced the collapse of 'the rich and extensive realm of Ermanaric, a warlike king whose many exploits had made him a terror to his neighbours' in the Ukraine. Although the remnants of Ermanaric's Greuthungi continued to resist, even hiring Hunnic mercenaries, the Tervingi of Athanaric were next to be defeated. Gothic elites faced an uncertain future, pressure from the Huns in the northeast was matched by Roman pressure in the southwest. In the 360s and 370s Valentinian and Valens had expended considerable energy and resources campaigning along and beyond the Rhine and Danube frontiers, destabilising the extant pattern of barbarian political leadership with an interventionist military policy, and a decrease in the quantity of diplomatic gifts. As the first emperors since the beginning of the century not to be descended from the house of Constantine, Valentinian and Valens needed military victories and a hard line on barbarians to maintain internal support. They also faced civilian pressure to reduce military spending.[18]

One result of this new Roman policy was that Gothic influence across the frontier was curtailed. To enter the empire, Goths needed to go through the official channels and enter Roman service. And by 376, presumably as a result of the disturbed conditions beyond the Danube, some Gothic groups were pressing hard for admission into the empire, to serve as soldiers or settlers and so regain Roman favour. Such recruitment and settlement was common, and one of the key mechanisms through which the empire replenished its military manpower. There were well-established processes through which such immigrants were processed and integrated into the Roman world, and Goths had been frequent Roman allies since at least their involvement in support of Licinius in the civil wars of the early fourth century. The Roman response in 376 was thus to accept some groups – notably those whose homelands were distant – but to refuse entry to others who were neighbours. Tried and tested strategies were used to maintain control over the entrants, ensuring their reliance on the imperial government and its agents, and despatching them away from the immediate vicinity of the frontier.

The reception of these Gothic immigrants soon, however, went awry. Problems began because of corrupt and incompetent officials on the ground, which meant that some were not 'processed' properly but were able to smuggle weapons across the border, along with their belongings and families piled on wagons. Shortages of supplies allied to profiteering incensed the immigrants. Eventual rebellion was followed by the dispersal of the Goths, who now simply disappeared into provincial society, with which they presumably had long-standing ties. Roman garrisons maintained control of the key strategic points along the frontiers and roads, and the Roman field armies from the east and west were soon converging on the Balkans. By 378 matters were under control and the Gothic rebels would have been mopped up and reprocessed were it not for the decision of the eastern emperor, Valens, to attempt to tackle the Goths alone rather than wait for the forces despatched by Gratian from the west, in the confident hope of gaining the credit unshared. But Valens fatally miscalculated and the Goths at their encampment just outside Adrianople decimated his army and killed him.[19]

Adrianople was a serious defeat, but the decision of Ammianus Marcellinus to use it as the end-point of his narrative, and thus avoid a potentially delicate discussion of the reign of the current emperor Theodosius, should not lead us to exaggerate its long-term significance. Ammianus sets up Valens as an object of criticism, and builds up a sense of foreboding by beginning his account of Goths and Huns with omens of death and disaster, and working up the defeat to round off his work: 'No battle in our history except Cannae was such a massacre, though more than once the Romans have been the playthings of fortune and suffered temporary reverses.'[20] In fact, the Goths, even in victory, sought to do no more than settle on their own terms within Roman provincial society in the Balkans, across the Danube from their previous homeland. And even the destruction of the eastern field army and emperor did not leave Rome at the mercy of the Goths: the remaining Balkan units plus the field army sent from the west were soon able to contain the Goths and slowly mop up Gothic resistance. Theodosius, a member of a celebrated western military dynasty from Hispania and the most senior Roman military officer available, was raised to the eastern throne in 379. The praetorian prefecture of Illyricum, who governed the Danube frontier and the Balkans, was transferred from its traditional subordination to the western emperor to the eastern court at Constantinople as part of the deal. Throughout the 380s Roman control of the frontier was maintained, with treaties with different Gothic groups reached in 380 and 382, and further Goths who had sought, and been refused, entry into the empire being defeated in 386.

Those Goths who had already entered the empire were allowed to settle in the Balkans. Unfortunately, relatively little is known about the terms agreed. Traditionally, they have been seen as marking a crucial new departure, as the first time a barbarian grouping was allowed to settle wholesale and maintain its own political structure within the empire. This view is influenced by hindsight, in that the descendants of the Goths settled in the 380s were, by the fifth century, to become a 'federate' people settled within the empire. The terms may have been less revolutionary than is normally suggested, with Gothic settlement in the Balkans acknowledged in return for military service, a pattern that had been practised, successfully, with many other defeated barbarian groups in the past. The Goths had forced Rome to allow their settlement in an area with which they had long-standing ties, but even this was not unprecedented: groups of Franks had been settled in a similar manner along the lower Rhine earlier in the fourth century, for example. In any case, the settlement of 382 marked a final clearing up of the mess left over by the mishandled Gothic immigration of 376, and the definitive re-establishment of the frontier. We cannot trace a direct link of cause-and-effect between the disaster at Adrianople, or the decision to settle what remained of the Goths who crossed the frontier in 376 in the Balkans, and the fatal problems faced by the western empire in the fifth century.

The eagerness with which Theodosius came to terms with the Goths after 376 highlights the size of the real problem posed by the defeat at Adrianople: the decimation of the core of the eastern army and the resultant shortage of soldiers. Theodosius' armies came with him from the west, and were supplemented by adopting the traditional practices of campaigning along and beyond the frontiers to defeat and then recruit battle-hardened barbarian warriors into the Roman army. Thus the eastern forces were replenished, but at the expense of the west. The Goths settled in the Balkans, indeed played a significant part on Theodosius' side in civil wars in 388 and 394. This demonstration of the fact that as barbarians they were relatively trustworthy, and unlikely to involve themselves in internal plots, meant that Theodosius had no interest in driving them back beyond the frontier.

Emperors, usurpers and barbarians: the crisis of the western empire

The last decades of the fourth century saw continued internal crisis within the empire, with recurrent usurpers in the west and heightened tension between west and east. The end result, in the context of limited Roman military resources, was the erosion of Roman defences in the west until, by the end of the first decade of the fifth century, the western provinces ignited in a blaze of usurpations and barbarian invasions. The first sign of crisis was the overthrow of the western emperor, Gratian, in 383 by the usurper Magnus Maximus, a military leader who claimed to be one of Theodosius' kinsmen. Beginning in Britain, Maximus' revolt soon gathered support in Gaul and Hispania, with Gratian being defeated and killed. Theodosius attempted to come to terms, acknowledging Maximus' control of Britain and Gaul, but attempting to have Gratian's son, Valentinian II, acknowledged emperor in the western Mediterranean.

But in 387 Maximus invaded Italy and then marched east through Pannonia; his eventual defeat in 388 involved the further decimation of the western army, which had been the bedrock of his support. It also left the western empire vulnerable, as barbarians took advantage of the denuding of Roman frontier defences and the political vacuum in the provinces to exert their sway across the frontier. The savage reprisals meted out on those involved in a further attempted western usurpation in 392–4, when the master of the soldiers Arbogast, himself of barbarian extraction, backed Eugenius in opposition to Theodosius' infant son Honorius, left military resources in the west stretched thinner still. Political pressure, meanwhile, made spending on the army an obvious target. The imperial court's concern with dynastic security and the primacy of internal conflicts with Constantinople left the western provinces denuded of military protection. As a result, provincial elites backed usurpers who could offer patronage and effective protection. In response, emperors and would-be emperors became reliant on the ability of military leaders to recruit and reward barbarian armies to prosecute civil war. These problems had not been caused by Adrianople and its aftermath, but were a result of structural problems within the western empire.

Military weakness in the west was a result of imperial politics, and particularly the dominance within the empire of Constantinople, seat of Theodosius' regime, over the west. What is striking already in the 380s is the evident dissatisfaction of western elites who backed the usurpers Maximus and Eugenius. Western aristocracies had always been wont to revolt when they were not granted an able, adult, emperor, active militarily and politically in their provinces. Whilst Theodosius' own family and military roots gave his regime considerable western support, he was geographically distant, and the dynastic succession of the infant Valentinian II did not meet provincial expectations. Theodosius' own determination to found his own dynasty further highlighted this mismatch. Dynastic concerns, and particularly the increasing importance of Constantinople, meant that western emperors were increasingly based in northern Italy – Milan emerged as Theodosius' favoured place in the west – rather than in the provinces beyond the Alps.

It may have been the demands of dynastic security and the ending of imperial presence beyond the Alps which led to the rise to political prominence of a new figure, who was to become typical of the last century of western Roman politics: the master of the soldiers. Under inexperienced infant or civilian emperors, the key imperial role in military leadership had to be delegated, hence the emergence of new, more powerful, generals, such as Arbogast, the dominant political figure in the west under Valentinian II. That Arbogast and his successors were overwhelmingly of barbarian origin may reflect the increasing role of barbarians within Roman armies, but it also had important political implications. A barbarian military leader, no matter how successful, could not aspire to the purple and so was not likely to become another Magnus Maximus. Hence the promotion of barbarian masters of the soldiers provided the imperial dynasty with a measure of political security. Barbarian masters could indeed be made honorary members of the imperial dynasty through marriage, as was the case with Theodosius' favoured eastern general, Stilicho, who was married to the emperor's daughter.

The success of this strategy in securing Theodosius' dynasty is self-evident: on his death in 395, the succession of his sons – Arcadius in the east, Honorius in the west – was uncontested. Power turned on control of their courts, and above all on control of Constantinople, whose political dominance within the empire as a whole was assured: Stilicho thus claimed to have been asked by the dying emperor to act as guardian for his sons. Struggles within the court establishment led to the exclusion of Stilicho from Constantinople. Thereafter, Stilicho's effective control of the west thanks to his military command was subordinated to recurrent attempts to gain control of Constantinople and thus the empire as a whole. The denouement of the political struggle between Stilicho and the eastern regime reflects the extent to which imperial politics was now played out in the Mediterranean, between Italy and Constantinople. It also underlines the extent to which east–west division had become a profound reality, and struggles for control of two strategically key provinces, the Balkans and Africa, played a central role in the rivalry. Just as control of Africa centred on the figure of the military leader Gildo, in the Balkans, the leaders of the eastern regime – the eunuch Eutropius and the Gothic general Gainas – used the Gothic leader Alaric to mobilise against Stilicho. But a shaking out within the eastern regime in 399–400, with first Eutropius deposed, and then Gainas and his Gothic soldiers massacred, found Alaric removed from Roman employ. Apparently, the eastern regime was now strong enough politically and militarily to lessen its reliance on barbarian contingents, and those who staged the coup were roundly critical of the reliance on barbarian military allies which had underlain Roman strategy for the previous decade. The rich and populous Near Eastern provinces allowed the regime to fund and recruit a regular army which was supplemented but not replaced by barbarian warbands.

Significantly, after the upheaval of 399–400, Alaric and his followers felt unable to return to the previous arrangement of settlement in the Balkans, as by now they were wholly reliant on employment in Roman military service. As a result, once negotiations with Constantinople had failed, in 402 Alaric staged an invasion of Italy, seeking office for himself and supplies for his men from the western regime, but was driven back into the Balkans. His campaign caused sufficient panic to lead to the removal of the court of the western emperor, Honorius, from Milan to Ravenna, where it was to remain, safe behind an almost impregnable screen of marshes, until the end of the western empire. By 407, Stilicho had hired Alaric as a Roman general, offering the legitimacy, cash and supplies which were always Alaric's goals, with an eye on launching an attack on Stilicho's enemies in Constantinople. Although we describe Alaric's army as 'Goths', there were clearly significant differences between a traditional warband recruited beyond the frontier by a native Gothic leader seeking wealth and glory in war against Rome in time-honoured fashion, and Alaric's troops. We cannot know precisely who followed Alaric, although those Gothic immigrants settled in the Balkans in the 370s and 380s and their descendants clearly played a dominant role. Alaric first rose to prominence in 392, as the rebellious leader of one group of Goths garrisoned on the Danube frontier, which sought to plunder the plains they were meant to protect. We do know, however, that a kaleidoscope of other groups – provincials seeking fame or fortune through a military career, runaway slaves, the remnants of defeated armies and barbarians groups – were swallowed up in the 'Goths' in the course of the 390s, 400s and 410s. And Alaric's position was essentially that of a military commander, reinforced by military success and based on military discipline and the recognition, at various times, of various Roman regimes. It must have borne little resemblance to Gothic traditions of political leadership beyond the empire, before 376. In the Roman sources, when Alaric had the recognition of a legitimate source of Roman authority, he was a Roman general leading his followers within the Roman army; he was only 'king of the Goths' when Roman legitimation was lacking. Alaric's Goths may have identified themselves with reference to those men and women who crossed the Danube in 376, but in reality they were shaped by the experience of militarisation and mobilisation at the behest of the Roman government and under the leadership of Alaric.

The prominence of Alaric and his following in the struggle between Stilicho and the eastern government, once again underlines the lack of Roman military resources. At several points in Alaric's career – in 392, 395 and 397 – he was effectively defeated by Roman troops, but he was too valuable as an ally against rivals to be simply eliminated. What Roman army there was in the west – essentially Stilicho's own forces – was itself made up of a heterogeneous mix of provincials and barbarians recruited in the civil wars of the 380s and 390s, often from the remnants of defeated forces. The primary difference between Alaric's and Stilicho's armies was in identity, not infrastructure or origin: in spite of his barbarian origin, Stilicho's status as master of the soldiers was unambiguous, and new recruits were absorbed into a force with a long-established identity as a Roman army. The denuding of the Roman field army in the west led to further estrangement between provincial elites and the imperial government, already presaged in the eager provincial support for local usurpers in the 380s and 390s. Whereas in the fourth century military emperors of provincial origin had ruled from the frontier, now provincial elites lacked both imperial patronage and military protection, as generals used their military followings to win political influence at the courts of Ravenna and Constantinople.

The dangers of such a situation were obvious. The political vacuum in the provinces invited both barbarian intervention, and encouraged provincial backing for usurpers. In the winter of 406–7 – as Stilicho and Alaric planned an expedition against Constantinople – the imperial government's tenuous hold on the western provinces collapsed. A series of barbarian warbands – Vandals, Sueves and Alans – crossed the Rhine, taking advantage of the absence of any meaningful Roman military presence. This is often seen as the inevitable result of abnormal climatic conditions, with the freezing of the Rhine unleashing a horde of barbarians into the empire. What is far more relevant is that just the year before, Stilicho had used barbarian contingents of a similar derivation to defend Italy against a barbarian invasion led by the Goth Radagaisus, and that the leaders of these groups may have been hungry for further service and supplies. The military crisis coincided with a new wave of attempted usurpations, beginning in Britain in 406. By 407 the military leader Constantine III crossed from Britain to Gaul, where he attracted considerable support, as he did from Hispania, where there had been unrest since 404. He was to remain *de facto* ruler of the west until 411, with the active support of bishops and provincial elites as well as barbarian allies. The Vandals, Alans and

Sueves were called into Hispania in the course of a dispute between Constantine's supporters, a rival faction which supported Honorius, and another usurper, Maximus, whilst Constantine himself allied with Gaul's immediate barbarian neighbours, the Franks and Alemans. His defeat at Arles in 411 was thus a battle between three rival Roman claimants to the purple, each using barbarian allies to supply military muscle.[21]

The provincial support offered to Constantine was compounded by imperial inaction on account of a long-drawn-out power struggle at the heart of the western government. The Roman Senate, wary of Stilicho's military power, refused to approve the funds (4000 pounds of gold) necessary to ensure the continued service of Alaric's Goths. The senate's intransigence shows how marginal the provinces appeared to the rulers of Italy by the beginning of the fifth century. After the murder of Stilicho in 408, and an attempted purge of the barbarian troops on whom he had relied, Alaric attempted to reopen negotiations himself, blockading Rome in an attempt to secure supplies and Stilicho's former position as master of the soldiers. When the title was not forthcoming – the Emperor Honorius, safe in Ravenna, was immune to the pressure – Alaric returned to Rome, seized the emperor's sister, Galla Placidia, and had the Senator Priscus Attalus, proclaimed emperor. Alaric, desperate for the supplies necessary to maintain his troops, considered securing them by embarking to North Africa, the source of the grain and other supplies that fed Rome and central Italy. When this ploy failed, Alaric turned his troops on Rome, which was sacked for three days and nights. But it still proved impossible to reach any permanent deal with the Roman government, and, after a further attempt to cross to Africa, the Goths finally left Italy in 412 under the leadership of Alaric's successor and brother-in-law, Athaulf.

The so-called 'sack of Rome' sent shockwaves through the contemporary world, and remains one of the best-known events in world history.[22] Yet in fact its destructive impact was relatively limited. Rome was not razed, nor did it suffer sustained damage, as Alaric maintained control of his troops, who were allowed three days plundering of the city. The shock caused by Alaric's actions arose from the symbolic significance of Rome, and the lack of any precedent for its seizure by an enemy. It was deepened by the ideology of eternal victory – the idea that Rome was by definition always and eternally victorious – that had long been promulgated by emperors, and was rooted deep in Roman identity as a justification for world empire. In fact, the most important effect of Alaric's actions in 410 was to provoke a bout of soul searching, and a controversy between those who saw the calamity as the result of the loss of the protection of Rome's traditional gods, and their Christian opponents. Hence Orosius, with whom this book began, argued that Rome had suffered disaster in pagan times, too, and the empire had been created by God to facilitate the universal spread of Christianity. His teacher, Augustine, in his *City of God* likewise dismissed the view that paganism, rather than God's will, had led to Roman success, but sought to present the universal Christian church – the city of God – as something which was not reliant on any merely temporal order or earthly city.

In fact, the events of 410 graphically show how different the realities of late Roman politics were from the traditional view of hordes of barbarians smashing their way into the empire bent on destruction. Alaric's career, after all, was spent either in, or seeking, official service as a Roman general. Throughout, his primary aim was the provisioning of his troops, where possible by negotiation with the imperial government but when this proved impossible through plundering. In spite of his unquestioned military dominance, Alaric's wholesale dependence on the Roman infrastructure for supplies, allied to the impregnability of the Emperor Honorius at Ravenna, allowed the imperial government to remain unmoving and tough out the crisis until the Goths had no choice but to leave Italy.

It was Constantius III, the Roman general who was appointed by Honorius to serve as master of the soldiers after Stilicho, who played the crucial role in re-establishing order. Constantius and his allies had been victorious over the usurpers Constantine III and Maximus at Arles in 411. Soon after, a further rash of usurpers appeared in the troubled western provinces. The most successful, the senator Jovinus, was proclaimed emperor on the Rhine frontier in 411, with the backing of another barbarian grouping, the Burgundians. The western government relied on the Goths, by now under the leadership of Alaric's successor Athaulf, to eliminate Jovinus in 413. Unrest in the province of Africa culminated in 413 with a failed invasion of Italy led by Heraclianus. The Theodosian dynasty was now unchallenged by provincial usurpers. But the position of the various barbarian groupings that remained the dominant military powers in the provinces needed regularising. In 414–15 an agreement was reached with Athaulf and the Goths in which they became effectively the Roman government's preferred barbarian allies: this was the context for Ataulf's marriage to Galla Placidia. Constantius, meanwhile, secured his links with the imperial dynasty through his own marriage to Galla Placidia in 417 (Athaulf having died in the meantime), effectively ruling the western empire and briefly serving as co-emperor before his death in 421.

The crisis of 407–13 was severe, and the western empire as effectively re-established under Honorius by Constantius III looked very different from that of Theodosius. It is natural to attempt to explain such a drama with reference to the sudden intervention of an external force, in this case the barbarian invasion of 406–7. Modern historians have tended to go back beyond the immediate events of 406–7, seeing barbarian success then as indicative of Roman military weakness in the west, and an over-reliance on barbarian recruits and increasingly barbarian allies. The defeat at Adrianople in 376 is frequently seen as the immediate root of both phenomena. In many interpretations, the image of the Huns relentlessly marauding through the barbarian world, driving their victims west and thus increasing pressure on Roman frontiers, unites both the events of 376 and 406. Relentless Hun pressure, however, rests on fragmentary and so necessarily inconclusive evidence. Whilst it might explain the predicament of the Goths in 376, it cannot explain subsequent Roman strategy, which maintained the integrity of the frontier, and no contemporary source makes a direct link between Hunnic campaigning and the invasion of 406–7.

As for Roman military weakness in the west, there is little doubt that there were real problems here. But the endemic western usurpations of the late fourth century must have played a more direct role than Adrianople in leading to such a state of affairs, as must problems with the regular mechanisms of recruitment and replenishment. And it may have been as much a lack of will as a lack of forces on the part of the Roman government that allowed the invasion of 406–7: witness the initial success of Frankish federates in resisting the invaders, and the fact that the forces of a handful of local aristocrats could hold back the Vandals and Sueves from crossing into Hispania for some considerable time in 409. It is certainly worth comparing the lack of concerted governmental action to defend the western provinces after 407 with the successful defence of Italy against the barbarian invasion led by Radagaisus in 405. When the western empire's Italian heartland was threatened, the imperial court and the senate were willing to do what was necessary to ensure their security. When it was the provinces which were under pressure, civilian distrust of military men with their barbarised ways came to the fore, and so in 408 the purging of Stilicho and his barbarian troops took precedence over the clearing of barbarians from the western provinces, which in any case supported the usurper Constantine III. When the imperial government did react to events in the western provinces, it was in response to the threat posed by the usurper Constantine III, who by 410 was in a secure enough position at Arles to challenge Honorius' control of Italy.

The real problem facing the western empire was the disjuncture between the senatorial elite, with its interest focused on Italy and its Mediterranean hinterland, and the provinces. When, after the 380s, emperors increasingly retreated to the Italian centre that was crucial in maintaining their hold on power, and increasingly left military leadership in the hands of the generals, they became part of this civilian elite. Military leaders, schooled in a provincial, barbarised frontier culture, remained necessary, but looked out of place in the world of the palace and the senate. In 382, the wearing of military dress within the city of Rome had been outlawed; in 397 and 399, the wearing of trousers, a barbarian habit adopted within the army, was likewise banned; and in 416 another aspect of barbarian-military fashion, long hair, was likewise prohibited on pain of exile.[23] And the retreat of the imperial court into civilian society in Italy left the provinces denuded of patronage and protection, hence the endemic problem of provincial usurpers. The fact that the invaders of 406–7 were not the empire's immediate neighbours, but groups whose homes lay further within the barbarian world, suggests that they too may have been reacting to the withdrawal of the imperial court to Italy. Barbarians along the frontier sought to maintain the status quo and the links and influence across the frontier this allowed. Meanwhile the withdrawal of the imperial court and the field army to Italy left barbarian rulers in the interior denuded of opportunities of reward by the empire and service in the empire, eventually forcing them to attempt to enter the Roman world.

All in all, then, we can see the crisis of the western empire at the beginning of the fifth century as the result of a series of problems within the western regime, an internal crisis into which barbarians, so long the objects of Roman diplomacy, were sucked. The fracture between the imperial court and senatorial elite on the one hand, and the provinces on the other, with the military and its barbarian allies straddled between, was peculiar to the west. In the east, a homogenous ruling class and a more harmonious interface between the imperial centre and the provinces allowed the government to maintain a viable military and control barbarian allies. Hence the eastern government was able to eliminate Gainas' Goths quite ruthlessly in 399–400 without leaving itself lacking adequate military protection, having the Goths rounded up and butchered in Constantinople. Contrast the pained western crisis of 407–12, centring as it did on imperial and senatorial distrust of Stilicho, Alaric and the barbarian military establishment, tempered by the lack of any alternative source of military power in the west.

Bibliographical essay

Translated sources

Ammianus Marcellinus (see bibliography for previous chapter) is by far the best contemporary account of political and military dealings with the barbarians, not least as Ammianus himself had served on the western frontier. The classic work for previous generations, Tacitus' *Germania*, ed. and tr. M. Winterbottom (Oxford, 1986), needs handling with care on account of its first-century date and polemical use of ethnography to criticise contemporary Roman mores. Other than that, there is little other than asides in panegyrics recounting imperial victories, and in narrative sources. J. Matthews and P. Heather, *The Goths in the Fourth Century* (Liverpool, 1992) collects what is available for the best documented sector of the frontier.

Barbarian society and barbarian invasions

H. Wolfram, *The Roman Empire and its Germanic Peoples* (Chicago, 1998) is by far the best survey, by an acknowledged expert; the uninitiated reader should know that Wolfram himself has devoted a lifetime to developing the theories presented here, and his views on the essential continuity of barbarian elites and their identities and cultures probably occupy a middle place in the spectrum of current opinion. P. Geary, *The Ethnic Origins of Europe: The Peoples of Europe in the Early Middle Ages* (Princeton, 2001) gives a brilliantly suggestive overview, whilst older studies such as E. A. Thompson's *Romans and Barbarians* (Madison, WI, 1982) and L. Musset, *The Germanic Invasions* (London, 1975), although useful, are now seriously flawed on account of their dated understanding of the nature of barbarian groupings.

On the ideologically charged presentations of barbarians in Roman historical writing see G. Ladner, 'On Roman attitudes towards barbarians in late antiquity', *Viator* 7 (1986); also W. R. Jones, 'The image of the barbarian in medieval Europe', *Comparative Studies in Society and History* 13 (1971); B. Shaw, '"Eaters of flesh, drinkers of milk": the ancient Mediterranean ideology of the pastoral nomad', *Ancient Society* 13/14 (1982/3); P. Heather, 'The barbarian in late antiquity: ideal, reality and transformation', in R. Miles, ed., *Constructing Identities in Late Antiquity* (London, 1999).

The work of W. Goffart is fundamental in having exploded a number of received ideas: see particularly 'The theme of THE barbarian invasions in late antique and modern historiography', in E. Chyrsos and A. Schwarcz, ed., *Das Reich und die Barbaren* (Vienna, 1989), reprinted in his *Rome's Fall and After* (London, 1989).

The main focus of recent controversy has been the extent to which ethnic identities were reshaped by the process of migration and settlement. On 'ethnogenesis', most debate has centred around the case of the Goths and the literature cited on them, as well as the work of Amory on Burgundians and Ostrogoths (see bibliography for next chapter); but see also on Alemans and Franks H. Hummer, 'The fluidity of barbarian identity: Alemanni and Suebi, AD200–500', *Early Medieval Europe* 7 (1998) and his article 'Franks and Alemanni: a discontinuous ethnogenesis?', in I. Wood, ed., *Franks and Alemanni in the Migration Period* (Leiden, 1999). The best general discussions are H. Wolfram, 'Gothic history and historical ethnography', *Journal of Medieval History* 7 (1981), H. Wolfram and W. Pohl, eds, *Typen der Ethnogenese* (Vienna, 1990); and in particular the work of W. Pohl: 'Conceptions of ethnicity in early medieval studies', *Archaeologia Polona* 29 (1991), reprinted in B. Rosenwein and L. Little, eds, *Debating the Middle Ages* (London, 1998), and W. Pohl and H. Reimitz, eds, *Strategies of Distinction: The Construction of Ethnic Communities 300–800* (Leiden, 1998). For an archaeologically informed approach see also G. Halsall, 'Mover and shakers', *Early Medieval Europe* 8 (1999). It is also instructive to compare the debate amongst specialists on barbarian 'peoples' with the parallel arguments about the nature of ethnicity being advanced by late Roman historians: see S. Mitchell and G. Greatrex, eds, *Ethnicity and Culture in Late Antiquity* (London, 2000).

Another important strand of recent thinking has stressed the transformative effect of interaction across the Roman frontier. Two important essays on these lines are P. Heather, 'State formation in Europe in the first millennium AD', in B. Crawford, ed., *Scotland in Dark Age Europe* (St Andrews, 1994) and D. Miller, 'Frontier societies and the Transition from late antiquity to the early Middle Ages', in R. Mathisen and H. Sivan, eds, *Shifting Frontiers in Late Antiquity* (Aldershot, 1994).

On the realities of barbarian society see M. Todd, *The Barbarians* (London, 1972, 2nd edn, 1987); E. A. Thompson, *The Early Germans* (Oxford, 1965); E. A. Thompson, *The Visigoths in the Time of Ulfila* (Oxford, 1966); although all are now superseded by W. Pohl, *Die Germanen* (Berlin, 2000).

Barbarian kingship is discussed by M. Wallace-Hadrill, *Early Germanic Kingship in England and on the Continent* (Oxford, 1971), first chapter; H. Wolfram, 'Athanaric the Visigoth: monarchy or judgeship?', *Journal of Medieval History* 1 (1975).

Archaeology is continuing to transform our knowledge of barbarian society. On the key issues of relations with Rome, and barbarian state-formation, fundamental treatments are M. Fulford, 'Roman material in barbarian society, 200BC–AD400', in T. Champion and J. Megaw, eds, *Settlement and Society* (Leicester, 1985); 'Roman and barbarian: the economy of the Roman frontier system', in J. C. Barrett, A. Fitzpatrick and L. MacInnes, eds, *Barbarians and Romans in North West Europe*, British Archaeological Reports International Series 471 (Oxford, 1989); L. Hedeager, 'A quantitative analysis of Roman imports to Europe north of the limes (0–400AD) and the question of Roman-Germanic exchange', in K. Kristiansen and C. Paludin-Muller, eds, *New Directions in Scandinavian History* (Copenhagen, 1978), and her 'The evolution of Germanic society, 1–400 AD', in R. F. Jones *et al.*, eds, *First Millennium Papers* (Oxford, 1988). See also A. Bursche, 'Contacts between the late Roman Empire and north-central Europe', *Antiquaries Journal* 76 (1996).

On barbarian elite settlements see W. Pohl, 'Germania, Herrschaftssitze östlich des Rheins und nördlich der Donau', in G. Ripoll, ed., *Sedes Regiae* (Barcelona, 2000). P. Nielsen *et al.*, eds, *The Archaeology of Gudme and Lundeborg* (Copenhagen, 1994) includes some excellent discussion on the startling discoveries from Gudme and Lundeborg, and also useful accounts of other northern European elite sites. On hillforts and the Roman frontier, H. Steuer, 'Höhensiedlungen des 4. und 5. Jhts. im Südwestdeutschland', in *Archaeologie und Geschichte des ersten Jahrtausends in Südwestdeutschland* (Sigmaringen, 1990), J. Werner, 'Zu den alamannischen Burgen des 4. und 5. Jhts', in W. Mueller, ed., *Zur Geschichte der Alemannen* (Darmstadt, 1970) (first in *Speculum Historiale: Festschrift für J. Spörl* (Freiburg, 1965)). For rural settlement in general H. Hamerow, *Early Medieval Settlements: The Archaeology of Rural Communities in Northwest Europe 400–900* (Oxford, 2002) provides an excellent overview; see also C. J. Becker, 'Farms and villages in Denmark from the late Bronze Age to the Viking period', *Proceedings of the British Academy* 73 (1987); H. Parker, 'Feddersen Wierde and Vallhager: a contrast in settlements', *Medieval Archaeology* 9 (1965); P. Schmid, 'New archaeological results of settlements studies (Roman iron age) in the north-west German coastal area', and W. H. Zimmerman, 'The economy of the Roman iron age settlement at Flogeln, Kr Cuxhaven, Lower Saxony: husbandry, cattle farming and manufacturing', both in B. Cunliffe and T. Rowley, eds, *Lowland Iron Age Communities in Europe*, British Archaeological Reports International Series 48 (Oxford, 1978). Several of the essays in K. Randsborg, ed., *The Birth of Europe: Archaeology and Social Development in the First Millennium AD* (Rome, 1989) are also relevant, e.g. S. Hvass, 'Rural settlements in Denmark in the first millennium AD' on the settlement of Vorbasse.

Roman frontiers

This has been another real growth area in recent research. The best overall survey is C. R. Whittaker, *Frontiers of the Roman Empire* (Baltimore, 1994); see also H. Elton, *Frontiers of the Roman Empire* (London, 1996). B. Isaac, *The Limits of Empire* (Oxford, 1990) is a model study, dealing with the east. Note also the stimulating suggestions of J. F. Drinkwater, 'The Germanic threat on the Rhine frontier: a Romano-Gallic artefact?', and H. Elton, 'Defining Romans, barbarians and the Roman frontier', both in R. Mathisen and H. Sivan, eds, *Shifting Frontiers in Late Antiquity* (Aldershot, 1996).

Work on military strategy and the army discussed in the previous chapter is also directly relevant: H. Elton's *Warfare in Roman Europe, AD350–425* (Oxford, 1996) is the best starting point, in addition to recent work by T. S. Burns (see bibliography on the Goths and Adrianople, below). See too B. Issac, 'The meaning of limes and limitanei', *Journal of Roman Studies* 78 (1988).

On the practicalities of Roman dealings with barbarians, see P. Heather, 'The late Roman art of client management', in W. Pohl, I. Wood and H. Reimitz, eds,

The Transformation of Frontiers (Leiden, Cologne, and Boston, 2001); P. Heather, 'Foedera and Foederati in the fourth century', and G. Wirth, 'Rome and its Germanic partners in the fourth century', in W. Pohl, ed., *Kingdoms of the Empire* (Leiden, 1997). A. D. Lee, *Information and Frontiers* (Cambridge, 1993) studies information gathering and frontier policy.

Finally, for differing views on the 'Germanic' consciousness of the new rulers of western Europe compare L. Hedeager, 'Migration Period Europe: the formation of a political mentality', in J. Nelson and F. Theuws, eds, *Rituals of Power* (Leiden, 2000) and M. Innes, 'Teutons or Trojans? The Carolingians and the Germanic past', in Innes and Y. Hen, eds, *Uses of the Past in the Early Middle Ages* (Cambridge, 2000).

Barbarians and frontiers from Valentinian to Constantius II

There is a large volume of high-quality material on the Goths after their entry into the empire, and strangely little on the crisis of 407–13 in the west, but two new books centre on this as the crucial period, in the context of wider-ranging discussions of the transformation of the Roman west: P. Heather, *The Fall of Rome: A New History* (Oxford, 2005) and B. Ward-Perkins, *The Decline of Rome and the End of Civilisation* (Oxford, 2004). Both are excellent, but controversial in attempting to reverse the trend of much recent scholarship in their emphasis on barbarian agency and destructiveness. Compare the classic paper by W. Goffart arguing for the primacy of Roman internal politics, with the barbarian invasions in the west an experiment which went tragically wrong: 'Rome, Constantinople and the barbarians', *American Historical Review* 86 (1981), reprinted in his *Rome's Fall and After* (London, 1989). Roman politics over the entire period is well discussed in J. Matthews, *Western Aristocracies and the Imperial Court, 375–425* (Oxford, 1975), whilst T. S. Burns offers a convincing study of Roman military strategy in *Barbarians within the Gates of Rome* (Bloomington, IN, 1994). There are important studies of events in Constantinople, and the anti-barbarian reaction and shifts in military strategy there, in J. H. W. G. Liebeschuetz, *Barbarians and Bishops* (Oxford, 1990), and A. Cameron and J. Long, *Barbarians and Politics at the Court of Arcadius* (Berkeley, 1993).

On the Goths see the high-quality accounts of P. Heather, *Goths and Romans 332–489* (Oxford, 1991) and *The Goths* (Oxford, 1996); H. Wolfram, *History of the Goths* (Berkeley, 1988); J. H. W. G. Liebeschuetz 'Alaric's Goths: nation or army?', in J. F. Drinkwater and H. Elton, eds, *Fifth-Century Gaul: A Crisis of Identity?* (Cambridge, 1990). On Adrianople see T. S. Burns, 'The battle of Adrianople: a reconsideration', *Historia* 22 (1983).

Notes

1. Tacitus, *Germania*, ed. M. Winterbottom (Oxford, 1986). Ammianus, 31.2 and cf. the discussion of the Saracens, 14.4. Jerome, *Letters*, nos 9, 123.
2. Jordanes, *Gothic History*, tr. C. C. Mierow (Princeton, 1915), esp. 25 for Scandza and cf. Procopius, *Gothic Wars*, ed. and tr. H. Dewing (Cambridge,

1939), II: 15 for Thule; for bibliography on the complex issues raised by Jordanes see chapter 4 below.

3. For the archaeology see P. Heather and J. Matthews, *The Goths in the Fourth Century* (Liverpool, 1991), pp. 51–101.
4. H. Parker, 'Feddersen Wierde and Vallhager: a contrast in settlements', *Medieval Archaeology* 9 (1965); S. Hvass, 'Rural settlements in Denmark in the first millennium AD', in K. Randsborg, ed., *The Birth of Europe* (Rome, 1989).
5. See the description by the Byzantine ambassador, Priscus of Panium, tr. R. C. Blockley, *The Fragmentary Classicising Historians of the Later Roman Empire* II (Liverpool, 1983).
6. See e.g. Paul the Deacon, *History of the Lombards*, tr. W. Foulke (Philadelphia, 1907), 1.1.
7. H. Heidinga, 'Frankish settlement at Gennep: a migration period centre in the Dutch Meuse area', and H. Steuer, 'Handwerk auf spätantiken Höhensiedlungen des 4./5. Jhts in Südwestdeutschland', in P. Neilsen *et al.*, eds, *The Archaeology of Gudme and Lundeborg* (Copenhagen, 1995).
8. Ammianus, 16: 12.
9. Ammianus, 30.5 (Quadi); 27.5, 31.3–4 (Athanaric's rule).
10. Tacitus, *Germania*.
11. Ammianus.
12. Ammianus, 16.11.
13. Ammianus, 16.12.
14. E.g. Ammianus, 17: 1–2, 8–10.
15. Ammianus, 17.1; Heather and Matthews, *The Goths in the Fourth Century*, note esp. the *Passion of St Saba*.
16. Ammianus, 20.2, 20.8, 14.10, 15.5.
17. Ammianus, 20.4.
18. Ammianus, 30.5 (Valentinian's campaigns), 31.4 (Hunnic advances).
19. Ammianus, 31.4–13.
20. Ammianus, 31.1, 13.
21. The fullest continuous narrative of the events leading up to the fall of Stilicho and the sack of Rome is that offered by Zosimus, *New History*, tr. R. Rapley (Canberra, 1982) books 5–6, writing a hundred years later; see also Orosius, *Histories against the Pagans*, tr. I. Raymond (Washington, 1936); insights on provincial matters, particularly in Hispania, in the *Chronicle of Hydatius*, tr. R. W. Burgess (Oxford, 1983); see also the surviving fragments of Olympiodorus of Thebes, tr. R. C. Blockley, *The Fragmentary Classicising Historians of the Later Roman Empire* 2 (Liverpool, 1982).
22. The sources are astoundingly thin given the event's impact. The fullest account is that of Olympiodorus, fragment 3, tr. Blockley, and see Zosimus, 5: 38–43, tr. Rapley, drawing in part on Olympiodorus; most of the other contemporary sources (Jerome's letter 123, Orosius) articulate the shock-waves felt around the Roman world as a result more than the actual events.
23. Theodosian Code, 14.10.1–4.

3

The fifth-century west and the 'fall of Rome'

Contents

Summary
Chronology
List of emperors
Reinventing the western empire: barbarian federates and Roman warlords
Map 2: Barbarian settlements and the fifth-century empire
The age of Aetius and the Huns
Going it alone: Gallic elites and empire after 454
The Vandal problem: Africa and the western Mediterranean
Essay: Vandals, *villas* and poets
The end of the western empire: Italian generals and the imperial title
How did the western empire end?
Bibliographical essay

Summary

The political crisis in the west in the decade after 400 left the old military infrastructure and frontier system abandoned. Roman strategy increasingly turned on using barbarian warbands, who were settled within the empire as federates, to safeguard the western Mediterranean heartland. Regular Roman army units all but vanished, as military power increasingly devolved onto barbarian warleaders and personal military retinues recruited by Roman generals. Any direct presence in outlying provinces was effectively ended, as the imperial court retreated to Italy.

In this new world, the dominant political figure became the master of the soldiers, the individual best able to manipulate barbarian warbands and Roman generals to provide security for Italy and southern Gaul, the heartlands of the fifth-century empire. From 433–54 Aetius was able to use this position to maintain order of a kind, above all thanks to his close relationship with the Huns, who had established overlordship over the barbarian peoples outside the empire.

In 451–4, the collapse of the Hunnic alliance, the eventual overthrow of the Hun Empire and the resultant coup against Aetius, led to political chaos in the west. As the Roman government increasingly found itself preoccupied with the security of Italy, provincial elites in the west opted to deal direct with the military leaders, mostly barbarian, who offered effective power and protection; thus by the end of the 460s the Roman government effectively ruled only the Italian peninsula. And Italy's security was under increasing threat from the Vandals, who between 429 and 438 had established a kingdom in Africa whilst Roman attentions were diverted towards Gaul and the Huns. Recurrent raiding meant control of Italy increasingly devolved to the master of the soldiers, as emperors came and went with alarming regularity. When, in 476, the last western emperor was finally deposed, and the army elected its leader king of Italy, it occasioned little comment.

Chronology

411–21	Constantius III, master of soldiers, dominant figure in west
413	Burgundians settle in Rhineland; Sueves, Alans and Vandals in Hispania
418	Goths settled as federates in southern Gaul, capital at Toulouse
418	Council of the seven provinces of Gaul established at Arles
429	Vandals under Gaiseric invited to Africa by Roman rebels
433–54	Master of soldiers Aetius dominant in the west
*c.*435–7	Burgundian kingdom destroyed by Huns on Aetius' orders
439	Vandals take Carthage; conquest of Africa complete
*c.*442	Vandal kingdom recognised by treaty
442	Burgundians resettled as federates in Burgundy
450	Marcian ends annual payments to Huns who invade Gaul
451	Huns defeated at Catalaunian Fields by barbarian federates
452	Hun invasion of Italy
453	Death of Attila
454	Huns defeated by subject peoples at Nauko; end of Hun Empire
454	Valentinian III has Aetius murdered
455	Valentinian III is murdered in revenge for Aetius' death
455	Vandals sack Rome
455–76	End of political stability: nine emperors in 21 years
457–73	Master of soldiers Ricimer dominant figure in the west
461	Execution of Majorian, last emperor with effective presence in Gaul
461–5	Aegidius, master of soldiers in Gaul, in revolt
468–9	Arvandus, praetorian prefect in Gaul, tried for treason
469	Anthemius' campaign against Vandals ends in failure
474	Constantinople makes 'eternal treaty' with Vandals
476	Military revolt over pay; Odoacer ousts last western emperor

List of emperors (simplified)

West	East
Honorius, son of Theodosius, 393–423	Arcadius, son of Theodosius, 383–408
Valentinian III, son of Honorius, 425–55	Theodosius II, son of Arcadius, 408–50
Western 'Shadow emperors'	Marcian, 450–7
Petronius Maximus, 455	
Avitus, 455–6	
Majorian, 457–61	Leo I, 457–74
Libius Severus, 461–5	
Anthemius, 467–72	
Olybrius, 472	
Glycerius, 472–4	
Julius Nepos, 474–5	Zeno, 474–91
Romulus Augustulus, 475–6	

Reinventing the western empire: barbarian federates and Roman warlords

In 417, the aristocrat and poet Rutilius Namatianus could wax lyrical about a journey from his estates in southern Gaul to Rome: as he saw it, the very fact that he was able to make the journey at his leisure indicated the renewal of Roman order.[1] However much we might be tempted to see the crisis of the 400s as marking the beginning of the end for the empire, we must take the testimony of contemporaries like Rutilius seriously. A quarter century of conflict and crisis had wrought profound changes, changes that are apparent in both the redrawing of the political map of the west, and in the redistribution of political and military power within the empire. But the Roman Empire survived as the ultimate framework of political power in the west for another half century. The imperial court at Ravenna and office within the Roman system continued to be the object of the political ambitions of local elites across much of western Europe until the final decades of the fifth century.

Geopolitically, the result of the crisis was a fracturing of the old frontier system. Militarily and politically, garrisons and fortifications no longer marked the edges of the effective power of the Roman state. Instead, we might see the western empire as being composed of a series of concentric zones. Direct Roman government on the traditional model continued in Italy, southern Gaul and, until the 430s, Africa. Beyond these old heartlands, in Hispania, Britain and northern Gaul, lay provinces which were still understood as being part of the Roman world, but in which there was no effective Roman military presence, and where local elites had no regular administrative contact with the imperial government. Here barbarian warbands were settled as military protectors, sometimes by the imperial authorities, sometimes by local leaders. Landowning elites may have wanted to remain part of the

Roman world. But in reality ties with Rome were of limited use in providing political security or social stability.

Fourth-century emperors had worked assiduously to maintain the Rhine and Danube frontiers as political and military divides. Here the withdrawal of direct Roman military and governmental action to the imperial core left the barbarian rulers who had emerged around the periphery of the empire in the fourth century free to exercise their power across the frontier, as they had in previous periods of Roman introspection. Paradoxically, Roman withdrawal here led to stability of a kind, as local political systems were able to evolve unimpeded, without the disruptive intervention of the Roman army. In contrast the collapse of the frontier system brought the civilian societies of the Mediterranean, previously insulated from their distant military protectors, into direct contact with the barbarised provincial culture of the Roman military. As a result political and cultural tension between the military and the civilian elites of court and senate was endemic.

In place of the old frontier system, barbarian warbands were formally settled within the empire. The Franks, Roman allies along the Rhine, had mounted just about the only effective resistance to the invaders of 406–7; in its aftermath they were pulled into the alliances surrounding the conflict between Constantine III and Honorius, and in the ensuing political vacuum in northern Gaul they established polities which straddled the old frontier. The Burgundians had been pulled into the empire when they allied with the usurper Jovinus in 411, and after his defeat they founded a kingdom in the Rhineland. Those groups who had crossed the Rhine in 406–7, the Vandals, Alans and Sueves, had been quickly invited across the Pyrenees and into the Iberian peninsula by local factions eager for military muscle to promote usurpers. By 413, they had negotiated a series of agreements with provincials to settle, although convoluted factional politics kept them out of the northeast, where the local elite had raised military forces from their estates to resist the barbarians hired by their rivals. The Goths, by now long-term Roman allies, were used by the imperial government against these Iberian settlements which had taken place without central authorisation; the Alans and one group of Vandals were defeated, clearing the wealthy, Romanised areas of the Meseta and the Mediterranean coast, and leaving just the Sueves in the remote northwest and the remnants of the Vandals and Alans in the south. The Goths were then settled, in 418, in southwestern Gaul, in a kingdom centred on Toulouse, from where their military force could be used by the Roman authorities to control both Gaul and Hispania.

This settlement of barbarians within the empire, although it had very long precedents, was new in scale and implications. Previous incomers had normally been processed through the regular Roman army, and thus assimilated, or, on occasion, settled as military colonists in troubled frontier regions, as groups of soldier-farmers within provincial society who were to complement regular military units in defending the frontier. By the 410s, however, regular Roman field armies in the west are more or less invisible in the sources; barbarian federates were their effective replacement. Although the policy of settling barbarians as poachers turned gamekeepers met with considerable success – the empire ended

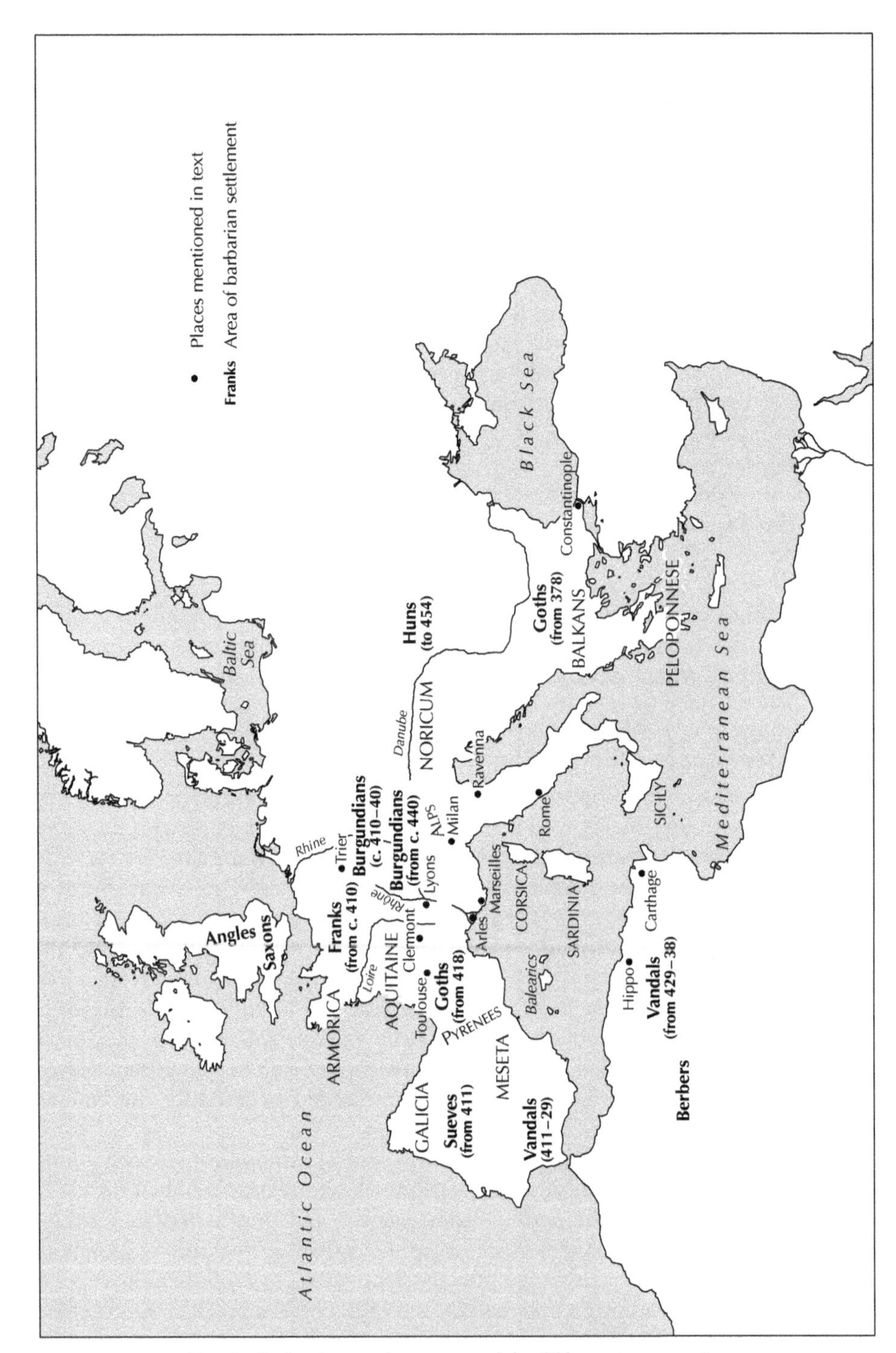

Map 2 Barbarian settlements and the fifth-century empire

through internal collapse not external conquest – it was also recognition of a chilling military reality.

Initially, the leaders of groups such as Alaric's Goths within the empire had been paid direct in cash and supplies by the Roman government, or where necessary had their forces raise cash and supplies direct by ravaging and foraging provincial society. The precise mechanisms of their subsequent settlement are controversial, and are destined to be so given the lack of good evidence. It used to be assumed that this settlement took place on the basis of the granting of land to the newcomers, mainly on the misplaced assumption that it was landhunger that drove the barbarian incomers. The historian Walter Goffart, however, has argued that the barbarians were not granted land, but handed over the right to a share of tax receipts. This hypothesis certainly explains why the process of barbarian settlement could be negotiated with so little controversy or large-scale social upheaval, and also accounts for the continuing influence of local landowning elites who through their control of city councils were responsible for the actual operation of the tax system. Where groups of barbarians did seize land, chroniclers squeal with complaint, whereas organised settlements negotiated with provincial landowners are normally described as 'divisions' with barbarian groupings receiving 'shares' (*sortes*).[2]

The problem is that we lack a full description of how a barbarian settlement was organised, and so argument about the nature of the 'shares' barbarians received is complex and indirect. By the time we have legal evidence, in the laws issued by barbarian kings in the decades around 500, barbarians were landowners, and barbarian 'shares' consisted of farms, fields, woods and slaves. Sixth-century chroniclers projected this reality back and saw barbarian settlement as a matter of land transfer, but barbarian landholding probably emerged gradually, not through wholesale acts of expropriation. Several fifth-century Gallic sources also refer to barbarians receiving 'hospitality' on the estates of wealthy Roman landowners: Sidonius Apollinaris, for example, memorably complained to his friend of the raucous singing and ravenous eating of the detachment of Burgundian 'guests' at his *villa*. These practices distributed barbarian warriors across the countryside on a semi-permanent basis, and so differed from the mechanisms that had been used to support the regular Roman army; they placed barbarian detachments in direct relationships with Roman landowners, and in all probability involved a significant lightening of tax demands. The best interpretation of the available evidence is that in time second and third generation 'guests' were able to acquire interests in the provincial countryside through a variety of mechanisms – including land gifts from kings or from Roman patrons, purchases from provincial landowners, the clearance of forest or waste, as well as violent expropriation and scams involving litigation.[3]

Information about the political organisation of the barbarian settlements is similarly scarce. Unlike earlier barbarians, who were admitted to the empire as either settlers within Roman provincial society or soldiers within the regular army, these incomers were allowed to develop their own, freestanding, traditions of leadership, independent of the official structure of the Roman state. The vocabulary used to describe these structures differentiated them from the Roman tradition. The rulers of barbarian 'peoples' were 'kings', given the Latin title *rex*, possibly drawing on an indigenous terminology using terms such as the Gothic *reiks*, although the philological evidence is difficult. 'King' was a term never applied to Roman leaders because in Roman political culture it had resonance of dictatorship and tyranny, and it remained clearly differentiated from imperial rule. The kings who ruled these barbarian peoples must have drawn on indigenous traditions of warleadership, but they were ruling heterogeneous and often fissiparous groups that had come together on the wartrail, and crystallised in the process of settlement. The process of negotiation with Roman authorities, central and local, both bound a new 'people' together, and enabled leaders to consolidate their royal status.

It is clear that barbarian rulers, particularly federates within the empire, quickly learned to express their rule in a language borrowed from Rome. Sidonius Apollinaris, in a poem on the court of the Gothic king Theodoric II (453–66) at Toulouse, presented a thoroughly Romanised picture of Gothic kingship. Theodoric, far from being the stereotypical barbarian, a wild and uncontrolled slave to his emotions, in Sidonius' depiction demonstrated the virtues of self-discipline, sobriety and regular order.[4] Although this was a panegyric, the fact that it was felt plausible and profitable to praise a Gothic king in these terms speaks volumes.

The kingship of Theodoric and his peers was not based on control of a state or rule of a territory. He was leader of an army that was coming to see itself as a people; king of the Goths not prefect of Toulouse or prince of Aquitaine. On the level of political theory, then, the settlement of barbarian federates did not remove the provinces concerned from the empire or place them under barbarian rule; there were no internal boundaries as one entered regions under barbarian control. Rather, barbarian kings were military protectors of provincial societies that remained within the empire. Of course, in practice the military muscle of this style of leadership, and the pull of a powerful court, meant that barbarian kings were influential figures in the provinces in which they settled: Sidonius describes the crowds of petitioners flocking to Theodoric's palace each day. The proximity of an effective ruler was often far more of a reality than the distant Roman government. The likes of Sidonius spent much of the fifth century maintaining a delicate political balancing act between the ultimate, theoretical, authority of the imperial government and the practical power of the Burgundian or Gothic king. Although there were recurrent but intermittent outbreaks of hostility, when barbarian kings marched on cities and received their submission, and presumably their tax revenues, we should think of a subtly changing orientation of complex allegiances and loyalties rather than the expansion of a self-evident boundary between Gothic and Roman territory. Whilst they continued to exercise the prerogatives of provincial governors as judges applying and interpreting Roman law with expert advice, barbarian rulers did not issue laws, or claim any form of independent sovereignty, until the later decades of the century when the western empire had ceased to be a practical reality.

The settlement of barbarian federates within the empire needs to be understood as a direct response to the crisis of the Roman military system in the west which was so evident in the decades around 400. Regular Roman military units are almost invisible in the narrative sources from this period. The civil wars of the

380s and 390s had been prosecuted with western armies topped up by barbarian recruits, and the practice of victors recruiting the surviving forces of their defeated rivals meant that these troops found their way into the forces of Theodosius and then Stilicho. The net effect had been to denude the western provinces of a military presence, as soldiers who had followed Magnus Maximus, Eugenius, and the usurpers of 406–13 were removed from the provinces to the Roman field army in Constantinople or Italy. The Rhine frontier was all but unguarded before 406, and the usurpations and civil wars of 407–13 saw the remaining regular troops from Britain and Hispania following their chosen imperial candidates to southern Gaul, where they were absorbed into the army of Constantius II. The primacy of the struggle for political legitimacy within the imperial system, and the well-known tendency of armies based in the western provinces to go native and back provincial usurpers meant that attempting to restore the western garrisons was scarcely a priority for the imperial court. At least barbarian 'kings' enjoyed no ambitions on the imperial purple, and could be handled by a mixture of force and diplomacy. From the point of view of an imperial court withdrawn for Italy, whose primary concern was internal security, barbarian federates were probably a safer means to garrison the western provinces than regular armies.

In any case, the re-establishment of the regular fiscal mechanisms that had sustained the regular Roman army was probably not really a possibility. Already in the last decades of the fourth century, the close bonds of personal loyalty between armies and their leaders had been increasingly noticeable. Military leaders were no longer generals who could be hired and fired, but warlords who could count on the devotion of their followers whether they were in or out of favour with the imperial government. It was precisely this kind of loyalty that had underpinned Stilicho's political dominance, allowing him to negotiate with both eastern and western courts, and with the senate, secure in the knowledge that he enjoyed the ultimate allegiance of what was left of the western Roman army. And military leaders like Stilicho took on direct responsibility for securing the pay and provisions to maintain their troops, through direct negotiation with the government, and established practices of foraging and billeting. The difference between this kind of 'Roman' army moulded by personal loyalty to its general, and a barbarian 'people' following its 'king', is a fine one indeed.

The gradual personalisation of military organisation is most visible in changing patterns of recruitment. By the fifth century, there is increasing evidence that here the traditional mechanisms were giving way to the personal power of landowners. With the denuding of the western army, local landlords increasingly relied on their own military followings for both protection, and local policing. In Hispania in the 400s, for example, there are several examples of groups of local landlords raising armies from their estates, and often meeting with considerable military success.[5] This was not just a crisis measure. There is a significant body of legislation from the late fourth century on, discussing *buccellarii*, soldiers maintained by great landowners in personal military retinues. These retinues were recognised, in legislation, as being legitimate entities, and given that landlords had traditionally been responsible for raising state imposts and supplying recruits from their own estates, their emergence could be seen as a natural outgrowth of the long-standing symbiosis between landlord power and government authority; in Egypt, the papyri suggest that it can be understood in this context. But in the political context of the fifth-century west, where regular military units had all but vanished from the provinces, the rise of personal retinues marked the effective breakdown of the divisions between civilian and military, and between landowning and office, which had been central to the Roman political culture. The institutions of the state were ceasing to mediate, even in theory, between those who exercised military power and the civilian society that they protected and by which they were paid.

One result of these changes was that the boundary between legitimate and illegitimate use of force became increasingly difficult to draw. Traditionally, weapon-bearing and the use of violence were restricted to members of the army, whose equipment was technically the property of the state. Those who used military force and were not members of the legitimate Roman army were by definition living outside the laws of the empire and so Roman civilisation: they were thus characterised as bandits or barbarians, two categories which easily merged. Of course, the categorisation of the use of force as legitimate always depended on the viewpoint of the observer: one man's usurper was another's legitimate emperor. But the new style of military organisation which emerged in the fifth-century west, and the decay of the state infrastructure of recruitment and supply for the military, made the differentiation of legitimate Roman troops from illegitimate military forces almost entirely a matter of subjective debate. It is therefore no accident that this period sees the emergence of a new scale of complaints about banditry and illegitimate militias. Often these 'bandits' may have been nothing more than forces raised by local landowners to protect themselves and their communities, whose resistance to the forces of barbarian kings or Roman generals recognised by the imperial government led to their being presented in our sources as illegitimate. The 'bandits' which met the Goths as they crossed the Alps in Honorius' service were in all probability a force of this type, aiming simply to prevent the destructive foraging of another army as it passed. Similarly, the 'revolutionaries' in Britain and Gaul who were said by later eastern historians to have thrown off the yoke of the Roman state in the aftermath of the barbarian invasion of 406 were probably similar militias raised by local landowners who threw in their lot with usurpers who at least offered military protection.[6]

In Gaul north of the Loire and Hispania in particular, these problems seem to have been particularly severe. The sources, writing from the perspective of the imperial government in southern Gaul and Italy, identify movements of *Bacaudae*. The term 'Bacaudae' had already been used in the third century to denote rebel movements in the difficult-to-control western provinces, and the re-emergence of the term reflects the recurrence of troubled conditions where the control of the imperial heartland over the provinces was tenuous. Traditionally, scholars have seized on the Celtic origins of the term, and the complaints of some Roman authors about a breakdown in social order, to see the *Bacaudae* as a quasi-revolutionary movement of social rebellion. In fact, complaints about the rejection of Roman order were part of the standard invective used against 'bandits' and illegitimate users of force. The term *Bacaudae*, then, may have been used by some Roman writers to disparage local landlord-led militias which emerged in areas where the Roman state was proving ineffective in providing military protection. Given the scarcity of evidence, particularly from the areas in which the *Bacaudae* were active, it is difficult to offer any definite conclusions, and in any case in the disturbed conditions of the fifth century matters may have differed significantly from region to region. In any case, the term is not used consistently or universally to refer to local self-help movements of whatever complexion. Certainly in Gaul north of the Loire the leaders of *Bacaudae* were the objects of later veneration, and the handful of known leaders of local militias are of respectable social origin. On the other hand, the term *Bacaudae* is particularly used of groups active in upland or forested areas which were notoriously difficult to control and had long been peripheral to the activities of the government, such as Armorica (modern Brittany) and so may have had some connotation of genuine rejection of social and political order.[7]

In fact, the problem of the *Bacaudae* demonstrates the way in which the relationship between outlying provinces and the imperial government had changed, with the rise of 'internal frontiers' dividing the core provinces from those areas notionally subject to imperial authority but lacking any direct governmental presence. The settlement of barbarian federates was organised so as to maintain the security of the heartland of the empire, Italy and Gaul south of the Loire, but also provided the imperial government with a military force capable of cowing provincials wanting to go it alone. Within the Italian and Gallic core of the empire, some semblance of Roman order was maintained, as military leaders enjoyed official Roman military rank, and legislation attempted to maintain a distinction between those soldiers who made up the warbands led by these generals and civilian society.

Viewed from the perspective of the southern Gallic and Italian heartland, and the priorities of the Roman government, the new system created in the 410s was a success: it enabled the continuation of the Roman social and political framework, with no further problems of barbarian incursion or pitched civil war until the middle decades of the century. The dynasty of Theodosius, in the person of Honorius, remained secure in its legitimacy. The imperial court at Ravenna continued to function on traditional lines, standing at the centre of a web of patronage and preferment as the ambitious sought office and status through proximity to the emperor. The care taken to integrate the elite of Gaul in particular into this system is evident in the increasing importance of the ancient Council of the Seven Provinces of Gaul, meeting at Arles from 418: here Gallic landowners found an accessible political forum through which they could be tied into the Roman system. The need for such an institution was a tacit admission of the decreased pull of the imperial court beyond the Alps. The shifting balance between regional concerns and imperial politics for the Gallic elite is also reflected in the appointment, as a rule, of locals to provincial governorships. But through such strategies it was possible to integrate regional interests into the Roman system. Tensions between landowning elites and the imperial court also had to be smoothed over in Italy, still dominated by the senate but now also home to the emperor. Emperor and senate ruled Italy in partnership and, in a dramatic but often unremarked development, senators increasingly took on permanent roles in the imperial administration, including key military commands. The increasingly direct relationship between military power, political authority and landowning enabled the senatorial aristocracy once again to function as a true ruling class.

The age of Aetius and the Huns

The political renaissance of the senatorial aristocracy had been clear already in 407–13, when the various usurpers who challenged Honorius for the purple were all senators now exercising direct military leadership. The resolution of the crisis saw Constantius III, another prominent Roman landowner, emerging as the militarily crucial figure and Honorius' master of the soldiers. Constantius' dominance allowed him to gain the purple, whilst allaying eastern fears by associating himself with the Theodosian dynasty. After marrying Galla Placidia, Honorius' sister, Constantius was briefly to rule as co-emperor with Honorius in 421. His almost immediate death, closely followed by that of Honorius himself in 423, left a political vacuum at the centre. The master of the soldiers, John, was unable to make good his bid for Honorius' throne, and Galla Placidia emerged as the effective ruler, regent on behalf of her son, Valentinian III, from 425. Galla Placidia's success, and the failure of the attempted military coup of John, were only possible thanks to military assistance from Constantinople, anxious to maintain the position of the Theodosian dynasty in both east and west, and to prevent the emergence of a western military leader as a potential rival to the civilian eastern emperor, Theodosius II. But Galla Placidia was now able to attempt to create a political system modelled on that in the east, carefully using her patronage to maintain a balance of power between the various military leaders active in the west, and promoting an imperial court dominated by civilians as the ultimate political arbiter in the west.

In the event, the attempt was unsuccessful. The realities of power in the west meant that military leaders were difficult to manage as they enjoyed the personal loyalty of their troops to an unprecedented degree. By 433, the general Aetius had established himself as the ultimate military power in the west, operating often uneasily alongside the imperial court of Valentinian III and Galla Placidia. Aetius was of provincial origin, his father a native of the Danube frontier who had risen through the Roman army and married a woman of senatorial rank; owing to his father's position, Aetius himself had been brought up as a hostage amongst the Huns beyond the Danube, before following in his father's footsteps as a Roman military leader. Aetius had been a key backer of Galla Placidia's opponent John, using his youthful contacts to raise a force of Huns from beyond the Danube frontier. Returning to Italy, he made a timely switch of sides and was rewarded with an official position under Valentianian III, as master of the soldiers in Gaul. In an effort to become supreme military leader in the west, and overcome the imperial court's tactic of divide-and-rule, Aetius murdered his main rival, Felix, and attempted to force himself on the imperial government in 430. Galla Placidia responded by summoning one of Aetius' rivals, the African military leader Boniface, who invaded Italy and defeated Aetius in 432; only Boniface's sudden death allowed Aetius' eventual triumph in 433.

Aetius' career graphically illustrates the changing nature of the Roman military, and of Roman politics in the west. Throughout his career his success rested on the personal loyalty demonstrated by his own troops, the core of which were the crack troop of Huns recruited in 424–5. His frontiersman background is typical of the late Roman officer class, and his career demonstrates the way in which a military aristocracy of provincial background, culturally and socially interleaved with their barbarian neighbours, was able to rise to dominance within the western empire as a whole, and eventually ally with the traditional rulers of Italy and southern Gaul, the senatorial aristocracy. Aetius' rise, and his dominance of the west for two decades until his death in 454, was based on his military might. The western court with its civilian leadership could attempt to work with his military command in an often uneasy relationship, but it could not make or break the basis of his power; Aetius, in return, needed the veneer of legitimate authority accorded by the recognition of the emperor, but designed and pursued his own political strategy. He was careful to cultivate good links with the resurgent senatorial aristocracy, many of whom were now exercising direct political power and military leadership in a manner that had not been seen since the early days of empire. Indeed, it seems that Aetius consciously promoted a cadre of Gallic and Italian senators as his generals, men like Litorius and Petronius Maximus.

There can be no doubting the military effectiveness of Aetius and his generals. In the late 420s and early 430s Aetius and his allies had enjoyed success against the Franks. In 435–7 Litorius used a force of Huns to re-establish direct Roman control north of the Loire, clearing the region of *Bacaudae*, and in 437 defeating the Burgundians and destroying their Rhineland kingdom. By 439 these Huns had been turned on the Goths in Aquitaine, where they were defeated. Nonetheless, the strategy of using one barbarian force from beyond the empire to keep barbarian settlements within the empire in check and under control should be seen as a success, and one which had minimal costs. Gothic expansion in southern Gaul was quashed. In 442 the leaders of the Burgundians were resettled along with an assortment of defeated barbarian troops as federates in the area in central-eastern France today known as Burgundy, where they could play an analogous role to the Goths in the southwest in ensuring the security of southern Gaul. Alan settlement in Valence, probably in 440, provided Aetius with yet another strategically placed federate people. The use of barbarians as the agents of Roman 'order', in opposition to provincials north of the Loire, underlines the extent to which the empire of Aetius essentially rested on a tangled web of alliances. The *Life of Germanus of Auxerre* describes the saintly bishop lobbying the emperor on behalf of the provincial landowners of the lower Loire valley, on whom Aetius had unleashed the Alans to crush 'rebellion'. The campaigns in northern Gaul, beyond the Loire and along the Rhine – where Aetius himself had been active in 428, and there is some archaeological evidence for refortification in the area that had been occupied by the Burgundians – may provide a context for the copying of the document known as the *Notitia Dignitatum.* This document is a memorandum of Roman military organisation that clearly looked back to the west's fourth-century heyday, and cannot have been an accurate reflection of fifth-century realities, as opposed to ambitions. Certainly, it speaks volumes for Aetius' success that provincials well beyond the effective reach of the Roman government, in Galicia (the northwest corner of modern Spain) and southern Britain, appealed to him for assistance – albeit without success.[8]

It is for his focus on Gaul that Aetius and his contemporaries have been subjected to harsh criticism from successive generations of historians. In particular, the loss of North Africa to the Vandals in the 430s was tacitly accepted, and no attempt was made at reconquest. Yet North Africa played a crucial economic role in the Roman system, as the supplier of grain and other staples to Italy in general and Rome in particular. In fact, the initial loss of Africa had resulted from continued internal strife within the Roman regime. Africa had been a bone of contention between east and west since the late fourth century, and military and political leaders of the province were periodically pulled into conflicts over the imperial title. Gaiseric, the leader of the Hasding clan of Vandals who had established himself as 'king' of the barbarians in southern Hispania, was invited into Africa in 429 in the course of one such episode of internal conflict. The failed invasion of Italy staged by the African Roman leader, Count Boniface, in 433–4, made any concerted attempt at their removal from the province impossible, and in 435 an agreement on Vandal settlement in the western portion of Roman Africa was agreed. Gaiseric's forces, in a politically peripheral area, were still seen as posing little by way of threat, but in 439 in a surprise attack the Vandals were able to take Carthage, and establish control of the province as a whole.

In 442, in response to Vandal raids on the Italian coast, Vandal control of Africa was recognised by treaty, and Gaiseric's son Huneric was betrothed to Eudocia, the daughter of Valentinian III, in return for the regularisation of the movement of grain and other supplies. The lack of Roman concern for Africa may seem odd to modern historians, writing with the benefit of hindsight, but it was the result of a conscious strategic decision. Politically, a Vandal king in Carthage was no threat to the western empire, so long as the flow of African supplies could be continued; presumably the calculation was based on the reliance of Carthage and its hinterland on the supply of Italy, which was a powerful lever for political accommodation. The imperative for the military leadership and the imperial court was the securing of southern Gaul and northern Italy precisely because these areas were home to those key constituencies of senators and aristocratic landowners on whom they relied for support.

And by the 440s, there was a real need to watch carefully and maintain the security of Gaul and Italy. Aetius' rise and early career had been based on the friendly relationship he had established with the Huns. The Huns were a federation of nomadic groups from the steppe. Some have sought their origins in a group known as the Hsiung Hu who formed in Mongolia, on the frontiers of the sedentary Chinese Empire, in the first century AD, but any direct link between this group and the federation that advanced into central Europe in the fourth century AD has proved impossible to make. The success of the Huns lay in the creation of a loose confederation of nomads on the steppe, which slowly snowballed as it swallowed up more and more nomadic tribes. The archaeology strongly suggests that Hunnic conquest led to relatively little long-term disruption at a basic agrarian level, but rested on the subjection of barbarian elites, who were forced either to flee into exile in Roman service or to enter into the Hun federation. This flexible and polycentric political organisation was the key to Hun success, which by the 420s was beginning to pose a real challenge to Roman strategy. Before the 420s, Hun conquests in central Europe were made by a succession of often competing groupings under different leaders, but by the 430s at the latest a unitary political leadership emerged with the supremacy of Rua. Rua was succeeded by his nephews Bleda and Attila in the 430s, and by 444 Bleda had been murdered leaving Attila as sole ruler. In the meantime, the Huns had abandoned their nomadic lifestyle as they settled north of the Danube, Attila founding a palace and a sedentary court whilst an elaborate system of confederate leadership to tie the various conquered barbarian tribes to the Hunnic ruler was developed; presumably these social changes encouraged the move to unified leadership.

The Huns' relationship to the Roman Empire was complex. There was no attempt at conquest and subordination of Roman territory. Indeed, the Huns were careful to stay outside the empire, demarking their territory from that of the Romans with a devastated 'no man's land'. Politically, the key Hun goal was the elimination of rival barbarian leaders who might weaken their hold over their subject peoples; one recurrent demand made of the empire was the return of barbarian hostages and exiles, who were then put to death by crucifixion or similarly horrific means. Beyond that, Hun ambitions centred on milking the empire for its wealth, particularly in gold, which could then be passed on from the Hun ruler to his confederates and their leaders, reinforcing his supremacy and binding subject peoples into the Hun confederation. Where possible, Roman wealth was tapped by the taking of tribute, through treaty. Where necessary, raids could be threatened or carried out to gather tribute direct and ensure that it would be freely given in future. The Hun Empire, then, relied on the Roman Empire in the same manner that a parasite lives off its 'host'.

Paradoxically enough, then, it was possible for Roman leaders like Aetius to attempt to ride the Hun tiger. The Huns eliminated or subsumed other barbarian groupings, so making the frontier easier to control and define; so long as the flow of tribute could be maintained, the Hun court could guarantee order of a kind. Aetius saw the possibilities of using the Huns to control more local barbarians, allowing them to enrich themselves at the expense of the western government's enemies; his personal ties to the Hun court enabled him to maintain good relations there. In any case, Constantinople was a far richer and more attractive target to the Huns than the west, and paid increasing annual tributes to maintain peace. From a western perspective, this situation led to some stability and peace, with the Huns quiescent, thanks to their eastern tribute, and a valuable source of troops for Roman campaigns in the west, propping up Aetius' dominance.

It was the escalating cost to Constantinople of the annual tributes – which had grown from an initial annual 350 pounds of gold to 2,100 pounds per annum plus 6,000 pounds back payment by 448 – demanded by Attila that upset this delicate balance. In the overall context of the eastern empire's budget, such sums were not unthinkably vast. But they did leave a political aftertaste. With the death of the eastern emperor, Theodosius II, in 450, the general Marcian seized the purple and resolved to deal with the increasing Hun demands, ending the annual payments.

Attila, rightly realising that an aggressive eastern emperor had the manpower and resources to move against him, thus had no alternative but to look to the weaker west in the hope of maintaining the flow of tribute and plunder. Aetius, however, was able to bring together an alliance of barbarian federates led by the Goths which defeated the Huns at the Cataulanian fields in Burgundy in 451: a telling vindication of the strategy of settling barbarians as federates to protect Gaul.[9]

Attila, retreating, headed to the rich pickings of Italy, and here it proved harder to organise meaningful resistance. There were no federates who had a vested interest in protecting Italy, so Attila was only faced with the personal followings of Italian landlords and the remnants of the regular Roman military. In the event, it was only the effects of an epidemic on his army, and the increasingly desperate diplomatic offers of the Romans, which persuaded Attila to withdraw. His death, in 453, was quickly followed by the collapse of the Hun Empire, as the regular flows of plunder and tribute that held the system together were turned off. In 454, the subject peoples of the Huns united and defeated their erstwhile masters, and central Europe reverted to a kaleidoscope of barbarian peoples and kings, attempting to revive earlier identities and carve out new kingdoms. With the collapse of the Huns, the empire had to face a whole new set of problems.

Going it alone: Gallic elites and empire after 454

Aetius and his relationship with the Huns had informed a successful military strategy for almost a quarter of a century. The poet Merobaudes could even celebrate Aetius' career with the stereotyped praise of panegyric.[10] But the empire Aetius inherited and preserved was based on the continued desire of the landowning classes of Italy and southern Gaul to structure their world around the patronage and rank bestowed by the imperial court and the senate. Provincials in Africa, Britain, Hispania, and along the Rhine and Danube frontiers were left to defend their own, provincial, versions of the Roman system in isolation, through conflict and negotiation with barbarian warlords who were simultaneously neighbours, protectors and conquerors. In such a world, what it meant to be Roman, and what made a province a part of the Roman Empire, was no longer clear.

And the empire of the fifth century no longer exercised an unquestioned or unthinking hold over the loyalties of its subjects: a world without Rome was no longer unthinkable. Whilst the authors of official panegyric presented their patrons in traditional tones, some Christian writers turned to criticism of contemporary mores. The priest Salvian, writing at Marseilles in the 440s, saw in the Roman Empire of his day only corruption and disorder, not the civilising gifts of law and justice upon which Roman claims to bring order to the world had been based. Salvian was a refugee from Trier in northern Gaul, which had only a generation earlier been a favoured imperial residence. Thanks to the theological foundations laid by Augustine's refusal to identify the Roman Empire with the City of God, Salvian could argue that throughout history God had intervened to punish the impious and unjust, and thus see in the empire's current misfortunes the governance of God (the title of his tract). Such, indeed, were the vices of Roman society that many fled to the barbarians or the *Bacaudae*: 'they would rather live as free men, though in seeming captivity, than as captives in seeming liberty; hence the name of Roman citizen, once not only much valued but dearly bought, is now voluntarily repudiated and shunned, and is thought not merely valueless, but even almost abhorrent'.[11]

Salvian's eastern contemporary, Bishop Priscus of Panium, although a loyal servant of the emperor, could debate the merits of empire in similar terms. In his description of his embassy to Attila's court, he uses an account of a meeting with a merchant of provincial Roman origin who had joined with the Huns to weigh the relative merits of Roman and Hunnic rule. The merchant turned warrior argues that his new life was better than his old, as he was able to defend himself and was very little harassed by his rulers, whereas in the Roman Empire he had been forced to rely on the government for protection, as civilians were banned from carrying arms, and had in return been subjected to taxation and injustice. Although Priscus defends the division of labour in Roman society as the invention of the 'wise and good men' who created the Roman state, the debate does not, as is normal in a literary text of this kind, end with the merchant seeing the error of his ways and applauding the benefits of imperial rule. Rather, he 'shed tears, and confessed that the laws and constitution of the Romans were fair, but deplored that the governors, not possessing the spirit of former generations, were ruining the state'.[12]

This crisis of confidence was not accidental: it was both a response to, and the inevitable result of, changes in the nature of Roman power in the provinces. The empire was no longer an overarching entity that defined and legitimated the power of local landowners and military leaders; it was becoming a matter of personal allegiance as local position was no longer reliant on the infrastructure of the Roman state. Such allegiances rested on the accessibility and availability of imperial patronage, through grants of rank and office. In this world of blurred dividing lines, all parties were reliant on barbarian allies for military protection, and the necessities of provincial politics often conflicted with the wishes of the imperial government and its generals. The 'fall of Rome' was not a dramatic collapse, but a gradual dissociation of provinces from the centre, a slow and steady unravelling of the authority of the imperial court.

The collapse of the Hun Empire triggered an internal crisis within the empire, where Aetius' entire career had been based on his ability to manage the west's relationship with the Huns. It was no accident that the death of Attila was thus quickly followed by the assassination of Aetius by his Roman rivals, in the imperial palace at Ravenna, allegedly on the orders of the emperor, Valentinian III. But Aetius' supporters were unwilling to let his bloody end lie unavenged. Petronius Maximus, a military commander and senatorial leader allied to Aetius, had Valentinian III murdered in retaliation for the death of Aetius. Petronius then had himself declared emperor by the senate at Rome: the landed wealth and military power of the senatorial aristocracy was now occupying the political centre stage. In an attempt to bolster his legitimacy, Petronius seized and married Valentinian's widow, and had his son wed to Valentinian's daughter, Eudocia, thus marrying his family into the Theodosian dynasty. But Eudocia had already been betrothed to Huneric, son of the Vandal king Gaiseric, who took the marriage as an affront and used it as a pretext to take advantage of the political vacuum and military weakness of the Roman government. In 455 Gaiseric launched a series of raids on Italy that culminated with the sack of Rome, this time with far more 'vandalism' than Alaric and his Goths had caused in 410. Petronius' regime collapsed. His successor, another senatorial general with links to Aetius, Avitus, enjoyed a similarly short and disastrous career. Stability was only restored by Ricimer, a barbarian who had been promoted to master of the soldiers by Aetius.

Under Aetius, the emperor and his court had played a vital role as a source of office and rank, pulling together military leaders and aristocratic landowners who were exercising an ever more direct power in the regions. This legitimating cultural veneer was possible because the western imperial court at Ravenna was stable, and the Theodosian dynasty unchallenged. Civilian emperors were thus locked in an uneasy but necessary partnership with the military leadership. After the murders of Aetius and Valentinian III, this changed radically: the 21 years from 455 to 476 saw no fewer than nine emperors, several reigning only a matter of months, the longest a bare five years. Rather than civilian figures concerned with court politics, these were almost all military leaders trying to outrank their peers, and so likely to be opposed and overthrown. The careers of Valentinian III's immediate successors Petronius and Avitus are emblematic of this lack of political stability. Although Ricimer was to remain the crucial military figure for 16 years, from 457–73, and on account of his barbarian descent was unacceptable as an imperial candidate, even his position was rarely unchallenged, for the emperors he notionally served were often also rival warlords. The result was, inevitably, that the imperial court was no longer able to act as an effective focus for landowners and generals, and the cultural, social and political cohesion that imperial patronage had previously supplied was gradually eroded. To the extent that there was stability, it was tied up with the efforts of Ricimer, as leader of the Italian army, to maintain the security of the peninsula.

Just as seriously, the events of the 450s undermined the ability of the imperial government to maintain military control of Gaul, and the frontiers in the north of the Alps and along the Danube that were essential to Italy's security. Aetius' close ties to the Huns had provided him with the military muscle to keep Gaul and the northern approaches to Italy in order through the 430s and 440s, and prevent federates settled within Gaul from becoming over-mighty. With the collapse of the Hun Empire, the key to Roman military strategy was destroyed; the fragmentation of the barbarian world beyond the frontier into a mass of competing kingdoms inevitably resulted in serious barbarian raids over the Alps.

The combination of crises in military strategy and in the emperor's political authority led to the increasing detachment of the empire's remaining provinces in the west. By the 470s, Roman Gaul was a thing of the past, as the interests of Gallic elites pulled them away from Roman politics. This outcome was far from evident in the 450s. In the aftermath of the fall of Attila and Aetius, ties between Gaul and the empire were, if anything, closer than they had been since the fourth century. Petronius, as a general under Aetius, had campaigned in Gaul, and after the Vandal sack of Rome the southern Gallic aristocracy – who had been relatively immune from the ravages of Huns and Vandals – rallied behind one of their own number, the senator Avitus, who had served as a general under Petronius, as candidate for emperor. Avitus counted on military backing from his federate neighbours in Gaul, the Goths. But on arriving in Rome, it quickly became clear that more reliable military backing that would be acceptable to an Italian aristocratic audience was necessary if Avitus was to last; ultimately as Avitus' Gothic allies were more interested in extending their influence in Gaul and Hispania than in defending Italy for the new emperor.

In the event, by the end of 456 Avitus had been deposed in a military coup, and in 457 another senator, Majorian, who along with Ricimer had led the Italian army to victory against renewed Vandal raids, was emperor. Majorian's political priorities reveal the continued importance of Gaul in the Roman system. From 458–61, he campaigned there, preventing Gothic and Burgundian expansion and overcoming initial reservations from adherents of Avitus. With hindsight, Majorian's brief reign appears as the swansong of Roman power in the west, with expeditions north of the Loire, and in Hispania. But Majorian's activities in the west were only possible because he left the defence of Italy to Ricimer: this was a *de facto* arrangement of power-sharing between two military leaders, the Roman Majorian enjoying the imperial title. And when Majorian's planned campaign against Vandal Africa was pre-empted by a disastrous defeat before his forces had even left Hispania, the defence of Italy – the province most endangered by the activities of the Vandals – was compromised. When Majorian attempted to return to Italy in 461, Ricimer saw his presence as a threat. Majorian was tried for treason and executed; he was replaced by the more pliable civilian emperor Libius Severus, who was to reign from 461–5 as Ricimer's puppet.

Ties between Italy and Gaul were now stretched to breaking point. Aegidius, the key Roman military leader in Gaul, rebelled, and the regime of Libius Severus and Ricimer found little Gallic recognition. The politics of the immediately following period are almost impenetrably cloudy. The military power of Gothic and Burgundian federates in the southern and central Gaul, and various groups of Franks in the north, made for a confused political situation. Aegidius was not removed until 465, when the imperial government persuaded the Goths to move against him. It is significant that Ricimer and his Italian generals did not engage on a large-scale campaign across the Alps to deal with the revolt, whilst Aegidius did not back a rival imperial candidate and attempt to conquer Italy, but operated independently in Gaul. Italian and Gallic interests were becoming increasingly divergent, and political horizons regional, even for those who inherited the rhetoric of Roman universalism.

After the falls of Avitus and Majorian no emperor visited, or campaigned in, Gaul. It is no surprise that in the course of the 460s, the ambitions and horizons of the Gallic aristocracy became increasingly localised. The shift of focus, away from imperial politics encompassing Italy and Gaul and focused on the imperial court, towards more local concerns, is apparent in the fate of Arvandus, the southern Gallic landowner who had been appointed praetorian prefect (i.e. governor) of Gaul by the Italian government in 464. Arvandus owed his position to a Roman government in Italy that could offer him precious little practical help in governing Gaul. Here, often delicate dealings with the barbarian federates who were the main providers of military muscle were necessary. But Arvandus' Italian masters saw these essential accommodations as constituting a real and present danger. In 468, he was called to Rome, following accusations from fellow Gauls, and tried for treason, his dealings with the Goths and Burgundians being interpreted as a conspiracy to overthrow the emperor.[13]

By the time of Arvandus' trial, Gallic aristocrats were so few and far between in Italy that Sidonius Apollinaris, who had visited Rome in the hope of reducing the tax on the city of Lyons, was made prefect of Rome by a new emperor in a desperate attempt to win Gallic support. Even Sidonius – our key source for this period, thanks to his voluminous poems and letters – eventually recognised that the imperial government in Italy was increasingly marginal to the political situation at home in Gaul. After serving his year as prefect of Rome, he returned home to his native Auvergne. In 470, he was to become bishop of his home city, Clermont, at the request of its citizens. In that role, he was able to hold out against and eventually negotiate a settlement with the Gothic king, after leading three years of resistance in which the Roman government could offer him no help. In taking up episcopal office, Sidonius was responding to the demands of the local populace that he take on the role of patron and protector of Clermont that his family had long exercised. But such patronage was traditionally exercised through secular office, and mediation between the locality and the imperial court. The office of bishop gave the demands of the city an exclusive hold, and by combining aristocratic patronage with spiritual authority gave it a legitimacy based on the supernatural, not on the Roman Empire. As Sidonius' world increasingly came to be dominated by the Gothic kings who were busy expanding their power across southern Gaul, so a distant emperor who could offer no military assistance became an irrelevance.

The path taken by Sidonius has come to be seen as exemplary by modern historians explaining the end of Roman Gaul. Aristocrats were forced to abandon the allurements of extensive politics based on office granted by the imperial court as Rome ceased to provide military protection in the provinces. To deliver to their local clients, they took up episcopal office, which now often combined secular and spiritual leadership of a city. In this position, their local power was made legitimate in new ways, enabling them to enter into agreements with barbarian military leaders. Certainly most of our written evidence concerns men who followed this course, and an aristocratic episcopate ruling their cities became typical of Gaul. But we should expect the overwhelming mass of our evidence to concern bishops who were revered as protectors and saints in their cities, and so commemorated for posterity. And not all aristocrats became bishops. Landowning and patronage networks could easily mutate into secular, military power as landlords were transformed into warlords. Trier, the old imperial capital, for example, was ruled by a count named Arbogast, whose name suggests some barbarian ancestry but whose military power was used to maintain the provincial landowning elite in the Moselle valley. Even in the south some Roman provincials became warlords with only a tangential link to the imperial government. Ecdicius, son of the emperor Avitus, established himself as a provincial leader in the Auvergne, recruiting a private army from his estates and clients, and in 470 and 474 entered into contact with Italian emperors wishing to establish a foothold in

Gaul, even receiving the largely meaningless title of praetorian prefect in Gaul.[14] But by the 470s, all the Roman state could do was offer titles to provincial aristocrats and attempt to play off barbarian leaders. Arles, the capital of fifth-century Gaul, was lost to the Goths by the 470s, in spite of shortlived reoccupations in 471 and 474. The sphere of the imperial government was restricted to Italy. Sidonius' letters show that contacts with the imperial court in Italy, or even with landowners in the territory of a different group of barbarians, were dangerous, and were likely to lead to the displeasure of barbarian kings who were the real holders of power.

In this new world, the landowning elite was able to maintain their position by throwing in their lot with the barbarian regimes that offered practical protection. The infrastructure of cities and their hinterlands, which in spite of inevitable dislocation survived in Gaul south of the Loire, switched their loyalties from Roman emperor to barbarian king. For the likes of Sidonius, 'Roman' was no longer a political allegiance but a cultural identity, tied up with the traditional attainments and refinements of the landowning elite: cultural virtuosity thus replaced honorific rank as a marker of status. It was through influencing the courts of barbarian rulers that aristocrats could best preserve their world. Sidonius teased his friend Syagrius of Lyon that thanks to his role as a close advisor to the Burgundian king, he now spoke better Burgundian than the Burgundians. But he also acknowledged that he was thus better able to preserve the underpinnings of Roman order, to be compared to the ancient lawgivers through his work as a 'new Solon among the Burgundians'.[15]

The Vandal problem: Africa and the western Mediterranean

This shrinking of the imperial government's sphere of influence was a direct result of its increasing problems in maintaining the security of Italy itself. Here, the 450s, with Attila's last campaign of 452–3 and the succession of Vandal raids on the Italian coast after 455, were arguably the most destructive decade of the entire late Roman period. Legislation from Majorian's reign indicates that the government was forced to recognise the need of civilians to arm themselves in self-defence against Huns and Vandals, and faced insuperable difficulties in recruiting soldiers. Raising tax to fund the military posed similar problems. The government even wrote off arrears owed from aristocratic estates in the hope of gaining some cash in the short term.[16] Given that the settlement of federates in Italy on the model of the Goths and Burgundians in Gaul was unacceptable to senatorial opinion, the Roman government had little alternative but to bulk up the remainder of the regular army as best it could, from whatever sources of manpower were available, barbarian and Italian. Fiercely loyal to their leader, Ricimer, these forces do seem to have been sufficient to repel the major threats faced by Italy through the 450s and 460s. Ricimer was able to defeat Vandal raiders in 455–6, and defend the northern frontier against Alemans in 457 and Alans in the early 460s. This ensured stability of a sort, and ensured that Ricimer remained the key political figure, controlling Italy to such an extent that on the death of his puppet, Libius Severus, in 465, he was to rule without a western emperor at all for two years. The leader of the Italian army enjoyed an increasingly uncontested political dominance.

Whilst Ricimer could drive barbarian raiders away from Italy, he could not campaign beyond the peninsula itself. In Gaul and along Italy's northern frontier, the playing off of one barbarian group against another was the necessary expedient. But endemic raiding of the peninsula's coastline from Vandal Africa proved impossible to stop. Any attack on Africa needed the organisation of a complex and costly naval operation, and Gaiseric's kingdom was bordered by no potential barbarian rivals with whom Rome could play divide-and-rule as in Gaul.

Whilst previously there had been occasional Vandal raids on Italy, from 455 these took on a new regularity and were conducted with a new impunity. Gaiseric was able to conquer a veritable western Mediterranean empire, establishing bases in Sicily, Sardinia, Corsica and the Balearics. Following the Vandal rout of Majorian at Carthagena in southern Hispania in 458, by the 460s the western government simply lacked the military resources to attempt to launch another attack. Roman efforts centred on negotiation, in the hope of establishing peace and securing the necessary supplies of African grain in return for the recognition of Gaiseric's conquests. Gaiseric himself was keen to regularise his position, and marry his son, Huneric, to Eudocia, daughter of the emperor Valentinian III, as had been promised in the treaty of 442. But protracted negotiations made little progress, and by the 460s Gaiseric was even backing the cause of the blue-blooded senator Olybrius as a potential emperor. Olybrius was married to Placidia, another Theodosian princess, and Gaiseric raided the Italian coast demanding that he be acknowledged as the heir of Valentinian III.

The alliance between Olybrius and Gaiseric raised the possibility of the Vandals establishing control of both sides of the western Mediterranean, and so led to the intervention of the eastern emperor in western politics. In 467 the Vandals had ventured as far as the Peloponnesian islands, off the south coast of Greece, where they had plundered, and seized hostages and craftsmen in their normal way. In retaliation, the eastern emperor Leo despatched the military leader Anthemius to fill the vacant western imperial throne. Anthemius, an outsider in the west, immediately set about wooing Ricimer through a marriage alliance, and courting the senate. In 469, an all-out attack was launched on Africa, on three fronts simultaneously: Anthemius' naval forces were co-ordinated with those of his kinsman Marcellinus and an eastern land army in Libya. There were striking initial successes, with the recovery of Sardinia and much of Sicily, and rapid advances in Africa itself. The Vandals had relied on raiding, and the inability of the western government to mount a serious campaign against them, and when faced with concerted action backed by the superior fiscal and military resources of Constantinople appeared to be on the brink of crumbling. But there was fatal hesitation, on account of internal rivalries within the Roman camp, and a successful Vandal offensive that destroyed Anthemius' fleet led to the humiliating collapse of the invasion.

The Vandal victory is strong testimony to their leadership of the African navy. But disunity among their Roman opponents made it possible, and proved fatal to

Roman ambitions in Africa. Anthemius had been a potential rival to Leo when the latter ascended to the eastern throne in 457, and his despatch to the west was designed to remove him from influence in the east. The political capital and strategic and military advantages that a resounding victory in Africa would have given Anthemius and his generals may have been a greater price than the court at Constantinople was prepared to pay for the defeat of Gaiseric. When, in 470, Leo renewed operations against Gaiseric, he did so without involving Anthemius, and with the more limited ambition of forcing Gaiseric to negotiate. Anthemius' adventure had cost a fortune, and it was not until 529 that another expedition was launched against Vandal Africa. But the campaign also revealed the weakness of Vandal power in the Mediterranean in the face of concerted military opposition. The logistical difficulties of co-ordinating and funding an attack on Gaiseric's kingdom were such that the problem was getting onto a battlefield against the Vandals, not defeating them once there: after all, in their conquest of Africa the Vandals had only faced local garrisons, not a full-scale conflict with Roman field armies. Throughout the period of conflict Gaiseric had sought a legitimate position within the Roman world, and in particular the marriage alliance that had been promised in his initial treaty with the Romans in 442. It is thus no surprise that the Vandals were soon back in negotiation with the empire, culminating in 474 in a treaty of 'eternal friendship' in which Constantinople recognised the Vandal kingdom in Africa.

The Vandals had caused real headaches on account of the difficulty of anticipating and defending against naval raids around the western Mediterranean. But the pressures on Gaiseric to find an agreed place in the Roman world are all too easily overlooked because of the bad press that the Vandals have received in contemporary sources and modern historiography, and the partial view of Vandal Africa that results. Pride of place here goes to the highly rhetorical work of the African bishop Victor of Vita, whose outspoken condemnation of the religious policies of the Vandal kings was designed to mobilise opinion in the empire, and within the Vandal realm, against the regime. Victor condemns the Vandal regime as heretical and predatory, painting life under Gaiseric (429–77) and his successor Huneric (477–84) in lurid terms, informed by the expectations of persecution which were deeply embedded in the history of the African church. His testimony is difficult to counterpoint with alternative perspectives, however, because our other extended discussions rest on similar, and likewise hostile, sources: the sixth-century Byzantine historian Procopius wrote to denigrate the Vandal kingdom and justify its conquest, whilst the neglected material associated with the churchman Fulgentius of Ruspe stems from the circles of aristocratic and ecclesiastical exiles from Africa who spent much of the fifth and early sixth centuries lobbying for Roman intervention.[17]

Victor's complaints were not directed at the Arianism of the Vandal kings *per se*, so much as the active measures taken against the Catholic church. The Vandal conquest had been followed by appropriations of property and wealth, focused on large landlords of senatorial rank and bishops, and used to reward the followers of the Vandal king and establish them in Carthage and its hinterland. Victor seems to show us here a class of Vandal landlords taking over Roman estates wholesale and relying on provincials to oversee their day-to-day running, a system which in time, judging from Procopius, led to some degree of acculturation and intermarriage. After the exiling, voluntary or involuntary, of major senatorial landowners, bishops became the increasingly obvious targets for further expropriation, and here Huneric was to turn the legislation against heretics contained in the Theodosian Code on the Catholic church. These policies clearly did threaten the infrastructure of the African church, and had the effect of generating a class of exiles – Fulgentius' peers, and the anonymous figures whose lobbying produced imperial legislation demanding compensation or the restoration of confiscated African estates – whose interests played a large part in determining the tenor of our surviving sources. But they took place in a context of long-standing sectarian conflict within African Christianity – even Augustine had struggled to get provincial governors to move against the Donatists and other heretics – and in a society where huge landholding by frequently absentee Italian senators was the norm. The injustice of Vandal expropriation may have appeared less clear-cut in some provincial circles than our sources, particularly Victor, would suggest.

The Vandals also faced their own 'barbarian' problem. The Roman province of Africa had its own long frontier, on the edge of the fertile and settled Mediterranean coastal fringe, beyond which lay Berber pastoralists and nomads, who posed a recurrent threat to sedentary, agrarian, Roman order, and were condemned as barbarians and bandits. In classic Roman fashion, military emplacements and garrisons along the frontier were co-ordinated with a vigorous policy of client management. Some Berber allies were used to supply military muscle against their rivals. Tribal coalitions on the fringes of the Sahara learnt to express their power in new terms. These could draw on the language of Roman political legitimacy: it was later claimed that kings among the Moors were only recognised if they had received regalia from the Romans. They also made use of indigenous cultural forms represented by the Djedars, a series of 13 magnificent stone mausolea in the form of square pyramids, found on two sites dating from the late fifth and sixth centuries. With the Vandal takeover, the careful balancing that Roman policy had entailed – which may have becoming increasingly problematic in any case – proved impossible to maintain, hence the increasing ideological assertiveness. By the last quarter of the fifth century, there is evidence for over half a dozen Berber dynasties setting up their own frontier kingdoms ringing Vandal Carthage, and claiming to exercise legitimate power over provincials: inscriptions commemorate the activities of Berber leaders such as the self-styled 'emperor' Masties, whilst in 508 another Berber leader, Masuna, was styled 'King of the Moors and the Romans'.[19]

Gaiseric's predatory policies, centring on aggressive expansion in the Mediterranean and the expropriation of senators and bishops at home, must have led to an influx of plunder and tribute, and a significant repatriation of wealth formerly controlled by absentees, in the short term. But state piracy was not a viable long-term policy, and internal problems, not least the growing threat of Berber kings on the fringes of the Vandal kingdom, needed addressing. Maritime raiding might raise cash, captives and hostages in the short term, but ultimately Africa relied on the wealth generated by control of Carthage and the exports that were so important to Italy and much of the rest of the western Mediterranean. The cities and

Essay

Vandals, *villas* and poets

Thanks in particular to the archaeology, there is growing evidence for the flourishing of African provincial society under Vandal rule; here the material culture enables us to read the neglected but rich literary culture of Vandal Carthage in new terms. Whilst digging has inevitably been determined by modern developments, the picture that has emerged from those sites that have been subjected to excavation is one of a thriving and functioning late antique city, with no indications of decline until the sixth century. The circus, for example, which was, according to Victor, 'vandalised', seems to have functioned through the fifth century, which makes sense of descriptions of the circus performance in the large corpus of surviving Latin poetry from Vandal Africa. Beyond Carthage, the evidence of inscriptions – many dated, like the coinage, after the 'Vandal era' beginning with the conquest of Carthage in 439 – likewise indicates a flourishing late antique society. Landowners used traditional Roman titles to advertise their status, and some even record with pride their official roles in the traditional civic and imperial cults, now no longer tied up with pagan religion but still an important means of asserting local power. Excavated *villa* settlements have traditionally been dated to the fourth century, on the basis of traditional views of the violent impact of the Vandals, but recent work on sites such as Sidi Ghrib, near Carthage, and Pupput, Keliba and Thubarbo in the rural hinterland, have suggested occupation through the fifth century. A remarkable cache of 34 wood documents from 493–6, written in full Roman legal tradition, show the continued functioning of the estate of Catullinus at Bir Trouch, worked by a large number of peasant smallholders cultivating olives, figs and nuts, and thus presumably integrated into a wider economic system. Here, then, is good evidence for continuity in the structures of provincial landowning, with *villa*-owners consuming traditional classical culture, and maintaining their local dominance within the Vandal kingdom. This milieu of thoroughly Romanised provincial elites serving a barbarian ruler at Carthage is vividly illuminated in the surviving poetry of Dracontius and Luxurius, and tacitly admitted by Victor in his condemnation of those provincials who were happy to serve at the Vandal court, even adopting Vandal dress and the Arian faith.[18]

Figure 3.1 The Lady of Carthage

estates of coastal Africa had been fully integrated into the Mediterranean economy of the Roman state: the large-scale export of African goods, particularly to Italy, rested on the infrastructure of the state and its annual shipments to feed Rome, and on the large-scale ownership of African estates, many geared to export, by Italian landowners. The Vandal conquest involved the removal of Africa from the Roman state: this, along with the expropriation of senatorial estates, compromised the mechanisms of Africa's economic dominance in the western Mediterranean. The archaeology makes it clear that Mediterranean exports continued on a lower level: the characteristic African Red Slip pottery continues to be found right around the Italian coasts in the second half of the fifth century, but in lesser volumes. Economic dislocation within the Mediterranean, combined with the diminished demand for luxuries in a period of political uncertainty in Italy, thus posed a real threat for the Vandal regime. Indeed, one of the objects of Vandal raiding seems to have been to take craftsmen as hostages back to Carthage, where they were presumably put to work, thus augmenting the kingdom's economic muscle, as well as to establish control over the islands of the western Mediterranean and so attempt to monopolise trade. But the economic reality was that some eventual political accord was necessary for the Vandal kingdom's continued existence.

The problem for the Vandal kings was that such accord was not necessarily popular with their followers, enjoying the fruits of plunder and the otiose lifestyle of landowning luxury. Indeed, the 'eternal treaty' of 474 provoked a serious revolt by Vandals unhappy both with the shift in policy, away from raiding towards symbiosis, and with the monarchical prerogatives claimed by the Hasding kings. Vandal kingship was a novel institution: Gaiseric's 'people' had only coalesced from a variety of Vandal and other groups following their defeat at Gothic hands in Hispania, and his role as 'king of the Vandals and Alans' rested on the riches and prestige that had come with the conquest of Africa. Internal tensions within the barbarian confederation led by Gaiseric are clearly reflected in the complex succession system adopted: the eldest surviving male member of the Hasding clan was to succeed on the current king's death, a system designed to minimise the possibility of vigorous adult claimants being excluded in favour of young sons in a direct line, and so prevent internal strife. Victor describes bloodthirsty political manoeuvring within the barbarian elite that helps explain the need for a succession system that favoured mature males, and hints at a dramatic process of political centralisation set in motion by the adaptation of a loose confederation of warbands to the rigid hierarchies of a wealthy Roman province. But the revolt of 474 failed, and after Huneric's death a softer religious policy was gradually adopted, with the legal measures taken against the Catholic church dampened down, as second generation immigrants who had grown up within African provincial society came to the fore.

The end of the western empire: Italian generals and the imperial title

The structural weaknesses of the Vandal regime made it possible for Constantinople to tame Gaiseric and his successors without conquering Africa.

But the resolution of the Vandal problem had been achieved at the price of destabilising what remained of the western empire. Remember, the collapse of the Hun Empire had brought in its aftermath the overthrow of Aetius and in retaliation that of Valentinian III. With the murder of the last male member of the Theodosian dynasty, the tacit trade-off between the civilian authority of the emperor and the military power of the generals, which had underpinned political life in the first half of the century, was no longer possible. Now, military leaders contested political supremacy directly, those of Roman background claiming the imperial title whilst their barbarian counterparts backed rival claimants. The rapid succession of emperors in 455–61 was largely a result of the destabilising effects of Vandal raiding, but left the legitimacy of the imperial office more tarnished than ever. By the mid-460s, the western empire seemed to be heading towards a quiet retirement, as Ricimer as master of the soldiers ruled through a puppet emperor and then, after 465, dispensed with the position altogether. The revival of the imperial title was a direct result of eastern intervention, and a response to the Vandals championing of various candidates for the throne. The result was a renewed political crisis that was resolved by the final abandonment of the western imperial title.

Anthemius, the eastern general who had been despatched from Constantinople to serve as emperor in the west in 467, did not last long. His credibility fatally damaged by the inglorious collapse of his campaign against the Vandals, he was soon in conflict with Ricimer, the real power-broker, and by 470 was accused of conspiracies by the senate. In 472, the eastern emperor Leo despatched Olybrius, the western senator and general whom the Vandals had backed as a potential emperor in the 460s, to arbitrate. Ricimer did not hesitate to set up Olybrius as emperor in opposition to Anthemius. The new regime rested on the support of two barbarian warlords and their followings. Gundobad, son of the king of the Burgundians in Gaul, was Ricimer's nephew, and enjoyed the title of master of the soldiers in Gaul. Odoacer was a military adventurer, the son of a barbarian king who had been an ally of Attila; after the destruction of his father's Scirian kingdom in modern Hungary he had fought as a Roman ally in Gaul.

The new regime proved short-lived: Olybrius died a little over a month after his accession, shortly after Ricimer's own peaceful death. Now there was real political crisis, as the northern approaches to Italy were threatened by Gothic federates led by Euric in Gaul, and by an unrelated Gothic warband led by Vidimer on the Danube. The leader of the imperial bodyguard, Glycerius, was hurriedly chosen as emperor, but Gundobad and Odoacer were in effective control of Italy. Once again, however, Constantinople intervened to prevent the political power of barbarian warlords in Italy becoming absolute. The eastern emperor Leo appointed Julius Nepos, a native of the Dalmatian coast facing Italy, as emperor in the west, and Nepos' forces were sufficient to force Glycerius to surrender, and retire to become a bishop, in 474. By now, the pull of Italian politics and the imperial court was waning to such a degree that Gundobad voluntarily gave up the position of master of the soldiers, to return to Burgundy and make good his claim to the Burgundian throne on his father's death: carving out an independent kingdom in Gaul was a more attractive prospect than exercising a Ricimer-style domination of what remained of the western empire. Gundobad was replaced by the general Orestes, a provincial from the Danube frontier who had served as Attila's secretary; Orestes drove out Nepos in favour of his own son, Romulus Augustulus, in 475. But Odoacer was not willing to back Orestes and in 476 his followers rebelled against the government, wanting regular pay on the model of a regular army, not the one-off subsidies on which they currently relied. Orestes was defeated, and his forces absorbed into Odoacer's following, which thus became the regular Roman army in the west. Romulus Augustulus was deposed and survived as a private citizen for a further quarter of a century, and Odoacer, acclaimed a king by his troops, ruled without a western emperor.

This political settlement confirmed the reality of the past quarter of a century, with the leader of the increasingly barbarised Italian army exercising practical political power. In fact, the attraction of the western imperial title for eastern adventurers like Olybrius, Anthemius or Nepos, or Roman generals like Petronius Maximus, Majorian, Glycerius or Orestes, had done much to cause instability by providing a political means by which the military supremacy of the master of the soldiers could be challenged. In this sense, the events of 476 were anything but catastrophic, and promised a return to the stability within Italy that Ricimer's regime had delivered in the 460s. Certainly, to the leaders of Italian society, and above all the senate at Rome, it presented no real threat; rather, it facilitated senatorial domination of Italian society in partnership with the military leadership. Indeed, one marked feature of the politics of the 460s and 470s was the lack of imperial aspirants from amongst the Italian aristocracy. Odoacer's royal title was seen as reflecting his relationship with his troops, not his power in Italy, where he simply served as military leader on the lines established by Ricimer.

Given the continued existence of an emperor at Constantinople, the events of 476 were not seen as revolutionary. Odoacer was keen to play on these constitutional niceties, negotiating with Constantinople to legitimate his position as ruler of Italy. The presence of the senate at Rome offered further possibilities, with grants of the largely honorific positions of consul and the like continuing as before. The despatch of the western emperor's regalia to Constantinople, and Odoacer's official titulature, as master of the soldiers, underlined the continued existence of the empire in constitutional theory. Constantinople, which had never recognised Romulus Augustulus, but continued to back the claims of Julius Nepos, may have been less than happy about Odoacer's actions, but it had been an interested and often disapproving observer of western politics for well over half a century. The current events constituted yet another western coup, not a threat to Roman sovereignty. In the event, after the murder of Nepos in 480, Constantinople chose not to raise up another claimant in his place, but instead to open somewhat uneasy negotiations with Odoacer. The eastern emperor Zeno faced a dangerous combination of barbarians and usurpers, making any attempt to deal with the situation in the west not only impossible, but also potentially disastrous, in that it might create a dangerous and legitimate rival.

Odoacer's coup, and the deposition of Romulus Augustulus in 476, remains indelibly etched in the chronology of world history as marking 'the fall of Rome', or, in more sober language, 'the end of the Roman Empire in the west'. Yet, embedded in immemorial authority though they are, this date and event are anything but a neutral 'fact' which is self-evident from the historical data. Rather, they are based on an amalgamation of medieval and modern interpretations that have fundamentally shaped our perception of the transition from Roman to barbarian Europe. There is absolutely no evidence that any contemporary of Odoacer's and Romulus saw the events of 476 as ending the Roman Empire in the west. Indeed, given the troubled succession of short-lived imperial dreams since 454, and the endemic conflict between military leaders and emperors, this was yet another coup at the top, the latest in a depressing succession which all too easily merged into one another. Even Odoacer's determination to rule without a western emperor was anything but revolutionary: Ricimer had made tentative moves in a similar direction in the 460s. Such a state of affairs made eminent sense precisely because the reassuring presence of a durable and potent imperial regime at Constantinople meant that the 'end of the Roman Empire' or 'the fall of Rome' was not at issue.

It was only around half a century after Odoacer's coup that observers in both east and west began to discern 'the fall of Rome', inaugurating a great set-piece historical debate which enjoys a continuous history down to the present day. It was very early on in this historical debate, in the second quarter of the sixth century, that the events of 476 came to be interpreted as marking 'the fall of Rome', and modern historians' reliance on these early discussions meant that 'the fall of Rome' and 'AD 476' quickly became reified as 'historical facts' as critical historical scholarship developed in the eighteenth and nineteenth centuries. In fact, the very first commentator to voice such an interpretation was the Byzantine chronicler Count Marcellinus, writing early in the sixth century. His sparse account of the fifth century offered both the deposition of Romulus and the fall of 'the last of the Romans' Aetius in 454 as possible dates for the end of the western empire. In the event, it was the later date which won favour with Marcellinus' successors, in spite of the fact that it involved reversing the official line of the late fifth-century eastern government, in both recognising Romulus, and ignoring Julius Nepos, whom Constantinople had continued to back as legitimate western emperor until his death in 480.[20]

Like many of his contemporaries in the early sixth-century east, when he looked west Marcellinus recognised that western Europe was made up of a series of effectively independent barbarian kingdoms. It seemed clear that somehow the Roman Empire in the west had ceased to exist, and it was now necessary to identify a sharp dividing point at which it had ended. History was thus reshaped with the benefit of hindsight, foreshortening the complex processes by which territorial kingdoms emerged around barbarian warlords in the late fifth- and early sixth-century west. This history of 'the fall of Rome' had a political dimension, offering an historical justification for the Emperor Justinian's policy of military intervention in the west by presenting it as 'reconquest'. But it also allowed western Mediterranean elites to understand how they had come to live in a world without a western emperor. Fundamentally it rested on a gradual recognition of political discontinuity, as the inhabitants of the sixth-century Mediterranean slowly recognised that their political world could no longer be adequately interpreted within the hitherto unquestioned and unquestionable framework of Roman world-empire.

The conservatism of the mental frameworks within which late fifth- and sixth-century elites thought about politics, and of the legitimising political ideologies with which they transformed power into authority, is underlined by the respect shown by the barbarian rulers of western Europe for the prerogatives of empire. Perhaps mindful of the sensitivities of the provincial elites who continued to exercise practical control in the localities, certainly informed by both diplomatic exchange with Constantinople and Romanised advisors who helped them build their regimes, barbarian kings continued to observe the constitutional niceties well into the sixth century. In coinage, for example, golden issues bearing the name or image of the ruler were avoided as an imperial prerogative until the late sixth century. Official recognition by Constantinople, and the gifts which went with diplomatic contact with the east, were similarly important as markers of legitimacy to the west's new rulers. To attempt to construct binding and clearly defined constitutional relationships between barbarian 'kings' in the west and the Roman emperor in Constantinople from all of this is to force the evidence too far. Much of this was the mutual deference typical of diplomacy, and the vagueness and vacuousness of the exchanges was intentional, in that it allowed rulers in east and west to place different interpretations on the same activity. But the constitutional vocabulary of the Roman Empire remained dominant in the post-Roman west, and played a central role in the gradual development of new forms of political legitimacy by barbarian kings.

How did the western empire end?

The problems of identifying the end of the Roman Empire in the west themselves tell us something important about the nature of the changes taking place. The 'fall of Rome' could only be identified with hindsight because it was a process that could only be recognised after its completion. It was not an event, self-evident and instantly understood by contemporaries, as a political rival announced the destruction of the Roman Empire and erected a new political infrastructure in its place. The ending of the process proved all the more difficult for contemporaries to identify as it coincided with no large-scale military or political crisis, no central drama on which attention could easily be focused. Rome in the west went out with a series of barely audible whimpers, rather than a single bang. The big 'bangs' had taken place in the late fourth and early fifth century, most notably with the collapse of the frontier system in the midst of the sustained political crisis in the west of 406–13. Alaric's sacking of Rome in 410 was the type of event to excite debate and reflection, and it coincided and interacted with the effective secession of much of western Europe from the direct control of the Roman state. But contemporaries were quite clear that these events did not mark the end of Rome, which successfully reinvented itself; nor did the Hunnic and Vandal raids of the 450s mark a caesura. Rather, provincial elites increasingly found themselves compelled to come to terms with local political realities that made traditional ties with Rome redundant. This process was eventually replayed in Italy itself, as practical power devolved into the hands of barbarian generals and the imperial office was eventually abandoned.

To this extent, we are dealing with a series of interconnected but individual shifts in the various provinces of the west. One fundamental problem for the historian is that the nature of the surviving evidence means that the further we move from the political centre of gravity, in Italy, the less we can say from the written evidence, and the harder it is to hear the 'whimpers' of provincial elites; and whilst archaeology can provide priceless insights into changes in social structure and cultural expression, it remains difficult to use as a source for political identity. Thus most modern scholarship has focused on the 'bangs' of the late fourth and early fifth centuries, often tacitly suggesting that Rome 'fell' then, in spite of the continued existence of western emperors for three-quarters of the fifth century. The result has been to foreshorten modern historians' understanding of the 'fall of Rome', presenting a short and dramatic crisis after which barbarian incomers take centre stage, and to encourage discussion of the difficult yet crucial middle decades of the fifth century in terms of the formation of barbarian kingdoms, rather than the continued efforts of Roman leaders.

In fact, listening for the fifth-century 'whimpers' with which the empire ended is vital, for it is in these protracted negotiations between barbarian warlords and provincial elites that a new social and political order was formed. In most frontier provinces, accommodation with a post-Roman political reality probably began soon after 406–13. Along the Rhine and Danube frontiers, long-term barbarian neighbours were no strangers, whilst in Britain the collapse of much of the basic framework of Roman society in the first half of the fifth century led to similar reorientation. But when and why elites came to see themselves as no longer part of the empire is harder to detect. The same is true of Hispania. The evidence from southern Gaul, thanks to Sidonius, allows us to identify the 460s and early 470s as the crucial period, but even here, at the heart of the western empire, the move away from a Rome-based political order was drawn out and gradual.

Sidonius' testimony can be complemented with Eugippius' *Life of St Severinus*. Severinus was a charismatic Holy Man who was active in the second half of the fifth century in his native province of Noricum, along the middle Danube in modern Austria. Eugippius, a disciple of Severinus, had fled Noricum for southern Italy after his hero's death; it was here, in circles close to the families of the last two western emperors, Julius Nepos and Romulus Augustulus, that he wrote up his hero's career as an argument for a particular model of asceticism, but also as a reflection on how Roman rule in Noricum had ended. Eugippius' picture of the frontier society in which Severinus had operated is fascinating: the Holy Man acted as a mediator and arbitrator between the provincial population, clustered behind the walls of the Roman cities along the Danube, and their long-standing barbarian neighbours, the Rugians and their king, with whom relations were friendly and basically symbiotic. Eugippius claimed that the definitive end of Roman Noricum came when the imperial government could no longer pay the remaining frontier troops: a party which left for Milan to return with their pay never returned, rumoured to have been murdered by barbarians, and as a result the garrisons drifted away leaving the cities undefended. The crucial break may in fact have come with the destruction of this provincial–Rugian symbiosis on which stability of this frontier had rested: here, political conflict between Odoacer and Constantinople had stirred up unfamiliar, hostile barbarians from the interior, whose depredations destroyed the delicate balancing act which Severinus had worked tirelessly to maintain.[21]

The important point to be made is that the 'end of Rome' was not a matter of barbarian armies defeating Roman opponents by force of arms, smashing their way into the empire and setting up a new political system. Indeed, with the exception of Valens' defeat by the Goths at Adrianople, it is remarkable how rarely in the fourth and fifth centuries barbarian forces defeated Roman armies in pitched battle. The typical form of military conflict remained that between rival Roman parties allied with different barbarian allies; barbarians fought to gain their leaders and ally a position within a Roman political framework. The move from 'Roman' to 'barbarian' rule was thus a matter of accommodation and negotiation between provincial elites and their military protectors, as the regular Roman army was replaced by barbarian warbands, and the patronage system of the imperial court slowly lost its pull, forcing provincial elites to narrow their political horizons.

Traditional views of Rome's 'fall' being wrought by barbarian invasion and conquest have been dominant through the millennium and a half since the end of the western empire. First developed in response to the perceptions of political discontinuity felt in the sixth-century Mediterranean, and reinforced by Justinian's 'reconquest' ideology, the need of early medieval kingdoms for foundation legends encouraged the further elaboration of a picture of barbarian invasions carving out new kingdoms. By the seventh and eighth centuries, these invasions were presented increasingly not only as conquests, but as wholesale replacements of population, as historians attempted to explain why the people of northern Gaul now called themselves 'Franks', those of Burgundy 'Burgundians' and so on. These histories became the origin legends of medieval kingdoms, and were used to explain the ethnic basis for the nation-states of modern Europe. They encouraged historians to see the 'fall of Rome' as a clean break, marking a fresh start as new peoples brought new customs with which they replaced the Roman society they overwhelmed and swamped.

In fact, once we avoid the presumption that the fall of Rome was an easily identifiable event, and examine the drawn-out process of political change in the fifth century in its entirety, continuity should no longer be a surprise. Barbarian warbands, even in the so-called 'great invasion' of 407–13, faced very little sustained local opposition. Militarily, they expanded into a vacuum, and provincial elites were thus soon willing to establish alliances with them to pursue their own ambitions. Whilst we should not sanitise the experience of invasion, civil war and political dislocation, or forget the associated plunder, pillage and destruction, it would be a mistake to see this type of conflict as leading to the outright devastation of Roman order, and a wholesale social collapse. Italy in the 450s probably suffered more than any other province in a comparable short span, and whilst imperial legislation makes it clear that there was an acute crisis, with power increasingly passing directly into the hands of landowners, it is also abundantly apparent from both written and archaeological evidence that Italian society did not collapse.

The fact that barbarians did not smash past Roman field armies, but entered a military vacuum, and soon established themselves as allies of provincial elites and Roman leaders, means that we have no need to see barbarian invasion and settlement as bringing with it a wholesale change of population based on the migration of entire peoples. This is reinforced if we look at the evidence for the actual scale of barbarian immigration. Numerical reports by ancient historians are notoriously inaccurate, and it has become deeply unfashionable to make any use of them whatsoever. Whilst they must be labelled 'handle with care', the estimates we do have are worth discussion. In the case of Vandal Africa, we have a number of different reports that clearly draw on contemporary debates over the size of the Vandal threat. Victor of Vita gives the number 80,000, claiming that it was based on a headcount taken by Gaiseric as his followers crossed the Straits of Gibraltar, but adds that this included women, children and the aged, not just warriors as some claimed. Victor was partly writing to mobilise Roman opinion against the Vandal regime, and here he is best seen as trying to explain figures that had become customary estimates of Vandal strength. Almost a century later, the Byzantine historian Procopius clearly drew on the same tradition, as he claimed that the Vandal army was made up of 80 units of 1,000, although he adds that this figure was a matter of controversy, as some earlier writers had believed Gaiseric's forces numbered 50,000. Whilst none of these figures should be taken as accurate, they have the same validity as the estimates of Roman military strength we derive from sources such as the *Notitia Dignitatum*; indeed, they are of the same scale, presumably because they derive from the same kind of strategic discourse. Given that the figures relate to an exceptional circumstance – the lock, stock and barrel migration of all the barbarians, bar the Sueves, in Hispania – it suggests that we should think of the biggest population movements as involving tens of thousands, with more normal barbarian bands numbering in the thousands. Ammianus' estimate, of 300,000 Goths, women and children included, crossing the Danube in the wholly exceptional circumstances which led up to the battle of Adrianople, seems to suggest barbarian movements of a similar order. The conclusion must be, then, that barbarian 'peoples' were of a similar size to fully mobilised Roman field armies; whilst militarily imposing, they were not sizeable enough to drive out the provincial population or swamp Roman society.[22]

Given the imbalance in weight between the barbarian incomers and their 'host' societies, continuity in the basics of social organisation in the post-Roman world is hardly surprising. Of course, the encounter between barbarian warriors and provincial civilians differed from region to region. For one thing, Roman society survived to varying degrees in different regions. In Britain and along the Gallic frontier, the infrastructure of provincial society seems to have rapidly collapsed once the Roman army and government withdrew at the beginning of the fifth century, whereas in Hispania, although abandoned at the same time, the landowning elite was able to maintain the cities and tax system. And different regions encountered barbarians in different ways. Along the Rhine frontier, barbarian rulers were well-known neighbours who had long been a part of a homogenous frontier society, whereas in Italy barbarians arrived as warbands providing military protection, but had long been painted as an uncivilised and uncontrolled Other, with barbarian dress outlawed and marriage between citizens and barbarians prohibited. But right across the former western empire, barbarian newcomers were integrated into societies that had emerged from Roman provinces; they did not start afresh, importing a social model from the forests of Germany.

The barbarians are often said to have brought their own legal customs with them, inaugurating a system of 'the personality of the law', whereby the remaining provincial population continued to use Roman law but Burgundians, Goths and Franks were all judged by their own, special, laws. The evidence for this, on close examination, is flimsy. In the decades around 500, barbarian rulers – the Visigothic king Euric in the 460s or 470s and the Burgundian Sigismund in the 510s – began to promulgate law-codes, provincial imitations of the great Theodosian Code. These collections were designed to demonstrate to the populations of the new kingdoms that Roman respect for law as the guarantor of civilisation would continue, much as Ataulf had promised at his wedding banquet a century earlier; the issuing of laws quickly became a central aspect of barbarian kingship. These law-codes consist largely of collections of edicts and judgements made by barbarian rulers, just as the Theodosian Code collected imperial edicts; they thus show the continuation of Roman structures of appeal and ruling on difficult issues on a provincial level, and rest on the advice and draftsmanship of Roman advisors at barbarian courts. This concern with utilising the techniques and traditions of Roman legal practice to deal with new problems in a new context explains why both Visigothic and Burgundian legislation was complemented by handbooks of Roman law, with the abridgement of the Theodosian Code in the Breviary of the Visigothic king Alaric becoming the standard text of Roman law in the early medieval west. In content, the law-codes of the barbarian kings primarily deal with difficult issues raised by the integration of barbarian newcomers into provincial society; they thus focus primarily on current problems regarding the relations between barbarians and Romans, and were territorial in their application. We certainly cannot read them as collections of the ancestral customs of a particular people, although there is some – albeit surprisingly little – material on the adaptation of barbarian 'custom' concerning matters of personal injury and compensation. They thus bear witness to a process of social transformation among both barbarian incomers and Roman provincials.[23]

Transformation is certainly visible in the identities of the barbarian incomers: look at the case of Odoacer, the son of a Hun general who had set himself up as king of the Scirians, was also described as a Rugian, and served both as a Roman general and 'king' of a heterogeneous barbarian warband, most of whom ended up joining Theodoric's Goths. In fact, the barbarian leaders who carved out the new kingdoms of the post-Roman west were themselves members of an international military aristocracy that had been shaped by service of the Roman state. In Gaul, for example, the Burgundian king Gundobad, and the Frankish ruler Childeric had both begun their careers as Roman generals within the official hierarchy of imperial command, whilst in Italy Theodoric, the Gothic king who defeated Odoacer, had been raised as a hostage in Constantinople. In such circles, barbarians of diverse origin intermarried with Roman leaders, as a hybrid Roman-barbarian military cadre emerged. The Hun Empire of the first half of the fifth century had left a clear imprint on this class: Roman generals like Aetius or Orestes had benefited from their personal links to the Huns, whilst barbarian leaders like Odoacer and Theodoric emerged in the aftermath of the Hunnic collapse of the 450s as leaders of former 'subject peoples'. It is no accident that the archaeology suggests that badges of Roman military command, and a style of military equipment derived from that associated with the Hunnic Empire, served as symbols of political legitimacy in the late fifth and early sixth centuries. Swords and helms harking back to the military culture of the Danube frontier, along with brooches issued as insignia to Roman generals, are found in rich burials from this period in northern Gaul and along and beyond the Rhine and Danube frontiers, most famously in the grave of Childeric but also in the 'Flonheim-Gültlingen' graves of northern Gaul and the Rhine frontier with which it is so closely associated.

The history of the fall of the Roman Empire in the west is in many ways the story of the formation of this hybrid military elite in the late fourth and early fifth centuries, and its subsequent rise to political dominance, until its members ruled the provinces of the west directly, without the mediation of the imperial government. In the fifth century, the challenge facing the Roman state was the need, given the cost of maintaining a huge standing army through the tax system, to utilise barbarian warbands as Roman armies, without leaving barbarian warleaders directly in control of Roman provinces.

In the east, the government at Constantinople was able to meet the challenge, helped in part by the fact that the Danube was the eastern empire's only frontier with the barbarians, but primarily by the stability of the rich, tax-paying and recruit-producing, eastern provinces which meant that barbarian recruits complemented regular Roman armies. Hence it was possible in 399–400 to sack and destroy Gainas' Goths. Hence subsequent barbarian leaders who served as eastern generals, such as Aspar, were never independent of the Roman state, with even Aspar eventually executed on the orders of his imperial master. Hence Gothic leaders in the 470s demanded that Constantinople disband its army and divert the tax revenue freed to hiring the Goths instead but were ignored.

In the west, there was no need to make such demands because imperial armies had vanished. The severe problems of maintaining the loyalty of the western provinces, always ready to back provincial usurpers, and the tension between the imperial court and the senate in Rome, were to prove fatal. Funding and recruitment for the western army remained difficult, and military units stationed in the western provinces quickly became potential political threats to the emperor. Thus by the first decade of the fifth century the western army had vanished, the frontier system collapsed, and the outlying western provinces were abandoned. Nonetheless, in the first half of the fifth century, the western government was to develop a new method of integration, with the settlement of barbarians within the empire as federates to provide a military shield, and the use of Hunnic allies and mercenaries in Roman service as a means of keeping order amongst the barbarians. The crisis of this system came in the 450s and 460s, as the collapse of the web of alliances and understandings centred on Aetius and the Huns, and the spectre of Vandal dominance in the western Mediterranean left the Roman government unable to keep military or political order. The result was, inevitably, that the barbarian military leaders on whom the western government had relied increasingly started to deal directly with the provincial societies they protected. The outcome was a new style of political organisation, as barbarian military leaders carved out territorial states based on kingship of a people. But the initial attempts at barbarian state-building – the kingdoms of the Vandals in Africa, the Goths and Burgundians in Gaul and, after the overthrow of Odoacer by Theodoric the Ostrogoth, the Goths in Italy and its appendages – proved short-lived. To understand why, we must look at the ebb and flow of Constantinople's dominance in the sixth- and seventh-century Mediterranean, and at the lasting successor states created in the course of the sixth century by Franks in Gaul, Lombards in Italy, and Goths in Hispania.

Bibliographical essay

General works

In general, the fifth-century empire has received less attention than it deserves. In part, of course, this is a function of the difficulty and fragmentary nature of the sources, but it has the unfortunate tendency of encouraging historians to see 'the fall of Rome' as a single phenomenon to be debated in terms of grand theories and monocausal explanations, instead of offering a proper analysis of the complex and interlocking processes at work in the fifth century.

P. Heather, *The Fall of Rome: A New History of Romans and Barbarians* (Oxford, 2005) offers an informed political narrative of this period, whilst Averil Cameron, *The Mediterranean World in Late Antiquity, 395–600* (London, 1994) is an insightful discussion of the structures of fifth- and sixth-century Mediterranean society. There is no shortage of works advancing a grand theory accounting for the fall of the Roman Empire: barbarian invasions, the socio-psychological effects of Christianity, over-taxation and manpower shortage have all been advanced. Most recent commentators would stress changes in military organisation, and particularly the replacement of the western army by barbarian federates and private militias: see the bibliography below. For the most successful recent attempt at a 'grand theory', focusing on the role of the aristocracy and the collapse of the tax system, see C. Wickham, 'The other transition: from the ancient world to feudalism', *Past & Present* 103 (1984), and see also P. Wormald, 'The decline of the western empire and the survival of its aristocracy', *Journal of Roman Studies* 66 (1976).

For reactions to 476, which only gradually and with hindsight came to be seen as marking the 'fall of Rome', see B. Croke, '476: the manufacture of a turning point', *Chiron* 13 (1983), E. Demougeot, 'Bedeutet das Jahr 476 das Ende des römischen Reichs im Okzident?', *Klio* 60 (1978), A. Momigliano, 'La caduta senza rumore di un impero nel 476', *Concetto, storia, mitti e immagini del Medio Evo* (Florence, 1973).

Translated sources

Fifth-century sources are more difficult, and fragmentary: there is no vivid narrative comparable to Ammianus. Nonetheless, the sources that there are deserve more attention for the insights they provide into reactions to changes within the western empire. Probably the most vivid accounts are Salvian, *On the Governance of God*, tr. J. F. Sullivan, *The Works of Salvian the Presbyter* (Washington, 1972); Victor of Vita, *History of the Vandal Persecution*, tr. J. Moorhead (Liverpool, 1992); Eugippius, *Life of Severinus*, tr. L. Bieler (Washington DC, 1965); and Sidonius Apollinaris, *Poems and Letters*, tr. W. B. Anderson (London, 1967). Note also the collection of C. D. Gordon, *The Age of Attila* (New York, 1966), and the excellent coverage in the relevant sections of A. C. Murray, *From Roman to Merovingian Gaul* (Peterborough, Ont., 1998).

Chronicle material is terse and often frustrating, but most is available in translation, e.g. R. W. Burgess, *The Chronicle of Hydatius and the Consularia Constantinopolitana* (Oxford, 1993); Zosimus, *New History*, tr. R. Rapley (Sydney, 1982); Count Marcellinus' *Chronicle*, tr. B. Croke (Sydney, 1995); R. C. Blockley, *The Fragmentary Classicising Historians of the Later Roman Empire*, 2 vols (Liverpool, 1981–3), which includes Priscus and Olympiodorus. Prosper and the 'Gallic Chronicle of 452' are accessible in Murray's *From Roman to Merovingian Gaul*. See also S. Muhlberger, *The Fifth Century Chroniclers: Prosper, Hydatius and the Gallic Chronicler of 452* (Leeds, 1990); R. Markus, 'Prosper of Aquitaine: theology and history', in C. Holdsworth and T. P. Wiseman, eds, *The Inheritance of Historiography 350–900* (Exeter, 1986); B. Croke, *Count Marcellinus and his Chronicle* (Oxford, 2001); M. Maas, 'Ethnicity, community and identity in Salvian', in J. Drinkwater and H. Elton, eds, *Fifth-Century Gaul: A Crisis of Identity?* (Cambridge, 1992); D. Lambert, 'The barbarians in Salvian', in S. Mitchell and G. Greatrex, eds, *Ethnicity and Culture in Late Antiquity* (London, 2000); and W. Goffart, 'Zosimus: the first historian of Rome's fall' and 'An empire unmade, 300–600', both in his *Rome's Fall and After* (London, 1989). For secondary reading on Sidonius and Eugippius – the two star witnesses for debate on the 'fall of Rome' – see below.

Letter collections are one genre of source material deserving of more study: as well as the classic collection of Sidonius' letters see the fifth-century collections of Ruricius of Limoges, tr. R. Mathisen (Liverpool, 1999) and Avitus of Vienne, tr. D. Shanzer and I. Wood (Liverpool, 2002).

Political history

Heather's work is far and away the best starting point. H. Wolfram, *The Roman Empire and its Germanic Peoples* (Berkeley, 1997) tells the story of the barbarian incomers: this work is in many ways the culmination of a lifetime's study on these themes, and Wolfram's exhaustive and critical understanding of the sources is used to argue that tribal traditions and myth played a central role in the making of the barbarian west. E. A. Thompson, *Romans and Barbarians* (Madison, 1982) is also a useful overview, but predates recent debate about the nature of the barbarian 'peoples' entering the empire.

The problems of sparse narratives as a basis for the source material, and the historiographical tendency to write off the western empire after 410, means that a full account of the age of Aetius has yet to be written, and the later fifth century poses a greater challenge still. For some comments on Aetius' strategy, viewed less positively than here, see J. R. Moss, 'The effects of the policies of Aetius on the history of western Europe', *Historia* 22 (1973). A. Gillett, 'Rome Ravenna and the last western emperors', *Papers of the British School at Rome* 69 (2001) is important on the imperial court. Other than that, detailed studies of the prosopography of the fifth-century elite offer important insights: e.g. R. Mathisen, 'Resistance and reconciliation: Majorian and the Gallic aristocracy after the fall of Avitus', *Francia* 7 (1979) and, for the links between the Vandal takeover of Africa and internal Roman politics, 'Sigisvult the Patrician, Maximinus the Arian, and political stratagems in the western Roman Empire 425–50', *Early Medieval Europe* 8 (1999).

Regional studies

In fact, the best way into the problems of the fifth century has proved to be a regional approach, focusing on one individual or area and their experience of the dramatic changes taking place.

On North Africa the classic study is C. Courtois, *Les Vandales et l'Afrique* (Paris, 1955), but the best recent work, luckily in English, is in the collected essays of F. M. Clover, *The Late Roman West and the Vandals* (Aldershot, 1993), which also cover the fourth century, and see now A. Merrills, ed., *Vandals, Romans and Berbers* (Aldershot, 2005). The archaeological finds from Carthage are transforming our knowledge: the most recent discussion (also including the art historical evidence of mosaics) is A. Ben Abed and N. Duval, 'Carthage, la capitale du royaume et les villes de Tunisie a l'èpoque vandale', in G. Ripoll, ed., *Sedes Regiae* (Barcelona, 2000). The precise economic trajectory of fifth- and sixth-century Carthage is a matter of debate: it is not in dispute that the fourth century was a period of prosperity, nor that there was serious decline by the seventh, but the chronology of the change is both important and difficult to unpick. For bibliography see chapter 5 below.

On Hispania, where fifth-century evidence is scarce and difficult, there is a series of articles by E. A. Thompson on 'The end of Roman Spain', *Nottingham Medieval Studies* 20–3 (1976–9); also J. Arce, 'The enigmatic fifth century', in J. Jarnut, H.-W. Goetz and W. Pohl, eds, *Gentes and Regna* (Leiden, 2002).

Gaul is probably the best-studied region, although the vast majority of the work has been done on the south, whose elite has left us a (relative) wealth of evidence. E. Wightman, *Gallia Belgica* (London, 1985) remains a classic and covers the north, whilst R. van Dam, *Leadership and Community in Late Antique Gaul* (Berkeley, 1988) is a brilliant discussion of the changing face of the aristocracy of the south. The best modern study of the fifth century concentrates on the eloquent testimony of one individual navigating a course through political changes: J. Harries, *Sidonius Apollinaris and the Fall of Rome* (Oxford, 1993), with the plentiful earlier bibliography on Sidonius; see also Harries' 'Sidonius Apollinaris and the frontiers of *Romanitas*', in R. Mathisen and H. Sivan, eds, *Shifting Frontiers in Late Antiquity* (Madisen, 1996), and W. M. Daly, '*Christianitas* eclipses *Romanitas* in the life of Sidonius Apollinaris', in T. Noble and J. Contreni, eds, *Religion, Culture and Society in the Early Middle Ages* (Kalamazoo, 1987). The essays collected in J. F. Drinkwater and H. Elton, *Fifth Century Gaul: A Crisis of Identity?* (Cambridge, 1992) and in R. Mathisen and D. Shanzer, *Culture and Society in Fifth-Century Gaul: Revisiting the Sources* (Aldershot, 2002) are varied and valuable. For a sophisticated view of changing political identities see P. Amory, 'Ethnographic rhetoric, aristocratic attitudes and political allegiance in post-Roman Gaul', *Klio* 76 (1994).

Detailed prosopographical investigations of the southern Gallic aristocracy were begun by K. F. Stroheker, *Der senatorische Adel in spatantiken Gallien* (Tubingen, 1948) and *Germanentum und Spätantike* (Zurich and Stuttgart, 1965), and continued by R. W. Mathisen, most recently in *Roman Aristocrats in Barbarian Gaul: Strategies for Survival in an Age of Transition* (Austin, 1993), which is perhaps of more value for the wealth of information than the interpretative framework. Much of the prosopographical work has concentrated on aristocratic control of bishoprics as a strategy for adaptation and survival: see M. Heinzelmann, *Bischofsherrschaft im Gallien* (Munich, 1976); R. Mathisen, *Ecclesiastical Factionalism and Religious Controversy in Fifth Century Gaul* (Washington DC, 1989).

On the Danube frontier, a key and often neglected area, unfortunately there is little in English, but see R. Markus, 'The end of the Roman Empire: a note on Eugippius' *Vita S. Severini* 20', *Nottingham Medieval Studies* 31 (1982); on this crucial text see now W. Pohl and M. Diesenberger, eds, *Eugippius und Severin. Der Autor, der Text und der Heilige* (Vienna, 2001), and for the wider context F. Daim and H. Wolfram, eds, *Die Völker an der mittleren und unteren Donau im fünften und sechsten Jahrhundert* (Vienna, 1980).

Oddly enough, there is very little in the way of regional studies of this key period in Italy, in part a result of a general lack interest in the political history of the fifth-century empire; attention has tended to focus instead on the barbarian rulers, and so work on the end of Roman Italy has tended to focus on Theodoric's regime. The dramatic reassertion of senatorial power and the continuing pull of the patronage of the imperial court are two themes in fifth-century Italian history which deserve serious study.

For reading on fifth-century Britain, see chapter 6 below, noting the reservations concerning the construct of 'withdrawal' and the historiographical isolationism favoured by most British historians.

The end of the western army: barbarians, *bucellarii* and *Bacaudae*

For the late Roman army and the *Notitia Dignitatum* see the bibliography to chapter 1, above. The key recent study of Roman military strategy and the barbarians is Burns, *Barbarians within the Gates of Rome*. On the fifth-century transformation of the western military see J. H. W. G. Liebeschuetz, 'The end of the Roman army in the west' and C. R. Whittaker, 'Warlords and landlords in the later Roman Empire', in J. Rich and G. Shipley, eds, *Warfare in the Roman World* (London, 1993); see also J. H. W. G. Liebeschuetz, 'Generals, federates and buccelarii in Roman armies around 400', in P. W. Freeman and D. L. Kennedy, eds, *The*

Defence of the Roman and Byzantine East, British Archaeological Reports International Series 297 (Oxford, 1986). H. J Diesner, 'Das Bucellarietum von Stilicho und Sarus bis auf Aetius', *Klio* 54 (1972) is an exhaustive study of the legislation, whilst J. Gascou, 'L'institution des bucellaires', *Bulletin de l'Institut Français de l'Archaeologie Orientale* 76 (1976) uses the Egyptian papyri to study the impact of these changes in the east.

For exciting recent developments in our understanding of the *Bacaudae*, see the relevant sections of van Dam, *Leadership and Community*, and a series of articles by J. F. Drinkwater: 'Peasants and Bagaudae in Roman Gaul', *Classical Views* 3 (1984); 'Patronage in Roman Gaul and the problem of the Bagaudae', in A. Wallace-Hadrill, ed., *Patronage in Ancient Society* (London, 1989); 'The Bacaudae of fifth-century Gaul', in Elton and Drinkwater, *Fifth-Century Gaul*. See also A. Giardina, 'Banditi e santi: un aspetto del folkloro gallico tra tarda antichita e medioevo', *Athanaeum* 61 (1983). The key work on legitimate and illegitimate violence is B. Shaw, 'Bandits in the Roman Empire', *Past & Present* 105 (1984).

Barbarian 'federates': settlements and kingship

On the handling of barbarian 'federates', debate has centred on Alaric's Goths, and touches on a series of key points of controversy in understanding the nature of the barbarian 'peoples' who entered the empire and the mechanisms by which they were settled. On the mechanics of barbarian settlement, W. Goffart, *Barbarians and Romans: The Techniques of Accomodation* (Princeton, 1980), launched the 'tax or land' debate; for response see M. Cesa, 'Hospitalitas o altere "techniques of accommodation"?', *Archivo storico italiano* 140 (1982), S. Barnish, 'Taxation, land and barbarian settlement in the later Roman Empire', *Papers of the British School at Rome* 54 (1986); M. Innes, 'Land, freedom and the making of the early medieval west', *Transactions of the Royal Historical Society* (2006) suggests a different perspective.

H. Wolfram and A. Schwarcz, eds, *Anerkennung und Integration* (Vienna, 1988), E. Chyrsos and A. Schwarcz, eds, *Das Reich und die Barbaren* (Vienna, 1989) and W. Pohl and H. Reimitz, eds, *Kingdoms of the Empire: The Integration of Barbarians in Late Antiquity* (Leiden, 1997) all discuss the integration of barbarians from a variety of perspectives. The integration of barbarian leaders into the late Roman military establishment is surveyed by E. Chyrsos, 'The osmosis of the late Roman and Germanic military aristocracies', in Chrysos and A. Schwarcz, eds, *Das Reich und die Barbaren* (Vienna, 1989); on Roman-barbarian marriage see J. H. W. G. Liebeschuetz, 'Citizen status and law in the Roman Empire and the Visigothic kingdom', and H. Sivan, 'The appropriation of Roman law in barbarian hands: Roman-barbarian marriage in Visigothic Gaul and Spain', both in W. Pohl and H. Reimitz, eds, *Strategies of Distinction* (Leiden, 1998), and H. Sivan, 'Why not marry a barbarian? Marital frontiers in late antiquity', in R. Mathisen and H. Sivan, eds, *Shifting Frontiers in Late Antiquity* (Madisen, 1996).

The various barbarian 'kingdoms' are studied by Wolfram and Thompson, as above, general reading; various contributions to J. Jarnut, H.-W. Goetz and

W. Pohl, eds, *Gentes and Regna* (Leiden, 2002) also offer the latest thinking e.g. Liebeschuetz on the Vandals, Wood on the Burgundians. On the Vandal kingdom see the bibliography on Africa above. On the Burgundians, P. Amory, 'The meaning and purpose of ethnic terminology in the Burgundian laws', *Early Medieval Europe* 2 (1993), 'Names, ethnic identity and community in fifth and sixth century Burgundy', *Viator* 25 (1994), I. Wood, 'Ethnicity and the ethnogenesis of the Burgundians', in H. Wolfram and W. Pohl, eds, *Typen der Ethnogenese* (Vienna, 1990). On the Visigoths and the kingdom of Toulouse see the reading on the Goths, chapter 2 above, plus P. Heather ed., *The Visigoths from the Migration Period to the Seventh Century* (Woodbridge, 1999).

Important studies of the evolution of barbarian kingship within the empire are H. Wolfram, 'The shaping of the early medieval kingdom', *Viator* 1 (1970), and 'The shaping of the early medieval principality', *Viator* 2 (1971). On the law, there is Wormald's important contribution to Jarnut, Goetz and Pohl, eds, *Gentes und Regna* (Leiden, 2002), and compare J. Harries, 'Legal culture and identity in the fifth-century west' with J. Matthews, 'Roman law and barbarian identity in the later Roman Empire', both in R. Mathisen, ed., *Law, Society and Authority in Late Antiquity* (Oxford, 2001); also A. Sirks, 'Shifting frontiers in the law: Romans, provincials and barbarians', in R. Mathisen and H. Sivan, eds, *Shifting Frontiers in Late Antiquity* (Madisen, 1996). P. Heather, 'Literacy and power in the migration period', in A. Bowman and G. Woolf, eds, *Literacy and Power in the Ancient World* (Cambridge, 1994) is important on the role of Roman advisors. P. S. Barnwell, *Emperor, Prefects and Kings: The Roman West 395–565* (London, 1992) argues for wholesale administrative continuity; see also his 'Emperors, jurists and kings: law and custom in the late Roman and early medieval west', *Past & Present* 168 (2000).

Attila and the Huns

On the Huns, E. A. Thompson, *A History of Attila and the Huns* (Oxford, 1948, reprinted 1996) is the best guide; Heather's afterword to the new edition gives a good guide to recent work, although there is more to be done. P. Heather, 'The Huns and the end of the Roman Empire in western Europe', *English Historical Review* 110 (1995) argues that the arrival of the Huns had cataclysmic effects on their barbarian neighbours and ultimately the Roman Empire. D. Sinor, 'The Hunnic period', in D. Sinor, ed., *Cambridge History of Eurasia and Inner Asia* (Cambridge, 1986), provides the wider background of developments on the steppes; see also his 'The historical Attila', in his *Studies in Medieval Inner Asia* (Aldershot, 1997). There is also the unfinished work of O. Maenchen-Helfen, *The World of the Huns* (Berkeley, 1973), and, in German, two archaeological treatments: I. Bona, *Das Hunnenreich* (Budapest, 1991) and the still classic J. Werner, *Beitrage zur Archaeologie des Attila-Reiches* (Vienna, 1956). D. Sinor, 'Horse and pasture in inner east Asian history', in his *Inner Asia and its Contacts with Medieval Europe* (Aldershot, 1977), and R. P. Linder, 'Nomads, horses and Huns', *Past & Present* 92 (1981) are important treatments, applying modern understanding of the workings of nomadic and semi-nomadic societies.

Notes

1. Rutilius Namatianus, 'On his return', tr. H. Isbell, *Last Poets of Imperial Rome* (London, 1971); extracts in A. C. Murray, *From Roman to Frankish Gaul: A Reader* (Peterborough, Ont., 2000).
2. See for example the terse entries in the 'Gallic Chronicle of 452', tr. A. C. Murray, *From Roman to Merovingian Gaul* (Peterborough, Ont., 2000), where *divisiones* between provincials and barbarians stand in marked contrast to the forcible seizures made by the Alans. See also Hydatius' *Chronicle*, tr. R. W. Burgess (Oxford, 1993), s.a. 411 for the negotiated division of Spanish provinces into *sortes*.
3. Sidonius Apollinaris, *Poems and Letters*, tr. W. B. Anderson (London, 1967), poem 12. The variety of mechanisms of land acquisition is clearest in the Burgundian Code, a collection of earlier decrees published *c.* 517 by King Sigismund: K. F. Drew, tr., *The Burgundian Code* (Philadelphia, 1971).
4. Sidonius Apollinaris, *Letters*, I: 2.
5. Hydatius, *Chronicle*, s.a. 409.
6. Zosimus, *New History*, tr. R Rapley (Sydney, 1982), 6.5.
7. Although the word is used in several sources, particularly the 'Chronicle of 452', the only extended discussion of the *Bacaudae* is in Salvian, *On the Governance of God*, tr. J. F. Sullivan (Washington, 1976), 5.6, which is highly rhetorical and needs handling with care.
8. Note that traditional chronologies of Aetius' activities are largely dependent on the Gallic 'Chronicle of 452', whose internal structures and dating systems may be less reliable than is often assumed; the normal dates, given here, need to be treated as if they are in inverted commas. For Auxerre, Constantius of Lyon, *Life of Germanus*, tr. T. Head and T. Noble (London, 1998); for the appeals of Britons and Gallicians, see Gildas, *On the Ruin of Britain*, ed. & tr. M. Winterbottom (London, 1978) 20.1, Hydatius, *Chronicle*, s.a. 431.
9. Here we are dependent on Jordanes, *Gothic History*, tr. C. C. Mierow (Princeton, 1915), pp. 197–215, which is dependent on a century of myth-making.
10. Merobaudes, *Poems*, tr. F. Clover (Philadelphia, 1971).
11. Salvian, *On the Governance of God*, quotation from 5: 5.
12. Priscus, fragment 4, ed. & tr. R. C. Blockley, *The Fragmentary Classicising Historians of the Later Roman Empire*, vol. 2 (Liverpool, 1983).
13. Sidonius, *Letters*, 1: 7 (Arvandus) and see also the 'conspiracy of Marcellus', 1: 11.
14. Sidonius, *Letters*, 3: 3 (Ecdicius); 4: 17 (Arbogast).
15. Sidonius, *Letters*, 5.5 (Syagrius) and for culture replacing rank see also 2: 10, 4: 17.
16. See the Novels of Majorian, tr. C. Pharr, *The Theodosian Code* (Berkeley, 1956).
17. Victor of Vita, *History of the Vandal Persecution*, tr. J. Moorhead (Liverpool, 1992); Procopius, *Wars*, esp. Book 3 (= Book 1 of the two-book *Vandal Wars*), tr. H. Dewing (Cambridge, MA, 1939); Fulgentius of Ruspe, tr. R. Eno (Washington, 1997).

18. Archaeology: A. Ben Abed and N. Duval, 'Carthage, la capitale du royaume et les villes de Tunisie à l'époque vandale', in G. Ripoll and J. Gurt, eds, *Sedes Regiae (400–800)* (Barcelona, 2000); documents: C. Courtois *et al.*, eds, *Tablettes Albertini* (Paris, 1952); for the poetry see Dracontius' *Satisfactio*, tr. M. Margeret (Philadelphia, 1936) and see M. Rosenblum, *Luxurius: A Latin Poet among the Vandals* (New York, 1961).
19. Regalia: Procopius, *Wars*, 3: 25. Djeders: A. Rushworth, 'State formation and regional identity in the pre-Saharan zone', in A. Merrills, ed., *Vandals, Romans and Berbers* (Aldershot, 2005), at pp. 79–86. Inscriptions: see e.g. G. Camps, 'Rex gentium Maurorum et Romanorum. Recherches sur les royaumes de Mauretanie des VIe et VIIe siècles', *Antiquités africaines* 20 (1984).
20. See B. Croke, '476: the manufacture of a turning point', *Chiron* 13 (1983).
21. Euggipius, *Life of Severinus*, tr. L. Bieler (Washington, 1965).
22. Victor of Vita, *History of the Vandal Persecution*, I: 2; Procopius, *Wars*, 3: 5; Ammianus, 31.1–4.
23. The complex issues are best addressed by a direct look at the legislation itself, which simply does not read as codification of ancestral customs. See Drew, tr., *The Burgundian Code* for the Burgundians (though take care with her introduction; her view of the code's origins predates recent work, e.g. by Ian Wood); Euric's code survives only in one erased manuscript, and is unfortunately untranslated, but it gave rise to the tradition of royal law-giving and codification evident in S. P. Scott, tr., *The Visigothic Code* (Boston, 1910).

Part II

The End of the Ancient Mediterranean

4

The western Mediterranean in the age of 'reconquest'

Contents

Summary

Chronology

Italy under Gothic management

Gothic identities and Italian allegiances

Essay: Gothic identity and material culture

The Christian empire and the 'reconquest' of the western Mediterranean

The paradox of 'reconquest'; the Gothic wars and the transformation of Italian society

The new social order: Italy as a frontier province

Bibliographical essay

Summary

The third quarter of the fifth century saw the growing dominance of the military in Italian politics. This trend culminated after 476 in the rule of Odoacer, leader of the Italian army, as an effectively independent king, albeit one exercising power in the name of the eastern emperor. In 489–93, Theodoric, leader of the Balkan Goths, invaded Italy at the request of the eastern emperor, defeated Odoacer and absorbed the remnants of the Italian military into his Gothic army. Theodoric ruled as king but worked through the structures of the Roman state and Italian society; civilian society was to be protected by the Gothic army funded through taxation. Although never claiming independence of the empire, Theodoric's was effectively a sovereign kingdom, the dominant power in the west.

Because the Gothic kingdom co-existed with a continuing Roman Empire in the east, senators and churchmen maintained contacts with the imperial court at Constantinople as well as Theodoric's at Ravenna. And when, under Justinian (527–65), a militarily and ideologically reinvigorated eastern empire was able to assert its prerogatives over the barbarian kingdoms of the west, the Mediterranean was once again united under the direct rule of the emperor, as Vandal Africa quickly fell, strategic outposts were made on the islands of the western Mediterranean and the south-eastern Spanish coast, and after a generation of war Italy likewise was reincorporated into the empire. This renewed Roman order was in fact a novelty. The result of the drawn-out Gothic wars was the final eclipse of the great landowners of the Roman Senate as the defining political, economic and social force in the western Mediterranean, and the direct rule of Constantinople over western provinces for the first time. Italian politics now rested on the interaction between the governor or exarch at Ravenna, the pope at Rome, and the emperor in Constantinople. The historic seat of empire was now a frontier province.

Chronology

476	Odoacer, master of soldiers, deposes Emperor Romulus Augustulus
489	Theodoric, king of Goths, invades Italy at request of eastern emperor
493–526	Theodoric ruler of Italy
524	Execution of Boethius
524–5	Mission of Pope John to Constantinople
527–65	Justinian eastern emperor
527–33	Justinianic Code
527–34	Amalaric, Theodoric's infant grandson, king; power in hands of his mother Amalaswintha
533–4	Byzantine armies led by Belisarius take Africa from Vandals
535	Murder of Amalaswintha
535–54	'Gothic wars': Byzantine armies campaigning in Italy
537–8	First siege of Rome
540	Rule of St Benedict; Belisarius receives Gothic surrender at Ravenna
551	Byzantine enclave established in southwestern Hispania
552	Gothic king Totila defeated and killed by Narses at Busta Gallorum
553	Council of Constantinople condemns the 'three chapters'; western bishops object
554	Overthrow of last Gothic king, Teia
554	Pragmatic Sanction: meant to end disorder in Italy
562	End of last Gothic resistance in Verona
590–604	Gregory the Great Pope

Italy under Gothic management

Between 523 and 526, a man named Anduit appealed to his king, Theodoric, to safeguard his freedom. Anduit was a former soldier, who had served in the Gothic army that had secured control of Italy for Theodoric, but he was now blind, and Gudila and Oppa had made him their slave, in spite of a court hearing at which he had been declared a free man. Anduit's problems – the oppressiveness of powerful neighbours and their ability to manipulate or ignore the legal system – had long precedents in the Italian past, but his voice, with its insistence on his personal relationship with his king and his warrior status as badges of his freedom, speaks in a new world. His is a distinctively Gothic freedom: he claims to enjoy 'the liberty of our army' and is bowed down because 'he cannot defend his freedom with his right arm, which is the proven help and patron of the brave'.[1]

In the course of the sixth century, Italy was to be conquered in the name of a Roman emperor ruling from Constantinople. What was at stake in these conquests was the shape of Italian society. According to Anduit's king, the freedom of the Gothic army, a reward for their military service, protected the ancient structures of Italian society, enabling the traditional freedoms of civilian society, security of title and the rule of law, to continue. Integration into Constantinople's new version of Roman order was fundamentally to alter this balance.

Crucial to the transformation of Italian society was the changing relationship between civilian landowners and the army. By the second half of the fifth century, effective political power in Italy had devolved to the military leadership. As the empire's western provinces passed beyond the control of the imperial government and fell under the domination of barbarian warlords who created new kingdoms, so too in the old heartland of Italy military leaders came to rule the roost, raising up and bringing down candidates for the imperial title almost at will. The western imperial court thus ceased to function as a meaningful political centre. Italian landowners looked directly to the senate in Rome for the representation of their views, and Italian politics rested on negotiation between the senate and the army. The army itself remained a heterogeneous mixture of provincials and barbarians who nonetheless demonstrated increasingly strong personal loyalties towards their generals, making it for practical purposes an agglomeration of individual warbands; the easiest means of recruiting more troops was to defeat a rival and absorb his following. This military leadership itself was increasingly mixed, consisting of ambitious barbarian warlords who brought retinues with them, and landowners who recruited from their estates and their clients; increasingly the two groups fused into a new elite. And this new elite desperately needed cash and supplies to ensure the continued loyalty of the military followings that guaranteed its position. These could only be gained by negotiation with, and coercion of, the civilian government. The need for the material means to reward personal warbands, along with the continued existence of the senate at Rome, and the continuing anxiety of the eastern emperors in Constantinople about Italy, meant that these warlords had to observe the constitutional niceties and rule through puppet emperors.

After 476, the new master of the soldiers, Odoacer, began to rule without a western emperor. Both the senate in Rome and the emperor in Constantinople realised that this was simply a recognition of the political reality. From the point of view of the senate, Odoacer was an effective military protector with whom direct dealings were possible, and whose regime was more malleable and so more acceptable than an ambitious imperial candidate with eastern backing or political designs of his own. From the point of view of Constantinople, concerns nearer to home made intervention in Italy an impossibility. Odoacer's regime was thus tolerated, although its precise constitutional position was never clarified.

Whereas through the 460s and 470s Constantinople had backed and funded a series of eastern generals as imperial candidates in the west, by the 470s and 480s the eastern emperor Zeno was primarily concerned with establishing order in his own Balkan backyard. The collapse of Attila's empire in the 450s had resulted in chaos in the Roman provinces south of the Danube and the formerly Hunnic lands beyond, the political map – as in contemporary Gaul – a constantly shifting kaleidoscope of barbarian warbands. Barbarian warleaders whose activities had previously been shaped by their place in Attila's confederate empire now had to establish themselves in a new political framework, and to maintain the flow of gifts that ensured the loyalty of their military followings. In response, they rediscovered pre-Hunnic political traditions of ethnic kingship, and sought employment, subsidy or plunder from Rome. Within the Balkan provinces of the empire, two armies of 'Goths' emerged as powerful allies and dangerous enemies for Constantinople: one, settled in the eastern Balkans by Aspar, the master of the soldiers in Constantinople, was led by Aspar's kinsman Theodoric Strabo ('the Squinter'); the other, settled along the middle Danube by the emperor Marcian, probably as a counterweight to Aspar and Strabo, fell under the domination of Theodemar, and, following his death in 471, his son Theodoric 'the Amal'.

Competition between the two Theodorics was intense in the 470s, because following the downfall of Aspar in 471 the supreme military position over Constantinople's western armies was up for grabs. The rival Balkan generals sought to make Constantinople totally militarily reliant on their troops and thus recreate the political dominance that Aspar had enjoyed for four decades. In 481, Theodoric Strabo demanded that Constantinople disband its western armies and use the tax revenue saved to hire his Goths in their place. Zeno – who had an independent military following from his native Isauria in Asia Minor – was able to resist. Anxious to avoid becoming reliant on any one Balkan warlord, and thus replicating the over-powerful position of Aspar, he pursued a strategy of divide and rule. By taking first one Theodoric, then another, into his service as a Roman general, and thus offering both legitimacy and pay, Zeno was able to ensure that no one military leader in the Balkans grew too powerful.

This delicate political balance ended with the death of Strabo in 481, and his son in 484, which left Theodoric 'the Amal' in uncontested dominance of the Balkans. Theodoric's goal remained that of attaining Roman service, which would legitimate his standing and guarantee a regular income for his followers: negotiations with Zeno ended in 487 with Theodoric threatening Constantinople in the hope of acquiring the position of master of the soldiers in the Balkans. Zeno attempted to remove Theodoric from the Balkans. He suggested that Theodoric invade Italy to remove Odoacer. Once tacit recognition of Odoacer was removed, Theodoric's invasion of Italy could be presented as a campaign to restore imperial rule to the peninsula. This abstract constitutional logic, however, obscured the fact that Zeno sought not to restore the western imperial title, but to replace the extant Italian military leader with a similar figure. In any case, on several occasions previously eastern emperors had encouraged potentially over-mighty generals to intervene in the west: rather than backing an attempt on the western imperial throne as his predecessors had, Zeno was now encouraging a bid for leadership of the Italian army. Constantinople had reason to expect stalemate between Theodoric and Odoacer, and may have planned to extend the policy of 'divide-and-rule' from the Balkans to Italy. If so, the strategy failed. Theodoric and his Balkan army met with rapid military success, winning a stunning victory at Verona in 489, and proceeding to 'reconquer' Sicily from the Vandals in 490. Nonetheless, it took four years of negotiation and skirmishing before Ravenna, the nigh-on impregnable seat of the Italian government, fell – and even then it fell by trickery rather than force, as Odoacer was invited to a banquet to treat for peace and treacherously murdered. But Theodoric was now unrivalled ruler of Italy.

Theodoric's precise constitutional position remained unclear. The terms of his initial agreement with Zeno are unknown, and in any case by 493 Zeno had died, and the new eastern emperor Anastasius refused to recognise Theodoric until 497. From then on, Theodoric ruled as, in theory, a viceroy, representing the emperor in the west. But, given that Theodoric's position in Italy was in no real way dependent on Constantinople, this theory was always apt to be overlooked. Italian reactions to Theodoric's rule were certainly more ambiguous and complex. Thus the celebration of Theodoric's *tricennelia* (the 30th anniversary of his rule) in 500, with a formal ceremony of welcome (*adventus*) in Rome, was something which previously only emperors had enjoyed. In fact, here Theodoric may simply have been courting Italian public opinion by behaving as an Italian ruler was expected to behave. Certainly his lavish patronage of public buildings, and the resumption of free bread and circuses for the population of Rome, was designed to advertise a self-conscious return to the Roman past and thus win support for the new regime. Whilst Theodoric went out of his way not to usurp imperial rights, the difference between a powerful ruler of Italy and an emperor was a fine one indeed. Hence Theodoric's repair of a stretch of the main road south from Rome, the *Via Appia*, as it crossed the notorious Pontine marshes was compared by his subjects to the work of the Emperor Trajan, and commemorated by one senator in an inscription celebrating 'Our lord the glorious and famous king Theodoric, victorious and triumphant, emperor (*Augustus*) forever'.[2]

Theodoric was the direct heir of the warlords who had dominated Italian politics for a century. His reign saw an Italian military and political resurgence in the western Mediterranean world, which was furthered by the careful cultivation of diplomatic ties with the new rulers of northwestern Europe on both sides of the former Roman frontier. In addition to the reconquest of Sicily in 490, the northern and eastern approaches to Italy – to which Odoacer had devoted much attention – were secured by the conquest of Pannonia and the eastern Adriatic coast. Most dramatic of all was the submission of the Gothic kings of Toulouse, who had dominated southern Gaul for half a century: after a calamitous defeat by the

Franks in 507 they submitted to Theodoric's rule. Contacts between the two Gothic groupings led to the adoption of the label 'Visigoths' ('western Goths') for the Goths of southern Gaul and Hispania, to differentiate them from Theodoric's 'Ostrogoths' ('eastern Goths') in Italy. These labels did not map onto ancient tribal identities. Theodoric claimed descent from the Amal dynasty which had ruled those Goths who remained outside the empire in the late fourth century, whereas the Goths of Toulouse were descended from those who had crossed the Danube then to flee the Huns, but there was no continuity of tribal identity or nomenclature: hence the need to coin the new terms Visigoth and Ostrogoth. Theodoric's intervention in the Visigothic realm was justified by his role as 'protector' of his infant grandson Amalaric, heir through his mother to the kingdom of Toulouse. But it rested on power politics more than hoary genealogies or pan-Gothic loyalty. Direct Italian rule of southern Gaul and Hispania had last been known in the days of Stilicho and Theodosius. Theodoric's rule was indirect, exercised through the agency of his trusted general, Theudis, despatched to act as regent at the court of Amalaric. Provence, however, was integrated into the Italian polity, with the Italian Liberius even appointed as the first non-Gallic praetorian prefect in Gaul since the fourth century. No military and political system on this scale had existed in the west since the days of Aetius and Galla Placidia.

Theodoric created a complex system of familial ties to bind this system together. Formal agreements of friendship were cemented by marriage alliances such as that contracted with the Vandals in Africa and the Visigoths in southern Gaul and Hispania, and complex rites of gift-giving, some of which involved Theodoric 'adopting' the offspring of neighbouring kings. Here, the end of the western empire allowed Theodoric to construct new diplomatic rites suited to an age of military kings of barbarian origin. This was a new political order in the west, centred on Theodoric's court in Italy: perhaps the seeds of a decentralised western empire on the fifth-century model, but one now directly under barbarian management.

Gothic identities and Italian allegiances

The basis for the political resurgence of Italy was continuity of its administrative, social and political fabric. We know an unparalleled amount about Theodoric's Italy, and can view Theodoric's government in action in a manner that is impossible for any other post-Roman state in the west until the eighth century. This knowledge rests on one source alone, the collection of almost 500 official letters, or *Variae*, made by Cassiodorus, a Roman senator who had served Theodoric and his successors in a succession of high-ranking posts. They are a far from neutral document, issued in 537 when the future of the Goths in Italy was unclear and Theodoric's reign the subject of fierce political polemic. But they do offer a priceless insight into the structure and rhetoric of the government of the Gothic kings.[3]

The *Variae* bear eloquent testimony to the continuation, in Italy, of the ornate hierarchy of office and rank that defined late Roman elites and underwrote the late Roman state. Cassiodorus wrote in the highly complex and formal Latin favoured by late Roman bureaucrats, and closely observed the careful etiquette which gave office-holders special titles of rank and prescribed correct forms of address according to those ranks. This was more than a culturally conservative veneer. In content, too, the *Variae* demonstrate the continuity of the fundamental structures of late antique Italian politics and society, with cities remaining the basic local units, and landowning elites seeking office to consolidate their local position and in turn meeting the demands of the state in their localities. At the centre, the government continued to be based in Ravenna, and the civilian administration and the opportunities for social advancement it allowed ensured the active participation of landowning elites. The continuing pull of office and its role in integrating Gothic king and Italian elites is indeed shown by the career of Cassiodorus himself, a southern Italian provincial landowner and intellectual who rose to membership of the senate, thanks to his activity in Theodoric's administration. Theodoric had no qualms about drawing on the services of those who had embarked on an administrative career under his predecessors. Two of his key ministers, Cyprian and Liberius, were Roman provincials who had risen through civilian office-holding under Odoacer. Indeed, under Theodoric, the appeal of the court at Ravenna and of administrative office, for those who sought wealth and power, rose to a degree not seen since the end of the Theodosian dynasty.

Into this intensely status-conscious milieu came Theodoric's military following: the Goths. As with the other barbarian 'peoples' who replaced regular Roman armies and eventually established political dominance in the provinces of the west, Theodoric's 'Goths' were not a homogenous group. Of this mixed bag, the critical mass were probably military followers recruited in the Balkans, but following the defeat of Odoacer Theodoric also absorbed his predecessor's troops, and the remnants of the Italian army, into his 'Goths'. This mixture of personal retinues, professional soldiers, and new recruits from the Balkans and beyond, was absolutely typical of the armies in whose hands Italy's fate had lain for a century. But Theodoric, rather than assimilating his following into the Italian army as Odoacer had before him, represented himself as 'king of the Goths', leader of the 'army of the Goths' (*exercitus Gothorum*), as the Italian military was now known.

There may have been political reasons for this choice of nomenclature. Theodoric played repeatedly, and almost certainly disingenuously, on his alleged descent from the semi-legendary Amal dynasty that had ruled the Goths before the advent of the Huns. This choice implies that the Gothic past was a powerful means of garnering support from his troops. But, whilst the bulk of Theodoric's army may have been Balkan warbands attached to a Gothic identity, this identity had a far from continuous history, and the Goths in Italy were made rather than born. Indeed, the manufacturing of Gothic history was one central concern of Theodoric's regime. Cassiodorus tells how at the king's behest, he 'made the origin of the Goths into Roman history' in a now lost work, which was used as a source in the *Gothic History* of Jordanes, written at Constantinople in 551. The significance of Cassiodorus' work has tended to be obscured by a long and convoluted scholarly controversy about its precise relationship to Jordanes'. Because Cassidorus' *History* is lost, it has been tempting to try to reconstruct it from Jordanes, and it has even been argued that Jordanes' work is a virtual paraphrase of Cassidorus'. In fact, the precise debt Jordanes owed Cassiodorus' lost work remains a puzzle, as does Jordanes' identity and purpose. Jordanes' work quite inaccurately presents the Goths as a single people, united all along under the rule of the Amal dynasty, Theodoric's alleged ancestors. But it includes very little that could not be found in Roman ethnography and history, and whilst it acknowledges the existence of oral traditions amongst the Gothic army it certainly cannot be read as a compilation of indigenous Gothic traditions preserved over generations, but rather as an attempt to remould Gothic tradition so as to explain the deeds of Theodoric's Amal regime. Cassiodorus' own comments suggest that his own lost *Gothic History* was similar in its sources and content, and whatever the precise debt Jordanes owes it, there can be little doubt that Jordanes' work was a similar project to Cassiodorus'. By such means, the Goths could thus acquire a history parallel to, and comprehensible to, their Roman hosts. Theodoric thus became the fourteenth king of his dynasty since the legendary ancestor Amal, just as Roman legend traced fourteen generations from Romulus and Remus. Creating a version of Gothic history that stressed unity and the leadership of Theodoric's legendary ancestors must also have helped unite the disparate elements of the 'army of the Goths', and legitimate Theodoric's kingship. In fact, given the disunity, diversity and fluidity of the various groups of Goths in the fourth and fifth centuries, Gothic history needed to be remoulded at Theodoric's court to reflect new-found unity.[4]

Cassiodorus' letters show how the army, with its Gothic identity, was grafted onto Italian society. On Theodoric's behalf, Cassiodorus essayed a rhetoric of co-existence based on *civilitas*. *Civilitas* centred on the recognition of the mutual benefits that would accrue if Goth and Roman were to live together in harmony. These benefits were possible because of the different functions fulfilled by the two groups: Roman civilians had their peace guaranteed by the Gothic army. Here was the civilian–soldier distinction so beloved of the late Roman state, but given an ethnic dimension: Goths were soldiers, Romans civilians. This division was in turn based on the continued operation of obligations to the Roman state. It was tax-paying which allowed civilians to maintain their civilised, non-military life by funding the Goths to provide military protection. Thus tax-payers were forbidden to bear weapons, a preserve of the Goths, who were in turn immune from tax and public burdens. This division was reinforced by the imposition of separate jurisdictions for Gothic soldier and Roman civilian, with the former answering to military commanders and agents of the Gothic king called *saiones*, the latter the traditional agencies of Roman law. This did not involve placing the Goths under a separate 'Gothic law'; but as soldiers had always been first subject to the separate jurisdiction of military courts, so the Goths answered to Gothic military judges. Thus the traditional divisions between soldier and civilian were dramatically reasserted after a century in which recurrent crisis had increasingly seen warlords with their personal retinues become the dominant figures in Italian society. The *civilitas* ideology which runs through the *Variae* was, indeed, firmly based in Roman legal culture, justifying the division between Gothic soldier and Roman civilian in terms of the preservation of Roman freedom (*libertas*) and the service of the Gothic army to the Roman state (*utilitas*). The rule of law, as the guarantor of civilisation, thus stood as the key element of Theodoric's ideology. In the *Variae*, the Goths are never referred to as barbarians, as they observe the rule of law; their role can be juxtaposed with the undisciplined and wild behaviour that is seen, in Roman ideology, as typifying barbarians elsewhere in the west. The *Variae* clearly show Theodoric and his successors giving judgements and making law in full Roman tradition, whilst a short tract known as the Edict of Theodoric likewise shows law-giving as both a practical response to the problems involved in the Gothic settlement, and an ideological restatement of the tradition of Roman order. In stressing the service of Theodoric's military following to the needs of the Roman state, and reasserting traditional legal categories, *civilitas* ideology was designed above all to foster acceptance of the new regime among the Italian population.

The *Variae* may allow a vivid insight into Theodoric's government, but they can also suggest a misleadingly static picture to the unwitting reader. The documents cover 30 years but are selected on grounds of rhetorical elegance, selected at the end of Cassiodorus' career – perhaps as a practical manual on statesmanship, coupled with Cassiodorus' Christian tract on ethics, *On the Soul*, which was appended to the *Variae*; perhaps as a justification of the Gothic regime and its Roman collaborators which, by the time the *Variae* were published, were under threat. Above and beyond the problems of selection and hindsight implicit in such a collection, the *Variae* represent the government's pronouncements. In fact, arrangements on the ground were more complex than the seamless co-operation suggested by the ideology of *civilitas*. Both narrative sources and in places the *Variae* themselves show that Goths, in addition to receiving payments and supplies as soldiers, were sometimes granted land for settlement, so it is no surprise that they soon became enmeshed in the civil society from which *civilitas* ideology attempted to keep them clearly differentiated. The *Variae* also include letters dealing with the cases of Goths who married provincials, or acquired land, or obtained a discharge from the army and retired to a life of leisure, and so began to cross the rigid divide between Gothic soldier and Roman civilian suggested by *civilitas* ideology; indeed claims about 'Gothic liberty' allowed warriors-turned-landowners to claim freedom from taxation, state imposts and civilian jurisdiction, and so enjoy a privileged status which irked Roman neighbours who complained of expropriation and intimidation. One letter deals with the case of the children of the 'ancient barbarians' (*antiqui barbari*) who had been settled long ago on the Danube frontier, married provincial women and been thoroughly integrated into the local community: should they pay tax and were they liable for military service? Ambitious Roman provincials who rose in the service of the Gothic king might also transgress the divide between Goth and Roman. Not only did able and experienced Romans like Liberius – who had served as a general under Odoacer – hold military commands in the 'army of the Goths'; but an ambitious Roman like Cyprian could also learn Gothic to further his career at court, and have his sons educated as Gothic-speaking soldiers so that they might follow in his footsteps.[5] The ideology of *civilitas* provided a powerful template for the initial settlement, and helped accommodate Italian society to its new military protectors. But it was not – and may not have been intended as – the blueprint for a lasting symbiosis, given the inevitable integration of the Gothic army into its host society and the blurring of distinctions that followed.

The puzzle facing the modern historian lies in understanding how the regime developed over time. Here there is an immediate problem. In addition to Cassiodorus' *Variae* there is a wealth of material from early sixth-century Italy thanks to the lively cultural life of Gothic Italy, encouraged by the patronage of Theodoric's court: philosophy, theology, the letters of the popes and of Ennodius, bishop of Pavia and the biography of Ennodius written posthumously by Epiphanius. But there is little that allows a developed political analysis or the tracing of political changes. In fact, the history of Theodoric's reign was not written until the middle decades of the sixth century, when the political situation had changed radically as Constantinople sought to destroy the Gothic kingdom in Italy and rule the peninsula direct. This prolonged struggle encouraged a pessimistic and often polemical view of Theodoric. The *Gothic Wars* of the Byzantine historian Procopius, for example, sought to justify imperial policy and blacken the reputation of the Gothic regime, presenting it as detrimental to Roman interests. The closest we have to a contemporary Italian chronicle of the reign, a fragmentary work written shortly after Theodoric's death known as the *Anonymous Valesianus*, likewise presents a pessimistic view of the last years of the reign, but is heavily influenced by hindsight in this. Modern historians, in any case strongly dependent on these sources, have been likewise heavily influenced by hindsight. Knowledge of the ultimate collapse of the Gothic kingdom after Theodoric's death has encouraged them to identify fatal tensions emerging in the years leading up to Theodoric's death in 526, and see the Roman–Gothic symbiosis attempted by Theodoric as ultimately doomed. Two events in particular have cast a long shadow over the reign: the execution of Boethius in 524 and the death of Pope John in 526.

Boethius was an intellectual from one of the oldest and most powerful families of the Roman Senate who had served as Theodoric's master of offices. Imprisoned following his conviction for treason in 524, Boethius wrote his *Consolation of Philosophy* – one the most important and influential works of theology and philosophy of late antique and early medieval Europe – whilst awaiting execution. His fall was brought about by the accusations levelled at him by a Roman rival, Liberius. The case for treason was heard in a full trial before the senate at which Boethius was condemned, his close relations with the imperial court in Constantinople leading to the claim that he was betraying Theodoric. Whatever the rights and wrongs of these suspicions, Boethius' fate was part of a savage factional conflict, centring on the disposition of high office and the political influence which went with it, which was absolutely typical of fourth- and fifth-century Italian politics: Boethius' execution was quickly followed by that of his father-in-law. The jealousy between Liberius, the provincial who had risen to prominence through an administrative career, and Boethius, the blue-blooded senator, was indicative of the recurrent tension within the late antique state in the west between the established senatorial families and parvenus who rose through the imperial administration. Similar tensions had led to the execution of two other senators for indulging in magical practices in 510. It was Boethius' literary reflection on his fate, rather than that fate in itself, which was unusual: his *Consolation of Philosophy* ensured that his was to become a *cause célèbre* for subsequent generations. But it is very difficult to see it as portending a political crisis or the breakdown of relations between Goths and Romans: Procopius' view, that this was Theodoric's only truly bad act, must be read as later propaganda.[6]

Boethius' was not the only death that was used to posthumously blacken Theodoric's reputation. Immediately after Boethius' execution, Pope John was ordered by Theodoric to travel to Constantinople to intervene on behalf of the Arian subjects of the emperor, notably the Gothic soldiers in imperial service at Constantinople and in the Balkans. In Theodoric's Italy, the Arian church was referred to as 'the church of the law of the Goths', as Ulfilas, the fourth-century missionary who had translated the Bible and liturgy into Gothic, had been a follower of Arius, and the Goths, Theodoric included, remained committed to Ulfilas' liturgy and Bible. When John returned, having failed to persuade the eastern emperor to shift policy, he was detained by Theodoric at Ravenna, where he died. By the middle of the sixth century, the Roman church, encouraged by Byzantine propaganda, was presenting Theodoric as a heretic who was responsible for the death of a pope; within a generation tales were even circulating of his torment in Mount Etna as a punishment for the deaths of Boethius and John.[7]

These verdicts have proved difficult to shake off, and religious differences have often been seen as indices of ethnic tension between Goths and Romans, and the fates of Boethius and John thus linked. In fact, Theodoric's attempt to protect Arians in the east through John's mission is virtually the only instance of Arianism becoming an issue of debate in his reign. Here it did so in response to a new and aggressively anti-Arian imperial policy in the east, not religious tension within Italy. Italian churchmen had long experience of working with Arians, and made little comment on Theodoric's Arianism; after all the barbarian generals who dominated fifth-century western politics had been Arians to a man. Within the Italian church the main ecclesiastical controversies in this period concerned western opposition to the eastern emperor's attempts to deal with theological divisions in the eastern church by reinterpreting traditional doctrine on the person of Christ: the so-called 'Acacian schism' of 484–519 saw Constantinople's theological pronouncements resisted by north Italian bishops in particular. Whilst Theodoric sponsored the building of a new Arian church, San'Apollinare Nuovo, in his capital at Ravenna, this did not preclude his working with the Italian church, nor indeed his worshipping the relics of St Peter on his visit to Rome in 500. Theodoric's handling of the 'Laurentian schism', an intermittently violent eight-year struggle between two rival popes following a disputed election in 499, adhered to this established pattern, and even won panegyrical praise from Ennodius of Pavia, a supporter of the eventually victorious pope, Symacchus.

Once the distortions of later propaganda are stripped away, then, there is little sign of escalating tension between Goth and Roman, Arian and Catholic. Indeed, before his death Theodoric had been preparing a campaign against the Vandal kingdom of Africa: hardly the action of a ruler whose kingdom was disintegrating because of raging sectarian struggles! Nonetheless, there are indications of social and political change, accompanied, inevitably, by tension. The letters dating from Cassiodorus' spell as master of the offices in 523–7, a position he took over from Boethius, provide the key to understanding what was changing: they use the language of *civilitas* rather less frequently than the letters from earlier periods in the reign, instead stressing the stature of Theodoric and his lineage, and the strength (*virtus*) of the Gothic regime. Now he was secure as ruler of Italy, Theodoric's concerns were no longer with the accommodation of his Gothic army, but with the fostering of an unequivocal loyalty to the Gothic kingdom and the Amal dynasty. The patronage offered by the immense pool of administrative positions so anxiously sought by the ambitious was used to create a ruling class devoted to Gothic and Amal *virtus*. Given this, it is probably no accident that the controversies surrounding both Boethius and Pope John turned on their relationship with the eastern emperor at Constantinople. Italy was effectively an independent kingdom under Gothic rule, and any residual loyalty to the emperor or contact with the court at Constantinople might come into potential conflict with the demands of the Amal ruler at Ravenna. The new stress on Gothic *virtus* was thus motivated by concerns about the potential influence of the emperor at Constantinople over office-holders in Theodoric's kingdom. It was also an attempt to shore up support for the succession, a potentially tricky issue as none of Theodoric's sons survived, and one in which Constantinople might be expected to intervene.

What was at stake was the identity of the ruling class: were they servants of the Gothic king or officials in a Roman Empire that, in the west, was under temporary Gothic management? This remained the key issue through the reign of Theodoric's successor, Athalaric (527–34), so far as the confused sources allow us to see. Athalaric was Theodoric's grandson, and closest surviving male heir. Because he was still a minor on his grandfather's death in 526, his mother, Theodoric's daughter Amalaswintha, was effective ruler as regent. Access to, and thus effective control of, the infant king were the objects of the political struggles of the seven-year reign. On Athalaric's death in 534, Amalaswintha, as a woman who was incapable of military command, was deemed unacceptable as a successor. She backed Theodehad, a nephew of Theodoric's, for the succession, and attempted to maintain her status by marrying him. Theodehad, like Amalaswintha, was a thoroughly Romanised civilian, a participant in the cultured literary and philosophical circles of early sixth-century Italy. He could not rule, however, without the support of the Gothic military leadership, which promptly had Amalaswintha killed.

Procopius, writing in the 550s, presented these struggles as centring on Athalaric's education. Amalaswintha had sought to 'make her son resemble the Roman princes' through a classical Roman education. However three wise Goths to whom she entrusted her son pleaded, successfully, that he receive a barbarian upbringing and be taught to fight as 'they wished to be ruled by him more after the barbarian fashion'. Although Amalaswintha agreed to their request, the Goths then plotted against her, beginning a long-running feud.[8] Procopius set up a conflict between 'civilised' Goths like Amalaswintha and the Gothic army as a reason for the breakdown of the Gothic regime: he expressly claimed that

Amalaswintha's murder, the pretext for Byzantine invasion, was a revenge for her murder of Athalaric's tutors. Whilst his propagandist and highly telescoped history must be taken with care, it is clear conflict did centre on the direction of the regime and the nature of Gothic identity and Gothic relations with the Romans. *Civilitas* ideology, with its clean separation of Gothic army from civilian society, had always been an attempt to classify a messier situation on the ground. But the maintenance of a regime founded on the wholesale separation of Gothic soldier and Roman civilian was increasingly problematic in the second and third generations after Theodoric's arrival in Italy, as the descendents of Theodoric's military following put down roots and assimilated into Italian society. These processes threatened the solidarity of the Gothic army as Goths acquired divergent interests in the Italian countryside, and found diverse niches in the Italian social hierarchy: think of the veteran Anduit, reduced to slavery by two fellow Goths. 'Gothic' and 'Roman' were not simply professional identities that an individual could shed at will depending on whether they chose a civilian or military career, nor were civilian and military in reality wholly separate and mutually exclusive paths. Education, as it determined whether a child's future career would lie in the civilian or military sphere, was a live issue: hence Procopius' attempt to simplify the whole conflict in terms of Athalaric's education, and his claim that Theodoric had banned Goths from having their sons educated in the Roman manner as it would soften their courage.[9] Whilst the military leadership favoured traditional Gothic *virtus* as underpinning their privileged political position, other Goths – like Theodehad – had become large-scale landowners, and acquired the cultural accomplishments of the Roman elite. Which path was the regime to follow?

This was not a debate between pro- and anti-Roman factions, but a question of conflicting reactions to the inevitable process of assimilation following the initial conquest of Italy. Maintaining the integrity of the Gothic army would preclude the development of a Gothic landed aristocracy, leaving military rank and service to the Amals the determinants of political power: the Goths would be a fluid community within which rank was determined by *virtus*. Amalaswintha and Theodehad, on the other hand, were embracing the integration of the Gothic leadership into the Italian landed elite. The marriage of Maximus, a senator and grandson of an emperor, to an Amal princess in 535, seemed to suggest the emergence of a new ruling class, uniting the Gothic court with the cultural and economic resources of the Roman Senate. But this promise remained unfulfilled, for by the 550s the Gothic kingdom was a thing of the past, destroyed by armies loyal to Constantinople. The wars of conquest meant that the problems and possibilities of symbiosis between Goths and Romans were never resolved, but left intriguingly poised. The complex interplay between the court at Ravenna, the senate at Rome, the Gothic military leadership and the office-holding classes is nowhere paralleled in the late antique west. The processes of assimilation from which post-Roman kingdoms were born did not involve such a multiplicity of institutions and interests. As it was, the long and convoluted process of conquest was to destroy this institutional multivalency, and alter the parameters of post-Roman development.

Essay

Gothic identity and material culture

The ambiguities of Gothic identity are articulated in the archaeological record, where choices about burial ritual and burial monuments were means of claiming identities. Across northern Italy is a scattering of cemeteries marked by male burials with rich grave-goods including wargear. Such burials have clear links with the Danubian homelands of the Goths, and draw on a range of influences in material culture, including military fashions associated with the late Roman

Figure 4.1 Mausoleum of Theodoric
© Foto archivio comune di Ravenna

Figure 4.2 Mosaic depicting Theodoric's palace at Ravenna

army and with the fifth-century Hunnic Empire. Lavish martial burials are particularly concentrated in the north, around the key garrisons which in the 'Gothic wars' were the heartlands of support for Gothic warrior kingship; they articulate a warrior identity of Gothic *virtus* in which the distinctive eagle brooches served as key markers.

It would be mistaken to suppose that all Goths were buried in such a manner, and so we cannot see the distribution of such graves as an indication of the geography or density of Gothic settlement. The rites used should not be seen as simple ancestral customs the diffusion of which mirrors Gothic migration, but as reflecting a process of acculturation whereby some elements within 'the army of the Goths' chose to proclaim a separate identity, whilst others, through the process of settlement, were assimilated into landed society and adopted its customs and habits. The *Variae* include a letter of Theodoric's urging Goths to abandon the use of grave-goods, and instead give alms on behalf of the dead, so using wealth in a manner more useful to the living and more pleasing to God.[10] Theodoric's pleas do not present the use of grave-goods as a practice linked to any pagan belief system (his followers were in any case long-standing Christians, albeit of an Arian variety) or an ancestral Gothic culture. Here, the king of the Goths is urging his followers to adopt a burial rite accultured to the practices of Italian civilian society, and to demonstrate their standing in death through the forms of patronage used by their neighbours.

The assimilated Romano-Gothic identity that would result is vividly illustrated by Theodoric's own funerary monument. His mausoleum at Ravenna is consciously modelled on those of Roman emperors, and particularly that of Augustus at Rome. Here we see material culture used not to claim membership of a specifically Gothic ethnic community with a particular role in Italian society, but to inscribe Theodoric in the long continuum of Roman history. Ironically, though, Theodoric's imprint was all but wiped from the face of Ravenna in the aftermath of Byzantine 'reconquest'. The process is graphically illustrated by the magnificent mosaics in the church of San Vitale: here, images of Theodoric and his family in procession were replaced with depictions of the Emperor Justinian, the Empress Theodora, and their entourage, a tiny outline of Theodoric's hand all that remains of the public magnificence of the Gothic king. Ravenna was never visited by Justinian nor any of his successors, but as the seat of the governor of Italy it was still a city dedicated to the celebration of the emperor, the guarantor of divinely-ordained order in this world.

Figure 4.3 Mosaic showing Justinian at San Vitale, Ravenna

Figure 4.4 Mosaic showing Theodora at San Vitale, Ravenna

The Christian empire and the 'reconquest' of the western Mediterranean

The development of the Gothic kingdom of Italy was cut short by the resurgent power of the surviving part of the Roman Empire at Constantinople – referred to by historians as 'Byzantium' or the 'Byzantine Empire', although the Byzantines themselves saw their empire as the continuing Roman Empire. The intervention of Constantinople was no accidental or external factor. Theodoric's invasion of Italy was after all the most recent chapter in a long story of repeated eastern attempts to install a pliant regime in Italy. Not only had Italy never formally seceded from the empire, but also important elements of Italian society remained attached to social and cultural forms that recognised its continuation as the framework of legitimate authority. Each year, for example, the largely honorific title of consul was given to two individuals by senate and emperor. This active engagement and continuing entanglement with the court at Constantinople was not paralleled elsewhere in the west. In the decades around 500, when Constantinople was preoccupied with internal problems, the Gothic kingdom was free to develop regardless of the notional sovereignty of the emperor; but once Constantinople turned its attentions to the west the delicate and ambiguous issue of Gothic rule in Italy was always likely to become live once again.

By 500, Constantinople itself had grown to such a size – the best estimate of population puts it at a million – that it exceeded any city in the west, Rome included. Control of the city itself was essential for the successful exercise of the imperial office. In the first half of the fifth century, emperors of the Theodosian dynasty had stopped leading armies in person, choosing instead to secure their hold on the imperial office from the security of Constantinople, and the patronage offered by the governmental machine, like the court now sedentary and settled in the capital. The end of the Theodosian dynasty only confirmed this development: the imperial succession now went to those military leaders with the muscle necessary to secure control of Constantinople and so the court and the governmental machine. The accession of the general Marcian in 451 began a succession of soldier-emperors that was unbroken until the death of Tiberius II in 580. These emperors were, to a man, warlords of provincial origin in Asia Minor or the Balkans – that is, in the immediate hinterland of the capital. The support of the palace guard often played a crucial role in their succession; the military followings they were able to gather thus allowed them to control and protect Constantinople.

Constantinople's rapid growth, both in terms of population, size and buildings, was largely a result of the concentration there of governmental activity. Constantinople was becoming the hub around which the Mediterranean economy revolved. The continuous presence of the imperial court led to a huge influx of resources, and an outpouring of imperial patronage, whilst the imperial administration acted as a magnet for the talented and ambitious from across the eastern Mediterranean. The avoidance of potential blockages in this system of imperial patronage and social integration was thus of vital importance. The striking cultural differences between the different provinces of the east, often articulated through local versions of Christian doctrine and practice, thus posed a real threat to imperial survival. The emperor claimed to be God's representative on earth, and as such guarantor of Christian unity and orthodoxy. Provincial traditions thus inevitably led to fears of schism and heresy. Yet to espouse too narrow a definition of orthodoxy was to risk excluding and alienating whole provinces from the imperial system.

These dangers were becoming increasingly apparent in the late fifth and early sixth centuries. From 484, there were successive attempts to promote statements of orthodox Christian doctrine that were broad enough to include a number of subtly different definitions of the relationship between Christ and God that were popular in the east. Western opinion, and many in the east, were estranged by imperial interventions in theological matters, and remained loyal to the authoritative doctrinal statement agreed at the Council of Chalcedon in 451. The potentially explosive nature of these conflicts – which can seem abstruse to us – is demonstrated by the problems following the accession of Anastasius, a general whose family hailed from Dyrrachium on the Adriatic, in 492. Anastasius was an adherent of the monophysite doctrine that stressed the unity of Christ and God. As a result, he faced serious riots in Constantinople from the supporters of the Isaurian troops who had been the crucial backers of the previous emperors, Zeno and Leo, and the armed opposition of Vitalian, a rival Balkan warlord who led a mixed barbarian and provincial following but was of resolutely anti-monophysite theological views. With Constantinople's hold on the Balkans and the west weakened, Theodoric was able to capitalise. Anastasius could only oppose the extension of Theodoric's power into the Balkans through a series of alliances with barbarian groupings from beyond the Danube such as the Gepids.

On Anastasius' death in 518, the commander of the palace guard, Justin, was able to secure the succession. A military man of Balkan origin but orthodox theological views, Justin was soon able to set about repairing the fractured ties between Constantinople and its western hinterland. In 519, the theological differences between east and west were ended as a statement of doctrine firmly rebutting monophysitism was accepted by both. Communications between emperor and pope were thus reopened, reanimating the links between Constantinople and Rome that ultimately led to the souring of Theodoric's relationships with both pope and senate. The military position was also rectified. Justin was able to use his Balkan contacts to repair the ties between Constantinople and these key provinces, which quickly became the key military recruiting ground for the Byzantine army. A reinvigorated empire was inherited by his nephew Justinian, whose position in the palace guard allowed him to win out against rival relatives, becoming co-emperor in 526 before succeeding on Justin's death in 527. The vision of a united Christian empire was redoubled, based on the identification of the Roman Empire with the Christian faith that was commonplace in eastern political thought. This vision inspired new legal, military and religious initiatives which were to bring Constantinople into direct conflict with the barbarian regimes which had emerged in the west in the decades around 500 – most notably the two regimes that controlled the shores of the western Mediterranean, the Vandal kingdom of Africa and the Gothic kingdom in Italy.

Justinian's policies are difficult to access beneath the ideology of renewal that informs the treatment of his reign in contemporary writings. The key historical sources are the works of Procopius, a provincial intellectual who served as secretary to Justinian's favoured general, Belisarius, rising in the service of the state. Procopius wrote three works on Justinian, of apparently contradictory tones: the *Wars*, covering campaigns in Persia, Africa and Italy in a laudatory manner, initially strongly favouring Belisarius but eventually lapsing into disillusion with the writer's erstwhile patron; the *Buildings*, effectively a panegyric acclaiming Justinian and his policy of renewal; and the *Secret History*, a work of vitriolic criticism of Justinian in the most lurid of terms. The precise chronology of the works is unclear, as are the details of Procopius' own life. All three works are to be dated in their current form to the 540s and 550s, the work of an elderly and presumably distinguished figure looking back on the great events in which he had participated.

The apparent contradictions between Procopius' different writings can be baffling for the reader. They show the violence of political debate in sixth-century Byzantium, and the problems of articulating that debate in highly conservative literary traditions that could constrain an author's ability to describe new realities. Procopius slips between the panegyric of the *Buildings*, hailing Justinian as God's representative on Earth, the restorer of Christian Roman order, and the polemic of the *Secret History*, vilifying Justinian as a secret heretic and sexual deviant, a demon answering to the Devil. The two are different sides of the same coin, reflecting the difficulty experienced by Procopius in finding a literary form that allowed rounded discussion of a new style of absolute imperial power theoretically derived from the Christian God. Even in the *Wars*, the literary conventions of a genre of secular historical writing stretching back to Herodotus make it difficult for Procopius to give proper coverage to religion, so central to Justinian's policies. These problems were not peculiar to Procopius. His contemporary John the Lydian, likewise a provincial of modest background who was drawn to Constantinople by the social possibilities of a career in the imperial bureaucracy, wrote an historical account of the Byzantine administrative hierarchy that is marked by its archaising and antiquarian nature. The product of Justinian's legal initiatives, the *Digest*, similarly presents itself as a work of renewal, harking back to an ancient past. Even the initiatives, primarily military in inspiration, described in Procopius' *Buildings* are there presented as works of restoration.

For all the fact that Justinian's programme was consciously presented as renewal, inspired by the model of the ancient past, in reality it was a matter of radical novelty. It was rooted not in ancient precedent, but in a recently emerged understanding of the imperial office. The emperor was personally responsible to God for ensuring the unity of the Christian empire. Thus in law the commission set up under the leadership of Justinian's legal spokesman or *quaestor*, Tribonian, was charged with the production of a unified systematic statement of law, which produced in 527–33 the Justinianic Code. Similarly, imperial religious policy was predicated on the need to find a single statement of doctrine that could define orthodoxy without controversy. Inevitably, the search for unity went hand-in-hand with centralisation, and caused unavoidable tensions between the imperial court at Constantinople on one hand, and the provinces with their own regional cultural traditions on the other, most graphically in repeated theological quarrels that simply refused to go away.

In the political and military spheres, Justinian's programme of direct intervention in the west was similarly presented in terms of renewal, but actually pursued new objectives informed by an enlarged conception of a Christian empire. The very notion of 'reconquest' is itself misleading, in that the western provinces had never been directly ruled from Constantinople, nor formally seceded from the empire. Indeed, the barbarian warlords who now provided military protection to western elites needed the recognition, or at least acquiescence, of the emperor in Constantinople to legitimise their position. Procopius was careful to present the legitimacy of barbarian regimes in the west as coming from formal treaties with the empire, and to justify Justinian's interventions as responses to breaches of these treaties, and attempts to restore rightful barbarian rulers who had been overthrown by their rivals. In reality, though, the 'reconquest' of the west in fact involved a dramatic expansion of the areas under Constantinople's direct dominion, and the clarification of the constitutionally unclear status of the barbarian successor states. In this, it paralleled legal codification and efforts to impose doctrinal unity, in that it disguised novelty as tradition.

In the new world of one unified Christian empire, there was no room for Roman provinces ruled by barbarian kings whose position was explained with reference to the notional sovereignty of the empire. Rather, the new polities of the west were now seen as standing unequivocally outside the empire, and the perception that the western provinces had been 'lost' quickly spread in court circles in Constantinople. It was Justinian's secretary, Count Marcellinus, who, in his *Chronicle*, first identified the loss of the west as having taken place with the deposition of Romulus Augustulus in 476. The Balkan origins of Justinian himself and his associates must have contributed to this interest in the west. And the new perception of the status of the west was certainly encouraged by a small but influential clique of westerners who had fled to Constantinople – a number of Italian senators who maintained good contacts with the eastern court, and a smattering of influential and vocal exiled churchmen such as the Catholic African bishop Fulgentius of Ruspe. Such opinion-formers had self-interested reasons for encouraging direct intervention in the west, and their lobbying may have encouraged some misconceptions, particularly about the religious policies of the Arian barbarians who ruled the west. In Vandal Africa, for example, Hilderic (523–30) had removed legal restrictions against Catholics and allowed Catholic bishops to return from exile, but in Constantinople the portrayal of the Vandals as heretical persecutors was unbudged.

For all these ideological underpinnings, the decision to intervene in the west was deeply controversial. Procopius stresses the opposition of many of Justinian's advisors, who harked back to previous disasters, most notably the failed attack on Vandal Africa in 468–70 and its disastrous financial and military costs; African campaigns had such a poor reputation that under Zeno barbarian recruits had been enlisted on condition that they were not asked to serve in any such adventure.[11] Some historians have seen the western campaigns as a ploy to divert attention from internal problems, and particularly the severe unrest in Constantinople that had boiled over in the Nika riot of 532. Sparked by an attempt to impose order on the Circus factions of blues and greens, which served as mafia-like organisations offering aid and protection to the population of Constantinople, the riot saw the government losing effective control of the city as the factions proclaimed a new emperor, Hypatius. Justinian survived only through holding his nerve and winning over the wavering palace guard, as well as the military forces loyal to the two key military leaders Belisarius and the barbarian Balkan warlord Mundo. It seems unlikely, however, that this deep-seated internal dissent could act as an encouragement or incentive for a controversial and potentially disastrous military adventure. The connection between the Nika riot and the western campaign more likely lies in the changes wrought to the composition of Justinian's court. John the Cappadocian, previously praetorian prefect, and the *quaestor* Tribonian, were removed from office as a sop to public opinion during the riot. By making John, an over-mighty courtier associated with taxation policies, the scapegoat, Justinian was able to use the unrest to reshape the balance of power at court and remove the most influential opponent to intervention in the west. In fact, it may be that the events of 532 saw the triumph within the court of a clique committed to a united Christian empire, and whose Balkan origins and close connections to influential westerners left them predisposed to intervention.[12]

In any case, following the agreement of peace with the Persians and the quashing of the Nika riot, Belisarius was despatched to conquer Africa with an army of fifteen thousand (if we can trust Procopius' figures). Success was unexpectedly rapid. The internal politics of the Vandal kingdom gave Justinian a clear constitutional pretext for intervention: the Vandal king Hilderic had been overthrown in 530 by Gelimir in a palace coup, and Hilderic's party sought aid from Constantinople to uphold the rightful succession. The concern to play to the letter of the Vandal law, and to present this as a restoration, not a conquest, helped persuade the Vandal fleet and army in Sardinia to switch its allegiance. A similar lack of concerted opposition is clear throughout the campaign. Loyalty to the Vandal kingdom was not strong enough to overcome internal dissension, and the promise of preferment within a new Roman order. As the Vandal fleet was busy dealing with the Sardinian revolt, Belisarius' forces were able to land unopposed and defeat the remaining Vandal forces outside Carthage before seizing the city and defeating the returning Vandal army. Gelimir fled to the interior but soon surrendered, preferring a modest position within the Roman system to last-ditch resistance. Vandal soldiers were offered terms and recruited *en masse* into the Roman army in 533–4. Africa was to be reintegrated into the empire, with full imperial backing given to the Catholic church against its Arian and other rivals, the estates of the Vandals and their kings seized as imperial land, and full-scale taxation reintroduced over the province as a whole, where previously Vandal landowners and their estates had been exempt.

This version of restored Roman order was not immediately or universally popular with the inhabitants of Africa: reconquest was rapidly followed by serious provincial revolt. Procopius gives us an intriguing account, presenting the ringleaders as Arian priests and the wives of the Vandals, both groups whose property rights and social status were overturned by the terms of imperial conquest. The role of the wives of the Vandals is particularly interesting: they quickly remarried the members of the new Byzantine garrison, urging them to claim the lands of the defeated Vandals as their just rewards for victory, for as conquerors surely they deserved to receive the property of the vanquished rather than to remain as servants of the emperor?[13] Procopius' story implies that Vandal identity rested on serving the Vandal king militarily, but that inevitably close links had formed between these macho warriors and the provincial society in which they owned land through marriage; after the Vandal defeat the expectation was a continuation of a similar order, with the mixed bag of barbarian and provincial recruits that made up Belisarius' army encouraged by provincials to see themselves as a warrior-elite who might inherit the socially privileged position of their Vandal predecessors. To establish Roman order, it was necessary to unpick the matrix of interests surrounding Vandal landowning and warrior status: hence a careful series of investigations and deportations of groups with a vested interest in the status quo. When unrest arose again in Africa in 535–6, the army did not try to resuscitate Vandal kingship or seize imperial estates, but drove out the governor in a protest over arrears in pay.

After the fall of Africa, Justinian's attention turned immediately to Italy. Again, care was taken to gain a clear constitutional pretext for intervention, in this case the bitter struggle for control over the Gothic throne which burst into the open following the death of Theodoric's son Athalaric in 534. Justinian claimed to be intervening to avenge the murder of Amalaswintha, Theodoric's daughter and the effective power behind the throne since her father's death. Like the ousted Vandal king Hilderic, she attempted to gain the support of the emperor, seen by her senatorial supporters as the guarantor of constitutional legitimacy. When Amalaswintha was murdered in 535 she was in negotiation with Justinian for support against her Gothic opponents, and on the verge of leaving Italy for Constantinople. The Gothic king Theodehad continued to negotiate with Justinian, and Procopius was even to claim that he considered handing Italy over to the eastern emperor. The Goths, for their part, were happy to acknowledge the theoretical overlordship of the emperor but stressed the legality of their position as federates, rooted in binding agreements. Conflicting spheres of interest in the Balkans, however, brought negotiations to an end when a Gothic army stationed on the Adriatic coast raided imperial territory and killed Mundo, the barbarian warlord whose allegiance ensured Justinian's power in the Balkans.[14]

Belisarius was then despatched to Sicily, an obvious target given the fall of the other islands of the western Mediterranean with the overthrow of the Vandal kingdom, and its strategic importance for control of the western Mediterranean. Initial gains mirrored the rapid fall of Africa, with cities and landed elites shifting allegiance to Belisarius in the absence of any concerted Gothic resistance; this in spite of the relatively small size of Belisarius' army (Procopius claimed just 7,500 men, half the size of that which had taken Africa, but he was trying to justify Belisarius' lack of outright success). It was only at Naples that Belisarius was forced to wait. The population of this important regional centre, in spite of its seaborne links across the Mediterranean, remained attached to the restored order they had enjoyed under Gothic protection. Belisarius' eventual seizure of Naples led to the overthrow of Theodehad by the Gothic army. Theodehad's policy of cultural and social assimilation into Italian society, allied to his unwillingness to fight Justinian's army, made him politically suspect to the Gothic army, who raised a tried and tested officer who embodied military *virtus*, Wittigis. Wittigis took care to legitimate his position by linking himself to Theodoric's blood and so the legendary Amal dynasty, marrying Amalaswintha's daughter. After Belisarius advanced as far as Rome, Wittigis was able to bring about a near stalemate, besieging Belisarius in the ancient capital of the empire for over a year in 537–8. It was only the arrival of a new force from the east, which arrived by sea to outflank the besiegers, that shifted the balance back against the Goths.

After a complex series of campaigns in Tuscany and the northern Italian plain, by 539 Wittigis himself was besieged at Ravenna, since the beginning of the fifth century the capital of Italy. A stalemate of a very different kind resulted. Ravenna was renowned for its impregnable site in the marshes, and continuing north Italian loyalty to the Goths as well as the depredations of Wittigis' Frankish allies remained serious problems for Belisarius. The division of Italy along the line of the Po, with the Goths holding the north (always the area of strongest military and governmental activity) against the barbarians beyond, and central and southern Italy integrated into Justinian's Mediterranean empire, seemed a real possibility in the resulting negotiations. But, unofficially, a very different solution was also mooted: the effective resuscitation of the western empire, with Belisarius ruling through the support of both Gothic and Roman armies to maintain a distinctively Italian political order in the west. In 540, the Goths surrendered Ravenna to Belisarius in the hope of enticing him to proclaim himself emperor of the west, thereby maintaining their position as the *de facto* Italian army. But Belisarius took Ravenna only to demonstrate his loyalty to Justinian by sending Wittigis to Constantinople. (It is an odd but important feature of the Gothic wars that the Gothic leadership to a man ended up enjoying an honourable retirement in Constantinople; indeed by 540 all the remaining Amals were in the east.) Gothic garrisons in the north, focused on Verona and Pavia, searched for an able leader as they sought to maintain their status in Italian society, rather than facing absorption into Justinian's army. Belisarius continued to refuse the appeals of the Goths, and was soon recalled to Constantinople.[15] After the collapse of two short-lived Gothic candidates for the kingship, Totila rallied the remnants of the Gothic army. Totila was to lead Gothic resistance for over a decade of continuous campaigning in northern and central Italy; in 546–7, and again in 550, the Goths were once more to lay siege to Rome. It was not until 552 that Narses, Belisarius' replacement as leader of Justinian's forces in Italy, finally defeated and killed Totila at Busta Gallorum. Gothic kingship did not formally end until the defeat of Totila's successor, Teia, in 554. Even then, the attempted invasion of northern Italy by the Frankish king Theudebert I played a large role in persuading the Gothic army to throw its lot in with Justinian's armies, as by now Frankish conquest posed a still greater threat to their position in north Italy than the surrender to the Byzantines.

The paradox of 'reconquest': the Gothic wars and the transformation of Italian society

Procopius was to hint that the long-drawn-out wars were the result of Justinian's jealousy of Belisarius, and the unwillingness of Constantinople to commit adequate troops to Italy out of fear of a revived western empire. Here, Procopius' personal agenda and complex relationship with his patron Belisarius need to be taken into account. Nonetheless, the repeated offers of rule over Italy that were made to Belisarius before his recall in 540, and the fact that his replacement, Narses, was a eunuch and therefore not an acceptable candidate for such a role, indicate the real problem with 'reconquest'. Italy, quite simply, had never been ruled direct from distant Constantinople, and had its own complex set of political traditions, centred on the barbarian military on one hand, and the senatorial landowners on the other. Any lasting political solution would have to acknowledge these groups. In fact, the inconclusiveness of the campaigns of the 540s points to a lack of Italian enthusiasm for rule from Constantinople; and to the willingness of cities, particularly in the traditional seats of army and government in the north, to lend their support to an able Gothic ruler who could claim to be acting to preserve the status quo. Whilst Procopius' account works unquestioningly within the framework of Byzantine claims to be 'restoring' Roman order, it is worth remembering that adherents of the Gothic cause could remind Italian provincials of the benefits they had enjoyed in a Gothic kingdom within the Roman Empire under Theodoric, and that the Byzantines could be castigated as 'Greek outsiders' who sought to impose themselves over an historic Italian order. In the course of the first siege of Rome, Belisarius had been forced to move against powerful Roman landowners whose loyalty was suspect: the senator Maximus, husband of a Gothic princess, was exiled from the city, as was the pope. Byzantine actions could add fuel to such tensions and alienate Italian opinion. The arrival from Constantinople in 540 of Alexander 'the Scissors' resulted in attempts to bleed Italy dry of tax revenue, with demands being made for taxes owed to the Goths in the period predating the 'reconquest'. On the other hand, the insecurity of the Gothic position likewise led to drastic measures. In 537, Wittigis had all the senators who were with him in besieged Ravenna executed, rather than risk their changing sides. In fact, as the wars grew ever more vicious through the 540s, the increasingly localised loyalties of Italian populations became ever more visible. Both the Byzantine vision of a 'restored', united empire, and the Gothic appeal to the traditional alliance of barbarian generals and Italian civilians must have come to look like empty rhetoric.[16]

Justinian's ideology saw the 'reconquest' as creating a Christian empire united in faith, a political unit that was coterminous with the Christian church. Here, too, western responses were ambivalent. The Italian church itself was far from united, and Justinian's own determination to drive through a theology around which all parties could unite drew considerable opposition. In 544, attempting to win the support of monophysite communities in the Near East, Justinian issued a new statement of orthodoxy on the key issue, the nature of Christ, which included a condemnation of the work of three theologians whose work had previously been considered orthodox, but was unacceptable to the monophysites; this condemnation of the 'three chapters' was confirmed by an universal church council held at Constantinople in 553. It was in the west that opposition to the 'three chapters' containing the denunciation was most marked. In many western eyes, Justinian's statement seemed to water down the statements of the Council of Chalcedon of 451, which was seen in the west as the touchstone of orthodoxy, and was especially valued by the church of Rome in its statement of the ultimate spiritual authority of the pope. Western disquiet was particularly marked in northern Italy, where the politically powerful bishops of Milan and Aquileia were vehemently opposed to Justinian's ecclesiastical policy, but was led by Pope Vigilius. Whilst there is no suggestion in the sources that ecclesiastical policy and theological differences had direct consequences for political loyalties, the situation was serious enough for Vigilius to be taken as a prisoner to Constantinople where he was forced to negotiate a compromise (albeit one which was not accepted across much of north Italy). What the outbreak of the 'three chapters controversy' clearly demonstrates is western unease at Justinian's view of a Christian unity rooted in a coterminous church and state. Justinian's theological manoeuvrings were motivated by the need to find a way of making this vision real in a context where a substantial part of the east remained wedded to monophysitism. In the west, however, although churchmen expected rulers to prevent open disorder within the church, there was no tradition of direct political intervention in theological matters, nor of a unity imposed from above.

It was not just the church and civilian populations that demonstrated shifting allegiances in the face of the competing claims of Gothic kings and Justinian's generals. Even more striking – and just as important in ensuring the continuation of war – was the tendency of troops themselves to swap sides. Whatever the ideology said, this was no clash of civilisations, barbarian against Roman. In fact, in terms of personnel, Gothic and Roman armies were less different than their names suggest. Theodoric's 'Goths' were a conglomeration of professional warbands who had coalesced in the Balkans and along the Danube frontier, where they had rallied to the banner of whichever warlord had been able to force his way into Roman service and to accrue the material gains that went with it. In Italy, they assimilated a similar pick-and-mix assortment of professional soldiers of barbarian and Italian origin, whilst gradually putting down roots in provincial Italian society. Belisarius' army was itself initially recruited largely from the professional, personal followings of Balkan warlords and landlords, supplemented by barbarians seeking riches in Roman service. As the campaign for Italy drew on, Byzantine armies, like Gothic, counted on increasing numbers of recruits with Italian ties, and became increasingly entangled with the local loyalties, and the politics of land and self-interest. Given these similarities, the criss-crossing of loyalties and changing of sides is hardly unexpected. The Balkan warlord Herodianus, for example, had supplied a sizeable part of Belisarius' initial force, and was left garrisoning Naples in the south. When the tide changed he swapped sides and surrendered Spoleto to the Goths, Procopius pointing to the fact that his Balkan origins meant that he was a kinsman of leading Goths.[17]

By the 540s the extent to which both armies were embedded in Italian society became increasingly evident. Barbarians and recruits with no Italian interests might have effected a conquest of Italy, had a quick victory been possible in Belisarius' initial campaign, as in Africa; similarly, had Gothic ties with Italian society been shallow, as Vandal links with their host communities seem to have been, 'reconquest' might have been rapidly effected. But as mercenaries with cares at home, such troops were not an effective force for a drawn-out war of attrition. In the 540s, for example, troops recruited from the Balkan province of Illyricum returned home without permission once they heard that their homeland, left defenceless, was being ravaged by Huns who had crossed the Danube. With mercenaries and outsiders unreliable, the war increasingly became a struggle for the allegiance of recruits with lands and interests in Italy, whether they were provincial men seeking to defend their own, or Goths and other barbarians who had married and bought their way into Italian society. Goths frequently surrendered on condition they were recruited into Justinian's armies on equal terms with Romans. Gothic leaders could play the same game, as in 542 when after victory over the Romans at Mugello Totila enlisted defeated prisoners as full-status members of his 'Gothic' army.[18]

Allegiances were fluid and difficult to enforce: already in 540, Belisarius had tried to ensure the continued loyalty of the leaders of the surrendering Goths by shipping their children to Constantinople as hostages. The key motivators were the desire for security of home and family in a world where enslavement and the expropriation of land and goods were ever-present threats. Here, Byzantine actions in the period of Belisarius' initial success may have prevented the quick stabilisation of military gains. The imposition of the full administrative and fiscal apparatus of the Byzantine state threatened the local interests of Italian populations, with goods and lands requisitioned against tax demands, and those who had fought in danger of having their title to land challenged at law. Some of the Gothic garrisons of the Cottian Alps, for example, had held out against Belisarius in 539–40, but quickly changed sides when their wives and children were threatened with enslavement by the local Byzantine general, whose forces controlled the countryside. Justinian recognised the problem of entangling local loyalties in legislation of 542 which banned soldiers from owning property, but in the context of the Italian war this proved impossible to enforce, and in any case could not have worked in a context where most soldiers on both sides already harboured claims to land.[19]

Eventually, the chronic instability of loyalties and insecurity of title threatened to overturn the social hierarchy: in Bruttium, the Roman landowner Tullianus raised a peasant militia to resist the Goths, and Totila retorted by offering the peasants outright ownership of the land if they deserted to him.[20] Large landowners like Tullianus were uneasy allies for either side as they might cut deals with opponents to ensure continued local pre-eminence. As early as 537, both Belisarius and Wittigis had purged their camps of senators, and both sides continued to demonstrate suspicion of senatorial loyalties, periodically executing or exiling those of dubious loyalty throughout the two decades of war. A lasting conclusion to the conflict was only possible once the need to reach a settlement to the tenurial chaos was recognised. The Pragmatic Sanction, issued by Justinian in 554, sought to draw a line under a generation of conflict by confirming title in the hands of those who had held it before the wars. But Italian society in the intervening period had changed out of all recognition, and any attempt to turn the clock back was doomed to failure.

In fact, the lasting impact of the Gothic wars lay in the calamitous effects of three decades of intermittent disorder on the Italian social order. Above all, the Gothic wars wrought two fundamental changes which augured the end of the established Italian social order: the collapse of any meaningful distinction between civilians and soldiers with the merging of military and political power; and the destruction of the senatorial aristocracy, the dominant class whose interests had determined the character of Italian society, economy and culture. The division between civilian and soldier had been central to the Roman vision of a political order resting in the rule of law, and likewise the underpinning of the ideology of *civilitas* used to legitimise Theodoric's regime. Although the categories had been crossed by the military emperors and barbarian warlords of the fourth and fifth centuries, and in times of crisis landlords had used their local muscle to raise militias – Cassidorus' grandfather, also called Cassiodorus, was celebrated for organising the defence of Calabria against the Vandals in 455 – the exigencies of the Gothic wars brought any effective division between salaried soldiers and tax-paying civilians to an end. At the beginning of the Gothic wars, Cassiodorus had written to provincials pondering their reaction to the approach of Belisarius' army, urging them to stick to their normal routine of harvesting and tax-paying so that they could supply the Gothic army to defend them, rather than abandoning the fields and organising themselves into militias.[21] Two decades in which both Gothic and Byzantine commanders urgently sought troops, and in which self-help quickly proved the best option for both cultivators and landowners, soon meant that any division between civilian and military power was a thing of the past.

The Gothic wars also saw the decimation of the power of the class that had been the determining influence on western Mediterranean society and politics right through late antiquity: the senatorial aristocracy. The senate still continued in name for half a century. But the scale of extensive landowning scattered across the Italian peninsula and beyond, and the staggering wealth thus generated for the senatorial aristocracy, was now a thing of the past. Endemic disorder, along with the periodic purges of senatorial landowners carried out by both sides in the Gothic wars, was the most immediate challenge to continuing senatorial prosperity. How could landowners keep control of their tenants at a distance, or indeed claim the fruits of the land which guaranteed their wealth, in a situation of long-term attritional warfare, which allowed the peasantry the opportunity to claim title to the land they worked, perhaps in return for military aid to one side or other? It is extremely difficult to trace any concentration of landed property on a more than regional scale by the later sixth and seventh centuries. Popes maintained connections with estate administrators in Sardinia and Sicily, but their title was closely tied to the state's control of land and resources, and was, in any case, exceptional. Concentrated property holding was undermined by demographic change too. The effects of the plague that came from the east in 541 are difficult to quantify and easy to exaggerate, but in any case there is clear evidence that this epidemic reinforced a longer-term contraction of the rural population, which would have further altered the balance of power in favour of labourers over landowners.

Archaeologically, the sixth century was the crucial watershed in longer-term patterns of settlement change. Field surveys, and excavations of rural sites, show dramatic changes in the countryside in the sixth and seventh centuries, with the structure and material culture of rural settlement altering out of all recognition. First and foremost, a definitive move away from the *villa* economy is clearly visible, with lavish stone-built aristocratic residences and their associated farms far harder to find. In their place, we find new settlements on new sites, often hilltops, with domestic building in wood or reclaimed stone from abandoned Roman sites. The material culture of these new settlements is far less lavish and complex: locally-made, sometimes hand-made, pottery comes to dominate. These changes, indeed, make early medieval settlements far less visible in the coutryside than their classical predecessors: although the population clearly was contracting, the poorer material culture of many early medieval sites makes comparison with ancient populations difficult. What the archaeology shows above all is the dramatic simplification of the social hierarchy. Elites are far harder to see either as landlords, organising the countryside, or consumers enjoying lives of rural leisure. The central places we do find are of a new type, small fortifications (*castra*) which enjoyed an administrative and political function, often associated with stone churches, as at Castelseprio in Varese, an enclosed hilltop centre with public buildings and roads built in the late fifth century; elsewhere, for example at S. Cornelia in the Lazio just north of Rome, churches themselves seem to have acted as foci for settlement. None of these developments are dramatic or sudden, and most are the culmination of trends reaching back into the fifth century. The archaeology thus serves as an important reminder that the conflagerations of the Gothic wars accelerated and confirmed longer-term trends rather than causing change on their own. But it also confirms the extent of change in the course of the sixth century.

The paradox of Justinian's career is that the Italian campaign, self-consciously styled as 'reconquest', actually marked the fundamental break with the social order of antiquity in the Italian peninsula. The established patterns of Italian – and indeed western – politics, resting on the negotiation between barbarian military leaders, the landowning aristocracy, and the civilian administration, were swept aside, as indeed was the developing synthesis between barbarian and senatorial elites. Ultimately, in the course of decades of civil war, it became clear that senatorial power on the ground was a potential threat to both Gothic and Byzantine commanders, so neither side intervened to prop up senatorial power. The result was a new social and political order, no longer structured by the patterns of senatorial landowning which had defined the basic patterns of Italian society, and tied together the shores of the western Mediterranean. And Constantinople's vision of an empire coterminous with the Christian faith conflicted with the traditions of western churchmen who saw the church as something which could not be wholly identified with any merely terrestrial political order. The final victory of Justinian meant that, for the first time for a millennium, Italian society lacked any central political forum, whilst western bishops had to react directly to the ecclesiastical policy of the imperial court at Constantinople. Italy was now a province, not the seat of empire.

The new social order: Italy as a frontier province

Italy was never fully pacified after the Gothic wars. The northern plain was repeatedly threatened by the barbarian mercenaries who had effected reconquest; it remained a frontier zone, imperfectly integrated into the imperial system. In the decades around 600, imperial crisis allowed the slow crystallisation of an alternative political system in the north, centred on the Lombard warlords who set themselves up as dukes of the major cities. But it would be a mistake to write off Italy as a province of the seventh-century empire and tacitly dismiss reconquest as short-lived, misguided and wholly destructive.

Italian politics revolved around two cities, Ravenna and Rome, which are also well documented thanks to their respective churches. Ravenna, more or less impregnable behind a ring of marshes on the northern Adriatic coast, was the seat of the governor of Italy. As such, it enjoyed regular contacts with Constantinople: a run of surviving papyrus documents registering property transactions show a cosmopolitan society with international links in the sixth century, with imperial soldiers jostling alongside Goths, merchants alongside civil servants, and the holder of an imperial shipping franchise owning land. The main movements of personnel centred on the person of the governor, or exarch, who combined military and civilian power, like his counterpart at Carthage: in the reconquered west, distant from the capital, one man on the spot, not ornate and overlapping hierarchies, were needed. Exarchs were appointed from the bevy of ambitious easterners who flocked to the imperial court at Constantinople, and normally brought with them a staff of relatives and retainers. The archbishops of Ravenna pointed to their city's status as a former imperial capital and the seat of government in the west, and sought to limit the influence of the popes in Rome over their province, an ambition in which they were encouraged by emperors from Justinian onwards, which culminated in the grant of total independence from Rome (autocephaly) in 666.[22]

For Rome, although it was no longer the official seat of government, remained central to Italian politics. As the former capital of the Roman Empire, and thanks to the pre-eminence attributed to its bishop, it enjoyed a huge symbolic importance. In spite of its dramatic shrinking in the sixth and seventh centuries, when its population may have fallen as low as 100,000, it remained the biggest city in Italy. But in the aftermath of the Gothic wars the basis of its former political muscle, the senate, was gone. Even under Theodoric, the senate had remained the central political forum in Italy, voicing the concerns of a hyper-rich aristocracy with far-flung interests. In spite of the calamitous effects of the wars of the sixth century on the wealth of the senatorial class, the senate was still the political voice of wealthy landowners as late as the 580s. But in the last decades of the sixth century and the first of the seventh it disappeared. Gregory the Great, himself a senator, never mentions it except to lament its disappearance, and in the 620s the Senate House, its *raison d'être* gone, was converted, significantly, into a church by the pope, now the dominant power in Rome.[23]

Crucial in the emergence of the papacy as a real political power in Rome and its environs is the rule of Gregory the Great, from 590 to 604. Gregory himself came from a senatorial family, although not one of the first rank; it owed its position to its tradition of service within the Roman church. Gregory had served as prefect of Rome in his youth, before retiring from public life and turning his family home, on the Caelian Hill, into a monastery, an aristocratic home devoted to asceticism and learning. Having entered the papal bureaucracy, Gregory served a spell as papal representative at the imperial court in Constantinople, before being persuaded to take up the papal throne in 590. Gregory's career itself mirrors the papacy's slow takeover of the duties formerly undertaken by the city's civil government. In a shrinking city, which no longer focused as the seat of an increasingly regionalised Italian aristocracy, the papacy was the major institution able to maintain the city. Whereas in the Gothic wars, and in the face of renewed incursions by new groups of barbarians in the 560s and 570s, the senate had spoken for Rome and negotiated with passing armies, by Gregory's reign that role had become the pope's. By Gregory's day, the rich papal estates of southern Italy, Sicily and Sardinia supplied food for the city's population. In the course of the seventh century, the city's physical infrastructure came to rely on papal care. The buildings and renovations of successive popes recorded for posterity in the reign-by-reign biographies of the *Book of Pontiffs* (*Liber Pontificalis*) show traditional papal investment in ecclesiastical buildings slowly coming to redefine the topography of the city in the seventh century – as with the redevelopment of the Senate House – and by the eighth century the fabric of the city – walls and aqueducts – was being repaired by the popes.[24]

Gregory's pontificate did not only mark a crucial stage in the establishment of papal government within Rome. His characteristic brand of piety, so typical of late antique aristocratic asceticism, stressed self-control; in Gregory's hands, self-rule was to be placed at the centre of a programme for the rule of human society, advanced through a series of popular theological works. In his *Pastoral Care*, directed at bishops but equally applicable to all those holding power in this world, Gregory presented rule in thoroughly Christianised terms, as an activity centred on the care and salvation of souls, and offered a rule of conduct for those exercising power based on monastic rules designed to discipline the self; in his *Morals from the Book of Job* Gregory's reading of one book of the Bible was animated by a series of allegorical reflections on the cares and tribulations that went with the exercise of power. Not only were Gregory's 'bestsellers' to remain profoundly influential templates for bishops and kings in centuries to come, they offered a mechanism to transform the internal workings of the Roman church to enable it to take on its new tasks. Gregory's legacy was to introduce a cadre of monks, and a monastic discipline, as a potent force within the Roman church, but one which was also potentially controversial: the posthumous biography in the *Book of Pontiffs* is lukewarm, and it is no accident that Gregory's life was first written up as saintly in distant Whitby on the British North Sea coast.[25]

Gregory's posthumous glorification in distant Whitby points to another important new development. Popes had long enjoyed a somewhat intangible preeminence in the western church, but in the late sixth and seventh centuries they came to be seen as spokesmen and representatives of western Christians. Here, Gregory's careful cultivation of diplomatic links with bishops, kings and queens beyond the imperial frontiers, in Gaul and Hispania, went hand-in-hand with his sponsorship of missions to the lost Roman province of Britain. This should not be seen as an attempt to build up an independent, western, power base beyond the emperor's reach. The Christian Roman Empire remained the ultimate framework of authority in this world for Gregory and his contemporaries, and the identification of the empire as God's chosen vehicle to spread Christianity and ensure orthodoxy underwrote claims to universality; so with his involvement in western Europe beyond Italy Gregory was actually acting as a loyal imperial servant. But Gregory's initiatives – and his status as the pre-eminent Latin theologian of the age – guaranteed the continued authority of the pope as the ultimate point of appeal on matters of doctrine and discipline, and as a crucial mediator between the western churches and the Christian empire.

The importance of the pope as mediator between east and west made it imperative that an individual with the right pedigree and contacts filled the office. In the late Roman and Gothic periods, the personnel of the Roman church had come primarily from the ranks of ambitious middling landowners, and popes had been chosen 'in house'. Although Justinian and his successors did not make papal appointments, simply approving Roman elections, the need to find a candidate acceptable to the imperial court, and able to engage with the theological disputes of the Greek-speaking east, was paramount. Through to the middle of the eighth century, these necessities led to the election of a succession of Greek-speakers, immigrants and exiles who had fled to southern Italy and Sicily, and who were well represented in the numerous Greek monasteries of Rome. Their dominance also reflects the economic and social ties between Rome and the great estates of the south.

We might expect these social changes to augur a papal takeover of Rome and its environs. In fact, the nexus of imperial influence and social and economic ties with the south and its cadre of educated exiles was not the only check. The sources for Rome, written as they were from within the papal administration, may overstate the extent and rapidity of ecclesiastical domination over the city. If we look at the only non-papal written sources, the legendary accounts of the deeds of the Roman martyrs, we are transported to a world of wealthy lay patrons directly supporting and celebrating martyr cults with a piety far less refined than Gregory's. The fourth, fifth and sixth centuries had seen recurrent conflicts between the Roman church and wealthy lay patrons and patronesses, particularly over control of Rome's parish churches or *tituli*, and the cults of the many legendary martyrs which sprang up around the city. Exciting new archaeological discoveries show the continued presence of wealthy laypeople within seventh- and eighth-century Rome, housed in luxury stone complexes such as those unearthed at the Forum of Nerva or the Crypt of Balbus, where they consumed high-status imported goods, many from Rome's central Italian hinterland, but some imported. The inhabitants of these private aristocratic compounds, which abutted and enclosed previously public spaces and imperial possessions, no longer enjoyed the scale of wealth, the spread of interests, and the political dominance that had typified the senatorial aristocracy. They emerge only rarely, as faces in a crowd, in our written sources, but the largesse showered on the Roman population by popes in their building programmes and food and welfare distributions needs to be placed against the backdrop of the likelihood of competing structures of aristocratic patronage.

Gregory's piety was typical of his time and class in his attachment to monastic discipline as a means of acquiring self-control. Traditions of asceticism had long roots in the social and religious practice of high-status Roman men and women, and in the late fourth and fifth centuries teachers like John Cassian had imported the mortifications of eastern monks in the desert to the west and domesticated them into practices which could mark out aristocratic households as places of spiritual excellence. The idea of taking a vow to follow a set regime of discipline and so converting a household into a monastery – as Gregory himself did in his youth – quickly caught on, and the sixth century saw the circulation of a number of 'rules', templates for monastic discipline from which those considering taking a vow could pick and mix to set a suitable regime for their household. In this milieu, the rule associated with Benedict, founder of Monte Cassino south of Rome, quickly gained popularity, partly because it was intended as an easy introduction, a 'rule for beginners' which those with spiritual expertise could augment.[26] Monasticism, though it had long historical precedents, appealed because it allowed a partial disengagement from the compromises and horrors of sixth-century Italian public life: in creating a microcosm of spiritual perfection in their households, landowners were not rejecting terrestrial order outright, but neither were they enthusiastically embracing the claims of the Christian empire to be God's chosen vehicle for mankind. Cassiodorus, for example, whose family history and public career had lain in service of the state, abandoned public life in the aftermath of the first sieges of Rome and Ravenna, the cities around which his world had previously revolved; he spent the last four decades of his life until his death in 580 in a monastery founded on his Calabrian estates, named Vivarium after the fishpond of the family *villa* of Squillace by which it stood. This was no 'retirement' by a now discredited statesman: as he explained in his *Institutes* Cassiodorus saw it as a 'conversion', as he now worked in the service of God to promote divine order in the world. Hence the role of Vivarium as a cultural centre, preserving the classical learning of antiquity for a new Christian world, and translating Greek texts for a Latin audience in 'self-help' guides comparable in their aims to Benedict's 'beginner's rule'.[27] The monastic culture shared by figures as diverse as Cassiodorus, Gregory and Benedict was essentially one in which the classical culture of antiquity was repackaged in explicitly Christian terms for an audience who, compared to the senators of the fourth and fifth centuries, were middlebrow readers of middling wealth; in the siting of Benedict's Monte Cassino, a hilltop church with wooden farm buildings huddled around it, overlooking the main road south from Rome to Naples, we see the new social context of this new landed elite.

It was the members of this reshaped landowning elite that were the agents of a crucial social transformation. In the seventh century, in a largely invisible process, a new elite of relatively modest but militarised landowners emerged as the crucial class in Italian society. Even in Justinian's time, Italian armies had never been big: hence the recurrent use of barbarian allies and mercenaries to fight on behalf of the emperor. The financial pressure of recurrent war in the east made the supply of western armies a real problem in the last quarter of the sixth century, and Italy was of necessity left to make the best use of its own resources. In 578 and 580 the senate, making what was to be its final appearance as the voice of Italian society, petitioned the Emperor Tiberius for additional military help, but all that was forthcoming was advice on buying the support of barbarian warlords. When Gregory the Great opened talks with Lombard leaders to protect Rome in the 590s, he was accused of treason by the exarch, but the Emperor Maurice accepted his actions as necessary.[28]

By 700 the empire had become ever more focused on Constantinople. Provincial elites competed for position at Constantinople, their identities enmeshed in their participation in the elaborate court ceremonial that defined their rank, and the shared cults that bound together the fate of city and empire. Lacking the independent landed and military muscle to form strong regional aristocracies, provincial landowners were tied into a court society writ large as the imperial city. Italian elites, however, stood largely outside of this system. Geographically distant from Constantinople, the structures of power in their society made them less dependant on the rank and office bestowed by the imperial court: the governor at Ravenna exerted some patronage, but had little choice but to work through local landowning elites, which continued to identify with their cities and regions. In Sicily and the south, things may have differed: the lack of documentation makes social structure difficult to unpick, but there are clear indications of a relatively cosmopolitan society with close links across the Mediterranean sea lanes in the large numbers of wealthy immigrants from the east and the emergence of Greek as the spoken language. The pull of Constantinople across the sea should not be underestimated: the panegyrist of Justinian's successor, Justin II, was Corippus, a north African poet whose move east speaks loudly of the magnetic pull of the imperial court.[29] But in central and northern Italy, even ambitious youngsters from Ravenna or Rome had little occasion to travel to Constantinople or become enmeshed within the hierarchy of the imperial court.

Bibliographical essay

General works

General works have tended to focus on Italy, or on Byzantium (usually meaning, in effect, Constantinople and its immediate hinterland); for guidance on these, see chapters 5 and 6 below. But for a thought-provoking treatment of the sixth-century Mediterranean as a whole see Averil Cameron, *The Mediterranean World in Late Antiquity* (London, 1996). M. Maas, ed., *Cambridge Companion to the Age of Justinian* (Cambridge, 2005), although focused on the east like most Byzantine history, is also an invaluable introduction and point of reference.

Primary sources

Theodoric's reign is richly served. The key source is Cassiodorus, *Variae*, selection tr. S. Barnish (Liverpool, 1992). Jordanes' *Gothic History*, a controversial text but crucially important, is available translated by C. C. Mierow (Princeton, 1915). Ennodius, *The Life of St Epiphanius*, tr. G. Cook (Washington, 1942), gives valuable insights into Ostrogothic Italy. The pessimistic chronicle of Anonymous Valesianus on Theodoric is ed. and tr. J. C. Rolfe as an appendix to the Loeb edition of *Ammianus Marcellinus: Res Gestae* vol. 3, pp. 531–69 (Cambridge, MA, 1939). Boethius' *Consolation of Philosophy* is available in Penguin Classics, tr. V. Watts, or Oxford Worlds Classics, tr. P. Walsh (1999).

The crucial sources for the age of Justinian come from the pen of Procopius, and are available in a number of translations. The eight books of his *Wars* consist of the Persian Wars 1–2, the Vandal Wars 1–2 and the Gothic Wars 1–4. The Loeb edition of H. Dewing contains a full translation (Cambridge, MA, 1939). The lurid *Secret History* is available in Loeb, ed. and tr. H. Dewing (Cambridge, MA, 1935), or in Penguin Classics, tr. G. Williamson, which also includes Procopius' account of Justinian's *Buildings*. Subsequent Byzantine historians were remarkably uninterested in the west, an important phenomenon which deserves proper study: for details of later sixth- and seventh-century Byzantine sources, see chapter 5. For the Byzantine state see John Lydus, *On the Magistracies of the Roman State*, tr. A. C. Bandy (Philadelphia, 1983); for Justinian's legislation *Institutes*, tr. P. Birks and G. McLeod (Ithaca, 1987), and *Digest*, tr. A. Watson (Philadelphia, 1998).

A number of works give a local perspective on post-Roman development. Pride of place must go to the collection of papal biographies known as the *Liber Pontificalis*, tr. R. Davis, *The Book of Pontiffs: The Ancient Biographies of the First Ninety Roman Bishops to AD 715* (2nd ed. Liverpool, 2000), which are full of information on Rome. Compare Agnellus of Ravenna's *Book of the Pontiffs of Ravenna*, tr. D. Deliyannis (Washington, 2004).

For cultural changes, pride of place goes to the works of Gregory the Great, of which surprisingly there is no programmatic translation other than those in the relevant volumes of the *Select Library of Nicene and Post-Nicene Fathers* (London, 1890–1900). The *Dialogues* – containing stories of Italian churchmen and saints – are tr. O. Zimmerman in the Fathers of the Church series (New York, 1959). The wave of rule-writing in sixth-century Italy produced the Rule of Benedict (many tr., e.g. T. Kardong, Collegeville, MI, 1996); for the cultural and religious changes of the sixth century see also Cassiodorus' *Institutes* (tr. L. Jones, *An Introduction to Divine and Human Readings*, New York, 1946, or M. Vessey, Liverpool, 2005).

Theodoric and the Gothic kingdom

There are a number of good treatments of the Goths: see in particular H. Wolfram, *History of the Goths* (Berkeley, 1988); P. Heather, *The Goths* (Oxford, 1996); T. S. Burns, *A History of the Ostrogoths* (Bloomington, IN, 1984). On Theodoric's reign in Italy, J. Moorhead, *Theodoric in Italy* (Oxford, 1993), gives a solid introduction. The most important work by far, with a radical reinterpretation of the period as a whole, is P. Amory, *People and Identity in Ostrogothic Italy, 489–554* (Cambridge, 1997). See also Heather's important study of Theodoric's regime, 'Theodoric, king of the Goths', *Early Medieval Europe* 4 (1995). P. Heather's contribution to J. Jarnut, H.-W. Goetz and W. Pohl, eds, *Gens und Regna* (Leiden,

2001) is a good way into the debate. Other useful recent conferences, although with little in English, are *Teoderico il Grande et I Goti d'Italia*, Atti del XIII Congresso internazionale di studi sull'alto medioevo, Milan 1992 (Spoleto, 1993), and G. P. Caratelli, ed., *Magistra barbaritas: I barbari in Italia* (Milan, 1984); the contributions by V. Bierbrauer are the most useful introductions to traditional views of the archaeology, but need treating with care in light of the more recent work on material culture summarised here. Also M. Johnson, 'Towards a history of Theodoric's building programme', *Dumbarton Oaks Papers* 42 (1988).

The seminal discussion of the cultural context of Ostrogothic Italy is A. Momigliano, 'Cassiodorus and the Italian culture of his time', in *Proceedings of the British Academy* 41 (1955) reprinted in Momigliano, *Studies in Historiography* (New York, 1966); see also S. Barnish, 'Maximian, Cassiodorus, Boethius, Theodehad: literature, philosophy and politics in Ostrogothic Italy', *Nottingham Medieval Studies* 34 (1990). Boethius' writings are covered in M. Gibson, ed., *Boethius: His Life, Thought and Influence* (Oxford, 1981), which includes an important chapter by J. Matthews on his social and political context.

There is ongoing debate about the key primary source, Jordanes. The relevant chapter of W. Goffart, *The Narrators of Barbarian History (AD 550–800): Jordanes, Gregory of Tours, Bede and Paul the Deacon* (Princeton, 1988), suggests a very different reading from the traditional interpretation exemplified by Wolfram; Heather and Amory each suggest interesting alternative readings; see also P. Heather, 'Cassiodorus and the rise of the Amals: genealogy and the Goths under Hun domination', *Journal of Roman Studies* 79 (1989). The other sources are less well treated. On Cassiodorus, there is a biography by J. O'Donnell, *Cassiodorus* (Berkeley, 1979); R. Macpherson, *Rome in Involution: Cassiodorus' Variae in their Literary Setting* (Poznan, 1989) places the *Variae* in the context of late antique administrative practice. Ennodius' writings are neglected, although B. Näf, 'Das Zeitbewusstsein des Ennodius und der Untergang Roms', *Historia* 39 (1990) discusses perceptions of 'the fall of Rome'. On *Anonymous Valesianus* see S. Barnish, 'The anonymous Valesianus II as a source for the last years of Theodoric', *Latomus* 42 (1983).

Justinian and reconquest

Justinian's reign has inevitably attracted biographical treatment such as J. Moorhead, *Justinian* (London, 1994) and R. Browning, *Justinian and Theodora* (London, 1971). See also J. A. S. Evans, *The Age of Justinian: The Circumstances of Imperial Power* (Oxford, 1996). The essays in P. Allen and E. Jeffreys, *The Sixth Century: End or Beginning?* (Brisbane, 1996) give a sense of the Byzantine context.

Arguably the most innovative and important work has come, however, through close treatment of the primary sources in their own right. See in particular the insights into the world of Justinian in A. Cameron's magisterial *Procopius and the Sixth Century* (London, 1985), a short taster of which is available in 'History as text: coping with Procopius', in C. Holdsworth and T. P. Wiseman, eds, *The Inheritance of Historiography, 350–900* (Exeter, 1986). For the work of one of Procopius' contemporaries, and its insight into Justinian's programme, see M. Maas, *John Lydus and the Roman Past: Antiquarianism and Politics in the Age of Justinian* (London, 1992); also Maas, 'Roman history and Christian ideology in Justinianic reform legislation', *Dumbarton Oaks Papers* 40 (1986). T. Honore, *Tribonian* (London, 1978), esp. first chapter, provides the essential introduction to Justinian and the law. On the progress and problems of reconquest there is, surprisingly, a need for more work. J. Teall, 'The barbarians in Justinian's armies', *Speculum* 40 (1965), discusses recruitment to Byzantine forces, and the crucial issue of Italian loyalties in the Gothic wars is discussed in most of the major works on Ostrogothic Italy, notably Amory's book.

Ravenna, Rome and Byzantine Italy

Byzantine Italy in the seventh and eighth centuries is the subject of an excellent study by T. S. Brown, *Gentlemen and Officers: Imperial Administration and Aristocratic Power in Byzantine Italy, AD 554–800* (Rome, 1984); Brown's prosopographical appendix has now been updated by S. Cosentino, *Prosopografia dell'Italia bizantina* 2 vols (Bologna, 1996, 2000). Similarly excellent is the recent Italian study of E. Zandini, *Le Italie bizantine. Territorio, insediamenti ed economia nella provincia bizantina d'Italia (VI–VIII secolo)* (San Spirito, 1998). See also T. S. Brown, 'The church of Ravenna and the imperial administration in the seventh century', *English Historical Review* 94 (1979), and his 'The interplay between Roman and Byzantine traditions and local sentiment in the exarchate of Ravenna', *Settimane* 34 (1988). On ecclesiastical politics see R. Markus 'Ravenna and Rome, 554–604', *Byzantion* 51 (1981). Sicily and the south, whose importance is a recurrent theme in recent work, remain understudied, largely due to lack of sources: L. Cracco Ruggini, *La Sicilia tra Roma e Bisanzio* (Naples, 1980) is the most useful survey, whilst P. Charanis, 'On the question of the Hellenisation of Sicily and Southern Italy in the Middle Ages', *American Historical Review* 52 (1946–7), is the classic discussion of a key issue.

There is inevitably a large bibliography of general works on Rome and the papacy: for full guidance see chapter 5 below. Gregory the Great has attracted most discussion of the early medieval popes, much of it focusing on his thought. The best starting point is R. Markus, *Gregory the Great and his World* (Cambridge, 1997), which has a full bibliography. See also the biographical studies of C. Straw, *Gregory the Great: Perfection in Imperfection* (Berkeley, 1988) and J. Richards, *Consul of God: The Life and Times of Gregory the Great* (London 1980), and, for discussion of Gregory in his full cultural milieu, J. Cavadini, ed., *Gregory the Great: A Symposium* (Notre Dame, 1995) and C. Leyser, *Authority and Asceticism from Augustine to Gregory the Great* (Oxford, 2000). For discussion of the extent to which Gregory's career augured a new, more western, papal world view, see Markus, 'Gregory the Great's Europe', *Transactions of the Royal Historical Society* 31 (1981), J. Hillgarth, 'Eschatological and political concepts in the seventh century', in J. Fontaine and J. Hillgarth, eds, *The Seventh Century: Continuity and Change* (London, 1992), P. Delogu, 'The papacy, Rome and the wider world in the seventh and eighth centuries', in J. M. H. Smith, ed., *Early Medieval Rome and the Christian West* (Leiden, 2002).

The nature of the source material is discussed by T. Noble in 'A new look at the Liber Pontificalis', *Archivum Historiae Pontificiae* 23 (1985), for the *Liber Pontificalis*, and 'Literacy and papal government in late antiquity and the early Middle Ages', in R. McKitterick, ed., *The Uses of Literacy in Early Medieval Europe* (Cambridge, 1990), for documentary traditions. On the institutional basis of papal power, and the role of the popes in Roman society, see a series of important articles by P. Llewelyn, 'The Roman church in the Laurentian schism: priests and senators', *Church History* 47 (1978); 'The Roman church in the seventh century: the legacy of Gregory the Great', *Journal of Ecclesiastical History* 25 (1974). On papal use of relics, see J. McCulloh, 'The cult of relics in the letters and the dialogues of Gregory the Great', *Traditio* 32 (1976). Two important recent articles try to test the papal perspective of the most commonly used sources against the power of other groups in Roman society: K. Cooper, 'The bishop, the martyr and the matrona', *Early Medieval Europe* 8 (1999) and C. Leyser, 'Gregory the Great and the Roman martyrs', *Early Medieval Europe* 9 (2000).

For the rich archaeological material, and the development of Rome as a city, see P. Delogu in R. Hodges and B. Hobley, eds, *The Rebirth of Towns in the West 700–1050* (London, 1988) and in G. Ripoll, ed., *Sedes Regia* (Barcelona, 2000), the best two introductions. Important new finds opening new perspectives on urban society in Rome are discussed by R. Coates-Stephens, 'Housing in early medieval Rome', *Papers of the British School at Rome* 64 (1996) and 'Dark-Age architecture in Rome', *Papers of the British School at Rome* 65 (1997). See also J. M. H. Smith, ed., *Early Medieval Rome and the Christian West: Essays in Honour of Donald A. Bullough* (Leiden, 2000), esp. Augenti, Marazzi, Noble and Valenziani; also Noble's 'The making of papal Rome', in M. de Jong and F. Theuws, eds, *Topographies of Power in the Early Middle Ages* (London, 2001). R. Krautheimer, *Rome, Profile of a City 312–1308* (New Jersey, 1980) is still the classic on the city's topography and the 'papal takeover'. Also important on the economic ties between the city and its hinterland are S. Barnish, 'Pigs, plebeians and potentates', *Papers of the British School at Rome* 55 (1987) and P. Arthur, 'Early medieval amphorae, the duchy of Naples and the food supply of Rome', *Papers of the British School at Rome* 61 (1983).

Ravenna, by comparison, has been relatively neglected, although there is now some high-quality work utilising Agnellus' ninth-century collection of Ravennese tradition. See J. M. Pizarro, *Writing Ravenna* (Princeton, 1989) and his discussion of urban violence in Agnellus in J. Hill and M. Swan, eds, *The Community, the Family and the Saint* (Turnhout, 1998), as well as T. S. Brown's discussion of Agnellus in C. Holdsworth and T. Wiseman, eds, *The Inheritance of Historiography 350–800* (Exeter, 1988).

Archaeological evidence for settlement change covers the late Roman to Lombard period, and can be approached through much of the general reading on Lombard Italy in chapter 6 below. A good introduction is R. Francovich, 'Changing structures of settlements', in C. La Rocca, *Italy in the Early Middle Ages* (Oxford, 2001), with an excellent bibliography; compare P. Arthur, 'From vicus to village: Italian landscapes, 400–1000', in N. Christie, ed., *Landscapes of Change: Rural Evolutions in Late Antiquity and the Early Middle Ages*

(Aldershot, 2004), with a welcome emphasis on the south; for a good case-study from one region, G. Barker, *A Mediterranean Valley: Landscape Archaeology and Annales History in the Biferno Valley* (London, 1995). For interpretation of the settlement archaeology see C. Wickham, 'Italy and the early Middle Ages', in K. Randsborg, ed., *The Birth of Europe* (Rome, 1989), reprinted in his *Land and Power* (London, 1994) and updated in 'Early medieval archaeology in Italy: the last twenty years', *Archaeologia Medievale* 26 (1999), and compare R. Francovich and R. Hodges, *Villa to Village* (London, 2003).

Notes

1. Cassiodorus, *Variae*, 5: 29; tr. S. Barnish (Liverpool, 1992); 5: 30 suggests the equation of the 'freedom of our army' with the 'freedom of our Goths'; direct appeal to the ruler bypassing the tangling intermediary structures of government is what marks this appeal as distinctively 'Gothic' rather than more generally 'late Roman'.
2. *Tricennalia*: *Anonymous Valesianus*, tr. J. Rolfe in the Loeb *Ammianus Marcellinus: Res Gestae* vol. 3 (Cambridge, MA, 1939), 65. *Via Appia*: *Corpus Inscriptionem Latinarum* 10, no. 6850, conveniently tr. by Barnish, *Cassiodorus: Variae* (Liverpool, 1992), pp. 36–7, and *Anonymous Valesianus*, 60.
3. Barnish's translation offers a good selection; for the entire collection, although with much condensation, there is an older tr. T. Hodgkin, *The Letters of Cassiodorus* (London, 1886).
4. Jordanes, *Gothic History*, tr. C. Mierow (Princeton, 1915); Cassiodorus *Variae* 9: 25 is the only source for his now lost history. For the complex issue of the relationship of these texts, see bibliography.
5. 'Ancient barbarians': Cassiodorus, *Variae*, 5: 14; sons of Cyprian: *Variae*, 8: 21–2.
6. Boethius, *Consolation of Philosophy*, tr. P. Walsh (Oxford, 1999) I: 4; *Anonymous Valesianus*, 65–7; Procopius, *Wars*, tr. H. Dewing (Cambridge, MA, 1935–9), 5.1.
7. *Liber Pontificalis*, tr. R. Davis, *The Book of the Pontiffs* (2nd ed. Liverpool, 2000), John; Gregory the Great, *Dialogues*, tr. E. Gardner (London, 1911) or O. Zimmerman (New York, 1959) 4: 30–1.
8. Procopius, *Wars*, 5.2, 4.
9. Procopius, *Wars*, 5.2.
10. Cassiodorus, *Variae*, 4.34 (not in Barnish).
11. Malchus fragment 2, ed. and tr. R. Blockley, *The Fragmentary Classicising Historians of the Later Roman Empire* 2 (Liverpool, 1983).
12. The only account of the Nika riot is Procopius, *Wars*, 1: 24.
13. Procopius, *Wars*, 4.2–3.
14. Procopius, *Wars*, 5.6–7.
15. Procopius, *Wars*, 6.29–30, is a careful and guarded account of the negotiations.
16. Expulsion of Maximus and pope from Rome: Procopius, *Wars*, 5.25. Alexander's tax demands: Procopius, *Wars*, 7.1 and see also *Secret History*, 18: 13–15. Wittigis at Ravenna: Procopius, *Wars*, 5.26.

17. Herodianus' changing sides: Procopius, *Wars*, 7.21, and compare his *Secret History*, 56.
18. Illyrian recruits returning home: Procopius, *Wars*, 7.11. Goths surrendering and joining Byzantine armies on 'equal' terms: Procopius, *Wars*, 6.11, 19, 27, 29. Mugello: Procopius, *Wars*, 7.5 and see also e.g. 7.36.
19. Cottian Alps: Procopius, *Wars*, 6.28. Justinian's legislation: *Novels of Justinian*, 116, unfortunately untr., ed. R. Schöll and G. Kroll, *Corpus Iuris Civilis*, vol. 3 (Berlin, 1928).
20. Bruttium: Procopius, *Wars*, 7.18.
21. Cassiodorus, *Variae*, 1.4, 12.5.
22. Documents: J.-O. Tjäder, ed., *Die nichtliterarischen lateinischen Papyri Italiens aus der Zeit 445–700* (Lund, 1954). For the institutional identity and memory of the Ravennese church, see the ninth century *Books of the Pontiffs of the Church of Ravenna* by Agnellus, tr. D. Deliyannis (Washington DC, 2004).
23. Gregory, *Sermons on the Prophet Ezekiel*, 2.6.22, ed. M. Adriaen (Corpus Christianorum Series Latina 157, Turnhout, 1971); Conversion of Senate House: *Liber Pontificalis*, tr. Davis, Honorius I.
24. For Gregory's political role and the economic infrastructure of the Roman church, see his Register of Letters, a full selection tr. in P. Schaff, ed., *Select Library of Nicene and Post-Nicene Fathers* 11–12 (London, 1900; now online at www.ccel.org/fathers2); for papal patronage in Rome, the biographies in the *Liber Pontificalis.*
25. *Liber Pontificalis*, Gregory I; Anonymous of Whitby *Life of Gregory the Great*, tr. B. Colgrave (Cambridge, 1985).
26. Benedict's *Rule*, tr. T. Kardong (Collegeville, MI, 1995); the key source on his career is Gregory, *Dialogues*, tr. Zimmerman, book 2.
27. Cassiodorus, *Institutes*, tr. L. Jones (New York, 1946) or M. Vessey (Liverpool, 2005).
28. Embassies to Tiberius: Menander the Guardsman, fragments 49, 62, tr. R. C. Blockley (Liverpool, 1985); accusations against Gregory by the exarch Romanus: Gregory, *Register of Letters*, 5: 36,40.
29. Corrippus, *In Praise of the Emperor Justin*, ed. & tr. A. Cameron (Oxford, 1976).

5

Arabs, Avars and amphoras: causes and consequences of imperial collapse

Contents

Summary

Chronology

List of emperors

Map 3: The Mediterranean world in the sixth and seventh centuries

Imperial collapse and the rise of Islam

Mediterranean exchange: the economics of decline

Collapsing frontiers: the Balkans

Fracturing allegiances: Constantinople, Rome and Ravenna

Bibliographical essay

Summary

The success of Justinian had raised the possibility of a new Mediterranean order centring on Constantinople, with diplomatic subsidies and selective intervention furthering imperial influence in the barbarian kingdoms of the west. But the practical problems of rule from Constantinople soon became apparent, not least the huge military expenses. Attempted cost-cutting led to military unrest which undermined political stability in the first decades of the seventh century: as a result of civil strife, Byzantine frontiers in the Balkans and the Near East collapsed. In spite of military recovery under Heraclius (610–41), the military and political vacuum in the Near East was filled by the rapid emergence of a dynamic new force in the 630s and 640s, the Arab tribes united under the banner of a new religion, Islam. By 642, Constantinople had lost the rich eastern provinces, and with them approaching three quarters of the imperial budget. Meanwhile, following civil war and the withdrawal of troops, the Balkans were left more or less undefended, as sixth-century raiding by two new groups, Avars and Slavs, escalated into full-scale settlement in the former Byzantine provinces in the seventh century.

Intimately related to these dramatic political developments, economic and cultural linkages around the Mediterranean were changing. Long-distance exchange, already troubled by declining demand in the west and the impact of plague in the sixth century, was dramatically affected by the loss of the Near Eastern provinces. The ending of the regular state-led transfers of goods to Constantinople further divorced the Near East from the western Mediterranean economy. As the potential for regular long-distance trade atrophied, regional or even sub-regional economic networks increased in importance. With these adjustments, long-distance contact and communication became harder too, and cultural differences within the Mediterranean, above all between the new imperial heartlands in Constantinople's hinterland and the remaining western provinces, emerged into the clear light of day. Throughout the sixth and seventh centuries, imperial interventions in matters of Christian doctrine had been a matter of lively debate and intermittent conflict, with the popes acting as representatives of western opinion. By the beginning of the eighth century, however, the new imperial policy of iconoclasm combined with political crisis in Italy to sever the ties between Constantinople, Rome and Ravenna.

Chronology

590–604	Gregory I the Great Pope
602	Emperor Maurice overthrown as Balkan armies rebel
610	Heraclius leads African army to Constantinople; seizes imperial throne
610–41	Heraclius eastern emperor
610–28	Heraclius wars with Persia: loss of eastern provinces
617	Annual state shipments from Egypt to Constantinople end
c. 570–632	Life of Prophet Mohammed
626	Persians and Avars besiege Constantinople
630	After victory over Persians, Heraclius rides in ceremony into Jerusalem
636	Arab victory over Byzantines at Yarmuk; Syria evacuated
638	Arabs take Jerusalem
640–2	Arab conquest of Egypt
646	Arabs defeat Persian army
649	Lateran Synod: western condemnation of imperial theological policy of monotheletism
651	Final Persian resistance to Arabs ends
662–6	Constans II in Italy
674–7	Arab naval blockade of Constantinople
695–717	End of political stability: seven emperors in 22 years
698	Fall of Carthage
717–41	Leo III emperor
717	Siege of Constantinople
726	Imperial policy of iconoclasm begins; Italian revolts
751	Ravenna falls to Lombards

List of emperors

Justinian 527–65
Justin II 565–78
Tiberius 578–82
Maurice 582–602
Phocas 602–10
Heraclius 610–41
Constans II 641–68
Constantine IV 668–85
Justinian II 685–95
695–717: seven emperors in 22 years including return of Justinian II 705–11
Leo III 717–41

Imperial collapse and the rise of Islam

Amongst the correspondents of Pope Gregory the Great was one Rusticiana, a descendant – probably the granddaughter – of the senator and philsopher Boethius who had been executed by Theodoric the Great. Gregory and Rusticiana had meet at the imperial court in Constantinople, even though both were descended from prominent Roman families. In Gregory's case, Constantinople had been a temporary abode, as he served five years as the papal representative at the imperial court; his family remained in Italy. For Rusticiana and her kin, however, the move to Constantinople was permanent, the result of a decision to abandon a now insecure Italy for the centre of a new Mediterranean order. The imperial court acted as a magnet for the able and ambitious from right across the Mediterranean world. Rusticiana's father had served Justinian as prefect of Africa. And it was through the links of the court that Rusticiana's daughter contracted a marriage into the richest family in the richest province of the empire, the Apiones of Egypt, whose interests are so well documented thanks to the survival of the Oxyrhynchus papyri. Thanks to the survival of the empire, Rusticiana and her family were able to continue to manage sizeable Italian estates from Constantinople, as well as develop their interest in Egypt.[1] These webs of personnel, and of property and kinship, were underpinned, and in turn reinforced, by economic ties. Constantinople and its court were fed by Egyptian grain, and the imperial government redistributed tax revenue from the wealthy African and Near Eastern provinces across and around the Mediterranean: in their wake these state activities made long-distance exchanges, witnessed by the mute testimony of amphorae, possible.

For modern historians, influenced by Procopius' vivid accounts of Justinian's reign and struck by the failure of Byzantium to establish control over the entire Italian peninsula, debate has centred on whether Justinian's reconquests were misguided, leaving the empire doomed to failure. Such debate has its validity, but

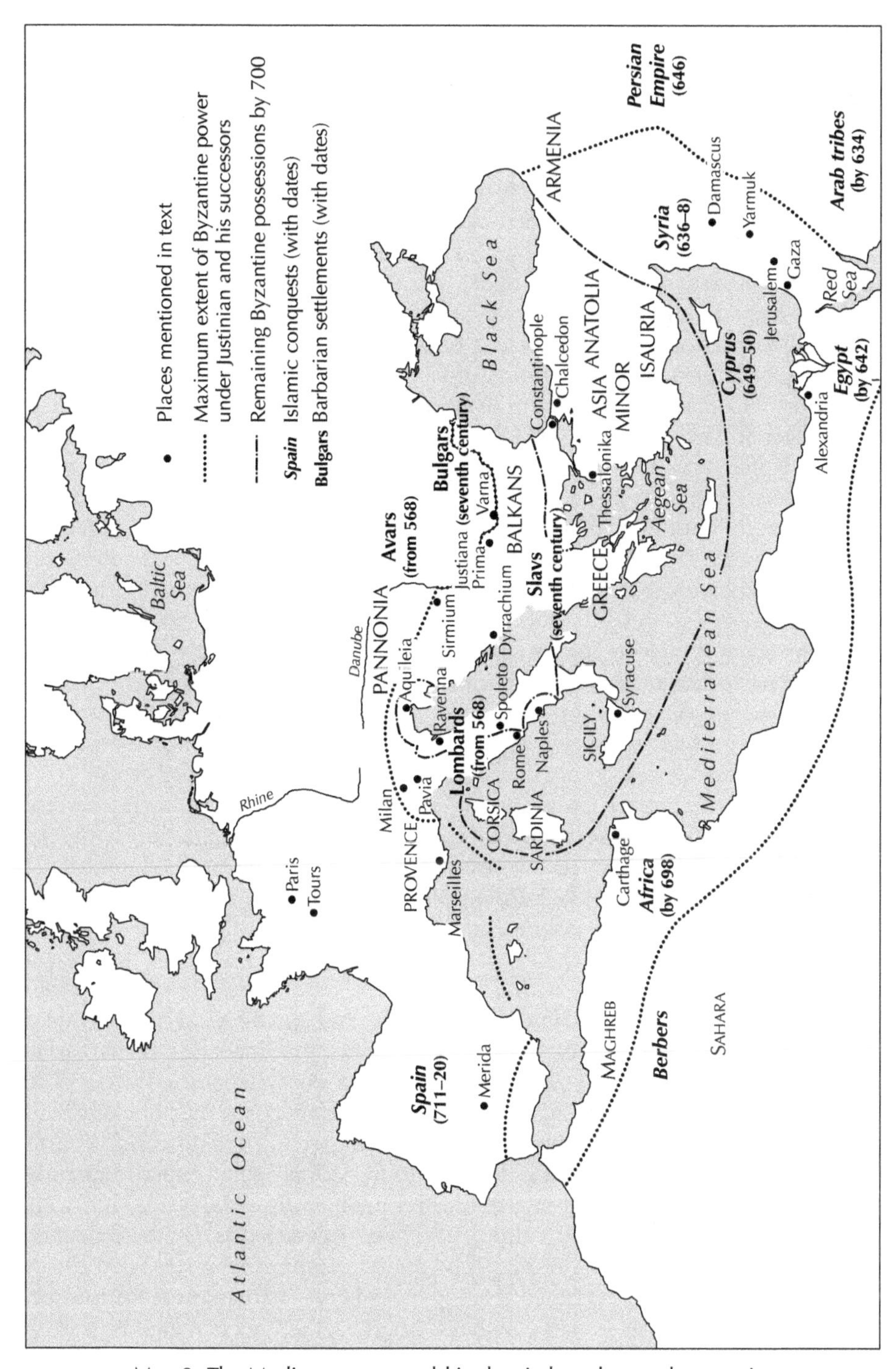

Map 3 The Mediterranean world in the sixth and seventh centuries

it has tended to obscure the viability and importance of sixth- and seventh-century Byzantium as a Mediterranean empire. True, by the beginning of the eighth century the networks which underpinned Rusticiana's world were shattered: the crucial Near Eastern and African provinces were part of a new political and religious system, the Islamic caliphate which had been established following the Arab conquests of the last two thirds of the sixth century; the Balkans had largely slipped from imperial control under the domination of Slavs, Bulgars and Avars; and the remaining Byzantine toeholds in Italy were rebellious and increasingly independent-minded. But to see this collapse as the inevitable result of military overstretch and financial overcommitment caused by Justinian is to write off the best part of two centuries as a long and preordained decline. It involves ignoring the importance and intensity of interactions around the Mediterranean in a century which saw the imperial throne at Constantinople seized by the son of the prefect of Africa, Heraclius (610–41), and his grandson, Constans II (641–68), visiting Rome – the only Byzantine emperor to do so – and setting up court in Sicily. The result has been to allow historians of western Europe and of Byzantium to work in relative isolation, their interests and stories not interacting due to the belief that Justinian's reconquest was a mirage which made no meaningful impact on the reality of Mediterranean division. This owes much to modern perceptions of east–west division within Europe, and an understandable search for their roots. However, contemporaries of Rusticiana would have adopted a different perspective, stressing Constantinople's rapid rise to dominance in the Mediterranean basin from the fourth century to the sixth; it was only sustained crisis that meant that by the early eighth century the new Mediterranean order had fragmented into a series of only intermittantly connected regional systems.

The transformation of Constantinople's European provinces in the western Mediterranean and the Balkans cannot be understood in isolation from the profound crisis suffered by the empire as a whole as a result of developments in the Near East. Throughout late antiquity, the safeguarding of the Near Eastern frontier with Persia was the political and military priority of Byzantine emperors. To enter into conflict with the Persians, the other 'Great Power' of the ancient world, was to enter into war with a sophisticated state whose huge tax revenues supported a professional army; qualitatively and quantitatively, it posed a different order of threat to campaigns in European provinces against barbarian warbands. The long frontier zone, stretching from the Caucasus in the north to the Sinai peninsula in the south, was dotted with ancient cities, the populations of which were long familiar with the processes of taking refuge and negotiating terms as invading armies advanced. Particularly in Syria, the region most frequently contested, these cities nestled in a fertile and prosperous countryside, and were cradles of a strong and vibrant culture. The Near East acted as a kind of magnet, attracting not only the fiscal resources of the two empires who struggled for its control, but also armies recruited from its periphery – barbarians from Europe, tough mountain peoples from the Balkans, Anatolia, the Caucasus and the Iranian plateau, and nomads from the Eurasian steppe and the Arabian peninsula. Indeed, Byzantine policy in the west was determined by the need to raise manpower to fight in the Near East, and to conserve cash and supplies to serve these armies:

large-scale redeployment of armies to the west, with all the expense involved, was nonsensical when the fragmented barbarian groupings around Italy and the Balkans could easily be recruited to fight in the east.

The sixth century was an age of escalating conflict in the Near East: war, not peace, was the norm. By the first decades of the seventh century, the toll of this near constant warfare began to tell on both empires, and military fortunes began to fluctuate dramatically as they staggered in a desperate and deadly embrace. Maurice's attempted reforms of the Byzantine army were a direct response to these problems, and they in turn led to military unrest culminating in his overthrow by Phocas in 602. Phocas, unable to deal with the structural problems that had beset Maurice, was in turn overthrown by the son of the exarch of Africa, Heraclius, in 608–10, whose success rested on the ability to hold Constantinople to ransom by withholding vital African fiscal resources.[2] The results of this internal crisis were startling: the Byzantine frontier collapsed in 610 and the empire's eastern provinces were quickly captured, with even Egypt, the main exporter of both tax revenue and grain to Constantinople, lost in 616. As Persian armies moved at will through the eastern provinces, Heraclius managed to effect a stunning turnaround, by the daring tactic of leaving Constantinople, by now all but synonymous with the empire and the fount of imperial legitimacy, in the hands of the patriarch Sergius. Campaigns across Anatolia and Armenia allowed him to outflank the Persians and conquer the heartlands of their empire in modern Iraq from the north. By 628, it was the Persian regime's turn to disintegrate: as Heraclius' army approached the Persian capital Ctesiphon, the shah was murdered and a peace treaty offered. There followed political chaos in Persia, with no fewer than eight rulers in four years. Heraclius was able to restore the frontier, amid considerable confusion as some Persian forces attempted to hang on to their gains.

Although Heraclius was to stage a ceremonial entry into the reconquered Jerusalem in 630, the vulnerabilities visible in both regimes were quickly exploited by a wholly unexpected source: the Arab tribes. Like the barbarians on Byzantium's northern and western frontiers, tribes such as the Ghassinids had proved an invaluable source of manpower in recurrent Near Eastern wars. Indeed, the search for soldiers and support had drawn the different Arab tribes into closer and closer contact with the Byzantine and Persian Empires. Trade routes criss-crossed the Arabian peninsula, leading to the Red Sea and the Gulf. And along these trade routes also travelled the religions of the two empires, Christianity and Zoroastrianism, encouraged by imperial authorities who sought to politicise the issue of religious allegiance amongst their allies and neighbours. But, in spite of this growing prosperity and cultural complexity, imperial diplomacy combined with the tribal structures of society and the ecology of the Arabian peninsula to ensure the political fragmentation of the Arabs. Imperial eyes need not look south, to the desert, when invading armies massed in Syria or Mesopotamia.

It is into this fertile melting pot that the career of the Prophet Mohammed needs to be placed. Each and every issue of Mohammed's life is the subject of intense controversy, as the sources for that life are themselves not contemporary, but the products of successive religious controversies over the true nature of the Islamic faith he founded.[3] Islam was based on Mohammed's visions in which the One God,

Allah, spoke to him, the latest and last in a long line of Prophets including Moses and Jesus to whom He called out; Allah's words, memorised by Mohammed's close-knit band of companions, were written down as the Qur'an a generation later. Based initially at Mecca, a multi-tribal cult centre and market, Mohammed's followers adopted a new identity, united by faith. When they aroused opposition from the authorities in Mecca, they were able to establish control in Medina thanks to Mohammed's ability to act as an arbitrator between competing tribes, before returning to Mecca, thanks to the economic muscle afforded by control of Medina and the success of Mohammed and Islam in building a new confederation of cities and tribes. Little is known of the mechanisms by which Islam spread, but it did so amazingly quickly in this world of camel caravans and small-scale raiding. Speaking directly to the tribes, in their tongue and drawing on their cultural heritage, Islam was a potent faith, promising success and presenting the Arabs as the vehicle for God's will, the culmination of earthly history.

Although the period immediately following Mohammed's death in 632 was marked by dispute among his followers and the rise of a number of rival prophets, remarkably soon his successors as leaders of the faithful were leading Arab armies to military successes along the Byzantine and Persian frontiers. In 635, the second caliph, 'Umar, took Damascus, in Byzantine Syria; in the following year, Heraclius was forced to abandon Syria entirely following a catastrophic defeat at the battle of Yarmuk, and in 640–2 Arab armies overran Egypt. It was not only Byzantium which suffered: the Persian Empire had dramatically collapsed and its heartlands passed into the hands of the caliph by 646, with the final independent Persian ruler defeated in 651.

Older views about an Arab population explosion spilling out into the Near East have no evidential basis, and in any case cannot explain the sudden expansion of Arab power in less than a decade. Clearly, the fragility of both the Byzantine and Persian regimes, and their concentration on each other, allowed a rapid, unexpected, and often more or less unopposed advance from the south. Clearly, too, the lack of prolonged resistance from local populations and city authorities from Egypt to Mesopotamia points to an underlying weakness in the hold exerted by both empires on their provinces. Whilst it would be a mistake to see the anti-Jewish legislation promulgated by Heraclius, or the doctrinal differences between the official imperial church and the largely monophysite populations of much of Syria, as creating fifth columns of religious dissidents anxious to throw off Byzantine rule, the tensions that did exist clearly did create a certain distance between the imperial government and local authorities. The experience of three decades of military and political chaos must have similar loosened provincial ties to Constantinople; the degree of control exercised over provinces only returned to imperial hands for a handful of years, and then by truce rather than conquest, must be a moot point, and a cash-strapped government in Constantinople may have used the reconquest to reassess and reassert its fiscal rights. In the circumstances, it is easy to understand why city councils, faced with an Arab army offering favourable terms for submission, accepted rather than resisting.

Nonetheless, even when it is admitted that concerted resistance only occurred where the imperial government was able to confront the Arabs with field armies, the fact remains that the Arabs were able to win decisive victories against both the Byzantine and Persian military in short order, to the extent that no real counter-attack was attempted by either. However decimated the campaigns of 610–28 had left the Byzantine and Persian armies, their defeats in major battles in 636 and 637 respectively would not have been possible had Arab society not undergone revolutionary change. The extent to which the Arab conquests, and the early caliphate, can be understood in terms of a centralised movement subject to a single chain of command is a matter of intense debate, and some campaigns, such as the conquest of Egypt, are subject to conflicting traditions which are difficult to disentangle but which suggest an element of unconcerted opportunism by individual commanders. But whether one takes the maximist or minimist line on centralisation, it is clear that this was political and military action on a new scale. The transformation from fragmented tribes serving as imperial allies prized for their mobility and their adeptness at desert raiding, to a coherent military force able to win set-piece engagements can only be explained with reference to the unity provided by the new faith.

Of course, Islam was new for most of the participants in the initial runaway successes, and must still have been crystallising as a separate religion sharply differentiated from the previous beliefs of at least some of its followers; the rapid successes of the 630s and 640s, and the new-found power, wealth and status that resulted, were important factors in embedding the new faith and in the cohering of a new Islamic identity which transcended Arab tribalism. Nonetheless, in the medium term, the astounding unifying strength of Islam was vital in ensuring that the initial conquests created a coherent single state, the caliphate; the moment of Byzantine and Persian weakness could easily have seen piecemeal conquest, followed by fragmentation and some form of imperial recovery. In fact, conquest meant little immediate change to provincial society. Established elites continued their dominance through long-established city structures, tax revenue, collected as before, now passing into the hands of Islamic governors and garrisons. No pressure was put on provincial populations to convert to Islam, although non-believers were subject to a poll tax. The Islamic faith thus defined membership of a tax-consuming elite, and the economic basis of its power in tax revenue meant that it was an elite which, initially at least, was relatively unimplicated in local social relationships and landownership; over time, of course, local notables converted to Islam and conquerors built up landholdings, but the tax system remained intact, a potent mechanism for the extraction of wealth, and elites remained resident in cities and relatively abstracted from the land. Whilst a high proportion of tax revenue was distributed locally, the caliph claimed the title to a cut, and so the state sat at the centre of a web of practices which redistributed surpluses over vast distances. Islam held together a geographically vast but socially thin elite, and Arab tribal identities survived as badges that could define factional identities which transcended localities and criss-crossed Eurasia, providing routes of access to the court at Damascus and the holy places in Arabia.

In the west the barbarian peoples beyond the empire's European frontiers had been transformed by the experience of acting as allies and armies for their Roman neighbours, and then pulled into provincial society as a military elite once imperial government began to implode. In the east, the transformation of Arab society had similarly been accompanied by the military takeover of imperial provinces as the grip of the Byzantine and Persian regimes over the Near and Middle East began to slip. If the decimation of imperial armies, the draining of imperial treasuries and the dislocation of provincial allegiances provided the opportunity for Arab success, a combination of the disruption to the economic tendrils reaching down through Arabia and the dislocation of the politics of alliance whereby imperial influence was maintained may have provided a powerful impetus pulling Arab tribes into Syria and Mesopotamia. But, whereas in the west barbarian coalitions soon fragmented and dislocated provincial structures could not provide enough revenue to create a single successor state, here long-standing city structures and rhythms of tax assessment and collection were robust, and Islam provided a potent point of unity for a conquering elite.

Mediterranean exchange: the economics of decline

The endlessly fascinating – and vitally important – debate over the reasons for the creation of a vast new empire over such a short span of time are beyond the immediate scope of this book, but the consequences are vital for understanding the transformation of the late antique Mediterranean. Since the pioneering work of the Belgian economic historian Henri Pirenne in the early twentieth century, it has become customary to see the Islamic conquests around the Mediterranean as dealing a death-blow to the trading networks which had bound together the Roman world in antiquity; for Pirenne, the transformation from an interconnected ancient economy of cities and trade to the agrarian and land-locked eighth-century west marked the fundamental change from the ancient to the medieval. It is vital to remember that Pirenne *was* a pioneer: without any meaningful archaeological data, he had to work from mentions of eastern traders in written sources from the west, and evidence for eastern goods – the Egpytian papyrus on which ancient documents were habitually written, oriental spices and wines and so on – reaching the west. And Pirenne believed he was looking for genuine market-driven long-distance commerce of a kind familiar in his modern milieu, whereas historians nowadays see long-distance exchange in late antiquity as driven by the state systems which requisitioned supplies and transferred surpluses around the Mediterranean, providing an infrastructure on which long-distance trade piggy-backed. Given the strides that have been made, then, it is time to kick the habit of discussing the economic transformation of the sixth to eighth centuries in terms of the 'Pirenne thesis'.

In fact, it is becoming increasingly difficult to see the integration of the former Roman provinces on the eastern and southern shores of the Mediterranean into the Islamic caliphate as the direct cause of economic collapse. For one thing, although the Arabic sources remain remarkably underused, there is no evidence that political and religious division led to some form of trade embargo across the Mediterranean. And Arab pirates, often invoked to explain diminishing trade, are in fact more or less absent in our sources before the decades around 800. Waspish swarms of pirates feed on the jam of regular trade, and the increasing visibility of piracy by the end of the eighth century must be directly related to the clear revival of Mediterranean trade in this later period.

Whilst the archaeology is beginning to offer clear confirmation of diminishing exchanges between east and west, the bold picture of eastern goods simply disappearing from western markets because of a cut-off in supply needs revising. Take the example of papyrus. Only produced in Egypt, in antiquity it had been widely available and cheap, used for packing and candle wicks as well as for producing documents, travelling on the back of an extensive trade in bulkier items. Whilst it never wholly vanished from the west, by *c.* 700 it was a luxury item, rare and subject to specialised shipments, as the efforts of the Merovingian kings to maintain supplies through Marseilles make clear; and though it fell out of use in late seventh-century Gaul following a royal decision to switch to parchment for official documents in the 670s, it was still used in Italy, particularly in centres like Rome and Ravenna whose political clout maintained international links. These changes took place precisely because there was no regular system of high-volume exchange between the eastern and western Mediterranean, within which small and light bundles of papyrus could travel as incidental additions to holds bulging with grain, or jars of oil or wine. The widespread change to parchment, easily locally produced from animal skins, thus partly reflects changing patterns of supply, and a shift to local networks organised through monastic landholdings across much of the west. But there is also a cultural element. Papyrus was fragile and best suited to short-lived documentation with a short-term rationale, such as late antique states with their regular routines of tax assessment, land registration and administrative letters required. Parchment could survive far longer, and was thus ideally suited to the kind of documents increasingly required by western elites, establishing titles and privileges granted in perpetuity and commemorating land transactions tying secular landowners to ecclesiastical institutions. Rather than an old-fashioned 'clash of civilisations' explanation, a more complex picture of interconnected cultural, economic and political change is needed to understand our expanding database of evidence for changing patterns of long-distance exchange.[4]

The crucial impetus for change came with the collapse of the tax base of the Byzantine state and the associated system of long-distance transfers in the course of the seventh century. By the time of Justinian II at the end of the seventh century, the notional annual budget of the empire was perhaps a quarter of that enjoyed by the first Justinian a century and a half earlier.[5] This was the direct result of the loss of provinces in Africa and the Near East, but the financial crisis predated the advances of Arab armies. The eastern provinces and Egypt had already been lost to the Persians in the 610s, and were never regained for a fiscally meaningful time-span prior to their passing into Arab hands. The consequences were not just financial: Constantinople itself had been fed by the annual transport, on state initiative, of Egyptian grain, a transfer so vital that the civil war of 608–10 had largely turned on control of the *annona*, the annual grain shipment. In 617, after the loss of Egypt, the *annona* ended, never to be resumed: no wonder that Heraclius considered abandoning Constantinople and moving the capital to Carthage in his native North Africa.[6] These calamities took place 20 years before the Arab conquests, which simply ensured that the state transfers from Egypt and

Syria, and the trade which piggy-backed on them, would never be resurrected; and any Egyptian or Syrian traders now seeking to export to Constantinople would be subject to tolls, whereas previously a commitment to carry the *annona* had brought with it exemption and a whole string of other legal privileges.

The loss of Egypt and Syria had particularly severe consequences as these regions had grown increasingly dominant within the Mediterranean economy. Changes in the rhythms and flows of exchange around the shores of the Mediterranean had a long history. The fourth-century foundation of Constantinople and its subsequent rapid growth fed by Egpytian grain created a potent economic nexus. By the sixth century, the traders serving the coasts of Gaul and Hispania were Syrians and Egyptians. The testimony of thousands of pottery shards found at Marseilles, the valve linking Gaul to this international economy, can be coloured thanks to the anecdotes of the historian and hagiographer Gregory of Tours on the conspicuous consumption by Gallic elites of wine from Gaza and other oriental goods, and the shops of Paris; and Gregory's testimony can be combined with the complementary evidence of the vivid account of the connections of a Spanish city in the *Lives of the Fathers of Mérida*.[7] The exact chronology of the growth of this new nexus is still a matter of debate, but the broad outlines can be clearly discerned. The west as a whole had seen a contraction of settlement and a decreasing population from the third century onwards, and correspondingly the evidence for the large-scale export of Spanish or Gallic products decreases. Trade in the western Mediterranean became more and more a matter of relatively small-scale imports of luxury goods, which travelled much less far inland from the major ports, instead increasingly being consumed in a few centres where elites and their wealth were concentrated. Now that western traders had more or less vanished, this demand was increasingly met by easterners, who were still conducting bulk trade across the Mediterranean to serve the state. When Byzantium lost Egypt and Syria in the early seventh century, the incentives encouraging traders based in the Near East to serve the western Mediteranean were dramatically reduced.

In any case, the connections between the Near East and the western Mediteranean were already dwindling in the second half of the sixth century. The reason lies with one of those unexpected events that appear to be random but, on closer inspection, turn out to be intimately connected to social, political and economic changes: the outbreak of bubonic plague in 542. The plague spread from Pelusium, the port where the trade routes leading down the Red Sea to the African coast and ultimately the Indian Ocean met the shores of the Mediterranean, and ravaged the cities ringing the sea. Its spread, in fact, closely mirrors the economic connections reaching around and across the Mediterranean: it reached deeply and quickly into Syria and Egypt, prosperous provinces whose cities and villages were closely tied into the economics of long-distance exchange, whereas it left little trace in the west. This itself is no surprise: the black rats which carried plague themselves were unwelcome passengers on the ships which plied trade, and so the spread of plague closely mirrors the economic rhythms of the sixth-century empire. In fact, even the outbreak of plague must be linked to the stimulus that imperial renewal and the rise of Constantinople had granted the eastern Mediterranean economy, and the contacts that had thus been forged down the Arabian peninsula and beyond: the epidemic was not native to Europe, but originated in India or central Africa. Whilst written accounts of the plague need handling with care, as these authors saw natural disasters and prodigies as God passing judgement on the affairs of humans and thus wrote them up in polemical terms, recent work, particularly using the evidence of inscriptions, has confirmed that the outbreak had a significant and lasting effect on urban populations in those areas most closely connected with long-distance exchange. And plague hit trade particularly hard, because those most vulnerable were the sailors with whose cargoes the epidemic spread, and the ports through which these cargoes were moved.

There is one complication to this picture of long-distance trade, already damaged by plague, collapsing alongside the imperial frontiers in the early seventh century: the role of Carthage. It is an important complication. The third and fourth centuries had seen the growth of Africa as the bread-basket of Italy, with the western Mediterranean economy revolving around a Carthage–Rome axis: the Spanish pottery typical of imports to Rome in the early empire was slowly replaced by a new type of pottery reflecting a new set of economic connections, African Red Slip ware. The axis between Rome and Carthage was dislocated by the political changes of the fifth century, and particularly the Vandal conquest of Africa. The economic consequences remain unclear in their details. Carthage remained a major port whose connections with the Mediterranean economy were intimately linked to the 'foreign policy' of the Vandal kings and their control of the major islands of the western Mediterranean, and may have enjoyed a short-term boom as a result of this aggressive political backing. But regular state grain shipments from Carthage to Rome ended. In the meantime, Rome's population slowly declined through the fifth and sixth centuries, with the Gothic wars in particular dislocating the city's economy. Thus even when Rome and Carthage were again part of the same political system following Justinian's reconquests, Rome's need for large-scale imports of African grain had gone. A much smaller city of a few hundred thousand now relied on local and regional networks for its food supply. At the end of the sixth century the Rome of Gregory the Great was supported by the papal estates in Sicily and southern Italy; even at the beginning of that century, Cassiodorus' Rome had been increasingly reliant on regional networks created by aristocratic landowning.

In fact, Justinian's reconquest of Africa served not to reconnect the Rome–Carthage partnership, but to tie Carthage to the needs of Constantinople and the eastern Mediterranean economy, and to make the Carthage–Constantinople route the primary valve between the eastern and western halves of the sea: hence the wide distribution of African Red Slip pottery in the east as well as the west. Initially, this must have further strengthened the hand of Near Eastern traders, some of whom even served the Constantinople–Carthage route picking up African goods to add to their eastern cargoes. Africa is a much longer and more difficult voyage from Constantinople than Egypt and Syria, meaning that Egyptian and Syrian ships enjoyed a competitive advantage. But Carthage and its North African provincial hinterland remained in imperial hands after Egypt and Syria were lost. An enigmatic tract from the 640s, describing the forced baptism following imperial orders of a

Jewish trader from the Near East in 632 and his subsequent defence of his new faith, describes regular return voyages from Constantinople to Carthage, with trade an inevitable result. In the context of a global shrinkage in exchange, Carthage may actually have been growing in its relative significance in the Mediterranean economy in the seventh century.[8]

The story of seventh-century Byzantium is perhaps better told from the perspective of a linkage reaching diagonally across the Mediterranean, from Constantinople to Carthage via southern Italy. Connections also led to Rome, a short hop up the western Italian coastline, and Ravenna either by the heavily fortified overland corridor from Rome, or down the eastern Italian coast. These links underlay the basic patterns of politics in this period. They also explain the continued presence of African goods in seventh-century sites in Constantinople and Rome, even a trickle reaching the northern shores of the Adriatic around Ravenna. The volume of long-distance exchange may have been near the end point of a long downward curve, but the connections which made exchange possible were still functioning. They are given a human face by the very visible traffic of voluble churchmen, many of Near Eastern origin but now settled in Sicily or Africa, loudly debating the theological issues which were so central to Byzantine public discourse with the pope in Rome and the emperor in Constantinople. This Indian summer for a Roman Empire which, although diminished, still straddled the Mediterranean from its southwestern to its northeastern corners may have only lasted for three or four generations, but it should not be ignored, as it so easily is if Justinian's reign is seen as the starting-point of a steady and preordained decline. Certainly our understanding of western European history has suffered from the tendency to divorce it from the history of the Byzantine Empire at far too early a date.

One tacit acknowledgement of the continued importance of long-distance connections in the Byzantine world was the concerted effort made by the caliphs to challenge Constantinople's command of the sea. The inevitable result of the Arab conquest of Syria and Egypt was the development of naval power, which from the middle of the seventh century began to contest Constantinople's maritime hinterland. Cyprus was first targeted in 649, whilst by 655 the caliph's fleets were operating in the Aegean; by 674–7 Constantinople itself was subjected to a siege underpinned by a naval blockade. But ultimately Constantinople's seapower proved durable: the siege itself was abandoned and followed by a thirty-year truce, and Byzantine control of the islands of the eastern Mediterranean was relatively unscathed, although Cyprus was the subject of a complex set of agreements whereby revenue and sovereignty were shared between emperor and caliph.

In fact, the final death knell of such long-distance exchange as remained came not from the sea, but from the land. Although there had been initial attempts to conquer Byzantine North Africa after the fall of Egypt in 642, the long and barren route along the North African coast from Alexandria to Carthage saw relatively little military activity until the closing decade of the seventh century. The Berber tribes of the interior, however, had been increasingly assertive since the fourth century, as their rulers adopted the trappings of Roman legitimacy and acted as the linkmen between the coastal plains and the desert. Berber state-formation on this ecological and political frontier had led to the emergence of a series of kingdoms in the period of Vandal rule, and after 'reconquest' the exarch of Carthage invested in stone fortifications and garrisons in an attempt to police these alternative sources of authority. Crucial to the eventual fall of Roman power in Africa was the gradual infiltration of Islam into this tribal milieu, in many ways so similar to that of the Arabian peninsula. Economic change played a part too: in late Roman times the African economy had been fully integrated into the Mediterranean world, geared to the production of olive oil, figs and other bulk exports by the prevalence of large-scale landholding and the fiscal pressures of the Roman state. Fifth- and sixth-century contraction – above all the collapse of Italian demand which had stimulated these exports – hit hard, and loosened the ties which had bound the plains to the coastal ports which were the hubs of Roman civilisation and the gateway to the Mediterranean. In the new economic context, it made more sense to look to the tribes of the uplands and the margins of the Sahara, and to seek out new strategies geared to local exchanges, than to remain tied to the cities of the coastal strip. So the Berbers, now united by Islam, were slowly to gain the upper hand in the second half of the seventh century, as the coastal cities held out but slowly fell.

Carthage, on account of its connections with Sicily and Constantinople across the sea and the protection offered it by the imperial navy, was to hold out for most of the 690s, but a civil war within the empire led to the mutiny of a force destined to relieve the pressed city in 697–8, and by the beginning of the eighth century Africa was definitively lost. Tellingly, Carthage itself, in the fourth and fifth centuries arguably the most prosperous city in the west, was subsequently abandoned, the most spectacular case of urban failure in the early medieval period; its *raison d'être*, its linkage with the imperial sea lanes, was gone, and an inland site, at nearby Tunis, was more suited to the new economy centred on the Maghreb. Whilst the causality is difficult to unpick, it is also no coincidence that the fall of Carthage coincided with a period of prolonged political chaos within the empire, with no fewer than seven emperors in the period 695–717. Nor is it accidental that these same decades see the final petering out of African Red Slip imports in Rome and Constantinople, and the collapse of the previously stable gold currency minted in the emperor's name in the administrative centres of Byzantine Italy. At one site, an aristocratic house built in the Crypt of Balbus in Rome, we even get a sense of an elite adjusting its patterns of consumption and display in the face of diminishing contacts: imported Egyptian raw glass diminishes in the later seventh century and ancient glass begins to be remelted and remade on an increasing scale.[9]

As we move into the eighth century, we move into a new Mediterranean world and a new Byzantine Empire. Constantinople, its population dramatically diminished since its sixth century heyday in spite of the influx of refugees fleeing from the Balkans and the Near East, now stood at the heart of an essentially regional system. Its immediate hinterlands – the Anatolian peninsula (modern Turkey) and the Greek coast and islands – were naturally tied by a series of short sea hops to the southern tip of Italy and thence Sicily, which had witnessed a steady influx of Greek speakers and Greek culture right through the early medieval period. This region – a Greek diaspora in the ancient world – remained cohesive, its connections rooted deep in the cultural landscape. Constantinople dominated its society, politically and economically. Already in the seventh century we see locally produced Aegean ware emerging in the archaeological record, as relatively low-volume local networks took over the task of supplying a much smaller urban population. The political and administrative structures of the empire emerge, by the eighth century, in a dramatically simplified form, the old network of provinces with their complex hierarchies of civilian and ecclesiastical office swept away, and replaced by new units, themes, with a single governor combining military and civilian authority. Governors commanded the army of the *theme* consisting of locally recruited and locally supplied farmer-soldiers. At the heart of this new empire we can detect a new elite, soldiers of diverse origin, many of provincial background or even from beyond the empire's frontiers, coalescing within the walls of Constantinople, united in the service of the Christian emperor.

Collapsing frontiers: the Balkans

These fundamental changes were played out most dramatically in the Balkans. Control of the Balkans was vital to the maintenance of Byzantine interests in the sixth century. Not only was maintenance of the Danube frontier vital to safeguard both Constantinople and Italy, but control of the Balkans made possible land travel between Constantinople and Italy, whilst the sea route relied on the safety of the Adriatic and Aegean coasts. Perhaps more importantly still, the barbarian groupings along and beyond the Danube frontier were the vital recruiting grounds for the Byzantine army. It is no accident that every eastern emperor from Anastasius in the late fifth century to Phocas in the early seventh had family roots in the region.

In the last days of the western empire the control of Balkan provinces had been a major bone of contention between eastern and western courts. Such squabbles continued, indeed were intensified, when Theodoric assumed control of Italy. In the late fifth century, in the aftermath of the collapse of the Hun Empire, Theodoric had established dominance over the various groupings in the Danube basin, along the Roman frontier; continued control was vital to safeguard Gothic power in Italy, but also inevitably led to tension with Constantinople. Justin and Justinian exercised an active diplomacy among the groupings beyond the frontier, following traditional Roman divide-and-rule tactics and cultivating alliances which might also provide much needed military manpower. With the defeat of the Goths in Italy, care was taken to establish a finely-tuned balance of power, with the city of Sirmium, vital to controlling the middle Danube, the major prize in this manoeuvering. Imperial interest extended beyond the bribing and befriending of barbarian leaders. Procopius' panegyric, the *Buildings*, trumpeted Justinian's fortifications, and archaeology is now confirming the scale of imperial investment in the cities and forts of the Balkans, still recovering from the raids of a plethora of barbarian groups during the Gothic wars.[10]

Justinian's buildings not only fortified the frontier proper; they were distributed throughout the Balkan peninsula in a series of three lines, thus ensuring control of the countryside and particularly the roads, if the frontier defences were breached. They also acknowledged and entrenched far-reaching social changes which had taken place in the region during the disruption of the fifth and sixth centuries, as many of the old centres of social life and provincial administration in the cities had been replaced by fortified military strongholds. Those Balkan cities that did survive did so through transformation into defensive centres offering security – witness accounts of the population of seventh-century Thessalonika not daring to leave the city walls to collect the harvest because of marauding Slavs. This new system was heavily dependent on the state for its continued operation, as the garrisons could not be supported from the surrounding countryside. In fact, in 536 Justinian had created the new office of 'prefect of Scythia' with jurisdiction over some of the territories previously subject to the prefect of the East, precisely to safeguard the Balkans. This new administrative unit, centred on the prefect's court at Varna, combined inland frontier provinces with eastern Mediterranean coastlands and islands, thus placing provinces 'which were almost the most prosperous of all' at the disposal of the official charged with securing the Danube frontier, and providing the fleet to bring supplies from the eastern Mediterranean to the Danube. Simultaneously, the bishop of Justinian's birthplace, a village rebuilt by the emperor as the city of Justiniana Prima, was granted ecclesiastical jurisdiction over the churches of the frontier provinces.[11] The archaeology makes the importance of this state infrastructure abundantly clear.

The re-establishment of the Danube frontier in the sixth century changed the political balance of power in a region which had been the point of conflict between the Roman Empire and recurrent groups of barbarians since the fourth century. Justinian's successors were able to campaign aggressively beyond the Danube, the first emperors to do so since the death of Valens at Gothic hands at Adrianople two centuries earlier. This pre-emptive frontier warfare, aimed at maintaining a balance of power amongst various barbarian groupings, is even reflected in a military textbook written by an anonymous officer, the *Strategikon*. But it was also expensive: the *Strategikon* offers advice on plundering the enemy's lands as a means to gain supplies, whilst archaeological evidence shows garrisons relying on hunting and market gardening to complement state supply. The strain on the system was such that by the end of the sixth century it was necessary to cut costs, but this could only cause disquiet amongst the Balkan garrisons, and the political muscle of the army made this a serious matter, with mutiny breaking out in 588.[12]

This disquiet reached its head when the Balkan army revolted and marched on Constantinople to overthrow the Emperor Maurice in 602, in response to his order that they leave the safety of its garrisons and winter on the barbarian side of the Danube, where they could live off the countryside.[13] Maurice's replacement by the military officer Phocas, however, did not resolve the problem of how to find the resources to maintain the frontier. Far-reaching changes within the empire meant that by the second quarter of the seventh century the system of redistribution which had maintained a Roman army in the Balkans was a thing of the past. Pressing threats on the eastern frontier saw units transferred, the first as early as

605, so that by 620 there simply were no regular Roman units left to safeguard the frontier; at the same time, as we have seen, in response to the same developments in the east, the system of grain shipments, the *annona*, ended, and with it the infrastructure which had allowed the empire to garrison its frontiers.

What was the effect on the Balkans? Traditionally, the collapse of Byzantine control has been seen in dramatic terms of conquest by waves of marauding barbarians, with the frontier a dam which finally burst once pressure had built to an intolerable level; the key development is thus usually seen as the emergence of new groupings of barbarians. We have, however, only the most fragmentary and laconic of written sources, with the exception of a detailed but chronologically jumbled account of events at Thessalonika in the *Miracles of St Demetrius*; these are insufficient to support a model of invading armies and sod-busting settlers. Archaeologically, it is notoriously difficult to tell how and why a site was abandoned, but at the majority of Roman fortifications there are no signs of any large-scale destruction as opposed to simply abandonment. We know of one Byzantine garrison in seventh-century Italy which, on receiving the news that it must winter in the countryside as state supplies were not forthcoming, simply 'went barbarian' and joined the nearest Lombard warband.[14] Certainly after the collapse of the Roman infrastructure which allowed the redistribution of surplus over vast distances in the name of the state, the alternatives were stark: farming or force. It is no accident that the two groupings which emerge in Constantinople's former Balkan provinces in the seventh and eighth centuries, the Slavs and the Avars, are each primarily identified with one of these different social strategies.

Groupings referred to as 'Slavs' or '*Antae*' first emerge in our written sources in the first half of the sixth century. Procopius' claim that 'the Slavs and Antae are not ruled by one man, but have lived from of old under a democracy, and consequently everything which involves their welfare, whether for good or ill, is referred to the people' voiced a clear perception of difference between Slav social organisation and Byzantine monarchy.[15] Whilst we should beware of painting early Slavic society as a model of egalitarian primitive democracy, both the archaeological and written sources from the seventh and eighth centuries suggest an extremely decentralised organisation, with a multiplicity of competing local leaders and a lack of any fixed or long-lasting political hierarchy. Slav society was overwhelmingly agrarian; the basic economic, social and political unit seems to have been the individual 'Sclavene', perhaps corresponding to large and largely self-sufficient settlement areas. When Slav leaders attempted to create more hierarchical forms of political organisation than traditional, largely elective chieftaincies cemented by feasting, they did so with reference to external models and often under external pressure: Byzantine sources describe how one Slav leader used the plunder from a successful raid on Corinth to create an imitation of the canopied throne used by the Avar ruler or khagan, whilst Perbundos 'king of the Rychines' adopted the dress of a Byzantine official and spoke Greek.[16] But judging from the archaeology, it was not until the ninth century that internal social differentiation had progressed far enough to sustain a social elite which was able to live off the labour of others, abstracted from village life, living in hillforts and fortified residences with wooden palisades, and priding themselves on their martial equestrian lifestyle. Byzantine sources of the sixth and seventh centuries comment on the fierce independence and antipathy to any extended form of political power on the part of the Slavs, the ease with which different groups and leaders might be played off against one another, and the difficulty of contracting lasting treaties in such a fluid state of affairs; but whilst Slav bands were reluctant to unite as one on the battlefield, they were adept at the warfare of ambush, skirmish and raid. This made the Slavs difficult to bring into the imperial orbit.

The sixth, seventh and eighth centuries saw the rapid and wholesale 'Slavicisation' of central and eastern Europe from the Baltic to the Adriatic. Modern historians from both eastern and western Europe have often been tempted to read back political and social differences between east and west to contrasts between Slavic and Germanic peoples in this period. This reading of the past has all too easily been used to justify attempts to present racial difference as a fundamental divide in the present. In the academic world, the notion of a strong and long-standing difference between Slavic and Germanic peoples has led archaeologists, linguists and historians to search for the 'origins' of the Slavs deep in the period before any source refers to any groupings as 'Slavic'. In fact, as we have seen, such searches only make sense if we see the 'peoples' referred to in our sources as homogenous and distinct groups, and the evidence of both archaeological and written sources makes such a reading impossible. Slavic identity cannot be seen as something continuous and unchanging since time immemorial; it emerges out of a variety of sources in sixth-century central Europe. If we are to understand social differences across Europe, we need to look at the different contexts in which new social structures coalesced in the aftermath of Roman rule. In the empire's western provinces, barbarian warlords took fractured but functioning provincial societies, and barbarian leaders already accultured to the world of the Roman military quickly coalesced with provincial elites to create new ruling classes. 'Slavicisation', on the other hand, operated entirely outside the social hierarchies of the Roman world and the surpluses they generated. Slav culture arose in a context where the crisis of the empire had pulled successive generations of warrior elites into the Roman world. Where former Roman provinces were 'Slavicised', in the Balkans, the structures of provincial society had collapsed in the fifth and sixth centuries, in a countryside detached from the apparatus of taxation, trade and town life (and, it should be added, primarily in areas whose geography and ecology encouraged such detachment: it is no accident that it was along the coast, and on the plains of Greece, where 'Slavicisation' was checked). That these circumstances, rather than any innate racial characteristics, best explain the particularities of early medieval Slavic society is underlined by the fact that the closest comparison to the 'Slavicisation' of southeastern Europe comes in the spread of an unambiguously 'Germanic' culture in another former Roman province, with the creation of early Anglo-Saxon society in eastern Britain.

The breadth and speed of 'Slavicisation' is best understood in terms of the appeal of a culture of independent and self-sufficient agrarian settlement for provinces adjusting to a retracting Mediterranean economy and the Roman state, and cut off from mechanisms for the acquisition of surplus wealth and social status. But the processes which saw the rapid spread of the Slavic language, or of particular forms of domestic settlement, across such a vast swathe of Europe, much of it never formally part of the Roman Empire, cannot be understood apart from their political context. This political context was the brief dominance of a consciously non-Roman Empire across central and eastern Europe: that of the Avars.

The Avars were in origin a steppe-nomad group like the Huns, which had emerged in response to political changes on the Eurasian steppe, in particular Turkic expansion. Nomadic life on the steppes required extensive territory regulated according to a complex system of grazing rights embedded in a fragmented political and social system. But in a recurrent process, it was possible for larger federations to emerge as successful and ambitious leaders moved beyond their original ecological niche and the inevitably fissiparous tendencies of a pure nomadism, and raised plunder and tribute from the sedentary empires of Eurasia to pass on to their followers. Like the Huns, the Avar federation was pulled into central Europe by the lure of the wealth of the Roman world. As with the Huns, the immediate context for the establishment of this steppe-nomad polity in the middle Danube basin came with the disruption of the complex system of alliances along the Roman frontier in the aftermath of the Gothic wars. In 558–9, the Avar khagan requested an agreement with Justinian whereby in return for annual payments the Avars would fight on behalf of the empire. By 567 the Avars moved into central Europe, reaching an obscure agreement whereby they took over the Lombards' former homeland in Pannonia. In 582 they took the crucial city of Sirmium. Like the Huns, the Avars devoured the surpluses tapped by the Roman state without integrating into Roman society, using force or the threat of force to generate plunder, subsidy and tribute. As with the Huns, that polity took the form of a core area which sustained an Avar military elite, from which branched out a wide-reaching system of tribute from subject peoples.

Avar domination of central Europe provided an umbrella under which 'Slavicisation' could proceed apace. Whilst there are cases of Avars using military force to subject individual Slavic groups, within the Avar polity a basically tributary system which allowed Slavic groups autonomy in return for supplies, hospitality and military aid, as required, prevailed. In many ways, these relationships could be symbiotic; to some observers Avars and Slavs looked like allies working in partnership. When the Avars rode on Constantinople in 626, they did so alongside Slavs troops and with a Slav navy. In the event, despite the seige being co-ordinated with a Persian attack from the east, the Avar-Slav army was defeated, and a half-century of ever-increasing tribute payments ended. The flow of plunder and tribute had allowed the khagan to bestow the gifts and favours that had held the Avar federation together. Its turning off – and the lack of later seventh-century coin finds in Avar territories show that it was definitely turned off – fundamentally undermined that system. Whilst the Avar khagan was able to maintain control of the heartlands beyond the Danube, where the archaeology shows the survival of a powerful warrior elite, after 626 the outlying areas of the Avar federation splintered away. Tellingly, the new groups which emerged were characteristically made up of Slavs under the leadership of outsiders. On the western edge of Avar power, in the modern Czech Republic, the Frankish trader Samo was elected king by Slav groupings who had rebelled; he had twelve wives, marrying into the various tribes of his kingdom to cement his rule; but after his death there is no sign of the continuation of his 'kingdom'.[17] More lasting were those constellations which adapted the structures of Avar rule to their own ends, drawing on steppe-nomad traditions: most successfully, the Bulgars, who were able in the decades around 700 to carve out a state of their own on the lower Danube, in symbiosis with local Slav groups and oscillating between alliance and conflict with their Byzantine neighbour; more obscurely, the Croats and Serbs. Constantinople, anxious to help stabilise these new groupings and so undercut the Avar khagan, as well as cultivate potential sources of military manpower, engaged in a careful diplomacy which offered the rulers of these new groupings legitimation and attempted to tame them in the process. Thus by the end of the seventh century the Bulgarian polity which coalesced around the mouth of the Danube, a fertile and strategically important area, had entered into a treaty of peace with Constantinople, and Bulgarian troops were fighting in Byzantine civil wars.

Fracturing allegiances: Constantinople, Rome and Ravenna

A standing army of sorts remained in Gregory the Great's Italy, concentrated in the cities, above all Ravenna and Rome, its supplies increasingly provided through local networks. By the first half of the seventh century, even those transfers of tax which provided military pay were falling into local hands. Imperial crisis, with the fall of the eastern provinces and the resultant drying-up of tax revenue, meant that Italian soldiers revolted over arrears in their pay in 616 and 619, and again in 640–2. The great churches, above all those of Rome and Ravenna, stepped into the gap, using their landed wealth to act as bankers for the provincial government. After 642, soldiers' pay is not even mentioned by the sources, and taxation as an issue takes a far lower profile too. In Ravenna, the provincial capital, the seventh-century papyri show the coalescence of a homogenous elite combining local landowning with military titles; elsewhere, we lack the run of documentation, but the written sources reflect parallel developments when they talk of the soldiers (*milites*), tribunes and dukes of specific cities. Quite how this came about is unclear: the inherent flexibility in the tax system, the tax exemption enjoyed by soldiers, and the obligations of great ecclesiastical landowners like the churches of Ravenna and Rome must have allowed local systems of supply to grow up within the framework of an official accounting of tax liabilities and allocations. The end-point of the process is shown by a plea made by the inhabitants of Istria to their new ruler, Charlemagne, at Rivana in 802: the 172 'captains' (*capitanei*) of the province rehearsed the obligations they had previously owed the emperor at Constantinople, enumerating specific military services in the locality and tax liabilities which took the form of fixed sums paid by each city.[18] As the apparatus of the state ceased to play a significant role in the circulation of wealth or the provision of military protection, and Italian society fell under the domination of militarised elites of local landowners, political allegiances became more and more an issue of cultural identity. Italian allegiances and Italian identities, however, differed from those in the empire's other remaining provinces.

The different horizons of Italian elites and the imperial court did not mean the immediate uncoupling of Italy from the empire. But Italian loyalties were primarily a matter of ideological allegiance to the Christian Empire. Here, the role of the pope as both a source of authority on doctrine, and spokesman for the western church, led to repeated tensions. Controversy centred on the doctrinal issues regarding the relationship between Christ the Son, God the Father, and the Holy Spirit. The theological disputes mattered, because on a fundamental level they concerned issues of power: in the late antique Mediterranean, talk about the relationship between Christ the Son and God the Father, and the relationship between the human and the divine in the person of Christ, was ultimately talk about God's power in this world. In a world where emperors were not only God's viceregent on earth, but also closely linked to Christ – from Heraclius they styled themselves as '*basileus* faithful in Christ', linking their position to Christ's royal ministry – these issues also had immediate political repercussions. And the politics were further complicated by the cultural differences between the western and eastern provinces of the Roman Mediterranean. Emperors drew on the tradition of identifying the Roman state as God's chosen vehicle on earth which dated back to Eusebius, and was deeply rooted and widely accepted in the east. They thus felt able to intervene in issues of doctrine. To most westerners, however, the relationship between the Roman Empire and the Christian church seemed more complex, and imperial involvement in doctrinal issues more ambivalent. In a world of barbarian warlords, where the boundaries of Roman order were far from clear, it was far harder to place hopes for mankind's salvation in the Christian empire, as opposed to the community of Christians, embodied in the church. This distinctively western take on ecclesiology – the nature of the church – had intellectual roots in Augustine's works, above all in his refusal to identify the city of God with the Roman state, but its force came from the social and political conditions that prevailed in the west. Theological debate on Christology, led by imperial initiatives aimed at correct doctrinal unity, thus also touched on fundamental issues regarding the nature of imperial power and the identity of Christian society: this was in a very real sense public, political, debate.

Tensions over doctrinal issues had rumbled since the days of Justinian's conquests. But they broke out into the open with a new ferocity in the middle decades of the seventh century, as the political map of the empire was being dramatically redrawn. In 638, following drawn-out talks aimed at establishing formal unity between the quarrelling eastern churches, Heraclius issued a new doctrinal statement, the Ekthesis, which pushed a compromise position designed to be acceptable to those who favoured a monophysite position without abandoning orthodoxy as defined in the councils of the church. Given the political situation – the imperial hold on the Near East had been shaky for a generation, and Syria had just been evacuated following the Arab victory at Yarmuk in 636 – appeasing the monophysites, and encouraging them to identify their church with the Christian empire was a real imperative. In the west, however, Heraclius' intervention met with outraged opposition, and encouraged further heated theological debate over the doctrine of monothelitism, which identified a single will or energy uniting the Holy Trinity, expounded in the Ekthesis. Heraclius' position, however, was upheld by his grandson and successor Constans II (641–68). Following a series of public debates in which western opposition to the imperial line was led by a refugee from the east, Maximus the Confessor, a series of church councils was held in North Africa in 646 which condemned the Ekthesis as heretical; simultaneously, the exarch Gregory launched a rebellion, seizing on western military unrest over pay and hoping to emulate Heraclius by using the wealth of Africa – in many ways the most secure imperial province – to seize the imperial throne.

Gregory was killed fighting Arab raiders in 647, but direct opposition to imperial monothelitism had by now spread to Italy. Constans attempted to close down theological debate, issuing a decree known as the Typikon, which banned 'any discussion of one will or one energy, two wills or two energies', whilst recognising western sensibilities by ordering the removal of the Ekthesis from the church of Hagia Sophia in Constantinople. This attempt to shut down the issue was a recognition that there was little immediate hope of recovering the lost provinces in the Near East, and that the wealth and relative security of the coasts and islands of the western Mediterranean were vital if the empire was to have a viable future. But the seriousness of the situation in the west was such that ordering an end to debate was no longer a possibility. In 649, following the death of his predecessor, a new pope was elected, significantly without imperial approval being sought. Martin, although he had served as his predecessor's envoy in Constantinople, broke with the pattern of his immediate predecessors, in that he was of Italian rather than eastern origin. He proceeded to rally western opinion against monthelitism, holding a council of 105 western bishops in the Lateran in Rome. The 649 Lateran Synod, orchestrated by Maximus the Confessor, formally condemned both the Ekthesis and the Typikon. Western loyalties were stretched to the extent that the governor of Italy, the exarch Olympius, was unable to arrest Pope Martin when ordered to do so by Constans: instead, he attempted to harness popular opposition by plotting a rebellion from Sicily. Olympius' death in an epidemic in 652 ended the immediate threat, and Constans was able to appoint a new exarch – tellingly, the only Italian ever to be raised to the position – who arrested Martin and Maximus and dragged them to Constantinople. The charges against them were political: Maximus claimed to be innocent of conspiracy with the rebellious exarch Gregory, but denied the emperor any right to intervene in matters of doctrine, whilst Martin was accused of treason, and forbidden from speaking on the theological issues. Martin was deposed, his sentence of death commuted to exile; Maximus was repeatedly offered a pardon if he would admit the emperor's authority on matters of doctrine, but refused and was mutilated and exiled.[19]

The loss of the eastern provinces meant that the wealthy and relatively secure coasts and islands of the western Mediterranean enjoyed an increased political and economic importance within the empire. Indeed, those churchmen and wealthy landowners who fled Arab rule in the east sought out Sicily and southern Italy, which further shifted the empire's centre of gravity. Constans' attempt to shut down the whole monothelite issue was, indeed, a recognition of the changed political imperatives: there was now no urgent need to placate the monophysite churches of the Near East, and Constans' handling of Martin and Maximus focused on their challenge to crucial imperial prerogatives – approval of papal elections, involvement in doctrinal matters – not on theology. Above all, it was the links between the western ecclesiastical campaign against the Ekthesis and the Typikon, and the revolts of the exarchs of Carthage and Ravenna, which spelt danger: Maximus at his trial was accused of loving the Romans but hating the Greeks, and having visions of the exarch Olympius acclaimed emperor by a choir of western angels whose chanting drowned out their eastern rivals. It was thus both natural and necessary for Constans, as he sought to reforge the basis of imperial power, to look west, and in 661 he launched an expedition to Italy. In part, the rationale was military, and Constans, the only Byzantine emperor to campaign in person in the west, won some initial success against the Lombard duchies in the south. But Constans came not only at the head of an army, for the imperial court also moved with him, and eventually found a home at Syracuse in Sicily. Constans' five years in the west eased pressure on the authorities in Constantinople by removing the major focus of consumption in the city, and also avoided the dangers of civil unrest in a city where Constans was remembered as the 'second Cain'. His move west had precedents in the plans of Maurice – who had considered dividing the empire and setting up one of his sons as emperor in Italy and the west with his brother ruling the Near East from Constantinople – and Heraclius – who had mooted moving his court to the west as a means to ease pressure on Constantinople.[20] Constans' Italian sojourn in fact demonstrated the extent of regional differences within the Roman Mediterranean, for even in an area awash with refugees from the east, where Greek was rapidly becoming the spoken language, the presence of the imperial court quickly caused tension. Constans' efforts to squeeze every possible penny of tax from the western provinces inevitably jarred in a region unused to the kind of aggressive fiscality necessary to supply the imperial court. Hence Constans' visit to Rome, the first imperial visit to the city since the ending of the western empire in the fifth century, was remembered as an exercise in looting to raise revenue.[21] Local unrest over the possible permanent presence of the court in Sicily culminated in Constans' assassination by a member of his bodyguard in 668.

The aftermath of Constans' assassination demonstrated that the centre of political gravity remained firmly and unequivocally in Constantinople. His son and successor, Constantine IV, was raised to the purple in traditional fashion in Constantinople, with no objections from the west. Indeed, the politics of Constantine's reign, which saw a three-year naval blockade of the city by an Islamic fleet in 674–7, reaffirmed the centrality of Constantinople within the imperial system. The western provinces remained loyal to the notion of the Christian Roman Empire. The sixth ecumenical council, held at Constantinople in 680, saw the final disavowal of monothelitism, and led to a flurry of activity in the west; the papacy played a central role in relaying its acts, translated into Latin and debated at a synod in Rome in 680, to the churches of the west, with provincial councils held beyond the empire's frontiers in Hispania and Britain.

This coincided with formal peace treaties being concluded with the Bulgars and Lombards, and can be seen as part of an attempt to pacify the empire's western provinces. But this political quiescence disguised the fact that the ability of the emperor to impose his will in the west was slowly ebbing away. When renewed ecclesiastical controversy broke out, it no longer focused on the major ideological issues of the previous century, but on differing cultural practices between east and west. A further council held at Constantinople in 692 (known as the 'Quinisext' or 'fifth-sixth' as it aimed to iron out issues left unresolved by the fifth and sixth ecumenical councils) aroused western opposition on a range of issues of ecclesiastical discipline, notably clerical marriage, where eastern and western practices differed.

Once again, imperial attempts to promote unity backfired, now because they highlighted cultural practices which had long co-existed without causing controversy. When the Emperor Justinian II (685–95) attempted to arrest Pope Sergius I (687–701) for his opposition to the council, the limits of imperial power in Italy became abundantly clear. Whereas in the 640s, the emperor had been able to impose his will and arrest Pope Martin in spite of a rebellious exarch, half a century later western opinion was resolutely behind the pope, and it proved impossible for the emperor to impose his will. The army in Ravenna mutinied against the exarch and marched to Rome to support Sergius, who had to intervene to protect the emperor's emissaries.[22] Justinian's problems in Italy may have been exacerbated by links between Ravenna and the emperor's opponents in Constantinople, but when a coup was staged in 695 it was an affair of the capital and court, in which Italian affairs were incidental.[23] Now, political insecurity at the centre, with seven emperors in 22 years, left imperial power in Italy in shreds. Sergius' successor, Pope John VI (701–5), again had to intervene to protect the exarch from his own troops, and John VII (705–7) promoted his predecessor Martin, whose death in exile and treatment in imperial hands were the subject of lurid rumours in the west, as a saint. Even the peace-making visit of Pope Constantine to Constantinople in 711 (where Justinian II had regained the throne in 705) led to nought, as in its immediate aftermath another coup brought the monothelite Phillipicus to the throne.[24]

The empire which emerged under Leo III (717–41) was, more than ever, focused on Constantinople and its immediate hinterland, and on the loyalties of the new elite of ambitious provincials which had crystallised around the imperial court at Constantinople: Leo's rise, indeed, came in the course of the third major siege of the city in a century. The role of western bishops and landowners within this palace society, focused on the imperial city, was unclear. In the event, Leo's new religious policy, of iconoclasm, gave rise to renewed, and fatal, conflict. The recurrent crises of the late sixth and seventh centuries had seen the growth of popular devotional practices in which Byzantine men and women had sought security, and contact with the divine, through the adoration of images of Christ and the saints. Opponents of these practices saw in this use of icons a form of image-worship, and could draw on long-standing theological worries about the possibility of depicting the divine, and, perhaps, point to the opposition of the caliphs to image-worship among all their subjects, Christian as well as Muslim.

Leo, influenced by these critiques, ordered the destruction of icons throughout the empire in 726.

The precise forces at work within iconoclasm are difficult to reconstruct, for the supporters of icons were eventually, by 843, to win out, and the surviving sources are largely written with hindsight from their perspective. Nonetheless, imperial opposition to icons probably reflected the prevailing current of opinion amongst those in the imperial service, and enjoyed considerable support both in Constantinople 'and in the imperial armies' particularly in Asia Minor. The cultural logic of opposition to icons in this milieu seems to have drawn on a series of complementary arguments. Traumatised by a century or more of military disaster, it was difficult for the inhabitants of Constantinople and its hinterland, and the soldiers of the imperial armies, to hold on to a self-confident identity as subjects and servants of the Christian emperor, God's viceregent on earth, in the face of repeated Islamic advance; crises such as the 717 siege of Constantinople, in their thought-world, must be expressions of God's displeasure. By laying the blame on the use of images in worship, iconoclasm allowed past imperial failures to be interpreted as God's judgement on idolatrous practices, and explained why the pained efforts of the populace to appease their God and seek succour through icons had failed. For those whose careers hinged on their place within the intricate web of office within the imperial system, iconoclasm made it clear that God's will was only manifested through the proper channels. Veneration of manifold icons of diverse religious figures suggested the possibility of many channels of access to the divine, some of them unmediated by those holding authority. Iconoclasm, however, allowed a ruling elite whose careers were wholly implicated in the service of a Christian empire governed by God's viceregent to mould their society into a hierarchy with the emperor at the apex. Iconoclasm thus articulated a legitimating identity for the new imperial elite.

The bishops and landowners of Italy, distant from the hierarchical ceremonial of the court and the hopes of advancement in the imperial service that brought provincial landowners from Greece and Asia Minor to Constantinople, stood outside the new elite and its ideological milieu. To them, iconoclasm was yet another misjudged imperial intervention in doctrinal issues, and one which threatened the religious practices which expressed their identity in terms of their local, city-based, saints' cults and shrines; it brought back memories of western opposition to monothelitism, which, through the cult of Pope Martin, could be potentially understood in terms of martyrdom in the face of heresy. In an Italy whose allegiances to the empire were increasingly strained, iconoclasm brought a crucial ideological element into play. Imperial power had never been properly re-established in the aftermath of the revolts of the 690s: officials beyond Ravenna's hinterland were increasingly being chosen by local landowners, not appointed by the exarch. Meanwhile Leo, immediately on his accession to the imperial throne in 717, had ordered Italian tax liabilities to be reassessed and increased, and despatched easterners to rule the key cities. From the viewpoint of Constantinople, this made sense in a shrunken empire that had lost most of its tax base in the seventh century. But the inevitable result was revolt: in Italy, tax liabilities had tended to fossilise, and become embedded within local patterns of landholding and obligation; imperial attempts to reimpose a fully-working fiscality cut across these local solidarities and loyalties. With the emperor's power in Italy already withering away, then, the proclamation of iconoclasm in 726 brought the emperor's very authority into question. Pope Gregory II (715–31) refused to back a Tuscan landowner who was raised as emperor in opposition to Leo, but roundly condemned not only iconoclasm, but also the whole principle of imperial involvement in matters of doctrine. This went far further than any of his predecessors, in that it undercut the emperor's own view of his authority. Leo attempted, in a series of letters and embassies, to threaten and cajole Gregory into line, with no success. His threats of arrest and deposition rang hollow, given the lack of any agency in his Italian possessions willing to follow his orders; all he could do was seize the papacy's sizeable Sicilian estates. Eventually, in 732, a fleet was despatched, only to be wrecked before it even reached Italy. In the meantime, the cities of Byzantine Italy had elected their own dukes from among their own numbers, driving out Leo's appointees, their revolt gaining in confidence and legitimacy from the papacy's stand on iconoclasm.[25]

These events marked a fundamental break in Italian politics. In the north, the exarchs struggled until the final fall of Ravenna in 751 to hold territory against the increasingly confident and now Catholic Lombard kings, as landowning elites saw little hope in fighting their neighbours in the name of a distant emperor. In the south, in the absence of a concerted military threat, cities like Naples remained nominally part of the empire, but were effectively self-governing under their own dukes. Only in the far south, in Calabria and Apulia in the 'toe' and 'heel' of the Italian peninsula, and in Sicily, was imperial authority meaningful: these coastal provinces remained closely tied into the networks of communication and exchange around the Aegean and the eastern Mediterranean which fed back to Constantinople, and had undergone rapid 'Hellenisation' thanks to sixth- and seventh-century immigration from the east.

The most remarkable, and most important, developments took place in central Italy, with the transformation of the political status of Rome. In the first half of the eighth century, the popes themselves can be seen playing an increasingly active role in providing direct political leadership in central Italy, effectively independent of the emperor. It would be misleading to see these developments as the result of a conscious plan to create a central Italian polity headed by the pope, the 'republic of St Peter'. Gregory II and his successor, Gregory III (731–41) remained unhesitatingly loyal to the ideology of a universal Christian Roman Empire. Their difficulties were with specific policies of the emperor here and now, not with the ultimate shape of proper imperial order. They saw their role in time-honoured terms as acting as a 'bridge between east and west' and as advisor to the emperor. Gregory II, moreover, had resolutely refused to play any part in Italian attempts to raise a rival emperor to Leo. It was this refusal to raise a usurper, not any decision to secede from the empire, that ultimately, and in all probability unintentionally, left the pope as an effectively independent ruler. Committed to working through the established framework of imperial power, the popes were unwilling to see the creation of any Italian successor-state ruled by a local, Italian, emperor; but in a situation where Constantinople was unable to offer military help or re-establish political control, the established framework was doomed.

The inevitable result was that the papacy filled the void. Political necessity, and the pope's authority as the ultimate guarantor of ecclesiastical order in the west, meant that there were long-standing links between Rome and the courts of the Lombard and Frankish rulers. The popes were able to build on these links in an attempt to safeguard the imperial provinces in Italy.[26] This involved not only negotiating with Lombard kings to safeguard Rome, with treaties signed in 742 and 752, but also intervening on behalf on the exarch, with the pope stepping in and successfully halting Lombard attacks in 743 and 749. Nor was papal diplomacy based on spiritual capital alone. The Lombard dukes of Spoleto, just south of Rome, were neighbours likewise resistant to the ambitions of the Lombard kings in Pavia, and as such potential allies. And Gregory II and his successors built on their continuing links with the Frankish court, and their role as sponsors of missions on the Frankish frontier, to cultivate an alliance. To the leaders of the Franks – Charles Martell (714–41), and his sons Carloman (741–7) and Pippin (741–68) – ties of spiritual kinship, and honorary titles from the Roman past, generated a charisma that they, not being of royal blood, otherwise lacked. It was the papacy that was to legitimate Pippin's accession to the kingship, with Pope Stephen even visiting Francia and blessing Pippin and his family in 754. And, whereas emperors did not respond to appeals for military help, the Franks did, with Pippin besieging Pavia and forcing the Lombard king to hand over central Italian territories in 756. That these territories were returned, not to the emperor, but to the 'patrimony of St Peter' underlines the extent to which the pope was now ruler of an effectively independent polity, but one which presented itself as simply an agglomeration of rights and properties, not as a sovereign state in its own right.

The attempted integration of the 'reconquered' western provinces into an empire centred on Constantinople had led to recurrent doctrinal conflict. This conflict was inevitable, given not only the pronounced theological differences between east and west, but also very different views regarding the relationship between church and state, and the extent of imperial jurisdiction in matters of doctrine. But it would be a mistake to see a slow escalation of conflict from Justinian's leaning on Pope Vigilius in the course of the 'three chapters' dispute to the final breach over iconoclasm. The theological disputes of the age of Justinian, Heraclius and Constans were disputes over matters of high theology, above all Christology, and they were debates conducted across the Mediterranean as a shared cultural space. The leaders of western opposition to monthelitism were, after all, Greek-speaking immigrants like Maximus the Confessor, so they cannot be seen as representatives of a monolithic Latin west defined in opposition to the east. And the progress of these debates was determined by a combination of coercion and negotiation within the unquestioned framework of the Christian empire: hence Martin and Maximus could, eventually, be arrested and tried for treason. By the time of Leo III, the parameters of debate had changed: conflict arose over matters of practice, not doctrine, and the emperor had ceased to be able to wield coercive power over bishops in his western provinces, indeed no longer supplied a political framework within which Italian bishops and landowners necessarily worked. As Italy slipped away from imperial control, the combination of political self-interest and ideological attachment to the ideal of empire that motivated Pope Gregory II and his successors prevented the formation of a narrowly Italian imperial successor state. But it left an imperial tradition which was to be revived in the new political circumstances created by Charlemagne.

Bibliographical essay

General works

There have been few attempts to write a history of the Mediterranean in late antiquity, as opposed to treating Italy, Byzantium and the caliphate separately. But for what can be achieved see Averil Cameron, *The Mediterranean World in Late Antiquity* (London, 1996), particularly focused on the sixth century. See also the discussion of cultural changes, and particularly the growing distance between east and west, by J. Herrin, *The Formation of Christendom* (London, 1989), which is the best introduction to the theological issues, on which it gives a full bibliography. General works on Italy are discussed in chapter 6 below.

Primary sources

After Procopius, the Byzantine historiographical tradition continued through to the beginning of the seventh century. See Agathias, *Histories*, tr. J. Frendo (Berlin, 1975); Menander the Guardsman, *History*, surviving fragments tr. R. C. Blockley (Liverpool, 1985); and Theophylact Simocatta, tr. M. and M. Whitby (Oxford, 1985). Thereafter, we are dependent on the traditions collected in the chronicle of the early ninth-century abbot, Theophanes, tr. C. Mango and R. Scott, *Byzantine and Near Eastern History 284–813* (Oxford, 1997). None of these works devotes much attention to the western provinces, a phenomenon that deserves proper study. For insights into sixth-century military organisation, particularly in the Balkans, see G. Dennis, tr., *Maurice's Strategikon: Handbook of Byzantine Military Strategy* (Philadelphia, 1984). Italian perspectives are available primarily through the papal biographies and Agnellus of Ravenna: see bibliography chapter 4 above.

Byzantium and the west

For the general context of Byzantine government and society, although concentrating on Constantinople, the best introductions are J. Haldon, *Byzantium in the Seventh Century* (Cambridge, 1990), L. Brubacker and J. Haldon, *Byzantium in the Iconoclast Era* (Cambridge, 2005) and the relevant sections of M. Whittow, *The Making of Orthodox Byzantium, 600–1025* (London, 1996); there are a wealth of other political surveys. Averil Cameron, ed., *The Byzantine and Early Islamic Near East III: States, Armies and Resources* (Princeton, 1995) gives useful comparative essays on Byzantine military organisation.

W. Goffart, 'Byzantine policy in the west under Tiberius II and Maurice', *Traditio* 13 (1957), suggests the extent to which Byzantine policy could encompass the barbarian kingdoms of the west as a whole in the decades around 600. The role of the western provinces in the late sixth and seventh centuries, particularly under Maurice, Heraclius and Constans II, deserves more consideration. M. Whitby, *The Emperor Maurice and his Historian* (Oxford, 1988), and J. Howard-Johnston, 'Heraclius' Persian campaigns and the revival of the eastern Roman Empire', *War in History* 4 (1999) are the best studies of these two emperors, whilst for Constans II in the west see P. Corsi, 'Constante II in Italia', *Quaderni Medievali* 3, 5, 7 (1977, 8, 9), giving rise to his *La spedizione italiani di Constante II* (Bologna, 1983), plus P. Llewellyn, 'Constans II and the Roman church', *Byzantion* 46 (1976).

Other than Italy (on which see chapter 4 above) the other major western province was Africa. Important studies here are Av. Cameron, 'Gelimer's laughter: the case of Byzantine Africa', in F. Clover and R. Humphreys, eds, *Tradition and Innovation in Late Antiquity* (Madison, 1989); Cameron, 'Byzantine Africa: the literary evidence', *Excavations at Carthage 1982* (Michigan, 1982); R. Markus, 'Religious dissent in North Africa in the Byzantine period', *Studies in Church History* 9/D. Baker, ed., *Schism, Heresy and Religious Protest* (Cambridge, 1972); R. Goodchild, 'Byzantines, Berbers and Arabs in seventh-century Libya', *Antiquity* 41 (1967); compare W. H. C. Frend, 'The end of Byzantine North Africa: some evidences of transitions', *Bulletin archéologique du Comité des Travaux Historiques et Scientifiques* 19 (1985). M. Fulford, 'Carthage – overseas trade and political economy, AD 400–700', *Reading Medieval Studies* 6 (1980) is of great importance for understanding the province's role in the Vandal and Byzantine periods, whilst A. Leone and D. Mattingly's chapter in N. Christie, ed., *Landscapes of Change* (Aldershot, 2004) is important on rural settlement.

For the Arab conquests there is a huge and growing bibliography. M. Cook, *Mohammed* (London, 1983) is a useful introduction to the Prophet, whilst H. Kennedy, *The Prophet and the Age of the Caliphates* (London, 1986) is the best introduction to early Islamic history, with excellent bibliographical essays. See also F. Donner, *The Early Islamic Conquests* (Princeton, 1981), W. Kaegi, *Byzantium and the Early Islamic Conquests* (Cambridge, 1992, rev. 1995). Controversy has centred on attempts to unravel the complex layers of later tradition and religious controversy in the sources, thereby questioning the main emphases of the Islamic historiographical tradition: see e.g. P. Crone and M. Cook, *Hagarism: The Making of the Islamic World* (Cambridge, 1977). But studies such as R. Hoyland, *Seeing Islam as Others Saw It* (Princeton, 1997) show that there are only limited disagreements between Islamic and non-Islamic traditions; see also G. Hawting, *The Idea of Idolatry and the Emergence of Islam* (Cambridge, 1999). Traditional interpretations of the economic context are similarly questioned in P. Crone, *Meccan Trade and the Rise of Islam* (Oxford, 1987), whilst P. Crone, *Slaves on Horses* (London, 1980) is a challenging but rewarding investigation into the structure of early Islamic politics. For differing perspectives on the nature of the Arab conquests, the nature of Arab armies and the state of the Byzantine and Sassanian opponents, the best starting-point is the essays in Averil Cameron, ed., *The Byzantine and Early Islamic Near East III: States, Armies and Resources* (Princeton, 1995).

The Balkans

For the collapse of Byzantine power in the Balkans, the 'Slavicisation' of central Europe, and the establishment of the Avar Empire, there are two challenging recent works: W. Pohl, *Die Awaren: Ein Steppenvol im Mitteleuropa, 567–822 n. Chr.* (Munich, 1988) and F. Curta, *The Making of the Slavs* (Cambridge, 2001). See also P. M. Barford, *The Early Slavs* (London, 2001) for a thorough overview, particularly of the archaeological evidence. D. Obolensky, *The Byzantine Commonwealth* (London, 1974) remains a classic on interactions between the Slavs and the Byzantine world, but its treatment of the early periods needs setting alongside these more recent works, as does the narrative assembled by J. Fine, *The Early Medieval Balkans* (Ann Arbor, 1983). Pohl's ideas are attractively synthesised in a number of shorter pieces e.g. in P. Urbancyck, ed., *Origins of Central Europe* (Warsaw, 1997), or in his contribution to J. Jarnut, H.-W. Goetz and Pohl, eds, *Regna and Gentes* (Leiden, 2003); for the rich archaeological evidence see also F. Daim's contribution to the latter, and to W. Pohl and H. Reimitz, eds, *The Transformation of Frontiers* (Leiden, 1999), which make available the findings of his fundamental work on the archaeology to the Anglophone; see also the contributions by Hardt, Urbancyck and Gassowski to W. Pohl and H. Reimitz, eds, *Integration und Herrschaft* (Vienna, 2002). On the wider effects of changes in east-central Europe and the Balkans there is surprisingly little, given the centrality of the region to the late empire and the more or less total cessation of land communication between Constantinople and the west in the seventh and eighth centuries. For archaeological perspectives see A. Dunn, 'The transition from polis to the kastron in the Balkans (III–VII cc.): general and regional perspectives', *Byzantine and Modern Greek Studies* 18 (1994), and chapters by Christie and Poulter in N. Christie and S. Loseby, eds, *Towns in Transition* (Aldershot, 1996), and by Bowden and Hodges, Sanders and Poulter in N. Christie, ed., *Landscapes of Change* (Aldershot, 2004).

Economic change

Debate still centres around H. Pirenne, *Mohammed and Charlemagne* (London, 1937), published posthumously from unfinished notes. But, in spite of the revolutionary character of Pirenne's work, the growing body of archaeological evidence and increasingly sophisticated uses to which it is being put means that debate should now move on from the framework adopted by Pirenne. Thus subsequent work has tended to be presented as correctives to Pirenne: R. Hodges and D. Whitehouse, *Mohammed, Charlemagne and the Origins of Europe* (London, 1983).

For the most exciting recent attempt to develop a global explanation for economic changes see M. McCormick, *The Origins of the European Economy: Commerce and Communication AD300–800* (Cambridge, 2001); discussion in *Early Medieval Europe* 12 (2003). Similarly important is the attempt by N. Purcell and P. Hordern to develop a universal model of pre-industrial Mediterranean society: *The Corrupting Sea* (London, 1999), which pays homage to Pirenne amongst others; for students of the early Middle Ages, the best way into this complex treatment of long-term historical structures is P. Squatriti's important critique, 'Mohammed, Charlemagne and the early medieval Meditteranean', *Early Medieval Europe* 12 (2003). Compare the emphasis on social changes suggested by C. Wickham, 'Italy and the early Middle Ages', in K. Randsborg, ed., *The Birth of Europe: Archaeology and Social Development in the First Millennium AD* (Rome, 1989), reprinted in Wickham, *Land and Power* (Rome, 1994). Important in attempting to adopt an alternative, long-term perspective based on the archaeology, is K. Randsborg, *The First Millennium AD in Italy and Europe* (Rome, 1989), whilst an intriguing alternative vista onto Italian society is opened up by P. Squatriti, *Water and Society in Early Medieval Italy* (Cambridge, 1998). Finally, important on the function of coin and the changing nature of exchange is M. Hendy, 'From public to private: the western Barbarian coinages as a mirror of the disintegration of late Roman state structures', *Viator* 19 (1988).

Two recent volumes arising out of one working group funded by the European Science Foundation's Transformation of the Roman World project give region-by-region treatments of economic changes, integrating the archaeology fully and covering the eastern as well as the western Mediterranean: they should be the starting-points for any future discussion of the economic changes and show what can be achieved by properly managed international collaboration. See R. Hodges and W. Bowden, eds, *The Sixth Century: Production and Demand* (Leiden, 1998) and C. Wickham and I. Hansen, eds, *The Long Eighth Century* (Leiden, 2001). For the data on the pottery, see P. Reynolds, *Trade in the Western Mediterranean AD 400–700: The Ceramic Evidence*, British Archaeological Reports International Series 604 (Oxford, 1995). The bibliography on changing urban life gives a wealth of case-studies: it is best approached through two further ESF volumes, G. Brogiolo and B. Ward-Perkins, eds, *The Idea and Ideology of the Town from Late Antiquity to the Early Middle Ages* (Leiden, 1998) and G. Brogiolo, N. Christie and N. Gauthier, eds, *Towns and their Territories from Late Antiquity to the Early Middle Ages* (Leiden, 2000); further bibliography chapters 1 and 6. R. Balzaretti's work advances persuasive models of increasingly regional economies: e.g. his contributions to N. Christie and S. Loseby, eds, *Towns in Transition* (Aldershot, 1996) and G. Ausenda, *After Empire* (San Marino, 1995).

On demographics, and particularly the potential role of epidemics in the sixth century in changing Mediterranean society, there has been lively debate: the best introduction is P. Horden's contribution to M. Maas, ed., *Cambridge Companion to the Age of Justinian* (Cambridge, 2005) with excellent bibligraphy. See also M. McCormick, 'Bateaux de vie, bateaux de mort. Maladie, commerce, transports annonaires et le passage economique du bas-empire au moyen age', *Settimane* 45 (1998) and his 'Rats, communication and plague: towards an ecological history', *Journal of Interdisciplinary History* 34 (2003).

Notes

1. Rusticiana: Gregory, *Register of Letters*, 2.27, 9.83, 11.25–6, 13.26 and see Brown, *Gentlemen and Officers: Imperial Administration and Aristocratic Power in Byzantine Italy, 554–800* (Rome, 1984), pp. 29–30.

2. Response to Maurice's reforms: Theophylact Simocatta, 7.1, 8.6.2; Heraclius' withholding African shipments: Theophanes, 6100. Note also his reliance on an army largely recruited from the Berber tribesmen on the fringes of his father's province.
3. For discussion of the sources for early Islamic history, their problems and conflicting schools of interpretation, see bibliography.
4. On papyrus imports to the west see now McCormick, *Origins of the European Economy*, pp. 704–8.
5. The calculation is based on M. Hendy, *Studies in the Byzantine Monetary Economy, 300–1450* (Cambridge, 1985), pp. 619–20.
6. See the account of the *Chronicon Paschale*, tr. M. and. M. Whitby (Liverpool, 1989).
7. See Gregory of Tours, *Histories*, tr. L.Thorpe (Harmondsworth, 1974), 6.32 (shopping in Paris), 7.29 (wine of Gaza), 10.2 (shopping in Carthage on voyage to Constantinople), *Glory of the Confessors*, tr. R. van Dam (Liverpool, 1988), 64 (Gaza wine again); *Lives of the Fathers of Mérida*, tr. A. Fear, *Lives of the Visigothic Fathers* (Liverpool, 1997) and S. Loseby, 'Marseille: a late antique success story?', *Journal of Roman Studies* 82 (1992) and 'Marseille and the Pirenne Thesis I: Gregory of Tours, the Merovingian kings, and "Un grand port"', in W. Bowden and R. Hodges, eds, *The Sixth Century: Production, Distribution and Demand* (Leiden, 1998).
8. See the *Doctrina Jacobi nuper baptizandi* ('The doctrine of Jacob the newly-baptised'), ed. G. Dagron and V. Déroche, 'Juifs et chrétiens dans l'Orient du VIIe siècle', *Travaux et Memoires* 11 (1991), on which see McCormick, *Origins of the European Economy*, pp. 107–8.
9. African exports: McCormick, *Origins of the European Economy*, p. 102; Italian coinage: P. Grierson, ed., *Catalogue of Byzantine Coins in the Dumbarton Oaks Collection* (3 vols, Washington, 1966–73), vol. 2 pp. 46–51, vol. 3 pp. 84–94. Crypt of Balbus and glass: see the debate between D. Whitehouse, '"Things that traveled": the surprising case of raw glass' and M. McCormick, 'Complexity, chronology and context in the early medieval economy', *Early Medieval Europe* 12.3 (2003) (pp. 301–6, 322–3).
10. Procopius, *Buildings*, tr. Dewing; for a synthesis of the archaeology, F. Curta, *The Making of the Slavs: History and Archaeology of the Lower Danube Region 500–700* (Cambridge, 2001), chapter 3.
11. *Novels of Justinian* 11, 46, ed. Schöll and Kroll; John Lydus, *On the Magistracies of the Roman State*, tr. A. Bandy (Philadelphia, 1983), II. 28–9.
12. See G. Dennis, tr., *Maurice's Strategikon: Handbook of Byzantine Military Strategy* (Philadelphia, 1984); Theophylact Simocatta, tr. Whitby and Whitby, 7.1.
13. Theophylact Simocatta, tr. Whitby and Whitby, 8.6.2
14. *Life of Floridus* cited and discussed by Brown, *Gentlemen and Officers*, p. 89; *Miracles of St Demetrius*, ed. P. Lemerle, *Les plus anciens recueils des Miracles de Saint Démétrius* (2 vols, Paris, 1979–81).
15. Procopius, *Wars*, tr. Dewing, 7.14.22.

16. Michael the Syrian, *Chronicle*, 10.21 (and for the Avar khagan, Menander the Guardsman, tr. Whitby, frag. 27); *Miracles of Demetrius*, ed. Lemerle, 2.4; for discussion of the Byzantine sources on Slav political organisation see Curta, *Making of the Slavs*, chapter 7.
17. Fredegar, *Chronicle*, tr. J. M. Wallace-Hadrill (Oxford, 1962), 4: 48, 68.
18. Ravenna papyri: Tjäder, ed., *Die nichtliterarischen lateinischen Papyri Italiens*. Rizana plea: C. Manresi, ed., *I Placiti del Regnum Italicum 776–995* (Rome, 1955), pp. 50–6. Excellent analysis: T. S. Brown, *Gentlemen and Officers: Imperial Administration and Aristocratic Power in Byzantine Italy, 554–800* (Rome, 1984), pp. 82–108.
19. Material relating to Maximus' career and his sensational trial is tr. G. Berthold, *Maximus the Confessor: Selected Writings* (New York, 1985); for Martin see his life in the *Liber Pontificalis*.
20. Constans as a 'second Cain': Theophanes, *Chronicle*, tr. C. Mango and R. Scott, *Byzantine and Near Eastern History 284–813* (Oxford 1997); Maurice's succession plans: Theophylact Simocatta, *History*, tr. M. and M. Whitby (Oxford, 1985), 7.11.9. Heraclius: Theophanes, *Chronicle*, 6153, 6160.
21. See the account in the *Liber Pontificalis*.
22. *Liber Pontificalis*, Sergius I.
23. For the links see Agnellus of Ravenna, tr. Deliyannis, chs 119–20, 137, 141, 146; on Johannicus, Agnellus' great-great-grandfather.
24. *Liber Pontificalis*, John VI, John VII, Constantine; John VII's promotion of the cult of Martin is evident in the frescoes in Santa Maria Antiqua in the Roman Forum.
25. *Liber Pontificalis*, Gregory II, for his backing of the revolt against Leo's taxes but his refusal to acknowledge the usurper Tiberius in southern Etruria; see the account of the early ninth-century *Chronicle* of Theophanes for the view from Constantinople, and note his stress on Gregory's denunciation of any imperial prerogative to make doctrinal statements.
26. For what follows, see the papal biographies in the *Liber Pontificalis*.

Part III

Kingdoms and Communities in the Post-Roman West

6

Hispania and Italy: contrasting communities

Contents

Summary

Chronology: Visigothic kingdom and Umayyad al-Andalus

Chronology: Lombard Italy

Visigothic kings and Hispanic landlords

Map 4: The Iberian peninsula in the early Middle Ages

Court and regions: the seventh-century Visigothic kingdom

The making of al-Andalus

The Lombard alternative

Map 5: Italy in the early Middle Ages

Italy as a warrior society

Bibliographical essay

Summary

In the Iberian peninsula, the fifth and early sixth centuries saw landowning elites negotiating with a changing spectrum of barbarian protectors. It was the Visigothic king Leovigild and his sons Hermenegild and Reccared who were to create a unified kingdom embracing the peninsula as a whole in the last third of the sixth century through a series of successful military campaigns. Most importantly, after the formal conversion of the kingdom to Catholicism in 589, a potent alliance between the Hispanic church and the royal court at Toledo was formed. In the seventh century, politics was focused on the royal court. With no single dynasty able to establish a monopoly on the kingship, the royal office was the goal of aristocratic competition which churchmen attempted to regulate. This system, however, rested on more or less untrammelled landlord power in the regions, and the destruction of palace and kingship by Islamic armies in the 710s inaugurated a half-century of political fragmentation and chaos. The various Islamic armies enjoyed coercive force but little internal unity, and it was only in the second half of the eighth century that 'Abd al-Rahmān was able to create a viable political system, the amirate of al-Andalus focused on Cordoba in the south. The crystallisation of this new political system led to the stabilisation of a political frontier in the Duero and Ebro valleys in the north, with a number of tiny Christian polities claiming to continue the Visigothic tradition in the north, whilst the rich provinces of Septimania and Catalonia in the northeast submitted to the Frankish kings.

In Italy, the northern plain gradually fell under the domination of a new group of barbarian warlords, the Lombards, in the last quarter of the sixth century; Lombard warlords also established the duchies of Spoleto and Benevento in central and southern Italy. In the course of the seventh century, the Lombard court at Pavia was able to fashion a kingdom from the city-based duchies of northern Italy, and gradually encroach on the Byzantine possessions that linked Ravenna to Rome. Italian society became increasingly an agglomeration of city units, dominated by bishops and military aristocracies; their landowning, now the basis of power, was local in its scope. But the reluctance of the Italian church to throw its institutional weight behind Lombard kingship – reluctance intimately tied up with the close relationship between the church of Rome and the empire – checked the progress of Lombard state-formation.

Chronology: Visigothic kingdom and Umayyad al-Andalus

411	Vandals, Sueves and Alans settled in Hispanic provinces
429	Vandals and Alans under Gaiseric conquer Africa
456	Visigoths defeat Sueves; begin domination of Hispania
507	Franks defeat Visigoths at Vouille, much of kingdom in southern Gaul lost
551	Byzantine occupation of cities of southeastern coast
569–86	Reign of Leovigild; military unification of peninsula
579–85	Revolt of Hermenegild
585	Kingdom of Sueves conquered by Leovigild
586–601	Reccared first Catholic king of Visigoths
589	Third council of Toledo; Recarred ends Arianism
602–30	Isidore bishop of Sevillc
624	Last Byzantine possessions in southeast conquered
633	Fourth council of Toledo; beginning of continuous run of Toledo councils
642	Accession of Chindaswinth, last king to take throne by force
698	Carthage, capital of Byzantine Africa, taken by Islamic armies
711	Defeat of Roderic by Islamic armies
715	Islamic governor 'Abd al-Azīz assassinated for acting like a Visigothic king
720	Islamic forces take Narbonne, end of Visigothic kingship
734	Islamic army defeated by Franks near Poitiers
739–57	Alfonso I king of Asturias
739	Berber revolts in Africa and al-Andalus
741–2	Syrian armies defeated by Berbers in Africa, cross to al-Andalus
750	Overthrow of Umayyad Caliphate by 'Abbasīds
756–88	Umayyad 'Abd al-Rahmān establishes self as amir of al-Andalus
759	Narbonne 'liberated' by Franks
777	Berber regime of imam Shaqya in Meseta ends
802	Franks take Barcelona
851–9	Cordoba martyrs movement

Chronology: Lombard Italy

568	Lombard king Alboin leads invasion of northern Italy
574–84	'Interregnum': no Lombard kings
589–620s	Queen Theudelinda dominant political figure
590–616	Agilolf king of Lombards
620s–640s	Queen Gundperga inherits role of her mother Theudelinda
643	Edict of Rothari
680	Formal peace treaty between Lombards and Byzantine Empire
698	Synod of Pavia ends 'three chapters' schism; Cunincpert celebrated as Catholic king
712–44	Liudprand king of Lombards; rapprochement with Rome and conquests of Byzantine territory
751	Ravenna taken by Lombards
754	Pope asks for Frankish assistance against Lombards
756	Frankish intervention; Aistulf promises to return Frankish territory to Lombards
774	Charlemagne conquers Lombard kingdom

Visigothic kings and Hispanic landlords

At the western extreme of the Mediterranean world, the former Roman provinces of Hispania, modern Spain and Portugal, remained connected to the imperial systems of the east. Thanks to its internal geography, the Iberian peninsula was subject throughout the ancient and medieval periods to poor internal communications: Roman government spread from the sea along the great river valleys, with the arcing coastline tying northeastern Spain closely to southern Gaul, and the southeast to Africa. In the aftermath of the barbarian invasions of Gaul and Italy in 406–7, a significant number of barbarian warbands found their way across the Pyrenees into Hispania, encouraged to do so by rival Roman governments anxious to establish control of southern Gaul. The initial settlement was negotiated directly between Hispanic landowners and the leaders of the diverse barbarian groups – Alans, Sueves and Vandals – and took place according to the drawing of lots, with each Hispanic province allotted to designated groups of barbarians as their 'share', whilst the area of richest senatorial landowning, Tarragonensis in the northeast (roughly modern Catalonia) was left free of barbarian 'guests'.[1] The precise meaning of this division, and the barbarian impact on Hispanic society, remain unclear. Our only Iberian source, the chronicle of Bishop Hydatius, gives a picture of shifting military balances.

In fact, the settlement of 411 recognised long-standing regional differences. The Catalan coast had long-standing social connections with the imperial court, and was closely connected with the coastlines of the western Mediterranean, whilst barbarian settlement took place in economically, ecologically and politically more marginal areas. After the majority of the barbarian warbands crossed to prosperous North Africa in 429 under the Vandal Gaiseric, the main area of barbarian domination was the mountainous northwest, dominated by a 'king of the Sueves' who attempted to assert control over the peninsula as a whole. Meanwhile in the western Pyrenees, an area long ambivalent to Roman 'order', the local population identified itself by the pre-Roman name 'Basques' and developed its own social structures. The Gothic kingdom based in Toulouse was, from 456, the major military power, and Gothic kings campaigned intermittently across the Pyrenees: by the end of the fifth century most of Spain, except the Sueve kingdom, nominally acknowledged the 'protection' of the Gothic kings. But it is difficult to see fifth-century campaigns as moving a clear political frontier, or as creating a Gothic kingdom. Rather, as direct ties with the imperial court withered, we have a hotchpotch of cities, landowners, and barbarian warlords. It is only hindsight – and the formation of a Visigothic kingdom in the later sixth century – that encourages historians to focus on the kings of the Goths.

The connections along the Mediterranean coasts of southern Gaul and eastern Spain thus remained a crucial nexus, tying the cities and landowners of the wealthiest Hispanic provinces to the court of the Gothic kings. The Gothic defeat by the Franks at Vouille in 507 is often seen as a crucial juncture, as it was followed by the absorption of much of southern Gaul into the Frankish kingdom. Certainly, Frankish conquest left the Goths more reliant on their Hispanic possessions than previously, but it is possible to overstate its impact: right through its

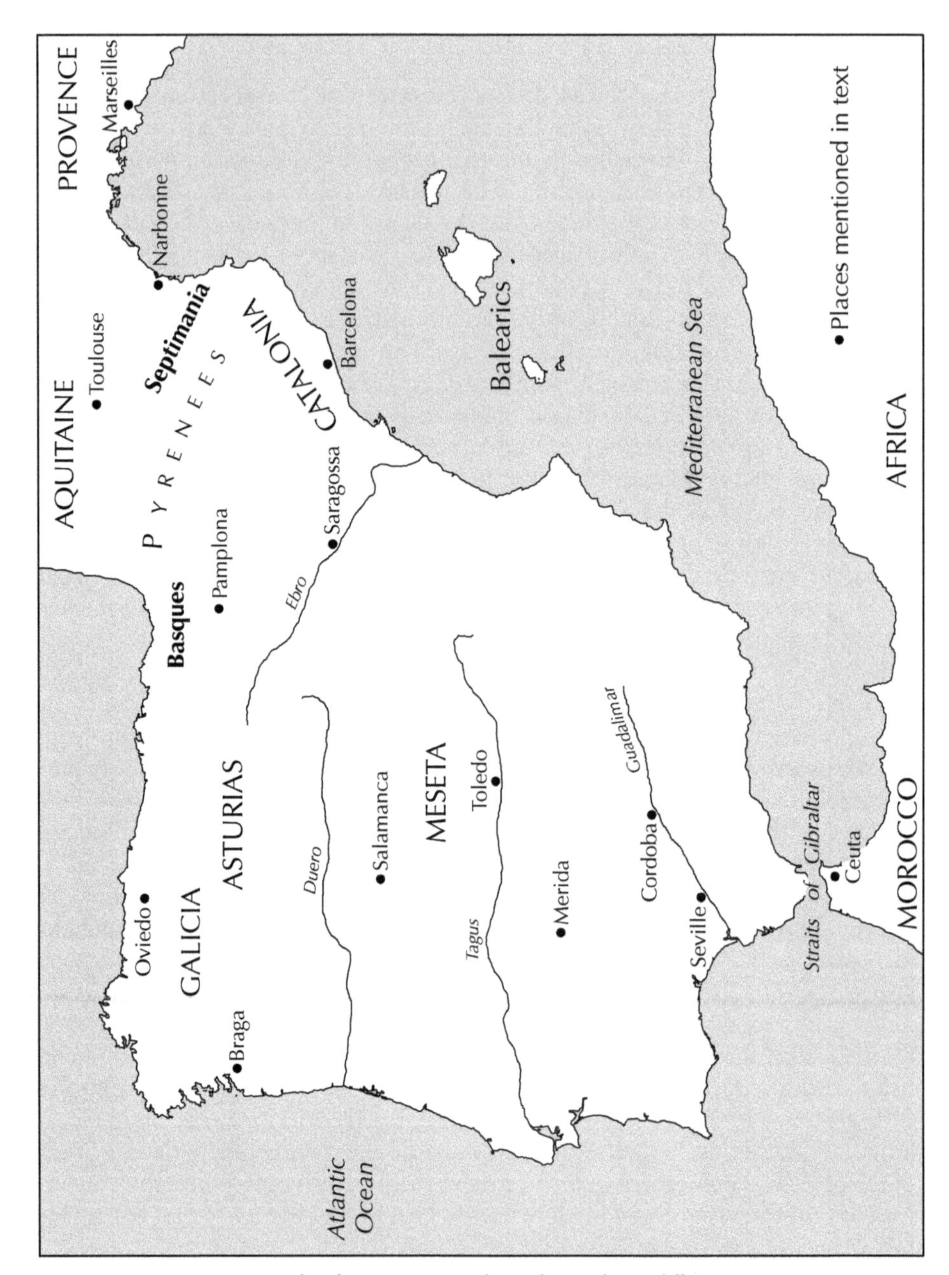

Map 4 The Iberian Peninsula in the early Middle Ages

history, the Visigothic kingdom was to include a significant part of Gaul north of the Pyrenees, Narbonne and its hinterland. Indeed, events after Vouille confirmed the continuing power of connections along the Mediterranean coast. The defeat had exterminated the Balt dynasty that ruled the kingdom of Toulouse, leaving the future of kingship unclear. Theodoric, in firm control of Italy and gaining a hold over the southern Gallic coast in Provence, intervened to support the claims of his grandson Amalaric, who was related to the Balts, against a rival faction that attempted to rally Vandal and Burgundian support. Theodoric was to present himself as ruler of a united Gothic people whose realm spread from the Danube to Hispania. Given that the various groups of Goths had no history of unity, but were made up of diverse groupings that had entered the empire at various stages in the fourth and fifth centuries, these claims were more a testimony to Theodoric's power than any pan-Gothic allegiance.

The Visigoths remained connected to the politics of Gaul and Italy after Theodoric's death. Amalaric attempted to win Frankish support through a marriage alliance, but in 531 the Franks had him murdered, and Theudis, the general who had been despatched by Theodoric as Amalaric's regent, was raised as king in his own right. Theudis' career demonstrates the essentially superficial and military nature of Visigothic kingship at this date. An outsider, he owed his elevation in 531 to a personal following of 2,000 troops, many recruited from the slaves on the estates of his wife, a member of a leading Hispanic senatorial family.[2] Indeed, in the crisis following Theudis' death in battle in 548, the fragility of the Visigothic kingdom made it seem likely that it would go the same way as Ostrogothic Italy and Vandal Africa, for civil war gave Justinian an opportunity to intervene, ostensibly (as in Italy and Africa) to uphold the rights of a claimant to the throne. In the event, Byzantine ambitions and Byzantine manpower did not stretch to the conquest of the Iberian peninsula as a whole, with Justinian instead garrisoning a string of strategically important cities along the southeastern coast, and so attempting to control Hispanic connections with the Mediterranean world.

The texture of sixth-century society is difficult to recreate. The *Lives of the Fathers of Mérida*, an account of the bishops of a southern city written just after 600, portrays a still Romanised world, with public life focused on the city, symbolised by its relationship with its patron saint, Eulalia. Here we meet Syrian merchants plying their wares around the Mediterranean, and a vibrant civilian community; the Goths that impinge on sixth-century Mérida are servants of the distant king, tied to the court, and clearly separate from the indigenous population on account of their military role and Arian religious affiliation. Our sources from elsewhere in the peninsula are sparse. The remarkable discovery of 150 or so legal deeds surviving on slate from the region of Salamanca should enable future researchers to build a detailed picture of social patterns. But the very existence of these documents confirms the continuation of a local world of property holding and law on the Roman model. Elsewhere, we learn that the 'senators of Seville' plotted the assassination of Theudis' successor as king, Theudegisel, and his replacement by Athanagild, whilst Cordoba was in 'revolt' – that is, running its own affairs independently of the Gothic kings – for two decades after 551, its quarrels with the royal court centring on the status of its local patron cult, just as the political ties between Mérida and the court were expressed through the interaction of individual kings with the cult of Eulalia.[3]

It is no accident that these scraps of evidence come from the cities of the south and the east, the heart of the Roman province and the key stage where Visigothic kings courted Hispanic landowners. Visigothic kingship here may bear comparison with that of the Merovingian dynasty of the Franks in sixth-century southern Gaul. This was a functioning city-based society, with the bishop the most prominent figure and relic-cults foci of local patriotism in landowning society. Kings simply plugged into this sphere of public action, fulfilling the expectations of the provincial population by acting as judges and lawgivers. In fact, the surviving legislation suggests that in this period kings attempted to maintain a clear distinction between Goths and the indigenous population, modelled on the Roman distinction between civilians and soldiers. Certainly, injunctions against intermarriage between Goths and non-Goths, first made in the kingdom of Toulouse, were maintained. Presumably the motive for this was to maintain the army as an institution firmly dependent on the king, and prevent the emergence of a Gothic landowning class independent of the royal court.

It was in the final third of the sixth century that Visigothic kingship was transformed into an institution with real roots in provincial society. Leovigild (569–86) was the key figure in this process: in a series of campaigns he effected the military unification of the peninsula, culminating in the conquest of the Suevic kingdom in Galicia. Leovigild's campaigning was not simply a matter of conquest: most of it involved the assertion of direct royal power over regional elites whose powers were effectively independent of the Visigothic court and army. Thus Leovigild's arrival in Cordoba in 572 marked the assertion of royal control after two decades of 'revolt', whilst elsewhere Leovigild campaigned against 'the senators of the Cantabrians'. The meagre evidence makes the implications of these campaigns difficult to work out. Isidore, writing a generation later, claimed that Leovigild's opponents suffered execution or the loss of hands and hair as a judicial punishment, along with the expropriation of property.[4]

Leovigild's efforts did not solely focus on the wartrail; he also attempted to create a new religious consensus that could help structure links between king and region. The *Lives of the Fathers of Mérida* recounts Leovigild's attempts to secure the relics of Mérida's patron, Eulalia, for the royally sponsored Arian church, thus attaching city to court with supernatural glue, much to the horror of the Catholic bishop who controlled Eulalia's cult. Leovigild's promotion of 'his' Arian church with its own infrastructure was coupled with attempts to win over Catholic opinion, with a council held at Toledo in 580 reinterpreting Arian doctrine to move it closer to Catholic 'orthodoxy' and removing the requirement for rebaptism by those who moved from one faith to the other. Paradoxically, though, Leovigild's efforts simply ensured more vocal opposition from Catholic bishops led by Bishop Leander of Seville, alarmed at the threat posed by active royal promotion of the Arian church.

The issues of embedded regionalism and religious division came to a head in the revolt of Leovigild's son, Hermenegild. Both Hermenegild and his brother, Reccared, had been established as kings under their father's tutelage in 573. In 579

Hermenegild rebelled, setting himself up as ruler of an independent kingdom centred on Seville in the south. Given the fact of coregency before 579, this may have been a largely symbolic act; it did not cause civil strife until Hermenegild negotiated for Byzantine support and staged a public conversion to Catholicism in 582. The fact that the leading Catholic opponents of Leovigild's religious policy – notably their spokesman, Leander of Seville – were based in Hermenegild's sphere must have been significant in this decision. Indeed, Seville's role as a centre for landed society in the south is suggested by the assassination, a generation earlier, of the Visigothic king Theudegisel by the 'senators of Seville'. As well as attempting to court this grouping in the south, and to win over potential backing from Byzantium, Hermenegild was also linked with the Frankish court through his wife. Eventually, though, Hermenegild's attempts to win Frankish or Byzantine support came to nought. In 584 the commander of the Byzantine cities of southwestern Spain negotiated a treaty direct with Leovigild that excluded Hermenegild, who was then exiled before being assassinated in 585. In any case, Hermenegild's appeal to Catholicism did not lead to a mass revolt against his father's Arian rule. Religious confession, whilst it had political implications, did not determine political allegiance. Indeed, all our sources written within the Visigothic kingdom denounce Hermenegild as a usurper and ignore the religious issue; it was only distant writers such as Gregory of Tours, with no experience of the reality of Arian–Catholic co-existence, who could see Hermenegild's career in black and white terms of orthodoxy and heresy.[5]

Although Hermenegild's appeal to the Catholic bishops failed, both he and his father had attempted to use religion as a unifying force to tie together the diverse communities of the Visigothic kingdom; here, they may have been reacting to Byzantine imperial ideology of the Christian empire, and also the political practice of the Frankish realm where the church played a central role in political life. The death of Leovigild and accession of his surviving son, Reccared, in 586 saw the religious policies of the previous decade reaching a conclusion with Reccared's public declaration of conversion to Catholicism. In 589, a council of the bishops of the kingdom was held at the royal capital of Toledo to oversee the formal ending of Arianism, an event symbolised by the burning of Arian books and the incorporation of the Arian church into the Catholic establishment. The bishops assembled at Toledo celebrated Reccared as the 'apostolic and orthodox king', echoing the model of Constantine as a convert-ruler comparable to the apostles in spreading the faith. In presenting the Visigothic king in terms of a Roman-Christian model of rule, consciously drawing on imperial ideology, the bishops at Toledo were following through initiatives whose origins can be traced back to the reign of Leovigild. It was Leovigild who had in 578 founded a city named Reccopolis after his son, as a dedicated royal centre: the model of Constantine and Constantinople is clear. Leovigild was the first Visigothic king to have gold coins minted in his own name, thereby contesting an imperial prerogative which had previously been punctiliously respected; he also consciously borrowed imperial victory imagery, notably in the coins issued to celebrate his capture of Medina. The coins suggest a series of wider changes in the ways in which Visigothic kings represented themselves to their subjects. Leovigild was depicted not wearing traditional Gothic robes, but attired with Roman-style regalia, which we know were used by seventh-century kings. The political message, that the Visigothic kingdom was an independent sovereign entity, not a federate kingdom of the empire, was certainly redoubled thanks to the support of the bishops as voiced at Toledo in 589. Leander of Seville, the leading churchman at the council, had spent time as an ambassador at Constantinople, so was well aware of the implications of these claims.[6]

Court and regions: the seventh-century Visigothic kingdom

In the fifth and sixth centuries Gothic warlords and Hispanic landlords able to raise armies of several thousand had been effectively independent political actors. For kingship to be effective, it needed to shift the balance of power towards the royal court at Toledo. Rule through a Gothic army that was distinct from its host society would have been a possibility if there were either continuous expansive warfare, or a strong taxation system, either of which would have supported a military establishment not tied to landed estates or with inherited interests in the localities. But in the course of the sixth century, the cohesiveness of the Gothic 'people' was eroded. Warfare was sporadic, internal and localised, centring around the ambitions of provincial elites courted by candidates for the throne. Indeed Leovigild's constant campaigning may have been in part an attempt to reactivate the loyalties of the Gothic army to its king through the plunder and tribute generated by the wartrail. As for tax, the scraps of evidence we have likewise suggest decentralisation: a court case from Barcelona in the last decade of the sixth century suggests that tax assessments and the processes of tax collection had become fossilised as customary dues, increasingly overseen by the bishop.[7] The collections of royal edicts which had been made since the time of Euric in the 460s are sometimes seen as collections of specifically Visigothic law, creating a separate legal system for a privileged group; their contents, however, make it more sensible to see them as record of royal judgement which dealt with problems on the ground, complementing Roman law by applying its principles to new situations. By the mid-sixth century, neither law nor tax can have functioned as dividing lines between Gothic settlers and provincial populations. Indeed, the sole evidence we have for any continuing sense of a distinct Gothic identity comes in a series of cemeteries containing lavish grave-goods demonstrating a distinctive 'barbarian' material culture: tellingly, these are concentrated on the plateau of the Meseta, close to Toledo, a favoured residence of the Visigothic kings, and so may indicate an attempt to maintain a distinct Gothic identity by royal retainers.

The problems posed by the assimilation of barbarians into provincial societies were implicit in the political systems set up right across the core provinces of the western empire in the fifth century. The power of Burgundian, Ostrogothic and Vandal kings rested on the ties that kept their 'peoples' firmly tied to them, and able to function as cohesive armies. But the reality of settlement inevitably encouraged barbarians to find a place in provincial society and put down local roots which complicated their allegiances and identities. Even in the caliphate, where the conquering armies were united by the Islamic religion and able to maintain a functioning tax system that paid salaries, a similar process was well advanced within a hundred years of the initial settlements. Whilst kings elsewhere in the post-Roman west – notably Theodoric's successors in Italy – began to address these problems, the Visigothic kingdom was the only kingdom built on these foundations which survived beyond the mid-sixth century: the Frankish and Lombard realms originated in more fluid situations. The development of Visigothic kingship thus illustrates the potential and limits of one model for post-Roman political settlement.

How did Visigothic kings respond to a situation where military power was embedded in the hands of landowning elites, and so regionalism was a very real social fact? The dynasty of Leovigild may have envisaged a system similar to that practised by the Merovingians in Gaul, with a broad royal kindred enjoying a dynastic monopoly on royal status, but dividing the constituent city and provincial units of their kingdom between royal males – including child-kings – of appropriate political standing. Ties with the Merovingian realm were close in the decades before 600, in part because of the ties of Brunhild, the Visigothic princess who as queen, mother and grandmother of successive Merovingians was a dominant figure in Frankish politics in this period. With the Merovingians in Gaul, political division within an exalted dynasty tied regions to the kingdom and dynasty by allowing them access to their own king who could guard their local interests. Leovigild himself had succeeded to a divided kingdom which reflected the regional divisions of the realm, with his brother Leova ruling from Narbonne over the Pyrenees, an effective buffer to intensive Frankish interest in the region, until his death in 573. Leovigild's policy of elevating his sons as coregents with regional bases, and founding new cities, dedicated royal places tied to the memory of the dynasty, in newly conquered regions such as Galicia rested on a similar logic. But such a dynastic solution failed, with Recarred survived only by an infant son who lasted a mere two years on the throne. In part, this was a result of the weakness of dynastic traditions. The rulers of the fifth-century kingdom of Toulouse claimed descent from the Balt dynasty, but the defeat of 507 and the subsequent political crisis meant that forcible seizure of the throne by the able and powerful had become the norm in the sixth century. The continued existence of Byzantine enclaves in the southwest, and intense Frankish interest in the Gallic provinces of the Visigothic kingdom, made the elevation of a proven warleader paramount.

These concerns made a dynastic solution on the Merovingian model impossible. Instead, in the seventh century Visigothic kingship developed into a formally elective institution. The impetus came not from any archaic Gothic tradition but through the attempts of the church to regulate conflicts over the royal succession. The agency came via the regular councils of the bishops of the kingdom at Toledo, the royal capital. Whilst the foundations of this alliance between bishops and court was laid under Recarred, it was not for almost another half-century that the run of Toledo councils began, under the auspices of Leander's relative and successor as bishop of Seville, Isidore (600–36). The fourth council of Toledo, held under Isidore's auspices in 633, following the accession of Sisenand after a bitter civil war, stood at the head of a rich tradition of conciliar activity, with no fewer than 15 subsequent councils down to 702. The acts of the council of 633, strongly influenced by Isidore, begin with the Biblical lesson that a kingdom divided against itself was doomed to fall; it went on to condemn the seizure of the throne by force, and laid down that royal successions should be based on the consensus of bishops and nobility. This was an attempt to settle the succession on the grounds of negotiation rather than armed conflict. The very verb used for king-choosing, *electio*, was resonant of the choosing of bishops, and the efforts of successive Toledo councils down to 702 to set down regulations about the eligibility of candidates for the kingship and the conduct of kings are likewise reminiscent of the legislation of earlier councils on episcopal election.[8] Election in this sense was not a process of choice between rival candidates with distinct programmes, but the culmination of a political process through which an individual emerged as acceptable to the collectivity of bishops and aristocracy, and was given a formal legitimacy by 'election'. Nor was the ideology of election incompatible with the current efforts of kings and their supporters to maintain the political status quo by securing father–son succession: five of the 17 seventh-century kings followed their fathers on the throne.

Conciliar notions of election were inevitably, then, often a means of legitimating a prior political reality, sometimes even a *post hoc* justification of the acquisition of the throne by naked force. Of 17 seventh-century kings, ten were deposed, forcibly converted to monasticism, or assassinated, leading one Frankish observer to refer to regicide as 'the Gothic disease'.[9] Here, the Toledo councils were frequently concerned with managing bitter and often bloody conflicts that emerged into the open in the context of succession. Not that the efforts of bishops were always successful. Chindaswinth was said to have executed 700 nobles and others on his accession in 642, and there is evidence for both the forcible tonsure and long-term imprisonment of backers of failed royal candidates.[10] After 642, however, outright military force was never again the naked means of gaining the kingship, as councils were convened explicitly to settle the succession issue, rather than to endorse the outcome of political conflict. All parties in the political community had an a priori interest in the creation of consensus, as any might find themselves on the losing side in any future dispute. Thus legislation attempting to prevent retaliation against the kin of previous kings, or against rival factions, could attain wide theoretical support. Although in practice any new king determined to exact revenge was difficult to stop, and there was ultimately no mechanism other than military force to impose royal power on malcontents, it is significant that the elite, secular and ecclesiastical, of the Visigothic kingdom chose to organise themselves around a template of consensus, and to develop institutions designed to tie the political community together. Theological explanations of collective decision-making as a manifestation of God's will gave an ideological gloss to their social and political values.

Much of the conciliar legislation concerning kingship and the succession was at best the expression only of pious hopes. But the cumulative effect of these injunctions, allied to the fact that the elective system ensured that kingship circulated between the dominant groups within landed society, created a very real sense of kingship as an office granted by God. In fact, the precocity of Visigothic kingship lay in developing a sense of a royal mission or ministry, according to which the king was answerable to God, and in the elaboration of royal ritual and ideology, and was rooted in the fact that each new king needed to state his claim from fresh, as his position had not been inherited. Thus the councils' distinction between the public lands attached to the office of king, and the private estates of the individual who happened to be king at any one time, was eminently necessary in a system where the kingship rarely passed from father to son. Thus too the elaboration of coronation rituals, culminating in the anointing of the new king with holy oil by the archbishop of Toledo, first documented in 672 but possibly beginning earlier in the seventh century, was likewise necessary to transform the status of an individual who had previously been just one noble among many, but was now an actor on a different plane as king. The elaborate inauguration, most fully described in the *History of King Wamba*, was vital in allowing the new king to remake his relationships with his erstwhile equals, and thus reforge the political community.[11]

Along with the articulation of a sense of kingship as an office, implicated in the church like that of a bishop, went the development of a sense of Hispania as a political community, the 'Gothic nation'. Isidore was the key figure here. His *History of the Goths, Sueves and Vandals*, written in the 620s, provided a remarkable historical justification of Gothic rule in Hispania.[12] This, unlike the work of Cassiodorus or Jordanes focusing on the Ostrogoths, did not even claim to collect indigenous Gothic tradition, or link back contemporary rulers to heroes of the pre-migration period. In all probability, by the beginning of the seventh century, after almost two centuries of assimilation into the landowning elites of southern Gaul and Hispania, those groups who identified themselves as Gothic had lost all contact and all use for a separate Gothic past, whilst the failure of the various families which tried to establish themselves as royal dynasties meant that there was no court-based family tradition which might look back to legendary heroes of the fourth and fifth centuries. For Isidore, it was Hispania which mattered, and Gothic kingship was to be celebrated for its barbarously martial past, now tamed and dedicated to the protection of the fatherland, *patria*, above all the church, now purged of heresy and unified in Catholic orthodoxy. Isidore's projection of the kingdom as a geographical entity united in faith under Gothic rule was only possible given the successful campaigns against the remaining Byzantine enclaves in the southwest in the first quarter of the seventh century: it is telling that the run of Toledo councils began only after the fall of the last Byzantine toehold in 625. Isidore's political theology has, indeed, even been seen as explicitly anti-Byzantine, rejecting the identification of imperial power with the Christian faith, and developing the notion of Hispania as a sovereign political unit, with Gothic kings answerable directly to God on behalf of their people. This model of a peninsular political community, identified as the 'Gothic nation', is echoed in the conciliar legislation, which condemned the use of foreign – that is, Frankish or Byzantine – support, and restricted the kingship to those of noble Gothic blood, which in practice by the seventh century meant the landowning elite.

What this political vision meant on a local level is unclear, given the paucity of sources other than the laws and the decrees of the councils. It is evident from the laws that by the seventh century the Visigothic army consisted of levies recruited by the landlords, an impression confirmed by the scarce narrative sources; as well as bands of personal retainers, these military contingents could also include slave-soldiers fighting on their owner's orders.[13] Whatever remnants of the Roman taxation system had survived into the sixth century were certainly no longer operative in the seventh. The laws and councils are unambiguous in dealing with the politics of land. The language of taxation is used only for dues collected from fiscal land, that is land owned by the state. Here there are indications that we are sometimes dealing with the estates of rebels and losers in succession disputes, who were enslaved and whose land was forfeit to the fisc as punishment, but who might one day seek rehabilitation and regain their freedom. The implicit notion – that taxation was something which was incompatible with the status of being a free man, a member of the 'Gothic people' – suggests that the withering away of tax went hand-in-hand with the creation of a new identity for the landowning elite, in a process paralleled in seventh-century Gaul.[14] Theoretical prohibitions against intermarriage between Goths and Romans were abandoned by the time of Chindaswinth (642–53), but they had relied on divisions which had been slowly eroded on the ground long before.

What is wholly unusual about seventh-century Spain is the absence of any strong link in the legislation between free status, Gothic identity, and military service. In contrast to Merovingian Gaul and Germany, Lombard Italy or Anglo-Saxon England, where weapon-bearing was the badge of legal freedom, the Visigothic laws made no connection between freedom and fighting.

Ultimately, these contrasts related to differences in social structure. In practice, elsewhere in the post-Roman west, it was impossible for all, and probably for most, free men to perform military service for the king regularly, and alternatives were negotiated. The notion of a class of free warriors informed ideas about social status, though, because kingdoms like those of the Lombards and the Franks had been forged in the context of a crisis in landlord power and a simplification and shallowing of social hierarchies in the countryside. In the Visigothic kingdom, however, provincial landowners had continued to exert local power in something approaching a political vacuum in the fifth and sixth centuries: seventh-century kings had to acknowledge their formal, legal, power over the countryside in a manner unparalleled elsewhere. The legislation again and again underlines the importance of slaves and freedmen to landlords, tending to depress the legal status of dependent peasants and accentuate the importance of legal unfreedom. This did not make the Visigothic kingdom a world of huge plantations cultivated by gangs of slaves. Rather, the subjection of peasant cultivators who cared for family farms and passed on rent was confirmed by their legal rights over them held by their landlords: the closest comparisons here may come, unsurprisingly, from southern Gaul where we can see similar structures in eighth-century documentation.[15]

Given the reality of landlord power in the countryside, some historians have even gone so far as to characterise seventh-century kingship in terms of 'theoretical strength and practical weakness'.[16] But what is remarkable is that the regions held together. In spite of recurrent conflict over the royal succession, there were no attempts to break away from the political system, or to set up self-standing regional polities. Here, the elective nature of the kingship was crucial: regional aristocracies had the hope, at least, of seeing one of their number elevated to the throne and so had an interest in engaging with the politics of Toledo and the royal court. Julian of Toledo's *History of King Wamba* gives a vivid account of the failed attempt of Paul, based over the Pyrenees in Narbonne as *dux* or provincial governor, to seize the throne in 673. Paul's claims rested on his ability to raise a considerable army from his provincial power base, which he ruled from what must have seemed a quasi-regal court at Narbonne, where he had himself elevated to the kingship and anointed by local bishops. Julian, justifying and commemorating his close links as archbishop with King Wamba, launched a shocking invective against Paul, a verbal parallel to the rituals of humiliation and degradation used by Wamba's supporters to label Paul as a usurper. Julian concludes his account with a vivid invective, echoing the injunctions of the Toledo councils banning outsiders from aspiring to the throne, condemning Paul as unfit to be king because he was not truly Gothic, but allied to foreigners and reliant on Basque troops from the mountains. Here Paul's regional power is laid bare, but had he remained loyal or been successful he would have been seen as unambiguously Gothic; no qualms were raised in the sources about Wamba's successor, Erwig, whose father had been an immigrant from the Byzantine Empire.[17] Paul's rebellion is an episode onto which we have a unique spotlight, but there is good reason to suppose that similar regional constellations underpinned the bids for royal power, some successful, some not, which littered seventh-century politics. The legislation limiting the retribution which could be taken against those associated with previous regimes, and the fears that landowners would not always rally with their followings to the royal standard when the army was mobilised, suggests as much. The inability of any one faction or family to establish a monopoly over the kingship thus served an important political function, in that it made it worthwhile for all sections of the aristocracy to continue to engage with the politics of the Toledo court and the royal succession.

Paul's rebellion ultimately failed as he was unable to seize Toledo, where Wamba had built up strong support. Chindaswinth in 642 was the last successful claimant to the throne to have himself declared in the provinces and then seize Toledo. Subsequent kings won the support of the archbishop and court at Toledo and then imposed themselves over provincial malcontents such as Paul. In fact, there are clear hints that by the middle decades of the seventh century at least, court office and position in the palace at Toledo had become crucial resources in the political strategies of regional landowners. Wamba himself, for example, owed his elevation to the throne to his inside knowledge of the Toledo establishment gained through 20 years holding various offices at the royal court, but he also had links with the province of Galicia, acting on occasion as representative of the archbishop of Braga at the court.[18] Social status, judging by the language of the sources, was clearly linked to office-holding, and some individuals seem to have combined office at court with regional governorships, thus creating clear links between regional groups and the royal court at Toledo, or acted as representatives of the interests of their 'home' regions at the court, as with Wamba and Galicia. Little is known about the degree to which kings controlled office in the regions, in particular the crucial role of *dux*, governor and military leader in a province, as exercised by Paul. By the seventh century, this role seems to have eclipsed that of the counts, attached to cities, who had been the key royal officials in the sixth century, a reflection of both urban decline and the regionalisation of landed elites. There can be little doubt that such positions needed to be filled by men with local muscle, based on land and the military following this made possible, given the tenor of the laws. But the fact, acknowledged again and again in the legislation, that kings were likely to move against those who had opposed them and failed, hints at the possibility of royal intervention in the dispensation of power within the landed elite. In other words, in spite of the reality of landlord power, the circulation of the royal office kept aristocracies engaged with regnal politics, and enabled the creation of a palace-centred polity in which the social and military power of regional aristocracies was politically articulated through the royal court at Toledo. In fact, the political negotiation, factionalism and alliance-building which determined recurrent debates over the succession played an important role in preventing regional aristocracies from emerging as distinct, self-standing entities without interests, kin or connections outside their own areas. Chindaswinth's purge of his opponents on gaining the throne may have eliminated any potential rival constellations – even Wamba had begun his career at Chindaswinth's court – but it is clear that by the second half of the seventh century court politics were binding regional aristocracies together into more broadly-based political factions. Indeed, the emergence of these court-centred factions must have played an important role in lessening the frequency of armed conflict over the succession, and enabling the prevalence of successions negotiated through the bishops and nobility at Toledo.

The centripetal role of Toledo and the royal court is particularly evident in the church. Here, the succession of Toledo councils laid down kingdom-wide practices in the practicalities of ecclesiastical discipline, religious observance and above all in the performance of the liturgy, which was to be carried out throughout the peninsula according to the rites of Toledo. The concerns of these 'national' councils were followed through at a local level in provincial councils. Centralisation would be the wrong term to describe this state of affairs: the Toledo councils brought together bishops from across the kingdom, whose 'home' churches enjoyed widely differing endowments and environments, from the former Roman cities of the south and the seaboard to the more rural foundations of the mountainous north. By laying down common patterns of observance, particularly liturgical, the councils created a veneer of cultural unity tying together the churches of the kingdom. Shared observance created a common identity, rooted in common cultural practice but also on occasion articulated in political terms, through the adoption of regular prayers for the king and kingdom, and in celebration of royal victory. The conciliar legislation also reiterated the view of the Visigothic kingdom as a Christian society. One marked feature was the repeated attacks on the social and civil status of the Jews, culminating in legislation requiring forcible conversion in 694, which may have drawn on seventh-century Byzantine legislation scapegoating Jewish communities, but which was pursued by the Visigothic church with shocking insistence. As always with legislation, the relationship of the anti-Jewish rhetoric of the Toledo councils to provincial practice is impossible to unpick, but the extent to which the national church was wedded to a vision of a Christian Visigothic kingdom is clear. Representing Jews as pagan outsiders was a way of defining the boundaries of Christian society, just as banning 'foreigners', exiles or those reliant on external support from the kingship defined the boundaries of the political elite.[19]

Just as office at palace pulled together the regional aristocracies of the kingdom, so the conciliar tradition ensured that churches with their own rich cultural traditions, and their own schools, such as Seville under Leander and Isidore, fed into a larger whole. Although Toledo was technically one of five metropolitan bishoprics within the kingdom, in practice after the inauguration of the tradition of Toledo councils the supremacy of the archbishopric of Toledo was acknowledged in practice, there even being cases where bishops of other sees were translated to Toledo, contrary to canon law. There were tensions here, particularly when, as in the late seventh century, the importance of the Toledo councils tended to accentuate the pre-eminence of the archbishopric of Toledo, and ties between the palace and the government of the church. The presence of the royal court and the slow shrinkage of urban life allowed Toledo to be redefined as a 'new Jerusalem', a complex of churches nestled around the royal palace, its permanent inhabitants largely dependent on the episcopal and royal households, but with a regular and sizeable influx associated with the festivals of the church and the pull of the royal court. The archbishopric of Toledo was in the control of the king, and palace officials were frequently given plum offices in the church, including the role of bishop. Wamba even created a 'bishop of the royal chapel', institutionalising royal control of the church and the use of the church as a means of patronage for bright young men from the palace.[20]

With the church, as with political and social life, we must not forget that the initiatives of the small but highly visible elite tied into the court life of Toledo were essentially concerned with unity, not uniformity. Common liturgical practice created bonds of prayer that tied together the Christian communities of the peninsula. But on the ground, religious practices differed, as communities had shaped Christian practices in the light of their local concerns and experiences. In Galicia in the northwest, there is good evidence for a distinct religious culture, looking back to Martin, the sixth-century bishop of Braga, whose work included rules reflecting and regulating local monastic life, and *On the Castigation of Rustics,* a tract dealing with the Christianisation of a rough countryside, a slow piecemeal battle against customary practices embedded in an agrarian cycle and a distinctive landscape.[21] Traditions of pactual monasticism, with whole settlements agreeing on common religious observances that gave them a monastic status, likewise rested on a social structure of cohesive communities and weak landlords. The religious experience of these regions must have differed dramatically from those of the plains of southern Spain. Indeed, it is no accident that we have no Hispanic equivalent of Gregory of Tours' hagiography in Gaul or Gregory the Great's *Dialogues* in Italy, describing an extensive cultural landscape defined by an interlocking web of saints' cults: the several Visigothic saints' lives we do have point to a resolutely regional topography of holiness.[22]

The making of al-Andalus

The role of Toledo, a royal city dominated by palace and archbishop, in creating a thin but bright lustre that held together the regions of the Visigothic kingdom, is underlined by the sudden political changes of the eighth century. Military defeat by an Islamic force from Africa led to the sudden collapse of the Visigothic kingdom in the 710s. The killing of Roderic, who had only come to the throne in 710, the defeat of the royal army and the capture of Toledo destroyed the bonds that had held the kingdom together: although there were attempts to continue the tradition of Visigothic kingship across the Pyrenees at Narbonne, these had been quelled by 720. The date of Roderic's defeat – 711[23] – has become instrumentalised as an emblem of wholesale change and tied up with the identity of the modern Spanish state. The ideological significance attached to the events of 711 results from the claims made by the nascent Spanish state in the later Middle Ages and the early modern period: its origins were portrayed as lying in a centuries-long process of 'reconquest', in which the territory of Spain was redeemed from Islamic rule, and the Spanish nation defined as the Christian followers of the rulers of Aragon and Castile who were to succeed in creating a unified monarchy. In modern times, the historiography of 'reconquest' continued to play a central role in legitimating the Spanish state, creating as it did a template of an united 'Catholic Spain' which left no space for the regionalism or secularism that were such live political issues in the nineteenth and twentieth centuries: it is only in the last generations, following the end of the Franco regime, that it has begun to be questioned. In such a scheme of interpretation, Islamic rule is negated as an alien other, existing simply to define Christian Spain, whilst the Visigothic kingdom is essentially disconnected from 'national' history, with the honourable exceptions of the Toledan councils with their championing of a kingdom united in faith. These shadows continue to fall over much modern scholarship.

In fact, a careful look shows that these traditional schemes rest on shaky foundations. The ideology of Christian reconquest is very difficult to find before the twelfth century at the very earliest. And the reality of Christian–Islamic relations both within al-Andalus, the Islamic polity ruled from Cordoba, and across the frontier, which remained centred on the Duero and Ebro valleys until the twelfth century, was more complex and multi-faceted than presuppositions of constant conflict between monolithic and united groupings on either side of the religious divide allow. The real problem for those seeking historical understanding of these interactions lies in the nature of the source material. There is a huge volume of Islamic historiography, but aside from the inevitable linguistic difficulties it poses for the non-Arabist, its nature is wholly different from the kind of source material western historians are trained to handle, resting as it does on the accumulation of tradition (*hādith*) by compilers often writing centuries after the events they record; these traditions need careful handling, as they often had a particular role as historical precedent in Islamic legal and political thought, and so were reshaped according to present concerns at various points in the chain of transmission. Christian narrative sources, however, are meagre before the twelfth century, and even the documentary survivals that shed rich light on the societies of northern

Spain from the tenth century onwards are lacking for our period. For the formative period, we are dependant on a single, spare, narrative, written by a Christian inhabitant of al-Andalus, the *Chronicle of 752*;[24] this is primarily useful as a control on the far richer but far harder to use Islamic material.

The fact that the Visigothic kingdom followed fast on the heels of the Byzantine provinces of North Africa in succumbing to Islamic conquest underlines the significance of the far-reaching changes wrought across the seventh-century Mediterranean for events at its western extreme. After all, the period in which the Visigothic kingdom was able successfully to present itself as the framework for legitimate political power in the Iberian peninsula – the period between the crucial reigns of Leovigild and Reccared and the Islamic conquest – corresponds closely with the collapse of Byzantine authority and power beyond Constantinople's immediate hinterland. In concrete terms, this meant far more than the ending of the Byzantine military presence on the southern coast of the peninsula and the establishment of Visigothic control of a narrow strip of the Moroccan coastline around Ceuta; the cultural achievements of the seventh-century church are at least partly to be explained by an intensification of traditional contacts with nearby North Africa, the movement of ideas facilitated by an influx of refugees from Byzantine provinces under severe pressure. Thanks to these same geographical and social links, armies serving the Islamic governor of a new province of Africa, Ifrīqiya, came into contact with the Visigothic kingdom within a decade of the fall of Carthage in 698.

The crucial groupings in this process were the Berber tribes of the North African interior, who since the fourth century had been creating increasingly powerful polities. Their conversion to Islam in the second half of the seventh century had effectively undermined the remaining Byzantine hold on the cities of the modern Tunisian coast, and the first decade of the seventh century saw them receiving the submission of the cities and inhabitants of the western part of the North African coastline, in modern Morocco. From here, an expedition was launched across the Straits of Gibraltar in 711, under Ṭāriq ibn Ziyad, a freed slave (*māwla*) of Mūsā ibn Nuṣayr, the governor of Ifrīqiya, with immediate and surprising success. Berber forces were to play the central role in the subsequent conquest of the Visigothic kingdom. The itinerary of these Berber warbands strikingly reverses that of the Vandals under Gaiseric almost three centuries earlier; as with the Vandals, these movements were not the spontaneous 'wanderings of peoples', but the result of internal tensions within imperial systems that spanned the Mediterranean.

In the case of the conquest of the Visigothic kingdom, the tensions resulted from the internal structures of the Islamic polity ruled by the Umayyad caliphs of the late seventh and early eighth centuries. In establishing government over the former imperial provinces they had conquered in the course of the seventh century, the caliphs had attempted to prevent the conquering armies from putting down local roots that would encourage them to merge with provincial society and disengage from the wider Islamic polity; care was taken to keep governorships in the gift of the caliph, as appointments were circulated rather than being made for life. Religion played an important role here: there were no forced conversions, as the other 'religions of the book', Christianity and Judaism, were tolerated, their adherents paying a poll tax to the Islamic conquerors. So too did the insistence on the role of the Islamic state in collecting and distributing the proceeds of provincial taxes (those inherited from predecessor regimes as well as the dues paid by non-believers) and income from public lands: for this, an annual 'salary' (*dhīmma*) was paid to the Islamic conquerors and their descendants. The effect of this practice was to create a privileged elite, whose membership was effectively restricted to the Arab tribes who had been the first converts to Islam. Yet Islamic conquests after the initial successes of the first half of the seventh century were increasingly carried out not by Arab armies, but by more recent converts under Arab leadership, their energies turned outwards: even Mūsā was only a second-generation Muslim, a Syrian whose father become a client of the caliph. In Ifrīqiya, tensions between the small Arab administrative elite, mainly consisting of appointees from Damascus with widespread contacts but limited local roots, and the Berbers were soon simmering; further conquest was one way of dealing with them.

These tensions should warn us against seeing Islamic conquest as part of a homogenous or monolithic movement masterminded by the caliphs, a manifestation of a latent 'clash of civilisations'. In fact, both Islamic traditions and the *Chronicle of 752* agree that Islamic expeditions were successful because they interacted with internal conflicts within the Visigothic kingdom. Roderic had been elected king only in 710, and a rival ruler, Achila, was recognised in the northeast; Roderic's army, indeed, had to abandon a campaign against Basque rebels, presumably encouraged by Achila, to turn south and deal with Tāriq. Other discontented elements within the regime are also identified in both historiographical traditions. John, the *dux* controlling the Visigothic possessions in Morocco, was opposed to Roderic and aided Islamic troops in crossing from Africa, and the relatives of the previous king, Wittiza, are also named as conspiring against Roderic, perhaps even fighting alongside an Islamic force; in doing so, they were following several previous Visigothic royals and usurpers in drawing on external help. In this context, Roderic's army must have consisted of little more than his personal following, and was roundly defeated by Tāriq. The defeat and death of the king was rapidly followed by the capture of Toledo and execution of what remained of the palatine nobility: the heart of the Visigothic polity had been removed at one stroke, and resistance centred on Narbonne, long a centre of regional feeling and the seat of several usurpers in the seventh century.

The conquest of the Visigothic kingdom was unlike previous Islamic expansion, which had absorbed former Byzantine and Sassanian provinces into a new Islamic polity, rather than taking over an independent state. As such, it posed an immediate threat to the structure of the caliphate: namely, that its conquerors might graft their rule onto Visigothic kingship and prove effectively independent. The speed with which Mūsā, leading a separate Islamic force, humiliated Tāriq after the defeat of Roderic, is striking here; so too the equal speed with which Mūsā was recalled by his master, the caliph. By 712 Mūsā's son, Abd al-Azīz, was the official governor, but he took to acting like a Visigothic king, wearing a crown and demanding that rituals of supplication be performed by his 'subjects': in 715 he was murdered by his followers for these breaches of Islamic political traditions.[25]

Thereafter, the caliphs appointed a rapid succession of governors serving for a handful of years each, and Toledo was abandoned as a political centre. This made any continuation of the structure of the Visigothic monarchy impossible, but in all probability there was no real centralised administrative machine to take over by right of conquest. With the complex web of bonds that had bound regions to Toledo destroyed, the allegiance of provincial elites did not follow automatically, and through the 710s and 720s politics was primarily a matter of the movements of diverse Islamic armies. In other words, the Islamic conquest destroyed Visigothic regnal structures, and left regional societies with little to hold them together.

For many landowners, coming to terms with the new conquerors, who did not force their conversion or threaten to overturn the social order, made sense. Like Islamic armies elsewhere, those which conquered the Visigothic kingdom offered cities which stood in their path two choices: either submit, and have religious freedom and local governmental structures confirmed in return for an agreed payment of tax, or resist and face enslavement. The text of one treaty, made in 713 by Theodemir, the Visigothic *dux* of seven cities on the southern coast, is preserved in a later Islamic work; this agreement structured power in the region for at least half a century, and gave it its modern name, Tudmir.[26] Although the terms of this type of agreement were familiar right across the caliphate, the societies of the Visigothic kingdom differed from those of the imperial provinces subjected to Islamic conquest elsewhere. Most importantly, there was no regular mechanism of land tax on which Islamic governors could draw, and although there were tax-lists drawn up in the 720s, tolls on trade and the head-tax on Christians were the main sources of fiscal income, overseen by a new administrative structure of *qādis* or governors based in the major cities likes the counts and *duces* of the Visigothic kingdom. As a result, the seizure and distribution of land was probably far more important than in other Islamic conquests: certainly, the Islamic historiographical tradition is unanimous that the normal conventions were not followed here, and the frequent use of expropriation and enslavement for 'political' crimes in the Visigothic kingdom may have acted as a precedent.

In this situation, it would be a mistake to see any of the rapid succession of governors exercising any meaningful form of central authority. The closest parallels for the situation of landowning elites negotiating with marauding armies may lie in the fifth and sixth centuries, but the Islamic conquerors had a very different political culture from their barbarian predecessors. The Islamic conquerors maintained their tribal identities, rooted in the landscapes and historical traditions of the Arabian peninsula. Not that this was a tribal society in its proper sense of a system of multi-family groupings whose social and economic unity was articulated in terms of a belief in a shared descent and history; the Islamic armies were not made up of tribes recruited wholesale, but of individuals who were members of tribes, whose solidarities were rooted in extended clan units. But tribal identities were fundamental to the structure of Islamic politics, signalling allegiances and alliances which could be maintained within the Islamic elite right across the vast provinces of the caliphate, and also defining the dividing lines in times of internal conflict. These complex systems of allegiance, kinship and identity, and their central political role, stand out against anything else we meet in the early medieval west: they should remind us that for all the importance of kinship in the successor-states to the western empire, western European kinship even in this period was relatively fluid and loose as a social and political bond compared to the extensive and cohesive systems we find elsewhere.

The presence of large numbers of Berbers, whose strong sense of separate identity was tied up with the maintenance of their own system of tribal allegiances rooted in the Maghreb, added further to the complex internal divisions of Islamic society in al-Andalus. The Berbers seem to have preferred to settle in ecological niches in the uplands of the Meseta and the north where they could attempt to reproduce the economy and society of their native Africa, and so remained geographically distinct from the Arab armies based in the cities of the south. Tensions between Arabs and Berbers finally erupted in a serious revolt in Africa in 739, fuelled by resentment against the privileges of the Arabs and religious movements insisting on the equality of all Muslims. Inevitably conflict quickly spread to al-Andalus. An Arab army from Syria was sent to put down the revolt, but was defeated in Africa and fought its way to al-Andalus, where its constituent units or *junds* quickly established itself as the dominant political force and settled in the cities of the south. This fragmentation was paralleled elsewhere in the caliphate, as a series of revolts resting on similar tensions to those in Africa and al-Andalus, led to the overthrow of the Umayyads and their replacement by the 'Abbāsids. One member of the Umayyad family, 'Abd al-Rahmān, fled to Africa, to seek the support of his mother's Berber tribe, and thence to al-Andalus in 756; here, he was able to use Arab tribal politics to rally support from some of the Syrian forces in the south and seize the capital, Cordoba.

It is 'Abd al-Rahmān's reign (756–88) that marks the real creation of a new Islamic political system in al-Andalus, and with it the crystallisation of the northern frontier of the *dār al-Islam*, the Islamic world. The creation of an Umayyad state in al-Andalus formalised its political division from the caliphate, probably inevitably given its social difference and geographical distance. Although 'Abd al-Rahmān styled himself simply *amir*, and his successors did not take the title of caliph or commander of the faithful until the tenth century, al-Andalus was now an independent political entity, not a province of the caliphate. The slow process of re-establishing control over fragmented and militarised societies confirmed that the heart of al-Andalus would lie in the south, whose cities had seen the heaviest Arab settlement: hence the development of the major southern city of Cordoba as a site of courtly ceremonial and cultural patronage, begun by 'Abd al-Rahmān but reaching its apogee in the ninth and early tenth centuries. Even in the south, 'Abd al-Rahmān faced prolonged opposition, including 'Abbāsid-inspired revolts and tribal conflicts among the Arab troops. Further north, control was not established over the Berber settlers in the Meseta, the central plateau which had been the heartland of the Visigothic kingdom, until the end of the 770s. Legitimacy here was difficult to establish thanks to the influence of the strand of Islamic thought which was to become Shi'ism, and which sought the restoration of the direct line of the Prophet as imams combining spiritual and temporal authority: it was only the assassination in 777 of Shaqya, who had been proclaimed imam, that allowed 'Abd al-Rahmān to establish himself here.

The amirate of al-Andalus established by ʻAbd al-Rahmān was to endure as the framework for political life in the southern half of the peninsula for two centuries. For all the magnificence of the court at Cordoba, whose fame as a cultural centre rested on the revenue-raising activities of a sophisticated financial administration, the political culture of ninth- and tenth-century al-Andalus was one in which recurrent provincial revolt was accepted, indeed expected. In part, this was a result of a tribal political culture which was legitimated by long-running feuds. These tendencies were exacerbated by the strong roots which Berber tribesmen and Arab *junds* put down in their localities, and the landed interests they acquired; by the ninth century the growth of landed elites of indigenous converts to Islam, *muwallads*, further complicated matters, with complicated struggles breaking out between *muwallads* and the descendents of the Islamic conquerors in the south. Whilst these local political struggles between tribal groupings were common across the Islamic world of the ninth century, here they arose in a particular context, rooted in the unusual importance of land seizure as opposed to fiscal structures in the process of settlement. By creating a dominant and cohesive class of wealthy consumers concentrated in a small number of cities, some long-established and some new foundations, settlement was an important stimulant for the rebirth of urban life in the ninth century. But politically, these strong local ties meant that major cities like Mérida, Saragossa and Toledo were the sites of repeated and recurrent revolts against central interference. This fraying of ties between the Islamic conquerors and the central government made it necessary for amirs to look for independent sources of military power. Al-Hakam I (796–822) was said to have recruited a slave (*mamlūk*) army of 6,000, as well as inaugurating the custom of regular military pay to his soldiers: this use of the fiscal resources of the state to recruit professional armies of outsiders was common across the ʻAbbasīd Caliphate from the middle of the ninth century, with slave-armies primarily recruited from eastern European captives sold on by their Christian western European captors the prime source of manpower for the rulers of al-Andalus.[27]

In the meantime, a series of tiny Christian polities had emerged in the northern part of the Iberian peninsula. Lack of interest on the part of the Islamic traditions makes their origins shadowy in the extreme, recorded only in much later and ideologically coloured sources. The origins of the kingdom of the Asturias in the mountainous far north, for example, were written up towards the end of the ninth century in a series of chronicles connected with the court of King Alfonso III: this tradition portrayed the kings of the Asturias as leading Christian resistance to Islam almost from the moment of conquest, claiming that the kingdom originated in a victory over forces of the Berber governor at Covadonga in 718. That this battle is mentioned in none of our Islamic sources, nor in the contemporary, albeit southern narrative of the *Chronicle of 752*, warns us that at best we are dealing with interested myth-making around a distant memory of a local conflict. In fact, the crucial period seems to have been the reign of Alfonso I (739–57), which coincided with the most chaotic phase of the civil wars amongst the Islamic conquerors: with the rebellious Berber garrisons of the north sucked into these southern conflicts, Alfonso I was able to campaign successfully in Galicia, creating a stable kingdom which, under Alfonso II (791–842) claimed to recreate 'the order of the Goths as it had been in Toledo, in church and palace alike', pretensions also expressed in the palace complex at Oviedo.[28] The Visigothic roots of the Asturian kingdom were hardly continuous: this was an aristocratic coalition fuelled by successful plundering which crystallised around the palace, harking back to the Visigothic past to legitimate its hold on Galicia and encourage immigration from the Meseta.

In the northeast, matters were more complex still. The strong attachment of the powerful landed elite of Catalonia and Septimania to the Visigothic monarchy meant that it was an urgent target for the Islamic conquerors: immediately after the defeat of Roderic and the fall of Toledo, one Islamic force had marched to Saragossa. Attempts to continue a Visigothic monarchy in the region finally failed with the conquest of Narbonne, north of the Pyrenees, in the 720s. Islamic garrisons here inevitably saw the opportunity to seek further tribute and plunder in the south of a Frankish kingdom which was engaged in civil war: attempted attacks on Aquitaine, however, were successfully resisted, and through the 720s Islamic activities here need to be understood as part of a series of complex and shifting regional coalitions which pitted the ruler of Aquitaine against the Frankish court. The famous Islamic attack on Aquitaine which culminated in defeat by the Frankish ruler Charles Martell near Poitiers in 734 cut across these coalitions, in that it forced the Aquitainians into temporary alliance with the Frankish court: it certainly cannot be seen, as it so often is, as a decisive turning-point marking the end of a conscious and centralised strategy of Islamic expansion. What it did mark was the start of a resolutely Frankish political order in southern Gaul, where previously there had been a delicate balance between Aquitaine and Visigothic Septimania. By the 740s and 750s the combination of civil war in al-Andalus and the reassertion of Frankish royal control in Aquitaine and Provence saw the landowning elites of formerly Visigothic territory giving their allegiance to the Franks: the arrival of a Frankish army to 'liberate' Narbonne in 759 articulated the new order.

South of the Pyrenees, in Catalonia and the Ebro valley, the last quarter of the eighth century saw locals increasingly forced to choose between the amir of Cordoba, now able to assert his power in the region having finally established control of the Meseta in 777, and the Franks, from 781 represented by a subking based in Aquitaine. In 778, the *qādi* of Saragossa offered to submit to the Frankish king Charlemagne in return for assistance against the amir. The deal fell through, and the Frankish army suffered a humiliating ambush by Basques as it returned north. The episode demonstrates the pressures on locals to align themselves with one side or another, and the Frankish allegiance of the southern foothills of the Pyrenees was slowly established, with Barcelona taken in 801. With the traditions of the Visigothic monarchy dead, landowners nonetheless maintained a Gothic identity, notably in their continuing use of Visigothic legal traditions, and monopolised countships in the region; immigrants from al-Andalus, *Hispani*, were actively settled in the frontier regions.

These pressures – the growing assurance of the Umayyad regime at Cordoba in the south and the creation of alternative foci for Christian political loyalties in the north – led to the crystallisation of the frontier of al-Andalus along the river valleys of the Duero and the Ebro. Here, the ideology of reconquest has continued to cast a long shadow, with the frontier depicted as a First World War-style no-man's-land of devastation, across which the only form of contact was military conflict; subsequent 'reconquest' thus becomes a process of physical resettlement in an empty landscape devoid of contact with Islam. In reality, the evidence for such a view is difficult and sparse, a few phrases in ninth-century Asturian chronicles referring to the 'devastation' of the countryside in the course of campaigning. In fact, it seems that rather than a depopulated countryside riven by war, these frontier zones were marked by an absence of the regular structures of government; when government was slowly reimposed in the tenth century, it required claims to land, now being more intensively exploited, in terms of new colonisation. And in political terms, the frontier was anything but a sharp or impermeable divide. Its proximity gave the holders of local power options in their relationship with amir and king. Thus Mūsā ibn Mūsā, leader of the Banu Qasī clan which dominated the upper Ebro valley through the middle and later ninth century, could rely on support from his Christian neighbour the king of Pamplona when in 'revolt' against the amir, and claimed descent from the Visigothic aristocracy; similarly, Christian rulers in the north could solicit support from their Islamic neighbours, or even become clients of the amir, when they needed help against internal opponents. This was a world of effectively independent warlords, who lived in a complex symbiosis which secured a delicate political balance.

The stabilisation of the frontier established a rough-and-ready divide between the territories of Islamic and Christian rulers. But within these territories, religious divisions were anything but sharp or sudden. In al-Andalus, although there was a slow increase in the Islamic population as generation by generation some of the Christian population took on the religion of their rulers and became *muwallads*, converts to Islam, Christians remained in the majority through the tenth century at least. The history of the Mozarabs, as the Christians of al-Andalus came to be known, remains obscure. Attention has too easily been swayed by the one spectacular instance of religious conflict, the 'Cordoba martyrs' movement of the 850s. This involved over 50 well-to-do Christians making repeated public denunciations of Islam in the knowledge that by doing so they would bring legal retribution and eventually execution upon themselves. The highly stylised Latin accounts of the priest Eulogius, whose own execution in 859 marked the end of the movement, presents these actions as martyrdom on the model of the persecuted Christians of the third-century Roman Empire. There certainly were earlier precedents for small groups of Christians who felt uneasy at collaboration with the Islamic regime. The followers of Migetius, for example, had been condemned by Archbishop Elipandus of Toledo, the chief architect of the policy of co-existence, in the 780s for their refusal to suffer contaminating contact with unbelievers, which Elipandus linked to heterodox theological views, and at a church council in 839 a similar sect seeking 'pure Christianity' was condemned. The changing social makeup of the amir's court at Cordoba, the focal point of the martyrs' movement, also played a role: the government had always relied on a significant number of Christians in its administration, but a century and a half after the Islamic conquest, there was a ready pool of *muwallads* –

indigenous converts – able to take on these roles. The amir Mohammed I (852–86) seems to have restricted the recruitment of Christians to some posts, creating the context where a the close-knit grouping of Christians commemorated by Eulogius felt the necessity to make a stand for their faith. For all their high profile, and the interest in the Cordoban martyrs north of the Pyrenees at the Frankish court, the co-existence of Christian and Muslim remained the norm.[29]

Ultimately, the political conflicts of the eighth century ensured the political fragmentation of the Iberian peninsula. The strong regional elites which had underlain the Christian lustre of the Visigothic monarchy of Toledo were transformed by the process of Islamic conquest. Uncoupled from the court, they found their local power in urgent need of legitimacy, and were unable to resist Islamic armies. Internal divisions within the conquering elite, common across the Islamic world, proved particularly fierce in al-Andalus on account of the strong ethnic and tribal divisions among the Islamic conquerors, and the land-based process of settlement necessitated by the relative weakness of Visigothic systems of taxation. Internal conflict and the inability of the conquerors to draw on the structures of loyalty that had animated the Visigothic kingdom left the shape of the state up for grabs. Ultimately, although 'Abd al-Rahmān was able to weld together the fissiparous Islamic forces and create an Islamic polity in the south, northern elites found other solutions. Whereas Visigothic kings had lacked the coercive force consistently to cow regional elites, Islamic leaders possessed military power of a different order. But their political imperative was the maintenance of control over the forces who supplied that military muscle; ultimately, this led to the creation of a sophisticated Islamic state in the south, and a kaleidoscope of local polities in the north.

The Lombard alternative

Visigothic kingship, limited as it was by the continuing extent of landlord power in the countryside, relied on the practical and ideological support of the church, moulded through the Toledo councils into an institution coterminous with the kingdom. In Italy, the continuing ties between key groups within society and the imperial court at Constantinople had meant that Theodoric's Ostrogothic kingdom had been unable to establish itself as the only possible framework for political life, and the resulting ambivalence ended in the Gothic wars. In spite of Justinian's eventual victory, however, the Byzantine state was similarly unable to establish itself as the uncontested framework of power. Within two decades of the final collapse of the Gothic kingdom, a new barbarian 'people', the Lombards, crossed into Italy from the middle Danube plain, and established control over the former heartlands of Gothic support in the north. In the resulting settlement, the Italian peninsula divided between Lombard and Byzantine control: it was to remain politically fragmented until the nineteenth century. Constantinople was too distant to function as a meaningful political centre for the landowning elites of the regions of Italy, but neither the Lombard capital of Pavia, nor the seat of the exarch at Ravenna, were able to create a network of regional allegiances. Competition between Ravenna and Pavia, and doctrinal tensions between church and secular authorities in the Lombard kingdom and the Byzantine Empire,

Map 5 Italy in the early Middle Ages

meant that the Italian church was unable to underwrite state-formation on the model of the Visigothic kingdom. In the eyes of Italian churchmen, Lombard kings were tainted by Arianism, whilst recurrent imperial initiatives to determine doctrine so as to weld together the kaleidoscope of doctrinal traditions of the churches of the empire aroused constant opposition.

Historians have long seen the Lombards as a 'second wave' of barbarian invasions, a new impulse from over the Alps destroying the momentary achievement of Justinian's generals in establishing control over the Italian peninsula. Lombard invasion, particularly in the north, the area know to this day as Lombardy, has often been seen as a process of more or less total meltdown, with the arrival of the people who gave the region its name traced in place names, linguistic terminology and archaeological artefacts. In fact, the Lombards emerged in a context of Byzantine diplomacy, and had been intimately tied into Italian politics through the wars of the sixth century; and the process in the second half of the sixth century which saw the emergence of Lombard rule over a sizeable portion of Italy is far more complex and messy than a simply military invasion and subsequent occupation, for, as we saw, Italian society and its ruling elites were undergoing wholesale transformation.

The problem for historians is that they are highly reliant on a single source, Paul the Deacon's *History of the Lombards*, written after the end of the Lombard kingdom, in the 780s, and so strongly influenced by hindsight. Strictly contemporary sources are frustratingly fragmentary, and do not tell a continuous history of Italy in the late sixth and seventh centuries: we have snippets of information about Italian affairs in Byzantine and Frankish histories, and the letters of Italian churchmen, particularly Pope Gregory the Great. Paul's *History of the Lombards* continues his earlier *Roman History* in telling the history of Italy, and he handles Lombard history as a strongly linear narrative, beginning with origin legends and prehistoric migrations, and presenting the Lombards as a united people who carved out an Italian kingdom. This story needs handling with care, because Paul was writing in the best ethnographic tradition which treated its subject, the Lombards as a people, as a unity which could be traced back in the classical and legendary past, whereas modern historians now see ethnic identities being created and recreated to tie often diverse groups of people together as they encounter new situations.[30]

Paul, although a Lombard by birth, was writing at Charlemagne's court around a decade after the Lombard kingdom had been conquered and incorporated into Charlemagne's realm. So his history, in tracing the Lombards from their beginnings, could be seen as an attempt to preserve their traditions after their demise as a sovereign people, and perhaps to thus provide the Frankish conquerors with an explanation of their historical context. In fact, this may be why Paul's work makes compelling and entertaining reading. Far more than most other early medieval historians he includes colourful anecdotes and legends, such as the story of how the Lombards got their name from the long beards of their womenfolk. These were the pegs around which the historical traditions which informed ethnicity were woven. Paul's careful integration of this kind of material into his plot is precisely where the value of his work for modern historians lies. And Paul was particularly well placed to draw such material together. Born in Friuli in the north, where his family had close links with the ducal court, he also had contacts with the independent Lombard dukes in the south and the royal court at Pavia, and came to enjoy Charlemagne's patronage following a journey to the Frankish court to attempt to secure the release of his brother, who was held hostage there. But Paul also clearly had to take care that his history was not seen to include too explicit a political message, given the recent conquest of the Lombard kingdom and the continued existence of effectively independent Lombard duchies in central and southern Italy. He actually ended his history with the reign of Liudprand (712–44), safely before any Frankish involvement in Italy, and although his work may include some coded comments on the fate of the Lombard kingdom, particularly in a number of prophecies, it cannot be seen as explicit propaganda for any one party.

If we put aside Paul's vision of the Lombards as a single and homogenous group trekking over the centuries from a Scandinavian homeland to Italy, it becomes clear that the Lombard 'invasion' of Italy cannot be seen as a new process, with a definite beginning in 568, and therefore separate and separable from events of the earlier sixth century, in particular the Gothic wars. The Lombards are first mentioned by Procopius, as one of a number of barbarian groups settled in the middle Danube, the region where successive barbarian groupings had been formed and then pulled into the politics of Roman and post-Roman Europe since the fourth century. Since the collapse of Attila's Hun Empire in the 450s, the middle Danube had seen a dizzily changing kaleidoscope of ethnic groups appear and disappear as warrior-elites competed to establish their dominance by attracting the attention of the Byzantine and Italian courts, and thus enjoying subsidies or military employment. The Lombards may not have been an entirely new people – there is an earlier mention of Lombards by Tacitus in the first century AD, who places them on the Elbe in central Germany – but the archaeological evidence points to the strong influence of the cultural milieu of the middle Danube, and suggests a new group coalescing in this melting pot, under the leadership of a warrior-elite with central German links. As allies of Justinian, they were to play an important role in the decisive campaigns of the Byzantine general Narses in the 550s. With the defeat of the Goths, the Lombards were settled as federates of Constantinople in the former Roman provinces of Noricum and Pannonia on the Danube, to secure the approaches to Italy and the Balkans; their ruler was granted subsidies and married to a Gothic princess who had been taken hostage to Constantinople.[31]

This situation changed dramatically in the 560s, as a result of changing Byzantine policy. Justinian's successor, Justin II, radically changed Byzantine policy on this central European frontier: in the case of the Lombards, this led to the ending of subsidies and the abandonment of traditional alliances in favour of a rival group, the Gepids. The Lombards allied with another group of barbarians who had fallen from Byzantine favour, the Avars, to defeat the Gepids, but then vacated the middle Danube in favour of the militarily dominant Avars, who sought to establish dominance in the region. The Lombard king Alboin gathered together an army consisting of a veritable tribal flotsam and jetsam – displaced groups of provincials and barbarians from the middle Danube alongside warrior groups, such as several contingents of Saxons, who sought plunder – and marched into northern Italy, just as a succession of barbarian leaders had since the fifth century. In Italy, there was little to no military resistance – hardly surprisingly, as the groups that Alboin had gathered owed their very existence to Constantinople's need for barbarian fighters in Italy and the Balkans.[32]

If, as seems likely, Alboin and his army were following in the footsteps of a succession of earlier barbarian leaders in northern Italy, and attempting to force the Roman government to negotiate a settlement whereby they gained federate status, military employment, and the cash and supplies that went with it, they were disappointed. Italy no longer had a government of its own, but was a province ruled from Constantinople: from there, these north Italian troubles looked like a frontier flare-up, or worse still a potential distraction and diversion of resources. In fact, it was not until 680 that a formal treaty was to be agreed between Constantinople and the Lombards, although the intervening century saw plenty of negotiation. But a lack of interest from Constantinople did not preclude informal agreements with Italian provincials, the papacy and Byzantine officials on the ground.

In the course of the 570s and 580s, Lombards came to control much of the north, with the exception of the area around Ravenna, the residence of the exarch, and a string of cities leading south and west to Rome. Beyond this Byzantine enclave, Lombard control stretched across much of central and southern Italy from Spoleto to Benevento. Quite how this came about is unclear. It certainly was not a result of any large-scale military campaign or extensive war of conquest. Indeed, the extent to which 'Lombardisation' was almost wholly decentralised and localised is truly remarkable. Alboin supplied some military leadership in the north until 572, when he was assassinated by elements of his army who had reached an agreement with the Byzantine governor in Ravenna; his successor, Cleph, was assassinated in turn in 574, following which the sources mention no further Lombard kings for a decade. Alboin's army itself quickly split apart, hardly surprisingly given its composite nature. Some Saxon contingents, having enriched themselves with plunder, returned to their northern German home, whilst other groups enriched themselves through raiding over the Frankish frontier. Quite which groups established Lombard rule in Spoleto and Benevento and their hinterlands is even more unclear, but there are certainly no accounts of sizeable armies streaming past Rome into the south, and the first attested Lombard leader in Benevento, Duke Zotto, had previously served as a Byzantine general. 'Lombardisation' involved subjection to a Lombard ruler, or a switch of allegiance into a new political system. Within Alboin's hotchpotch army, some groups were happy to align themselves with Italian provincial elites and Byzantine officials very early on. The so-called 'interregnum' – the decade from 574 to 584 when there was no Lombard king – has even been seen by some historians as a result of a Byzantine strategy to split up Alboin's force into its constituent parts. Certainly the exarch at Ravenna, and city authorities in the provinces, negotiated with various Lombard leaders, although there is no indication that we should see this as part of a grand strategy agreed in Constantinople rather than sensible local authorities seeking their own security in the face of a fissiparous and unstable barbarian army.

In fact, the key to understanding 'Lombardisation' lies in the almost total lack of military opposition from either the Byzantine administration or Italian provincials. Individual cities might raise enough troops for the local population to remain safe behind their walls when Lombard troops approached, as Rome did in 579 and Naples in 581, but there was no resistance on a larger scale. This was, quite simply, because there was no real Italian army to resist Alboin and his followers, only garrisons attached to important cities, and local militias. This was largely a result of Byzantine priorities, which lay in the Near East and the Balkans, not Italy. But in any case, since the fifth century Italy had relied for its security on barbarian troops from the Danube frontier; in the Gothic wars, Byzantine cash had increasingly been used to pay barbarian warriors from those same areas to reconquer Italy. It was precisely the remnants of these groups, militarised in response to Roman needs and now left without employ, that Alboin mobilised in 568. In other words, if Constantinople was to maintain the newly reconquered Italy without a client barbarian warlord comparable to Theodoric in the north, it needed to stabilise those frontier regions which had traditionally supplied the barbarian manpower for Italian armies: Justinian and Justin II ordered the first Roman campaigns north of the Danube since the reign of Valentinian in the fourth century. The long-term problem here was the constant need of barbarian warleaders for plunder and prestige to ensure the continued loyalty of their followers. Constantinople needed deep pockets to keep subsidies flowing, and skilful diplomacy to maintain a balance of power between the various groupings, and by Justin's reign the financial and political costs were more than could be afforded, whilst Roman military aggression simply disturbed the political status quo beyond the frontier. So those groups who had come into being in response to the need for military manpower in Italy were left with no alternative but to march into Italy.

And in much of Italy, the arrival of a barbarian force with a strange name but an oddly familiar feel, if not exactly welcomed with glee, did suggest a future which made sense in terms of local experience. The regions in the north that were to become the heartland of the Lombard polity were precisely those where barbarian troops had long been stationed, and which had demonstrated a continuing attachment to the Gothic political system that rested on the presence of a barbarian army and king as protector of provincial Italian society. These areas had scarcely been pacified since the Gothic wars, when they had suffered from repeated invasions by the Franks, who had not been finally driven out until 561; Verona had remained Gothic as late as 562. Vulnerable and still recovering from the disruption of war, northern Italian society had hosted generations of soldiers recruited from over the Alps, and in many cases assimilated them and their descendants. The possibility of accepting the army which had followed Alboin over the Alps, and settling and taming a barbarian contingent, offered an alternative to the new post-reconquest world of Byzantine governors where military protection, whilst paid for dearly through taxation, was distant and dependent on political whim. Ecclesiastical politics had created a sense of distance between Italian provincials and the empire, with northern Italian bishops remaining steadfastly opposed to the official imperial line on ecclesiastical doctrine as espoused by Justinian in 544 in the so-called 'three chapters' controversy. Whilst these ecclesiastical matters did not lead bishops and their congregations to welcome Alboin with open arms – the leading opponents of imperial policy, the metropolitan bishops of Milan and Aquileia, fled from Alboin's army – it did make it easier for many to consider a return to an older order of barbarian warlords.

In any case, to make a local agreement with a Lombard warband was not to secede from the empire – many Lombards pledged allegiance to the exarch at Ravenna – but it was to move outside the rigid system of Byzantine administrative and taxation. In fact, for most of Italy other than those areas which had lain on Alboin's direct path in 568–72, the 570s and 580s posed awkward questions about the future. Given that local elites could always remain safe behind city walls and wait for warbands to move on in search of new provisions, they had real choices: to remain with the newly established status quo of exarchs and tax-collectors, or to opt out of the Byzantine state and into a world of local agreements with barbarian warriors who could hopefully be tamed or settled. In the unsettled north, with its long-standing acquaintance with barbarian warlords, and down the mountainous Apennine spine of Italy into the Lombard regions of central and southern Italy around Spoleto and Benevento, it made sense to take the barbarian option; around Rome, along the north Adriatic coast around Ravenna with its seaborne links east, and along the southern coasts looking to the far shores of the Mediterranean, ties to Constantinople were stronger.

Taking the barbarian option did not necessarily involve becoming the subject of a barbarian king, not least as between 574 and 584 there was no barbarian king! Northern Italy in the 570s and 580s must have looked like developing into a society not unlike sixth-century Spain, with barbarian contingents merging into city-based elites, which were effectively self-governing. But, just as from the 570s Leovigild and his successors were together a Visigothic kingdom, so in the decades around 600 a Lombard kingship was created which slowly established itself in northern Italy. The dynamics of kingdom-creation differed, but the common context was political crisis in Byzantium: with civil war, struggle with the Persians, and the collapse of the Danube frontier meaning that Constantinople had precious little energy or resources to spare on intervening around the western hinterland of the Mediterranean basin.

The collapse of the Lombard kingship after Alboin's invasion of Italy reflects the extent to which the institution itself was a novelty, a warlordship based on the need for a rag-tag army, some of whose contingents included migrating women, children and dependants, for a strong military leadership. Once Alboin had reached northern Italy, his followers had no need for such leadership, and the fission of his army inevitably proceeded. Indeed, Gisulf, the first duke of Friuli, was allowed to choose which *farae*, the extended households led by warrior-males that were the constituent parts of Alboin's army, he wished to settle with him.[33] Ravenna encouraged Frankish incursions in the hope that it would drive cities and their Lombard dukes into the arms of the exarch, and weaken the Lombard leadership; certainly, some Lombard bands seem to have submitted to the Franks. In any case, the weakness of the Roman administrative context in northern Italy meant that there was no institutional base that could be used to ensure the continuity of the kingship established during the migration from the Danube. It is striking that Lombard royal documents, the first of which survive from the seventh century, are based on the forms used for private deeds and contracts in the late Roman and Gothic period, not on the usage of state chanceries. The refusal of the Byzantine authorities to confer any formal position, either as federate or as a Roman general, such as had been granted barbarian leaders from Alaric to Theodoric, meant that Lombard kingship could not be welded onto a Roman administrative base.

In fact, it was the basic unit of Italian society, the city and its hinterland, which structured Lombard settlement. In the 570s and 580s a mosaic of city-units emerges, each with its Lombard duke (*dux*), whose followers had merged with local militias as bishops and landowners made agreements with barbarian 'protectors'. Paul claims that many Roman nobles were killed 'for love of gain' – claims apparently confirmed by contemporary sources – and that others were subjected to Lombard 'guests' as 'tribute-payers'.[34] The long experience of north Italian cities in settling and assimilating warriors from beyond the Alps must have provided templates for a process that worked on a local level. There were no longer larger, regional, levels of political and social life, no wider ties based on administrative circumscriptions or landholding that could structure barbarian settlement or political allegiance. In this situation, each of the 35 or so Lombard dukes simply allied with the exarch at Ravenna, or with Frankish invaders, or ignored both, as it suited them.[35] Presumably Ravenna's strategy of divide-and-rule aimed at the submission of the Lombard cities, and their absorption into the empire. The integration of barbarian federates on what was now the imperial frontier must have seemed a likely outcome to many observers.

That the Lombard duchies were not assimilated into Constantinople's Italian province reflects both the ultimate military weakness of Ravenna, and the inability of the empire to provide a framework within which these barbarised and militarised societies could comfortably fit. In 584, those Lombard dukes who had submitted to the latest Frankish invasion elected Authari, the son of the king who had been murdered in 574, as their king. The political context for the renewal of the kingship is unclear: the Frankish invasion had been encouraged by the Byzantines, but it was the Frankish invaders who encouraged the dukes to elect Authari, and the Lombard kings continued to pay an annual tribute to their Frankish 'overlords' until 616. What functions the dukes initially assigned to Authari, other than warleader, is unclear. Paul the Deacon reports that the dukes agreed to give up half of their *substantiae* – literally, 'substance' – to the king, but as always he writes with hindsight and the story of an agreement over the division of revenues at the inception of the kingship must have served as a historical template legitimating arrangements once a fully-fledged kingdom was established. Clearly some transfer of resources to allow the creation of a viable kingship was agreed, but Paul's choice of terminology, in a passage probably based on the now lost early seventh-century history of Secundus of Trento, may suggest a transfer of moveable wealth derived from plunder and tribute to create a royal treasury, the crucial institution for the functioning of any warrior kingship.[36] Byzantine blandishments and renewed Frankish invasions were Authari's primary obstacles through the last decades of the sixth century, but we must take care with Paul the

Deacon's suggestion that Authari maintained central control over the dukes as they submitted, constituting as it does a foundation charter for Lombard kingship rooted in hindsight. Certainly the duchies of Spoleto and Benevento in central and southern Italy remained aloof and uninvolved, and in the northeast revolts and rebellions by individual cities and their dukes punctuate Paul's narrative of the seventh century.

Authari's campaigning ensured that the revived kingship survived, but it was under his successors that the Lombard kingdom developed as a viable political system for northern Italy. The crucial role here seems to have been played by Authari's widow, Theudelinda, and then continued by her daughter, Gundperga. Theudelinda was a daughter of Garipald, king of the Bavarians, a new grouping that was coalescing from the remnants of the former Roman provincial population on the Danube frontier, like the Lombards under loose Frankish overlordship. She had married Authari in 589 to confirm an alliance between the two formerly neighbouring peoples. These Bavarian contacts were to prove important in stabilising the nascent Lombard kingdom: the alliance secured the route across the Alps and into northern Italy that had been used by generations of barbarian warlords since the fourth century.

Theudelinda's primary importance, however, was in transmitting and developing the office of king. On Authari's death in 590, the succession was peacefully managed as Theudelinda married the duke of Turin, Agilolf, who thus became king. Theudelinda was able to ensure the succession of her and Agilolf's son, Adaloald, at the age of 14 in 616, ruling jointly alongside him until his death in 626. After 626, Theudelinda's role in managing the succession was taken up by her daughter Gundperga: a political crisis over the succession was averted in 626 by her marriage to Arioald, duke of Turin, who thus became king; and on Arioald's death in 636, the crown passed to Gundperga's new husband, Rothari duke of Brescia. The peaceful management of the succession was vital, given the potential danger of civil war in a system where individual duchies might easily secede. Theudelinda's initial role in Agilolf's succession must have been helped by the fact that as a newcomer and outsider to the Lombard political scene she was in a position to broker an agreement acceptable to all parties. Certainly, the events of 626 involved Gundperga playing a central role negotiating with several rival factions. The roles of Theudelinda and Gundperga in stabilising the kingship echo that of Amalaswintha, Theodoric's daughter, in the last years of the Ostrogothic kingdom. As women whose informal influence included the supervision of the royal household, they were well placed to build ties amongst the elite, and by their marriages they were able to ensure that the kingship passed to the most able adult warleader, whilst guaranteeing continuity at the heart of the kingdom. In fact, Lombard kings continued to associate themselves with Theudelinda's progeny down to 712, usually by marrying into the line after coming to the throne on account of their political power. Thus the coherence of the kingdom, at least in northern Italy, was established, as the dukes could aspire to the kingship, and so were drawn into the politics of the palace through competition for royal office, whilst the creation of dynastic continuity through association with Theudelinda's line ensured that the circulation of kingship did not create instability at the centre.

Hence Lombard Italy, like the Visigothic kingdom, quickly evolved into a court polity with a fixed focal point, the royal palace at Pavia. But the Lombard practice of association within a single dynasty meant there was no need for the complex attempts to regulate the struggle for the succession through legislation that was such a feature of the Visigothic kingdom.

These royal women were far more than 'peace-weavers' working informally in the background. Theudelinda, in particular, is credited in the sources with agency independent of her husbands and sons. Her correspondence with Pope Gregory the Great shows her both managing the international relations of her kingdom, and managing the sensitive but vital issue of relations with the church, divided as it was not only between Arians and Catholics, but also between those Catholics who supported the imperial line in the 'three chapters controversy' and those, like Theudelinda, who were Catholic but opposed imperial policy. The foundation of a royal palace at Monza, complete with a basilica dedicated to St John the Baptist, was also Theudelinda's initiative. This was Theudelinda's royal place, where part of the royal treasury was permanently kept, and for which she procured from Rome phials of holy oil that had touched the relics of Roman martyrs. Paul the Deacon, doubtless seeking to explain the fall of the Lombard kingdom to Charlemagne, reported that it had been prophesied the Lombards would survive as long as the basilica did: that is, at Monza Theudelinda had ensured that her people enjoyed the supernatural protection of St John the Baptist. It was also Theudelinda who first sought to record a Lombard past which could underwrite Lombard identity in the present. Her close advisor Secundus, bishop of Trent, recorded the history of the Lombards under her patronage. This work is now lost, but possibly followed the model of Theodoric and his commissioning of a written history that gave the Goths a past to rival the Romans from Cassiodorus. The palace at Monza was decorated with frescoes recording the deeds and customs of the Lombards, which were studied by Paul the Deacon almost two centuries later. This queenly role in commemorating the past and securing supernatural protection may relate to the responsibility of women to nurture family identity through prayer and commemoration, but here it was transposed into a public role that made the queen responsible for her people. It was continued through the seventh century, judging by the actions of Queen Rodelinda in 670 in founding the monastery of St Maria in Pavia, by then the royal capital, to commemorate those Lombards who died far from their families and whose memory was therefore in danger of neglect.[37]

Theudelinda's career carved out a public role for the queen, which her daughter and later successors could draw on, and it was also in Theudelinda's time that the public image of the king was developed. There are consistent traditions in a number of sources which present the spear as a symbol of royal status, and which must have their roots in the pre-Italian period of Lombard history, but in the decades around 600 regalia instantly recognisable across the Mediterranean world were adopted. Now that the constitutional fiction that had presented earlier barbarian regimes as in some sense 'kingdoms of the empire' was no longer tenable, kings like Agilolf could take on the trappings of sovereignty. It was to the royal treasury at Theudelinda's basilica in Monza that Agilolf gave a votive crown, now lost, in which he was styled 'king of all Italy', and a depiction of Agilolf on a reliquary shows the adoption of the status symbols of Roman and Byzantine rulers – throne, crown, orb with cross, and the insignia of divinely granted victory – as well as war gear and barbarian long hair, beard and moustache.[38]

Italy as a warrior society

The Lombard political system as it evolved into the seventh century stands out amongst the barbarian kingdoms of western Europe on account of its urban nature. Throughout the kingdom's existence, its basic units were the duchies, each centred on a city and its hinterland. As a result, it was made up of a network of compact and tightly organised units right through the seventh and eighth centuries, when the Visigothic and Frankish kingdoms saw the emergence of a smaller number of looser regional units. The high profile of the duchies was possible because of the continued importance of cities as focal points for the social activity of local landowners, even as urban populations declined and the fabric of urban life was transformed. Not every Roman urban centre survived as a Lombard duchy: we are dealing with a process of selective and competitive adaptation, most obviously with the large southern duchies of Spoleto and Benevento, which were effectively principalities encompassing many Roman *civitates*.

Given the importance of cities in Lombard political life, so evident from the sources, it is surprising that the survival of urbanism in early medieval Italy was ever a matter for debate. Yet it is only in the last generation or so that scholarship has moved on from arguing about whether urban life survived to examining the specific ways in which cities were transformed. In large part, earlier reservations about early medieval urbanism were a result of the long shadow cast over Italy's past by the Roman past, and the city-states of the later Middle Ages and the Renaissance. Archaeologists and historians were conditioned to look for a particular kind of city life, and trained to analyse particular forms of evidence – such as monumental public buildings and equally monumental and public inscriptions – that were the key to understanding classical cities. Early medieval urbanism produced very little tractable evidence of this form, and its remains simply did not look like anything that matched classical or Renaissance preconceptions about city life. As a result, early medieval remains were described as evidence for ghost towns of impoverished settlers huddling in ruins they could not repair, or garden cities which were no different from the surrounding countryside. Some smaller towns did go under: Roman Italy was highly urbanised and a number of sites had a single *raison d'être*, the disappearance of which was fatal, as at Luni where the collapse of the marble trade and the silting of the harbour led to abandonment. But Italy remained an urban society with a dense network of cities, the functions and structure of which we are slowly beginning to understand. Changing perceptions have partly been shaped by developments in excavation, which have allowed early medieval adaptation, division, reuse and indeed redevelopment of Roman buildings to be more fully understood, and improved our awareness of construction in wood, which became more common in our period. Early medieval cities looked different from their predecessors. Churches increasingly defined their topography, and within city walls we often find clusters of habitation with some cultivation around them, with urban space effectively privatised and the urban economy having very little role in terms of intensive or specialised production. But cities were still the focal points of public action, which is why they underpinned the basic structures of Lombard state and society.

The context for the emergence of the duchies was the collapse of the intermediate layers of government that had stood between city councils and the courts of Roman emperors and Ostrogothic kings, and of the patterns of extensive landowning which had underpinned senatorial power. We have no Lombard equivalent to Cassiodorus' *Variae* precisely because the forms of political communication represented – instructions and petitions passed between the ruler, the functionaries of the central administration and the senatorial class – had ceased. Lombard laws and royal documents simply issue royal instructions, made at the court or in public assemblies: they are not addressed to an administrative machine, but simply assume an audience of local landowners and a system of local courts and city notaries embedded in the urban fabric of Italian society.

The process of 'Lombardisation' in the decades around 600 had not even involved the takeover of what survived of the infrastructure of provincial government: that remained answerable to the exarch in Ravenna. Instead, we simply have contingents of Lombards led by their dukes, attached to their cities and answerable to their king. Thus there is no sign of any real continuation of Roman taxation. The politics of the seventh-century Lombard kingdom were the politics of land: when Paul discusses the origins of ducal power, he refers to their *substantiae*, a term more closely aligned with income from landholding than with tax allocation. The duchies, in other words, adjusted the urban traditions of Italian society to new administrative and political structures that were necessary given the collapse of provincial government. This lack of direct administrative continuity, resulting in a conscious adaptation of a surviving urban landscape, is eloquently shown by the pattern of residences of the Lombard kings. Palaces were established in a number of northern cities, but Lombard rulers favoured new palaces, as at Monza, or new developments on old sites as at Milan. Even Pavia, which emerged as the fixed centre for the kingdom by the reign of Rothari at the very latest, was a city whose Roman past was modest, and devoid of a special administrative or political role.

Quite how cities were administered is unclear. Italian bishops were far less dominant within their cities than their counterparts in Gaul and Hispania. There, the political crisis of the fifth century had encouraged the senatorial class to take up episcopal office to preserve its position, whilst in Italy senators had by and large remained tied into the politics of the imperial and Ostrogothic courts and aloof from episcopal office. Whilst bishops were significant landowners and powerful players in local politics, on the level of the city Lombard dukes were able to establish oversight over local courts and justice – a lucrative source of income as well as patronage – as well as military leadership. Ultimately, in Italy it was the Lombard dukes, not bishops, who took over the functions traditionally associated with city councils; when the cities of Byzantine Italy united in revolt against Leo III in the 720s, they likewise elected their own dukes as their leaders, where before governors had been appointed by the exarch in Ravenna.

The continued attachment of landowning elites to city life meant that local politics was city politics, and city politics was essentially secular. The absence of strong episcopal leadership was paralleled at the regnal level. There is no Lombard equivalent to the rich synodal tradition of the Visigothic kingdom, or the active and collective involvement of the church in Frankish politics. Whilst bishops were inevitably influential figures who might act as royal advisors, on a structural level the church did not underpin the kingdom. The proximity of Rome and continuing imperial interests in Italy prevented the church from uniting to underwrite the Lombard kingdom. Whilst bishops might happily operate within the Lombard kingdom or even serve the Lombard kings, the papacy remained loyal to the empire and vehemently anti-Lombard because of the military threat to Rome, and many Italian bishops remained uneasy about the possibility of secession into a local church serving a particular kingdom, rather than an universal church tied, however indirectly, to the empire. Thus in negotiations with the papacy in 591, bishops in Lombard-controlled Aquileia raised the very real fear shared by all parties that theirs might become an *ecclesia in gentibus*, a church of barbarian peoples outside the empire.[39] So the institutional weight of the Italian church could not be placed behind the court of Pavia, precisely because the Italian church was not coterminous with the Lombard kingdom.

In any case, the rhetoric of popes and imperial officials condemned the Lombards as Arian heretics, which made co-operation difficult. Claims about Lombard Arianism may mask a far more complex situation, and continued to be pressed after the official end of Arianism. Procopius, writing before Lombard power in Italy made Lombard religion a political issue, presented the Lombards as orthodox Catholics, whilst it is clear that amongst the elite of the late sixth- and early seventh-century Lombard kingdom confessional allegiance had no impact on political affiliation, and that there were a variety of religious persuasions, often even within the same family. The Catholic Theudelinda played an important role in negotiating Lombard relationships with the church, as is shown by her correspondence with Pope Gregory the Great, and this role may have been continued by her daughter Gundperga, also Catholic, whilst kings such as Agilolf were Arian. Indeed, the slow erosion of Lombard Arianism in the seventh century is more or less invisible, to the extent that any notion of conversion or of any concerted campaign or dramatic action, as had been the case with the Visigoths, is impossible.

The religious issue had political relevance not because of Lombard antipathy or otherwise to the Catholic church of northern Italy, but because of divisions within the Italian church that predated the Lombard settlement, and particularly the opposition of northern Italian bishops to what they saw as imperial meddling in matters of doctrine. The so-called 'three chapters controversy' in particular meant that sections of the northern Italian church remained in formal dispute with the imperial position through the late sixth and seventh centuries. The possibility of these ecclesiastical divisions feeding through into politics was a real threat to Byzantine interests, and also potentially to the papacy. The papacy remained committed to the empire, if wary of imperial intervention in doctrinal matters, and so attempted to heal the division, but it also made it difficult for Lombard rulers to deal with the church, in that it forced them into the anti-three chapter camp, on the opposite side to the pope. Indeed, from 606 to 698 there was a formal schism in the northeast – which closely mirrored the political frontier between Lombard and imperial possessions – between bishops who were in favour of or in opposition to the imperial position on the 'three chapters', the former loyal to the bishop of Byzantine-controlled Grado, the latter to Aquileia in Lombard territory. By reinforcing these political divisions, this dispute may have aided the consolidation of the Lombard kingdom, but it also ensured that the north Italian episcopate remained fundamentally and bitterly divided throughout the seventh century.

Lombard kings, like their contemporaries elsewhere in the west, were avid founders of monasteries and endowers of churches, who styled themselves as rulers by divine grace. But their political system remained largely insulated from doctrinal controversy. Perhaps this was largely because of a deliberate policy of non-alignment, and a refusal to make religious allegiance a live issue, given its potential to divide opinion within the church, and also within the court at Pavia and the Lombard establishment. But this insulation was ultimately only possible because of the survival of a strong network of city-units led by secular figures in the duchies. It was the continuity of this local infrastructure that underpinned the involvement of Lombard kings in that most Roman of ruling activities, law-giving. In 643 Rothari inaugurated a rich tradition of law-giving that continued to the reign of Aistulf in the mid-eighth century, whilst the Lombard laws continued to be copied and used down to the eleventh century. The edict of Rothari was promulgated in the royal palace at Pavia. Whilst in its prologue it presented itself as a collection of useful and wise customs which had been passed on by elders and agreed by the Lombard army, Rothari's Roman advisors with their legal expertise played a central role in drafting the law-code. There was a strong ideological element in law-giving. Rothari's edict included the first written version of the Lombard origin legend, and a genealogy which made him the seventeenth king of the Lombards, just as Cassiodorus had claimed Athalaric was the seventeenth king of the Goths, drawing a comparison with Roman history in which Romulus, founder of Rome, was the seventeenth king since Aeneas. But this was not just a piece of ideological window-dressing. The regular issuing of new laws by Rothari's successors indicates a continuing demand for practical legal rulings in a society in which a system of local courts, judges and scribes survived.[40]

Royal law-giving did not aim to draw distinctions between Lombard and Roman subjects by creating a separate regime of Lombard law for one segment of the population. Lombard kings declared that 'the law of the Lombards ... is well known to be open to all', whilst surviving charters (documents of legal practice) from the eighth century indicate that individuals could appeal to either traditional Roman legal practice or the Lombard law of the kings.[41] The thickening of the evidence for social organisation at a grass roots level with the survival of charters through monastic and episcopal archives from the eighth century points to a society which, in its basics, rested on traditional Roman practice in matters of property law and the establishment of title. And not only churches kept archives: Ghittia, a widow turned nun, had an inventory of her effects which listed 88 legal documents relating to her family drawn up and preserved, whilst the childless landowner Totto of Campione left his family archive of around 20 documents relating to a handful of villages in the Alpine foothills around Lake Como, along with the church he had founded on his estate, to the archbishop of Milan.[42] The law-codes likewise reflect the continuation of centuries-old Roman practices on this grass roots level. It is in matters of criminal law that Lombard terminology, and legal ideas with no roots in Roman practice, emerge, with for example the tariffs of compensation with which amends could be made for everything from scandalous insults to horse thieving.

When we come to the eighth century, it is possible to begin to reconstruct the social structures that gave these ideas their currency, thanks to the thickening of documentary evidence. What emerges quite clearly is the limited scale of the landowning and local focus of even the richest echelons of landowning society. In our surviving records, estates tend to cluster in the hinterland of one city, and individual families may even have identified themselves with a particular city or locality. The royal retainer (*gasindus regis*) Taio, for example, owned a dozen land parcels, some little more than tenant farms, concentrated around Bergamo, the city with which he identified himself, and Verona; his royal connections meant that he also had a residence close to the court at Pavia. Entrance into the world of court politics and patronage could lead to considerable mobility, as Paul the Deacon's career spanning Friuli, Monte Cassino, Benevento and Pavia shows even before the admittedly exceptional circumstances which led to his presence at Charlemagne's court, but there is little evidence for the acquisition of property interests on a similar scale. Paul's attachment to his family's primary residence, a townhouse in Friuli, is clear from the story he tells of its rebuilding by his grandfather's friends and relatives after an Avar raid in the seventh century. By the eighth century, some large landowners may have been resident in country seats supported by rural estates: for example, the Lombard aristocrat Walfred founded a monastery on his country seat at Monteverdi in Tuscany in the middle decades of the century. But these estates existed alongside urban dwellings, and the relatively small scale and narrow range of aristocratic landholding meant that the public life of the city could not be bypassed as a means of exercising local power. When Aistulf attempted to differentiate in his legislation between different levels of the landowning elite, the minimum holding for a member of the highest stratum was seven farmsteads: a far cry from the scattered estates and huge incomes enjoyed by Roman senators, or even the far-flung and large-scale landholdings of the most powerful members of the contemporary Frankish aristocracy.[43]

In the context of these relatively small-scale landholdings, gifts of royal land played a central role in binding together the polity. The Lombard kings, and the dukes of Benevento in the south, were far and away the largest landowners in Italy, with the possible exception of the popes; indeed, they were effectively the only large-scale landowners, controlling perhaps ten per cent of the countryside of the northern plain. Relatively little of this land was exploited directly: the royal household and palaces needed supplying, but Lombard courts were urban, and kingship relatively sedentary at Pavia. So most royal land was made up of small-scale parcels, no different from those that were the basis of aristocratic wealth, and kings operated a closely defined system of gift-giving, binding local landowners to them. Some landowners even became royal retainers (*gasindi*) like Taido, or *gastalds*, who ran royal estates. Neither *gasindi* nor *gastalds* were royal officials in the sense that either we, or an afficionado of late-Roman administration like Cassiodorus, would understand the term: they were bound into the service of the king, and might perform specific missions to guard his interests or manage his estates, but they were not responsible for the operation of government. A hint at the scale of royal gift-giving comes from family archives like those of Ghittia or Totto, both of whom preserved documents of this nature. That Ghittia's family could receive a dozen tiny gifts close on the heels of one another, and that a small-time landowner who dominated a few villages like Totto was a recipient of royal patronage, helps us understand how royal gift-giving tied the polity together, connecting local landowners to the Lombard king as well as their city and region. And gift-giving was not disinterested. It is no accident that Lombard laws gave uniquely detailed injunctions on the loyalty and service expected in return from the recipients of gifts, and detail the means of redress when these obligations were not met: here the professional legal culture of Italian notaries led to social expectations being set up in legal form.[44]

Alongside this shallow social hierarchy went a decentralised structure of landholding and estate management. Lombard estates were characteristically made up of small parcels of land, interleaved with similar parcels belonging to other landowners. Large-scale estate complexes where huge domains were cultivated by dozens of peasants were a thing of the past, as even aristocratic holdings often consisted of relatively scattered agglomerations of small parcels, farmed by peasant tenants, free or unfree. The only qualitative, as opposed to quantitative, difference between aristocratic and peasant estates in the Lombard period is the appearance, in the documentation from the eighth century on, of labour services: that is, the obligation of peasant tenants, free or unfree, to perform fixed duties for the landlord. The origins of these services remain obscure: precedents are scarce, consisting of one sixth-century papyrus. The process of Lombard conquest *may* have played a role here, if we are to trust Paul's enigmatic account of Roman senators and other Roman landowners being made 'tributaries', or divided up between, their Lombard conquerors. But whatever the origins of these services, there importance was primarily social rather than economic, as demonstrations of subordination: few landlords had holdings large or concentrated enough to adopt a classical manorial structure, with a large demesne or reserve cultivated for the lord by the labour services demanded from their tenants. The combination of relatively weak landowners and the continuing importance of urban life had important economic consequences: it meant that economic networks centred on cities as the centre of aristocratic consumption and the destination of rural produce and rent never disappeared. Even at the absolute low point of long-distance exchange, in the second quarter of the eighth century, we have indications of inter-regional economic connections and relatively sophisticated systems of exchange, such as those recorded in a document of 715 dealing with the relationships between the landowners of the Lombard cities of the Po valley and Byzantine settlements at the Po's outlet into the Adriatic.[45]

Whilst the frameworks of urban life and property law which structured Lombard Italy had been inherited from Roman antiquity, the basic ideas according to which society was organised had changed. Social status ceased to be defined in terms of civilian versus solider, Roman versus barbarian. This was a warrior society, and for all their Roman precedents, the Lombard laws are predicated on the identification of Lombard identity, legal freedom, the right to carry weapons and the obligation of free men to serve their king. Carrying weapons was now the norm, unquestioningly accepted, and legislators had to deal with the consequences of accidental or unintentional harm, and the boundaries of legitimate recourse to interpersonal violence. Given that physical coercion had underpinned the power of late Roman state and landlord, this need not be seen as pointing to an increase in violence, but it did mark the embedding of violence, and the right to exact legal revenge, throughout male free society – the worries of legislators focused on active female violence, not male weapon-bearing.

Universal military service by all adult free men was, inevitably, impossible to meet in practice. Eighth-century laws identified divisions within the free population, but continued to insist that all free men owed the king military service: those who owned a warhorse and so had warrior status (they were *exercitales* or *arimanni*, literally 'army-men') were to serve in person, but 'lesser men' were still obligated to serve the king and his army in a variety of ways. Legislators had to deal with a stratified society, but their injunctions were structured around an identification between freedom and fighting. This identification animated social structure and was the mechanism whereby individuals articulated their social status: hence the lavish display of weaponry (spears enjoyed a particular symbolic importance) and even on occasion horses amongst the grave-goods buried in a number of late sixth- and seventh-century cemeteries in the north. Weapons and wargear symbolised free status in their ritual uses among the living too. The laws of Rothari were confirmed, after a process of consultation and deliberation, 'by *gairethinx*', that is in a public assembly of free males, representatives of the Lombard army, who waved their spears in acclamation. Transfers of title to land and everyday legal transactions on the most local of levels could likewise be confirmed by the rite of *gairethinx*: that is by the performance of public rituals with weapons.[46]

The Lombard kingdom in the north provided an open political framework which landowners of all complexions could embrace. In the new Italian society born in the sixth and seventh centuries, made up of small militarised landowners, Lombard political culture was an attractive option, and the law- and gift-giving of Lombard kings tied landowning elites into a wider north Italian political system. But Lombard state-formation was ultimately compromised by the lack of active and enthusiastic structural engagement by the Italian church. Here, Lombard Arianism and ecclesiastical divisions may have played a part, but the major block was the role of the church of Rome, and its continuing ties to the imperial ideal. Even in the first half of the seventh century, when Liudprand (712–44) was carefully courting the Roman church even whilst his armies absorbed most of the remaining Byzantine territories in the north, the popes were unwilling to throw their weight behind an able and successful north Italian ruler. Papal attachment to empire and unease about their Lombard neighbours continued under Liudprand's successors, although relations between Rome and Pavia remained intermittently cordial. Ultimately, it was papal Rome which, through the agency of its Frankish allies, was to prevent the Lombard state-formation in Italy from reaching its conclusion.

Bibliographical essay

General works

On Italy, there is an excellent survey by C. Wickham, *Early Medieval Italy: Local Power and Central Authority, 400–1000* (London, 1981). The first chapters of G. Tabacco, *The Struggle for Power in Medieval Italy* (Cambridge, 1989) give a lively account of the changing derivation of political power. C. La Rocca, ed., *Short Oxford History of Italy in the Early Middle Ages, 476–1000* (Oxford, 2001) is thematic, concise and excellent, with good bibliographies, particularly on the Italian material. On Iberia, the starting-point is R. Collins, *Early Medieval Spain: Unity in Diversity, 400–1000* (London, 1983).

Primary sources

The crucial source for the Lombard kingdom in Italy is the *History of the Lombards* by Paul the Deacon, which makes for an entertaining read: tr. W. D. Foulke (Philadelphia, 1907). The Lombard laws are translated by K. F. Drew (Philadelphia, 1973). Legal documents are unfortunately unavailable in translation; for sources for Rome and the papacy, see chapter 4 above.

Visigothic narratives are much earlier and less full than Paul. Isidore of Seville's ideologically charged *History of the Goths, Sueves and Vandals* is tr. G. Ford (Brill, 1970) or by K. Wolf, *Conquerors and Chroniclers of Medieval Spain* (Liverpool, 1992); Wolf also includes the sixth-century chronicle of John of Biclar, and two crucial chronicles written in the Christian north after the Islamic victory of 711 and therefore permeated with myth-making, the *Chronicle of 752* and that of Alfonso III. The monumental Visigothic Code, which gives an impression of the sophistication of the Visigothic court, is tr. S. P. Scott (Boston, 1910), and available online at http://libro.vca.edu/vcode/visigoths.htm. For a regional perspective, the hagiographical is helpful: A. Fear, *Lives of the Visigothic Fathers* (Liverpool, 1997); for a fuller selection of writings shedding light on the Iberian church, C. W. Barlow, *Iberian Fathers* vols 1–2 (Washington, 1969). See also Julian of Toledo, *History of King Wamba*, tr. J. M. Pizarro (Washington, 2005). There are nineteenth-century translations of the some of the major Islamic accounts of al-Andalus, but this material needs handling with care: a useful selection can be gleaned from C. Melville and A. Ubaydli, *Christians and Moors in Spain* 3 (Warminster, 1992).

Visigoths

The best introduction is R. Collins, *Early Medieval Spain: Unity in Diversity, 400–1000* (London, 1983), and now his *Visigothic Spain* (Oxford, 2004); also the excellent short summary by P. Bonassie, 'Society and mentality in Visigothic

Spain', in Bonnassie, *From Slavery to Feudalism in South Western Europe* (Cambridge, 1991). A. Ferreiro, *The Visigoths in Gaul and Spain, 418–711: A Bibliography* (Leiden, 1988) is an invaluable work of reference. The older treatment of E. A. Thompson, *The Goths in Spain* (Oxford, 1969), is still useful, although there are problems with the attempt to detect precise changes in law and administration from omissions and inclusions in the law-code. P. D. King, *Law and Society in the Visigothic Kingdom* (Cambridge, 1972) also gives an excellent overview, whilst some of the essays in E. James, ed., *Visigothic Spain: New Approaches* (Oxford, 1980) still offer new approaches a quarter of a century later. Two more recent collections also include much important material: A. Ferreiro, ed., *The Visigoths: Culture and Society* (Leiden, 1999) and P. Heather, ed., *The Visigoths from the Migration Period to the Seventh Century* (Woodbridge, 1999), both of which also provide useful archaeological as well as historical studies. Collins' articles are collected in *Law, Culture and Regionalism in Early Medieval Spain* (Aldershot, 1992).

For the fifth century, see the discussions of Hydatius by R. Burgess in J. Drinkwater and H. Elton, eds, *Fifth-Century Gaul: A Crisis of Identity?* (Cambridge, 1990) and in R. Mathison and H. Sivan, eds, *Shifting Frontiers in Late Antiquity* (London, 1996); also J. Arce in J. Jarnut, H.-W. Goetz and W. Pohl, eds, *Gentes and Regna* (Leiden, 2003). The sixth century remains little studied, although the *Lives of the Fathers of Mérida* has inspired good work on that city and its relationship to the kingdom: see the papers by Collins in E. James, ed., *Visigothic Spain: New Approaches*; Wood in P. Heather, ed., *The Visigoths* and J. Arce in I. Wood and E. Chrysos, eds, *East and West: Modes of Communcation* (Leiden, 2000), and now S. Castellanos, 'The significance of social unanimity in a Visigothic hagiography: keys to an ideological screen', *Journal of Early Christian Studies* 11 (2003). On Leovigild and Hermenegild, see J.N. Hillgarth, 'Coins and chronicles: propaganda in sixth-century Spain and the Byzantine background', *Historia* 15 (1966), now in J. N. Hillgarth, *Visigothic Spain, Byzantium and the Irish* (London, 1985), and M. Girves, 'Commentiolus, Magister militum Spaniae missus a Mauricio Augusto contra hostes barbaros. The Byzantine perspective on the Visigothic conversion to Catholicism', *Romano-Barbarica* 14 (1996–97). For the Byzantine enclaves in the southeast see G. Ripoll in W. Pohl, H. Reimitz and I. Wood, eds, *The Transformation of Frontiers from Late Antiquity to the Carolingians* (Leiden, 2000).

On identity, and relations between Goths and the provincial population (called Hispano-Romans by historians, but not by contemporaries), see G. Ripoll Lopez, 'The arrival of Visigoths in Hispania: population problems and the process of acculturation', and D. Claude, 'Remarks about Visigoths and Hispano-Romans in the seventh century', in W. Pohl and H. Reimitz, eds, *Strategies of Distinction* (Leiden, 1998); also W. Liebeschuetz, 'Citizen status and law' and H. Sivan, 'The appropriation of Roman law in barbarian hands: Roman-barbarian marriage in Visigothic Gaul and Spain' in the same volume. For a different, literary approach see S. Teillet, *Des Goths au nation gothique* (Paris, 1984).

The fundamental work on the political culture of the Visigothic kingdom is now P. Diaz and M. Valverde, 'The theoretical strength and practical weakness of the Visigothic monarchy of Toledo', in J. Nelson and F. Theuws, eds, *Rituals of Power from Late Antiquity to the Early Middle Ages* (Leiden, 2000); see also Diaz, 'Visigothic political institutions', in Heather, ed., *The Visigoths* (1999), and I. Velazquez in H.-W. Goetz, J. Jarnut and W. Pohl, eds, *Gentes and Regna* (Leiden, 2001). For the tax system see S. Castellanos, 'The political nature of taxation in Visigothic Spain', *Early Medieval Europe* 12 (2003), and for the army D. Perez Sanchez, *El ejército en la sociedad visigoda* (Salamanca, 1989).

The approach from the legislation can be usefully juxtaposed with a rare insight into Visigothic political practice allowed by Julian of Toledo's highly polemical account over the succession to Wamba: see R. Collins, 'Julian of Toledo and the royal succession in seventh-century Spain', in P. Sawyer and I. Wood, eds, *Early Medieval Kingship* (Leeds, 1977) and M. De Jong, 'Adding insult to injury: Julian of Toledo and his Historia Wambae', in Heather, ed., *The Visigoths.*

The legal emphasis of the source material can make social history difficult to access, but for attempts to use the law-code see e.g. D. Claude, 'Freedmen in the Visigothic kingdom' in James, ed., *Visigothic Spain*; L. Garcia Moreno, 'Legitimate and illegitimate violence in Visigothic law', in G. Halsall, ed., *Violence and Society in the Early Medieval West* (Woodbridge, 1998), and his 'From coloni to servi: a chapter in the history of the Visigothic peasantry', *Klio* 83 (2000). A different approach, based on the hagiography, is attempted in a number of recent studies by S. Castellanos, e.g. *Poder social, aristocracies y hombre santo en la Hispania visigoda: la Vita Aemiliani de Braulio de Zaragoza* (Logrono, 1998).

It is only very recently that full use has begun to be made of the archaeological evidence. See now the important new study by K. Carr, *Vandals to Visigoths: Rural Settlement Patterns in Early Medieval Spain* (Michigan, 2002). See also the new synthesis of archaeological and documentary evidence advanced in S. Castellanos and M. Viso, 'Local articulation of central power in the northwest of the Iberian peninsula, 500–1000', *Early Medieval Europe* 13 (2005).

For the bishops, ecclesiastical organisation and social integration, see now R. Stocking, *Bishops, Councils and Consensus in the Visigothic Kingdom, 589–633* (Michigan, 2000), and her, 'Martianus, Aventinus and Isidore: provincial councils in seventh-century Spain', *Early Medieval Europe* 6.2 (1997). On Christianisation the fundamental article is by J. Hillgarth, 'Popular religion in Visigothic Spain', in James, ed., *Visigothic Spain*, reprinted in his *Visigothic Spain, Byzantium and the Irish* (London, 1985). On monasticism, see P. Diaz in A. Ferreiro, ed., *The Visigoths*, and in M. De Jong and F. Theuws, eds, *Topographies of Power in the Early Middle Ages* (Leiden, 2001). Anti-Jewish legislation is discussed most recently by W. Drews, 'Jews as pagans', *Early Medieval Europe* 9 (2001).

Much work has been done on the cultural achievements of the Visigothic kingdom, and particularly the work of Isidore of Seville. The classic treatment is still J. Fontaine, *Isidore de Seville et la culture classique dans l'Espagne wisigothique* (Paris, 1959–83: 3 vols); see also M. Reydellet, *La royauté dans la littérature latine de Sidoine Apollinaire à Isidore de Seville* (Rome, 1981). In English, J. N. Hillgarth's collected essays *Visigothic Spain, Byzantium and the Irish* (London, 1985) are useful. On historical writing, Hillgarth's collection includes 'Historiography in Visigothic Spain'; also P. Bassett, 'The use of history in the chronicle of Isidore of Seville', *History & Theory* 15 (1976), R. Collins, 'Isidore, Maximus and the Historia Gothorum', in A. Scharer and G. Scheibelreiter, eds, *Historiographie im frühen Mittelalter* (Vienna, 1994). On the laity and written culture see R. Collins, 'Literacy and the laity in early medieval Spain', in R. McKitterick, ed., *The Uses of Literacy in Early Medieval Europe* (Cambridge, 1989).

Al-Andalus and its neighbours

For the wider Islamic context, see bibliography for chapter 5 above; the historiographical ramifications of 711 are best followed through P. Linehan's essays collected in *History and Historians of Medieval Spain* (Oxford, 1993), and in *Past and Present in Medieval Spain* (Aldershot, 1992) esp. ch. 1. On the 'Arab conquest' and its aftermath, the best introduction comes in the first chapters of H. Kennedy, *Muslim Spain and Portugal* (London, 1996) and R. Fletcher, *Moorish Spain* (London, 1994). R. Collins, *The Arab Conquest of Spain, 711–97* 2nd edition (Oxford, 1994) is a fuller account; compare two recent articles by A. Christys, in J. Jarnut, H.-W Goetz and W. Pohl, eds, *Gentes und Regna* (Leiden, 2001) and W. Pohl and H. Reimitz, *Integration und Herrschaft* (Vienna, 2002). E. Lévi-Provençal, *Histoire de l'Espagne musulmane*, 2 vols (Leiden and Paris, 1950) remains classic.

A selection of useful articles on a variety of topics is translated into English in M. Marin, *The Formation of al-Andalus I: History and Society* (Aldershot, 1998); this makes a good starting-point for serious study. T. Glick, *Islamic and Christian Spain in the Early Middle Ages* (Princeton, 1979) offers an interesting approach to economic and social differences, whilst P. Guichard, *Structures sociales 'orientales' et 'occidentales' dans l'Espagne musulmane* (Paris, 1977) investigates the impact of Arab and Berber social organisation.

For the Christian majority and their Muslim rulers, there is now A. Christys, *Christians and Muslims in al-Andalus 711–1000* (Aldershot, 2001). The flashpoint of conflict between Christians and Muslims, caused by the Cordoba martyrs movement of the mid-ninth century, has been far better studied than the normal situation of co-existence: see J. Coope, *The Martyrs of Cordoba* (Oxford, 1995) and K. Wolf, *Christian Martyrs in Muslim Spain* (Cambridge, 1988); for Frankish interest, J. Nelson, 'The Franks, the martyrology of Usuard and the martyrs of Cordoba', *Studies in Church History* 30 (1993). For Cordoba as a court city, see Christys in M. de Jong and F. Theuws, eds, *Topographies of Power from Late Antiquity to the Early Middle Ages* (Leiden, 2001).

On the nature of the frontier between al-Andalus and the Christian principalities of the north, there is important new work by E. Manzano Moreno, *La frontero de Al-Andalus en epoca de les Omayas* (Madrid, 1991), to which the author gives useful English introductions in D. Power and N. Standen, eds, *Frontiers in Question* (London, 1998) and in R. Hitchcock, ed., *Christian-Islamic Interaction in Medieval Spain* (London, 1991). On the Christian polities of the north there is surprisingly little, particularly in English, on the eighth and ninth centuries: scholarship has concentrated on the processes of social change and political expansion in the tenth and eleventh centuries, and has been overshadowed by grand narratives about regional and national identity. Collins' *Early Medieval Spain*, which has a good bibliography, is the best starting-point. On Carolingian Catalonia, the best English study is R. Collins, 'Charles the Bald and Wifred the Hairy', in J. Nelson and M. Gibson, eds, *Charles the Bald: Court and Kingdom* (Aldershot, 2000), and the classic work is that of R. d'Abadal, e.g. his *Els premiers comtes Catalans* (Barcelona, 1958).

Lombard Italy

The Lombards are well studied, in part because they gave their name to the north, economically and politically dominant within the modern Italian state, and the historiography has thus seen them as the makers of medieval Italy. In addition to the general treatments of Italy above N. Christie, *The Lombards* (Oxford, 1995) is a useful account of the archaeology. R. Harrison, *The Early State and the Towns: Forms of Integration in Lombard Italy 568–774* (Lund, 1993) exhaustively assembles the evidence for the importance of cities within the Lombard state. The current state of play – which is exciting and lively – can be judged from two recent conferences: W. Pohl and M. Diesenberger, eds, *Die Langobarden: Herrschaft und Identität* (Vienna, 2006) and C. Wickham, ed., *The Lombards from the Migration Period to the Eighth Century* (Woodbridge, 2007).

On Paul the Deacon, the key source, see W. Pohl 'Memory, identity and power in Lombard Italy', in M. Innes and Y. Hen, eds, *The Uses of the Past in the Early Middle Ages* (Cambridge, 2000) with references and summaries of the same author's work in German; responding to W. Goffart, *The Narrators of Barbarian History* (1988), chapter 5, and see also R. McKitterick, 'Paul the Deacon and the Franks', *Early Medieval Europe* 8 (1999), and D. Bullough, 'Ethnic history and the Carolingians: an alternative reading of Paul the Deacon', in T. P. Wiseman and C. Holdsworth, eds, *The Inheritance of Historiography AD 350–900* (Exeter, 1986). For Paul in proper intellectual and social context, see the essays in P. Chiesa, ed., *Paulo Diacono e il Friuli altomedievale (sec. VI–X)* (Spoleto, 2001).

On the Lombard settlement of Italy, see now W. Pohl, 'The empire and the Lombards: treaties and negotiations in the sixth century', in Pohl, ed., *Kingdoms of the Empire: The Integration of Barbarians in Late Antiquity* (Leiden, 1997); for the making of the Lombard people and kingdom, J. Jarnut in Jarnut, H.-W. Goetz and W. Pohl, eds, *Gentes und Regna* (Leiden, 2001). On Theudelinda, see R. Balzaretti, 'Theudelinda "most glorious queen": gender and power in Lombard Italy', *Medieval History Journal* 2 (1999). On Lombard identity and law, Pohl, 'Memory, identity and power in Lombard Italy' and B. Pohl-Resl, 'Legal practice and ethnic identity in Lombard Italy', in W. Pohl and H. Reimitz, eds, *Strategies of Distinction: The Construction of Ethnic Communities, 300–800* (Leiden, 1998). N. Everett, 'Literacy in Lombard government', *Early Medieval Europe* 9 (2000) and *Literacy in Lombard Italy 568–774* (Cambridge, 2001) look at the use of writing. R. Harrison, 'Political rhetoric and political ideology in Lombard Italy' and S. Gasparri, 'Kingship rituals and ideology in Lombard Italy', in F. Theuws and J. L.

Nelson, eds, *Rituals of Power from Late Antiquity to the Early Middle Ages* (Leiden, 2000), give accounts of Lombard political culture, although their identification of Germanic pagan influences could be contested.

On Italian society and the Lombard landowning classes, there is much exciting new work using the documentary evidence. C. Wickham, 'Aristocratic power in eighth-century Lombard Italy', in A. C. Murray, ed., *After Rome's Fall* (Toronto, 1998), is crucially important on the structure of the Lombard aristocracy; see also Wickham's 'Land disputes and their settlement in Lombard and Carolingian Italy, 700–875', in W. Davies and P. Fouracre, eds, *The Settlement of Disputes in Early Medieval Europe* (Cambridge, 1986), for law and justice. For the possibilities opened up by a detailed document-based study of rural society, see M. Costambeys, *Piety and Property in Early Medieval Italy* (Cambridge, 2007), drawing on the Farfa material.

On the complex issue of Lombard religious allegiance see S. Fanning, 'Lombard Arianism reconsidered', *Speculum* 56 (1981), W. Pohl, 'Deliberate ambiguity: the Lombards and Christianity', in G. Armstrong and I. Wood, eds, *Converting Individuals and Christianising Peoples* (Leeds, 2001). On the growth of rural monastic foundations see M. Costambeys, 'Innovation and Gregorian tradition in early medieval Italian monasticism', in Y. Hen and M. Innes, eds, *The Uses of the Past in the Early Middle Ages* (Cambridge, 2000).

Recent work on burial archaeology has similarly started to engage with some of the approaches pioneered by students of the northwestern European material. The best overview is now C. La Rocca, 'Segni di distinzione. Dai corredi funerari alle donazioni post obitum nel regno longobardo', in L. Paroli, ed., *L'Italia centro-settentrionale in eta longobarda* (Florence, 1997); see also for an interesting the case-study L. Jørgensen, 'Castel Trosino and Nocera Umbra: a chronological and social analysis of family burial practices in Lombard Italy', *Acta Archaeologica* 62 (1992)

The dominance of cities in Italian historiography is reflected in the fact that the major genre of local studies of this period consists of studies of urban evolution and continuity, with archaeology playing a large role, rather than histories of medieval societies. The debates of the past quarter-century are summarised by B. Ward-Perkins, 'Continuists, catastrophists and the towns of post-Roman northern Italy', *Papers of the British School at Rome* 45 (1997), which is the best starting-point. The classic arguments for continuity, which provoked debate, are those of C. La Rocca, '"Dark Ages" a Verona: edilizi privata, aree aperte e strutture publiche in una citta del'Italia settentrionale', *Archaeologia medievale* 13 (1986); in English see her 'Public buildings and urban space in northern Italy in the early medieval period' in J. Rich, ed., *The City in Late Antiquity* (London, 1992). For other case-studies see D. Bullough, 'Urban change in early medieval Italy: the example of Pavia', *Papers of the British School at Rome* 34 (1966); P. Arthur, 'Naples: a case of urban survival in the early Middle Ages?', *Mélanges de l'Ecole français de Rome* 103 (1986) and now his *Naples: From Roman Town to City-State* (London, 2002). B. Ward-Perkins, *From Classical Antiquity to the Middle Ages: Urban Public Building in Northern and Central Italy, AD 300–850* (Oxford, 1984), studies the changing face of cities. There are many useful essays in three recent collections: G. P. Brogiolo and B. Ward-Perkins, eds, *The Idea and Ideal of the Town between Late Antiquity and the Early Middle Ages* (Leiden, 1999), G. P. Brogiolo, N. Christie and N. Gauthier, eds, *Towns and their Territories from Late Antiquity to the Early Middle Ages* (Leiden, 2001), N. Christie and S. Loseby, eds, *Towns in Transition* (Aldershot, 1996).

Notes

1. Hydatius, *Chronicle*, s.a. 411, tr. R. W. Burgess (Oxford, 1993).
2. Procopius, *Wars*, ed. and tr. Dewing, 5.7.
3. *Lives of the Fathers of Mérida*, tr. A. Fear, *Lives of the Visigothic Fathers* (Liverpool, 1998); I. Velazquez, ed., *Los pizarras visigodicas* (Murcia, 1989); Jordanes, *Gothic History*, tr. C. Mierow (Philadelphia, 1915), 63, and Isidore of Seville's account of this period in his *History of the Goths*, tr. K. Wolf, *Conquerors and Chroniclers of Early Medieval Spain* (2nd ed., Liverpool, 2000).
4. The main sources for Leovigild's reign are the chronicles of John of Biclar and Isidore of Seville, both tr. Wolf, *Conquerors and Chroniclers of Early Medieval Spain* (2nd ed., Liverpool, 2000); plus *Lives of the Fathers of Mérida*, tr. Fear; for the 'senate of Cantabria' see Braulio of Saragossa's *Life of Aemilian*, tr. Fear, *Lives of the Visigothic Fathers*, 26.
5. In addition to John and Isidore's accounts see Gregory of Tours, *Histories*, tr. L. Thorpe (Harmondsworth, 1974), 5.38, 6.18, 6.40, and Gregory the Great, *Dialogues*, tr. O. Zimmerman (Washington, 1959), 3.31.
6. For the acts of III Toledo, see the translation of O. Constable, *Medieval Iberia: Translated Sources* (Philadelphia, 1997), pp. 12–20; for coins and royal images, M. Blackburn and P. Grierson, *Medieval European Coinage I: The Early Middle Ages* (Cambridge, 1990).
7. J. Vives, ed., *Concilios visigoticos e hispano-romanos* (Barcelona and Madrid, 1953), p. 54.
8. Conciliar legislation is edited by Vives, *Concilios*, but unfortunately very little is available in translation.
9. Fredegar, *Chronicle*, ed. M. Wallace-Hadrill (Oxford, 1962), 4.62
10. Fredegar, ed. Wallace-Hadrill, 4.82.
11. See Julian of Toledo, *History of King Wamba*, tr. J. M. Pizarro (Washington, 2005).
12. Isidore's *History* is tr. Wolf, *Conquerors and Chroniclers*, or by G. B. Ford (Leiden, 1970).
13. Military laws: Book 9 title 2 of the Visigothic Code, tr. Scott: tellingly not part of any longer discussion of fiscal practice or public dues, but with laws on runaway slaves and fugitives from justice.
14. S. Castellanos, 'The political nature of taxation in Visigothic Spain', *Early Medieval Europe*, 12.3 (2003) assembles the evidence from the conciliar legislation; for the Gallic comparison see chapter 7 below.
15. The major document from southern Gaul is the will of Abbo of Provence, see p. 294.

16. P. Diaz and M. Valverde in J. Nelson and F. Theuws, eds, *Rituals of Power from Late Antiquity to the Early Middle Ages* (Leiden, 1999).
17. The best insight into royal ritual and its functions, including anointing, comes in Julian of Toledo, *History of King Wamba*, tr. Pizarro.
18. Wamba's career at court: Julian of Toledo, *History of King Wamba*, tr. Pizarro, ch. 4; he acts as a representative of the see of Braga in the tenth council of Toledo.
19. The legislation is collected in Book 12 title 2 of the Visigothic Code, tr. Scott: 'On Jews and heretics'.
20. Wamba's new palace bishopric was condemned after the end of his reign at the twelfth council of Toledo.
21. Martin of Braga, *On the Castigation of Rustics*, tr. J. Hillgarth, *Paganism and Christianity, 350–700* (Philadelphia, 1986).
22. Visigothic hagiography is collected in Fear, *Lives of the Visigothic Fathers*; note that the activities of Leander and Isidore differed in their emphasis from those of the two Gregorys.
23. The date has the unanimous support of the Islamic historiographical tradition, which portrayed Visigothic collapse as instant and the result of a single campaign; but compare the more complex account given in the *Chronicle of 752*, tr. Wolf, *Conquerors and Chroniclers*, which has Roderick's defeat in 712.
24. Translated in Wolf, *Conquerors and Chroniclers*.
25. *Chronicle of 752*, tr. Wolf, a report paralleled in Islamic historiographical tradition.
26. See R. Collins, *Early Medieval Spain: Unity in Diversity 400–1000* (2nd edn, London, 2000), pp. 203–4 with notes for full references.
27. On al-Hakam see al-Maqqarī, tr. P. de Gayangos, *History of the Mohammedian Dynasties in Spain* (London, 1840–3), vol. 2, 6.3.
28. See the *Chronicle of Alfonso III*, tr. Wolf, *Conquerors and Chroniclers*, for the Asturian historiographical tradition about Covodonga and Oviedo; Alfonso II's recreation of the 'order of the Goths' comes from the *Albelda Chronicle*.
29. J. Gil, ed., *Corpus Scriptorum Muzarabicorum* (Madrid, 1973), pp. 68–78 (Elipandus letter 1, condemning Migetius), 139 (Council of Cordoba 839), and Eulogius' *Memoriale*.
30. Paul the Deacon, *History of the Lombards*, tr. W. D. Foulke (Philadelphia, 1907, repr. 2003).
31. Tacitus, *Germania*, tr. M. Winterbottom (Oxford, 1978), 40; Procopius, *Wars*, tr. Dewing, 6: 14–15, 7.25, 7.33–4.
32. For events in the Danube basin, see Theoplylact Simocatta, tr. Whitby and Whitby, 6.10.9–12, and Menander the Guardsman, tr. Blockley, frag. 12. Book 2 of Paul's *History of the Lombards* gives the Lombard tradition of their migration to Italy, but needs comparing with the passing references of contemporary sources, e.g. the chronicles of Fredegar and Marius of Avenches.
33. Paul, *History of the Lombards*, 2.9.

34. Paul, *History of the Lombards*, 2.31–2; note that this much-discussed passage concerns only Roman nobles; for contemporary witnesses of the exile or murder of high-status Romans see Marius of Avenches' *Chronicle*, ed. J. Favrod (Lausanne, 1999), s.a. 573.
35. The figure of 35 comes from Paul, *History of the Lombards*, 2.32, an account of the interregnum which names the five key dukes (of Pavia, Bergamo, Brescia, Trent and Friuli) but adds that there were 30 others; this should be treated as a loose indication.
36. Paul on Authari and the dukes: *History of the Lombards*, 3.36. Campaigns: 3.18, 27, 4.3, 13, 23.
37. For Theudelinda, Monza, and Secundus: Paul, *History*, 4.21–2, 27, and note 4.47 for Gundperga's church at Pavia 'in imitation of Theudelinda'. Secundus' lost history 3.29 and 4.40; Rodelinda: Paul, *History*, 5.34.
38. See F. Bougard, 'Public power and authority', in C. La Rocca, ed., *Italy in the Early Middle Ages* (Oxford, 2001), p. 36.
39. Gregory the Great, *Register of Letters*, 1.16.
40. Rothari's edict, tr. K. F. Drew, *The Lombard Laws* (Philadelphia, 1974).
41. Laws of Liudprand ch. 91, tr. Drew, *Lombard Laws*; B. Pohl-Resl, 'Legal practice and ethnic identity in Lombard Italy', in W. Pohl and H. Reimitz, eds, *Strategies of Distinction: The Construction of Ethnic Communities 300–800* (Leiden, 1998).
42. For Ghittia, L. Schiaperelli, ed., *Codice Diplomatico Langobardo*, 2 vols (Rome, 1929–33), vol. 2 no. 295; for Totto, S. Gasparri and C. La Rocca, eds, *Carte de Famiglia* (Rome, 2005); Italian charters, unlike those north of the Alps, survive overwhelmingly in the original; the continuous run begins *c.* 710, but around 75 per cent of pre-800 documents are preserved in the cathedral archive at Lucca; in the ninth century the transmission thickens.
43. Taido: Schiaperelli, ed., *Codice Diplomatico Langobardo*, vol. 2 no. 293; Walfred: K. Schmid, ed., *Vita Walfredi und Kloster Monteverdi* (Tübingen, 1991); social division: *Lombard Laws*, tr. Drew, Aistulf ch. 2 (750).
44. Gifts and countergifts (*launegild*) are pervasive in much of the legislation: for royal gifts specifically see e.g. Rothari 167, 177 and note 375 regulating 'private' gifts to royal agents; Liutprand 59; Aistulf 1.
45. Sixth-century labour service: Tjäder, ed., *Die nichtliterarsichen lateinischen Papyri Italiens* 2; Lombard settlement: Paul, *History of the Lombards*, 2.23 for senators being made 'tributaries' and note laws of Liudprand 59 for a royal property in the form of a 'tributary farm' (*casa tributaria*). Exchange networks in 715: L. Hartmann, ed., *Zur Wirtschaftsgeschichte Italiens im frühen Mittelalter* (Gotha, 1904), pp. 123–4.
46. Legal ritual 'by *gairethinx*': edict of Rothari 167, 172, 222, 224, 375, 386; laws of Liutprand 54, 77, 105, 140; laws of Aistulf 11, 12.

7

Gaul and Germany: the Merovingian world

Contents

Summary

Chronology

Franks and frontiers

Essay: The burial of Childeric

Conquest and conversion: the Merovingian unification of Gaul

Sixth-century society: cities, bishops and counts

The remaking of the kingdom

Map 6: Merovingian Gaul

Bishops, monasteries and aristocrats: social change in the seventh century

Courts and kingdoms in the seventh century

Bibliographical essay

Summary

In northern Gaul, it was a loose and decentralised group of tribes known to the Romans as the Franks who established themselves as the dominant military power after the middle of the fifth century. In the decades around 500, under the leadership of Clovis, one particular warband was able to establish its pre-eminence amongst the Franks, and to lead the conquest of both Roman Gaul and the regions east of the Rhine. Although the plunder and tribute generated by successful warfare was vital to the early Merovingians, the size, wealth and sophistication of the sixth-century Merovingian kingdom owed much to the Roman inheritance. The sixth and seventh centuries saw the consolidation of Merovingian and Frankish power, and also the emergence of new power structures, with the slow decay of Roman administrative institutions and the growth of a politics more directly dependent on the aristocracy.

Seventh-century kings successfully adapted to these changes, restructuring their kingdom as a series of self-standing units, the 'three kingdoms' of Neustria, Austrasia and Burgundy at the core, ringed by a series of peripheral principalities which developed under Frankish tutelage. The royal court, as the stage on which local factional struggles were settled, played a vital role in binding these units together. Throughout the seventh century, the Neustrian court in the Paris basin was politically dominant, but following prolonged crisis in the 670s the three kingdoms were effectively united under Pippin, an Austrasian aristocrat who controlled the key office of mayor of the palace. The final breakdown of this system came in the 710s, in a conflict in which one of Pippin's sons, Charles Martel, emerged victorious, but at the expense of severing the ties which bound local elites from Neustria and Burgundy, and the leaders of the peripheral principalities, into the political system.

Chronology

460s–470s	Childeric a military leader in northern Gaul
c. 481	Death of Childeric and his burial at Tournai; succession of Clovis
496	Clovis defeats Alemans at Tolbiac; traditional date for his conversion
507	Defeat of Visigoths at Vouillé; Clovis celebrates triumph at Tours
c. 511	Death of Clovis, fourfold division of his kingdom between his sons
534	Frankish conquest of Burgundy
536	Frankish takeover of Provence
561	Death of Chlothar I; fourfold division of kingdom between his sons
567	Revised threefold division following death of Charibert I
570s–600s	Recurrent civil war between rival Merovingians
594	Death of Gregory of Tours
590s–600s	Sons and grandsons of Brunhild dominant rulers
613	Austrasians and Burgundians abandon Brunhild for Clothar II
614	Council and edict of Paris
623	Dagobert I sent as subking to Austrasia
629	Death of Chlothar II; Dagobert moves to Neustria
633	Sigibert III sent as subking to Austrasia
638	Death of Dagobert; infant Clovis II succeeds in Neustria
640s–660s	Balthild, wife of Clovis II (+657), dominant in Neustria
656	Austrasian king Sigibert III dies; Childebert the Adopted succeeds
657	Neustrians capture and execute Grimoald, father of Childebert
662	Neustrians replace Austrasian king, Childebert, with Childeric II
664	Ebroin mayor of the palace in Neustria
673	Burgundians, led by Leodegar, rebel against Ebroin; civil war in west
675	Childeric II and pregnant wife murdered by Neustrians
679	End of Austrasian court and kingship; Ebroin murdered
687	Pippin and Austrasians intervene in Neustria, victorious at Tertry
687–714	Pippin dominant figure in kingdom; cultivates support in Neustria
714	Death of Pippin; Neustrians and Frisians back Chilperic II
714–19	Charles Martel defeats Neustrians

Franks and frontiers

Writing the preface to his history of his own times up to 591, Gregory, bishop of Tours, lamented the absence of any historian 'sufficiently skilled in setting things down in an orderly fashion to be able to describe the unfolding of events'.[1] The century before Gregory remains a yawning gap in our evidence: Gregory's treatment of the period before his entry into public life in the 570s is cursory, relying primarily on the reminiscences of his kin and therefore focused particularly on their aristocratic milieu in the Auvergne; for fifth-century Gaul we are largely dependent on the letters of Gregory's distant ancestor, Sidonius Apollinaris, and his circle. Gregory's pen looms large over our picture of Gaul: in addition to his rollicking *Histories*, he collected accounts of the lives and miracles of the saints of the Gallic church. Our perspective is thus essentially that of the senatorial aristocracy of southern Gaul, whose continued status in the sixth century relied on their dominance in the church. This viewpoint is very particular: Gregory's horizons were those of a bishop descended from a major landowning family in southern Gaul, and he wrote to delineate the active power of God in this world, acting through the saints and their relics which now dotted the southern Gallic countryside, and the bishops who were the preservers and protectors of saintly power. Whilst we cannot help but rely on Gregory, we also need to be aware of the extent to which we are reliant on him.

Gregory's political worldview focused on the kings of the Franks and their doings: their centrality was unquestioned, as was the fact that the position of those kings was transmitted through the blood, thanks to their membership of the Merovingian family. But about the origins of this political system, Gregory was less than well-informed: he himself expressed frustration at the lack of information on the early history of the Franks, and much of what he does tell us about the period before his own lifetime serves to explain and legitimate current arrangements.[2]

In fact, if we dispense with Gregory and use the written and archaeological fragments that survive from the fourth and fifth centuries, it is clear that the Franks emerged in northern Gaul in the context of interaction across the Rhine frontier and the eventual collapse of that frontier. Contemporary sources use the term 'Frank' intermittently, jostling alongside a series of tribal labels, to refer to the groups living on and beyond the lower Rhine. In the course of the fourth century individuals of Frankish origin played a series of high-profile roles in the Roman military from Antioch to Angers, underlining the importance of contact with Rome. The complexity of the diplomatic and political ties thus created are neatly encapsulated in the career of Silvanus, son of a Frankish general who had served Constantine: after finding success as a Roman military leader in Gaul, Silvanus was the victim of intrigues of the court, and so rebelled, proclaiming himself emperor at Cologne in 355 with support from both sides of the frontier, before being murdered. Men like Silvanus were, in origin, members of a social elite in the Frankish homeland, whose connections and status allowed them to follow a career within the empire: one of Silvanus' allies, Mallobaudes, who worked his way through the ranks to serve as a commander in the imperial bodyguard, was also reckoned to have royal status.[3]

About the Frankish society beyond the Rhine we know little. The fragments of now lost Latin histories of Renatus Frigeridus and Sulpicius Alexander that form the basis of Gregory's account of this period suggest essentially local political units ruled by petty kings.[4] What is clear is that in the course of the fifth century Frankish power was consolidated on both sides of the lower Rhine, and from there down into the northern parts of Roman Gaul. Formal agreements with the Roman authorities may have played a part in this, but Roman attentions were focused further south than this most northerly stretch of the frontier. In the resulting vacuum, established Frankish leaders from beyond the frontier would have been free to exert their domination across the Rhine, as they had done intermittently in periods of imperial weakness since the fourth century. The 'Francisation' of the frontier provinces may have simply been a recognition of the close ties that had developed across the frontier, and the military power of the Franks in a period of scant Roman resources. Roman leaders also continued to use Frankish generals in their military strategy in the west, but these generals brought Frankish warbands with them and so combined power over their Frankish followings with power within the Roman infrastructure.

One such leader was Childeric, whose activities in concert with Roman leaders in the 460s and 470s spanned Gaul from Angers to the Rhine. The sources for the activities of Childeric and his contemporaries are frustrating: bare notices of campaigns scattered in sparse contemporary sources, and confused traditions recounted a century later by Gregory of Tours. Childeric competed with Roman leaders, notably Aegidius and his son Syagrius. Some historians have taken a cue from Gregory's description of Syagrius as 'king of the Romans' to interpret this conflict as one between two well-established kingdoms, but the fifth-century reality seems more fluid. Aegidius had been appointed master of the soldiers in Gaul by the Emperor Majorian, but the bewildering changes of regime in Italy may have left him an apparently independent warlord. The Frankish warlord Childeric competed with his Roman counterparts for a loose military dominance which turned on official recognition, personal charisma and the ability to gain loyalty through success with its spoils, and was held together by a series of alliances brokered by the western military supremo Odoacer, who campaigned along the Loire in the 460s. Hence Gregory's lurid stories about Childeric's sexual excesses leading to his being forced to take refuge with the rulers of another group, the Thuringians, as his followers opted for the leadership of Aegidius instead; we know another Roman general, Count Paul, led a force of both 'Franks' and 'Romans'.[5]

Northern Gaul in the third quarter of the fifth century cannot be understood in terms of an expanding Frankish realm and a shrinking Roman frontier: rather, we see long-established barbarian leaders establishing themselves along the Rhine frontier, and a kaleidoscope of warbands of diverse origins, led by a range of warlords, some Roman in origin, some barbarian, within Gaul itself. These should be compared to the more formal political systems established by the Visigothic and Burgundian kings in the south, working in concert with powerful Roman elites and drawing on strong administrative continuities to maintain the apparatus of law-giving and tax-collection. The highly educated senatorial bishops to whom we owe our record of this world – men like Sidonius Apollinaris and Avitus of Vienne – would have been astounded to learn that, within a century, their descendants would serve a family descended from the rough frontiersmen of the north in a political system which embraced all of Gaul.

Essay

The burial of Childeric

Aside from Gregory's tales, Childeric's milieu is vividly witnessed by probably the most famous archaeology find from early medieval Gaul: his grave at Tournai. First uncovered in 1653, the grave was immediately identifiable as Childeric's thanks to the presence of his seal ring, making it almost unique in being the burial of an individual of proven royal status who is discussed in the written sources, and whose death can be dated to *c*. 481. Many of the actual objects with which Childeric was buried were subsequently lost or stolen, leaving us dependent on early modern depictions, but recent renewed excavation of the area immediately around the grave has shed new light on the burial, whilst advances in our understanding of early medieval cemetery archaeology allow us to attempt a tentative 'reading' of this public statement of newly won power.

The deposition of lavish grave-goods relating to the public role of the deceased – notably wargear, ornament and regalia – is a practice with a variety of precedents. Grave-goods of this type certainly were used beyond the Roman frontier, but they also have a prehistory within northern Gaul. In fact, Childeric's burial demonstrates a kaleidoscope of influences, rather than following an established tradition imported from the Frankish homelands. It stands at the beginning of a wave of similar burials which emerge across northern Gaul and into southern Germany in the decades around 500; what is not yet clear is whether we can see these burials, and the grave-goods they contain, as radiating out from the Frankish court and so marking Frankish influence, or whether they simply mark the final stage in the establishment of barbarian warlords as local rulers across a vast swathe of western Europe.

The burial evokes Childeric's membership of an international elite of barbarian warlords that had emerged in contact with, and often in the service of, Rome. There are significant contacts, both in the rite and in the origins and style of the wargear, with burials from the Danube and the Black Sea, and ultimately with the Huns. But the significance of Rome is also clear. For a start, the burial is situated by an important Roman road, in Tournai, a strategically important Roman site in northern Gaul. Amongst Childeric's grave-goods were around three hundred coins, the most recent dating from 476–7; Childeric's brooch, moreover, is of a type worn by high-ranking officers within the Roman army. Most remarkable of all is Childeric's seal ring, which implies that this barbarian warlord needed to authenticate official documents in the manner of a Roman provincial governor.

Childeric was also buried with a horse, complete with a magnificent harness decorated with gold and cloisonné bees. Recent excavations have uncovered the remains of no fewer than 21 more horses, in three graves, radiocarbon dated to 460–520; they are sited around Childeric's burial, probably at the foot of a mound which was raised over it. Horse-burial is not common, but there are a significant number of incidences, most between the Rhine, Elbe and Danube; the scale of Childeric's is unparalleled. And although Childeric's burial is close by the church of St Brice, which is thought to have late-Roman origins, later church leaders saw horse-burial as unambiguously pagan. Childeric's burial – presumably a public statement organised by his son and heir, Clovis – aimed at winning over the continued loyalty of his following by lavish public display in a shared warrior culture.

Conquest and conversion: the Merovingian unification of Gaul

The man who Gregory saw as responsible for this change was Childeric's son, Clovis. Clovis' reputation as founder of the Merovingian kingdom and his converter of the Franks to Christianity have made him a legendary figure in the French national memory to the current day. The fact that Gregory, as always our main source, was writing with hindsight, when Clovis already had the status of a founder figure, makes it particularly difficult to handle his reign. Gregory did an extremely good job at threading together a coherent narrative from the material available to him, and as we only have fragments of contemporary evidence, Gregory's plot of Clovis' reign has remained more or less unchallenged to the present day, but we must remember that it is essentially Gregory's version.

The story, as it is normally told, focuses on two issues: Clovis' conversion to Christianity, and his conquest of most of Gaul. The two have been repeatedly linked since the time of Gregory, who saw Clovis' choice of Catholic Christianity, as opposed to the Arianism favoured by other barbarian rulers in Gaul, as winning divine favour and so victory. Modern historians have often offered what is essentially a secularised version of the same story, arguing that Clovis' Catholicism made him more acceptable than rival barbarian rulers to the Roman population of Gaul, and played an important part in winning him local support and military success. Plausible as this may sound, the primary evidence is lacking, and the virulently anti-Arian invective of Gregory is a reflection of mentalities of his own time, not those of a hundred years earlier. The line between Catholicism and Arianism seems not to have been so hard and fast in the late fifth century (there was no need for rebaptism to mark transition from one allegiance to the other), and there is no real sign that religious affiliation was a live political issue. The stress on Clovis' Catholicism as an explanation for his success ultimately derives from Gregory's own view of history as a manifestation of God's will, and his personal theological interests, and whilst Clovis' conversion was one clearly vital element in the establishment of Frankish rule in Gaul, we should avoid assuming that on its own it can explain the Franks' political success.

The conversion of the king, and with him his people, were great set-piece occasions, and in keeping with the best literary traditions most accounts, medieval and modern, set up a dramatic moment of revelation when all changed. But the religious dividing lines of Clovis' world were far from being clear cut, and long-standing Frankish interaction with the Roman world, and indeed Frankish military and political power within Roman Gaul, meant that Christianity was scarcely strange or novel for Clovis and his followers. The key issues in looking at the conversion of the Franks are the relationships between the adoption of a new religion, the establishment of Frankish power within Gaul, and the changes to Frankish political organisation wrought by conquest and settlement within the former Roman frontier.

About the context and mechanism of Clovis' conversion we can piece together a suggestive quantity of information, from contemporary sources as well as from Gregory. The two key strictly contemporary sources are letters to Clovis from two powerful bishops, Remigius of Rheims and Avitus of Vienne. Remigius' letter was occasioned by Clovis' takeover of the administration of the Roman province of Belgica Secunda, either on his father's death or after a subsequent victory, and in either case early in the reign and so well before any of the conventional dates given by historians for Clovis' conversion: in it he warns Clovis to listen to the advice of the bishops, and gives sensible advice for a young barbarian ruler attempting to establish himself in a Christian Roman society in which bishops were the key local power-brokers. Avitus' letter, which may come from late in the reign, was written by the leading Catholic bishop of the kingdom of Burgundy (whose kings were Arians) and was a response to a report that Clovis was about to make a formal declaration of a new faith.[6]

It is telling to compare the discretion of the strictly primary sources with the story strung together by Gregory. By Gregory's time, at least two separate traditions about Clovis' conversion seem to have been in circulation, which even Gregory's master narrative does not quite succeed in co-ordinating: this in itself may reflect the gradual progress of conversion. One tradition, recounted with verve by Gregory and highly reminiscent of the conversion of Constantine, has Clovis turning to the Christian God when faced with a tight corner on the battlefield, fighting the Alemans: when, as a result, Clovis gains victory he keeps his word and undergoes conversion. Gregory places this victory at Tolbiac in 496, thus supplying the traditional date for Clovis' conversion, but we know of other campaigns against the Alemans later in the reign, and we should not place too much weight on Gregory's chronology. Once reliance on Gregory's dating is placed aside, it is possible to construct a strong case for a date late in the reign, perhaps as late as 508. Gregory, indeed, also gives an alternative version of the conversion to the victory over the Alemans: these are echoed in a letter of a sixth-century bishop of Trier, and centre on the influence of Clovis' wife, Clotild – a Catholic Burgundian princess – and particularly her desire to have her children baptised. Again, there are many early medieval parallels to the phenomenon of the queen-converter, the Christian princess marrying into a pagan royal family and bringing her faith with her. Clotild organised the burial of her husband, consciously reminiscent of Constantine's, in Paris, in a newly constructed church dedicated to the Holy Apostles.[7]

Clovis came into contact with Christianity, and under pressure to convert, as a direct result of his position as ruler of a significant proportion of northern Gaul: conversion was a part of the process of political settlement and the consolidation of the regime. For Gregory, Clovis' victories had to come after his conversion, as a result of God's backing, but we need not be so sure. The key to the consolidation of his father's power in northern Gaul came with the defeat of Syagrius, the son of the general Aegidius who had been Childeric's rival. Growing power in the barbarian world east of the Rhine may have been important in supplying the manpower and wealth which allowed Clovis to consolidate his power within Gaul: probably among the earliest of his political successes was the absorption of the Thuringians, whilst the significance of victory over the Alemans is reflected in its role in Gregory's conversion story. But it was Clovis' final major campaign, against the Visigothic kingdom in southern Gaul, which finally consolidated

Frankish domination within Gaul, and gave the Merovingian kingdom an outlet to the Mediterranean.

Frankish conquest resulted in a shifting of the allegiance of local elites to the Frankish king and his military muscle. In a world of local warlords, Clovis was the successful warleader *par excellence*, his military machine fuelled by the influx of plunder, and swollen by the defeated warbands it swallowed up; here, the wave of late fifth- and early sixth-century lavish burials, expressing martial power in an idiom similar to that adopted by Clovis in burying his father, points to the milieu which Clovis and his sons came to dominate. We have no need to think of large-scale Frankish settlement, particularly not outside the frontier zones of the north and east; and even there, settlement was in all probability a process which took place to a different rhythm, and at a different social level, from the coming and going of military success and political allegiance. Political integration was consummated by the slow symbiosis of the Frankish elite with the indigenous aristocracies of Roman Gaul. Religion certainly played an important role in this process: Clovis was proclaimed a new Constantine by supportive bishops, and Gregory's account of his Visigothic campaign makes clear the conspicuous respect he demonstrated for the patron saint of Romanised central Gaul, St Martin. The triumphal ritual, complete with acknowledgement from the eastern emperor, which was celebrated by Clovis at Tours as he returned from defeating the Visigoths, may have been imprecise in terms of its specific legal significance, but it was redolent of Roman symbolism, creating legitimacy by presenting a new regime in borrowed clothes.[8] The eastern emperor, indeed, remained an important figure of authority for a significant part of the sixth century: Clovis' successors took care to respect imperial prerogatives in the minting of gold portrait coinage, for example, and Roman coins may have been symbols of power, judging from their inclusion in many rich sixth-century graves. The key to the consolidation of the regime was its ability to command the support of the indigenous population. It was precisely the continuation of Roman social and political organisation on this level that allowed the eventual reunification of Gaul under the Merovingian dynasty, after almost a century of local warlordism and shifting military alliances.

The creation of a Frankish kingdom encompassing Gaul south of the Loire as well as the frontier provinces of the north necessitated the transformation of the structures of leadership within Frankish society. One of Gregory's most celebrated anecdotes hints at the process of political centralisation involved in the establishment of the Merovingian kingdom. It concerns the fate of plunder taken by Frankish warbands. Clovis, so Gregory tells us, whilst still a pagan was petitioned by a bishop to return a vase, one of the treasures of his church, which had ended up in Frankish hands. When his army assembled to divide the spoils of war into equal lots, Clovis asked that the vase be reserved for him so that he might return it; one Frank, however, objected, on the grounds that strict equality was the rule when sharing out plunder; Clovis removed his head for his pains.[9] The story was the stuff of folklore already in Gregory's day, but it contains an important message. The unfortunate Frank was voicing a tradition of a relatively egalitarian political organisation within the warband; Clovis was asserting a new order in which his regality removed him from his followers. And Gregory insists on Clovis getting his way through violence. The removal of opponents by killing them was to be a recurrent feature of the Merovingian political system through the sixth and seventh centuries. Gregory's image of Clovis suggests that indigenous men schooled in the savagery of late-Roman politics may have played an important role in legitimating this violence, and the uncontested ability of Merovingian kings to kill subjects may make most sense when viewed against the background of the late-Roman state, grafted onto Frankish kingship.

By Gregory's time, the Merovingian dynasty defined Frankish kingship: the two were synonymous. But as Gregory well knew, in Clovis' time there was a plethora of Frankish kings within northern Gaul, and cutthroat competition is as much in evidence as political co-operation between them. Gregory names members of a dynasty based at Cologne, as well as King Chararic, and the three brothers Ragnachar, king of Cambrai, Rignomar and Richar, and tells us there were other Franks with royal status. Although Gregory suggested that these kings were all linked by blood, this need be no more than his rationalisation of an earlier, alien, political order.[10] Whatever the basis of royal status amongst the Franks of the late fifth century, it seems clear that the family of Childeric and Clovis were relative newcomers, who had risen through military activity in fifth-century Gaul: dynastic traditions never reached back further than Childeric's father, Merovech, and he looks like a legendary figure.

The case of the Frankish kings of Cologne – in Clovis' time, Sigibert and his son Chloderic – underlines the extent to which Clovis may have been a pushy newcomer. The power of these rulers was effectively independent: Chloderic accompanied Clovis on his Aquitainian campaign in 507 as an ally, not a subordinate. Gregory tells an entertaining story of how Chloderic, on Clovis' prompting, had his father murdered in the woods outside Cologne, but was murdered in his turn by Clovis, who then decamped to Cologne and addressed the inhabitants, who 'clashed their shields and shouted their approval, then raised Clovis up on a shield and made him their ruler'.[11] Although Gregory's account is essentially a good story, contemporary written sources confirm the existence of a Frankish kingdom centred on Cologne and dominating both sides of the former Roman frontier in the Rhineland. Frankish kings from the Rhine's east bank had sought to expand their sway over the frontier since the third and fourth centuries, and Sigibert most likely represents a well-established dynasty which was able to expand over the Rhine following the ending of the Roman frontier in the fifth century. The archaeological record suggests continuous use of the public space at the heart of Cologne through the fifth and sixth centuries: the new rulers established their residence within the old Roman *praetorium*, and some were buried within the city. A series of graves of the first half of the sixth century in a privileged site beneath Cologne cathedral shows the pretensions of this elite. The most intriguing grave is that of an infant male, buried with lavish grave-goods, including a miniature set of adult wargear, next to an equally wealthy woman's grave. The child's burial includes two objects unparalleled from elsewhere in Merovingian Europe: the wooden remains of a chair and a bed. Both were seats of authority in early medieval society; their use as grave-goods here, in a boy's grave, points to an attempt to claim ruling status for the child's family.[12] Precisely whose blood gave rise to these claims must remain unclear: Gregory implies, but does not directly state, that after the murder of Sigibert and Chloderic the Cologne dynasty disappeared. From the reign of Theudebert I (511–34), Merovingian rulers with interests in the east used Cologne as a residence. But it is significant that sixth-century Merovingian rulers attempting to consolidate their interests in the Rhineland linked themselves to the memory of the preceding dynasty by naming their sons Sigibert, and it is probable that they also adopted other strategies of association. Even if the graves beneath Cologne cathedral show Merovingian attempts to establish their legitimacy in this crucial centre, their very existence serves as a reminder that Clovis and his successors had to win over Franks with allegiances to rival dynasties as well as cultivating the support of the leaders of post-Roman society in Gaul.

However much we may suspect Gregory's account of foreshortening, we simply lack the evidence from the north to be sure about the processes whereby Clovis and his descendants came to gain a monopoly on Frankish kingship. Even for the south, we are very poorly informed about events until the last third of the sixth century when Gregory's narrative thickens, but we do know that it was not under Clovis, but under his sons that the Burgundian kingdom, with its cultivated court boasting a sophisticated legal and literary culture, was conquered; similarly, too, much of the southern coast remained under the protection of the Ostrogothic kingdom in Italy until the wars of 'reconquest' allowed Frankish conquest. It makes more sense, then, to see the reigns of Clovis and his sons in terms of a single process, of expansive campaigning that allowed the consolidation of Frankish kingship in Gaul. It was this window of successful warfare that also created the political capital that allowed Clovis' dynasty to develop a mystique legitimating its hold on kingship.

Here, the unusual succession arrangement made on Clovis' death, normally dated to 511, may have played an important role in allowing his sons to build an unchallenged hold of power. Clovis' kingdom was divided into four, more or less equal, portions, one for each of his surviving sons. The practice of division has often been seen as a Germanic custom, resting on a notion of the kingdom as the private property of its rulers, but there is actually no evidence for earlier Frankish rulers dividing their kingdoms thus – hardly surprisingly, in that they were leaders of fluid configurations, not Roman provinces. Roman emperors had made good use of the practice of division, not least as it allowed the provision of effective local leadership to a political unit which was too big to be ruled satisfactorily by one individual: the division of 511 may have rested on similar concerns. It is likely that Clovis' widow and her episcopal advisors were calling the tune in 511, and their decision was probably designed to protect her sons Childebert and Chlothar, neither of whom had reached their majority, against their adult half-brother, Theuderic. It actually consolidated the Merovingian dynasty's hold on power by providing an accessible royal court to all the regions, and allowing local factions to find an outlet for their demands through partnership with a Merovingian, rather than raising a rival ruler, which must have been a real possibility in a fluid world where there were rival descent groups amongst the Franks, not to mention royal lineages among neighbouring peoples. Ties of blood between the kings ensured the integration of the individual kingdoms into a single political entity, defined by the Merovingian family. But although the division of 511 may well have been an expedient reaction to Clovis' transformation of the Frankish polity, it was one that was to cast a long shadow down the centuries; in 561, it provided the template for renewed division between Clovis' grandsons.

The strength of the Merovingian monopoly on power – right through the sixth and seventh centuries would-be usurpers claimed real or fictional Merovingian blood – makes it all too easy for us to forget that it must have been created, and that Clovis' reign marked the crucial stage in its creation. Seventh-century sources recounted that the dynasty's eponymous ancestor, Merovech, was descended from a sea monster. There is a very strong argument for seeing the sea monster story as a later literary creation, drawing on classical motifs – it was, after all, in the seventh and eighth centuries that stories of the Franks' descent from the Trojans of classical legend began to circulate. Whatever the precise dates that these classicising fictions of origin were developed – and it is striking that the first of Clovis' descendants to bear the name Merovech is a great-grandson born in the late sixth century – they clearly served to legitimate Frankish rule and Merovingian kingship, but have little value in explaining the origins of this system. Merovingian charisma was also articulated through a variety of strategies that marked off those of Merovingian blood from the elites of the kingdom. In their choice of wives, for example, they avoided the daughters of their own aristocracy, and married predominantly foreign princesses. Most famously, by wearing their hair long, in a distinctive hairstyle, adult males of royal birth demonstrated that it was Merovingian blood that ran through their veins. Long hair did not just project royal status: it encapsulated it, for when Merovingians were removed by their kin or rivals, they had their hair cut, or often tonsured if they were packed off into a monastery; letting it grow again was a means of declaring a political comeback.[13]

Clovis' sons and grandsons also embraced the Roman heritage of Gaul as a means of legitimising their rule. Already in the time of Clovis' sons, kings were issuing edicts, assisted by advisors learned in Roman law. Merovingian kings were educated in the literate traditions of late-Roman Gaul, and rulers like Clovis' grandson Chilperic I (reigned 561–84) aped the Christological initiatives of Byzantine emperors by dabbling in theology, as well as writing hymns, inventing new letters for the alphabet and founding circuses in Paris and Soissons. The dynasty as a whole followed in Clovis' footsteps in seeking an ever-closer alliance with the church, and using its supernatural power to bolster its own status, founding and patronising religious institutions. In Burgundy, the Merovingians were able to graft themselves onto the strong post-Roman royal tradition of the Burgundian dynasty they displaced. Of the third generation of Merovingian kings, Gregory gives the best press to Guntram (reigned 561–92), whose powerbase was Burgundy, and who was quasi-saintly, reputed to be capable of healing-miracles: here, he was following directly in the footsteps of his Burgundian predecessors, one of whose number, Sigismund, was the subject of a cult which was to become a model of royal sanctity. Other Merovingians created their own religious aura. Radegund, a Thuringian princess seized in campaign and married to Clovis' son, Chlothar I (reigned 511–61), fled her husband and founded a monastery at Poitiers, dedicated to a relic rich with symbolic reverberations, the relic of the Holy Cross, whose cult was strongly associated with Helen, the mother of Constantine. Chlothar, in spite of his problems with Radegund, seems to have been alive to the potential advantages of associating his dynasty with sanctity, in that he supported the foundation at Poitiers, granted it a special royal protection and placed two Merovingian princesses into his wife's care. This was to became a site where dynastic power merged with, and was replenished by, the supernatural power of a universal relic with strongly imperial associations; it was closely associated with royal women, through whom dynastic charisma was transmitted, just as Clovis' widow had been associated with churches in Paris and Tours.[14]

It is possible to tell the story of much of the history of the Merovingian realm in the sixth century in terms of actual and projected divisions, and the stratagems by which ambitious kings sought to increase their share at the expense of their kinsmen. As there were no fixed succession rules, with any male who could claim Merovingian blood in his veins considered throne-worthy, but needing to win over sufficient political support to make good his claim, intrigue was more or less constant. These struggles were the basis for Gregory's essentially negative view of the political history of the Merovingian kingdoms, which has been followed by most modern historians. But to see Merovingian history as a decline from the unity and expansion of Clovis' reign through civil war and internecine strife to weakness and division is misleading. Clovis' reign was wholly exceptional, in that unlike his successors' it took place in the context of a fluid political situation defined by the extensive links between a series of warleaders; it is only the carefully constructed narrative of Gregory which makes Clovis's reign appear as a model of unity. The internal strife and shifts of allegiance that are a recurrent feature of sixth-century politics owed much to the eagerness with which local elites across the kingdom sought an effective and wealthy Merovingian lord. In the pages of Gregory, political factions sought leaders with Merovingian blood: rivalries within Merovingian families thus allowed political conflict to be processed within a Merovingian framework, and so consolidated the position of the dynasty. And beneath these divisions at the top, the sixth century saw the consolidation of a new political system that was deeply rooted in the local societies that made up post-Roman Gaul.

Sixth-century society: cities, bishops and counts

Sixth-century divisions reflected the essential realities of sixth-century politics: that kingdoms were a conglomeration of local units, the *civitates* which had made up Roman Gaul, and negotiations between kings centred on the control of these *civitates* – or, rather, the right to take levies from them and appoint officials within them. Indeed, sixth-century divisions often created interleaved kingdoms, with neighbouring *civitates* owing allegiance to different kings, and on occasion regions were 'shared' between different kings. That divisions took these forms tells us something important about the nature of the kingdom, and the relationship between royal and local power: divisions were essentially allocations of tax revenue between different royal courts, and the whole system was possible because of the inheritance of a sophisticated administrative infrastructure on the level of the *civitas*. Kingdoms were actually ruled from royal seats within the *civitates* of a diamond roughly defined by the Oise and Meuse in the north and the Loire and Saône in the south: Paris, Soissons, Orléans and Reims were the key centres. This concentration of royal residence within a compact area – along with the division of the more highly Romanised areas of southern Gaul between different Merovingians, who often engaged in cutthroat competition for the lucrative rights involved – may have helped prevent the constituent kingdoms of the Merovingian realm from drifting apart.

We are best informed about the local level of political power in central and southern Gaul, thanks to the survival of the indigenous aristocracy, its domination of the church and its cultivation of literary culture and saints' cults, activities preserved for us above all thanks to the pen of Gregory of Tours. But we should remember that about the Merovingian heartlands north of the Loire, and even more so about the regions along, and to the east of, the former Roman frontier, we know next to nothing. We should clearly expect regional difference, not least given very different experiences within the Roman Empire and in the course of the fifth century, and the need to make allowances for regional difference in reaching an understanding of the Merovingian kingdoms as a whole should never be forgotten. In fact, sixth-century Merovingians themselves acknowledged as much: divisions primarily centred on the formerly Roman provinces where there was a local administration from which kings could profit, and aimed to ensure that each king had resources in different areas of Gaul. These patterns of division, indeed, aided the integration of these varied areas into a single polity, creating ties and shared interests between different regions. Kings were particularly interested in gaining interests in southern Gaul, and the Merovingian kingdom was sufficiently part of the Mediterranean world for the Byzantines to devote time and cash to diplomatic and political initiatives within it in the sixth century, notably supporting the pretender Gundovald in the 580s.

Within the *civitates*, two positions emerge as crucial: those of bishop and count. By the sixth century, kings enjoyed rights of appointment to both offices, and both were thus royal servants, albeit royal servants with powerful local powerbases and a significant degree of latitude (particularly in the case of bishops, who were difficult to remove from office once appointed). Bishops had become the central figures within their *civitates* after Constantine; in the fifth century, they were natural substitutes for distant and often ineffective rulers, and frequently the organisers of a city's defence, as local landowning families took up episcopal office to maintain their status. The family of Gregory of Tours, for example, effectively controlled their 'home' bishopric of Clermont-Ferrand from the fifth century onwards, as well as supplying bishops to a number of other sees, Tours included. It is in this period that bishops were able to mount a formal takeover of some of the most significant aspects of civic administration. With the Merovingian takeover of Gaul, royal rights to appoint bishops were acknowledged, although kings had to recognise and work through the local muscle which allowed families like Gregory's to dominate particular areas, and royal appointment may often have involved choosing between rival candidates championed by local factions. Nonetheless, this encouraged the growth of ties of patronage between the Merovingian court, the episcopate, and the local families who sought to place their sons on episcopal thrones.

Bishops were clearly important figures, but we should pause before assuming that they enjoyed a monopoly on local power, or indeed a uniform degree of local power at all times and places. Our evidence, overwhelmingly hagiographical, and episcopal in provenance, would inevitably tend to give a maximum view of episcopal power, but it also indicates the emergence of a new group of secular officials: counts. Within the empire, councils had ruled cities; the title *comes* ('count') denoted companionship of the emperor, a particular status within the imperial administration, usually reserved for military leaders. In the fifth century, however, the military title *comes* is used to describe their position of city 'governors', who offered protection, as in the famous case of the Count Arbogast, ruler of Trier in the late fifth century.[15] Counts, that is, emerged in the fifth century as a response to similar pressures to those which led to an increase of episcopal power, and it may be, again, that there was considerable variation from *civitas* to *civitas* in the precise functions taken on by count and bishop. But under the Merovingians counts became the norm in every *civitas*, the king's main secular officials, responsible for carrying out the king's will and overseeing local affairs; kings could occasionally group together a number of *civitates* under a kind of super-official, normally styled *dux*, whose role was normally primarily military. Sometimes this could lead to tension between count and bishop – Gregory of Tours' *bête noire* and principal local opponent was the count of Tours, Leudast – although we should not assume that such conflict was the rule.

What, precisely, did counts and bishops oversee? There is good evidence for the continuation of a fairly sophisticated civic administration. The literary evidence here is supplemented by that of formularies, collections of templates for documents used to record private legal transactions, from the late sixth and seventh centuries. The formularies demonstrate the survival of Roman habits of documentation through the agency of notaries; this continuity owed much to the regulation of property transactions according to long-established rules. Part of the appeal of this city-centred infrastructure of documentation was the need to trace ownership in the calculation of tax liabilities, and there is considerable evidence for the continued functioning of the revenue system on a local level into the sixth century. Indeed, it was these local civic structures, not royal courts at the centre, which were integral to the preservation and continued development of an essentially Roman fiscal system. Kings were unable to oversee the process of tax assessment, being met with howls of complaint and repeated claims from individuals and institutions about the liberties and immunities allegedly granted by their predecessors. Thus when Chilperic attempted to set new rates of tax on certain classes of property, he failed, eventually burning the registers detailing the new tax assessments. But royal agents could still count on collecting tax revenues if long-established liabilities, rooted in the fabric of provincial society, were accepted as the basis for negotiation. The degree of local initiative is reflected in the events of 589, when the bishop of Poitiers requested that the king send officials to draw up new tax lists for his city, as the extant ones were so far out of date that they contained anomalies and inequalities; when these same officials moved on to Tours, they were treated to a rehearsal of the church and city's ancient immunities and privileges.[16]

The changes to the wider political landscape were not without their consequences, of course. The late Roman state had enforced often onerous civic duties on frequently reluctant local elites, and with its disappearance the basis of the *civitas* inevitably changed: whilst the tax system continued, there was far less in the way of administrative demands placed on cities by a much smaller central administration. Archaeology suggests that there was widespread contraction in the population of towns, continuing the trend that had begun in third-century Gaul. Excavations at sites such as Tours suggest a transformation in the urban fabric, with the public monumental spaces of the Roman past losing their centrality, as the urban space splintered into smaller units, and new churches were founded on the margins of the Roman city – often outside the walls, near the cemeteries where the Christian dead were buried and the cults of martyrs centred. Within the city, too, space splintered into what were much more self-contained units, virtual compounds around the residence of aristocratic patrons. In part, these changes relate to a wider economic picture, of demographic decline and ruralisation, which have late Roman roots. But they also demonstrate the redefinition of the city in Christian terms, with the rise of new supernatural foci within the urban fabric. The presence of the bishop and his cathedral, after all, now defined city status, as Gregory showed, and episcopal patronage, notably through the establishment of doles and almshouses for the poor, played a dominant role in city life.

The promotion of the cult of the saints, venerated through the relics of Christian heroes, played a central role in defining the new urban landscape. Saints' cults were the typical form of piety, and the mechanism whereby Christianity established a cultural dominance, in post-Roman Gaul. Thanks to Gregory's recording of the stories of prodigies and miracles of the cult-centres of the central and southern Gallic countryside in his hagiographical works, we are uniquely well informed about these cultural transformations. Gregory presents holy relics as the crucial objects of veneration among the masses, urban and rural, and contrasts what he saw as their often vulgar piety of festivals and holidays with the proper reverence and awe that the well-bred and truly pious demonstrated. Reverence and awe were appropriate because the holy dead had proceeded to Heaven, and their bones and bodies were thus points of contact with the divine, radiating an energy which could transform the mundane and suspend the normal workings of the terrestrial world. The supernatural stood at the heart of Gregory's worldview, and it was bishops who were the proper interpreters of its meaning. The cultural transformation of the Gallic elite is reflected in the changing idioms in which its spokesmen worked. Although Gregory could write good, vigorous, Latin, and his contemporary, the poet Venantius Fortunatus, could win patronage from the elites of the Merovingian world, there is a sense in which the self-conscious classicism of the world of Sidonius Apollinaris was now a thing of the past: Gregory himself modelled his style on that of the Bible, and when Merovingian kings wished to demonstrate their cultural virtuosity they did so by composing hymns or through theological speculations of doubtful orthodoxy. In part, this reflects the decline of the public schools of late antiquity: the foyers of education were no longer the cities of the south, but the households of bishops. And the class solidarity of that elite, rooted in a belief in legitimate, legal, power as the basis of social order, was expressed in a new form, in the lively tradition of church councils – at which bishops developed the laws of the church to discipline their flocks – which are such a marked feature of the sixth century.

Gregory shows us cities as communities united by their shared veneration for a holy patron whose cult was cared for by the bishop. His picture points to the crucial mechanism by which landowning families like his were able to maintain their position as the elites in post-Roman society in central and southern Gaul. But his relic-centred piety may itself be a partial and self-interested view, for in the course of the post-Roman period bishops had established control over the relics of their holy predecessors and patrons as a means of legitimating their patronage over their cities: intercession at the site of a relic-cult to access the divine thus paralleled the structures of intercession with bishops as the means to power in the secular world. In his pages, we also find living holy men, like the ascetic Wulfolaic in the Ardennes, who sat on a pillar in the manner of Near Eastern stylites.[17] Whilst Gregory approved of Wulfolaic, who was after all dedicated to St Martin, such figures could be objects of suspicion where they threatened official ecclesiastical structures; they might even, in the case of popular religious leaders beyond episcopal control, be condemned as fakes and heretics. We should not forget the very obvious conflicts – between kings and bishops, and royal officials and bishops, but also between rival factions seeking to have their man appointed as bishop – that run through his narratives. Nor should we neglect the public, secular world of cities continuing to function as places where landowners had townhouses, and met to do business. Tours, indeed, as a relative backwater, may have been relatively easily dominated by its bishop; it certainly is striking that the cult of St Martin wholly dominates Tourainian society, whereas elsewhere competition, with rival factions forming around rival cults, is evident. And the cults of the holy dead which illuminated Gregory's world were housed in the senatorial landscapes of southern and central Gaul, their distribution reflecting the complex interactions between private family retreats and residences in the countryside, and the public role of episcopal patronage in the countryside: Gregory understood his life in terms of his relationship with the 'family' saint, St Julian, venerated by a relatively restricted familial group in a countryside of *villas* and visits, and his subsequent devotion to St Martin as the patron on whom his public career in Tours relied.

This picture of continuity, at the most basic level, of cities and local power is the case across a vast swathe of the Merovingian kingdoms, its northern boundary lying between the valleys of the Loire and the Seine. In that this zone, thanks to the sophistication of local administration and the value of the tax revenue it could produce, was central to the power of the sixth-century Merovingians, it deserves to be the focus of any discussion. The region to the north, where Roman patterns were more dislocated even on a local level, did not supply resources on the same scale; it is also only intermittently present in Gregory's pages, reflecting its at best partial integration into the topographies of holy power through which Gregory worked. About political organisation here we are less fully informed, the scarcity of the evidence largely a result of fifth-century dislocation which disrupted the kind of social circles which survived in the south, producing the lives and letters which are our primary sources. The degree of dislocation varied considerably, and in places cities could continue to function in a way not dissimilar to the world of Gregory: at Trier, for example, inscription and letter evidence shows bishops preserving much of the Roman infrastructure on a local level. Whilst as a rule bishops survived, they often survived only precariously, with bishoprics in areas such as the Rhineland effectively having to be refounded in the sixth century, and in some cases even changing location, as at Maastricht. Local government rested not so much on *civitas* units inherited from the Roman past, as on much larger, regional units, ruled by secular officials styled *duces*. Some of these units ('duchies'), such as Ripuaria, centred on Cologne, had tribal names; others, like the Hesbaye, along the Meuse, were referred to by geographical labels. The key figures on a local level were secular leaders referred to by the Franco-Latin title *grafio*, whose functions were essentially similar to those of a count in more Romanised areas. As a rule, the Roman heritage continued to play a defining role, with Roman cities and forts normally continuing to serve as the central places even on the Rhine frontier; but in the practice of administration, continuous contact was lost.

This pattern of disruption in the structures of local power probably went hand-in-hand with a more dramatic change in the makeup of local elites than was the case south of the Loire. Given the absence of written sources, the archaeology is the best avenue into this society. The most dramatic development here is the rapid spread of the culture of lavish funerary display exemplified in the grave of Childeric. In the first decades of the sixth century, the use of lavish grave-goods filtered down; initially used in the graves of warlords like Childeric and his anonymous late fifth-century contemporaries at sites like Flonheim in the middle Rhine valley and Gültlingen in Alemannia, this idiom of display was very quickly adopted by the population as a whole, in new cemeteries which clustered around and imitated the early graves of local leaders. The social meaning of this phenomenon is still unclear. It is not a practice imported wholesale from beyond the frontier, although it does have precedents there; it certainly cannot be seen as an indication of the migration of populations, not least as it shows no hard and fast geographical or ethnic divisions. Nor is ancestral 'pagan' religion a helpful explanation: whilst horse-burial, or cremation, were condemned by contemporary churchmen as 'pagan' practices, the use of grave-goods was accepted, and in the course of the sixth and seventh centuries there are numerous examples of lavishly accompanied burials being made in churches. What we can say is that these new burials were designed to symbolise idealised lives in the grave: corpses were buried not only with grave-goods, but fully clothed, and the wargear and jewellery that have tended to attract so much attention need to be understood as part of the costume and effects which were chosen to send a message to the living community of those participating in funerary ritual. This material culture, which is relatively international, drawing on diverse influences, may have been used in archaeologically invisible rituals of gift-exchange long before the decades around 500, but its visibility in graves from the late fifth century points to the increased importance of local audiences, with lavish burials the means of commemorating dead ancestors who legitimated present power. We should not confuse the sudden archaeological visibility of elite status symbols with the creation of a new elite, not least given the wealth of the earliest graves. Often the most lavish gifts were made for those whose death left the most difficult gap to fill in the community of the living. In these burials we can see the adoption of a new set of highly gendered social identities, the spread of a macho warrior culture and the resulting transformations of female identity. But we also get a sense of the relative fluidity of social structure, with status and community resting on a continuum of gift-giving that included the dead and aligning oneself with powerful ancestors. The evidence for feasting at the graveside, and the incidence of grave-robbing, confirms the picture of a culture of social competition pursued through rituals of consensus and conflict.

That this was clearly a very different world from Gregory's is underlined by the less spectacular but vitally important advances that have been made in our understanding of rural settlements. Here, the major change was the almost total dominance of building in wood: on some sites such as Mondeville in modern Normandy, wooden structures normally seen as 'Germanic' in their origin, notably sunken-floored huts built in association with larger and more complex houses, begin as early as the fourth century.[18] Wooden buildings have a fixed lifetime before they need remaking, and it is the necessity for periodic rebuilding – which must have been reinforced by the life-cycle, with households breaking up as children grew and married out before being passed on as parents died – that explains the 'shifting' nature of much Merovingian settlement, with the built area on a given site moving from generation to generation. Within these settlements – which are often relatively small – there is little evidence of strong internal hierarchies; the *villa* sites that had housed late Roman landlords were abandoned in the late fourth and fifth centuries. With the collapse of the infrastructure of Roman society, then, what we have emerging is a society of landowning farmers, relying on households which must have included free and unfree dependants as well as family, and competing for pre-eminence in the community through the feasting, raiding and gift-giving hinted at by the funerary evidence. This is the world reflected in the earliest surviving Frankish law-code, Salic law (*Lex Salica*), written up late in Clovis' reign but claiming to record the rules as they were remembered by four elderly and learned men from the Frankish settlements in northern Gaul, not as a statement of royal legislative authority.[19] In this it differed from the law-codes issued by the contemporary Burgundian and Visigothic rulers in southern Gaul.

What of government at the centre? It makes sense to spend so long looking at local government precisely because by the sixth century most government was local. Kings could issue orders, appoint officials, and give judgements on particularly contentious disputes, whilst there is a lively tradition of royal law-giving through Roman-style edicts. The royal court played a central role in the spread of personnel and ideas around the kingdom: senatorial bishops from the south, for example, were responsible for the rebirth of Rhineland towns and cities like sixth-century Mainz. The result was a process of acculturation: the strong sense of family honour which legitimated, indeed demanded, the violent seeking of vengeance in the Merovingian family soon influenced social practice even amongst the Romanised population of much of the kingdom, as can be seen in Gregory's stories of violent feuds amongst the populace of Tours.[20] But in terms of the actual business of governing, there was little that went on at a level above that of the city. If we compare Merovingian kings to the Roman provincial governors who they were in some ways replacing, what is immediately striking is the disappearance of a bureaucratic machine, and its replacement by a royal household which was much smaller, and whose rationale was social rather than administrative. Hence the complaints of Chilperic I: 'My treasury is always empty. All our wealth has fallen into the hands of the church. There is no one with any power left except the bishops. Nobody respects me as King: all respect has passed to the bishops in their cities.'[21] Thus, unlike their Roman predecessors, the Merovingians had no standing army, whether in the form of salaried soldiers or subsidised allies. The Frankish and other barbarian warbands that Clovis was able to unify doubtless provided the basis for his military efforts, but they increasingly merged into local societies as landowners and office-holders. They maintained a Frankish identity, and links with the Merovingian court, which created an obligation to perform military service, when it was needed. In central and southern Gaul, where Frankish identity spread more slowly, military obligations and royal service remained tied into some kind of post-Roman infrastructure: we know that cities put together levies from their inhabitants, whilst powerful aristocrats, much as they had in and after the empire, had bands of clients which could constitute private armies and might be placed in the service of friendly rulers. These were essentially *ad hoc* arrangements, and the common denominator in both north and south was the centrality of personal relationships of patronage between rulers and elites, even if the mechanisms of recruitment on the ground differed: there was no question of paying soldiers as state servants through tax income.

In that the Merovingians inherited a local administrative infrastructure that could deliver tax revenue from a vast swathe of Gaul, this left them incredibly rich. But if their wealth was not earmarked to fund a state bureaucracy or standing army, it was nonetheless soon spent, for holding together such a vast polity without a salaried administrative or military machine necessitated the intensive cultivation of the support of local elites, a costly trade in gifts and favours. Hence Chilperic I's complaints. The royal treasury and royal gift-giving have a high profile in all contemporary accounts of Merovingian kingship precisely because kings attracted and rewarded local supporters by granting away their wealth. Such munificence could take a variety of forms, from the patronising of circuses and public buildings in the cities of the more Romanised areas, to the pursuit of plunder and tribute on the wartrail beyond the Rhine. In a court-based politics of patronage such as this, royal women – queens and mothers – played a central role, able to act as patrons in their own right, and to build coalitions and cultivate conflict between their menfolk. It was through the brokering of personal relationships, and the redistribution of the wealth that flooded into the royal treasury, that the Merovingians ruled their kingdom. These processes allowed the development of a ruling class of diverse origins, whose interests were already widespread and large-scale by the time our documentation begins in the seventh century.

The remaking of the kingdom

As we move to 600 and beyond, we begin to escape from the problems posed by Gregory's dominance of the evidence for the sixth century, and the resultant skewing of our sources towards one particular milieu, and the period of Gregory's public life in the 570s and 580s. We are faced, instead, with a different problem: in the seventh century, we have a diversity of sources – saints' lives, official documents, and two important narrative histories – the *Chronicle* of Fredegar, written from a Burgundian perspective in the late 660s, and the *Book of Frankish History* (*Liber Historiae Francorum*), written in or near Soissons in the 720s – from which we can assemble a reconstruction, but we lack the anecdotal detail, and the master-narrative, that Gregory supplies for the sixth century. As a result, seventh-century history seems less colourful, and more technical, and the temptation to follow the propagandists of the Carolingian dynasty that eventually replaced the Merovingians in the eighth century, and write off the seventh century as a period of decline and disorder, is great. But we are now learning that this was a crucial period, which saw the transformation of Frankish society.

The experience of political division, and the factional conflicts of the latter part of the sixth century, led to the consolidation of distinct identities by the elites of the different regions of the Frankish realm. Neustria, literally 'new west land', was made up of the acquisitions of Childeric and Clovis, and had crystallised around the royal centres of Paris and Soissons, and the Merovingians who had ruled from them in the sixth century. Austrasia, the eastern kingdom, had been ruled through the sixth century from Rheims, but included a vast eastern hinterland, of which Metz was the key political centre. Burgundy, as its name suggests, had a slightly different genesis to its two northern counterparts, based in the Burgundian kingdom as developed by Merovingian rulers in the later sixth century. By the beginning of the seventh century, these 'segment kingdoms' (to use a literal translation of the indispensable German term for these units, *Teilreiche*) had emerged as the constituent parts of the Frankish polity, with their own political traditions: kings dealt with them as discrete political communities.

The significance of these political communities is nowhere better illustrated than in the downfall of Brunhild, the Visigothic princess who married Sigibert I (reigned 561–75) and dominated Frankish politics into the early seventh century, exercising her power through her familial ties to four generations of male Merovingians: her husband, son, grandsons and great-grandson. Brunhild's mastery of family politics was augmented by the fact that her men controlled Austrasia and so had easy access to those areas of the Merovingian realm best suited for lucrative offensive warfare. By the first decade of the seventh century, Brunhild's grandsons were firmly in control of Austrasia and Burgundy, leaving Chlothar II in Neustria the only

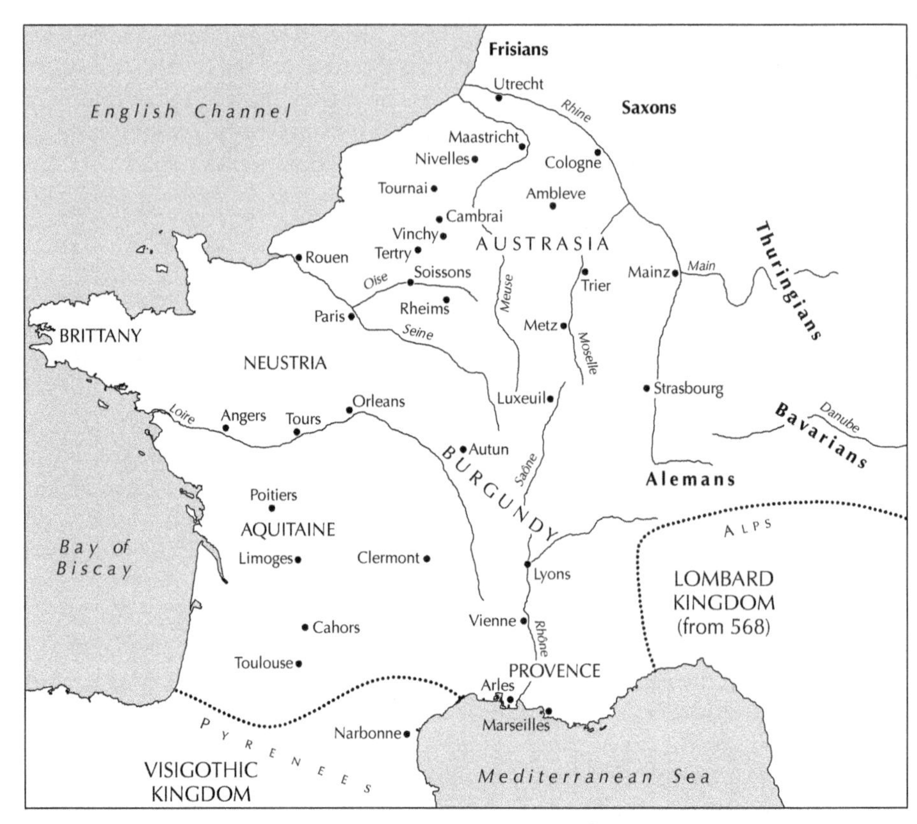

Map 6 Merovingian Gaul

surviving Merovingian not of Brunhild's progeny. In 613, however, in a stunning turnaround, Chlothar found himself the sole ruler of the entire Merovingian realm: following the death of her two grandsons, Brunhild had attempted to rule through her infant great-grandson, thus monopolising regality and overriding the discrete identities of the Burgundian and Austrasian aristocracies, which responded by turning to Chlothar.

In victory, Chlothar acknowledged the fears that motivated his new supporters, trying and executing Brunhild, then holding an assembly at Paris in 614, which promulgated both ecclesiastical and secular legislation. Under Chlothar, each of the three segment kingdoms was allowed its own 'mayor of the palace', through whom it was to interact with the king: in effect, each had its own political hierarchy and administration. The edict of Paris confirmed the privileges of the elites, secular and ecclesiastical, of each kingdom within that kingdom, most famously decreeing that only locals should be appointed to secular office. This is often seen as a royal capitulation to aristocratic demands. In fact, for the contents of the edict there are parallels in late Roman law, and the clause on local judges echoes Justinian's legislation. The appointment of outsiders was seen by contemporaries as a recipe for the abuse of office: insiders were far less likely to act arbitrarily as they were alive to local traditions and subject to local pressures. The edict acknowledged the importance of local elites as the representatives of royal power, and set down the proper relationships between these local elites and kings. It went hand-in-hand with moralising on the duties of a Christian king – to be pious, charitable, and exhibit justice – by the assembled bishops. Here was the template for a new political system.[22]

It was a system that was conspicuously successful. Conflict did not break out again between the different kingdoms until the last quarter of the seventh century. Co-operation between kings and elites was not, of course, always smooth, but this was a system which could cope with inevitable factionalism and political manoeuvring without outright revolt, or, indeed, the kind of inter-Merovingian politicking which had been typical of the sixth century. In 623, when the Austrasians desired a more accessible Merovingian, they were able to approach Chlothar II and have his son, Dagobert, appointed king in Austrasia, thus acknowledging the local interests of the Austrasians and tying them to the Merovingian dynasty. On his father's death in 629, Dagobert moved west, basing himself in the Neustrian heartland around Paris which his father had made home, but he continued to recognise the segmentary nature of the polity: in 633, when four years of royal absence had led to squabbling within the Austrasian elite and threats from peoples beyond the Franks' borders, Dagobert sent his son, Sigibert III, to act as Austrasian king, just as he himself had been sent east a decade earlier. In Burgundy, in contrast, the elite were content to access the Neustrian king; an arrangement which was such as success that in 626, after the death of the Burgundian mayor of the palace, the Burgundians asked not to be given a replacement but instead to deal directly with the Neustrian palace, and thus be effectively merged with the Neustrians. But Burgundy, although ruled jointly with Neustria, remained in important ways a distinct unit with its own political identity: hence, in spite of the increasing overlap in terms of personnel between Neustria and Burgundy, the Burgundian mayoralty could be revived in the 640s.

This new style of political organisation, of discrete regional units each bundled with their distinct identity, was not just adopted in the heartlands of the Merovingian realm: it also served as a template for the surrounding areas. It is possible to analyse the seventh-century realm in terms of three zones of Merovingian domination, each consisting of a series of interlocking segments: firstly, the three kingdoms of Neustria, Austrasia and Burgundy, each directly tied to the Merovingian dynasty, then the peripheral principalities, governed indirectly by a subordinate ruler, normally styled *dux*, and finally the surrounding peoples, over whom the Merovingians claimed overlordship. In creating such a system, the Merovingians not only reshaped the long-standing heartland of the Frankish realm in central Gaul, but also played a vital role in the development of regional political entities across western Europe as a whole. These changes were possible only because of wider geopolitical changes. The political drama played out in late sixth-century Italy, and related changes in central Europe and the Balkans, alongside the declining economic and cultural penetration of the Mediterranean in western Europe, gave the Merovingian heartland a new centrality.

The impact of these changes is most immediately apparent in southern Gaul. In the sixth century, Merovingian kings, although based in central and northern Gaul, had divided up the south between their kingdoms, and had fought with one another for the best share of the spoils of its Mediterranean trade and Roman infrastructure, but by the beginning of the seventh century the profile of the region was changing. Dagobert made an attempt to create a Merovingian-led kingdom on the model of Burgundy, Neustria and Austrasia, in southern Gaul, sending his half-brother Charibert there in 629; but on Charibert's death in 632 the attempt was abandoned, perhaps because of the difficulty of implanting a royal court in an area which was not used to hosting one, perhaps because the crucial royal interests in the south were now more or less confined to mint and toll rights at Marseilles and the trade route feeding it. Thereafter, effectively independent polities governed by indigenous aristocrats were allowed to emerge in Aquitaine and Provence, indirectly attached to the Merovingian crown and largely immune from its interference; in Aquitaine at least this went hand-in-hand with the development of a distinctive regional identity, as regional leaders began to adopt the title '*dux* of the Romans'. Aristocrats from across the Frankish world, but especially from Burgundy and Neustria, maintained links with the south, and southern leaders attended the Neustrian court until at least the end of the seventh century, but southern Gaul was bound into the Merovingian world in a style comparable to the provinces east of the Rhine, as a peripheral region made up of regional units whose leaders owed allegiance to the Frankish court.

It was not only in southern Gaul, however, that the changing geopolitical balance had important effects. Southern Germany, and in particular the upper Rhine and upper Danube, had traditionally been subject to profound political and cultural influence from beyond the Alps in northern Italy – this had, after all, been the frontline of Roman Italy against prospective barbarian invaders, and it remained a crucial area for the rulers of post-Roman Italy, many of whom entered Italy via the middle Danube basin. The political instability and eventual fragmentation of Italy meant that the maintenance of a balance of power in southern Germany to safeguard northern Italy was no longer possible. Although Lombard rulers in particular were to maintain close ties with southern Germany, and particularly the nascent Bavaria, the region across the Alps came increasingly into the Frankish orbit. This increasingly westward orientation was the result of political changes in Italy, the loss of Byzantine influence in south-central Europe, and the subsequent settlement of Slavs and Avars.

These shifts can be seen most clearly in the region most distant from the Frankish heartlands and in which Frankish influence was most intermittent: Bavaria. The very process by which the former Roman province of Noricum along the lower Danube became Bavaria is shadowy, as are the origins of the new name itself. In the fifth and sixth centuries, the region was an ethnic melting pot, its political fragmentation the result of frantic diplomacy from Constantinople and the various players in Italian politics; in the late sixth century a 'king of the Bavarians' emerged amongst the various competing groups.[23] In the seventh century, as a more cohesive polity emerged, under severe pressure from Avars and Slavs in the east, its inhabitants came to identify themselves as Bavarians. Frankish tutelage may have played an important role: certainly it was the Franks who gave the Bavarians a written law-code, probably in the early seventh century. The ruling dynasty, known as the Agilolfings, seem likewise to have owed their position to Frankish backing, and probably originated in Burgundy; Frankish sources styled them *duces*, although they enjoyed an effectively independent status, and Frankish influence was probably little more than the intermittent admission of overlordship.

Further west, along the upper Rhine and the upper Danube, genesis of a similar polity, that of the Alemans, is more obscure still: the Alemannic rulers of the former frontier provinces of the lower Rhine were defeated by Clovis, but the relationship between these Alemans and those of the seventh century is difficult to pin down. The archaeology suggests that Frankish conquest coincided with the systematic abandonment of the hilltop strongholds that had previously been the basis of princely power beyond the Roman frontier, after which, presumably, local elites were forced to buy into the Frankish system. The development of a new Aleman polity in southern Germany again took place under Frankish tutelage, with Frankish incomers and appointees playing a crucial role, and Merovingian rulers, in this case Chlothar II, capping the development with the issue of a written law-code.

Further north, but still east of the Rhine, we see a similar process at work in the creation of the Thuringian duchy, which again bore the name of a tribe subjugated by Clovis and his successors, but developed under the leadership of Frankish aristocrats set up with Merovingian backing. There is evidence for the payment of tribute in kind to the Frankish king, but the primary role of the duchy was military, particularly given the pressures caused by the political changes to the map of central Europe, and the threat posed by various Slavic tribes. Primarily a buffer, the Thuringian *dux* pursued an effectively independent policy, and could be pushed into opposition to the Franks by an over-active Austrasian ruler who threatened his freedom for manoeuvre, as in 639 when the Thuringian *dux* declared himself a king.[24] In spite of plentiful evidence for contacts with the Franks, it is likely that subsequently Thuringia's status was not unlike that of Bavaria, an effectively independent polity whose rulers entered into uneasy alliances with the Franks when necessary. As with Alemannia and Bavaria, however, the growing property interests of the Frankish aristocracy in Thuringia tied the region into the Frankish world, and may have lain behind a slow but steady Francisation of the area immediately to the east of the Rhine.

To the north, but still to the east of the old Roman frontier along the Rhine which remained such a fundamental political divide, lay the Frisians and Saxons, whose polities emerged not so much under Frankish tutelage as in response to Frankish pressure: significantly, whilst Bavaria, Alemannia and even Thuringia were nominally Christian, for all the missionary work that needed performing in them in the seventh and eighth centuries, the Frisians and Saxons expressed their opposition to the Franks through their pagan religion. We hear of Frankish campaigns against both peoples in the sixth century, and Frankish claims to overlordship. By the seventh century, Frisia, which stood hard on the Frankish frontier along the lower Rhine, on a flourishing trade route, seems to have become relatively centralised politically, with a single indigenous ruler: Dagobert utilised the Roman fort at Utrecht as a political and missionary centre in the region, and much of the seventh century seems to have been taken up with border squabbles. In the first decades of the eighth century, political pressure from the Franks went hand-in-hand with a shadowy process by which the Frisians along the lower Rhine at least shifted allegiance and merged into the Austrasian aristocracy. The Saxons, who dominated most of northern Germany, may have been rather less centralised politically, judging from both the accounts of their later, Carolingian, conquerors, and the tendency of Merovingian sources to refer simply to 'the Saxons' without identifying a leader: we may here be dealing with a tribal confederation which had not yet been subjected to the social and political pressures which led to the establishment of a unified hierarchy, which perhaps explains why its leaders were less prone to 'Francisation' than their western and southern neighbours. In the sixth century, we hear of Saxon 'rebellions', often in alliance with their Thuringian neighbours, and Frankish campaigning, which resulted in the establishment of an annual tribute of 400 cattle which was to be paid to the Franks; Dagobert was petitioned to commute this to military protection against Slav pressure, and after that we hear little except border raiding.

The sixth and seventh centuries, and particularly the decades around 600, were the formative period in the emergence of these new political identities, and the regional units they supported, across western Europe as a whole, from Saxony to Aquitaine. Even the Neustrians, Austrasians and Burgundians had their own 'ethnicities', as well as their own law-codes: the Neustrians, for example, saw the ethnonym 'Frank' and the territory 'Francia' as belonging exclusively to themselves, and in a crisis could dismiss the Austrasians as being 'almost pagans'; the Austrasians, although they were also Franks, did not use the term exclusively, but qualified themselves as 'eastern Franks' or, in the vernacular, 'eastern folk', differentiating themselves from the Neustrians, and had been given their own written law, *Lex Ripuaria*, early in the seventh century. What is striking is the way that the Merovingians were able to embrace the new politics of regional identity, and indeed play an active role in its development. The political system created in this period allowed the Merovingian court to emerge as the dominant political centre in northwestern Europe, exercising influence in England, northern Germany, Spain and Italy, overseeing the birth of a new political orientation east of the Rhine, and maintaining intensive contacts with southern Gaul. For all the intermittent nature of Frankish control east of the Rhine, the Merovingians were able to oversee the emergence of a new political order right across northwestern Europe, one which extended from the Thames to the Danube, but which had the Paris basin at its heart; through supplying technologies of law and leadership, the Merovingian court played a central role in the consolidation of the new identities which underwrote the principalities of the seventh-century world.

Bishops, monasteries and aristocrats: social change in the seventh century

Across the Merovingian world, the seventh century saw fundamental social changes that went hand-in-hand with the consolidation of these new identities.

The foundation stone of the sixth-century polity had been the preservation of an administrative system centred on the *civitates*, which allowed the redistribution of revenues and services. This was not wholesale continuity: as we have seen, what survived did so on a local level, and in an increasingly patchy manner. Claims for exemptions from royal imposts, encouraged by the church, further eroded the scope of taxation. Granting such exemptions to privileged individuals was a practice with very strong Roman precedents, and churches and priests, like Roman senators, had been exempt from most taxation since the fourth century. But increasingly bishops expanded their claims, acting as protectors for their cities as a whole: Gregory, for example, remembered how earlier Merovingians had granted Tours exemption from taxes out of regard for St Martin, and deployed his memory to force similar concessions out of subsequent kings. Another basis for exemption was the spread of Frankish identity north of the Loire, as Roman precedents for the non-taxation of soldiers linked to the special status of Frankish settlers. Certainly there existed a strong link between Frankish identity, military service and exemption from taxes in the early Merovingian kingdom: Gregory reports outrage against royal officials who taxed Franks, to the extent that they were sought out and lynched when their royal masters died. By the middle of the seventh century it was possible to define a 'truly free man' as one whose name was not inscribed in any tax-list.[25] As the population of Gaul north of the Loire increasingly came to see themselves as Frankish, it became increasingly difficult to levy tax from them. Rather, royal income lay in the incidents of the royal service for which, notionally, all free Franks were due: whilst Frankish armies in this period were made up of regional elites and their clients, it is no accident that fines for the non-performance of military obligations, the non-attendance of court when summoned, and other derelictions of service owed by Franks to their king, become increasingly important in the course of the seventh century. The result was a situation in which it became increasingly difficult for royal agents to levy tax. Tax-collectors were never popular figures, and already in the sixth century we find examples of their being greeted by riots, but in the course of the seventh century they simply disappear from the sources altogether.

There is very good evidence, however, for the continuation of many of the practices associated with the levying of imposts on a local level, in Gaul south of the Loire at least. This in itself should be no real surprise. The hold of major landowners over the actual extraction of fiscal obligations from those who worked the land rested on local practices that easily became the stuff of custom. A series of remarkable papyri from Tours – where, remember, claims about the city's immunity from tax on account of royal respect for its patron, St Martin, had been made in Gregory's day – show dues with distant roots in public exactions being collected from the peasantry in a routine manner.[26] Such evidence for continuity on local level encourages us to see seventh-century developments as, in part, a radical decentralisation of the fiscal system, consciously undertaken by kings. The best evidence for the continued existence of dues on a local level comes from the lands of the great churches of the kingdom, which is hardly surprising, given their monopoly of the surviving evidence – but it can be argued that they exercised these rights precisely because of the special privileges they were granted by Merovingian kings. After all, the church was a part of the Merovingian 'state', on account of both its involvement in local administration and its prayer for the stability of the kingdom. This argument can be buttressed by the coin evidence. Although there was a plethora of local agencies minting coin with no explicit reference to the king, analysis of the metal content suggests a degree of central oversight, and perhaps a controlled debasement in response to the contraction of the gold supply to western Europe. Given that the Merovingians had maintained a Roman-style coinage which had a high face value and whose primary functions were tied up with state finance, the delegation of rights over both coinage and taxation are likely to be related. Faced with increasing public resistance to the central levying of royal imposts, the fragmented rights that remained were granted to powerful local figures who exercised them directly; in the process, these privileged individuals and institutions were bound to the kings who acted as their patrons. A passage in the *Life* of St Eligius, Dagobert's goldsmith and chief moneyer, suggests indeed that there may have been close links between the granting of immunity and the delegation of what remained of royal rights of revenue extraction: on being granted the royal *villa* of Solignac near Limoges, Eligius was able to receive taxes collected there and use them to found and fund a monastery.[27]

It was individuals like Eligius who were becoming increasingly important in tying together the central and local levels of the polity. Whilst favoured courtiers and wealthy landowners had always been key figures, the dwindling of urban life and the gradual decline of administrative networks centred on the *civitas* allowed their role to take on a new openness and formality. Local government now lay directly in the hands of counts and bishops, offices now monopolised by local aristocrats. Above all, the gradual atrophy of royal taxation sidelined the role of the *civitas* in the redistribution of wealth and the creation of power. Even where the practices originally associated with the levying of state imposts survived, they did so as incidents on the land negotiated between those who worked that land and an individual or institution with a proprietorial or jurisdictional claim over them; these practices were effectively disentangled from the public life of the *civitas*, making them harder for kings to collect. Whilst the *civitates* did not wholly vanish – they continued to define episcopal sees, and so to function as both social and ecclesiastical centres from their hinterlands – they were no longer central to the redistribution of wealth or the creation of power, which had come to rest directly on the land. Whereas the sixth-century kingdom was still in important ways a conglomeration of *civitas* units, by the seventh century kings worked through local elites, which might often, but did not always, identify themselves with reference to *civitas* units. Counts in particular now found themselves able to exercise local domination without the checks and balances that the *civitas* infrastructure had previously supplied, nor the infrastructure of administration and taxation through which they had worked. Comital office was worth aspiring to it because it allowed its holders to claim they exercised legitimate power, but for such claims to ring true it was necessary to work through the public meetings which structured local opinion.

The changing structure of elites is clearly evident in the archaeology. In particular, in northern Gaul, and along and beyond the Rhine, there are strong indications of a more sharply differentiated social hierarchy in the countryside. This is evident in both burials and settlements. In burials, the emergence of a series of strategies to mark off a small group of elite graves from the mass of the population points to the emergence of a stronger sense of class difference. Elite status might be advertised by the creation of special structures over a grave – wooden huts which might serve as places of commemoration through feast or prayer, or, in the 'wild east' along and beyond the Rhine, huge barrows, either newly constructed or reused from prehistoric times. Most importantly, just as Merovingians from Clovis onwards had been buried, often with lavish grave-goods, in the favoured churches of the kingdom, so by the end of the sixth century at the latest aristocratic patrons sought burial within the church, close to the altar and relics which guaranteed access to Heaven. As aristocrats increasingly sought to invest in the church as a means of stabilising family power, so we meet the phenomenon of the 'founder-grave', a rich burial or family cemetery made beneath an aristocratic church: the lavish chamber grave of *c.* 600 at Morken in the Rhineland is a famous early example, but by the seventh and eighth centuries the phenomenon is ubiquitous in Austrasia and east of the Rhine. The emergence of separate aristocratic burial sites and strategies resulted in the fracturing of the common culture of public display evident in sixth-century cemeteries. Settlement patterns too show aristocratic families increasingly marking themselves off from their neighbours, constructing large halls which dominated a village like Laucheim in Bavaria.[28]

The thickening of the documentary record as we move past 700 allows us to investigate the sources of elite wealth. They reveal an elite of landowners with scattered holdings on a vast scale, often focused on one locality but reaching across a segment of the realm. The seventh-century noblewoman Ermentrude, for example, left land at several dozen locations around Paris and Meaux, and dealt with around 100 unfree peasant households, as well as a range of other effects from ornate jewellery and clothing to carriages and livestock, in her will. Ermentrude was a widow, living off her portion of inheritances; an aristocratic household at a different stage in its life-cycle would have had greater resources. But the structure of her estates is typical of what we see in other documents, made up of agglomerations of fairly small units, parcels of fields or individual vineyards rather than whole villages or tracts of the countryside, which were exploited by the peasant households, normally unfree, sometimes freed, who lived off them as family holdings. Landlord control, then, was relatively indirect, rooted in rights of ownership that translated as the ability to take a proportion of the surplus as rent. The prevalence of relatively broadly defined systems of kinship based on partible inheritance, and the need to build alliances to maintain status, encouraged the constant transfer of individual land units complete with peasants. Elite status, then, effectively rested on the transfer of the surplus as rent, not on the direct management of an estate run as a going concern and farmed by a disciplined mass labour force. There were of course regional differences. South of the Loire, in societies where elite power in the countryside had a continuous history from late Roman times, landlord power rested on practices of revenue and render collection which seem to have originated in the workings of the late Roman tax system, now fallen into private hands, as most famously at Tours. But even here, what was at stake was the transfer of rent and render, not direct estate management: the will of Abbo, the leading landowner in early eighth-century Provence, thus shows a series of estates scattered down the Rhone and along the coast, many held by freedmen, and some managed through rent-collectors (*cartularii*) active in specifically assigned territories on Abbo's behalf.[29] The only exceptions to this picture come on royal lands in the Merovingian heartlands of Neustria, where kings were able to develop a new form of estate, the manor. Here, peasant families still lived off plots on which they paid rent, but they were also required to cultivate the demesne, managed directly to support the landlord; this system drew on the king's ability to demand labour and other menial services, originally public obligations but here integrated with landownership to create a new structure.

The rise of local landed elites did not eclipse the position of bishops. But the relatively cohesive and coherent elite that found its spokesman in Gregory of Tours, and was able to dominate Gaul south of the Loire in the sixth century, dissolved into a series of regional aristocracies in the changed political and social context of the seventh century. Bishops now mattered, from the Rhone to the Rhine, because they were pivotal figures within these local elites: the complaints of eighth-century missionaries and reformers about their involvement in feasting, feuding and hunting underlines the extent to which they were part of the networks of landed society.[30] As local leaders administering huge resources of secular as well as supernatural power, in the shape of land and local patronage, bishops remained crucial. Indeed, the social and economic changes which left *civitates* essentially as centres of religious cults and collective action, without any real concentration of administration, population or production, enabled them to strengthen their hold on the running of their cities: the letters of Desiderius, bishop of Cahors, present an impressive model of episcopal leadership. Appointments to bishoprics were an important royal right, in that they bound the ecclesiastical centres of the localities to the court. The promotion of sometime courtiers, and trusted royal officials, indeed, was one of the key royal strategies throughout the seventh century. Desiderius' letters and a series of saints' lives, for example, allow us to reconstruct a circle of young men who rose through the courts of Chlothar II and Dagobert, and were later given episcopal office right across the kingdom thanks to the influence of Balthild, wife of Clovis II. The hagiography shows local factions attempting to have their own candidates appointed to episcopal office, and such conflicts gave kings room for manoeuvre, and made royal patronage crucial in local politics. Indeed, the hagiography associated with sainted bishops is perhaps the most plentiful, and potentially the most illuminating, source for seventh-century politics, not least when it is realised that the saints' lives themselves were often written in response to the controversy surrounding the career of a powerful bishop. It is no surprise that the tradition of church councils that had been so central to the life of the sixth-century church dies out with the ending of this network of courtier-bishops in the last quarter of the seventh century.[31]

These various themes – the changing role of the cities, the granting away of royal power into the hands of privileged churches, and the increased centrality of local elites in the political system – all come together in what is perhaps the most striking development of the seventh century: the large-scale foundation of monastic houses by landed elites on their rural estates, and the development of grants of immunity from royal administration and exemption from episcopal jurisdiction which gave such foundations a privileged status. It is worth remembering that precisely this development lies behind the survival of virtually all our sources, and also alters the kind of evidence which we have to work with: our surviving charters, legal acts by kings and private individuals, concern these monasteries and were preserved by them, and allow us to build up admittedly fragmentary pictures of regional and regnal networks. Monasticism was not a new phenomenon, but before the seventh century monastic foundations had tended to be urban or suburban, and thus relate in some way to the power of local bishops. The career of Columbanus, an Irish missionary active particularly in Burgundy and northern Italy in the decades around 600, was an important stimulus for the new fashion of rural foundation by great families. Columbanus brought a style of monasticism which was firmly based in the countryside away from the urban centres of post-Roman Gaul, and which was reluctant to submit to the power of local bishops. It is striking that the first of the waves of monastic foundations which marked the seventh century, at Meaux and Faremoutiers in central Gaul for example, were made by precisely those aristocratic circles most intimate with Columbanus, whose own foundation at Luxeuil enjoyed a high status, and it is no accident that the key narrative source for the period up to the middle of the seventh century, the *Chronicle* of Fredegar, is strongly associated with Columbanian circles. This new monastic culture profoundly influenced the court of Dagobert I, himself a patron of St-Denis, and spread from there through figures such as Audoin, bishop of Rouen, who founded important monasteries at Jumièges and St-Wandrille.[32]

The new rural monasticism had much to offer its supporters. Primarily, of course, to devote resources to a monastic foundation was a pious act, but this was a form of piety that offered real advantages in this world and was therefore quite compatible with aristocratic strategies of power. This was not only a matter of the prestige generated and demonstrated by founding a holy place, in direct and constant contact with the sacred, on familial estates. Rural monasteries could also act as family centres, focal points for the new, aristocratic, networks of power which were emerging in the place of the urban and administrative infrastructure of post-Roman Gaul: Columbanus even blessed the households of some of his aristocratic patrons, sanctifying the seat of family power. The hagiography offers vivid examples of monasteries as the key points in family politics, often run by widows or daughters, as at Nivelles, founded by the dominant aristocratic family in Austrasia, the forerunners of the Carolingian kings; such places could even be the object of attacks by local rivals. The thickening of the documentary evidence which gives us a fuller picture of the social hierarchy, particularly after 700, is itself a product of these social changes, not an accident of survival. In early Merovingian times, legal documentation establishing title to land and labour was the business of cities as the places of public business, and the preferred medium of documentation was papyrus; in the last quarter of the seventh century, the gradual slowing of Mediterranean trade to a trickle led to a shift to parchment, produced locally from animal skins and easier to preserve. Those parchments that survive do so because they were kept and copied by the new aristocratic monasteries of northern Gaul, recording as they do the building up of land and rights by these foundations, which acted as something like land 'banks' for landowning families, who sought to safeguard their rights by granting them to 'their' church. These archives also feature exemptions from episcopal interference and the royal grants of immunity that founders procured for their monasteries to help secure family control. The immunities granted by kings may have appeared to give away power, but they also created intimate ties between Merovingian rulers and the institutions they chose to patronise; when examined in detail, such grants, as used by a ruler like Dagobert, could serve as instruments to bind together the kingdom, tying local networks of familial power to the royal court. Indeed Balthild, the queen and royal mother who was the dominant political figure of the middle decades of the seventh century, was to bind the great churches of the Neustrian heartland tightly to herself and the Merovingian dynasty into which she had married through her patronage, and was able to exercise her power even beyond her official 'retirement' to the royal nunnery at Chelles through her religious network.[33]

The late Merovingian church was roundly criticised by later Carolingian reformers, and modern historians have been eager to repeat the negative judgements. We should beware of hindsight: to condemn the Merovingian church for the regional differences so apparent in its liturgies and rites is to adopt the standards of Carolingian reformers who sought to impose unity where none had previously existed. The seventh century was a golden age of church foundation, as elites engaged with new forms of piety that made sense of their world. Columbanus and his followers brought with them from Ireland a system of 'tariffed penance' which rapidly won widespread popularity. Based on the idea that for each sin, amends needed to be made to God through penance, this mirrored the secular world of family honour and feud, of favours to be reciprocated and wrongs avenged. Through the agency of the new monasticism, aristocratic families were able to invest in the economy of alms-giving, prayer and intercession that ensured God's favour. The *Vision* of the retired royal official and wealthy landowner Barontus gives a vivid insight into this world: having entered the monastery on Logoretum in his retirement for the good of his soul, Barontus aroused the suspicion of some fellow monks on account of his worldly past and the sins involving sex and money it had involved. Dangerously ill, and facing gossip about his conduct, in 679 he dreamt he was transported to the Other World. As his soul flew over the countryside of central Gaul, the bells and prayers of monastic life appeared, crystal clear, through the haze, points of contact between this world and the next which warded off the demons who fought with his angelic bearers for possession of him; on his return, he made a public repentance, and repeated the message he had been given about the cleansing effects of the medicine of penance, exemplified in the monastic life.[34] The old systems of gift-giving between living and dead through the burial of grave-goods slowly gave way to a new system in which the church acted as intermediary between the living and the dead, with gifts to monastic foundations linked to the commemoration of ancestors and the hope of salvation through prayer. There was no standard or single monastic rule – monastic patrons often operated a 'pick and mix' system, combining elements from the various rules on offer – but this reflects a period of experimentation and creativity, not a lack of discipline: there was no perceived need for centralised oversight or uniformity within monasticism. In fact, the most eloquent testimony to the engagement of the seventh-century church with Merovingian society was the export of Christianity into the old frontier areas along the Rhine and beyond. Again, whilst the propagandists of Carolingian reform sought to present the conversion of the provinces east of the Rhine as a Carolingian achievement, it was the seventh century which saw the development of a theology of mission, inspired by the example of Columbanus and the notion of a perpetual pilgrimage; on a practical level, the expanding interests of Merovingian bishops and elites resulted in waves of church foundations in the east.

What we see in the seventh century is the emergence of aristocratic networks of power, rooted in direct control over land, as the basis of politics. With the atrophy of the Roman administrative infrastructure, and the changing role of the cities, kings had no choice but to work through these networks. They did so remarkably successfully precisely because they acknowledged these facts and redefined their role, as patrons whose courts could become the focal point of local ambition and who could bind together those who held local power. To a large extent, this involved acknowledging the devolution of local power. Even the aristocracies of Neustria, Burgundy and Austrasia were allowed to develop their own hierarchies, headed by a leader who held the position of mayor of the palace for that kingdom. Although holders of a royal office, mayors were not royal appointments pure and simple: kings seem to have allowed elites to debate, and waited for a candidate to emerge rather than simply appointing on whim. The crucial point for the king was the maintenance of a political situation facilitating contact between court and locality, and encouraging local factions to aim for office within the court hierarchy. This was essentially a system of power-sharing between king and aristocracy. Within it, the inevitability of political conflict over the distribution of power was acknowledged, as was the king's role as final arbiter of that distribution.

Courts and kingdoms in the seventh century

Dagobert has traditionally been seen as the last effective Merovingian ruler, succeeded by generations of 'do-nothing kings', *rois fainéants*. Such a view is largely a result of the propaganda put out by their Carolingian successors in the first decades of the ninth century: now that historians are beginning to realise that such sources tell us more about the Carolingian court's willingness to use the past than they do about the realities of Merovingian politics, a radically different view, based on strictly contemporary sources, is emerging. The peaceful management of royal succession, the ease with which a succession of royal minorities was handled, and the continued ability of kings to exercise patronage over local elites, suggest a cohesive and successful political system based on power-sharing.

For the vast bulk of the seventh century – at the very least, from 613–87 – it was the western kingdom of Neustria that was the key to Merovingian politics. It is a testimony to the strength of the Neustrian hegemony that seventh-century Merovingians were able to base themselves and their court firmly in the Paris basin, and rule the kingdom without regular movements beyond this royal heartland. At potential flashpoints kings might travel to meet regional elites face-to-face, in their own backyards: Dagobert, for example, toured Burgundy in 628 and Austrasia in 629. But such journeys were the exception, not the rule: they intensified contact between king and local elites at key moments, but for most of the time such contact was maintained successfully without the king leaving the Paris basin. Here we find a royal landscape of palaces, many of them now rural or suburban where earlier kings had based themselves in Roman governmental residences within the cities. Here we also find a concentration of supernatural power. This took the form of royal patronage of holy places, above all the abbey of St Denis, spectacularly adorned by Dagobert, whose burial there marked the foundation of a royal necropolis, and a network of other monastic foundations such as Chelles, closely linked to Balthild. It was reinforced by the avid collection of holy objects in the royal relic collection, with the cloak of St Martin coming in time to define the royal chapel by the second half of the seventh century: Clovis II's enthusiasm was such that he even attempted to remove the arm of St Denis and add it to the collection. That important figures might have estates or dwellings at or close by the court, and young aristocrats were sent there for political training, only serves to underline the centrality of the court and the patronage networks leading out from it to the seventh-century polity. The centrality of the palace enabled the royal women whose job was to maintain the royal household to act as central brokers within this political system: Clovis II's reign (638–57) was dominated by two women whose influence was pervasive behind the scenes: initially his mother Nantechild and latterly his wife, Balthild, an Anglo-Saxon who rose from slavery through the patronage of his mayor of the palace, Ercinoald.[35]

In contrast to this detailed picture of the Neustrian court establishment, we are relatively poorly informed about the internal politics of Austrasia. Although proper allowance must be made for the differences in the evidence between the two kingdoms, and particularly the absence for Austrasia of anything comparable to the hagiography and letters associated with the circle of courtiers-turned-bishops on which our knowledge of Neustria is based, it may be that there were significant differences between the political structures of the two kingdoms. For one thing, Austrasian politics seems to have been less focused on a single royal heartland than that of the west. There was a series of important royal residences with associated estates and resources devoted to their upkeep: Metz on the Moselle, Cologne on the lower Rhine, and Strasbourg on the upper Rhine seem to have been the key royal centres. This series of centres reflects the political geography of a kingdom based along the long river valleys of the Rhine, the Moselle and the Meuse. Kings, however, must have moved further and more often than their western counterparts, and it may be no accident that in the sources that we do have there are mentions of kings visiting aristocrats in aristocratic residences: this may have been a polity in which royal power was dependent on the ability to bind together local elites through progress from locality to locality. It would certainly be unsurprising if the structuring of the relationship between king and aristocracy in Austrasia differed from that in Neustria. For one thing, unlike Neustria, Austrasia had a long open frontier, and a vast underdeveloped hinterland east of the Rhine: the documentary evidence from the seventh and eighth centuries makes it clear that aristocrats from right across Austrasia enriched themselves considerably through property holdings and political leadership east of the Rhine. The resultant close links between the Austrasian aristocracy and the leaders of the peripheral principalities beyond the Rhine could lead to political alliance, as in 639 when the Thuringian leader Radulf enjoyed considerable support from the Rhineland.[36] Throughout the seventh century factions within Austrasia were willing and able to call upon support from beyond the Rhine, as well as from Neustria: political conflict was thus significantly less centred on king and court than was the case in the west, because of the recurrent resort to the military might of outside backers. Neustrian intervention reflected the junior political status of Austrasia within the Merovingian realm as a whole, but it also meant that the Austrasian crown was discontinuous and the Austrasian court unable to create the kind of political centrality that we saw in Neustria.

The dominance of Neustria within the political system was a direct result of Chlothar II's triumph in 613, and both Chlothar and Dagobert used Austrasia as a political testing ground by granting sons subkingship there. The long reign of Sigibert III, from 633–56, may have allowed a court establishment comparable to that in Neustria to develop: certainly, the famous but shadowy events following Sigibert's death in 656, when the mayor of the palace Grimoald attempted to place his son on the throne, suggest so. Grimoald's son gained the throne not so much as an usurper as a surrogate Merovingian, taking the Merovingian royal name of Childebert and stressing that he was the adopted son of Sigibert's widow, who acted in concert with Grimoald to exclude Sigibert's son by an earlier wife from the throne, despatching him to a monastery in Ireland. Although they were designed to maintain the power of the court establishment, these actions would almost certainly have been unthinkable in Neustria. Indeed, outraged Neustrian sensibilities led to military intervention to restore 'order': Grimoald was captured and executed in 657, and Neustrian dominance re-established in 662, with a junior Merovingian from the Neustrian line, Childeric II, married to the daughter of Sigibert and established on the Austrasian throne. Although modern historians have often made much of the coup, pointing to the fact that Grimoald was an ancestor of the dynasty that eventually replaced the Merovingians, the Carolingians, it actually shows the continuing hold of the Merovingian dynasty on Frankish kingship, and the continued viability of the political system set up by Chlothar and Dagobert; in any case, the Carolingian kings were only indirect descendants of Grimoald and his heirs showed no will to attempt to repeat his attempted elevation.

The establishment of a new regime in Austrasia left the Neustrian court dominant once again. Aristocratic ambitions continued to centre around the patronage offered by the court: thus the death of the long-standing mayor of the palace in Neustria, Ercinoald, led to open conflict, before an aristocrat named Ebroin established himself as mayor in 664. Significantly, it was the growing power of Ebroin, and his attempts to exclude his rivals, and particularly those Burgundian aristocrats who had been prominent under his predecessor, from the court, that led to the first prolonged crisis of the seventh-century regime. Matters came to a head in 673, when Ebroin attempted to manage the royal succession in favour of his personal candidate. The Burgundians, led by Leodegar, bishop of Autun, were excluded from the process and attempted to establish a different regime; eventually the Austrasians, led by Childeric II, had to be called in. But in 675 Childeric and his pregnant wife were ambushed and murdered: their opponents feared the imminent possibility of a male heir to Childeric, which would have consolidated the hold of his Austrasian regime, which was already threatening the local interests of the Neustrian and Burgundian aristocracies. The ensuing power struggle involved rival factions within both kingdoms, and ended with the defeat of the Austrasians and abolition of the Austrasian court and kingship in 679.

Throughout the crisis, it is striking how the different aristocratic factions did not question the framework of Merovingian dynastic legitimacy, adopting men with Merovingian blood in their veins as their figureheads. The cluster of written sources (mainly hagiographical) describing the crisis articulate conflict in terms of norms about right and wrong political behaviour, and ideas about the proper ordering of political life. Thus Ebroin was charged by his opponents with having broken the basic rules of inclusiveness and power-sharing which had defined political life since 614 by excluding opponents from court through an 'unlawful edict'; Leodegar and his party, indeed, issued decrees in their turn which consciously evoked those issued at Paris in 614 as guaranteeing the ground rules of the political system.[37] This was not so much the failure of Merovingian kingship as a revolt against a court establishment that had alienated an important section of the aristocracy precisely because too much power had been concentrated in the hands of one figure, Ebroin, and the checks and balances in the system thus destroyed.

The long-term consequence of the crisis, however, was a significant change in the relationship between Neustria and Austrasia, with their final integration: after 679 they were never again ruled separately, but remained part of one kingdom with one court. As that court remained in Neustria, this left power within Austrasia directly in the hands of the aristocracy; Pippin, the son of Grimoald's sister, was able to emerge from the crisis of the 670s as the dominant figure. Political stability under the new king, Theuderic III, within the enlarged kingdom was elusive, in part because of the inevitable difficulty of giving factions from right across the unified realm a stake in the regime, and the danger that the mayor of the palace might prove over-mighty and exclude his opponents from the court – a fear that led directly to the assassination of the mayor Berchar in 680. Thereafter, peace was made, until another over-ambitious mayor provoked renewed internal conflict within Neustria and then renewed Austrasian intervention in the west, which culminated in Pippin's victory at the battle of Tertry in 687.

Thanks to the historical writings commissioned a century and more later by Pippin's royal Carolingian descendants, Tertry has often been seen as the end of the line for Merovingian kingship: thereafter it was Pippin who exercised real power, with the Merovingian kings little more than puppets, whilst Pippin's Austrasian followers were promoted over the heads of the Neustrian elite. Strictly contemporary writings offer a different perspective: the *Liber Historiae Francorum*, a concise historical narrative of the years up to 721, written from an explicitly Neustrian perspective, presents politics as continuing according to time-honoured norms of consensus, with the Merovingian court as the locus of power-sharing and consultation.[38] Pippin's political strategy suggests that this perspective is essentially accurate. Pippin's actions in Neustria were those of a newcomer finding his way into an embedded establishment. Initially he allied a leading Neustrian family, into which he married his son, Drogo; it was only in the late 690s, when his family had put down roots in Neustria, that he installed another son, Grimoald, as mayor of the palace in Neustria. Pippin's family was able to establish control over some key Neustrian bishoprics (such as Rouen) and monasteries (like St-Wandrille), but alliances with existing families were the mechanism through which this was achieved. Moreover, records of judgements made at the royal court, and particularly in the reign of Childebert III (694–711) show Pippin and his allies on occasion losing, and aristocrats from right across the realm, some of whom were Pippin's political opponents, in attendance.[39] In other words, although Pippin and his kin were the dominant faction, the court and the Merovingian king were still accessible to all, and royal patronage served to bind the kingdom as a whole together: hence the internal peace which seems to have marked the 690s and 700s. Nonetheless, we should not overemphasise continuity. The office of mayor, which already under Ebroin and Pippin's immediate predecessors had come to involve a significant amount of day-to-day governmental activity, was clearly a vehicle for the exercise of real political power, and whilst a ruler like Childebert III should not be dismissed as powerless, the functions of Merovingian kingship may have been increasingly bound up with brokering consensus and creating legitimacy. Whilst previous mayors had attempted to ensure their son's succession (almost always unsuccessfully), Pippin was able to grant mayoral office to his sons whilst he still lived, and thus establish a mayoral dynasty.

Nonetheless, it was probably in Austrasia, not Neustria, that these decades saw the most significant changes. Pippin had only emerged as the leading figure in Austrasia following the carnage and internal crisis of the 670s, and there is evidence for rival factions within Austrasia surviving well into the eighth century. The lack of a separate Austrasian court, alongside Pippin's dominance in Neustria, created an unprecedented situation which allowed him to overcome the normal laws of political gravity which meant that any family, after a certain period in the ascendant, would inevitably eventually lose out to rivals, ready to seize the moment created by a death, internal dispute or political crisis. For after Pippin had seized the reins of power in Neustria in 688, he returned to Austrasia, where he created a powerbase that surpassed that of any previous Merovingian aristocrat. The documentary record reveals that it was under Pippin that the dense network of land, clients and monasteries in Austrasia which were the foundation of Carolingian power were created: Pippin married into the dominant family of the Moselle valley, and later also acquired interests in the Meuse through a second liaison; the decades around 700 also saw moves against his main rivals within Austrasia, whilst the resources previously attached to the Austrasian court may have also found their way into Pippin's hands at this juncture.

The extent of Pippin's success is evident from the political conflict which followed his death in 714, which was to some extent a succession crisis within his family: Pippin's widow, Plectrude, and Charles Martel, Pippin's son by a second liaison whose status is unclear, struggled for control of Pippin's political legacy. Indeed, jockeying for position began as Pippin lay on his deathbed, with the murder of Grimoald, Plectrude's only surviving son, possibly at the instigation of Martel. Plectrude initially attempted to rule by appointing her infant grandchildren as mayors. The appointment of minors as mayors was wholly unprecedented, and provoked revolt from the Neustrians, who evidently felt that the political ground rules of consultation had been breached and moved against the establishment of a dynastic hold on the mayoral office. They selected a Neustrian aristocrat as their mayor, and, following the death of the reigning Merovingian in 715, raised a monk who claimed Merovingian blood and reigned as Chilperic II to the throne, giving them a Merovingian leader who was wholly independent of Pippin's family. Chilperic and his Neustrian followers allied with the Frisians, who had suffered militarily and politically at Pippin's hands; they met with immediate success, and it was not until 719 that they were finally defeated. That the descendants of Pippin were able to weather the storm in spite of their intra-familial differences was ultimately due to their dominance in Austrasia, and the absence of any focal point within Austrasia around which their rivals could rally. Martel was able to establish his dominance thanks to the strategic importance of the lands and followers inherited from his mother on the Meuse: it was in this region, at Amblève, that he was able to defeat a joint Frisian-Neustrian force which was ravaging Austrasia in 716. This victory, and a subsequent success at Vinchy, enabled him to establish himself as undisputed heir of his father and leader of the Austrasians. After acquiring a Merovingian claimant in whose name he could campaign, Martel's Austrasian army was able to force the Neustrians, now allied to the Aquitainians as well as the Frisians, to hand Chilperic II over in 719: without a Merovingian behind whom they could rally, Neustrian resistance collapsed.

The armed conflict of these years confirmed that the outcome of the earlier conflict of the 670–80s, namely Austrasian dominance within Neustria, was to continue; it was also the last explicit challenge to Pippin's implantation of his family at the heart of the kingdom as partners of the Merovingian dynasty. But whereas Pippin had been able to insinuate himself slowly, gracefully and peacefully into the Neustrian establishment, the events of 714–19 meant that Martel's coming to power across the realm as a whole was seen as far less consensual and far more abrupt. This led to real changes in the political system. True, Martel, although he was presented in increasingly regal terms, continued to rule through Merovingian kings and the Neustrian court. We certainly should not write off the Merovingian dynasty prematurely: the time and effort spent doing so by later Carolingian writers may in fact be an oblique testimony to their continuing role as a focal point for political allegiances, not least on account of their ritual functions. Nonetheless, if kingship remained important, the sense of a court establishment holding the polity together begins to falter in the 710s. Under Pippin the Merovingian court was the institution through which influence could be wielded throughout the kingdom; under Martel Merovingian blood legitimated the regime, but the subtle mechanisms through which the court had held together an array of local elites had begun to break down. This was not only the case in Neustria and Burgundy: the mechanisms which bound the peripheral principalities both east of the Rhine and in southern Gaul to the court – often delicately balanced and intermittent in their operation – likewise ground to a halt. As a result, Charles' nickname, Martel or 'hammer', is largely apposite: he literally had to hammer out his power across most of the Merovingian kingdom. But in doing so, he did not alter the segmentary and open nature of the Frankish political system, which continued to accommodate and legitimate the power of landowning elites, and was thus to provide a potent template for Frankish dominance of western Europe in the eighth century.

Bibliographical essay

Sources in translation

Most of the major sources for Merovingian history are now available in English translation. A. C. Murray, *From Roman to Frankish Gaul: A Reader* (Peterborough, Ont., 2000) is an indispensable companion, with all the major sources and much else too. In terms of individual authors, pride of place must be given to Gregory of Tours, whose *Histories* are translated under the title *History of the Franks* by L. Thorpe (London, 1974), and whose various works of hagiography appear in the Liverpool *Translated Texts for Historians* series: E. James, tr. *Lives of the Martyrs* (1985), R. van Dam, tr. *Glory of the Confessors* (1988), *Glory of the Martyrs* (1988). Gregory's two more 'private' works of hagiography, recording the miracles of his two personal patrons, Julian and Martin, are tr. as an appendix to R. van Dam, *Saints and their Miracles in Late Antique Gaul* (Princeton, 1993). The poems of Venantius Fortunatus are the other main source for sixth-century culture and politics: they are tr. J. George (Liverpool, 1995). The other major historical narratives are available in J. M. Wallace-Hadrill, *The Fourth Book of the Chronicle of Fredegar with its Continuations* (Oxford, 1962), and P. Fouracre and R. Gerberding, *Late Merovingian France* (Manchester, 1996), which includes the *Liber Historiae Francorum* and the Carolingian *Prior Metz Annals*, as well as several later Merovingian saints' lives. Other saints' lives are available: Jonas' *Life of Columbanus* in E. Peters, *Monks, Bishops and Pagans* (Philadelphia, 1981) or extracts in T. Head, *Medieval Hagiography* (London, 2000), which also includes Audoin's *Life of Eligius*; the lives of several female Merovingian saints, notably

Radegund, are tr. in J. McNamara, *Sainted Women of the Dark Ages* (Durham NC, 1982); the *Life of Amand* and the *Vision of Barontus*, tr. J. Hillgarth, *Christianity and Paganism, 350–700* (Philadelphia, 1986). Translations of Frankish law-codes are available in T. J. Rivers, *Laws of the Salian and Ripuarian Franks* (New York, 1986) and T. J. Rivers, *Laws of the Alamans and Bavarians* (Philadelphia, 1977).

General works

The past decades have seen the production of a surprising number of general works, many in English, reflecting the increased maturity of Merovingian history. I. N. Wood, *The Merovingian Kingdoms, 481–751* (London, 1993) is an excellent and exhaustive survey, based on an intimate knowledge of the written sources, whilst P. Geary, *Before France and Germany: The Making and Transformation of the Merovingian World* (New York, 1998) is full of insight and ideas. K. van Welck, ed., *Die Franken: Wegbereiter Europas*, 2 vols (Mainz, 1996) makes good use of the archaeological evidence, all too often ignored, and is well worth looking at for the lavish illustrations and maps even for those who cannot read the French and German articles. Although now dated, J. M. Wallace-Hadrill, 'The long-haired kings' in his book of the same title (Oxford, 1953) is still a good read and a sound introduction to the political narrative. E. James, *The Franks* (Oxford, 1988) is equally at home with archaeological and written sources, and the best read on the period up to Gregory of Tours. On the later Merovingian period, the introduction to Fouracre and Gerberding, *Late Merovingian France* (Manchester, 1996) is excellent, stimulating and succinct.

Work on the primary sources

As historians have grown more aware of the importance of the perspective and agenda of the writers of their primary sources, so the volume of work exploring the political and mental worlds of our guides to the period have expanded dramatically. This is particularly the case with Gregory of Tours, on whom the reading is voluminous and constitutes virtually a subdiscipline in itself: I. N. Wood's pamphlet, *Gregory of Tours* (Bangor, 1995), is probably the best place to start, and for a more detailed account of Gregory's political manoeuvring see the same author's 'The secret histories of Gregory of Tours', *Revue Belge d'Histoire et de Philologie* 71 (1993); on Gregory as an historian see W. Goffart, *The Narrators of Barbarian History* (1988), chapter 3, which demonstrates quite conclusively that Gregory aimed to write a history of Gaul in which God and his saints were centre stage, not a history of the Franks; Goffart's findings are reinforced by the work of A. Breukelaar, *Historiography and Episcopal Authority in Sixth-Century Gaul* (Gottingen, 1994); M. Heinzelmann, *Gregory of Tours: History and Society in the Sixth Century* (Cambridge, 2001), also his 'Heresy in Books I and II of Gregory of Tours' *Historiae*', in A. C. Murray, ed., *After Rome's Fall: Narrators and Sources of Early Medieval History* (Toronto, 1998); Gregory himself is placed in the tradition of Roman aristocratic culture and patronage politics by R. van Dam, *Leadership and Community in Late Antique Gaul* (Berkeley, 1985); whilst the

1200th anniversary of Gregory's death in 1994 led to N. Gauthier and H. Galinié, eds, *Grégoire de Tours et l'espace gaulois* (Tours, 1997) and K. Mitchell and I. Wood, eds, *Gregory of Tours* (Leiden, 2002). For one of Gregory's contemporaries, see J. George, *Venantius Fortunatus: A Poet in Merovingian Gaul* (Oxford, 1997). On Fredegar, see R. Collins' pamphlet, *Fredegar* (Aldershot, 1997), which has a good review of earlier debate, and Wood's, 'Fredegar's fables' in G. Scheibelreiter and A. Scharer, eds, *Historiographie im frühen Mittelalter* (Vienna, 1994). R. Gerberding, *The Liber Historiae Francorum and the Rise of the Carolingians* (Oxford, 1987) is an excellent detailed narrative of high politics, and a stimulating account of the political values of his source. On the use of saints' lives as sources for political history, P. Fouracre, 'Merovingian history and Merovingian hagiography', *Past & Present* 127 (1990) is a fascinating case-study.

Regional studies

There is a surprising amount in English. The best to start with is P. Geary, *Aristocracy in Provence: The Rhone Basin at the Dawn of the Carolingian Era* (Stuttgart, 1985), a detailed but easy to follow account of the regional politics and society of early eighth-century Provence, which also includes a full translation of the will of Abbo of Provence. Staying in the south, M. Rouche, *L'Aquitaine des Wisigoths aux Arabes* (Paris, 1979), is well worth the effort for those who can read French. On Burgundy and, further north, Neustria, there is relatively little: the conference proceedings *La Neustrie*, ed. H. Atsma, 2 vols (Sigmaringen, 1989) contain a number of important studies of all aspects of culture, society and politics, but the rich documentary evidence from the Merovingian heartlands in the Seine and Loire valleys could sustain detailed investigation of local structures; for the arrival of the followers of Pippin in this region see P. Fouracre, 'Observations on the outgrowth of Pippinid influence in the Regnum Francorum after the battle of Tertry, 687–715', *Medieval Prosopography* 5 (1984). There is more reading as we move east, into Austrasia. G. Halsall, *Settlement and Social Organisation: The Merovingian Region of Metz* (Cambridge, 1995) demonstrates the value of the archaeological evidence, but is less secure on documents and laws and misses the important contributions of German scholarship; compare here H. Hummer, *Politics and Power in Early Medieval Europe: Alsace and the Frankish Realm, 600–1000* (Cambridge, 2006). There is also a plethora of German studies, mostly concentrating on the late seventh and early eighth centuries: students should be aware of (even if they cannot read) two books by M. Werner on the Meuse and Moselle valleys respectively, *Das Lütticher Raum im frühkarolingischer Zeit* (Göttingen, 1980) and *Adelsfamilien im Umkreis der frühen Karolinger* (Sigmaringen, 1982); in French, A. Dierkens, *Abbayes et Chapitres entre Sambre et Meuse, VII–XI siècles* (Sigmaringen, 1985) is invaluable. M. Costambeys, 'An aristocratic community on the north Frankish frontier, 690–726', *Early Medieval Europe* 3 (1994) is a good short study, which gives an idea of the kind of work that can be done from the local evidence; in a similar vein, integrating the archaeology too, see F. Theuws, 'Landed property and manorial organisation in northern Austrasia', in N. Roymans and F. Theuws,

Images of the Past (Amsterdam, 2001). The eastern peripheral principalities have their own bibliographies, in German: H. Wolfram, *Die Geburt Mitteleuropas* (Vienna, 1987), is the best introduction to Alemannia and Bavaria, with full bibliography, whilst the most recent treatment is W. Hartung, *Suddeutschland im Merowingerzeit* (Sigmaringen, 1988); the bibliography on central Germany is more patchy, and best approached through R. Butzen, *Die Merowinger östlich des mittleren Rheins* (Wurzburg, 1987), who in my view makes Merovingian rule there far more institutionalised than was the case, and the older study of R. Sprandel, *Der merowingische Adel und die Gebiete östlich des Rheins* (Freiburg-im-Breisgau, 1957). I. Wood, 'The frontiers of western Europe: developments east of the Rhine in the sixth century', in W. Bowden and R. Hodges, eds, *The Sixth Century: Production and Demand* (Leiden, 1998), is an excellent treatment of political and other developments in these areas. On Frisia and Saxony there is very little in any language, largely due to the very sparse primary evidence, but the work of S. Lebecq, whilst primarily concentrating on economic history, gives invaluable insights into political and religious developments: see particularly *Marchands et navigateurs frisons du haut moyen age* (Lille, 1983), and his shorter study of political relations, 'Francs contre Frisons', in *La guerre et la paix au moyen age* (Paris, 1978). I. Wood's important pamphlet, *The Merovingian North Sea* (Alingsas, 1983), is the best treatment of Merovingian hegemony in northern Europe.

The making of the kingdom

I. Wood, ed., *Franks and Alemanni in the Migration Period* (Woodbridge, 1998), is an up-to-date guide to the making of the Frankish people and kingdom from the fifth to seventh centuries, with the latest thinking on both written and archaeological sources. For the fifth-century context, see esp. J. Drinkwater and H. Elton, eds, *Fifth-Century Gaul: A Crisis of Identity?* (Cambridge, 1992) and R. Mathisen and D. Shanzer, *Society and Culture in Late Antique Gaul: Revisiting the Sources* (Aldershot, 2001); on Childeric in particular, in addition to Halsall's contribution to the latter volume, see S. Lebecq, 'The many faces of King Childeric: archaeology, history, historiography', in W. Pohl and M. Diesenberger, eds, *Integration und Herrschaft* (Vienna, 2002). The conversion of Clovis is one of the great set-piece debates of historical scholarship. M. Spencer, 'Dating the baptism of Clovis', *Early Medieval Europe* 2 (1993) traces the development of the various arguments; the two most important recent contributions, both suggesting a radical reinterpretation, are I. N. Wood, 'Gregory of Tours and Clovis', *Revue Belge d'Histoire et de Philologie* 63 (1985) and D. Shanzer, 'Dating the baptism of Clovis: the bishop of Rheims versus the Bishop of Vienne', *Early Medieval Europe* 6 (1997). A good, up-to-date, discussion of Clovis' reign is W. M. Daly, 'Clovis: how barbaric, how pagan?', *Speculum* 69 (1994). I. Wood, 'Kings, kingdoms and consent', in I. Wood and P. Sawyer, eds, *Early Medieval Kingship* (Leeds, 1977) is the fundamental study of the division of 511. On Clovis, Byzantium and his reception at Tours, M. McCormick, 'Clovis at Tours: Byzantine public rituals and the origins of medieval ruler symbolism', in E. Chrysos and A. Schwarcz, eds, *Das Reich und die Barbaren* (Vienna, 1989).

Oddly, there is little on kingship in English, although J. M. Wallace-Hadrill, *Early Germanic Kingship* (Oxford, 1971), still has much of value, and A. C. Murray, '*Post vocantur Merohingii*: Fredegar, Merovech and "sacral kingship"', in Murray, ed., *After Rome's Fall: Narrators and Sources of Early Medieval History* (Toronto, 1999), is an important corrective; on the myth of Trojan origins, I. Wood, 'Defining the Franks', in S. Forde, L. Johnson and A. Murray, eds, *National Identity in Medieval Europe* (Leeds, 1995). On the political power of Merovingian women, see Nelson, 'Queens as Jezebels: Brunhild and Balthild in Merovingian history', *Studies in Church History Subsidia* 1 (1978), reprinted in her *Politics and Ritual in Early Medieval Europe* (Woodbridge, 1986). On royal hairstyles, Av. Cameron, 'How did the Merovingian kings wear their hair?', *Revue Belge de Philologie et d'Histoire* 43 (1965) remains the best discussion. E. James, 'Gregory of Tours and the Franks', in A. C. Murray, ed., *After Rome's Fall: Narrators and Sources of Early Medieval History* (Toronto, 1998), discusses the progress of Frankish identity in sixth-century Gaul.

The church

On the Merovingian church's political role, J. M. Wallace-Hadrill, *The Merovingian Church* (Oxford, 1983) is an excellent starting-point. The relevant sections of B. H. Rosenwein, *Negotiating Space: Power, Restraint and Privileges of Immunity in Early Medieval Europe* (Ithaca, 1998) give a stimulating introduction to the latest thinking on monasteries. The classic work on monasticism remains F. Prinz, *Frühes Mönchtum im Frankenreich* (Munich, 1965); there is also much of value in H. Clarke and M. Brennan, eds, *Columbanus and Merovingian Monasticism*, British Archaeological Reports International Series 113 (Oxford, 1981) and M. Lapidge, *Columbanus: Studies on the Latin Writings* (Woodbridge, 1997). Brilliant insight into the world of seventh-century family monasteries in R. Le Jan, 'Convents, violence and competition for power in seventh-century Francia', in M. de Jong and F. Theuws, eds, *Topographies of Power in the Early Middle Ages* (Leiden, 2001).

There are excellent treatments of the centrality of bishops to local politics by P. Fouracre, 'Merovingian hagiography and Merovingian history', *Past & Present* 127 (1990) and I. N. Wood, 'The ecclesiastical politics of Merovingian Clermont', in P. Wormald *et al.*, eds, *Ideal and Reality in Frankish and Anglo-Saxon Society* (Oxford, 1983); on the relationship between royal and episcopal power see P. Fouracre, 'Eternal light and earthly needs: practical aspects of the development of Frankish immunities', in W. Davies and P. Fouracre, eds, *Property and Power in the Early Middle Ages* (Cambridge, 1995). B. Jussen, 'Liturgy and legitimation, or how the Gallo-Romans ended the Roman Empire', in Jussen, ed., *Ordering Medieval Society* (Philadelphia, 2000) is the latest word on the origins of episcopal power; two important German monographs here are M. Heinzelmann, *Bischofsherrschaft in Gallien* (Zurich, 1976) and R. Kaiser, *Bischofsherrschaft zwischen Königtum und Fürstenmacht* (Bonn, 1981). J. Durliat, 'Les attributions civiles des évêques mérovingiens: l'exemple de Didier, évêque de Cahors', *Annales du Midi* 91 (1979) argues for episcopal power as delegated state power.

Work on religion has tended to move away from older views, which saw the church in a long-term and often compromised struggle against hardened paganism, and instead stress the changing definitions of Christianity after initial conversion, as the church gradually implicated itself in society; in this scheme of 'Christianisation', active pagan opposition plays a far smaller role, and the church's own attempts to define the boundaries of acceptable behaviour come centre stage. Vital here is R. Markus, 'From Caesarius to Boniface: Christianity and paganism in Gaul', in J. Fontaine and J. Hillgarth, eds, *The Seventh Century* (London, 1992); building on this, Y. Hen, *Culture and Religion in Merovingian Gaul 481–751* (Leiden, 1992). On 'popular' religion and Christianisation, see the contributions by Stancliffe, Wood and Fouracre to *Studies in Church History* 16 (1979); for the geographical expansion of Christianity in the seventh century see Hillgarth and Wood in M. Richter, ed., *Irland und die Christenheit* (Stuttgart, 1981).

On saints' cults, the starting-point was the work of Peter Brown, which placed Gregory of Tours at the end of late antique developments: esp. his *The Cult of the Saints: Its Rise and Function in Latin Antiquity* (Chicago, 1981) and his Stenton lecture, *Relics and Social Status in the Age of Gregory of Tours* (Reading, 1977), now reprinted in his *Society and the Holy in Late Antiquity* (Berkeley, 1982). R. van Dam, *Saints and their Miracles in Late Antique Gaul* (Princeton, 1993) is an excellent survey of Gregory; for some critical perspectives see P. Hayward and J. Howard-Johnston, *The Cult of the Saints in Late Antiquity and the Early Middle Ages* (Oxford, 1999) esp. Hayward. See also B. Beaujard, *Le culte de saintes en Gaule d'Hilaire de Poitiers au fin du VI siècle* (Paris, 2000). For the rise of penance and associated cultural changes, P. Brown, 'The decline of the empire of God: amnesty, penance and the afterlife from late antiquity to the early Middle Ages', in C. Bynum and P. Freedman, eds, *Last Things* (Philadelphia, 2000); for a different perspective on this source material, I. Moreira, *Dreams, Visions and Spiritual Authority in Merovingian Gaul* (Ithaca, 2000).

State and society

On royal and local government the fundamental work has been that of the German historian E. Ewig, most of which has been collected into *Spätantikes und fränkisches Gallien* 2 vols (Munich, 1976–9). Ewig's work is the starting-point for any serious study of Merovingian Gaul. W. Goffart, 'Old and new in Merovingian taxation', *Past & Present* 96 (1982), reprinted in his *Rome's Fall and After* (London, 1986), is an important analysis of the end of the Roman tax system; a different, but to my mind faulty, view of continuity has recently been developed by E. Magnou-Nortier and J. Durliat: see for example the latter's *Les finances publiques de Diocletian aux Carolingians* (Sigmaringen, 1990). On literacy and legal culture, see I. Wood, 'Administration, law and culture in Merovingian Gaul', in R. McKitterick, ed., *The Uses of Literacy in Early Medieval Europe* (Cambridge, 1990); on law in action, I. Wood, 'Disputes in fifth- and sixth-century Gaul' and

P. Fouracre '"Placita" and the settlement of disputes in late Merovingian Francia', in W. Davies and P. Fouracre, eds, *The Settlement of Disputes in Early Medieval Europe* (Cambridge, 1986). On administrative practice see D. Ganz, 'Bureaucratic shorthand and Merovingian learning', in P. Wormald, ed., *Ideal and Reality in Frankish and Anglo-Saxon Society* (Oxford, 1983), and W. Goffart and D. Ganz, 'Charters earlier than 800 AD from French collections', *Speculum* 65 (1990), drawing on fundamental work by P. Classen.

Specialised studies of local administration, emphasising continuity with Rome, are those of A. C. Murray, 'The position of the *grafio* in the constitutional history of Merovingian Gaul', *Speculum* 64 (1986); 'From Roman to Frankish Gaul: *centenarii* and *centenae* in the administration of the Merovingian kingdom', *Traditio* 44 (1988); 'Immunity, nobility and the edict of Paris', *Speculum* 69 (1994). K.-F. Werner, 'Les principautés périphiques dans le monde franque du VIIe siècle', *Settimane* 20 (1972) is the fundamental discussion of the structure of the later Merovingian kingdom; on the links between the court and aristocratic factions which held together the late Merovingian political system, see P. Fouracre, 'Merovingians, mayors of the palace and the notion of a "low born" Ebroin', *Bulletin of the Institute of Historical Research* 57 (1984).

Aristocratic and episcopal networks are emerging as central to the exercise of power on the ground, above all in regional studies. Like most work on social structure, though, much debate concentrates on formal issues of defining social 'classes', at the expense of a more three-dimensional view of how society actually functioned. A taster of German scholarship on the development of the aristocracy, showing exactly this pitfall, is translated in T. Reuter, *The Medieval Nobility* (Amsterdam, 1978); now see P. Fouracre, 'The origins of the nobility in Francia', in A. Duggan, ed., *Nobles and Nobility in Medieval Europe* (London, 2002). Compare R. Le Jan, *Famille et pouvoir dans le monde franc* (Paris, 1995), focusing on family and status, with the narrowly legal focus of A. C. Murray, *Germanic Kinship Structure* (Toronto, 1983).

Exciting new work on violence and feud offers a different way into social solidarities. Crucial here is N. Gradowicz Panzer, 'Degendering female violence: Merovingian female honour as an "exchange of violence"', *Early Medieval Europe* 11 (2002), summarising her *Sans peur et sans vergogne: de l'honneur et des femmes aux premiers temps merovingiens* (Paris, 2001); this bypasses tired debates about the definition and origins of 'feud'. Rural society needs more study, and archaeology and regional studies are leading the way, but there is important work on the structure of landholding: see W. Goffart, *Rome's Fall and After* (London, 1986), articles on 'Roman taxation to medieval seigneurie', and on 'Merovingian polyptyches'; and S. Sato, 'Merovingian accounting documents from Tours: form and function', *Early Medieval Europe* 9 (2000), and 'L'agrarium: la charge paysanne avant le régime domainal', *Journal of Medieval History* 24 (1998).

Archaeology

Much of the most exciting work on society has been based on the archaeology, although discussion has focused on the burial evidence and so the north. The best recent study of the origin and meaning of the increased use of grave-goods in early Merovingian times is F. Theuws and M. Alkemade, 'A kind of mirror for men: sword deposits in late antique northern Gaul', in Theuws and J. Nelson, eds, *Rituals of Power from Late Antiquity to the Early Middle Ages* (Leiden, 2000), whilst E. James, 'Cemeteries and the problem of Frankish settlement in Gaul', in P. Sawyer, ed., *Names, Words and Graves* (Leeds, 1979), remains a classic. Two books by B. Effros discuss the various interpretations of the archaeology: *Merovingian Mortuary Archaeology and the Making of the Early Middle Ages* (Berkeley, 2003) and *Caring for Body and Soul: Burial and the Afterlife in the Merovingian World* (Philadelphia, 2002); for discussion, H. Williams, 'Rethinking early medieval mortuary archaeology', *Early Medieval Europe* 13 (2005). Among the interpretations discussed by Effros, see particularly those of G. Halsall, linking burials to issues of gender, life-cycle and social structure: e.g. 'Burial ritual and Merovingian society' in J. Hill and M. Swan, eds, *The Community, the Family and the Saint* (Turnhout, 1998) and 'Female status and power in Merovingian central Austrasia', *Early Medieval Europe* 5 (1996), and building on the work of E. James, e.g. 'Burial and status in the early medieval west', *Transactions of the Royal Historical Society* 39 (1989); and those of B. Young on the diffusion of burial rites, e.g. 'Exemple aristocratique et mode funéraire dans la Gaule mérovingienne', *Annales: ESC* 41 (1986). H. Steuer, 'Archaeology and history: proposals on the social structure of the Merovingian Empire', in K. Randsborg, ed., *The Birth of Europe* (Rome, 1989), offers a different, but in some respects oddly similar, synthesis of burials and settlements. One way forward must be to consider the functions of material culture among the living as well as in the grave: B. Arrhenius, *Merovingian Garnet Jewellery: Origins and Social Implications* (Stockholm, 1985) is neglected, and could be built on. On royal burials, see the articles by E. James and P. Périn, in M. Carver, ed., *The Age of Sutton Hoo* (Woodbridge, 1994), and, for the Cologne graves, J. Werner, 'Frankish royal tombs in the cathedrals of Cologne and St-Denis', *Antiquity* 38 (1964). For the south, see E. James, *The Merovingian Archaeology of South-West Gaul*, British Archaeological Reports International Series 25 (Oxford, 1977).

More is needed on rural settlements, but on the French evidence see P. Périn, 'The origins of the village in early medieval Gaul', in N. Christie, ed., *Landscapes of Change* (Aldershot, 2004); on southern Germany, F. Damminger in Wood, ed., *Franks and Alemanni in the Migration Period*, whilst H. Hamerow, *Early Medieval Settlements: The Archaeology of Rural Communities in North-West Europe 400–900* (Oxford, 2002) synthesises northern Gaul and Germany, England and Scandinavia. On the written sources, M. Heinzelmann, 'Villa d'après les œvres de Grégoire de Tours', in E. Magnou-Nortier, ed., *Aux sources de la gestion publique* I (Lille, 1993), is fundamental.

On towns, again debate has concentrated on formal issues, particularly the classic problem of continuity, and neglected issues of urban function within this society; but it has been admirably interdisciplinary. The best recent work on cities is that of S. Loseby, e.g. his contributions to I. Wood, ed., *Franks and Alemanni in the Merovingian Period* (San Marino, 1998) and T. Slater, ed., *Towns in Decline, 100–1600* (Aldershot, 2000). Loseby's work also illuminates the changing role of

Marseilles, the major Mediterranean port of Merovingian Gaul: 'Marseilles: a late antique success story?', *Journal of Roman Studies* 82 (1992), plus his contributions to W. Bowden and R. Hodges, eds, *The Sixth Century* (Leiden, 1998) and I. Hansen and C. Wickham, eds, *The Long Eighth Century* (Leiden, 2000); note also Lebecq's contributions to the latter two volumes for trade and trading settlement in the north, and there is a huge bibliography discussed below, chapter 8. For case-studies on other cities see Loseby on Arles and Halsall on Metz in N. Christie and S. Loseby, eds, *Towns in Transition* (Aldershot, 1995); H. Galinie on Tours in R. Hodges and B. Hobley, eds, *The Rebirth of Towns in the West 700–1050* (London, 1988); S. Schutte on Cologne in G. Ausenda, ed., *After Empire* (San Marino, 1995); K. Böhner, 'Urban and rural settlement in the Frankish kingdom', in M. W. Barley, ed., *European Towns: Their Archaeology and Early History* (London, 1977). Important for cultural aspects is I. Wood, 'Topographies of holy power in sixth-century Gaul', in M. de Jong and F. Theuws, eds, *Topographies of Power in the Early Middle Ages* (Leiden, 2001).

Notes

1. Gregory of Tours, *Histories* (NB this, not *History of the Franks*, is the correct title), general preface.
2. Gregory, *Histories*, II: 9, which deserves a full study.
3. Ammianus, 15: 5–6 for Silvanus' rebellion; for Mallobaudes' later career, 30: 4, 31.10.
4. Gregory, *Histories*, II: 9; note the special pleading to relate these figures to the Frankish leaders of Gregory's own day.
5. Gregory, *Histories*, II: 11–12, 27 (Syagrius and Aegidius); for confused fragments on campaigns and alliances, surely copied from contemporary chronicles, II: 18–19.
6. Avitus' *Letters* are now tr. with a superb commentary by D. Shanzer and I. Wood (Liverpool, 2002), no. 46; Remigius' letter is transmitted in a later collection associated with the later Austrasian court, *Epistolae Austrasiae*, no. 2, and is translated along with Avitus' in J. Hillgarth, *Christianity and Paganism, 350–700* (Philadelphia, 1986) or A. C. Murray, *Roman to Merovingian Gaul* (Peterborough, Ont., 2000).
7. Gregory, *Histories*, II: 29–31, 43.
8. Gregory, *Histories*, II: 37–8.
9. Gregory, *Histories*, II: 27.
10. Gregory, *Histories*, II: 40–2.
11. Gregory, *Histories*, II: 40; for Chloderic as Clovis' ally in Aquitaine, II: 37 and note the presence of Ragnachar alongside Clovis in the campaign against Syagrius, II: 27 (Gregory glosses this with reference to bloodties, but he is at pains to have all the early kings he discusses sharing Merovingian blood).
12. J. Werner, 'Frankish royal tombs in the cathedrals of Cologne and St-Denis', *Antiquity* 38 (1964); for the city, see S. Schutte, 'Continuity and authority structures in Cologne' in G. Ausenda, ed., *After Empire* (San Marino, 1995).

13. The Merovech story is first recorded in the mid-seventh century *Chronicle* of Fredegar; Trojan origins first fully developed in the early eighth century *Liber Historiae Francorum*, although there are hints at a long prehistory in Gregory's story of migration from Pannonia (II: 9) and Fredegar; the Merovingians' special hairstyle is already clearly established for Gregory. See Fredegar, 2: 4–6, and *Liber Historiae Francorum* 1, both tr. Murray, *From Roman to Frankish Gaul.*
14. Childeric: Gregory, *Histories*, 5: 17 (circuses), 5: 44 (theological and literary interests). Guntram's miraculous healing powers: Gregory *Histories*, 9: 21. Clovis' widow Clothild: Gregory *Histories*, II: 43, III: 18, IV. Radegund: in addition to Gregory's account of her career (esp. *Histories*, III: 7, IX: 40, *Glory of the Confessors* 104) see her two *Lives*, by the poet Venantius Fortunatus and the nun Baudovina, tr. J. McNamara, *Sainted Women of the Dark Ages* (Durham NC, 1982).
15. Sidonius Apollinaris, *Letters and Poems*, ed. & tr. W. B. Anderson (London, 1967), 4: 17.
16. Chilperic's new taxes: Gregory, *Histories*, 5: 28, 5: 34. 589: Gregory, *Histories*, 9: 30.
17. Gregory, *Histories*, 8: 15–16.
18. C. Lorren, 'Le village de Saint-Martin de Mondeville', in P. Périn and L. Feffer, eds, *La Neustrie* (Sigmaringen, 1990).
19. See the preface to the earliest version of *Lex Salica*; it was Carolingian revisions which attributed the code to Clovis.
20. See emblematically Gregory, *Histories*, 5: 32, 7: 47, 9: 19; concerns about feud – that is, the legitimate pursuit of vengeance by the kin of the wronged – also pervade Merovingian legislation.
21. Gregory, *Histories*, 6: 46.
22. The edict and council acts are tr. in Murray, *Roman to Merovingian Gaul.*
23. Paul the Deacon, *History of the Lombards*, tr. W. D. Foulke (Philadelphia, 1907, reprint 2003), 3: 10: note his acceptance of royal status for the Bavarian ruler, something consistently denied by the Frankish sources, particularly in the context of Charlemagne's court where he wrote.
24. See Fredegar, *Chronicle*, ed. and tr. J. M. Wallace-Hadrill, *The Fourth Book of the Chronicle of Fredegar and its Continuations* (Oxford, 1962), 4: 87.
25. Gregory's claims: *Histories*, 9: 30; for resentment at taxation of Franks, 3: 36, 7: 15. 'Truly free man' he whose 'head was not assessed in the public polyptych': Marculf, *Formulary*, I: 19, ed. and French tr. A. Uddholm (Uppsala, 1962).
26. *Chartae Latines Antiquiores* 18, no. 659.
27. Audoin, *Life of Eligius*, tr. T. Head, *Medieval Hagiography* (London, 2000), 1: 15; also important for the minting of coin.
28. For an exhaustive listing of such status-markers, see H.-W. Bohme, 'Adelsgräber im Frankenreich', *Jahrbuch des Römisch-Germanisch Zentralmuseums Mainz* 40 (1995); note the wooden 'grave-house' at Mondeville (as n. 18 above). Laucheim: F. Damminger, 'Settlement structures in southwestern Germany in the Merovingian period', in I. Wood, ed., *Franks and Alemanni in the Migration Period* (San Marino, 1998).

29. Ermentrude: *Chartae Latines Antiquiores* 14, ed. H. Atsma and J. Vezin (Zurich, 1982), no. 592. Abbo: P. Geary, *Aristocracy in Provence: The Rhone Basin at the Dawn of the Carolingian Era* (Stuttgart, 1985).
30. See emblematically Boniface, *Letters*, tr. E. Emerton (New York, 1940), nos 50, 51, 57, 60.
31. See e.g. *Life of Audoin*, tr. P. Fouracre and R. Gerberding, *Late Merovingian France* (Manchester, 1996); Audoin, *Life of Eligius* (n. 27 above); Desiderius' letters are unfortunately untranslated.
32. Jonas, *Life of Columbanus*, tr. E. Peters, *Monks, Bishops and Pagans* (Philadelphia, 1981) and selections in Head, *Medieval Hagiography*; *Life of Audoin*, tr. P. Fouracre and R. Gerberding, *Late Merovingian France.*
33. For the milieu(x) see e.g. *Life of Gertrude of Nivelles* and *Life of Balthild*, tr. Fouracre and Gerberding, *Late Merovingian France.*
34. *Vision of Barontus*, tr. Hillgarth, *Paganism and Christianity.*
35. In spite of the rich evidence, no proper study of late Merovingian Paris or the Neustrian court exists. For the milieu of the court see *Life of Balthild*, *Life of Eligius*, *Life of Audoin*; for Parisian society see the rich documentary evidence collected in *Chartes Latines Antiquiores* vols 13–14, eds H. Atsma and J. Vezin (Zurich, 1981–2). Cloak of St Martin: Marculf, *Formulary*, ed. Uddholm, I: 39, and *Chartae Latines Antiquiores* 14 no. 567. Arm of St Denis: *Liber Historiae Francorum*, ed. Fouracre and Gerberding, *Late Merovingian France* 44.
36. Fredegar, IV: 87.
37. *Passion of Leodegar*, tr. Fouracre and Gerberding, *Late Merovingian France*, chs 4, 7.
38. The *Liber Historiae Francorum* is now tr. Fouracre and Gerberding, *Late Merovingian France.*
39. E.g. *Chartae Latines Antiquiores* 14, no. 587; the independence of St-Denis *vis-à-vis* the mayors is a theme running through the rich seam of surviving documents.

8

Britain and Ireland: kings and peoples

Contents

Summary

Chronology

Map 7: Britain and Ireland in the early Middle Ages

The end of the Roman province

Post-Roman consolidation: the 'Celtic revival'

Essay: Dunadd and Dalriada

Post-Roman crisis: the Anglo-Saxon settlement

Celtic kingships and Celtic churches

Anglo-Saxon kingship and conversion

Essay: Sutton Hoo and Anglo-Saxon kingship

Essay: Culture and identity in the age of Bede

Vikings and kings: Britain and Ireland in the ninth century

Essay: Repton: Viking warbands and Anglo-Saxon kings

Bibliographical essay

Summary

The late Roman province of Britain had backed a series of military usurpers who offered patronage and protection for the empire's outlying western provinces; the armies that followed them to the continent were never replaced, denuding the Roman garrison in Britain. In the political crisis of the first decades of the fifth century, the imperial government was forced to leave Britain to defend itself. The sparse written sources suggest that conventions inherited from the Roman and Christian past continued to shape the exercise of authority, whilst the archaeology demonstrates the rapid and complete collapse of the Roman power structure, with city life, coinage, and mass-produced pottery disappearing within a generation.

As a result, new forms of power developed. Along the former Roman province's frontiers, long-term raiders and neighbours, the Picts and Scots, were able to establish stable polities, and across much of the north and west potentates established themselves in reoccupied hillforts. In the southeast, the area most closely integrated into the Roman system, Saxons, who had raided Britain's coast since the fourth century, settled. These barbarian incomers were soon to establish themselves along the eastern and southern coasts from the Humber to the Solent, although the nature of their dominance remains unclear.

By the seventh century, when our written sources begin, right across Britain and Ireland we see broadly similar patterns of multiple layers of kingship and overlordship structuring society. With the conversion of the Anglo-Saxon kingdoms in the seventh century, post-Roman societies shared a common religion and a common political vocabulary. And the church was a crucial factor in changes in patterns of land tenure and local power that consolidated the position of landowning elites: as the most powerful rulers of the eighth and ninth centuries sought to monopolise royal authority, they had to come to terms with local landowning elites. In the course of the ninth century, Viking activity proved a catalyst for further change, exacerbating existing social and political trends.

Chronology

383–8	Magnus Maximus claims imperial throne with British troops
407–11	Constantine III campaigns on continent with British troops
429–35	Visits of Bishops Germanus and Palladius to Britain and Ireland
446–53	British appeal to Aetius for help against Saxons
Fifth century	Patrick taken as slave to Ireland; preaches and becomes bishop
Fifth/early sixth century	Ninian preaching in southern Scotland; founds Whithorn
First half of sixth century	Gildas *On the Ruin of Britain*
563	Columba founds monastery of Iona; later preaches to Picts
c. 580–618	Aethelbert king of Kent; issues first written Anglo-Saxon law-code
597	Mission of Augustine arrives in Kent
668–90	Theodore of Tarsus archbishop of Canterbury
688–704	Adomnan of Iona writes *Life of Columba*
716–57	Reign of Aethelbald of Mercia
731	Bede completes *Ecclesiastical History*
735	Bede's letter to Archbishop Egbert of York
757–96	Reign of Offa of Mercia
789–820	Constantine I king of Picts: beginnings of dynastic succession
789	First reports of Viking attacks in England and Scotland
793	Viking attacks on Iona and Lindisfarne
825	Monk Blathmac killed by Vikings at Iona
829	'Nennius' compiles *Historia Brittonum*
829	Egbert of Wessex receives submission of other Anglo-Saxon rulers
839	Vikings raid Fortriu, internal crisis and civil war in Pictland
c. 840–58	Cinead mac Alpin takes over kingship of the Picts
841	Vikings establish base at Dublin
843–77	Rhodri Mawr of Gwynedd 'king of Britons' overlord in Wales
846–62	Máel Sechnaill high king of Tara 'king of Ireland'
865–76	Viking 'great army' dominant military force in Britain
871–99	Alfred king of Wessex
876–80	Vikings take over and settle in Northumbria, Mercia and East Anglia
878	Alfred of Wessex defeats rump of 'great army' under Guthrum
886	Alfred stages entry to London and proclaimed 'king of Anglo-Saxons'
c. 893	Compilation of *Anglo-Saxon Chronicle* at court of Alfred of Wessex
c. 900	'Kingdom of *Alba*' official term for the new Scottish kingdom
902	Vikings expelled from Dublin

The end of the Roman province

To write an orthodox narrative account of fifth-century Britain is impossible: our written sources simply do not provide enough information. This is, in itself, telling. Fifth-century Britain stood on the very periphery of the Roman world. Passing mentions of British events in continental chronicles need handling with care. They reflect the ebb and flow of Roman power, and the resulting waxing and waning of Roman interest in British affairs; the events they record thus did not necessarily have central significance in British politics. From Britain itself, we have only two written sources, both from the end of the fifth century or possibly the beginning of the sixth, and both needing very careful handling. Given these problems, meaningful explanation and analysis is dependent on the archaeological evidence for important structural changes in British society.

Fourth-century Britain was a relatively stable and prosperous province, largely unscathed by the disruption associated with the third-century crisis in Gaul, although Allectus and Carausius created an effectively independent provincial 'empire' in Britain from 286–96. In the fourth century, there were significant social changes: a boom in the construction of rural *villas* corresponded with a decline in urban building. The landowners who inhabited these *villas* were fully integrated into the Roman infrastructure of office, and as such were important agents of Christianisation. Their expectations of promotion and protection led them, like their continental counterparts, to raise provincial military leaders as potential emperors when the imperial government was unable to meet its obligations towards its outlying provinces. In 383 the military leader Magnus Maximus was raised as emperor in Britain, ruling much of the western empire for four years before his defeat. Two decades later, in 406, as Honorius' regime at Ravenna proved too preoccupied with Italian affairs to address provincial needs, it was again in Britain that a series of military leaders were proclaimed emperor, with Constantine III crossing the channel and enjoying four years of relative success before his defeat in 411.

The unintended effect of these attempts to create an active imperial presence was the gradual loosening of connections between the Roman government and its British province. This was most evident militarily. Both Magnus Maximus and Constantine III had taken Roman field armies stationed in Britain across the Channel to make good their imperial dreams, and after their defeats their troops were swallowed into the military followings of their victorious opponents. Britain was left denuded of regular Roman troops. Talk of a Roman withdrawal, in terms of a conscious decision to remove troops for redeployment elsewhere and abandon the province, is misleading. Put simply, by 411 the direct Roman military presence in Britain was gone, and the imperial government was preoccupied with ensuring Italian security, and dealing with barbarians and usurpers in Gaul and Hispania, and revolt in Africa. In any case Britain, unlike Italy, Gaul and Hispania, was not under immediate threat from barbarian invasion.

The Byzantine historian Zosimus, writing around a century after these events, saw them as marking the effective secession of the province from the empire: after the barbarian invasion of Gaul in 407, he wrote, Britain and parts of Gaul had

Map 7 Britain and Ireland in the early Middle Ages

'broken away from Roman rule. Henceforth they lived independently, no longer obedient to Roman laws. The Britons took up arms and freed their cities from the invading barbarians by taking the hazards of war upon themselves ... they freed themselves by driving out the Roman officials and setting up their own administration.'[1] Zosimus' account needs careful handling: writing with the benefit of over a century of hindsight, and attempting to explain the fall of the Roman Empire in the west, provincial secession in response to barbarian pressure offered a neat explanation. It would be a mistake to argue that British elites actively sought independence from Rome, as opposed to seeking effective military leaders in preference to the distant Honorius. Zosimus' analysis does pinpoint the changing derivation of military power: no longer able to rely on the Roman army for defence, provincials took matters into their own hands, bypassing the mechanisms by which the infrastructure of the Roman state mediated between civilian society and the army, hence their actions were comparable to those of the *Bacaudae* in Gaul.

Although it is customary to identify the end of Roman Britain with Constantine III's defeat in 411, there is no evidence for any formal constitutional break. The fifth-century evidence is so sparse and fragmentary as to make British perceptions of the province's relationship to the Roman Empire impossible to recover, but the *Life* of Germanus, bishop of Auxerre in Gaul, hints at continuing contact. Written *c.* 480, the *Life* describes Germanus' two visits to Britain, in 429 and 435, to combat the heresy of Pelagius. Germanus' first visit was made at the pope's behest, and linked to the despatch of Palladius to the Christian communities of Ireland. Germanus' first visit led to the expulsion of the Pelagians from Britain, enforcing an imperial decree condemning heretics to exile. The perception that Britain was in a sense still a part of the Christian Roman Empire was shared by a continental chronicler who referred to the dual missions of Germanus, combating heresy in 'the Roman island' of Britain, and Palladius, spreading Christianity in 'the barbarian island' of Ireland, never a Roman province.[2] But the accusations of Pelagianism also suggest an awareness of increasing distance: such charges tended to be made against Christian communities that sought salvation independently of the universal church. The links between ecclesiastical and secular politics are underlined by Germanus' second visit to Britain, in which, according to Constantius, Germanus organised resistance to the Picts, Scots and Saxons, and won a miraculous bloodless victory by singing 'Alleluia'. The 'Alleluia victory' needs to be read in the literary context of stereotypical stories repeated in saints' lives to demonstrate their hero's sanctity: fifth-century Gallic bishops were frequently celebrated for saving their cities from the wrath of barbarians. It is tempting to read Constantius' account as an allegorised literary presentation of a diplomatic mission in which Germanus – a retired soldier who had negotiated settlements between provincials, barbarians and Roman generals in Gaul – met and advised British leaders. Roman authority in the west was no longer defined by a dedicated army and administration, but by alliances centred on the general Aetius, and Britain stood on the fringes of this network.

Germanus had met British leaders who demonstrated their power in Roman style, wearing Roman robes and bearing Roman titles. The continuing pull of

Rome is also suggested by the only internal account of fifth-century British history: the moral tract *On the Ruin of Britain* by Gildas. Gildas wrote in a highly rhetorical language of excoriating moral denunciation, making his work difficult and often frustrating for the modern historian, although surely an effective exhortation to his contemporary audience. The time and place at which Gildas was writing are a matter of dispute: the passages on which the traditional mid-sixth-century dating is based are open to variant interpretations, and Gildas' highly rhetorical Latin style, reminiscent of that taught in the late antique schools, might suggest an earlier, late fifth-century, context.

Gildas lavishes attention on the failings of the rulers of his own day, as he seeks to attribute political misfortunes to God's displeasure. His account of post-Roman politics is thus a moral parable of pride punished. Twice, Roman armies had saved the British from the raids of Picts and Scots; a third round led to a British appeal to the Roman general Aetius. When help proved unforthcoming, the British leader, a 'proud tyrant', hired three ships of Saxon mercenaries as federates, who soon demanded better terms and rebelled. Gildas named Ambrosius Aurelianus as the British leader in the wars against the Saxons: Ambrosius was the grandfather of the kings of Gildas' day, and his father 'had worn the purple'. This account needs careful handling. At points it is demonstrably mistaken: its story of two Roman missions against the Picts and Scots, for example, is an attempt to account for the existence of the Antonine and Hadrian's Wall, frontier fortifications from a much earlier period. Gildas' contemporary agenda shaped his story, with his recurrent stress on barbarian destruction as God's punishment for the vices of the Britons. It would be a mistake to try to build any narrative on this moral tale. For example, Gildas mentions the defeat of the Saxons at Mount Badon, which has thus been seen as a key event. But Gildas mentions Mount Badon either because it took place in the year of his birth, or because it had just taken place; on neither interpretation of this tricky text is there any need to see Mount Badon as militarily or politically crucial.[3]

The problems associated with using Gildas to construct a narrative should not obscure the priceless window he gives on the political culture of his day. The very fact that Gildas' wordy and moralising Latin rhetoric was a suitable vehicle for criticising rulers is significant, pointing to the survival of an elite Latin culture comparable in its highly moralising ethos to that of Gallic and Hispanic authors like Salvian and Hydatius. The letter appealing to help from Aetius, preserved by Gildas, similarly shows a good knowledge of formal political and rhetorical etiquette. Central to Gildas' criticism of the kings of his own day was the notion that they were tyrants: they lacked self-control and so were susceptible to personal and public vices and unable to govern justly. For Gildas these kings were successors to a long tradition of tyranny that originated with Magnus Maximus; here, he may have been contesting royal claims to be exercising legitimate authority derived from the Roman past, evident in royal names, and in claims of descent from Magnus and others which continued to be made for centuries.

That fifth-century political culture was shaped by the Roman past and Christian ideals is confirmed by the writings of St Patrick. Patrick's career is surrounded by an unusual degree of controversy, and his precise dates within the fifth century are impossible to establish. Because of the status he was to acquire as patron saint of the Irish his career was the subject of myth-making already by the seventh century, when material reshaping the past to legitimate present claims began to be produced, but we have two surviving works from his own pen, his *Confession*, a justification of his career in the face of criticism from British bishops, and his *Letter to the Soldiers of Coroticus*, a piece of moral invective against a British king who had raided Ireland and enslaved captured Irish Christians. Significantly, both are, like Gildas, pieces of polemic written in Latin (albeit simpler Latin than Gildas'). From them, we learn that Patrick had been brought up a Christian (and taught Latin) in Britain before being captured by Irish raiders, eventually winning his freedom and travelling to Britain or Gaul, and then returning to Ireland as a missionary and (apparently self-styled) bishop. Patrick's political vocabulary is very Roman, as in his references to his compatriots as citizens, and he compares the actions of Coroticus to the dealings of Gallic Christians with the Franks.[4]

If the written sources suggest the continuing influence of Roman political ideals, and, still more, the moral discourse of the Christian church, the archaeology indicates drastic social changes. Whilst Britain was integrated into the empire the state's system of taxation and requisition had supplied troops based in Britain, and also raised cash and produce from Britain to supply troops elsewhere, notably on the Rhine frontier. Archaeologically, the clearest traces of this infrastructure come in the distribution of coin (in this period not so much a medium for commercial exchange as the form in which the government took tax revenues from the cities and redistributed them to their recipients), and of mass-produced pottery (a good index of state supply for the military). In both these areas, the decades immediately following 400 witness sudden, dramatic and irreversible decline. The coin supply in Britain, disrupted in the later fourth century (presumably because of successive usurpations and their aftermath), dries up wholly after the first decade of the fifth century; pottery imports end at a similar date. The mass production of pottery in Britain itself, probably enabled by demand and distribution networks underwritten by the state, ended almost as precipitously as the import of continental pottery, within a generation. Cities likewise declined dramatically: decades of searching for signs of continuity have yielded only piecemeal evidence of the odd elite residence within the shell of cities in which urban life had clearly ceased. Since the fourth century the cities of Britain, as of northern Gaul, had seen little new building, and probably increasingly served as administrative centres without any real concentration of population or economic expertise: in the fifth century, they quite simply became redundant. Even the rural *villas* from which the landowning classes had enjoyed their social dominance ceased to be built, or repaired; even where there is evidence for the continued exploitation of the land, or continued settlement in the vicinity, the actual focus of habitation shifts. Without the infrastructure of the state to underwrite their position, elites no longer had the resources necessary to maintain a luxurious life of ostentatious leisure.

The collapse of Roman society in Britain was uniquely precipitous. In Hispania and southern Gaul, landowning elites were able to continue to maintain the local tiers of the Roman infrastructure of cities and revenue collection, and thus maintain their resources and lifestyle: cities, and some degree of economic specialisation, were deep rooted enough to withstand Roman withdrawal, and elites had sufficient resources to raise personal armies and maintain their local position. The closest parallels come from northern Gaul and along the Rhine frontier, but even here, in an area more troubled politically than Britain, and subject to invasion and colonisation from immediate barbarian neighbours, hybrid elites expressing their power in a shared idiom of military leadership were able to establish themselves in the fifth century. In Britain, landowners and churchmen seem to have been simply unable to maintain the social order that underwrote their dominance without the coercive and logistical power of the Roman state. The archaeology sheds some light on their fate. At Verulamium, where Germanus had met magnificently attired local potentates with Roman titles, amongst the general picture of abandonment, one urban building was repaired in the mid-fifth century; interestingly, the cult of St Alban, a Roman martyr who gave the city its modern name of St Alban's, is virtually unique in lowland Britain in its direct continuity from the Roman to the early medieval periods, suggesting that here Christian cult allowed adaptation and survival. At Wroxeter, careful excavation has shown the construction and repair of a wooden complex on one part of the site of the Roman baths and a late Roman basilica, the hall of a local leader able to adapt to the imperatives of a post-Roman society in the fifth and sixth centuries; elsewhere in the west, there is similar evidence for wooden buildings on Roman city sites which may have continued to be seats of power.[5]

By far the most successful strategy for survival must have been militarisation. Certainly, both Patrick's criticism of Coroticus, whose raiding made him indistinguishable from his pagan barbarian allies, and Gildas' charges of tyranny against the unrestrained coercive force of contemporary rulers, rest on concerns about the conduct of warrior-kings. With landowners no longer able to use the Roman state to anchor their position, and so forced to transform themselves into warlords, political unity within the former Roman province is likely to have become fragile, a matter of alliance not command. In Gildas, the 'proud tyrant' who first hires Saxons federates against the Picts and Scots does so after holding a council, and is presented as a national leader, as is the military leader Ambrosius Aurelianus, whilst among the contemporary kings Gildas condemns Maglocunus is 'first in evil, mightier than many both in power and malice': all of which suggests the slow dissolution of post-Roman provincial unity into a looser and more personal overlordship. This world of post-Roman warlords is that associated with King Arthur – but no contemporary source refers to a British warlord named Arthur, and the Arthur we meet in ninth-century and later Welsh collections of historical lore, and in the literature composed after Arthur's rise to international stardom in the twelfth century, is a legendary figure.

The social changes wrought by the collapse of the infrastructure of the Roman state were not the only problem faced by fifth-century elites. The third and fourth centuries had seen intermittent raiding by 'barbarians' from beyond the frontier: Picts in the Highlands of modern Scotland, Scots from modern Ireland, Saxons from the Germanic North Sea coast. Roman military activity in fourth-century

Britain concentrated on maintaining the northern frontier marked by Hadrian's Wall against the Picts and Scots, and on defence of the Channel coast, with the creation of a new post, 'count of the Saxon shore' and a series of new, large-scale, fortifications. The disappearance of the Roman army from Britain and northern Gaul at the beginning of the fifth century led to dramatic changes in the strategic balance: within Britain, there was no longer a fortified, linear, frontier defended by Roman troops, whilst the continental side of the channel was no longer under Roman control.

In this new situation, political linkages between post-Roman elites and their 'barbarian' neighbours quickly emerged, based on long-standing contacts and interactions across the frontier. In the north and west, Pictish, Scottish and British leaders competed for the allegiance of warbands by launching successful raids around the Irish Sea: witness Patrick's complaints about Coroticus' alliance with 'Scots, Picts and apostates' to raid Ireland. Patrick's own career and writings indicate more peaceful forms of cultural contact alongside endemic raiding, and there is good archaeological evidence for economic interaction around the Irish Sea. In the south and east, the Channel emerged as a similar zone, and here too it was not only Saxon 'barbarians' who profited from the economy of the wartrail. This was, after all, the period in which Armorica acquired its modern name of Brittany. Like Britain an outlying province increasingly distanced from the Roman government, post-Roman Armorica fell under the sway of military leaders from the British side of the Channel. The letters of Sidonius Apollinaris suggest endemic Saxon piracy along the Channel coastline, but also show us the British king Riothamus leading an expedition in Gaul as an ally of the emperor against the Goths, and eventually settling. The fabulous stories about Britain recorded by the Byzantine historian Procopius in the middle of the sixth century suggest a zone of seaborne raiding, the northern part of which was controlled by Saxon leaders and the southern part by Britons.[6] With the collapse of the apparatus of the Roman state in Britain, a new system based on plunder and tribute had emerged. Across much of the continent, the survival of the infrastructure of cities and office allowed provincial elites to come to terms with the military power of barbarian warlords in a more or less orderly fashion. In Britain, social collapse meant that there was no civil society onto which barbarian military protectors could be grafted: by the sixth and seventh centuries, this was a world of warlords competing for direct control over the spoils of the countryside.

Post-Roman consolidation: the 'Celtic revival'

The historian of post-Roman Britain faces one insurmountable problem: our surviving written sources overwhelmingly date from the period after *c.* 700. This historical horizon holds right across the British Isles. In the area that had fallen subject to Anglo-Saxon invaders in the fifth and sixth centuries, it was only in the aftermath of the re-establishment of an organised church by seventh-century missionaries that written culture was reintroduced. But even in the areas beyond Anglo-Saxon control, where Christianity survived intact from the Roman period, written histories do not survive from the period after Gildas. In the British areas of the west, in spite of the survival of Latin literacy evident in stone inscriptions, written sources are late and scarce. Research on works such as the collection of historical lore made by a Welsh writer known as Nennius, probably in 829, has shown that the stories it contains about the fifth and sixth centuries include a significant element of myth, and aim to explain and legitimate the present. In Scotland, the Picts in the Highlands and the British polities of the Lowlands have left no written traditions; historical information can be gleaned from the Anglo-Saxon historian Bede, and from works produced at the monastery of Iona in the Inner Hebrides, most notably the Latin life of its founder, Columba, written by his kinsman and successor Adomnan at some point during the years 688 to 704. Columba was a member of a royal elite whose interests straddled northern Ireland and northwestern Scotland: it was at Iona that the earliest sections of the *Annals of Ulster*, a year by year account of Irish events, were kept as a contemporary record from the late seventh century onwards. Our knowledge of Ireland does not, however, only come from overseas: indeed, the Irish source material is probably richer than that for any other part of the British Isles in the period before the tenth century, and includes a rich vernacular tradition of literary and legal material in Old Irish as well as Latin annals and legal tracts both ecclesiastical and secular, saints' lives, and liturgical and theological material. The dating and reliability of much of this material is a matter of complex and continuing debate, but what is clear is that the earliest layers of the legal material dates from the seventh and eighth centuries, whilst the literary works, although they draw on ancient tradition, in their current form reflect the interests of its ecclesiastical recorders in the eighth to twelfth centuries.

Archaeology, of course, is essential in relating the discourses of the sources to social organisation on the ground. The most striking aspect of the archaeological record is the difference in material culture between the lowland zone, the civilian heartland of the former Roman province in the south and east of modern England, and the highland zone, the military zone of the west and north of Roman Britain and the areas beyond the frontier in Scotland and Ireland. This difference is not simply one of the styles of the artefacts found in excavated sites in different areas; more significantly, it rests on a difference in typical forms of settlement and modes of burial. This division – which is never total or sudden – very roughly corresponds to linguistic and ethnic divisions apparent in the written sources of the seventh century and later, between the indigenous populations of the Celtic-speaking west and north, and the Germanic-speaking Anglo-Saxon communities of the south and east. But the archaeological division in the post-Roman period also emerges directly from a similar, and similarly gradual, divide in material culture in the Roman period, between the *villas* and cities of the civilian heartland, and the military culture of the frontier zone.

In western and northern Britain, the fifth and sixth centuries are marked by the use of hillforts as elite dwellings. This has striking parallels with developments along the former Roman frontier on the continent. As on the continent, it shows the leaders of a society that the needs of the Roman state had militarised quickly adopting the lifestyle of their long-standing barbarian neighbours once the Roman army withdrew. Traprain Law south of Edinburgh, for example, had remained inhabited right through the Roman period, the residence of an independent British leader; a rich early fifth-century hoard there, full of Roman goods, demonstrates the importance of access to Roman wealth, whether attained through friendly or hostile means, for potentates on the edge of the empire. By the end of the fifth century – precise dating is problematic because of the lack of coinage or mass-produced pottery after the Roman withdrawal – such redoubts had become common across northern and western Britain. Sites like Dinas Powys in southern Wales, or South Cadbury in Somerset, demonstrate an impressive control of manpower, implying the continued ability of elites to command and organise the majority of the local populace in spite of the Roman withdrawal. One recurrent feature of these centres is evidence of the activities of skilled craftsmen, particularly in metalwork such as jewellery and weapon-production. Another is the presence of long-distance imports from the Mediterranean, as evidenced by the presence of shards of pottery produced in the Mediterranean but also hanging dishes and similar exotic objects. Both phenomena suggest that the military leaders who resided in hillforts were able to control the production and circulation of high-status goods. In fact, the existence of a network of low-volume, and perhaps sporadic, exchange of such status symbols around the Irish Sea, some of native manufacture, some Mediterranean, is slowly emerging from the archaeology. From Tintagel in Cornwall to Dunadd in western Scotland access to this material, and its redistribution to ensure the loyalty of followers, was central to the creation of political authority.[7]

These potentates are often seen as the agents of a 'Celtic revival', returning to pre-Roman structures and identities. Certainly, some of the hillforts of the fifth to seventh centuries had originally been constructed in the pre-Roman Iron Age, before their subsequent abandonment following the Roman occupation of Britain. There is some evidence, too, for the survival of pre-Roman tribal names, with the ruler of Cornwall and Devon styled king of Dumnonia, that is of the territory of the Dumnonii. This hardly constitutes strong evidence for the suggestion of pre-Roman identities surviving underground through four centuries of Romanisation. In fact, Roman administrative geography drew on pre-Roman tribal names, as *civitates* were named after earlier tribal units, and so it is likely to have been Roman structures that led to the post-Roman kingdom which replaced the former *civitas* of the Dumnonii as Dumnonia. As for the reoccupation of ancient sites, elites had long been drawn into the Roman administrative and military infrastructure, which had guaranteed their standing; defensible hilltop sites had an obvious attraction as they sought to preserve their position once the Roman state collapsed. The spoken languages of western and northern Britain were variations of the language of Britain's pre-Roman Celtic inhabitants, for spoken Celtic had a continuous history in Roman Britain alongside Latin, although Latin remained the language of literacy in the post-Roman west and north. 'Celticisation' was thus a process of social adaptation, not the ideological abandonment of one cultural template for another.

In fact, the Roman inheritance remained central, far more so than any elusive 'Celtic' tradition. Witness the spread of Latin-inscribed stones in western Britain. The very notion of the Latin inscription drew directly on a tradition central to the self-expression of Roman elites, and some early Welsh inscriptions continued to use a Roman vocabulary of citizenship and status. They constitute a cultural medium of lasting commemoration drawing on Roman models. They also show the continuous spread of Christianity from the late Roman to the post-Roman period, for many inscriptions express Christian ideals, and many are located in churchyards; even where the church postdates the inscription this is still an indication of continuous Christian development.

Roman tradition did not only shape the culture of these areas on the fringes of the former Roman province; it was also an important influence beyond the Roman frontier in both Ireland and Scotland. Ireland, although never part of the empire, had been subject to Roman influence: excavations at Dalkey Island near Dublin have unearthed an entrepôt through which Roman culture percolated into Ireland. By the fourth and fifth centuries, when the written sources tell of raids by the Scots (as the inhabitants of Ireland were known), the archaeology shows increasing Roman influence on material culture. One aspect of this influence was the development of a native version of written script, ogam, which was, like the Latin alphabet, soon used for commemorative stone inscriptions: whilst the precise chronology of the development of ogam inscriptions and their relationship to their Latin counterparts remains a matter of difficult debate, there is little doubt that here is a local adaptation of the Roman model of the inscribed world. Contact with the late Roman and post-Roman world was influential enough to bring about a change of religion, in the now invisible process of gradual percolation by which Ireland was fully converted to Christianity in the course of the fifth and early sixth centuries. Christianity brought with it Latin literacy and learning, apparently spreading directly from the continent along the same routes as Mediterranean goods, but also from the British church. Early medieval Irish society, as it emerges in the written sources of the seventh and eighth centuries, was the product of a long and slow process of acculturation.

Elsewhere in the post-Roman north, similar processes of political consolidation and cultural transformation were at work. Dalriada, because of the relative richness of the evidence from Iona, and the fact that it was eventually to supply the identity around which the medieval kingdom of Scotland was formed in the ninth and tenth centuries, has always occupied a central place in scholarship. But British kings remained dominant across most of northern Britain through the fifth and sixth centuries. Here, the *Gododdin*, a Old Welsh poem commemorating the defeat of the eponymous Britons of the modern Scottish lowlands by Anglo-Saxon conquerors in the conventions of heroic verse, is a rare written source for this period: preserved in Wales by exiles lamenting the fate of their homeland, it claims to be the composition of the sixth-century poet Aneirin, a possibility which is inevitably much disputed.[9] The *Gododdin* gives a vivid insight into a warrior-elite measuring their worth by martial valour, and although its heroes were victims of Anglo-Saxon expansion, a process that continued through the seventh century, the powerful but unfortunately ill-documented British kingdom of Strathclyde existed right through our period. In the post-Roman period, these British kingdoms straddling the former frontier became Christian in a gradual process of acculturation that directly parallels the conversion of Ireland. The key

Essay

Dunadd and Dalriada

One consequence of the processes of interaction around the former frontiers of the Roman province was the foundation of a kingdom of the Scots (that is, Gaelic-speaking Irish immigrants) along the western sealanes of modern Scotland. Quite how the kingdom of Dalriada was formed remains murky, although it was close enough to the northern Irish coast to enjoy natural linkages. Traditions surviving in written form from the tenth century onwards credit its foundation *c.* 500 to Fergus Mor mac Eorc, a member of a royal lineage in Ireland who carved out a kingdom in this new territory. This legend underwrote the strong Gaelic cultural identity of the ruling elite, which in the sixth century was tied into the Irish political scene. Columba, for example, was a member of the Irish royal kindred of the Ui Neill, who came to Iona – within sight of the northern Irish coast on a fine day – when driven into exile by his rivals; in 575 he was instrumental in negotiating an agreement about the relationship between the king of Dalriada and the Ui Neill king of Ulster over the status of the sister kingdom of Dalriada in northern Ireland, whereby the Dalriadan kingdom in Ireland paid the king of Dalriada in Scotland an annual tribute, but acknowledged the overlordship of Ulster. The centre of the Dalriadan kingdom was a major hillfort complex at Dunadd, with two outlying provinces likewise centred on hillforts; these were not only royal residences, but also sites of craft production and exchange, and centres for

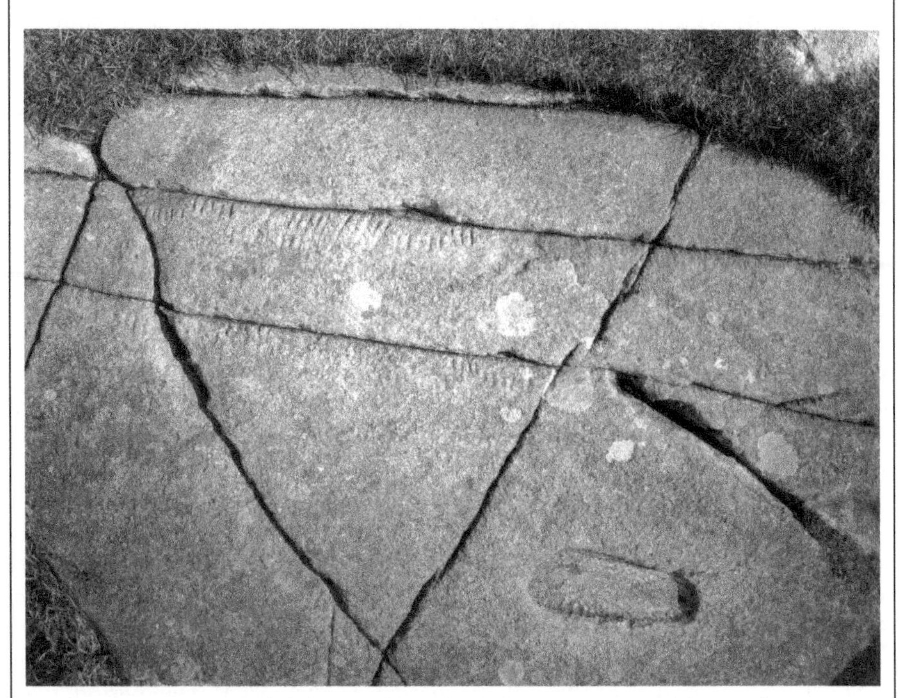

Figure 8.1 Dunadd hill fort, Ogham, showing inscription and footmark, 1963

Figure 8.2 Dunadd hill fort, seen from the southeast, 1988

the collection of dues from each household in the surrounding area, as recorded in a remarkable seventh-century survey; Iona, which in the sixth and seventh centuries established dominance over the churches and monasteries of western Scotland, fulfilled a comparable function in integrating outlying areas into the kingdom. Quite how centralised Dalriada was remains unclear. Our tenth-century traditions present its internal organisation as hierarchical, rooted in a legendary genealogy: Fergus Mor, it is claimed, had three sons, each of whom ruled a part of the kingdom from his own hillfort, with the eldest son succeeding to Dunadd. The fragments in the annals suggest, however, that the supremacy of Dunadd was contested, and we might see the story of Fergus Mor's sons as an attempt to stabilise a more fluid situation of political competition between relatively distinct groupings, each of which legitimated its position by claiming to be the true heirs of Fergus.[8]

figure here – and one even more shadowy than Patrick – was St Ninian, who was probably active sometime between 400 and 550. The written accounts of Ninian's career, sparse and garbled, can luckily be placed to one side thanks to recent excavations at Whithorn, the site of Ninian's cult and a major ecclesiastical centre. These show a site with its origins in the late fourth century, but with rich fifth- and sixth-century layers; sixth-century inscriptions in particular show close links with the continent via the Irish Sea, which perhaps explains Ninian's dedication of the church to the Gallic saint, Martin of Tours.[10]

Ninian's initial mission had also been to the southern Picts, whilst the northern Picts were converted in the second half of the sixth century by Columba of Iona.[11] The Picts have often been seen as the odd men out of early medieval British history: descendents of the original indigenous inhabitants of the island, therefore speaking a pre-Celtic tongue and creating an idiosyncratic polity based on matrilineal succession to the kingship. Whilst the Pictish language remains obscure, as it was extinct by the tenth century, it was most likely a divergent branch of the Celtic tongue shared by all the pre-Roman inhabitants of Britain. The Picts themselves first emerge in the written sources in the third century, as a federation of the barbarian peoples beyond Hadrian's Wall, and as such should be seen as one of the new confederate tribes that emerged in the late Roman period as an outcome of interaction between the empire and its neighbours. Like the Alemans on the continent, the collapse of the Roman frontier in the fifth century appears to have allowed them to consolidate their local position, rather than expand into former imperial provinces. The process of cultural fusion which resulted might explain even the oddest aspect of Pictish culture, the so-called symbol stones, with are inscribed with an as-yet-undecoded 'alphabet' of approximately fifty pictorial ornaments: like ogam in Ireland, this was an idiosyncratic and localised adaptation of the Roman practice of written script and the inscribed stone as guarantors of status and commemoration.

Notions of 'Celtic survival' or an archaic Pictish culture are of no value in explaining the specific trajectory of post-Roman western Britain and Ireland, for the changes that can be detected there owe little or nothing to the pre-Roman past. The continued cultural prestige of Rome is evident in the spread of both Christianity and stone inscriptions and the import of high-status goods from the Mediterranean. What is most remarkable is the lack of large-scale population movements, the coastal kingdoms carved out by Irish warlords notwithstanding. Here, Roman withdrawal allowed already militarised elites to consolidate their position and the social hierarchy to stabilise. The kingdoms that crystallised along the former Roman frontier on the fifth-century continent provide a close comparison. But on the continent, the barbarian warlords who were able to establish themselves as rulers of functioning Roman provinces, and so create strong, unitary kingships, were able to destroy these frontier kinglets: this was the achievement of Clovis along the Rhine, and Theodoric along the Danube. In post-Roman Britain, however, no unitary kingship was to seize and maintain provincial structures, and so the rulers of the frontier were allowed to establish their position unimpeded. To understand why this was so, we need to investigate how the south and east of modern England became 'Anglo-Saxon'.

Post-Roman crisis: the Anglo-Saxon settlement

The fundamental fact that does emerge from our seventh- and eighth-century sources is that of linguistic difference within Britain. The inhabitants of the north and the west spoke Celtic languages. Across most of what was to become England, on the other hand, Germanic dialects were the main spoken language by the end of the seventh century. These linguistic differences corresponded to contemporary perceptions of ethnic difference between the 'Anglo-Saxons' in the east and the surviving indigenous populations of the west. Historians have often seen language change in the Anglo-Saxon areas as evidence for mass migration of Germanic speakers, pointing out that Latin remained the basis of the spoken languages of post-Roman Italy and Hispania, and most of Gaul bar the frontier zones. In fact, this comparison is more complex than is often suggested, for nowhere in Britain did Latin survive as anything more than the language of the church: the alternative to Germanic was Celtic. In contrast, on the continent it was only in isolated and peripheral regions within the empire, such as the Basque region, that the languages of the pre-Roman indigenous populations survived. The triumph of Germanic in the Anglo-Saxon areas needs to be understood in the context of the disappearance of spoken Latin elsewhere in the province. For generations of historians, however, the perception of linguistic division between Celts and Anglo-Saxons has indicated a fundamental difference in the biological makeup of the population, from which divergent social and political traditions have been derived, prefiguring the present internal divisions of the British Isles. Only recently have historians begun to subject the evidence – and particularly the archaeology – to more critical scrutiny, leading to renewed debate about 'the making of the English'.

One written source has exercised a profound influence on the historical agenda. Bede, a monk at Jarrow in Northumbria renowned for his expertise as a Biblical commentator and interpretation of the complex arts of chronology and computation necessary to calculate the date of Easter, began his *Ecclesiastical History of the English People*, completed in 731, with an account of the fifth century based heavily on Gildas; when it came to discussing the sixth century, when he no longer had Gildas to rely on, Bede's account is a virtual blank. For Bede, Gildas' account had been valuable precisely because it offered an opportunity to explain how the Anglo-Saxons came to Britain. Gildas' moral diatribe against the rulers of his day presented barbarian invasion as a punishment sent by God. Bede, whose subject was the conversion of the Anglo-Saxons in the seventh century, was able to spin Gildas' presentation to suit his own ends: the Britons forfeited God's favour on account of their immorality, and failed to preach to the Anglo-Saxons, and so the Anglo-Saxons enjoyed God's favour and were converted directly from papal Rome. This Christian mission encouraged Bede to see his people, in spite of their political fragmentation, as united before God on the model of the Israelites of the Old Testament, although like other eighth-century writers Bede developed no consistent single term to refer to the groups we call the 'Anglo-Saxons'. Whether this sense of Anglo-Saxon identity was newly emerging in Bede's day, encouraged by the common culture of the church, or rested on older roots remains a matter of intense and important debate.

For Bede the 'advent of the Saxons' was a central event, which Gildas could explain, and for which Gildas could, if carefully handled, suggest a date. In Gildas, the Saxons were first invited as federates after the failure of Aetius to help the British: Bede correctly places the appeal to Aetius *c*. 449, thus providing a date that has remained standard ever since. But Bede was extrapolating from Gildas, no more, and there are internal inconsistencies in his reconstruction of the fifth century. In fact, Gildas and Bede both presented the arrival of the Saxons as a single momentous event because in their respective plots the Saxons were God's agents delivering punishment to the Britons. It is quite clear that Saxon settlement in England was the outcome of a long process, with raiding documented from the fourth century. Gildas' scenario, of one group of Saxons being hired by British rulers as federates, is highly plausible, but it does not explain the origins of the Saxon presence in Britain. Interestingly, Bede identified Gildas' story with one known to him from informants in Kent, adding names for the British king (Vortigern, which means 'proud tyrant') and the Saxon leaders (Hengest and Horsa), and commenting that contemporary kings claimed descent from them (a statement verified by surviving Anglo-Saxon royal genealogies) and that a monument survived to Horsa.[12] So there is strong reason to believe that in at least the southeast Saxon settlement occurred through a long process similar to that visible on the continent, with some barbarian raiders hired as federates and eventually able to use their military muscle to assert their power over their erstwhile hosts; but we should not attempt to encapsulate the history of the entire province within this Kentish story.

How were Saxon raiders and settlers able to create their own kingdoms? Here, the kind of written evidence which survives for the continent is simply lacking: Bede has more or less no information about the period between the end of Gildas' account and the arrival of Roman missionaries in Kent in 597. The *Anglo-Saxon Chronicle* written *c*. 893 at the court of King Alfred, fills out the gap with records of the battles of early Anglo-Saxon kings. Doubtless these figures and their victories were transmitted by oral tradition entwined around fictive genealogies linking current rulers to legendary forbears, but they are entered into the fifth- and sixth-century sections of the *Chronicle* under the entries for specific years with an entirely specious chronological precision. And some of these traditions are wholly spurious: the entry recording the capture of Portchester by the Saxon leader Port is clearly an attempt to explain the origins of a place-name.

If we can know next to nothing of the political specifics of the fifth and sixth centuries, can we trace the broad processes by which modern England became Anglo-Saxon? Traditional nationalist ideologies saw the 'English' as a distinct population from their 'Celtic' neighbours, and so posited a wholesale replacement of the indigenous population by Anglo-Saxon settlers. Gildas, with his stress on the Saxons as a divinely-sent punishment of the immoral British, and Bede, for whom the difference between the Anglo-Saxons and their British neighbours was axiomatic, can both be read as supporting this view. But Gildas and Bede need careful handling. On the continent, the writings of Gildas-style polemical moralists like Salvian likewise stress antagonism and conflict, but can be checked against writers with different agendas who give a very different picture. And

Bede's eighth-century continental contemporaries similarly wrote of mass migrations and wholesale changes of population in explaining the origins of their world, but can again be checked by modern historians against earlier sources which indicate more complex processes of cultural change, as indigenous populations came to identify themselves with their new barbarian rulers. It would be a mistake to argue from Gildas and Bede that in post-Roman Britain relations between the indigenous population and their new barbarian rulers were uniquely hostile. But if the continent shows the range of possibilities, only careful investigation of the archaeological evidence from England can help us understand the realities.

Bede famously claimed that the barbarian incomers were made up of three peoples from neighbouring areas of the north German and southern Danish North Sea coast: the Angles, the Saxons and the Jutes.[13] This reflected the political map of his own day, with the kingdoms from, roughly, East Anglia north being Anglian, those from the Thames estuary south being Saxon, and Kent being Jutish. Interestingly, this broad division corresponds roughly to regional differences in dress and material culture emerging in the generations immediately preceding Bede: in other words, to identities that were in the process of formation, not transplanted wholesale from continental homelands. We should not posit three distinct but coherent migrations, with populations from one area of the continent moving wholesale to a new home in Britain. Even Bede gives a much messier alternative view, in a later chapter when he explains that the British called their neighbours 'Germans', on account of their origins amongst several peoples in continental *Germania*, including the Frisians, Rugians, Danes, Huns, Old Saxons and Bructeri.[14] These diverse and heterogeneous immigrant groups presumably coalesced into new communities once they arrived in England. Archaeological evidence certainly confirms the picture of diversity: artefacts from late fifth- and sixth-century England are subject to a kaleidoscope of influences. But nowhere is there a simple direct correlation between the material culture of any single region of England and a continental 'homeland': there is a mixing of heterogeneous influences, including Scandinavian and Frankish.

Why migrate in the first place? The continental archaeology supplies some important insights. Along the North Sea coast, the fifth and sixth centuries were a period of rising sea level, the so-called Dunkirk transgressions, which must have placed coastal populations under ecological and economic pressure; many settlements along the Dutch and German coasts were abandoned in this period, in precisely those areas privileged in Bede's lists. But ecology, whilst it provides an impetus to move, does not explain a choice to migrate to Britain. Here, the economic ties between these populations and the demands of empire were crucial: at sites such as Feddersen Wierde, rising prosperity and social complexity are clearly evident results. With the collapse of the frontier, the rationale for the iron-working and the stock-raising which underpinned these developments was gone; new strategies were needed if emergent elites were to maintain their position. The most obvious, now Roman defence systems had gone, was seaborne raiding. For elites facing economic and political crisis, what could be a more inviting target than the fertile former Roman province of Britain, where the social collapse following Roman withdrawal had precluded the emergence of a strong post-Roman regime?

These opportunities may have encouraged lock, stock and barrel migrations, albeit on a small-scale; certainly the settlement archaeology suggests this. Whatever the case, here was an exceptional conjunction of ecological pressure on coastal communities already dislocated by the collapse of Roman power, and a power vacuum in lowland Britain. Continental migration to Britain is thus the extreme case of a more general phenomenon, as barbarian elites that had emerged by riding piggyback on the imperial system were pulled into former Roman provinces once the empire began to implode.

What effect had these migrations? There are very clear differences in material culture between excavated sixth- or seventh-century sites and those of Roman date. Since the pioneers of the nineteenth century, it has been customary to see these differences as reflecting the arrival of Anglo-Saxon culture from the continent, carried by an Anglo-Saxon population. In fact, detailed work on the archaeological record has shown that many of the traits seen as characteristic of Anglo-Saxon material culture need careful interpretation. There are three main areas of difference between Roman and early medieval sites in England. First, there is a general change in the nature of settlement and the associated techniques of construction, with the end of Roman stone building traditions of all types, and the prevalence of rural settlements made up of wooden halls surrounded by small huts with sunken floors (so-called sunken featured buildings). Second, burial practices undergo a similarly dramatic change, with the largely unfurnished inhumation graves of the late Roman period giving way to lavishly furnished burials, often in new cemeteries, some inhumations, some cremations housed in purpose-made pottery. Third, the traditions of manufacture and decoration of the artefacts found in both settlements and cemeteries change, with Roman-style mass-produced pottery replaced by homemade wares, and new styles of metalwork and jewellery rapidly growing in popularity.

None of these changes can be seen as a straightforward replacement of Roman tradition by a distinctively 'Anglo-Saxon' alternative imported wholesale from the continent. The wooden 'halls' of early Anglo-Saxon settlements differ in significant ways from the longhouses of the continental homelands. Changes in settlement types and building traditions need to be explained with reference to the dramatic crisis of British society following the Roman withdrawal: economic, logistical and technological imperatives must explain the gradual abandonment of existing stone buildings, and the shift to wood even where *villa* or city sites remained inhabited. Early Anglo-Saxon construction traditions actually have antecedents in the Roman countryside, where, as well as stone-built *villas*, there was plentiful wooden construction, and a vernacular building tradition out of which the wooden halls of the early medieval period emerge; even sunken featured buildings have clear parallels within the empire's frontiers. Early medieval material culture is simply of a different order to its Roman predecessor, and existing wooden building traditions were adapted and developed once building in stone became impossible.

Similarly, technical changes in pottery manufacture and metalwork reflect the ending of the Roman pottery industry with its carefully regulated insignia and close ties to state demands and resources. The new styles of decoration for both pottery and metalwork which emerge in the fifth century, long believed to be Anglo-Saxon in inspiration, are now seen as outgrowths of late Roman provincial and military traditions which had profoundly influenced barbarian taste: for example the so-called 'Romano-Saxon' pottery of the mid-fifth century fits into a provincial tradition that had been exported beyond the frontier. The belts and buckles characteristic of late fifth-century grave-goods have similarly been shown to be descended from designs which had functioned as insignia of office within the late Roman army, and had long been adapted as status symbols beyond the frontier.

Across a vast swathe of post-Roman Britain, south and east of a line roughly from York to Winchester, from the second half of the fifth century corpses were sent to the afterlife fully clothed, and accompanied by grave-goods. This marked a significant change from Roman practice, and the closest parallels are in the Germanic regions beyond the Roman frontier, although there were also precedents at sites such as the military cemetery at Lankhills near Winchester. In parts of eastern England, change was more marked still, as here cremation – a rite which had more or less vanished across the Roman world between the first and fourth centuries but which remained popular beyond the Rhine frontier – underwent a significant revival in the fifth and sixth centuries. Cremation burials, like inhumations, were furnished – clothes and grave-goods were either burned with the corpse or, where this was impossible, symbolically defaced – and so operated in a similar context of conspicuous display focusing on items of clothing and adornment. Neither cremation nor the inhumation rite can be seen as ancestral rites preserved by a new population articulating its ethnic difference from its neighbours. These rituals of death constituted a shared cultural idiom of conspicuous display, used by all sectors of the population, with no fundamental discontinuities of rite evident. There is significant local variation in material culture, which is particularly marked in the sixth century and in female burials. But within a common culture of funerary display, burial with wargear was a means of claiming full membership of the male elite, symbolised by the carrying of weapons: the ideological force is made clear by instances of the deposition of weapons in the graves of children, the infirm and disabled. These patterns suggest that standing in, and membership of, a local community was the paramount concern, not the racial divide between Anglo-Saxon and Briton that has been the obsession of modern scholarship. Burial rites did not articulate ethnic divides, but show new communities crystallising under the protection of new elites claiming Anglo-Saxon origin, and local status coming to be expressed in rites of display favoured by those elites.

Can we say more about the processes whereby these new communities were formed? Analysis of historical pollen deposits, of local boundaries in relation to Roman roads and estates, and of the rural landscape across Britain, have indicated that there was no large-scale break in the exploitation of the land, rather a gradual adjustment of agrarian strategies to the new economic realities of a world without markets. Careful excavation of settlements in relation to both local cemeteries and the surrounding rural landscape can begin to help us understand these transformations. At sites such as West Heslerton in Yorkshire, West Stow in Norfolk and Mucking in Essex this kind of detailed investigation has begun. In all three cases, early medieval settlements are related to predecessors from the Roman period, but there is a wholesale shift in the site of habitation in the immediate post-Roman period. What is less clear at present, but may be revealed by future work, are the mechanisms for this dramatic social reorganisation and the associated changes in burial rites, settlement patterns and material culture. It has been suggested at West Heslerton and Mucking that there may be phases where it is possible to detect the simultaneous presence of two distinct groups demonstrating archaeologically different cultural traits: if this is the case, it might be possible to investigate the reception of an incoming group, and the nature of the relationship between Anglo-Saxon incomers and the indigenous population. Similarly, careful analysis of the faunal record, and of animal bones found on settlement sites, reveal a shift to a less intensive, more subsistence-based, style of agriculture, with greater use of pasturing and low-level exploitation of natural resources such as woodland. The impression given by the settlement archaeology is one of a less intensively farmed, and less densely populated countryside; although there are references of varying trustworthiness to plague in some narrative sources, epidemic disease probably simply accentuated a demographic trend which resulted from practical decisions taken in the light of economic and ecological resources.

In assessing the scale of immigration, and the processes by which post-Roman society became Anglo-Saxon, we need to take account of regional differences within Britain: there was more than one path from Roman province to the Anglo-Saxon societies of Bede's day. Areas such as the Pennines, the West Midlands, and much of the Scottish lowlands were, by the eighth century, thoroughly and unambiguously 'Anglo-Saxon', but were also relatively recent conquests of the late sixth and seventh centuries. Here there is little evidence for population movement of any kind, and no question of mass immigration. British kingdoms such as Elmet in the Pennines, conquered by the Northumbrians in 626, were simply absorbed by their Anglo-Saxon conquerors. Yet the Northumbrian provinces in and over the Pennines and southern Scotland, and the Mercian heartlands of the West Midlands, were all Anglo-Saxon-speaking areas by the time Bede wrote in the early eighth century – a point which is often overlooked by scholars who see language-change as straightforward evidence for mass migration as opposed to the substitution of an Anglo-Saxon for a British elite.

It is unfortunate that controversy has centred on the scale of population change, with arguments ranging from large-scale migration that swamped the Britons to conquest by a small Anglo-Saxon elite that imposed its language and culture on its subjects. One problem with this kind of argument is that it focuses attention on the relative numbers of incomers, as if that alone determines patterns of cultural influence: in fact, the mechanisms of settlement, and the structures of power and authority which conditioned contact between Anglo-Saxons and Britons, are issues of vital importance. The most distinctive feature of early Anglo-Saxon history is the sheer scale of post-Roman change in lowland Britain. On the continent, provinces immediately within the old Roman frontier, where the language of barbarian neighbours must have always been familiar, became Germanic-speaking; elsewhere, Romance languages developed from the spoken Latin of the late Roman period. In Britain, Latin was replaced by indigenous

Celtic languages in the west, whilst in the lowland heart of the former Roman province the language not of the indigenous population, or of immediate barbarian neighbours, but of Germanic-speaking invaders from across the North Sea, came to dominate. On the continent, episcopal successions was disrupted in some frontier cities, but Christianity remained the religion of the barbarian kingdoms founded on Roman soil; in Britain, organised Christianity was replaced by pagan cults promoted by Anglo-Saxon kings. Whereas across the post-Roman Mediterranean, the survival of Roman administrative and legal structures through cities and bishoprics meant that barbarian incomers could be grafted onto a still-functioning provincial society, in post-Roman Britain wholesale collapse meant that new warrior-elites could reshape society to an exceptional degree.

Celtic kingships and Celtic churches

By the seventh-century horizon of our written sources, kingship was the basic political institution across the British Isles. Although it is customary to contrast 'Anglo-Saxon' and 'Celtic' kingship, this may owe much to the divergent academic traditions of Anglo-Saxonists and Celticists, and the different source material to be mastered in each field. In fact, close study of early medieval 'Celtic' societies has revealed not only that they shared a series of broad similarities with their 'Anglo-Saxon' neighbours, but also that there were significant differences between Ireland and Wales, not to mention Scotland and Brittany. The temptation to identify peculiarly 'Celtic' features of social organisation and a homogenous 'Celtic culture', sharply differentiated from that of Anglo-Saxon invaders, thus distorts the early medieval reality; it reflects a modern definition of the 'Celtic' in opposition to an Anglocentric norm.

Viewed against the backdrop of developments elsewhere in the post-Roman west, both Anglo-Saxon and Celtic societies share one striking feature: in both, there was a multiplicity of kings, and so a sense that there were different grades or levels of kingship. On the continent, the symbiosis between barbarian warlords and provincial elites ensured that there was thus a single locus of legitimate royal power; kings like Clovis and Theodoric were able to eliminate rival warlords with regal status both amongst their own 'peoples', and on and beyond their frontiers. In Britain, though, the collapse of the Roman province meant that there was no such dynamic; no process generating a single royal tradition took place among the Anglo-Saxons; and post-Roman kinglets proliferated around the fringes of the former Roman province. As a result, polycentric political traditions, with many layers of kingship, developed: among the Anglo-Saxons, a multiplicity of local kings overlaid by shifting overlordships; among the Britons, Irish, and Picts similar fluid pyramids of kings of varying power, and – among the Picts and Irish at least – competition for an overlordship or 'high kingship' which was more a potent ideal than an institutional reality. The geographical distribution of the source material in the seventh to ninth centuries means that these systems of kingship are clearest amongst the Anglo-Saxons and the Irish. Differences between the largely normative legal and literary traditions that dominate the Irish material, and the emphasis on practice in the Anglo-Saxon narrative and documentary evidence, mean that we have different – indeed, in some ways complementary – perspectives on these two political traditions.

The nature of the Irish evidence has encouraged an almost static image of early Irish society. Irish literary traditions were shaped by an astounding sense of continuity. Hence stories of prehistoric heroes were preserved in collections of Old Irish literature made by monastic scribes from the tenth century onwards, in which modern readers have been tempted to see a 'window on the Iron Age'.[15] This is too optimistic. Specialists on early Irish literature now argue that apparently archaic tales were reshaped by their early medieval Christian tellers so as to illuminate an early medieval Christian world. Tales about the legendary deeds of heroic ancestors clearly articulate values of loyalty, honour and valour; these values could be integrated into, and subtly transformed by, Christianity. The ethics thus transmitted could be made relevant to the tenth-century audience of the surviving version of *The Cattle Raid of Cooley*, the earliest great monument of Old Irish literature. The unique continuity of Irish cultural tradition should not be seen as evidence for a lack of social change, but for the peculiarities of Irish history in the Roman and post-Roman periods. Whereas elsewhere in Europe Roman and then barbarian conquest rendered tales about prehistoric heroes irrelevant to elites, in Ireland legends about mythical forbears flourished as ways to legitimate the current social order and explain the political landscape. In early medieval England and Francia, elites cultivated tales about the heroic leaders of the migration period; and though these traditions were a valued form of secular entertainment, from the eighth century there were recurrent worries, for priests in particular, about their suitability, on account of their association with the pre-Christian past and the polluting secularity of their role in feasting celebrations. In Ireland, however, there were no such worries about heroic traditions. The peculiar nature of the conversion to Christianity in Ireland, in a gradual and piecemeal process, meant that there was no real sense of dramatic confrontation between the needs of the Christian present and the cultural traditions of the pre-Christian past. Pre-Christian Irish society may, in any case, have been unusual in that it included a learned caste of legal experts, which may have facilitated this seamless process of transmission. But the fundamental reason for the continued preservation of heroic tradition was its continued relevance to an effectively stateless world: as Irish kings had no Roman models on which they could draw, and exercised personal rather than territorial power, so Irish social and political organisation had to be explained with a genealogical logic which linked current affairs to the actions of legendary heroes.

The timelessness of the literary material, then, is essentially an ideological projection; current leaders legitimated their position by linking themselves to a complex web of historical traditions. The image of a deeply conservative and highly regulated social system suggested by the law-tracts needs similarly careful handling. Aside from its inherent difficulties – the texts, dates and contexts of much of this material remains the subject of intense specialist debate – the rules collected in legal material can be used to create a neat and tidy model of a clearly defined hierarchy of kings, and the duties and obligations between different grades of king, and between kings and different grades of subject. On such a reconstruction, kings – indeed, individuals at each social level – appear to be tightly bound by law, which was archaic and unchanging. But this impression may be misleading. Irish law-tracts were systemising compilations made by the legally learned, and they thus delight in technical virtuosity and pay close attention to small intricacies; we have no records of law in action, however, and so no idea of how the law of the tracts interacted with actual practice. The image of an arcane and static legal order is largely an artefact of the particular source genre on which we are dependent. Nonetheless, the dominance of expert compilations is no accident: Irish legal culture was unique. Elsewhere in early medieval Europe, kings were law-givers and law-codes recorded the royal exercise of legislative authority. Irish kings, however, did not inherit Roman models, and so were participants in a legal tradition that was the recognised preserve of those with specialist knowledge.

In a society where kingdoms were personal rather than territorial, it is unsurprising that kings were not law-givers. But laws could be made in response to new social problems, and kings could be involved in their making, through mechanisms which are not reflected in the law-tracts. Written law itself was a new feature of the seventh and eighth centuries, encouraged by the use of writing in ecclesiastical matters. Inevitably, from the beginning ecclesiastical law-making spilled over into secular matters: the eighth-century Latin collection *Hibernensis* is concerned with both ecclesiastical and secular affairs, whilst the earliest dated vernacular tract *Caín Fhuitherbe* is the product of a mixed synod held *c.* 680. Indeed, in a politically fluid and fragmented world, the church played a central role in negotiating agreements, *cána* (singular *cáin*), which were guaranteed by kings and others through oaths and sureties, and seen as expressions of saintly will; these dealt with the kind of issues that were characteristically the concern of the earliest royal legislation elsewhere in Europe. The earliest surviving such agreement, *Cáin Adomnan*, dates from 697 but was reissued for over 200 years: it is mainly concerned with the protection of women; in return for its protection, its beneficiaries were to pay dues to Adomnan's churches and their representatives. The golden age of the *cána* was the eighth and early ninth centuries: there are over 33 recorded instances of their proclamation in the period up to 842, with no fewer than ten re-enactments of *Cáin Patrick*, which forbade the killing of clerics. But the role of the church as guarantor of order in a society organised around a principle of political division and resulting conflict also took other forms. Churchmen were the key arbiters and mediators seeking to end political disputes, and churches could be neutral sites for assemblies bringing kings together. Thus by the ninth century the abbots of Armagh, as the leading churchmen in Ireland, were repeatedly called upon to use their status, and their control of Patrick's relics, to broker agreements between quarrelling kings.[16]

Ecclesiastical mediation was necessary because Ireland was politically fragmented, with potentially upwards of 150 kings. The law-codes suggest an intricate hierarchy of kings, and develop a vocabulary to describe this hierarchy; in practice, what mattered was the ability of more powerful kings to establish overlordship over their neighbours, made visible through the payment of tribute. Central to Irish kingship was the ability to claim royal blood. Kingship was dynastic, dynasties claiming descent from the legendary figures of the distant past. But a king (*rí*) needed a constituency to rule: his *tuáth*, a vernacular term often but highly misleadingly translated as 'tribe'. In fact, what is remarkable about Irish political and social organisation – and stands in marked contrast to Anglo-Saxon England, and indeed the British kingdoms of the west – is the absence of any strong sense of self-identification by the 'peoples' over whom kings ruled: a king's *tuáth* tended to take its name from a dynasty or segment of a dynasty. Where we do see some sense of collective identity amongst the population, it tends to be in terms of a geographical regional label which did not necessarily coincide with fractured and changing political boundaries; rather we read of the men of Leinster, or Connacht, or Ulster, their identities rooted in legendary traditions of the five provinces of Ireland. There is some evidence, both in the annals and the literature, that the politically-active free populations of these regions may even have functioned as communities with shared local interests, with which kings had to deal through assemblies, and powerful kings increasingly came to style themselves as kings of Leinster, or Connacht, or another province. But it was essentially dynastic complexities that served to justify and legitimate kingship: one important function of the tales about legendary heroes that typifies Irish literature was to provide kings with a pedigree, whilst genealogical learning served to define relationships between different rulers in the present. Genealogy, not territory, was the basis of this political system.

This dynastic ideology can make Irish kingship appear the property of a closed and exclusive caste. Succession practices, however, ensured an endemic political fragmentation through a constant process of segmentation that meant that dynasties splintered as quickly as they could gain territory. This state of affairs meant that successful kingship was as dependent on the abilities and opportunities of a specific king, not on inherited or institutional position: dynastic identities continued but dynasties were fluid and constantly reshaping around able and successful rulers, with rules of succession constantly challenged and renegotiated. Fundamentally, kingship was implicated in and based upon a whole series of basically personal relationships of clientship: the glue of Irish society, whose intricacies are discussed at great length in legal tracts. Free clientship centred on military service: it was effectively a relationship between lord and retainer, of service for reward, and had a strong reciprocal element. Unfree clientship was essentially economic, centred on the extraction of surplus produce in annual renders that allowed the king to maintain his household. In an important sense, then, there was no distinction between political and social, or public and private, power: kings were quite simply those who exercised power over others, and there was no sense of sovereignty as a prerequisite for kingship. As a result, even kingship was a matter of relativities not absolutes, and there were many layers of kings, owing nominal or real obligations to royal overlords in a complex web of relationships again much-discussed by the lawyers.[17]

Kingship rested on the ability to exact tribute, and impose clientship, on those who worked the land, so as to maintain a household fitting for a king, and attractive to potential free clients. Archaeologically, there are many known royal centres, usually in the form of 'ringforts', whose nuclei of wooden halls and structures were surrounded by embankments and ditches: these range from substantial farms with rudimentary surrounding structures to large complexes ringed by several circuits of earthworks. These seem to have embodied a claim to royal status, and law-codes defined status in terms of the scale of defences around an individual's household; these were the material correlate to the elaborate genealogies that were central to political discourse. They were more than status symbols. Because there was as a rule intense competition between rival kings for tribute, clients and recognition, raiding and fighting were a necessity, although because one year's raider could be the next year's raided there were norms governing these activities. This endemic conflict characterised the life of the elite to such an extent that Irish society could be seen as resting on the constant struggle of kings and their military followings, constantly seeking to maximise their resource-base of subject farmers. Dynastic ideology thus played an important role in allowing the system to adjust to changes in the actual balance of power, as rising rulers in claiming the illustrious descent necessary to legitimate their position were integrated into the wider political system.

The dominant trend in the politics of the seventh and eighth centuries was the rise of the various groups who claimed descent from the legendary hero Niall of the Nine Hostages. The Ui Neill, like other Irish dynasties, should not be seen as a coherent entity following a united policy: internecine war was not unheard of within these segmented, fragmented and geographically diverse groups who shared a claimed legendary ancestor. By the seventh century, the Ui Neill kings of the province of Meath in central Ireland were able to capitalise on the success of Cormac mac Airt and claim a high kingship centred on their political centre at Tara. The 'high kingship of Tara' had no real institutional solidity: it was an ideological claim that needed to be backed up by military success. The antiquity of these claims is difficult to determine, given the problems of using our late sources: they may have been developing in the seventh and eighth centuries, as there is both literary and archaeological evidence that suggests that centres such as Cashell in Munster may have enjoyed significant ritual and political prominence in the effectively prehistoric period before the seventh century. But it was Tara that was to establish a lasting claim to pre-eminent status. Here, the ritual and cultural associations of a huge and complex site may have been strengthened by the social significance for the upper echelons of Irish society of the annual fairs and festivals held at Tara, centrally located close by the five great prehistoric trackways which defined Irish provincial geography.

The theory of power descending from above, with a clear hierarchy of kingship in which each ruler was notionally appointed by his superior, was attractive to the ecclesiastics and lawyers who developed it, but it remained no more than theory: local power remained the underpinning of kingship, and succession to the 'high kingship' tended to devolve to powerful overlords who had the military muscle to control Tara itself. Nonetheless, the lustre of the 'high kingship' was sufficient to attract claimants from across Ireland, the title thus encouraging the political integration of the island as a whole and preventing the development of firmly territorial regional polities. The lustre of the high kingship may also explain why the majority of the successful dynasties of the seventh and eighth centuries identified themselves as branches of the Ui Neill: not only the Clann Cholmain in Meath and the Eogain of Armagh, between whom the kingship of Tara tended to alternate, but also rulers with more local ambitions like the Ui Briuin kings who were establishing local dominance in seventh-century Connacht. The social dynamics underlying these political changes are difficult to detect, and more research is needed on the archaeological evidence; but the net effect was to consolidate the position of a strata of regional rulers with far-reaching interests at the expense of local petty kings, either by conquest, as in the Ui Neill takeover of Leinster in the last quarter of the eighth century, or consensus, as in Ulster, where by the ninth century local landowners were opting to become clients of the Ui Neill directly rather than entering the service of local dynasties. Our legal and literary sources' concern with norms and rules, then, does not reflect a static and highly-regulated system, but is a reaction to, and an attempt to order and regulate, an inherently dynamic and fluid system.

The very existence of written laws and moral tracts, ecclesiastical or secular, Latin or vernacular, bears eloquent witness to dramatic cultural changes wrought by the church. The Irish church was profoundly influenced by the ideals of monasticism, in part because traditional models of episcopal authority rested on the city-centred administrative structure of the Roman Empire and were thus difficult to adapt to Irish society. In spite of its origins as a movement of ascetic retreat, monasticism was easily adapted into the heart of Irish society: monasteries were able to build up rights to renders and tribute from huge swathes of countryside, and monastic settlements, enclosed in a manner reminiscent of royal residences and often located on former royal sites, were the greatest concentrations of wealth and population known to this society: the monastery of Kildare was famously described as a city.[18] The notion of a spiritual elite implicit in monasticism may have been particularly appealing to the royal class from whom leading churchmen were drawn. By the eighth century at the latest, monasticism had come to dominate the church in its entirety. Bishops were sometimes abbots, their power based on a monastery and its dependent churches; sometimes, as in the monasteries associated with Columba, founder of Iona, monks subordinate to the abbot were consecrated bishops to perform the acts reserved in canon law for the holders of episcopal office. Major monastic churches claimed rights over smaller foundations on the basis of involvement with founders and benefactors, resulting in a mosaic-like map of interwoven ecclesiastical 'empires', rather than strictly territorial dioceses: in this, the dynastic pattern of personal dominion which typified the secular world was reproduced in the church. Indeed, there was no clear distinction between the titulature of secular rulers and ecclesiastical potentates. The extent to which these ties – essentially modelled on personal ties of kingship and clientage transposed onto the church, and determined by the personal allegiances of the founders of monasteries – entirely replaced the territorial and administrative patterns of episcopal power based on dioceses and diocesan boundaries is unclear. Even in the eighth and ninth centuries, legal tracts still stressed the rights and jurisdictions of bishops, although it may be that episcopal status was simply appropriated by major abbots. Nonetheless, the pattern of extensive networks of monastic foundations clearly allowed the structures of the church to relate to those of kinship and kingship: strong episcopal administration of territorially defined dioceses would have been an impossibility in that it would have created a substantial power structure which crossed political boundaries, and was exercised with reference to principles in conflict with the genealogical logic of early Irish society, and would have thus been unacceptable to kings.

In fact, the structure of the early medieval Irish church did help consolidate the power of royal dynasties. Monasteries institutionalised claims to renders and to dependants which had originally been embedded in interpersonal relationships of clientship: in the eighth and ninth centuries there are even examples of monasteries going to war with one another over such claims! It is no accident that successful kings founded and cultivated close relationships with important monastic houses as a means of exercising their power, as the monks of Clonmacnois supported their patron, the high king Flann Sinna, in the decades around 900. Indeed, the increasing geographical range of the claims of the royal and ecclesiastical elites followed parallel paths. The rise of the high kingship of Tara to political pre-eminence is mirrored in the ecclesiastical sphere by the rise of the church of Armagh – a complex of monastic churches ruled by an abbot-bishop – to ecclesiastical pre-eminence in the seventh and eighth centuries. As with the high kingship of Tara, Armagh's position was more a matter of status than actual control: Armagh was no more the administrative centre of an institutionalised Irish church than Tara was the capital of an Irish kingdom. And as with the high kingship of Tara, Armagh's special status was explained with what was effectively genealogical logic, rooted in legendary founders: Armagh thus based its primacy on its claims to have been the centre of Patrick's mission. As a result, the seventh and eighth centuries saw the emergence of a lively 'Patrick industry', where Armagh's claims to jurisdiction over neighbouring churches, and to have been the centre of Patrick's mission, were documented through the creation of a series of written traditions about Patrick's life. As with Tara, though, these claims remained subject to the reality of a politically fragmented society, in which power rested on personal ties and so no one ruler or institution could claim direct and unmediated authority over the island as a whole. As a result, just as local kings might offer tribute or acknowledge the theoretical pre-eminence of the claims of Tara whilst consolidating their local position, so eventually monastic houses simply justified their own regional pre-eminence with respect to the Patrick legend. Successive rewritings of the life of Brigit of Kildare, for example, show that in the seventh century Kildare had initially harboured its own ambitions as an alternative centre to Armagh, linked to the political ambitions of its patrons in the Ui Dunlaige dynasty, but that its monks eventually settled for acknowledging the primacy of Patrick, simultaneously defining its limits by revising their account of Brigit's career and suggesting that Kildare had all along been an ally of Armagh and its Ui Neill royal patrons.[19]

The adaptation of the structures of the church to the fragmented societies of early medieval Ireland had far-reaching cultural results. Elite society in early medieval Ireland consisted of a weapon-carrying, horse-riding, cattle-rustling class of noblemen. Beneath the bewildering flux of early Irish politics lay a constant flow of ambitious young men, sent out to be fostered by powerful relatives in their youth in order to cement relations of patronage and acquire the prowess which would attract a following amongst their peers, in constant danger of being exiled from a particular kingdom if their rivals seized power. These structures of male elite mobility were determined by the generational cycles of the leading dynasties, and so they quickly found their counterparts amongst the ecclesiastical elite, which was likewise drawn from those dynasties. Hence the practice of *peregrenatio*, the 'voluntary' exile of churchmen from their kin and homeland as a form of pilgrimage in the service of God, was born. Soon, the ideology of *peregrinatio* could be used to describe not only movements between the kingdoms of Ireland, but to their closely-related counterparts over the Irish Sea; by the beginning of the seventh century, Columbanus, abbot of Bangor, could spend a career travelling through Gaul and northern Italy. Columbanus and his later followers brought with them another cultural adaptation born in the peculiar social context of early medieval Ireland, in a new form of penance. Penance – the performance of atonement for sins – had in the early church been a dramatic public ritual, acknowledging and repenting of a lifetime's mistakes before one's peers, in the hope of forgiveness from a distant but all-knowing God. In an Irish society built around the requirement that compensation be given for harm done, failing which revenge was extracted by a wronged kin-group and their allies, sins were easily seen as isolated acts of wrong for which specific amends could be made in a one-to-one relationship with God, just as enraged neighbours could be bought off for stolen cattle or offended kin: penitentials, listing potential sins and calibrating the correct penance to be performed by their perpetrator, thus offered a new form of religiosity which spread rapidly, speaking as they did to the landowning families of the post-Roman west.

The distinctive, and well-documented, patterns of political and ecclesiastical organisation discovered in Ireland have often provided the basis for a model of 'Celtic kingship' and the 'Celtic church' which have been used to understand the sparse and often late evidence from other 'Celtic' areas, most notably Wales. In fact, there were significant differences between Welsh and Irish society. In Wales, for example, whilst post-Roman kingship was localised and small-scale, there is little sense of the almost total relativism, with kingship based in dynastic title and embedded in a social hierarchy, which characterises Ireland. Whilst Wales was a country of many kings, some superior to others, and a developed genealogical tradition tying these kings to legendary ancestors, the basic political units had territorial labels – Powys, Gwynedd, and so on. So Welsh kings did not style themselves as leaders of peoples, as their Anglo-Saxon neighbours did, nor explain their position solely in terms of dynastic origin, as in Ireland, but as rulers of these territorial units. Not that there was a stable or fixed map of kingdoms: powerful rulers might seize the territories of lesser kings, enlarge their kingdom at the expense of its neighbours or rule over several kingdoms. But there was a territorial foundation to political organisation, perhaps a complex metamorphosis of Roman provincial geography: Powys, for example, may be derived from the Latin geographical term *pagus*. Genealogy remained important in justifying a royal pedigree, but unlike in Ireland genealogy did not legitimate current rulers with reference to a legendary Celtic past, but connected the present to a past in which Rome played a central role.

The long-term legacy of Roman rule probably also explains differences in organisation between the Welsh and Irish churches. The origins of the Welsh church remain obscure, recorded as they are in late saints' lives of the eighth to twelfth centuries whose value as sources for the immediate post-Roman period is dubious, but it seems to have developed directly out of late Roman Christianity. It was, after all, through the church that the most Roman of legal technologies, the written title deed, was preserved in west Britain, whereas in the Anglo-Saxon areas of the east writing in law as in other aspects of life disappeared: records from the bishopric of Llandaff preserve a series of texts beginning in the sixth century.[20] The Welsh church was unambiguously an episcopal church. Monks and monasteries were not unknown but they may normally have been attached to episcopal churches, and certainly did not determine the structure of the Welsh church. There is strong evidence for the presence of local churches and associated cemeteries as the basic ecclesiastical unit. There is little evidence for the building up of large-scale landowning by ecclesiastical institutions that is such a marked feature of monasticism in Ireland. Whilst by the eighth century a small number of churches – most notably St David's in the north, the see of the pre-eminent bishop in Wales – had succeeded in building up large-scale holdings, they did not create extensive networks of related monastic foundations scattered across political boundaries, the kind of constellations that became something close to monastic 'empires' in Ireland.

The differential impact of the Roman legacy explains not only the differences between 'Celtic' Ireland and Wales, but also the similarities between Ireland and the societies of early medieval Scotland. Here historians' keenness to see the Picts as an archaic curiosity from the pre-Celtic past has tended to distance discussion of their political and social organisation from that of their neighbours. In particular, the Pictish system of royal succession has been seen as evidence for a matrilineal society – that is one in which inheritance through maternal kin was of crucial importance in determining status – and thus a wholly different state of affairs from that found elsewhere in early medieval Europe. The evidence for Pictish matrilineage is thin, perhaps hardly surprisingly as the written evidence for Pictish society is next to non-existent. Bede records a legend of Pictish origins which is echoed in several later, tenth-century Irish texts: it tells how the Picts, after they had migrated to their lands in northern Britain, sought wives from the Irish, which they were granted on the condition that they chose their kings on the basis of their maternal rather than paternal parentage when the succession was unclear. The story in fact is not evidence for the structure of Pictish society as a whole, and in its earliest version it sees matrilineal succession as an emergency measure when normal practices had failed. Given that the Pictish kings we do meet in the written sources are often outsiders, whose paternal descent leads back to the royal dynasties of the neighbouring kingdoms of the Irish Scots in Dalriada, the British in southern Scotland, or the Anglo-Saxons in Northumbria, the legend of a Pictish promise to take on kings on account of their maternal descent must have served as an explanation and legitimation of this Pictish propensity to adopt outsiders as rulers, and suggested that these outside rulers married into the families of their predecessors to forge links with the Pictish polity; Bede's legend seems to have come from an Iona informant, so in emphasising Irish claims to Pictish kingship through female blood it may have reflected the ambitions of the kings of Dalriada.[21]

In any case, the matrilineal legend has tended to direct attention away from the nature of the Pictish kingship it discusses. The Irish annals which name Pictish kings most frequently identify kings with specific regions or seats, not with rule over the Picts as a whole. The kingship of Fortriu – Fife, the richest Pictish province – may have carried with it a notional overkingship of the Picts, reminiscent of the status of the kingship of Tara in Ireland. Later traditions of seven provinces of Pictland may record seven kingships within a broader Pictish confederation loosely held together through the kingship of Fortriu, although in the sparse written sources there is no explicit reference to kings for many of these provinces. Similarities between Irish and Pictish social structure may explain why the monastic traditions of the Irish church, as relayed through Iona, were rapidly adopted by the Picts. Nonetheless it would be dangerous to normalise Pictish political structure: the matrilineal story clearly rests on the contemporary perception that somehow Pictish political arrangements were different, and required special explanation. In the surviving Pictish king-list, there is no hint of kings following their fathers either directly or indirectly until the very last decades of the eighth century. The sources support the idea of a confederate, multi-centred political structure, with a variety of levels of kingship, and the position of king of Fortriu not the property of any one dynasty, but circulating within the polity, and on occasion to outsiders. In such a system, and particularly in a system that was open to the adoption of outsiders as kings of Fortriu, the role of royal women in tying different groups together, and managing the succession, is likely to have been crucial. In fact, even in avowedly dynastic systems elsewhere in early medieval Europe, where there was no obvious candidate for the succession, royal women often exercised the crucial political role. Lying behind the matrilineal legend must be the careers of Pictish equivalents to the Gothic queen Amalswintha, the Lombards Theudelinda and Gundperga, and the Merovingians Brunhild and Balthild, able to create a formal political role for themselves in a multi-layered system in which royal succession was a matter of negotiation.

Anglo-Saxon kingship and conversion

By the time we cross the threshold of our written sources in the seventh century, those areas of Britain subject to Anglo-Saxon settlement were likewise divided into a multiplicity of small and often overlapping political units whose rulers might harbour claims to royal status. The origins of Anglo-Saxon kingship, and of Anglo-Saxon kingdoms, are obscure. But the nomenclature of the political and social groupings that appear in the written sources suggests that most were formed in the immediate post-migration period, not imported from continental homelands. One striking feature of the surviving royal genealogies for the various

Anglo-Saxon kingdoms and of Anglo-Saxon heroic poetry, both of which first survive in ninth- and tenth-century manuscripts, is the lack of any detailed pre-migration continental tradition. These kings ruled new peoples, made in Britain even if they were defined by a belief in a common but distant continental origin.

Anglo-Saxon kings of the seventh and eighth centuries styled themselves as rulers of peoples: as, say, king of the East Anglians not king of East Anglia. But these peoples did not bear ancient tribal names brought from their continental homelands: instead, their names were determined by post-migration political geography. The *Cantware* (literally the 'men of Kent') were named after the Roman *civitas* of Canterbury in which they dwelled, as were the 'people' of Lindsey, around Lincoln. Other labels were purely geographical, and slowly shifted: the Mercians, who by the seventh century had established rule over the Midlands, began as the dwellers on a (now unknown) mark or frontier. The *Humbrenses*, 'the dwellers around the Humber', were transformed into the *North*umbrians by their sixth-century conquest of Deira and Bernicia, two territories with British names north of the Humber. Elsewhere, along the southern and eastern coasts in particular, there is less hint of interaction with pre-existing units, with different political communities simply referred to in relative terms, as the middle or eastern branch of a particular people; even these labels, however, may have emerged relatively late, as the outlines of the political map crystallised and so allowed the identification of southern, eastern and western Saxons, for example. The West Saxons, for instance, coalesced around a dynasty that claimed descent from Cerdic, whose name, like those of his successors into the eighth century, is of British origin; in their first appearances in the sources this 'people' were named the *Gewissae*. The various local political communities who had emerged in the sixth-century East Midlands were grouped together as the Middle Angles only in the early seventh century, when the Mercian king, Penda, attempted to carve out a kingdom of the Middle Angles for his son. As the names of many of these local groupings – communities like the Gwyre of the Fens, who still had their own princely family in the seventh century – advertise no Anglian pedigree, it may be that their Anglian identity was a relatively late political creation. These patterns of political nomenclature suggest that the distinction between Angles, Saxons and Jutes reported by Bede was commonplace by the end of the seventh century. The cases of Wessex and the Middle Angles could suggest that this division between Angle and Saxon was in fact only slowly winning currency; certainly it articulated seventh- and eighth-century political realities, with, for example, the area under Mercian domination corresponding to the 'Southumbrian' Angles, as both Bede and some eighth-century documents commented, and distinct from the Saxons and Jutes south of the Thames. The neat division into Anglian, Saxon and Jutish kingships might thus be seen as a means of legitimating a newly crystallised political dispensation.

The relations between different kings and kingdoms were hierarchal, with powerful kings acting as overlords, or establishing more or less formal rights over lesser rulers. In contrast to Ireland, there was no attempt to constitutionalise this political hierarchy in terms of different grades of kinship, and as we have seen even in Ireland law-tracts suggest a far more ordered picture than was the reality. Bede does give a list of seven kings who had 'held imperium over the English', a list copied at the end of the ninth century by the compiler of the *Anglo-Saxon Chronicle*, who gave these rulers the title *Bretwalda*, literally ruler of Britain. These two references do not point to any continuous tradition of overlordship, equivalent to the high kingship of Tara in Ireland. Bede's list is essentially concerned with placing his particular heroes, the seventh-century Christian Northumbrian kings Edwin, Oswald and Oswiu, in the tradition of other famous kings, whilst the compiler of the *Anglo-Saxon Chronicle* seizes on Bede's list to link the dynasty of his patron, Alfred of Wessex, to the golden names of the past.[22]

In fact, both the narrative sources and the documentary records when they begin in the eighth century reveal multiple layers of kingship and fluid systems of overlordship. The politics of seventh- and eighth-century England is best thought of in terms of a series of layers of political activity and allegiance beneath that of the kingships of the most powerful rulers who dominate the narrative histories. The fullest perspective on this multi-layered political system comes in a chance survival, the text called the 'Tribal Hidage' by modern historians. This is a listing of various groupings and territories, proceeding in a series of concentric circles from the heartland of the kingdom of Mercia in the West Midlands. This text – to call it a document implies an institutional context that is lacking – needs handling with care, but it confirms the impression of both documents and narratives. It shows Mercia as consisting of several dozen regional units, each given a rating, being said to consist of a number of 'hides', as are the other major Anglo-Saxon kingdoms south of the Humber. According to Bede, the 'hide' was the notional unit of land needed to support one family, and on which tributes and dues were assessed; in the 'Tribal Hidage' we have round numbers which would seem to reflect the order of tribute a Mercian king might expect from the constituent parts of his kingdom, and from his neighbours, just as Bede shows us kings reckoning newly conquered areas at a round number of hides.[23]

What were the origins and functions of these local units? There has been a strong urge to see the original building-blocks of Anglo-Saxon society as incredibly small-scale local communities with their own identities and political traditions, out of which the kingdoms that dominate the written sources emerged. According to many scholars, such was the level of political collapse and decentralisation in post-Roman Britain that the basis of society became the extended kin-group. On this model, political and social change from the fifth to the eighth century is characterised as a process of 'competitive exclusion' leading to the formation of the small number of major kingdoms we see in the eighth and ninth centuries, whereby conflict between expanding kin-groups over vital economic resources led to the swallowing-up of the weaker by the stronger. There is an attractive neatness in this model, which fits well with a long-established tradition of seeing early Anglo-Saxon history as the story of small groups of incoming pioneers. Certainly there is now an impressive range of evidence suggesting that these *regiones* – as they are often called in early documents – were basic units in early Anglo-Saxon society. However, there is actually next to no evidence to support the notion that they were in origin self-standing kin-based units. Some regions did have independent political traditions, most notably those with roots in Roman provinces and their sub-Roman successors: the area around Worcester, for example, was part of the kingdom of the Mercians but subject to a 'subruler of the Hwicce' in the eighth century. But others, like the 'kingdom of the Middle Angles' or Surrey, a *regio* with its own subking in the eighth century, were artificial creations carved out of larger kingdoms whose rulers aimed to consolidate local control in the hands of lesser members of their dynasties. The vast majority of such units recorded in the 'Tribal Hidage' and the documentary sources, have names rooted in local topography (the 'Chiltern-dwellers', the 'Wrekin-dwellers', and so on): these are best seen as regional units, rooted perhaps in horizontal bonds of community but also shaped by the vertical demands of kings for tribute and service.

Early kingdoms were not clearly defined and easily recognised sovereign entities. The claiming of tribute and overlordship by successful kings over their weaker neighbours was the basic process of early Anglo-Saxon politics; political scale must always have rested on the efforts of warrior-elites anxious to maximise their chances of ending as tribute-takers rather than tribute-payers, calculations which may have always encouraged regional conglomerations of the kind visible in the seventh- and eighth-century sources. Extensive overlordship, rather than intensive rule, was the essential mechanism through which kings built up their status, taking tribute and winning the renown that would enable them to attract the support of the cream of the warrior class. This was not a world of well-defined kingdoms with strict succession systems, but one of a wide class of potential kings, who needed the wealth and luck to build up a military following to make good their claims, in patterns not dissimilar from those we saw in Ireland. St Guthlac of Crowland, for example, was a member of a Mercian royal line who began his career as the teenage leader of a warband of aristocratic youths.[24] As with Ireland, it would be a mistake to try and assert the priority or precedence of any given level of political organisation, whether wide overlordships like those of Bede's heroes or the local units that have been emphasised by more recent historians. This society functioned through the layering of mutually dependant lordships slowly shading into kingship, not the assembly of distinct and self-contained building blocks. Just as many of the 150 or so *túáth*s of contemporary Ireland had doubtless never enjoyed meaningful independence but existed as the necessary corollary of ambitious overkingship, so in England the kind of unit visible in the 'Tribal Hidage' was the basis for a broadly royal elite to collect food and tribute from the those who cultivated the countryside.

By Bede's day, there was a social elite whose lifestyle clearly differentiated them from those who worked the land. Take Imma, a young retainer and distant kinsman of the Northumbrian king who, after a disastrous battle in which his master was killed, was taken captive by a close associate of the victorious Mercian king: fearing that his captor would kill him in vengeance for the kinsmen he had lost in the battle, he tried to pass himself off as a peasant who had been obliged to accompany the army with supplies, but was given away by 'his appearance, his bearing and his speech', and thanks to the church's efforts to limit revenge killing sold into slavery and ransomed. There could be no more vivid proof of the emergence of a warrior-elite, structured by bonds of kinship and lordship, which was developing its own technical vocabulary, with the youngster Imma serving in a royal court as a 'soldier and officer', or *thegn*, whilst his Mercian captor had moved on to preside over his own household but still remained a companion or *gesith* of his royal master.[25] The archaeology gives insight into the processes whereby this clearly stratified social order had emerged. In the areas of eastern England characterised by 'Anglo-Saxon' material culture, sixth-century settlement shows little sign of internal class divisions between different household units. The dead were buried in large cemeteries apparently serving a wide area, and whilst the quantity and nature of grave-goods varied from burial to burial, the variation was gradual. The most plausible interpretation is that this was a society marked by a relative lack of formal differentiation between the various household units; these households competed for pre-eminence within the community of the free, hence the importance of lavish funerary display. By the seventh century, on the other hand, we begin to see leading families attempting to mark themselves off from their neighbours, with greater stratification between household units evident in the settlement sites, and the emergence of special high-status cemeteries likewise marking the emergence of clearer class division within the community of the free. A corresponding decrease in the need for competition for local pre-eminence, now the preserve of an increasingly well-defined elite, is perhaps the explanation for the changes in the nature of grave-goods, which – with the exception of those used in some of most outstanding elite burials – are generally less lavish and show greater uniformity than previously.

The emergence of stable elites increasingly able to control rural labour and land explains the emergence of trading centres in the late seventh and eighth centuries. Imma, for example, was sold to a Frisian slave-trader who took him to London – described by Bede as a 'market (emporium) of many nations' – and sold into captivity in Kent. Archaeology has identified the hub of such activities in seventh- to ninth-century London as lying just outside the Roman walls, around the modern Strand and Aldwych: contemporaries differentiated London-wic, the site of the emporium, from London-burg, the area within the walls where the holders of political authority resided. Urban redevelopment in the late twentieth century led, unintentionally, to 'rescue' excavations at a series of similar sites, likewise prospering in the eighth century. Collectively referred to by modern historians as 'emporia' or 'wics' (the latter after the characteristic ending of their names, although *port* seems to have been the normal Old English noun), these were dedicated markets, part of a network that tied together the coasts of the North Sea, particularly Scandinavia, continental Europe and southern and eastern England. These sites were characteristically undefended, and located for ease of access for the relatively shallow draught ships which conducted the North Sea trade; they thrived into the ninth century, when a combination of Viking activity and environmental change (silting and changing sea levels allied to a shift to deeper draught vessels better able to carry bulk cargoes) led to reorganisation. The best understood of the English emporia, Hamwic near modern Southampton, exhibits a regular street plan and explodes ready-formed into activity *c.* 700, and so has been seen as a planned initiative on the part of the kings of Wessex, or possibly the bishop of Winchester. This interpretation of Hamwic as a result of a conscious economic policy has for a generation informed our understanding of the emporia as a group: through them, it has been argued, kings sought to control access to

Essay

Sutton Hoo and Anglo-Saxon kingship

The most famous and most spectacular of these new elite cemeteries is that at Sutton Hoo in modern Suffolk. Here, a total of 17 graves dating from the end of the sixth to the middle of the eighth century, most marked by barrows, marked a promontory near the mouth of the river Deben. Sutton Hoo's fame rests on the spectacular boat burial excavated in mound 1 in the late 1930s. Here were the magnificent effects of an early Anglo-Saxon king, which evoked a warrior culture of daring deeds and fabulous treasure made familiar through vernacular poems like *Beowulf*, whose eponymous hero was committed to the sea in a burning boat. In fact, precise connections between *Beowulf* and Sutton Hoo are trickier to make than is often imagined; the site is not a neutral reflection of the aristocratic values of heroic valour, but the result of conscious investment by an emerging elite anxious to legitimate its position. The grave-goods demonstrate a magpie-like eclecticism, some pointing to close contacts with the Franks, others originating in the Mediterranean world of Constantinople and evoking the Roman past, others still pointing towards Scandinavia, the inspiration for the rite of boat burial, paralleled at only a handful of other Anglo-Saxon sites close by on the Suffolk coast. They are deposited in a highly visible manner, at a site over-looking the major waterway leading to a documented royal estate, in the burial ground reserved for a restricted group of lavish graves – most alas plundered by

Figure 8.3 Original 1930s excavation of boat burial at Sutton Hoo

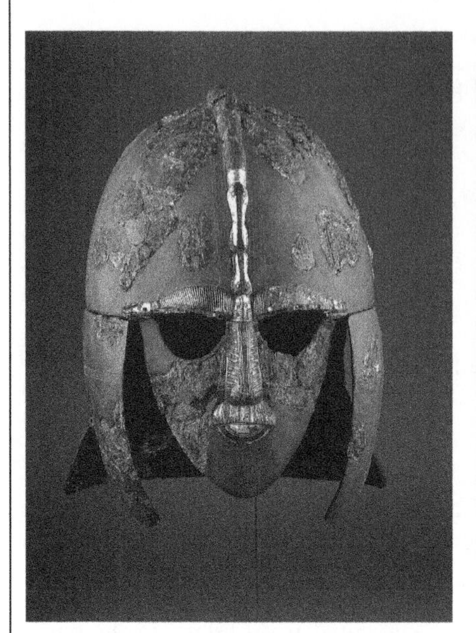

Figure 8.4 Ceremonial helmet found in boat burial in mound 1

Figure 8.5 Stag and staff – possibly a piece of royal insignia – found in mound 1

later grave-robbers – used for perhaps half a dozen generations. Attempts to pin down the identity of the individual in mound 1 – encouraged by a carefully assembled package of Merovingian coins which can be tied down to a very precise chronological moment around 630 – are probably inevitable, but ultimately problematical given the inadequacy of the information of early seventh-century East Anglian politics available to Bede, our only written source. We can similarly never know with certainty exactly what religious allegiance the burial in mound 1 was meant to profess; indeed, what is most striking is the continuity of the cemetery as a whole across the age of conversion, as Christianity embraced a culture of aristocratic conspicuous consumption. Ultimately, the Sutton Hoo cemetery articulated and advertised dynastic claims, claims that encompassed the right to judge and punish suggested by the execution burials recently discovered around mound 1.

high-status prestige goods, and so buttress their position. This emphasis on strong royal initiative may, however, need modifying: London or Ipswich, whilst certainly the object of strong royal interest, seem to exhibit a more organic pattern of growth, with intensifying exchange networks around the North Sea naturally focusing on sites where the powerful were close at hand, and Hamwic may be an attempt by the kings of Wessex to channel this growing trade through their kingdom. High-status status symbols had circulated around the North Sea before

– witness the elite fashions evident in grave-goods – but the second half of the seventh century in particular evidently saw a reorganisation and regularisation of the networks of exchange into regular markets: from the beginning, sites like Hamwic were centres of production, not just markets, where tradable commodities were collected and processed.

The archaeology thus encourages us to see an almost evolutionary process, whereby successful groups slowly established themselves as dominant in a locality, building class barriers which marked them off from the rest of the free population, and subsequently developing exchange networks whereby they were able to use their control of the agrarian surplus to participate in wider networks of consumption which marked their elite status. But this model is based on internal changes in the regions that underwent the deepest collapses and most profound changes in the immediate post-Roman period. It may be misleading. Just as the more stable stratification of seventh-century elites on the northern and eastern peripheries of the Merovingian world was facilitated by their interaction with their southern Gallic neighbours, so the successful Anglo-Saxon kings and kingdoms of the seventh century were those that had been able to absorb indigenous societies. The settlement archaeology underlines the importance of these links. The classic demonstration of the emergence of a clearer hierarchy among settlements comes in the spectacular excavations at the Northumbrian royal estate of Yeavering, mentioned by Bede. Here, Anglo-Saxon kings built on an older, British, political centre; in other words, the takeover of indigenous social hierarchies played a crucial role in the crystallisation of the Northumbrian kingdom.[26] Yeavering – where kings received guests and feasted in a magnificent hall, and met their people in a remarkable wooden amphitheatre – was not alone. Several other major centres of the Northumbrian kingdom – the coastal stronghold of Bamburgh, for example, but also former Roman cities at Carlisle and York – were important precisely because of their continuity as central places in a region where sub-Roman political systems of relative coherence had quickly emerged in the fifth and sixth centuries.

This phenomenon – the stabilisation of Anglo-Saxon kingships through the takeover of British political systems – was not confined to Northumbria. The other major kingdoms of the eighth century rested on similar patterns of expansion to that of Northumbria north of the Tees and west of the Pennines, with the Mercians advancing into the West Midlands and the Welsh borders, and the West Saxons into the southwest. These activities are usually seen as marking a shifting balance of power between the Anglo-Saxons and the British, as kings exploited the possibilities of plunder and tribute offered by this 'frontier'. In fact, patterns of alliance and conflict paid no heed to our division between Anglo-Saxon and British kingdoms, and the notion of a 'frontier' rooted in ethnic difference is a modern construction; there is no reason to believe that it was more profitable to expand at the expense of British rather than Anglo-Saxon neighbours. Northumbrian, Mercian and West Saxon political success probably rested on the fact that they were taking over regions that had not suffered the type of calamitous collapse seen along the eastern and southern coasts of England in the post-Roman period. A passage in the late seventh-century laws of the West Saxon king Ine hints at the circuits of rents and renders, similar to those we have already seen in the 'Celtic west', that kings were able to take over, detailing arrangements for the transport of food-rents of honey, loaves, ale, cattle, geese, hens, cheeses, butter, salmon, fodder and eels.[27] The stabilising effects of control over British areas cannot, of course, explain social and political change on its own: the widening social gulf, and dramatic growth of exchange networks, that were increasingly evident by the eighth century had their own dynamic, and it is striking that the one major kingdom of Bede's day distant from the ethnic 'frontier', Kent, was the major point of cultural, economic and political contact with the Merovingian world. But seventh- and eighth-century elites were able to rule more extensively because they had acquired and developed systems whereby they need not be directly involved in the exploitation of land.

This process of consolidation involved the appropriation of existing idioms of authority, hence the echoes of Rome in the material culture of early Anglo-Saxon kingship, evidenced in the Yeavering amphitheatre, the standard or *tufa* used by the Northumbrian rulers of Bede's day, or some of the objects found in the Sutton Hoo boat grave.[28] In this context, it is hardly surprising that Anglo-Saxon rulers begin to engage with Christianity as another means of articulating their expanding authority. The seamless narrative constructed by Bede profoundly influences the traditional account of the 'conversion of the English'. Bede's agenda here owed much to his involvement in the ecclesiastical politics of his time; his firm views on the proper ordering of the church emerge with particular clarity from a programme of reform he set out for Archbishop Egbert of York, and they shaped his reading of the past. Crucial here was the role of bishops exercising hierarchical authority ultimately derived from the senior bishop within the English church at Canterbury, and thence from the bishop of Rome. Bede's account of the seventh century past therefore concentrates on the role of Rome in inaugurating mission, and is organised around the conversion of kings and the foundation of bishoprics: it is the story of Augustine, the monk despatched to convert the English by Pope Gregory the Great in 597 and first archbishop of Canterbury, and his disciples and successors.

For Bede, the true progress of the English church was marked by its adherence to what he saw as Roman traditions: the Synod of Whitby in 664, which adjudicated on rival methods of calculating the date of Easter, thus becomes a central event, symbolising the triumph of proper Roman order. But Bede's perspective is highly personal and may distort. As an acknowledged authority on Biblical commentary and the arcane lore of calculating dates and dividing time, Bede cared profoundly about an issue like the Easter controversy, in which the latest methods of calculation outlined in the newest pamphlets transmitted via Rome stood opposed to the inherited traditions developed in isolation by the Irish church. It is normal to see the conflicts that led to Whitby in terms of an opposition between 'Celtic' practices and the teachings of the Roman mission. But such monolithic categories are misleading: as we saw above, the idea of a single institutional or spiritual template that we can label 'Celtic Christianity' is a modern illusion, and debate over the dating of Easter – and, indeed, over another cause célèbre: the correct way to perform the monastic haircut or tonsure – began within the Irish church, not as an attack on a static 'Celtic' tradition. Practical issues, above all the need to avoid confusion and safeguard unity within the nascent church, were more important than theological correctness at Whitby. And Bede here, as elsewhere, treats Wilfrid, the dominant figure of the seventh-century Northumbrian church, with cool detachment. This opposition was not rooted in conflicting ecclesiastical traditions but on factional conflict within the church that did not divide along Roman–Celtic lines. Wilfrid's turbulent career, for example, rested on far-flung political contacts which enabled him to build up a personal network of churches which crossed political boundaries, reminiscent of the dynamics of status among the secular elite and the ecclesiastical constellations which animated Irish politics. But Wilfrid also insisted on his institutional and territorial power as a bishop, controlling all aspects of ecclesiastical affairs within his diocese, in a thoroughly Roman manner. Bede's evident opposition to Wilfrid, and his eliding of the events of his own public career – his fifth and final book concentrates on moralising tales exploring the need to repent for sins and the nature of the afterlife, and says little about the ecclesiastical controversies and political events of the early eighth century, ending instead with a rose-tinted picture which pairs bishops with kings as the defining figures of English society at the dawn of the eighth century – underlines the extent to which his account needs treating with care.

Conversion was intimately related to the processes of change taking place within seventh-century society. Bede's emphasis on Roman initiative in inaugurating mission obscures the vital role of the Merovingian kingdoms of Gaul as intermediaries in the spread of Christianity in southern Britain: Augustine's mission, after all, followed from the marriage of the king of Kent to a Frankish princess. Although many of the leaders of the seventh-century church – Augustine, Hadrian, Theodore – were Mediterranean churchmen despatched from Rome, they travelled via the Merovingian realms and the cultural and material resources of the Frankish church played a vital role in the establishment of Anglo-Saxon Christianity. These cross-Channel links quickly worked both ways: witness the education of a string of Anglo-Saxon princesses at the Merovingian royal nunneries of Faremoutiers and Chelles near Paris, and the involvement of Anglo-Saxon churchmen, like their Irish neighbours, in the Frankish church from the late seventh century onwards. On one level, then, missionary activity in southern England was part and parcel of the same cultural processes as the Christianisation of the eastern peripheries of the Merovingian realm in the seventh and eighth centuries.

Contact with the indigenous Christian traditions of Britain was probably more important still than political relations with continental rulers. In Kent, Augustine moved into a landscape where the remains of Roman Christianity were still visible: Canterbury was a former Roman city, and Augustine and his followers operated out of an abandoned church building. Although there is no evidence for continuing Christian observance on this site, the very earliest layers of ecclesiastical legislation hint at the continuation of Christianity as a folk religion in at least parts of Kent. And once we move away from the southern and eastern coast, the existence of the British church was indubitable: even in Bede's account, one of Augustine's first actions was to meet with a council of 'British bishops' at an unknown location.[29] Bede, portraying the conversion of England as a clean process carried out under the authoritative auspices of the representatives of the

Roman church, avoided the complicating and contaminating factor of British Christianity wherever possible. But the political consolidation of seventh-century Anglo-Saxon kingdoms came through the integration of regions where Christianity survived: the Northumbrian kings, indeed, granted the British churches of the Pennines to favoured churchmen such as Wilfrid.[30] If Bede's account reflects distaste on the part of conquerors for taking on the religion of the conquered, then Irish Christianity was more appealing. The conversion of Northumbria in particular can be seen as the inevitable result of the close involvement of its sixth- and seventh-century rulers with the politics of the Irish Sea. Webs of alliance and marriage tied the dynasties of northern Britain, and Northumbrian royals encountered Christianity through their contacts with places like Adomnan's Iona. Even Bede describes in detail the involvement of churchmen from this milieu – men like Aidan and Cuthbert – in the early history of Northumbrian Christianity. Part of the historical landscape, in his account they become spiritual exemplars to be harnessed to the hierarchical tradition of the institutional church transmitted via the Roman mission.

In tracing the progress of Christianity in seventh-century England, it is still normal – probably inevitably so – to see a sharp dividing line between pagans and Christians, but religious affiliation did not determine political allegiances, nor was conversion a factor in political conflict. Given that the cults and practices we lump together as 'Anglo-Saxon paganism' were polytheistic, and that they made no claim to exclusivity, our categories in fact make the gradient of religious change steeper than it actually was: a king like Raedwald of the East Angles could make sacrifices to the traditional gods of his dynasty and people whilst acknowledging the power of the Christian God.[31] Notions of Christianisation, emphasising the longer-term process of cultural change as the church as an institution gained a hold on the population, are here more helpful than the vocabulary of conversion, encouraging us to expect a dramatic once-and-for-all moment of revelation. The dividing lines between Christian and pagan practices were blurred, and changed over time. Dealing with the queries of missionaries encountering a bewildering array of social practices wholly alien to the Mediterranean world from which they had come, Pope Gregory encouraged gradualism and pragmatism, in what was to become a template for missionary activity.[32] To see this as a 'compromise' which facilitated the 'survival of pagan practices' in the context of popular religion is misleading: when missionaries built churches on earlier cult-sites, celebrating Christian festivals on traditional dates, they were tying the new religion into an inherited calendar and landscape so as to detach established social practices from any association with the traditional gods. Traditional interpretations of early medieval Christianity which see in such 'compromises' the beginnings of a centuries-long war of attrition with a populace stubbornly wedded to pagan custom are profoundly shaped by the experience of a different form of Christian mission, in the colonial empires of nineteenth- and twentieth-century European states. In the early medieval context, there is no real evidence for continuing pagan belief or observance within two or three generations of the formal experience of conversion. It is easily forgotten that in those areas of the south and east where the social crisis of the fifth and sixth centuries had seen the ending of Roman Christian

Essay

Culture and identity in the age of Bede

Bede's privileging of Kent, and his lack of information on Mercia and Wessex, where we might expect similar processes to those visible in Northumbria to be at work, distorts our understanding of seventh-century cultural change. If we look at the patterns of influence and patronage suggested by other forms of cultural activity a far more varied picture emerges. The magnificent series of insular seventh- and eighth-century Gospel Books, for example, shows artistic idioms crossing political boundaries. The Lindisfarne Gospels, prepared to mark the exhumation of the grave of Cuthbert in 698 and his formal proclamation as a saint, articulate the cultural alignment of its audience with a northern British world embracing Christian communities of all complexions and profoundly influenced by the example of the Irish church as transmitted via Iona. The range of these influences is such that the provenance of the Book of Kells, named after the Irish dependency of Iona where it is today, remains unclear: it might have been commissioned by a Pictish as easily as a Northumbrian patron. The systems of patronage that funded such masterpieces were derived from secular traditions of

Figure 8.6 An evangelist page showing St Mark from the Lindisfarne Gospels

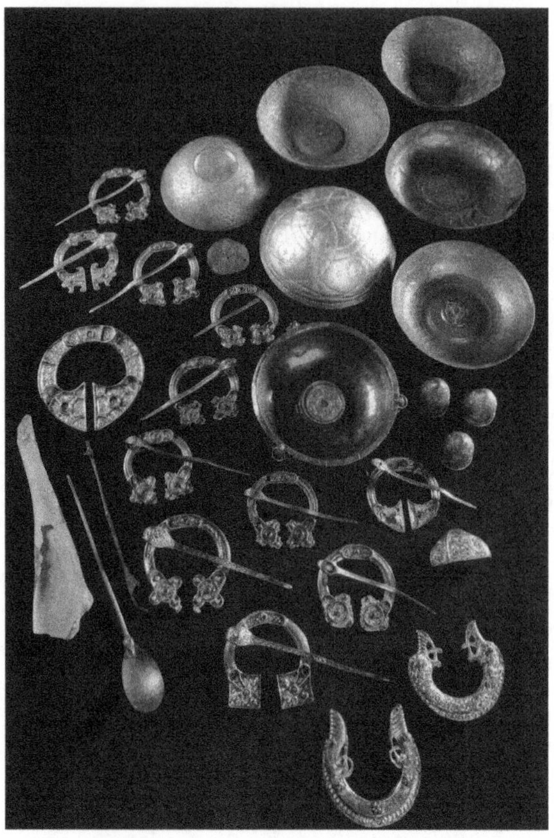

Figure 8.7 Secular patronage: the metalwork and treasure of an unknown Pictish potentate found on St Ninian's Isle

gift-exchange as a means of demonstrating prestige. Hence there is a certain crossover of artistic genres, with interlaced decoration of a type familiar from high-status secular metalwork adapted for the painted page and combined with a variety of traditions of artistic representation. Stone sculpture, notably in the remains of the imposing crosses which were found across much of seventh- and eighth-century Britain, shows the didactic function of Christian patronage: the Ruthwell Cross, for example, includes a series of illustrations of crucial Biblical figures, functioning as a visual mnenomic representation of the act of preaching. But it could also be adapted by ambitious rulers, like the unknown Pictish king buried in the highly classicising sarcophagus now at St Andrew's cathedral. Bede's essaying of a corporate identity for an English church ideologically and institutionally distinct from the earlier Christian communities of the British Isles, and so derived directly from Rome, needs locating in the context of the traditions of patronage and production developed at his monastery of Wearmouth-Jarrow. Intimately shaped by the activities and connections of its

Figure 8.8 Stone cross (south face) from Ruthwell in Dumfriesshire, modern Scotland, but in our period part of Anglo-Saxon Northumbria

founder, Benedict Biscop, these focused on the close emulation of Roman templates, most dramatically in the Codex Amiatinus, a magnificent Gospel Book whose imitation of a late Roman exemplar acquired by Biscop articulates a very different identity from the products of the monks of Lindisfarne.

Figure 8.9 The emulation of Rome as a statement of royal power: the central panel of St Andrew's sarcophagus

traditions, Anglo-Saxon culture was itself scarcely a century old by the time it encountered Christianity, and so Anglo-Saxon paganism can hardly have been deeply rooted in what was in any case a new and rapidly changing landscape. Ecclesiastical legislation and literature of the eighth and ninth centuries focuses on the inculcation of new, and ever stricter, standards of observance, first of all within the church hierarchy itself, not a continuing battle with pagan observance. Thus when a church council in 757 forbad priests from reciting the Christian liturgy as if they were a poet reciting the deeds of legendary ancestors, they were not seeking to clamp down on a living tradition of paganism, but imposing new standards which aimed to set priests apart as sacred figures mediating between man and God. The practices here frowned on by bishops were not part of a pagan counter-culture, but rested on a successful symbiosis between Christian practice and Anglo-Saxon society.[33]

This long-term process rested on the growth of the church's infrastructure. The appeal of the Christian God inevitably remains difficult for us to investigate: the set-piece speeches renouncing the old gods and acknowledging Christian superiority which structures conversion narratives need to be treated with care, reflecting as they do the expectations and preconceptions of their authors, writing in well-worn literary traditions at some remove, culturally and chronologically, from the events they describe. In fact, the message of Christianity, with its emphasis on the omnipotence of a single God, the king of Heaven, must have made sense to the ambitious warlords who were consolidating their hold on the seventh-century countryside. There is, indeed, good evidence that such rulers were closely involved with the cults of traditional gods as they sought to legitimate their newly-won power. Gold medallions depicting pagan gods, for example, were manufactured on royal estates in Kent, and circulated as precious and status-enhancing gifts.[34] The written evidence for Anglo-Saxon paganism is unusual in that it shows elements of organised cult, pagan temples served by pagan priests, and such structures are beginning to be identified in the archaeological record. This level of organised paganism is unparalleled in the early medieval evidence, a couple of celebrated cases in Scandinavia aside; it is probably no accident that it is found in the only western Roman province where organised Christianity collapsed, where the cultural memory of Christianity may have been a significant influence.[35] In any case, organised cults with temples and priests implies considerable investment and organisation, and where pagan cults appear in our written sources they are closely associated with kings. Royal patronage of paganism was thus one face of seventh-century political consolidation; buying into Christianity, which offered access to a wider idiom of established hierarchical authority, was another. Christianity offered the possibility of venerating successful royal ancestors, thereby sacralising a dynasty and legitimating its rule: much of Bede's narrative concerns the sainted kings of seventh-century Northumbria, Oswald and Oswiu. But even after conversion, the traditions manufactured by pre-Christian kings enjoyed a cultural hold: the genealogies detailing the legendary ancestry of royal dynasties continued to be copied and developed long after the gods they listed had become heroes whose stories no longer had religious significance. For continental kings, such traditions were redundant, because their royal status rested on their takeover of former Roman provinces in a process which coincided with that of conversion; their survival in England is reminiscent of the continuing hold of the legendary past as a template for Irish kingship, with the important difference that the Anglo-Saxon material cannot traverse the fifth and sixth centuries, centring as it does on shadowy heroes whose careers are set in the migration period, and a tiny handful of gods.

What implications had conversion for Anglo-Saxon society? Perhaps the most far-reaching consequence – and certainly the one that has most profoundly influenced historical perspectives – was the advent of a formal written tradition, encompassing not only the work of a scholar like Bede, but also more practical instruments, the acts of councils designed to ensure right order in the church, royal law-codes aiming first and foremost to protect the church, and royal documents guaranteeing the liberties and properties of the church. The first written law-code, issued by Aethelbert of Kent, was said by Bede to be made 'following the example of the Romans'; Anglo-Saxon law-giving, unlike Irish, was a royal prerogative and so a legitimating activity. But in content, these early law-codes were primarily concerned with 'giving king and God their due' by articulating royal protection for the church; they did not augur any structural changes in the relationship between kings and communities. The example of written law on a Roman model is normally seen as being transmitted from the continent via the church: it certainly is striking that our law-codes come from Kent and Wessex, and show the influence of Merovingian legislation. But in one important way, Anglo-Saxon legislation differed from its continental exemplar: it was written not in Latin, but in the vernacular. Writing in the vernacular for any purpose was more or less unprecedented, although continental law-codes could include the odd technical term in the vernacular. Where there were clear parallels with the Anglo-Saxon material, however, was in Ireland, where the tradition of secular and ecclesiastical law which began, like Anglo-Saxon law-giving, in the seventh century was written in the vernacular. For all the differences between the Anglo-Saxon and Irish legal traditions, it may make sense to place the issuing of law-codes by seventh-century Anglo-Saxon kings in the context of the cultivation of written legal learning in Ireland.

The ecclesiastical geography of early medieval England mirrored politics. Because mission had essentially been a process of converting kings and their entourages, the typical pattern was a bishop for each kingdom, that is for each 'people'. Whereas on the continent, even where city life faltered, the church continued to operate from inherited, once urban, seats of power and so adapt the map of Roman provincial administration to new realities, in England the loss of continuous contact with Roman city life and Christianity meant that the distribution of bishops simply mirrored the political dispensation of the age of conversion. A handful of former Roman sites which served as political centres – most notably York and Canterbury – were granted bishops, as was London, where a significant economic hub was emerging on the fringes of the former Roman city. But most bishoprics were founded thanks to royal patronage in new sites situated conveniently close to royal palaces, Lichfield in Mercia close by Tamworth, Lindisfarne off the Northumbrian coast near Bamburgh.

This process in all probability helped crystallise what were still fairly fluid political boundaries, not least as bishops notionally enjoyed territorial jurisdiction over the churches within their dioceses. But religious activity was not circumscribed by political boundaries: church councils bringing together bishops from southern England became 'national' occasions legislating for the Anglo-Saxon church as a whole. This regular synodal activity, which was a marked feature of the eighth century in particular, arose directly from the role of the Roman mission in co-ordinating the initial stages of conversion in the seventh century, and in particular the activities of Theodore of Tarsus, archbishop of Canterbury from 668–90; it went hand-in-hand with a strong sense of internal hierarchy focused on Canterbury. Ambitious overlords like the eighth-century Mercian rulers Aethelbald and Offa could attempt to work through this tradition, using these conciliar assemblies as major political occasions, through which royal initiatives and interests could be pursued. But unlike continental kings, they were not presiding over a church which was commensurate with their kingdom, whose structures could sustain royal administration. Offa's attempts to create a more malleable church hierarchy, through manoeuvring to have Lichfield raised to the status of an archbishopric, underline the extent to which the institutional church was something which kings could attempt to work with, but could not control: the scale of episcopal opposition to Lichfield's elevation meant that it was swiftly abandoned after Offa's death. Similarly, Aethelbald and Offa had to deal with concerted opposition to their determination to levy military service and associated dues – the so-called 'three necessities' which they were increasingly insisting were owed by all subjects to their king – from the land of the church. Ecclesiastical geography, moreover, by preserving the boundaries and identities of seventh-century kingdoms, meant that ambitious overlords had to work through these units. Canterbury, the seat of the southern archbishop, lay in a relatively small kingdom which increasingly fell under the domination of more powerful overlords in the eighth and ninth centuries; but as the church of Canterbury was embedded into local landed society, the archbishops were powerful mouthpieces for Kentish opinion, and struggled to safeguard the liberties of the churches of Kent against distant kings. The archiepiscopal opposition aroused by Offa's imposition of his men in Kent led to his difficulties with Canterbury: the doomed experiment with Lichfield was ultimately an admission of his inability to rule through the established traditions of the 'national' church.

At a level below that of bishops and councils, the structures of the church also defined the parameters of power. Conversion rested not only on the provision of a bishop and bishopric for each kingdom: kings and those close to them were soon founding churches through which the new faith could be spread. Monasticism, which had been such a powerful influence on the Irish church, and was rapidly spreading on the continent in the seventh century, proved an attractive model. The blurring of the boundaries between the formal hierarchies of church government, centred on bishops, and the ideal of pursuing a perfect life through membership of a religious community, particularly evident at Lindisfarne, a monastic community modelled on Iona but also the site of a bishopric, was far from isolated. In contemporary usage most ecclesiastical institutions were referred to by the vernacular term 'minster', which, although derived from the Latin 'monasterium', simply denoted a community of priests living together in a church, without necessarily following a monastic rule. Some historians, pointing to the evidence that in some areas minsters were founded on royal estates, have seen an ordered creation of an ecclesiastical infrastructure as an agency of royal power aiming at the provision of pastoral care for the population as a whole. But not all churches were founded by kings, and to see the planned creation of a network of royal minsters is to overestimate the extent of royal power in a society still characterised by fluid and overlapping social hierarchies; bishops, indeed, had to work hard to establish control over privately founded churches.

Bede criticises the practice of landowners founding 'family monasteries' on their lands as denuding the kingdom of crucial resources, in particular military manpower, whilst creating ecclesiastical institutions whose relationship to the formal structures of church discipline was problematic.[36] Bede's condemnation of such foundations as 'false monasteries' does not imply that their creation was a cynical strategy devoid of religious motivation; his criticism rests on a hardline insistence on the role of proper monastic discipline, an insistence that may have meant little to landowners eager to embrace the new faith. Nor was the primary function of such foundations the provision of pastoral care to the surrounding countryside, a point forcibly made by Bede. In fact, church foundation was a means of embedding power rooted in land: the kin of founders expected to enjoy continuing interests in 'their' church, which in turn became an anchor for family identity and family power, and also led to important changes in systems of land tenure. Inevitably given the horizon of our sources, patterns of landholding in the sixth and seventh centuries are obscure, but we should think not of outright ownership in our terms, but of elites enjoying rights to renders and services from extensive and sometimes scattered groupings of rural settlements; presumably the evident increase in social stratification in the seventh century was a result of the ability of a widely based warrior-elite to free itself from labour on the land and institutionalise such render circuits as a matter of status. The endowment of the church, which brought with it ideas of ownership rooted in Roman property law, and quickly insisted on the recording of its endowments in written deeds based on continental models, involved the creation of more absolute rights of control over these loose territories owing tribute. When kings 'booked' land by making a written instrument outlining the church's title to it, they were redirecting a series of rights to receive renders in food and produce to a new beneficiary, but by describing those rights in the language of inalienable possession in God's service, they effectively created property rights of a kind that had been unknown before. By the end of the seventh century, land was being 'booked' not just for churches, but also for favoured members of royal retinues, and the foundation of family churches further allowed warrior-elites to benefit from these changes in the nature of control over land. The result was the emergence of a less footloose social order based on landowning elites now firmly embedded in the countryside. Whilst society was still structured by the cycles of gift-exchange that radiated from royal courts, politics was no longer simply a matter of kings attracting able and ambitious retainers; it was a process of negotiation with entrenched local landowners rooted in the politics of land.

Vikings and kings: Britain and Ireland in the ninth century

In the course of the ninth century, the political map of Britain and Ireland was redrawn. Most dramatic was the establishment of Viking warlords at York, in the place of the Northumbrian court that had been the political focus of seventh- and eighth-century northern Britain; its rulers now attempted to maintain a loose dominance of Scandinavian warbands scattered across the former kingdoms of eastern England and northern Britain and around the Irish and Scottish coasts. To the north and south, rulers who styled themselves as 'king of Alba' and 'king of the Anglo-Saxons' respectively were creating new overkingships; further west, the growing range of the 'king of the Britons' in Gwynedd was forcing hard choices on petty kings in southern and central Wales, whilst even in Ireland the overlords of Tara were styling themselves as 'king of the Irish' even though they were still exercising overlordship of a long-established kind. Because these reformulated kingdoms were the seeds from which later nation-states grew, they have attracted much attention from historians. In contrast, the Viking nexus at the geographical centre of the insular world of Britain and Ireland has been neglected, in part because of the scarcity and extreme difficulty of the source basis, but also because of an unstated assumption that it was parasitical on, and a distraction from, the serious business of state-formation elsewhere. As a result, the Vikings appear in modern historiography as bolts from the blue who, by undermining existing political dispensations, enable entrepreneurial rulers – the likes of Alfred 'the Great' and Cinéad mac Alpin, the heroes of subsequent national historiographies – to forge new kingdoms legitimated by new identities. Debate has ultimately centred on the possibility of tracing back a continuous history for their political programmes before the Viking impact. Can we see political consolidation before the Vikings, with fewer, larger, kingdoms in England and the beginnings of the integration of the Dalriadan and Pictish kingdoms in Scotland? Can we see the new political constellations as in a sense the natural outcome of ethnic allegiances and geopolitical common sense?

The Vikings first appear in the written sources in the last decade or so of the eighth century: this chronology is shared by Irish annals, the *Anglo-Saxon Chronicle* and continental sources, and so must mark a real sea change. These early entries report raids on coastal monasteries such as Lindisfarne and Iona, and on ports of trade like Portland on the southern English coast. The sources are uninterested in Viking aims and motivations. Viking activity is God's judgement on the failings of those who suffered, an argument most eloquently essayed by the scholar Alcuin, reflecting on the first Viking raids on the monasteries of the Northumbrian coast from the safe distance of Charlemagne's court: the proper response was to impose stricter reformed standards of religious life and so placate God.[37] Scandinavian material dates from the eleventh and twelfth centuries, and looks back on a semi-legendary age of Viking derring-do; it cannot fill the gap. Given this, any explanation for the outbreak of Viking activity is ultimately no more than a plausible reconstruction of the patterns of raiding noted in the narrative sources, and the archaeological evidence for contact of varying kinds – trading as well as raiding – between Scandinavia and the British Isles. What is clear is that the context for the developments of the decades around 800 was one of increased exchange, most famously in the trade between southern Scandinavia and the Frankish and English North Sea coasts; Alcuin could even point out the similarities of Anglo-Saxon and Scandinavian fashions in elite consumption. Once peaceful exchange had reached a certain level in this context of political and cultural division, we might expect piracy to emerge, piggyback fashion; the chronology of its outbreak might also be linked to internal political pressures in southern Scandinavia. The Viking impact thus needs assessing with care: resting on new connections, it combined activities of plundering, trading and tribute-taking which to us might seem conceptually distinct and mutually exclusive.

Given its very complexity, it would be a mistake to seek a single cause for all facets of Viking activity in eighth- and ninth-century Britain. Our label 'Viking', a later term transformed into a universal label for Scandinavians of all shapes and sizes active in eighth- to eleventh-century Europe by Victorian sensibilities, lumps together diverse groups of differing origin, operating in different areas with different aims. Contemporary labels, although more various, similarly encourage us to see a homogenous mass defined as outsiders in both political and religious terms: Biblical language referring to 'gentiles' is the favoured usage of the Irish annals, whilst the *Anglo-Saxon Chronicle*, normally used as a neutral eyewitness to the pattern of Scandinavian activity in England, actually builds up a coherent narrative of escalation which forms the backdrop to the heroic activities of its patron, Alfred, again encouraging us to see a homogenous and linear 'Viking threat'. If we disaggregate Viking activity, we might tentatively distinguish two distinct spheres of activity with differing rhythms.

The first sphere, where Viking activity began in the course of the eighth century, and where Scandinavian connections and colonies continued to be of vital importance into the eleventh, encompasses the islands and coastline of northern and western Scotland, leading south into the Irish Sea and Ireland itself. The onset of Viking activity here was made possible by advances in seafaring, enabling the direct crossing from Norway, but it was motivated by internal change in Scandinavia, and in particular increased political competition as a more stratified society developed. The archaeology suggests that significant amounts of plunder and tribute found its way back from northern and western Britain to Norway in the eighth and ninth centuries; wealth and status acquired across the sea may have played an important role in stabilising the new social hierarchy. Control of the western and northern sealanes of the British Isles was facilitated by settlement in a landscape very similar to that of Scandinavia. The archaeological record, indeed, suggests that Scandinavian settlement at strategic sites off northern and northwestern Scotland took place in the mid-eighth century. The earliest written references to raids, in the decade before 800 on monasteries off the northern coasts of Britain and Ireland such as Iona, probably reflect the southward expansion of this zone of activity. Ninth-century Irish annals refer to raids led by the 'king of Lochlann', in all probability the military leader of the heterogenous Viking households and warbands of western Scotland, and identify hybrid groups of *Gal Gaedhil*; they also distinguish between 'black' and 'white' foreigners, that is 'new' Scandinavians and those settled in Britain. In the 830s, as raids began on inland Ireland, coastal settlements known as *longphorts*, fortified enclosures controlling major estuaries, were founded, many on the sites of future urban development as at Dublin and Waterford; here warbands could enjoy the fruits of their plundering and profiteering, and winter off the tribute they exacted from the surrounding countryside.

Viking activity used the sea as a means of linking together the disparate segments of this socially and politically fragmented world, operating largely in the spaces between existing institutions and polities. Irish politics and Irish society in particular had long been structured by the endemic warfare through which kings asserted their status and recruited clients. Viking warbands slotted into this pattern as a complicating factor, but did not threaten it, sometimes fighting for the kings of Tara, sometimes their opponents, sometimes plugging into old rivalries as allies or mercenaries, sometimes singling out targets as lucrative and untapped pots of plunder and tribute. Even their plundering of churches, prime sources of portable wealth, needs locating within long-established patterns: Irish rulers plundered their rivals' churches, and on occasion monastic confederations could go to war with kings, or plunder one another. If the plundering of churches was a familiar activity, however, when the perpetrators were Vikings it felt different, because Vikings were pagan outsiders, not Christian neighbours who would in all probability make amends whilst suing for peace, or suffer plundering in their turn, in the not-so-distant future. Whilst Viking plundering was neither religious in its motivation nor senseless in its violence, but strictly aimed at efficiently amassing portable wealth, because it took place across a religious divide its victims could be portrayed as martyrs. The death of Abbot Blathmac of Iona in 825, when he refused to show Viking raiders where the monks had hidden the riches of their abbey's shrine, thus occasioned outraged comment across Europe. Iona and its constellation of monastic settlements, a network uniting the islands and coasts of western Scotland before the Vikings arrived, suffered violence of such an intensity and scale – including the death of 68 monks in 806 – that they were eventually abandoned in favour of Kells in Ireland, founded in 807. This fate, however, was unusual, precisely because Iona was unusual in that it stood directly in the path of Viking sealords and threatened their control of the western seas; elsewhere, notably in Ireland, monastic communities continued in spite of Viking plundering. The key to understanding the Viking impact on Irish society lies in the extent to which it transgressed and transformed established norms about the acceptable limits of violence, especially when its victims were kings or churchmen. Irish warfare was traditionally low intensity, aimed at redistributing tribute and recalibrating honour. Vikings were less well accustomed to these norms than their allies and victims, and more interested in acquiring liquid wealth to transport elsewhere; it is no accident that Viking coastal bases were the starting-point of Irish urbanisation, tying the Irish countryside into a wider system of exchange for the first time.

In the second sphere of Viking activity, England, the Vikings impacted on a society where political authority had been consolidated in far fewer hands, and whose coasts were already connected to an extensive economic network around the North Sea. Viking activity here thus collided far more directly with existing social and political patterns. The context for the regular arrival of large warbands – Anglo-Saxon and Frankish sources are consistent here in suggesting an upsurge in the 830s, with the presence thereafter of forces of several hundred which might easily coalesce into armies of thousands – led by Scandinavians of royal status lies in the interactions between the Frankish Empire and its Scandinavian neighbours, and particularly in the pulling of rival claimants to power in Denmark into the Frankish civil wars of the 830s and 840s. Social, economic and political connections meant that struggles for dominance within southern Scandinavia and Francia were intimately connected, and the coasts of the North Sea became a shared political stage where a complex web of shifting alliances and rivalries was played out; southern England, economically and culturally tied to the Carolingian world, inevitably became a part of this world of ambitious warlords seeking status and wealth. This sphere of Viking activity was thus closely rooted to the politics of the Jutland peninsula and the coasts and islands of the southern Scandinavia. Its rhythms therefore differed from those of Scotland and the Irish Sea, more closely tied into Norway and the north Atlantic, although the two zones were never wholly separate: particularly in the second half of the ninth century successful warleaders might exercise a temporary magnetic pull on warbands of diverse origin operating across the British Isles as a whole.

Viking activity in southern and eastern England operated in an essentially parasitic manner, being predatory on existing mechanisms for the redistribution of surplus wealth. The primary targets were therefore ports – Hamwic was a regular target through the 830s, just like its continental partners Quentovic and Dorestad – and royal and ecclesiastical centres, the nodal points of well-oiled networks for the collection of renders and tributes. From 851, Viking warbands began to 'over-winter', initially on coastal sites reminiscent of Irish *longphorts*, such as the Isle of Sheppey in the Thames estuary, but soon by seizing existing central places and living off the countryside they dominated. The Viking impact, here as in elsewhere, cannot therefore be seen in terms of random violence or all-encompassing destruction. Whilst the coastal monasteries of Kent and Northumbria were abandoned, like Iona in Scotland, elsewhere the Vikings, by extracting both huge amounts of liquid wealth in plunder and tribute, tapped indirectly into existing structures of obligation and ownership. This might cause short-term crisis in terms of draining usable resources, but in the long run it did not turn over the existing social hierarchy; it hit particularly hard at small ecclesiastical communities because such demands, and the possibility of their sites being seized by Viking armies, endangered their stability and thus their institutional survival. The evident decline in the production of manuscripts and in Latin scholarship in the last three quarters of the ninth century should thus be seen as a result of this immediate crisis, not a symptom of any longer-term cultural decline: the run of legal documents from Canterbury eloquently demonstrates the consequences of institutional instability and its effects on the education of future generations of churchmen, with a decline in scribal standards evident from the middle decades of the ninth century and culminating in a situation where the community apparently relied on one elderly and seemingly short-sighted scribe, presumably as it had been impossible to recruit and train a younger generation of clerics.[38]

As in Ireland, Viking armies, once they were staying for years at a time and living off the countryside, inevitably became a part of the political scene. The Vikings thus exacerbated the internal fault-lines of existing systems of kingship and overlordship, allying with Welsh and Cornish victims of Anglo-Saxon expansion. Viking warbands were similarly exploitative of the internal rivalries into which they were sucked in Ireland and Francia, but this pattern of interaction had particularly far-reaching consequences in England. Whereas Ireland remained a world of many competing kingships, lacking the institutional scale and political coherence to make them tempting targets for takeover rather than tribute, Anglo-Saxon kingdoms were, by the eighth century, relatively extensive and stable territorial entities. In marked contrast to their Frankish counterparts on the continent, they proved susceptible to Viking conquest. In part, this was an issue of political scale: Anglo-Saxon kingdoms, while bigger than their Irish counterparts, were sufficiently small to be vulnerable to an agglomeration of Viking warbands, particularly when Viking leaders allied with one party in an internal struggle and so avoided uniting their opponents. Whereas on the continent, Viking leaders wherever possible avoided direct confrontations with royal armies and could be driven out through concerted action on the part of Carolingian kings when their activities threatened the dynasty's political control, in England there was no really tractable tradition of political coalition beyond the individual kingdom, so a Viking warband of several thousand intervening in an internal struggle might face a force of roughly comparable size.

The formation in 865 of what the *Anglo-Saxon Chronicle* called 'the great army', an agglomeration of warbands led by three brothers, Ivar, Ubba and Halfdan, thus led to an attempt to institutionalise the flow of tribute and plunder through the establishment of political control. Intervention in a Northumbrian civil war led to the killing of the king and the installation of a pliant Anglo-Saxon ruler in 866–7; the king of East Anglia and his army were comprehensively defeated in 869; the British kingdom of Strathclyde likewise overrun in 870–1; the king of Wessex killed and his brother and heir forced to buy peace through tribute in 871; and in 873–4 intervention in Mercia led to the partition of the kingdom with a pliant royal. Behind these dramatic successes lay a fluid and loose confederation based on personal charisma and military success: although Ivar could be described as 'king of the Northmen of Britain and Ireland', his death in 873 allowed the inevitably fissiparous tendencies of warbands which retained their own leadership, and had been on the wartrail for a decade, to unravel.[39] In part, the 'great army' was a victim of its own success: it had imposed puppet rulers and tributary status on the kingdoms of Britain from the Clyde to the Channel, but the maintenance of this type of domination, most close paralleled in the Hun and Avar empires of central Europe, required a dramatic centralisation of political leadership and the constant activity of a mobile and overwhelmingly large military force to maintain the flow of tribute from subject kings. In fact, the leaders of the various groupings within the 'great army' sought instead to cash in their political domination by taking over Anglo-Saxon kingdoms directly, replacing the landowning elites they had decimated with their followers. Thus in 876 Halfdan was to implant himself at York, in the place of the puppet Anglo-Saxon kings who had ruled for a decade, and share out lands amongst his followers, while in 878 settlement took place in the eastern half of Mercia, and in 880 Guthrum, the leader of the rump of the 'great army', set up court in East Anglia and shared out land to his followers; other Vikings may have returned home, or moved on to Ireland or Francia, enriched by their participation in the 'great army'.

These events fundamentally redrew the political map. The two dominant kingdoms of Bede's day, Mercia and Northumbria, were the primary victims of Viking conquest, whilst East Anglia vanished as an independent entity after 869; only Wessex, focused in the southwest but exercising overlordship over the southeast, survived. The Vikings, moreover, did not recreate long-established patterns of overlordship in new hands. Guthrum, for example, exercised nothing more than a loose overlordship over individual 'armies' with their own leaders, now focused on fortified boroughs from which they dominated the surviving countryside where they owned estates; although he minted coins in honour of the last East Anglian king, seen as a martyr by the English population, there is no hint at the continuation of any centralised political structures.

North of the Humber, where Viking kings exploited the traditional political centrality of York, and a system of regional dominance based on the archbishop was maintained, royal authority beyond the immediate hinterland of York, the ancient kingdom of Deira, was less stable. Partly this was the culmination of processes which long predated the Viking conquest: the aggressive Northumbrian wars of expansion against the Picts, Britons and even in the Ireland of Bede's day had ended as, in the second half of the eighth and the first part of the ninth centuries, Northumbria had seen a rapid and often bloody turnover of kings as rival factions with claims to membership of a broad group of families of royal blood coalesced around distinct geographical bases in Deira and Bernicia. But the court at York had remained the focal point of the political ambitions of all these groups, and the means to dominate not only Northumbria as a whole, but also to play a central role in a northern British political system extending from the Forth and Clyde to the Irish Sea and the Humber. This pattern of conflict within an extensive court establishment ended with the Viking takeover, as bonds of allegiance and authority tying the periphery to York were broken. Even Bernicia, which along with Deira had constituted the Northumbrian core, went its own way, under an Anglo-Saxon dynasty based at the ancient capital of Bamburgh, but Viking warlords were also a factor, as the wanderings of the monks of nearby Lindisfarne, whose peregrinations around their inland holdings in search of a new site suited to a changed political and economic geography ended at Chester-le-Street, demonstrated. Viking kings at York continued to be the crucial figures in north British politics, primarily because of their personal ties with Dublin, and the pull they could exert over Viking armies settled south of the Humber, but this nexus, though potentially powerful, was unstable and intermittent.

Broadly similar processes can be seen at work in Mercia, the dominant Anglo-Saxon kingdom through the eighth century. Like Northumbria, the Mercian court stood at the heart of an extensive system which combined loose alliances and overlordships on its fringes with tighter rule over its heartlands; like Northumbria, the price for holding this coalition together was a succession system which allowed a wide range of kin groups with distinct regional bases within the Mercian core to pursue their claims, often through violent means; like Northumbria, by the ninth century the recurrent conflict over the succession that resulted was blunting the ability of Mercian kings to enforce their will by the sword on the fringes of their overlordship. The career of Offa had marked the zenith of Mercian power, and demonstrated the limitations of the style of rule on which it rested. Offa's overlordship over the independent kingdoms to his east and south, established at sword-point, was fragile, and ensuring a smooth succession was central to its consolidation. Whilst Offa's efforts ensured that his crown passed to his son, Cenwulf, his attempts to establish a new style of dynastically rooted kingship – witness his adoption of the ritual of royal anointing developed by the Carolingians, and his attempts to elevate the status of his wife and daughters, having a Roman-style coinage issued in their name – failed: the Mercian coalition rested on the active participation of the landowning elite in the circulation of kingship within a wide group of claimants, and internal conflict here allowed those subjected to Offa's overlordship to escape. By 829, Egbert of Wessex was able to overcome Mercian dominance, and his successors were able to integrate England south of the Thames into a separate political system, whilst in the course of the ninth century the flow of plunder and tribute from Wales which had been such a potent element of Mercian power – Offa's Dyke, the earthwork along the Mercian–Welsh frontier, should probably be seen as an attempt to institutionalise Mercian exploitation of the Welsh – may have been slowing. As in Northumbria, Viking intervention took advantage of internal conflicts within a political system no longer fuelled by the spoils of expansive overlordship, and the result was a splitting of the former core of the kingdom. Here, though, the absence of any single political centre like York meant that the Mercian royal tradition itself was compromised: the east fell under the domination of a series of effectively independent Viking 'armies', whilst in the west a representative of a segment of the royal kindred ruled, behaving in a king-like manner by leading armies and issuing solemn judgements but apparently desisting from claiming royal status.

These political transformations left Wessex the sole remaining Anglo-Saxon kingdom, and as a result Alfred of Wessex has normally been cast as the key figure in English history, holding out single-handedly against the Vikings and thus providing the foundations on which his successors were to erect an unified kingdom in the tenth and eleventh centuries. This heroic view of Alfred's reign owes much to the needs of modern national identities, portraying a clean and linear process whereby a politically divided but ethnically homogenous people formed a precursor to the modern English state in response to external pressure. But it also rests on the views of Alfred's achievement propagated by contemporary sources that are all connected directly or indirectly with Alfred's court. Our two primary narrative sources – the year-by-year account of Anglo-Saxon history circulated *c.* 893, and subsequently updated in the major churches of the kingdom, in the

Essay

Repton: Viking warbands and Anglo-Saxon kings

The complexity of the Viking impact on Anglo-Saxon political structures is vividly illustrated by the archaeological riches of Repton. Here, a royal minster had been founded in the seventh century, one of the earliest Christian sites in Mercia. Located at a strategic point on the River Trent, Repton was the central place for the surrounding area, the 'region of the Hreppingas'; the church complex here likely doubled as a centre for the collection of royal dues and possibly a royal residence. Repton served as an important royal mausoleum following the burial there of Aethelbald, and in the ninth century the crypt was enlarged in a style redolent of Carolingian influence: its role as a place of commemoration nurturing the identity of one segment of the Mercian royal dynasty was reinforced by the burial there of Wystan, a boy-prince sanctified after his murder by a rival royal in 850 and soon the object of a dynastic cult. It was at Repton that the Viking 'great army' wintered in 873–4, in the course of a series of campaigns which drove out the Mercian king Burgred and a client king, Ceolwulf, imposed in the west. Occupation of Repton thus enabled the Viking leadership to plug into existing networks of tribute-taking within the East Midlands, which now passed under their direct control, and denigrate a crucial site in the construction of Mercian dynastic kingship. The archaeological traces of this occupation are visible not only in the construction of an earthwork rampart around the monastic complex, but also in a remarkable series of burials, some reported in the works of seventeenth-century antiquarians and others discovered in systematic excavation since the 1970s. A mass grave on the site of a stone chapel contained the disarticulated bones of some 249 individuals, about 80 per cent male, which seem to have marked a high-status burial: that of a man whose skeleton bore the signs of extensive wounds and possibly mutilation, and was accompanied by weapons, a Thor's hammer and a boar's tusk. Full scientific analysis of the bones makes it unlikely that this deposit was a Viking mass grave, as might initially be supposed: the range of radiocarbon dates is too great to be easily compatible with the casualties of one winter, and a more likely scenario is the conscious reuse of the remains found in an existing cemetery or charnel house as the backdrop for the burial of one or more Viking warlords whose identities remain unknowable thanks to the paucity of

Figure 8.10 Crypt of St Wystan's Church, Repton, Derbyshire, showing columns and probable site of Mercian royal graves

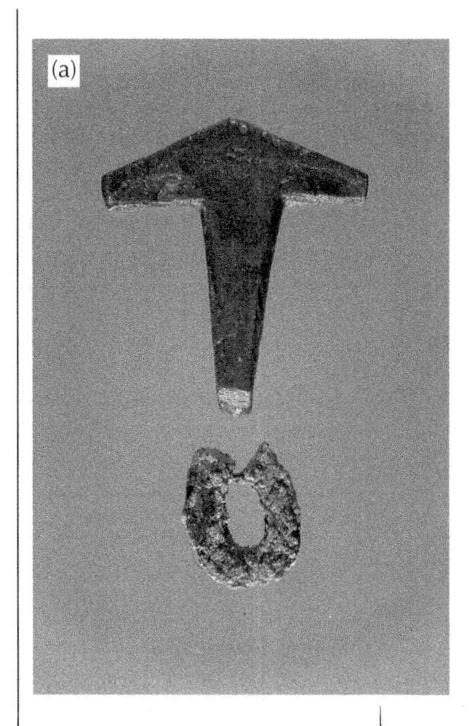

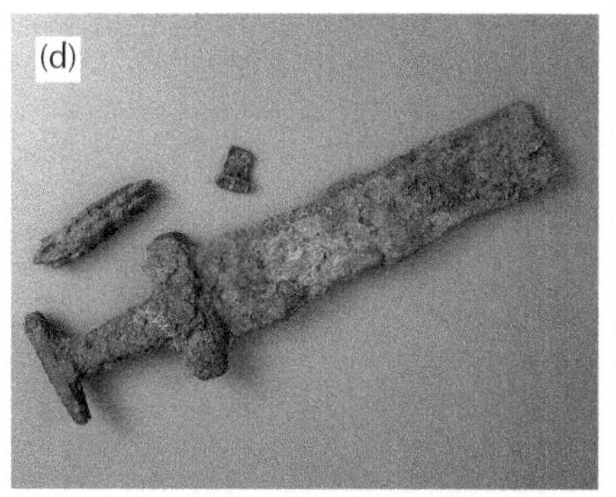

Figure 8.11 Grave goods found in Viking burials at Repton and Ingleby Wood
(a) Thor's hammer, Repton;
(b) Silver band (part of a ring), Ingleby;
(c) Iron buckles, Ingleby;
(d) Repton sword

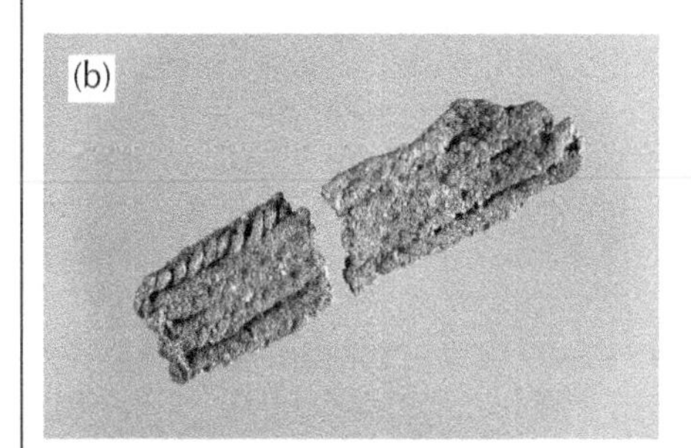

8.12 The 'Repton Stone': monumental representation of a Mercian ruler, possibly Aethelbald (716–57)

written sources.[40] But this symbolic appropriation of a Mercian royal centre in the name of a Viking warlord is striking, and it may be no accident that a series of over 50 cremations with barrows raised over them – unparalleled in an English context – is found nearby at Ingleby Wood. The rite clearly points to Scandinavian influence, and the inevitably sparse indications of date point to the decades around 900, but the topography of the Ingelby Wood cemetery suggests piecemeal growth over a generation or two, not a short, sharp burst of activity. It may therefore make most sense to see the burials here as belonging to the Scandinavian settlement of eastern Mercia after 878, rather than the few months in which Repton served as a Viking headquarters. Here was a highly visible hilltop cemetery close to a political centre where the Vikings had erased the physical mnenomic of Mercian kingship: did burial at this special site articulate the short-lived solidarity of those who claimed membership of the occupying Viking army in the generation or so that they remained distinct from the Anglo-Saxon population into which they were eventually integrated?[41]

Anglo-Saxon Chronicle, and the Latin biography written by the Welsh priest Asser – both emphasise Alfred's personal qualities, portraying his reign as a period of energetic military and cultural activity as politics and prayer were combined to deal with the Viking threat. Although the leading role in which Alfred has been cast in later historiography led some nineteenth- and twentieth- century historians to question Alfred's own role in shaping this narrative – the typically early medieval piety described in Asser's life, for example, fits so ill with the modern tradition of the muscular national hero that some have even suggested, in the face of all the contemporary evidence, that the biography must be a later forgery – it is quite clear that Alfred's court was manufacturing an image of a model Christian king, and attempting to create a shared past for his subjects, in order to legitimate the changed political landscape that had emerged in the aftermath of the Viking conquests of the 860s and 870s. Here, the line essayed by Asser and the anonymous compiler of the *Chronicle* is paralleled in a series of other sources closely associated with, and in some cases clearly produced at, Alfred's court: a law-code echoing Old Testament Biblical legislation but encompassing the laws of early Anglo-Saxon kings from Aethelbert to Offa, and translations of a series of key historical and theological works from Latin to the written form of the vernacular language, Old English.

Alfred's court thus sought to represent itself as the guardian of an inclusive Anglo-Saxon cultural and political tradition, not as the agency for the domination of Wessex over its erstwhile neighbours. Whereas Offa has been 'king of the Mercians' exercising Mercian domination over neighbouring peoples, Alfred was 'king of the Anglo-Saxons', ruler of all 'Englishkind'. Much has been made by historians of Alfred's adoption of continental models of kingship and cultural patronage here. There were certainly close and enduring links, particularly between Wessex and the Carolingian rulers, whilst Alfred himself attracted scholars not only from across Anglo-Saxon England, but also from the continent, to his court; Asser, indeed, could model his biography of his patron on that of Charlemagne written by one of his court scholars, Einhard. Whilst these links are important in understanding Alfred's cultural policy, they should not obscure important differences between Alfred and Charlemagne. No Carolingian ruler had consistently attempted to essay a shared past which informed a common ethnic identity for his subjects. And the concern with the correction of Latin to create a uniform pattern of Christian observance that was central to Charlemagne's cultural policy is largely lacking from Alfred's court. Alfred could lament – in a rhetorical passage frequently taken far too literally – about the collapse of Latin learning in English south of the Thames, seeing in Bede a hazily distant golden age against which the present could be judged and found wanting: the Vikings, here, were God's wake-up call, and the cultivation of a properly Christian culture was the way to appease Him. But this response took place in the written vernacular, through the translation of the central works of the Christian traditions into Old English, 'not word for word but sense for sense', so as to be accessible not to priests charged with liturgical correction, but to laymen.[42] Although Einhard had portrayed Charlemagne as a patron of secular culture transmitted in the Germanic vernaculars, and Alfred's contemporaries in the eastern Frankish kingdom in modern Germany were patrons of similar works of translation and high culture in written Old High German, the vernacular was never used in the Carolingian world as a direct replacement for Latin culture. Alfred's programme here fitted into an insular tradition that made extensive use of the written vernacular not only for practical purposes but also as a medium of cultural expression in its own right; this medium allowed him to essay a common Anglo-Saxon identity for his subjects.

Because Alfred's successors were able to build on the foundations he laid, it is easy to assume that the political programme of the unification of 'Englishkind' under a model Christian king was smoothly and unproblematically accepted. In fact, relatively little new territory fell under West Saxon rule in Alfred's reign: the expansion of Wessex was really an achievement of his tenth-century successors. The ideology of English unity seems to have been particularly important in legitimating Alfred's seizure of London in 886: it was after this event, so claimed Asser, that 'all Englishkind' submitted to their king, and special coins commemorating the event were minted. Here, Alfred may have been particularly keen to acknowledge the traditional Mercian alignment of London and its hinterland north of the Thames, now incorporated into his kingdom: although the rulers of late ninth- and early tenth-century Mercia were allied through marriage to the West Saxon dynasty, and shied from directly claiming royal status, they behaved as independent rulers to all intents and purposes. The notion of a 'kingdom of Anglo-Saxons' described a distinctive new political order in England south of the Humber, not a template for the modern English state. And, if the highly charged descriptions of the formation of this new dispensation produced by its architect are read with care, and complemented with the evidence of coins and documents, it becomes clear that the heroic view of Alfred the uniquely blessed general able to reverse relentless Viking progress cannot be sustained. Alfred's early years on the throne are shadowy, but he was forced to buy peace – that is, become a payer of tribute to the 'great army' – through the 870s; his survival through this period was particularly dependent on the southwest, crucial for its economic wealth and political loyalty. If we strip away the later perspective of our written sources, Alfred in this initial period was not so dissimilar to the Anglo-Saxon royals on the Mercian and Northumbrian thrones, condemned as 'foolish' puppets by the *Chronicle* and modern historians alike. Alfred's creation of a new political identity was only possible because he was able to inflict a decisive defeat on his Viking opponents in 878 and so ensure that Wessex avoided the fate of East Anglia, Mercia and Northumbria, and here, crucially, Alfred faced a weakened opponent. Viking attentions only turned to the imposition of direct rule on Wessex when the 'great army' was in an advanced stage of breaking up, following the settlement of Northumbria and Mercia; Alfred's retinue, plus royal levies (the *fyrd*) raised from the southwestern heartlands of Wessex thus had just enough muscle to defeat this Viking splinter force, and persuade its leader, Guthrum, to seek greener pastures in kingless East Anglia. Subsequent political consolidation owed much to the damage suffered by those major ecclesiastical communities that had borne the brunt of Viking ravaging: Alfred was able to utilise ecclesiastical land for royal purposes with little of the vociferous complaint that had been directed at the Mercian kings of the eighth century, whilst the need for defensible strongholds against the Vikings facilitated a renewed stress on the universal obligation to perform public works, enabling the construction of fortified centres (*burhs*), planned and organised by the royal court, several of which subsequently developed into towns.

Wessex's survival through the 870s thus owed much to the distance of its heartlands, in the southwest, from the main areas of Viking interest. Alfred's ability to capitalise on good luck may, however, have been helped by certain characteristics of Wessex's political structures. It certainly is a striking fact that the Vikings were unable to manipulate internal dissension over the succession in Wessex as they were in Mercia and Northumbria. In fact, in the ninth century the royal succession in Wessex was successfully limited to a single family, with a complex agreement reached whereby the sons of Aethelwulf (839–58) would each succeed in turn; in spite of the potential for fraternal friction, this settlement worked until Alfred sought to have himself succeeded by his son, Edward, and so provoked his nephew Aethelwold into seeking Viking aid to gain the throne. Aethelwulf's plans for the succession may have been aided by Viking pressure, and the resulting need for an able and active adult king to be quickly selected, but they allowed a single dynasty to act as a focal point for the political life of the kingdom. It certainly is striking that we have no equivalent in Wessex to the rival royal kindreds with distinct regional bases that are so apparent in Mercia and Northumbria, and so no saints' cults linked to dead – often murdered – members of royal kindreds. Even West Saxon control of the southeast, and in particular Kent, which after all had an independent political history, was maintained, in marked contrast to the fracturing of the Mercian and Northumbrian polities: here, the careful courting of Kent by West Saxon rulers through the ninth century, evident both in the degree of self-determination Kentish landowners were allowed in local affairs and in royal attempts to claim a Jutish pedigree, paid dividends.

It is almost natural to stress the English element in Alfred's programme, but the Viking activities shook up the existing political order in Wales too, with important implications for Wessex. Here, kings had long been pushed by Mercian plundering into the increasingly powerful arms of the rulers of Gwynedd in the northwest, safe from the immediate Anglo-Saxon threat and tied into a series of shifting agreements and alliances with the Mercians. The ninth century had seen the fracturing of Mercian systems of tribute-taking, allowing Rhodri Mawr of Gwynedd (king 843–77) to establish overlordship over the Welsh; but Gwynedd, nestling on the edge of the Irish Sea, was now dangerously close to the central axis of Viking activity in Britain, and Rhodri was forced into exile in Ireland in 876. In the last three decades of the ninth century, the kinglets of southern and central Wales, facing attempts by Rhodri's sons to reassert the overlordship of Gwynedd, were increasingly drawn into the sphere of the kings of Wessex. Asser, Alfred's biographer, was carefully headhunted for his Welsh connections, eventually receiving the plum West Saxon bishopric of Sherburne: a leading scholar from the pre-eminent ecclesiastical centre, St David's in Gwynedd, his life of Alfred at points seems to anticipate a Welsh audience to whom it advertises the benefits of Alfred's overlordship. We should thus take Asser's presentation of Alfred as 'king of all Britain' just as seriously as a political and ideological initiative as his carefully presented claim to be ruler of 'Englishkind': the *Anglo-Saxon Chronicle*'s coining of the term 'Bretwalda' to describe the position of his grandfather may echo Asser's perspective. But although Alfred's successors claimed imperial rule over their British neighbours, their interest in Wales was intermittent, and the kings of Gwynedd under Rhodri's grandson Hywel Dda were able to create a more lasting overlordship.

In England and Wales, then, sustained Viking pressure fractured the political system along existing points of strain, and as new orders legitimated by new political identities emerged. In Ireland, the Viking threat also led to the development of an ideology of Irish unity in the present, resting on claims for a shared ethnic identity of the Irish people projecting back to a common past; but, because the Vikings simply slotted into and exploited an already fragmented political system, these ninth-century initiatives did not immediately or directly lead to a new political dispensation. The Ui Neill king Máel Sechnaill, who was 'high king of Tara' 846–62, sought to present himself as leader of a common Irish cause, united in the face of the Viking threat. Mael's self-representation as *ri Erenn*, literally 'king of the Irish' is evident in the annals and the material culture; it is echoed in the claims of continental observers that victory in 848 saw Ireland 'liberated' from the Vikings. This notion of the high kingship as a title not only tied to dynastic title or the control of a particular ceremonial centre, but as resting in leadership of the Irish as a people against outside foes, remained current at the court of Mael's son and successor but one, Flann Sinna (king of Tara 882–916): in 885, the royal poet Máel Mara wrote a panegyric 'Flann for Erinn' not only presenting Flann as leader of the Irish people, but also tracing back a common origin myth for the inhabitants of Ireland in the legendary Tuathal Techtmar.[43]

This common identity could be sharpened in opposition to Viking 'foreigners': in 902 the Vikings were expelled from the *longphort* at Dublin. But the nature of the Irish political system made it impossible for the likes of Mael and Flann to transform the high kingship of Tara into a national kingship: the various layers of kingship were too deeply embedded in Irish political culture and practice, and the genealogical claims and legends associated with Tara's pre-eminence in fact legitimated a segmentary system of many kings. The kingship of Tara was not under the strict control of any one dynastic segment, but was the object of constant struggle between two strands of the Ui Neill dynasty with different regional bases, so that Flann did not succeed his father directly or automatically, but had to struggle to gain the throne which had been seized by a rival Ui Neill segment on his father's death, and mobilise allies in order to campaign against internal and external foes. In this context, whilst Viking activity might promote a clearer feeling of Irish togetherness, and on occasion high kings in their prime might lead joint actions against threatening Viking leaders, in general the Vikings remained deeply implicated in Irish social and political life, as allies and neighbours as well as enemies. After all, in Ireland the Vikings did not seriously threaten the continued existence of the current political order, but sat in their coastal settlements on its edges, acting in a manner as predatory as any indigenous Irish king, but also providing economic links and military allies within the Irish system. It is thus no surprise that the expulsion of the Vikings from Dublin was to prove short-lived, with Scandinavian settlement re-established on a new site by the kings of York in 917, and Dublin subsequently becoming a key ally for ambitious Irish kings.

In Scotland, in contrast, a new political dispensation uniting three distinct kingdoms was to emerge in the course of the ninth century, and by 900 the rulers of this 'kingdom of Alba' were encouraging their subjects to adopt a shared identity. As always with early Scottish history, the sources are scarce, late and difficult. Later tradition claimed that this new kingdom was created by Cinead mac Alpin (*c.* 840–58) utilising traditions of matrilineal succession to unite Pictish and Scottish dynasties and so create a new realm. National historiogaphies need founding figures, and Cinead's status in Scottish history is in many ways reminiscent of Alfred's in English. Scottish historians, however, have led the way in questioning later legends about the dramatic transformations of the eighth and ninth centuries, and have seen Cinead's reign as but one episode in a longer history of interaction.

In the eighth century, a single political framework centred on the palaces and churches of Fortriu in the Scottish east midlands was emerging. The sophistication and wealth evident in the St Ninian's Isle treasure, or the St Andrews sarcophagus, point to a powerful elite prospering within this framework. Although the balance of power in the north seesawed, the openness of Pictish kingship to outside claimants meant that northern rulers, of whatever origin, were increasingly participating in a common political culture. In this context, it is no surprise that kings in Fortriu seem to have been tempted to limit royal status and the royal succession to their own immediate kin; in attempting to pass on hard-won overlordships to their sons, they were behaving in exactly the same manner as their contemporary Anglo-Saxon Offa. The reign of Constantine I, from 789–820, seems to mark a watershed in the growth of dynastic power: his reign is the first documented case of the Pictish kingship passing, albeit indirectly, to the son of an earlier king, and he was succeeded in turn by his brother, his son and his brother's son. Constantine's dynasty was of Dalriadan origin, but it is not clear that its emergence represented the Dalriadan takeover of the Picts: the two kingdoms remained separate, and Constantine and his heirs did not always or automatically rule Dalriada; it is possible that they did not rule in Dalriada at all. Indeed, by the end of the ninth century, Dalriada had vanished as a separate political entity, and a new kingdom, based in Fortriu but ruled by a Dalriadan dynasty, from a court whose cultural idiom was Gaelic, through a Gaelicised elite, dominated northern Britain. The one hint we have at the Pictish ancestry of the new kingdom comes in its denomination from the end of the ninth century on as the 'kingdom of Alba' and its aristocracy as the 'men of Alba'. 'Alba' was in origin a geographical term for northern Britain: its adoption rested on its lack of ethnic connotations, making it a politically neutral term offering a shared identity for the ruling elites of an expansive northern British polity which encompassed Picts and Britons as well as Gaelic Scots.

The creation of the 'kingdom of Alba' was thus far more than a matter of dynastic change and military success. The disappearance of the Pictish language, and of Pictish cultural identity, was complete and remarkably rapid: we hear nothing of it after the ninth century. In part, this must rest on the – inevitably unquantifiable – losses suffered by the bearers of Pictish tradition, the aristocracy, in the ninth century. But identities may have been changing long before the advent of Viking raiders and Gaelic kings. As elsewhere in early medieval Britain, the establishment of the church had profound social effects, and Pictish Christianity had its origins and inspiration in Iona and St Columba. In terms of culture and personnel, the church was thus Gaelic, and its prestige may have given Gaelic culture a certain attraction for the Pictish elite. Already in the eighth century, for example, Pictish kings were adopting Gaelic names, and elites eager to express their status and entrench their position through founding and patronising local churches were tied into a new milieu of display, one no longer characterised by the distinctively Pictish medium of the symbol stones, but which aspired to the universalising Christian culture of the St Andrews sarcophagus. The temporary expulsion of the Columban clergy by King Nechtan in 717 certainly rested on the perception that they were agents of Gaelicisation, wedded to the 'Celtic' dating of Easter and so cutting off the Pictish church from the mainstream of ecclesiastical opinion in Britain. By the ninth century, the church was consciously used by kings to legitimate Gaelic rule. Churches founded at sites such as Dunkeld and St Andrews were part of the infrastructure of royal power: Dunkeld, for example, claimed to have received relics of St Columba from Cinead mac Alpin, in a tradition which legitimated its status as the seat of the 'chief bishop of Fortriu'. The past of the Scottish church was thus one in which the Picts had no place, and indeed the Pictish kings were denigrated as oppressors of the church. The cult of Columba was thus a crucial supernatural glue that held together the new political identity: royal armies carried the relics of Columba with them into battle, where they proclaimed their allegiance with the war cry 'for Alba!'.

The complex practices which had given rise to the legend of Pictish matrilineal succession, and frequent adoption of outsiders as kings of the Picts, clearly made the Dalriadan takeover possible. But they cannot explain why this takeover took place now, over three or so generations in the ninth century. Here, the Vikings once again clearly played a vital role as a catalyst for change. Both Dalriadan and Pictish kingdoms suffered at Viking hands in the course of the eighth and ninth centuries, weakening both. By the tenth century the northern Picts, for example, had formed an effectively independent lordship of Moray, probably under Viking influence, and this splintering away of northern support may explain why in the ninth century Fortriu, the traditional centre of Pictish power, was peculiarly vulnerable to outside conquest. Increasing Dalriadan involvement in Pictish politics in the late eighth and ninth centuries was itself probably a necessary reaction to Viking raiding and ravaging on the western seaboard. And Viking raids on Fortriu were also central to the establishment of a new Gaelic dynasty. Cinead rose to power in the aftermath of a calamitous Viking victory in Fortriu in 839, which led to the overthrow of that segment of the Dalriadan royal dynasty which had been busy attempting to establish itself on the Pictish throne in the preceding decades. Cinead's rise to power is obscure. The king-lists suggest that he had to overcome a string of Pictish kings to establish himself, perhaps members of older royal kindreds ruling locally as the complex political system splintered under Viking pressure. Cinead himself, however, was not a king before these campaigns, and his father, Alpin, remains a shadowy figure; later traditions, recounting Cinead's descent from the eighth-century Dalriadan king Aed mac Gabrain, legitimated his line, but we should not allow them to obscure the fact that Cinead was a successful warlord operating in a political crisis. The source of the military might that underwrote Cinead's success remains shadowy, but Irish as well as Scottish traditions consistently associate him with Viking allies and mercenaries. Although Cinead's successors were to suffer from serious Viking incursions, they too able to benefit from Viking disruption, notably colluding with Viking aggressors in the overthrow of the British dynasty which ruled the kingdom of Strathclyde: Strathclyde subsequently became a part of the kingdom of Alba, normally given as a subkingdom to the reigning king's favoured son. And it was Cinead's successors who were ultimately the main beneficiaries from the collapse of the Anglo-Saxon kingdom of Northumbria, the northern parts of which were conquered in the tenth century.

The ninth century was thus a formative one in British and Irish history. This was not because Vikings were outsiders, agents of wanton destruction forcing a new beginning. National historiographies might make useful play of pagan warriors as an alien threat which encouraged the political union of previously divided 'peoples'. But Vikings, in fact, rapidly became a part of their host societies. Their essentially parasitic activities placed existing systems under real stress and caused collapse where there were weaknesses. Their demands were a powerful force for the liquidation of wealth, which were to encourage the transformation of renders into rents and the adoption of more intensive systems of agrarian management by landowning elites; they fractured the carefully balanced systems which had created a delicately poised kaleidoscope of allegiances around a handful of major royal courts for much of the eighth and ninth centuries. Here, the tendency of national historiographies to isolate national histories obscures the interlocking nature of the changes taking place across Britain and Ireland. Viking activities, after all, did not respect such boundaries, and right across Britain they produced similar responses, as those groups best-placed to weather the storm created new overlordships legitimated by new political identities.

Bibliographical essay

Primary sources

Modern academic traditions and nationalist ideologies which have tended to separate 'English' from 'Celtic' history have affected the presentation of the primary sources just as deeply as they have the secondary reading. Translations of many of the most important sources are easily available on the web, e.g. via the major medieval websites listed in the introductory bibliography.

D. Whitelock, ed., *English Historical Documents* I: *500–1042* (2nd edn, London, 1979) is the essential starting-point for any serious study of Anglo-Saxon England. There are independent translations of a number of key sources, many of which are excerpted in Whitelock's collection. Of particular importance is Bede's *Ecclesiastical History*, which is available in many translations of which the 'standard' are the Oxford Medieval Texts versions by B. Colgrave and R. Mynors (Oxford, 1969); Bede's *Letter to Egbert* is an appendix to this volume. Also important are a number of saints' lives. From Northumbria there are lives of St Cuthbert by an anonymous monk of Lindisfarne and by Bede himself (tr. B. Colgrave, Cambridge, 1940) and the life of Wilfrid by Stephan of Ripon, translated by B. Colgrave (Cambridge, 1927); the lives of Wilfrid, Cuthbert and Bede's *History of the Abbots of Wearmouth-Jarrow* are also available in Penguin Classics under the title *The Age of Bede*. From Mercia there is an important and neglected life of Guthlac, written by Felix of Crowland (tr. B. Colgrave, Cambridge 1956). The other crucial narrative source, for all its difficulties, is the *Anglo-Saxon Chronicle*: there are many translations. Some of the letters of two Anglo-Saxon churchmen who found fame on the continent, Alcuin and Boniface, also shed light – normally critical light – on events in England: recent selections are Alcuin, *Letters*, selection tr. S. Allott (York, 1984) and Boniface, *Letters*, tr. E. Emerton (New York, 1940) or in C. H. Talbot, *The Anglo-Saxon Missionaries on the Continent* (London, 1954). S. Keynes and M. Lapidge, *Alfred the Great* (London, 1983) is the best way into the material associated with his reign. Anglo-Saxon royal law-codes are available in *EHD* or the older translation of F. Attenborough, *Laws of the Earliest English Kings* (Cambridge, 1922). *EHD* also translates a good selection of charters and synods, probably the key sources for the eighth and ninth centuries, whilst the Anglo-Saxon Charters website at www.trin.cam.ac.uk/wwwchart/ is an invaluable resource. There are numerous translations of the rich vernacular literary traditions, most surviving in written form from the tenth and eleventh centuries and so needing careful handling.

For early medieval Scotland, the crucial source is Adomnan of Iona, *Life of Columba*, Penguin Classics tr. R. Sharpe (1995) or A. and M. Anderson (1991); other than that, and comments in Bede and Irish Annals, evidence is sparse, late and best approached in tandem with the secondary literature. A. Anderson, *Early Sources of Scottish History I: AD500–1288* (Edinburgh, 1922) is best read alongside M. Anderson, *Kings and Kingship in Early Scotland* (Edinburgh, 1973); similarly J. Bannerman, *Studies in the Early History of Dalriada* (Edinburgh, 1974) includes texts as well as discussions, notably of *Senchas fer nAlban*, the origin legend of the Dalriadan kingdom which also includes a register of obligations due to the king.

The most recent edition and translation of the key source for the post-Roman British society is Gildas, *The Ruin of Britain*, tr. M. Winterbottom (London and Chicester, 1978). From the British kingdoms there is also Aneirin, *The Gododdin*, ed. J. T. Koch (Cardiff, 1997), although whether this is a genuine seventh-century poem about relatively recent events remains a matter of controversy. 'Nennius', *Historia Brittonum*, ed. and tr. J. Morris (London, 1978) is now universally seen as ninth-century Welsh mythmaking, combining legend and folklore. Legal material is later and difficult; the charters and inscriptions are the most promising source material, for which see, respectively, the work of Wendy Davies (below) and the database of the Celtic Inscribed Stones Project at University College, London: www.ucl.ac.uk/archaeology/cisp.

For Ireland, in comparison, there is a relative wealth of material, much of it requiring careful contextualisation (particularly the literary traditions). The writings associated with Patrick are available in *St Patrick: His Writings and Muirchu's Life*, ed. A. Hood (London and Chichester, 1978). The *Annals of Ulster*, ed. and tr. S. MacAirt and G. MacNiocaill (Dublin, 1983) are generally agreed to give a reliable narrative backbone from the seventh century. A number of other annalistic traditions, most of which need careful handling, are accessible, e.g. D. Murphy, ed., *Annals of Clonmacnoise* (Dublin, 1896); J. Radnor, *Fragmentary Annals of Ireland* (Dublin, 1978). A significant body of hagiography and law has been translated: for tasters, see e.g. Cogitosus, *Life of Brigit*, tr. S. Connolly and J. M. Picard, *Journal of the Royal Society of Ireland* 117 (1987), *Crīth Gablach*, tr. E. MacNeill, 'Ancient Irish law: the law of status and franchise', *Proceedings of the Royal Irish Academy* 36 C (1921–4). There are various translations giving a flavour of the literary traditions, e.g. T. Kinsella, *The Tain* (Dublin, 1977) or K. Jackson, *A Celtic Miscellany* (London, 1971), whilst L. Bieler, tr., *The Irish Penitentials* (Dublin, 1975) gives a flavour of religious life. There are excellent guides to the source material in K. Hughes, *Early Christian Ireland: An Introduction to the Sources* (London, 1972), which surpasses J. Kenney, *The Sources for the Early History of Ireland* (rev. L. Bieler, Dublin, 1979), which also covers ecclesiastical sources; law is best approached via F. Kelly, *A Guide to Early Irish Law* (Dublin, 1988). The Celtic Inscribed Stones database is also valuable. There is an invaluable online Corpus of Electronic Texts (CELT), many in translation: www.ucc.ie/celt/.

General reading

Once again, national divides permeate almost all the secondary scholarship: the new perspectives which can be opened up by avoiding them are shown by the most recent general treatment, the excellent E. James, *Britain in the First Millennium* (London, 2000). W. Davies, ed., *From the Vikings to the Normans* (Oxford, 2002), vol. 2 of the Short Oxford History of the British Isles, shows the value of properly comparative treatment; vol. 1, is ed. T. Charles-Edwards, *After Rome* (Oxford, 2004).

An indispensable resource for Anglo-Saxonists is Prof. Simon Keynes' online bibliography: www.wmich.edu/medieval/research/rawl/keynes/. The most accessible and best recent treatment, focusing on the politics in its social and cultural context, is J. Campbell *et al.*, *The Anglo-Saxons* (London, 1982). There are a number of recent political histories, e.g. B. Yorke, *Kings and Kingdoms of Early Anglo-Saxon England* (London, 1998); interesting from a wider perspective is P. H. Sawyer, *From Roman Britain to Saxon England* (London, 1978). None of these general works quite succeeds in integrating recent work on the archaeology, which is so central to our rapidly changing understanding of the fifth and sixth centuries in particular. Here, D. M. Wilson, ed., *The Archaeology of Anglo-Saxon England* (London, 1975) shows its age; R. Hodges, *The Anglo-Saxon Achievement: Archaeology and the Beginnings of English Society* (London, 1989) is an interesting and individual synthesis. D. Hill, *An Atlas of Anglo-Saxon England* (Oxford, 1981), and M. Lapidge, S. Keynes, J. Blair and D. Scragg, *Blackwell Encyclopaedia of Anglo-Saxon England* (Oxford, 2000) are valuable resources.

On Wales, there is an excellent treatment by W. Davies, *Wales in the Early Middle Ages* (Leicester, 1982); her *Patterns of Power in Early Wales* (Oxford, 1991) is a short and stimulating introduction.

On Scotland, A. Smyth, *Warlords and Holy Men: Scotland AD 80–1000* (London, 1984), is succinct and provocative; S. Foster, *Picts, Gaels and Scots: Early Historic Scotland* (London, 1996) is a good introduction.

On Ireland, there has been a flowering of scholarship encouraged by changing approaches to the sources. Older works like F. Byrne, *Irish Kings and High Kings* (London, 1973), took the laws and literature of early Ireland as evidence for an unchanging society with roots in the distant past. Now political and social development – even dynamism – are stressed by D. O'Croinin, *Early Medieval Ireland, 400–1200* (London, 1995) and the seminal work of T. Charles-Edwards, *Early Christian Ireland* (Cambridge, 2000). For the archaeology see N. Edwards, *The Archaeology of Early Medieval Ireland* (London, 1990) and H. Mytum, *The Origins of Early Christian Ireland* (London, 1992).

The use of regional studies to illuminate wider processes, which has been so successful on the continent, has been less widespread in British historiography. Although the sources are sparse and difficult, regional studies of Anglo-Saxon history at least are both possible and valuable, as is shown by J. Blair, *Anglo-Saxon Oxfordshire* (Stroud, 1994), which is excellent on the archaeology and on social developments, and P. Sims-Williams, *Religion and Literature in Western England, 600–800* (Cambridge, 1990), which is particularly strong on church and culture. N. Brooks, *The Early History of the Church of Canterbury* (Leicester, 1984) is effectively an ecclesiastical and political history of Kent.

The end of Roman Britain

The best study of the Roman withdrawal and its consequences is the excellent S. Esmonde-Cleary, *The Ending of Roman Britain* (London 1989), persuasively arguing for a cataclysmic view. Other recent attempts at synthesis include

N. Higham in *The English Conquest: Gildas and Britain in the Fifth Century* (Manchester, 1994), M. Jones, *The End of Roman Britain* (Ithaca, 1996).

On particular aspects of late Roman Britain, particularly the archaeological evidence, see the useful collection edited by P. Casey, *The End of Roman Britain*, British Archaeological Reports British Series 71 (Oxford, 1979); for Roman towns, R. Reece, 'Town and country: the end of Roman Britain', *World Archaeology* 12 (1980). C. Thomas, *Christianity in Roman Britain to AD500* (London, 1981), is the best discussion of Roman Christianity in Britain.

The written sources for fifth-century Britain, meagre though they are, have given rise to considerable controversy. The best treatment of the continental material is I. Wood, 'The fall of the western empire and the end of Roman Britain', *Britannia* 18 (1987), and on the ecclesiastical dimension see R. Markus, 'Pelagianism: Britain and the continent', *Journal of Ecclesiastical History* 37 (1986). On Gildas, M. Lapidge and D. Dumville, *Gildas: New Approaches* (Woodbridge, 1984), and see also P. Sims-Williams, 'Gildas and the Anglo-Saxons', *Cambridge Medieval Celtic Studies* 6 (1983). The material associated with Patrick is discussed by D. Dumville, ed., *St Patrick: 493–1993* (Woodbridge, 1993); see also E. A. Thompson, 'St Patrick and Coroticus', *Journal of Theological Studies* 31 (1980); *Who Was St Patrick?* (Woodbridge, 1985). A stunning deconstruction of the Celtic sources, particularly those associated with Arthur, is performed by D. Dumville, 'Sub-Roman Britain: history and legend', *History* 62 (1977).

The archaeological evidence for western British elites in the post-Roman period is assembled by L. Alcock, 'Message from the dark side of the moon: western and northern Britain in the age of Sutton Hoo', in M. Carver, ed., *The Age of Sutton Hoo* (Woodbridge, 1992), and 'The activities of potentates in Celtic Britain, 500–800', in M. Nieke and S. Driscoll, eds, *Power and Politics in Early Medieval Britain* (Edinburgh, 1988); see also E. Campbell, 'Trade in the Dark Age west: a peripheral activity?', in B. Crawford, ed., *Scotland in Dark Age Britain* (St Andrews, 1996). These can be combined with the often neglected inscription evidence now admirably discussed by M. Handley, 'The early medieval inscriptions of western Britain: function and sociology', in J. Hill and M. Swan, eds, *The Community, the Family and the Saint* (Turnhout, 1998), and 'The origins of Christian commemoration in late antique Britain', *Early Medieval Europe* 10 (2001), with reference to the work of earlier scholars. K. Dark, *Civitas to Kingdom: British Political Continuity, 300–800* (Leicester, 1994) offers an extreme interpretation of the archaeology in terms of wholesale continuity from Roman times. On the impact of Roman and post-Roman contacts on Irish society see L. Laing, 'The Romanisation of Ireland in the fifth century', *Peritia* 4 (1985) and R. Warner, 'Some observations on exotic material in Ireland', *Proceedings of the Royal Irish Academy* 76 C (1976).

The Anglo-Saxon settlement

J. Hines, ed., *The Anglo-Saxons from the Migration Period to the Eighth Century* (Woodbridge, 1997) gives a good taster of recent work using a wide range of evidence. The written sources for the Anglo-Saxon settlement are subjected to devastating dissection by P. Sims-Williams, 'The settlement of England in Bede and the Chronicle', *Anglo-Saxon England* 12 (1983), in addition to his article on Gildas; see also B. Yorke, 'Fact or fiction? The written evidence from the fifth and sixth centuries AD', *Anglo-Saxon Studies in Archaeology and History* 6 (1993). N. Higham has presented controversial arguments for a minimalist view of Anglo-Saxon conquest rather than immigration in *Rome, Britain and the Anglo-Saxons* (London, 1992). Two important papers by J. Hines cover both language and archaeology: 'Philology, archaeology and the adventus Saxonum vel Anglorum' in A. Bammesberger and A. Wollman, eds, *Britain 400–600: Language and History* (Heidelburg, 1990); and 'The becoming of the English: identity, material culture and language in early Anglo-Saxon England', *Anglo-Saxon Studies in Archaeology and History* 7 (1994). For language change see also M. Gelling, 'Why aren't we speaking Welsh?', *Anglo-Saxon Studies in Archaeology and History* 6 (1993); B. Ward-Perkins, 'Why did the English not become British?', *English Historical Review* 115 (2000).

For the archaeology, on which any interpretation of the Anglo-Saxon settlements must rest, the best guide, particularly for the archaeologically illiterate, is M. Welch's English Heritage guide to *Anglo-Saxon England* (London, 2000); try also C. J. Arnold, *From Roman Britain to Saxon England* (London 1984). C. Hills, 'The archaeology of Anglo-Saxon England in the pagan period', *Anglo-Saxon England* 8 (1979) remains an important discussion of the late Roman military precedents for 'Anglo-Saxon' material culture. The focus of recent argument has been the relationship between changes evident in the archaeological evidence, particularly in burial rituals, ethnic identity and the migration of population. See e.g. T. Dickinson, 'What's new in early medieval burial archaeology?', *Early Medieval Europe* 11 (2002); H. Härke, 'Warrior Graves? The background of the Anglo-Saxon weapon burial rite', *Past & Present* 126 (1990); H. Hamerow and J. Chapman, eds, *Migrations and Invasion in Archaeological Explanation*, British Archaeological Reports International Series 664 (1997), chapters by Crawford and Hamerow; C. Hills, 'Spong Hill and the adventus Saxonum', in C. Karkov *et al.*, eds, *Spaces of the Living and Dead* (Oxford, 1998); J. Richards, 'The archaeology of early Anglo-Saxon England', in G. Ausenda, ed., *After Empire* (San Marino, 1995); N. Stoodley, *The Spear and the Spindle: A Critical Enquiry into the Construction of Gender in the Early Anglo-Saxon Burial Rite*, British Archaeological Reports British Series 288 (1999); the bibliography could easily be expanded and continues to grow apace. There is a path-breaking reconsideration of building traditions, again stressing indigenous precedents, in S. James, A. Marshall and M. Millet, 'An early medieval building tradition', *Archaeological Journal* 141 (1984), and see now H. Hamerow, *Early Medieval Settlements* (Oxford, 2002), which places the Anglo-Saxon material in its proper continental context.

Anglo-Saxon kingship, conversion and the church

The crucial work on the documentary and written evidence for the emergence of Anglo-Saxon kingdoms is S. Bassett, ed., *Origins of Anglo-Saxon Kingdoms* (Leicester, 1992), whilst J. Campbell, 'Bede's *reges* and *principes*', Jarrow Lecture

1979, reprinted in his *Essays in Anglo-Saxon History* (London, 1986), is fundamental. There has recently been a wealth of important archaeological discussion. C. Scull, 'Archaeology, early Anglo-Saxon society and the origins of Anglo-Saxon kingdoms', *Anglo-Saxon Studies in Archaeology and History* 6 (1993) is crucial, and for a case-study see C. Behr, 'The origins of kingship in early medieval Kent', *Early Medieval Europe* 9 (2000). T. Dickinson and D. Griffiths, eds, *The Making of Kingdoms*, Anglo-Saxon Studies in Archaeology and History 10 (Oxford, 1999) offers a good selection of approaches in a broader north-European context, as does M. Carver, ed., *The Age of Sutton Hoo* (Woodbridge, 1992); on Sutton Hoo itself, M. Carver, *Sutton Hoo: Burial Ground of Kings?* (London, 1998) is the most recent word, whilst C. Kendall and P. Wells, eds, *Voyage to the Other World* (Minneapolis, 1992) has useful essays, including discussion of the impact of Anglo-Saxon studies on the initial dig in 1939. Finally, overlordship has its own special debate linked to the notion of the 'Bretwaldas': among a large bibliography see S. Keynes, 'Rædwald the Bretwalda', in Kendall and Wells, *Voyage to the Other World* and S. Fanning, 'Bede, imperium and the Bretwaldas', *Speculum* 66 (1991). Further discussion of the relationship between Bede's narrative and Aethelbald of Mercia's self-representation could prove invaluable.

Discussion of kingship and political change has inevitably been inextricably linked to debates around the interpretation of Bede and the implications of conversion. On Bede as a historian, the two discussions in Campbell's *Essays* are fundamental; amid a huge bibliography see now W. Goffart, *The Narrators of Barbarian History 550–800* (Toronto, 1988) chapter 4, and J. McClure and A. Thacker in P. Wormald *et al.*, eds, *Ideal and Reality in Frankish and Anglo-Saxon Society* (Oxford, 1983). One important strand of recent debate has been the role of Bede, and of conversion, in creating a shared 'Anglo-Saxon' identity: see N. Brooks, 'Rome, Canterbury and the English', in J. M. H. Smith, ed., *Early Medieval Rome and the Christian West: Essays in Honour of Donald A. Bullough* (Leiden, 2000); P. Wormald, 'The Venerable Bede and the church of the English', in G. Rowell, ed., *The English Religious Tradition and the Genius of Anglicanism* (Wantage, 1992); P. Wormald, 'Bede, the Bretwaldas and the making of the gens Anglorum', in Wormald *et al.*, eds, *Ideal and Reality in Frankish and Anglo-Saxon Society* (Oxford, 1983).

On conversion, start again with the two pieces on this topic in Campbell's *Essays*, which are responses to the book-length treatment by H. Mary-Harting, *The Coming of Christianity to Anglo-Saxon England* (3rd edn, London 1991); P. Wormald, 'Bede, Beowulf and the conversion of the Anglo-Saxon aristocracy', in R. Farrell, ed., *Bede and Anglo-Saxon England*, British Archaeological Reports British Series 46 (Oxford, 1978) is fundamental. Again, there is a wealth of recent work, e.g. R. Gameson, ed., *St Augustine and the Conversion of England* (Stroud, 1999), I. Wood, 'The mission of Augustine of Canterbury to the English', *Speculum* 69 (1994). The religious background to the Roman mission has been subject to vigorous rethinking from various directions: J. Blair, 'Anglo-Saxon pagan shrines and their prototypes', *Anglo-Saxon Studies in Archaeology and History* 8 (1995); R. Meens, 'A background to Augustine's mission to Anglo-Saxon England', *Anglo-Saxon England* 23 (1994); I. Wood, 'Some historical reidentifications and the Christianisation of Kent', in G. Armstrong and I. Wood, eds, *Converting Individuals and Christianising Peoples* (Turnhout, 2000). Two books by N. Higham, *An English Empire: Bede and the Early English Kings* (Manchester, 1995), *The Convert Kings* (Manchester, 1997), place Bede's story in the light of recent research. On the institutional growth of the church, J. Blair, *The Church in Anglo-Saxon Society* (Oxford, 2005) is inspiring, making full use of the archaeology; Blair's interpretation, however, rests on a much-debated hypothesis about the creation of an organised system of 'minsters', on which see J. Blair and R. Sharpe, eds, *Pastoral Care before the Parish* (Leicester, 1992); E. Cambridge and D. Rollason, 'The pastoral organisation of the early Anglo-Saxon church: a review of the "minster hypothesis"', *Early Medieval Europe* 4 (1995). See also A. Thacker and R. Sharpe, eds, *Local Churches and Local Saints in the Early Middle Ages* (Oxford, 2003). J. Hawkes and S. Mills, eds, *Northumbria's Golden Age* (Stroud 1999) is a good way into the cultural riches of the period, whilst M. Lapidge, ed., *Archbishop Theodore* (Cambridge, 1994) shows the cultural influences on the English church in its formative period.

Political histories have tended to focus on the overlordships created by the eighth-century Mercian rulers, and particularly on the reign of Alfred: both have a central role in English national historiographies. The northern British political system centred around the Northumbrian court remains neglected, largely because of Alcuin's negative views, essayed in exile: the best account is D. Rollason, *The Kingdom of Northumbria* (Cambridge, 2001). On Mercia, see now M. Brown and C. Farr, eds, *Mercia: An Anglo-Saxon Kingdom in Europe* (Leicester, 2001). Understanding of how Mercian overlordship actually worked is best gained through the case-studies offered by the regional studies by Sims-Williams on the West Midlands and Brooks on Canterbury. Brooks' work is also fundamental for royal relations with the church; C. Cubitt's study of *Anglo-Saxon Church Councils 650–850* (London, 1995) is also relevant here. R. Abels, *Lordship and Military Obligation in Anglo-Saxon England* (Berkeley, 1988) and N. Brooks, 'The development of military obligations in eighth- and ninth-century England', in P. Clemoes and K. Hughes, eds, *England before the Conquest* (Cambridge, 1971) illuminate the structure of royal power; see also J. Haslam, 'Market and fortress in England in the reign of Offa', *World Archaeology* 19 (1987). Fundamental for the differences between Mercian and West Saxon overlordship are N. Brooks, 'England in the ninth century: the crucible of defeat', *Transactions of the Royal Historical Society* 29 (1979) and S. Keynes, 'The control of Kent in the ninth century', *Early Medieval Europe* 2 (1993). On Alfred, R. Abels, *Alfred the Great* (London, 1998) is the best of the biographical treatments, whilst T. Reuter, ed., *Alfred the Great* (Aldershot, 2003) is a good way into recent work, much of which has focused on the cultural output of Alfred's court as a way into Alfred's understanding of kingship and his self-representation. Important here are a series of articles by J. Nelson, e.g., 'The political ideas of Alfred of Wessex', in A. Duggan, ed., *Kings and Kingship in Medieval Europe* (London, 1993), reprinted with other pieces in her *Rulers and Ruling Families in Early Medieval Europe* (London, 1999). Controversy has centred on A. Smyth's attempt to revive the older theory that the biography of Alfred by Asser is a later forgery in his *Alfred the Great* (London, 1995); for the issues at stake, see J. Nelson, 'Waiting for Alfred', *Early Medieval Europe* 7 (1998) and for Asser see now P. Kershaw, 'Power, prayer and illness in Asser's Life of Alfred', *Early Medieval Europe* 10 (2001) and M. Kempshall, 'No bishop, no king: ministerial ideology of kingship in Asser', in R. Gameson and H. Leyser, eds, *Belief and Culture in the Middle Ages* (Oxford, 2001). M. Blackburn and D. Dumville, eds, *Kings, Currency and Alliances* (Woodbridge, 1998) is important on the reconquest of London and Mercian relations, esp. S. Keynes, 'King Alfred and the Mercians', whilst J. Maddicott, 'Trade, industry and the wealth of King Alfred', *Past & Present* 123 (1989) demonstrates the importance of the southwest. For Alfred as 'king of the Anglo-Saxons' and the political use of English identity see S. Foot, 'Angelcynn: English identity before the Norman conquest', *Transactions of the Royal Historical Society* 6 (1996) and 'Remembering, forgetting and inventing: attitudes towards the past at the end of the first Viking age', *Transactions of the Royal Historical Society* 9 (1999).

Social history is less well served, and best approached via regional studies. Royal law-codes have been brilliantly discussed by P. Wormald: 'Lex scripta and verbum Regis: legislation and Germanic kingship from Euric to Cnut', in I. Wood and P. Sawyer, eds, *Early Medieval Kingship* (Leeds, 1977), is fundamental, and reprinted along with his other articles on early Anglo-Saxon law (e.g. 'Giving God and king their due') in his *Legal Culture in the Early Medieval West: Law as Text, Image and Experience* (London 1999); his monograph on *The Making of English Law* (Oxford, 1998) primarily deals with the tenth century and later. Crucial on social status is T. Charles-Edwards, 'The distinction between land and moveable wealth in Anglo-Saxon England', in P. Sawyer, ed., *Medieval Settlement* (London, 1976); also his 'Kinship, status and the origins of the hide', *Past & Present* 56 (1972). Aspects of aristocratic status can be approached through H. Loyn, 'Gesiths and thegns in Anglo-Saxon England from the seventh to the tenth centuries', *English Historical Review* 70 (1955) and S. White, 'Kinship and lordship in early medieval England: the story of Cynewulf and Cyneheard', *Viator* 20 (1989), whilst Wormald's 1978 Jarrow lecture, 'Bede and the conversion of England: the charter evidence', reprinted in his *Legal Culture in the Early Medieval West*, is the best discussion of the tricky topic of land tenure and the impact of written documents; on the latter topic see also S. Kelly, 'Early Anglo-Saxon lay society and the written word', in R. McKitterick, ed., *The Uses of Literacy in Early Medieval Europe* (Cambridge, 1990). R. Faith, *The English Peasantry and the Growth of Lordship* (Leicester, 1997) is the best discussion of estates and their organisation. The archaeological evidence for rural settlement urgently needs properly integrating into the historical debates: Hamerow's *Early Medieval Settlements*, and her 'Settlement mobility and the "middle Saxon shift": rural settlements and settlement patterns in Anglo-Saxon England', *Anglo-Saxon England* 20 (1991) here offer invaluable data.

Towns have been the subject of much specialised debate. S. Loseby, 'Power and towns in late Roman Britain and early Anglo-Saxon England', in G. Ripoll and J. Gurt, eds, *Sedes Regiae (400–800)* (Barcelona, 2000) is the most stimulating treatment, covering the fate of Roman cities as well as the role of the emporia.

Debate on the emporia and the North Sea trade was framed by R. Hodges, *Dark Age Economics: The Origins of Towns and Trade 600–1000* (London, 1982); two recent collections with discussion, some critical, of Hodges' views are M. Anderton, ed., *Anglo-Saxon Trading Centres: Beyond the Emporia* (Glasgow, 1999) and D. Hill and R. Cowie, eds, *Wics: The Early Medieval Trading Centres of Northern Europe* (Sheffield, 2001); see also C. Scull, 'Urban centres in pre-Viking England?', in J. Hines, ed., *The Anglo-Saxons* (San Marino, 1999), whilst R. Hodges and B. Hobley, *The Rebirth of Towns in the West 750–1050* (London, 1986) has good case-studies.

'Celtic' kingship and the 'Celtic' church

Notions of a uniform 'Celticness' shared by western British societies are now under sustained attack. See P. Sims-Williams, 'The visionary Celt', *Cambridge Medieval Celtic Studies* 11 (1986) and 'Celtomania and Celtoscepticism', *Cambrian Medieval Celtic Studies* 36 (1998). On kingship, see W. Davies, 'Celtic kingships in the early Middle Ages', in A. Duggan, ed., *Kings and Kingship in Medieval Europe* (London, 1993), and P. Wormald, 'Celtic and Anglo-Saxon kingship: some further thoughts', in P. Szarmach and V. Oggins, eds, *Sources of Anglo-Saxon Culture* (Kalamazoo, 1986). There has been important questioning of the notion of a shared 'Celtic' Christianity: in addition to the specialist literature on the Irish and Welsh churches, see K. Hughes, 'The Celtic church: is this a viable concept?', *Cambridge Medieval Celtic Studies* 1 (1981), and W. Davies, 'The myth of the Celtic church', in N. Edwards and A. Lane, eds, *The Early Church in Wales and the West* (Oxford, 1992). On social organisation, see T. Charles-Edwards, *Early Welsh and Irish Kinship* (Oxford, 1993). H. Pryce, ed., *Literacy in Medieval Celtic Societies* (Cambridge, 1998) is useful.

On Wales see the path-breaking work of W. Davies, most importantly *Patterns of Power in Early Wales* (Oxford, 1990). Davies argues that the documents preserved in the twelfth-century Book of Llandaff allow genuine insight into early medieval southwestern Welsh society in *An Early Welsh Microcosm* (London 1978); for the implications of this case for social and political history see her 'Land and power in early medieval Wales', *Past & Present* 81 (1978), and, on legal links with the Roman past, 'The Latin charter-tradition in west Britain, Brittany and Ireland' in D. Whitelock, D. Dumville and R. Sharpe, eds, *Ireland in Early Medieval Europe* (Cambridge, 1982). Compare J. Davies, 'Church, property and conflict in Wales, 600–1100', *Welsh History Review* 18 (1997). For the Welsh church, A. Lane and N. Edwards, *The Early Church in Wales and the West* (Oxford, 1992)

Work on early medieval Ireland has tended to analyse cultural artefacts and social structures rather than change over time, in part because the national historiography has privileged pre-Viking Ireland as a locus of 'Celtic origins' rather than, as in England or Scotland, state building. Many of the classic works on the law-codes and literature reflect this static view, but more recently cultural dynamism, and the reworking of traditions in the light of literate Christian culture, have been stressed. Compare, for example, K. McCone, *Pagan Past and Christian Present in*

Early Irish Literature (Maynooth, 1990) with K. Jackson, *The Earliest Irish Tradition: A Window on the Iron Age* (Cambridge, 1964). On the social impact of writing, see J. Stevenson, 'The beginnings of literacy in Ireland', *Proceedings of the Royal Irish Academy* 100 (1982) and her 'Literacy and orality in early medieval Ireland', in D. Edel, ed., *Cultural Identity and Cultural Integration: Ireland and Europe in the Early Middle Ages* (Dublin, 1995). A good example of the way in which our reading of the sources has changed is D. O'Croinin's discussion of the way in which royal genealogies were manipulated and manipulable means to advance political claims: 'Creating the past: the early Irish genealogical tradition', *Peritia* 12 (1998).

The major area of controversy has been the organisation of the church, with older views of a distinctively 'Celtic Christianity' with its separate traditions of monastic organisation increasingly questioned. The crucial works here are K. Hughes, *The Church in Early Irish Society* (London, 1966); D. O'Corrain, 'The early Irish churches: some aspects of organisation', in O'Corrain, ed., *Irish Antiquity* (Cork, 1980); R. Sharpe, 'Some problems concerning the organisation of the church in early medieval Ireland', *Peritia* 3 (1984); R. Sharpe, 'Churches and communities in early medieval Ireland' in J. Blair and R. Sharpe, eds, *Pastoral Care before the Parish* (Oxford, 1990), and now C. Etchingham, *Church Organisation in Ireland 650–1000* (Maynooth, 1999). On the overlap between ecclesiastical and royal authority, W. Davies, 'Clerics as rulers: some implications of the terminology of ecclesiastical authority in early medieval Ireland', in N. Brooks, ed., *Latin and the Vernacular Languages in Early Medieval Britain* (Leicester, 1982), has important implications. L. Bitel, *Isle of the Saints: Monastic Settlement and Christian Community in Early Ireland* (Cornell, 1990) is a highly accessible introduction to the role of monasteries in early medieval Irish society. T. Charles-Edwards, 'The social background to Irish peregrinatio', *Celtica* 11 (1976) and C. Stancliffe, 'Red, white and blue martyrdom', in D. Whitelock, R. McKitterick and D. Dumville, eds, *Ireland in Early Medieval Europe* (Cambridge, 1982), discuss traditions of exile as pilgrimage. Scholarship on the cultural achievements of the Irish church and its impact on Anglo-Saxon England and continental Europe continues to flourish. Here there is a series of useful conferences, e.g. M. Richter, ed., *Ireland and its Neighbours in the Seventh Century* (London, 1999), P. Ni Chathain and M. Richter, eds, *Irland und Europa* (Stuttgart, 1984) and *Irland und die Christenheit* (Stuttgart, 1987), H. Löwe, ed., *Die Iren und Europa im früheren Mittelalter* (Stuttgart, 1982).

Nowhere is the move away from static models of Celtic tradition more apparent than in recent work on kingship. Classic discussions of the relationship between kings and peoples are F. J. Byrne, 'Tribes and tribalism in early Ireland, *Eriu* 22 (1973) and D. O'Corrain 'Nationality and kingship in pre-Norman Ireland', in T. Moody, ed., *Nationality and the Pursuit of National Independence*, Irish Historical Studies 11 (Belfast, 1978). But see now B. Jaski, *Early Irish Kingship and Succession* (Dublin, 2000); also his discussion of 'Early medieval Irish kingship and the Old Testament', *Early Medieval Europe* 7 (1998). And for archaeological approaches to kingship, which are surely a vital way forward, B. Wailes, 'Irish royal sites in history and archaeology', *Cambridge Medieval Celtic*

Studies 3 (1982) and R. Warner, 'The archaeology of early historic Irish kingship', in M. Nieke and S. Driscoll, eds, *Power and Politics in Early Medieval Britain and Ireland* (Edinburgh, 1988). Social and economic history, however, remain in their infancy, as the archaeological material will need to be fully integrated to move away from a descriptive use of normative sources. On economics, see C. Doherty, 'Exchange and trade in early medieval Ireland', *Journal of the Royal Society of Antiquaries of Ireland* 110 (1980), and on monasteries as centres of redistribution his 'The monastic town in early medieval Ireland', in H. Clarke and A. Simms, eds, *The Comparative History of Urban Origins in Non-Roman Europe*, British Archaeological Reports International Series 288 (Oxford, 1985); on the decisive impact of the Vikings here, J. Bradley, 'Urbanisation in early medieval Ireland', in C. Karkov *et al.*, eds, *Spaces of the Living and Dead* (Oxford, 1998). On gender, viewed through literary traditions, see L. Bitel, *Land of Women* (Ithaca, 1996).

In Scotland, attention has tended to be focused on Dalriada, and on the eighth- and ninth-century developments that saw a Dalriadan dynasty take over the Pictish kingdom, creating the medieval kingdom of Scotland; here political devolution has encouraged a rethinking of early Scottish history. E. Campbell, *Saints and Sea-kings: The First Kingdom of the Scots* (Edinburgh, 1999) is an accessible introduction to the Dalriadan kingdom, of which there are good analyses by M. Nieke and H. Duncan, 'Dalriada: the establishment and maintenance of an early historic kingdom in northern Britain', in S. Driscoll and M. Nieke, eds, *Power and Politics in Early Medieval Britain* (Edinburgh, 1988) and R. Sharpe, 'The thriving of Dalriada', in S. Taylor, ed., *Kings, Clerics and Chronicles in Scotland, 500–1297* (Dublin, 2000). Archaeology, particularly at the hillfort of Dunadd, seat of the senior segment of the ruling dynasty, has added significantly to our understanding: see A. Lane and E. Campbell, *Dunadd: the Archaeology of an Early Dal Riadic Capital* (Oxford, 2000), also A. Lane, 'Trade, gifts and cultural exchange in Dark-Age western Scotland', in B. Crawford, ed., *Scotland in Dark Age Europe* (St Andrews, 1994).

Pictish history is complicated by the lack of any surviving indigenous written tradition: on this see K. Hughes, 'Where are the writings of early Scotland?' in her *Celtic Britain in the Early Middle Ages* (Woodbridge, 1980), and K. Forsyth, 'Literacy in Pictland', in H. Pryce, ed., *Literacy in Medieval Celtic Societies* (Cambridge, 1998). Thus most scholarship has focused on the matrilineal origin legend reported by Bede and in tenth-century Irish tracts: on this see M. Miller, 'Matriliny by treaty: the Pictish foundation legend', in D. Whitelock, R. McKitterick and D. Dumville, eds, *Ireland in Early Medieval Europe* (Cambridge, 1980) and most recently A. Woolf, 'Pictish matriliny reconsidered', *Innes Review* 49 (1998). New work, looking at the art history in relation to patterns of patronage and the establishment of identity, is beginning to produce important results: see e.g. the essays in S. Foster ed., *St Andrews Sarcophagus* (Dublin 1998) or M. Carver, *Surviving in Symbols: A Visit to the Pictish Nation* (Edinburgh, 1999). B. Crawford, ed., *Conversion and Christianity in the North Sea World* (St Andrews, 1998) is the best way into the thorny problems of early Christianity.

On the political changes associated with the integration of Dalriada and the Pictish kingship of Fortriu, the traditional emphasis on Cinead mac Alpin has been revised: for an important reassessment of the period immediately before Cinead, see D. Broun, 'Pictish Kings 761–839: integration with Dalriada or separate development?', in S. Foster ed., *St Andrews Sarcophagus* (Dublin 1998), and for debate over how a new political identity was forged in the ninth century compare P. Wormald, 'The emergence of a regnum Scottorum', in B. Crawford, ed., *Scotland in Dark Age Britain* (St Andrews, 1994) with D. Broun, 'The origins of Scottish identity in a European context', in B. Crawford, ed., *Scotland in Dark Age Europe* (St Andrews, 1996); note also M. Herbert, 'Rí Éirenn, Rí Alban: kingship and identity in the ninth and tenth centuries', in S. Taylor, ed., *Kings, Clerics and Chronicles in Scotland, 500–1297* (Dublin, 2000). On the influence of Iona and the cult of Columba see M. Herbert, *Iona, Kells and Derry: The History and Historiography of the Monastic Familia of Columba* (Dublin, 1996), T. Clancy, 'Iona, Scotland and the Céli Dé' in Crawford, ed., *Scotland in Dark Age Britain*, and D. Broun and T. Clancy, eds, *Spes Scottorum, Hope of Scots: St Columba, Iona and Scotland* (Edinburgh, 1999), esp. Broun's 'Dunkeld and the origins of Scottish identity'.

The Vikings

Introductory books on the Vikings abound, most retelling essentially the same story: perhaps the most interesting recent example of this genre is P. Cavill, *The Vikings: Faith and Fear* (London, 2000). H. Loyn, *The Vikings in Britain* (Oxford, 1994) is invaluable in considering Britain as a whole, whilst P. Sawyer, ed., *Oxford Illustrated History of the Vikings* (Oxford, 1997) is a good introduction to the major debates; see also chapter 10 below. The works of A. Smyth blazed a controversial trail, stressing the links between Viking activity in Ireland and Britain: see his *Scandinavian Kings in the British Isles 850–880* (Oxford, 1977) and *Scandinavian York and Dublin*, 2 vols (Dublin 1975–9), and the comments of D. O'Corrain, 'High-kings, Vikings and other kings', *Irish Historical Studies* 12 (1978–9), R. Frank, 'Viking atrocity and skaldic verse: the rite of the blood eagle', *English Historical Review* 99 (1984), and P. Wormald, 'Viking studies: whence and whither?' in R. Farrell, ed., *The Vikings* (London, 1982). Debate over the problems of Smyth's use of much later Scandinavian saga material has tended to overlook the crucial implication of his work: that Viking activity has to be understood in the context of the British Isles as a whole, not as an external factor impinging on individual regions.

For Viking activities around the Irish Sea, see H. Clarke, M. Ni Mhaonaigh and R. O'Floinn, eds, *Ireland and Scandinavia in the Early Viking Age* (Dublin 1998), and D. O Corrain, 'The Vikings in Scotland and Ireland in the ninth century', *Peritia* 12 (1998). The Viking impact on the Irish church is the subject of a classic paper by A. Lucas, 'The plundering and burning of churches, 7th to 16th century', in E. Rynne, ed., *North Munster Studies* (Limerick, 1967), and see now C. Etchingham, *Viking Raids on Irish Church Settlements in the Ninth Century* (Maynooth, 1996) and D. Dumville's pamphlet on *The Churches of Northern Britain in the First Viking Age* (Whithorn Lecture, 1997). On the political impact of the Vikings in Ireland, B. Jaski, 'The Vikings and the kingship of Tara' *Peritia* 9 (1995).

Recent work on the Vikings in England and Scotland has focused on their settlement, an important aspect of modern regional identity. For Scotland, see B. Crawford, *Scandinavian Scotland* (Leicester, 1987) and J. Graham-Campbell and C. Batey, *Vikings in Scotland, an Archaeological Survey* (Edinburgh, 1997); for England Brooks' work (above) is crucial on the cultural and political impact, and J. Richard's English Heritage guide *Viking Age England* (London, 2000) an accessible introduction to the archaeology, but see now two recent conferences, J. Graham-Campbell and J. Jesch, eds, *Vikings and the Danelaw* (Oxford, 2001) and D. Hadley and J. Richards, eds, *Cultures in Contact* (Turnhout, 2001).

Notes

1. Zosimus, *New History*, 6.5, tr. R. Rapley (Sydney, 1982).
2. Constantius of Arles, *Life of Germanus*, 14, tr. F. Hoare, *The Western Fathers* (Washington, DC, 1954); Prosper of Aquitaine, *Chronicle*, s.a. 431 tr. A. C. Murray, *From Roman to Merovingian Gaul* (Peterborough, Ont, 2000).
3. Gildas, *On the Ruin of Britain*, tr. M. Winterbottom (London, 1978), for Mount Badon ch. 26.
4. A. Hood, tr., *St Patrick: Writings and Muirchu's Life* (London, 1978).
5. P. Barker and R. White, *Wroxeter: Life and Death of a Roman City* (London, 1998); there is some evidence for similar post-Roman occupation at Silchester and Chester, and the *Anglo-Saxon Chronicle* annal for 577, although written three centuries later, is suggestive.
6. Patrick, *Letter to the Soldiers of Coroticus*, ch. 14; Sidonius Apollinaris, *Poems and Letters*, tr. W. B. Anderson (London, 1969), Letters 3.9; Procopius, *Wars*, tr. H. B. Dewing (Cambridge, 1935–9), 8.20.
7. See L. Alcock, *Dinas Powys* (Cardiff, 1963) and *Cadbury Castle, Somerset* (Cardiff, 1994); E. Campbell, 'Trade in the Dark Age West: a peripheral activity?', in B. Crawford, ed., *Scotland in Dark Age Britain* (St Andrews, 1996).
8. Adomnan, *Life of Columba*, tr. R. Sharpe (London, 1991); *Senchas fer nAlba*, tr. J. Bannerman, *Studies in the Early History of Dalriada* (Edinburgh, 1974), for the legend of Fergus and the seventh-century register of dues; E. Cameron and A. Lane, *Dunadd* (Oxford, 2000) for the archaeology.
9. J. Koch, *The Gododdin of Aneirin* (Cardiff, 1998).
10. P. Hill, ed., *Whithorn and St Ninian: The Excavation of a Monastic Town, 1984–91* (Stroud, 1997).
11. Bede, *Ecclesiastical History of the English People*, tr. B. Colgrave and R. Mynors (Oxford, 1969), III: 4.
12. Gildas, *Ruin of Britain*, ch. 23; Bede, *Ecc. Hist.*, 1.15.
13. Bede, *Ecc. Hist.*, 1.15.
14. Bede, *Ecc. Hist.*, 5.9.
15. The subtitle of the philologist K. H. Jackson's study *The Oldest Irish Tradition* (Cambridge, 1964).
16. These figures are based on L. Bitel, *Island of the Saints: Monastic Settlement in Early Medieval Ireland* (Ithaca, 1990), p. 165 n. 80; K. Hughes, *The Church in Early Irish Society* (Cambridge, 1975), p. 152.

17. The classic legal description of early Irish society in these hierarchical terms is *Críth Gablach*, tr. E. MacNeill, 'Ancient Irish law: the law of status and franchise', *Proceedings of the Royal Irish Academy* 36 C (1921–4).
18. Cogistosus, *Life of Brigit*, tr. S. Connolly and J. M. Picard, *Journal of the Royal Society of Ireland* 117 (1987).
19. L. Bieler, tr., *The Patrician Texts in the Book of Armagh* (Dublin, 1979); C. Doherty, 'The cult of St Patrick and the politics of Armagh in the seventh century', in J. M. Picard, ed., *Ireland and Northern France 600–850* (Blackrock, 1990); K. McCone, 'Bridget in the seventh century: a saint with three lives?', *Peritia* 1 (1982).
20. W. Davies, *An Early Welsh Microcosm* (London, 1978).
21. Bede, *Ecc. Hist.*, 1.1 and for the tenth-century Irish material, M. Miller, 'Matrilineany by treaty: the Pictish foundation legend', in D. Whitelock, R. McKitterick and D. Dumville, eds, *Ireland in Early Medieval Europe* (Cambridge, 1982), pp. 133–61.
22. Bede, *Ecc. Hist.*, 2.5, *Anglo-Saxon Chronicle*, tr. D. Whitelock, *English Historical Documents I: 500–1042* (London, 1979), s.a. 829.
23. Most conveniently tr. Whitelock, *English Historical Documents I*, no. 54; for the hide see T. Charles-Edwards. 'Kinship, status and the origins of the hide', *Past & Present* 56 (1972).
24. Felix, *Life of Guthlac*, tr. B. Colgrave (Cambridge, 1956).
25. Bede, *Ecc. Hist.*, 4.21, and see E. James, *Britain in the First Millennium* (London, 2001), pp. 126–7, for the vernacular terminology revealed by the ninth-century Old English translation.
26. B. Hope-Taylor, *Yeavering: An Anglo-British Centre of Early Northumbria* (London, 1977).
27. Laws of Ine ch. 70, tr. Whitelock, *English Historical Documents*, no. 32.
28. Bede, *Ecc. Hist.*, 2: 16; W. Filmer-Sankey, 'The "Roman Emperor" in the Sutton Hoo ship burial', *Journal of the British Archaeological Association* 148 (1996).
29. R. Meens, 'A background to Augustine's mission', *Anglo-Saxon England* 23 (1990); Bede, *Ecc. Hist.*, 2.2.
30. Stephen of Ripon, *Life of Wilfrid*, tr. B. Colgrave (Oxford, 1956) ch. 17.
31. Bede, *Ecc. Hist.*, 2.15 and cf. also 2.5.
32. Bede, *Ecc. Hist.*, 1.17.
33. Acts of the council of *Clovesho*, 757, conveniently tr. Whitelock, *English Historical Documents.*
34. C. Behr, 'The origins of kingship in early medieval Kent', *Early Medieval Europe* 9 (2000).
35. I. Wood, 'Some historical reidentifications and the Christianisation of Kent', in G. Armstrong and I. Wood, eds, *Converting Individuals and Christianising Peoples* (Turnhout, 2000); J. Blair, 'Anglo-Saxon pagan shrines and their prototypes', *Anglo-Saxon Studies in Archaeology and History* 8 (1996).
36. Bede, *Letter to Egbert* ed. & tr. as an appendix to Colgrave and Mynors' edition of his *Ecclesiastical History*.
37. Alcuin, *Letters*, tr. S. Allott, *Alcuin of York* (York, 1974) or in Whitelock, *English Historical Documents.*

38. N. Brooks, 'England in the ninth century: the crucible of defeat', *Transactions of the Royal Historical Society* 29 (1979).
39. Ivar's title: *Annals of Ulster*, tr. S. mac Airt and G. mac Nichoill (Dublin, 1970), s.a. 873.
40. On Repton see M. Biddle and B. Kyolbe-Biddle, 'Repton and the Vikings', *Antiquity* 66 (1992), and their 'Repton and the Viking "great army" of 873–4', in J. Jesch, J. Graham-Campbell and D. Parsons, eds, *Vikings and the Danelaw* (Oxford, 2001); my interpretation, although based on the data reported by them, differs.
41. J. D. Richards, 'Excavations at the Viking cemetery at Heath Wood, Ingleby', *Antiquaries Journal* 84 (2004); my interpretation, which differs slightly from that of the excavator, rests on the evidence from elsewhere in eastern England for the survival of an identity of belonging to the *here* articulated through participation in public meetings at specific sites well into the tenth century, for which see M. Innes, 'Danelaw identities: ethnicity, regionalism and political allegiance', in D. M. Hadley and J. D. Richards, eds, *Cultures in Contact* (Turnhout, 2001).
42. See Alfred's preface to the translation of Gregory the Great's *Pastoral Care*, tr. M. Lapidge and S. Keynes, *Alfred the Great* (London, 1983).
43. M. Herbert, 'Rí Éirenn, Rí Alban: kingship and identity in the ninth and tenth centuries', in S. Taylor, ed., *Kings, Clerics and Chronicles in Scotland, 500–1297* (Dublin, 2000).

Part IV

The Carolingian Moment: Western Europe in the Eighth and Ninth Centuries

9

'The invincible race of the Franks': conquest, Christianisation and Carolingian kingship

Contents

Summary

Chronology

Map 8: The Frankish world in the eighth century

Carolingian claims and Merovingian legitimacy

The expansion of the Frankish realm: Aquitaine and Italy

The expansion of the Frankish realm: east of the Rhine

Beyond plunder and tribute

Bibliographical essay

Summary

The eighth century saw the doubling of the size of the Frankish realm thanks to year-on-year campaigning. This process of expansion began out of necessity, following a civil war that raged from 714–19 following the death of the mayor of the palace Pippin, who had effectively controlled the kingdom for a quarter of a century. Pippin's son, Charles Martell, emerged victorious against his stepmother and half-brothers, and opponents of his father's regime, ruling in the name of a Merovingian figurehead. But the conflict had fractured allegiances right across the Frankish kingdom. Martell was able to reconstruct the traditional ties within the Frankish heartlands, but Frankish claims over the 'peripheral principalities' south of the Loire and east of the Rhine were reasserted at swordpoint over the next two generations. Successful campaigning allowed Martell and his descendants to win over aristocratic followers through the distribution of the spoils of the wartrail. The loyalty so generated allowed Martell's son Pippin to dispense with the fiction of ruling in the name of the Merovingians, and have himself made king in 751.

The second half of the eighth century saw an intensification of annual campaigning in a number of carefully chosen areas – Aquitaine under Pippin and Saxony under his son and successor Charlemagne – that were forcibly integrated into the kingdom. But Carolingian success was not solely a matter of military might, and other areas were integrated through less visible and more gradual processes. East of the Rhine in particular, Carolingian rulers worked hand-in-hand with missionaries seeking to integrate new and old converts into a properly institutionalised church hierarchy, and loyalty to the Carolingians brought with it lavish rewards for landowning elites. With the rapid conquest of the Lombard kingdom in Italy in 774, and the peaceful mastering of Bavaria in 788, Charlemagne ruled from the Elbe to the Tiber. Yet the loyalties of the wartrail could not last forever: the challenge now was to create a lasting framework to bind this vastly expanded realm together.

Chronology

690–739	Anglo-Saxon Willibrord active as missionary
714–19	Charles Martell emerges victorious from civil war after death of his father
716–54	Anglo-Saxon Boniface active as missionary
733	Charles Martell defeats 'Abd al-Rahmān just outside Tours
737	Charles Martell rules without a Merovingian king
741	Death of Charles Martell; succeeded by sons Carloman and Pippin
742	Pippin and Carloman hold first church councils for 70 years
742–67	Chrodegang, formerly clerk at Martell's court, bishop of Metz
743	Pippin and Carloman raise a new Merovingian king
746	Battle of Cannstadt and 'conquest' of Alemannia
747	Carloman travels to Rome, leaving his son Drogo in his place
747–53	Martell's son Grifo canvasses for support in Bavaria, Saxony and Aquitaine
748	Child Tassilo imposed as duke of Bavaria by Pippin under regency of Chiltrude
751	Pippin crowned king by Frankish bishops; last Merovingian sent to monastery
754	Pope Stephen travels to Francia, anoints Pippin and his family at Soissons
756	Pippin intervenes in Italy, Lombards promise to return territory to pope
757	Tassilo, now a major, visits Pippin at Soissons
759–69	Annual campaigns in Aquitaine
759	Former Visigothic territories around Narbonne submit to Frankish rule
768	Death of Pippin, succeeded by sons Carloman and Charlemagne
771	Death of Carloman, leaving Charlemagne sole king
772	Charlemagne destroys pagan shrine, the Irminsul; beginning of Saxon wars
774	Charlemagne campaigns in Italy, conquers kingdom of Lombards
776	Lombard revolt in Italy
778	Military disasters in Pyrenees and Saxony, where Paderborn sacked
781	Charlemagne visits Rome, appoints sons kings in Aquitaine and Italy
781	Tassilo visits Charlemagne at Worms and renews allegiance
783	Monks of San Vincenzo accuse Abbot Poto of insulting Charlemagne
786	Conspiracy of 'Thuringians' plots against Charlemagne
787	Tassilo refuses to answer Charlemagne's charges against him
788	Charlemagne marches on Bavaria; Tassilo deposed as duke
789	'General Admonition': beginnings of upsurge in legislative activity
790–3	Conquest of Avars led by Charlemagne's sons and generals
794	Council of Frankfurt

Carolingian claims and Merovingian legitimacy

We began this book with Orosius, writing against the claim that the sack of Rome in AD 410 was the result of the abandoning of traditional Roman religion for a new Christian God. Four centuries later, a new palace was constructed on the old Roman Rhine frontier at Ingelheim, making conscious borrowings from the Christian and imperial architecture of Orosius' world. Frankish engagement with the world of late antiquity was not simply a matter of status-boosting architecture and titles, designed to flatter a ruler who had, on Christmas Day 800, been crowned emperor by the pope at Rome. Attempting to explain the historical role of this new imperial order, courtiers turned to works like Orosius'. A court poet celebrating the conversion of the king of the Danes at the hands of the emperor Louis the Pious (ruled 814–40) describes the frescoes that adorned the throne room at Ingelheim. Here, a vast pictorial representation of the history of mankind as recounted by Orosius began with the Bible, the heroes of the ancient world, and the Christian Roman emperors, and culminated with the recent exploits of the Franks under the leadership of the Carolingian dynasty: Louis' great-grandfather Charles Martell (714–41) was shown defeating the pagan Frisians, his grandfather Pippin (741–68) vanquishing the Aquitainians, and his father Charlemagne (768–814) converting the Saxons at swordpoint.[1] For Orosius' teacher, Augustine, the possibility of identifying the Roman Empire wholly and unambiguously with the Christian faith had been a matter for pained and ultimately pessimistic debate: Rome was simply one of a series of constellations of earthly societies, none of which could be wholly identified with the community of Christians. Augustine's discussion of *The City of God* was the favourite reading of Charlemagne,[2] but for the intellectuals of the Frankish court there was no room for ambiguity in the identification of their empire with God's plans for mankind: for them, the Franks were God's chosen people, and the Frankish ruler was responsible to God for the creation of a truly Christian society. The military success of the Carolingian dynasty was thus justified in terms of the propagation of the Christian faith; the celebration of conquest and conversion presented Carolingian rule as an inexorable process, the inevitable end-point of Christian world history.

Most modern historians have presented the eighth century as a seamless succession of Carolingian victories. That they have chosen to do so is an eloquent testimony to the persuasiveness of the narrative of Carolingian success rehearsed in the Ingelheim throne room, which had been constructed at the court in the second half of the eighth century and the first half of the ninth. Already in the 760s, Charlemagne's father Pippin had the Frankish law-code, *Lex Salica*, revised and added a new prologue celebrating the 'invincible race of the Franks ... immune from heresy', who had rightly driven the Romans, persecutors of the early Christians, from Gaul. Soon the reworking of the past was taking the form of historical writing: Pippin's kinsmen Childebrand and Nibelung sponsored the addition of sections celebrating the victories of their family to the seventh-century *Chronicle* of Fredegar, whilst by the last quarter of the eighth century the court itself was the site of year-by-year recording of 'annals' covering the recent past. Given its most influential statement in the so-called *Prior Metz Annals*, composed

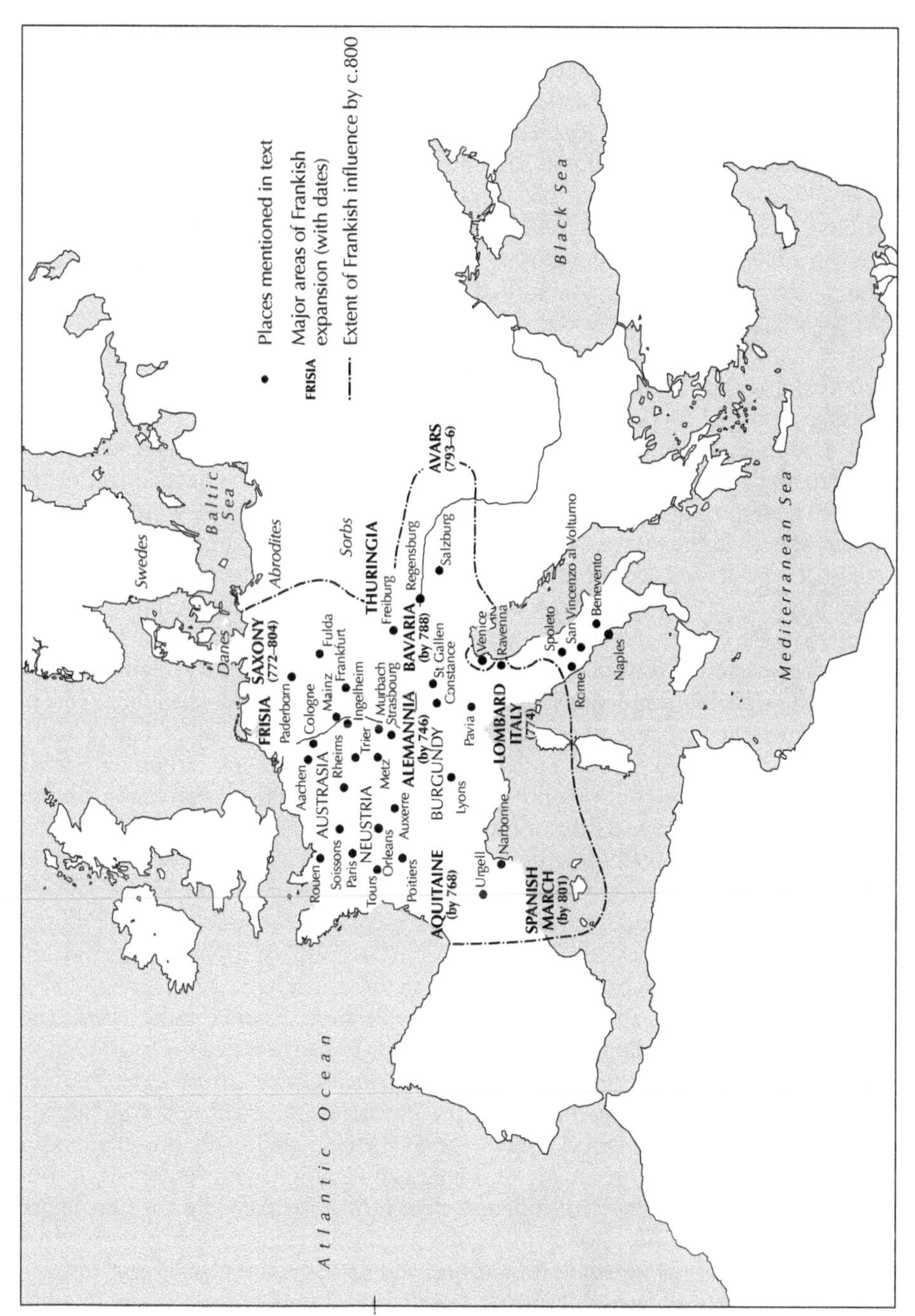

Map 8 The Frankish world in the eighth century

c. 806 under the auspices of Charlemagne's sister, Gisela, this construction of the eighth century created the impression that Merovingian kingship had long been little more than nominal, as Carolingian military leadership bypassed older sources of political legitimacy.[3] The replacement of the last Merovingian king by Charlemagne's father, Pippin, in 751, thus appeared as the inevitable final act of a drama whose ending had long been clear to all involved. Essayed with the benefit of hindsight, this narrative served to legitimate the current political order; but if we work from strictly contemporary sources, and look closely at the underlying complexity of events often simplified or simply misrepresented by Carolingian propagandists, a rather different view of the eighth century results.

The Carolingian reconstruction of the late Merovingians as literally 'useless' (*inutilis*) does not do justice to the significance of the royal court, and the legitimising power of Merovingian blood, in Frankish society in the decades around 700. The ancestors of the Carolingians were only able to rise to power in the late seventh and early eighth centuries by establishing themselves at the heart of this system through their position as mayor of the palace, without which their vast landed wealth in the east could not be translated into legitimate political authority. And their position was not assured. In 714 the death of the head of the family, Pippin, plunged the Frankish world into civil war, as rival groupings bid for control of the court, and the eventual victory of Charles Martell did not mark a smooth accession of power. Charles was an outsider – later writers claimed he was a bastard, probably importing later and much clearer standards than those current at the time – and he was not initially included in Pippin's plans: Charles had to triumph over his stepmother Plectrude, and win over his father's erstwhile followers, before he could turn to defeating rival Frankish aristocratic factions and their Aquitainian and Frisian allies in a civil war which raged from 714–19.

The civil war of 714–19 fractured allegiances and broke ties between the court and the localities. In many ways the key business of the reigns of Martell, his son Pippin, and his grandson Charlemagne, was 'reconquest': the subjection, by force, of the landed elites of western Europe who had been subject to Merovingian claims. In fact, Carolingian campaigning took place in three different stages, corresponding to the three concentric zones of Merovingian rule: first, the old Frankish heartlands of Neustria, Burgundy and Austrasia, where 714–19 had revealed the fragility of the Carolingian position; then the 'peripheral principalities' around the Frankish heartland, in particular the duchies of the Bavarians, Alemans and Aquitainians, whose ties to the Merovingian court were weakening; and finally the surrounding peoples such as the Saxons, many of whom had traditionally acknowledged some form of Merovingian overlordship, and were now potential allies for Carolingian opponents. Hence a new policy of regular aggressive campaigning is visible from the very beginning of Martell's dominance, and intensified under his successors in the second half of the eighth century. Writers noted with surprise years in which there was no campaign. This activity not only neutralised potential threats, but brought with it lucrative spoils in land and office, as well as plunder and tribute, which the Carolingians were able to redistribute as they chose; successful warfare thus generated charisma. Joining the wartrail was the easiest way to gain the goodwill and notice of the rulers. Through the shared experience of campaigning

Carolingian rulers were able to build bonds of association and loyalty that entrenched their dominance of the political community.

As well as tying landowning families into a political system centred on the Carolingians, campaigning enriched the Frankish aristocracy on an unprecedented scale. The systematic and self-confident harnessing of political violence by the eighth-century Carolingians created a snowball effect whereby this already hugely wealthy and wholly militarised elite expanded and consolidated its interests. It is here, in the political and social momentum that the Franks gathered under Martell, that the key to their eighth-century military success lies: aristocrats were eager to participate in warfare, and to bring their followers with them, because it offered status and spoils. As a result they were honed into a highly efficient and well-oiled military machine that simply dwarfed its opponents. One recent comparison, for example, has demonstrated how few landowners in Lombard Italy owned more than a dozen estates scattered around one or two city territories, a concentration of wealth easily equalled by families of the second tier within the Frankish aristocracy: no wonder Italy succumbed so quickly to Charlemagne in 774![4]

Viewed with hindsight, this continuous campaigning played a vital role in enriching and expanding the Carolingians and their followers. In origin, however, it was a matter of urgent political necessity. Our labelling of the polities south of the Loire and east of the Rhine, the principal victims of Carolingian expansion, as 'peripheral principalities' reproduces the perspective of the Frankish court and easily leads us to underestimate the viability of the opposition to the Carolingians. In the course of the seventh century, peripheral elites that had emerged as agents and allies of the Merovingian court became increasingly confident and assertive in their own right. Families like those of the dukes of the Alemans and Bavarians, justified their position with reference to the kings of the Franks, but in doing so created a distinct legitimacy of their own: thus both the Alemannia and Bavarian ducal houses promulgated law-codes for their subjects, constituted as 'peoples', which presented a hierarchy of authority, dukes being the representatives of a sovereign authority embodied by the king.[5] The importance of this veneer of legitimacy in binding the Merovingian world together grew ever greater as the economic and political systems which had underwritten the centrality of the Merovingian court – and in particular the flows of wealth associated with the remnants of the Roman fiscal system – metamorphosed into the politics of land. But the growing power of the Carolingians made this veneer ever thinner and flakier. Princes such as those of Aquitaine or Bavaria were unimpressed by the increasing pretensions of the Carolingian mayors of the palace. Whilst in the long run the Carolingians were able to mobilise the resources of the Frankish heartland to re-establish the traditional hegemony, we should beware of assuming that this outcome was preordained. Carolingian success was far from a simple or neat progression, and even the wooing of the Frankish aristocracy was a long and bumpy courtship punctuated by fits of pique and second thoughts.

It is, indeed, the establishment of Carolingian power in the Frankish heartlands that is the most shadowy, but also the most crucial, part of the process. It was long believed by historians that Martell's arrival brought about wholesale change in patterns of landholding and personnel. Certainly, saints' lives and histories of bishoprics and abbeys, most written well after Martell's career, suggest a world of regular political violence and the forcible redistribution of resources, above all land. But the mechanisms by which hardcore opponents of Martell were punished, and supporters rewarded, were varied. Most centred on the disposition of church land. The power of bishops, and the endowment of family monasteries, had resulted in the large-scale transfer of resources to churches deeply implicated in local webs of patronage and protection. In the hands of his opponents, the local dominance of a powerful bishopric or the wealth entrenched in a family monastery posed a very real threat to Martell. In response, appointments were closely controlled: in Neustria a relative of Martell's with local contacts, Hugo, was given no fewer than five bishoprics as well as the wealthiest monasteries. The landed wealth of the church was also carefully redistributed: at Auxerre, for example, where Bishop Savaric had forged something approaching an independent principality, Carolingian supporters were endowed with church land and a now independent local count created as a counterweight to the bishop.[6]

Later authors from the ninth century onwards presented such actions as despoliation, as Martell became a convenient fall guy on whom lost church lands could be blamed. But large-scale changes in the distribution of land such as those he oversaw inevitably aroused strong feelings. In the 740s, indeed, his sons Pippin and Carloman moved to regularise the handling of church land, attempting to remove the controversy whilst assuring their control of this vital resource: in a series of church councils from 742 to 747 agreement was reached that church land which was deemed 'excess' to immediate needs should be granted out on the word of the ruler, and the status of these grants as life-tenures, on which an annual rent of the ninth and tenth parts of the estates produce was to be paid, were confirmed. Whilst these arrangements were the subject of repeated discussion at church councils through the eighth and ninth centuries, the basic principle was never challenged. The result was to prove a foundation stone of the Carolingian political system, for the Carolingian rulers were now implicated in the distribution of key landed resources which had previously been dealt out in bilateral deals between regional elites and their favoured churches; those who wanted to rise socially needed to find a way to access the favour of the king to acquire an interest in church land. These arrangements ensured royal authority over the disposition of church land, but they did not involve large changes to the basic structures of landholding and power.

Martell's interventions were selective, not wholescale, and allowed the reshaping, not the replacement, of the Frankish elite. Whereas the Merovingian kings of Gregory of Tours' time did not hesitate to have their opponents legally killed, often with something approaching glee, by Martell's day being sent into internal exile, confined to a monastery to do penance for one's crimes, was the norm. Our major chronicle from the period confirms the care with which Charles dealt with his opponents within the Frankish heartlands of the Merovingian realm. The author of the *Book of Frankish History* (*Liber Historiae Francorum*), writing in the heart of Neustria (probably in Soissons) in 727 described a world where the Neustrians and only the Neustrians were true Franks, and politics was a matter of negotiation between Merovingian rulers and Frankish (i.e. Neustrian) magnates, as exemplified by the reign of Childebert III 'of blessed memory' (694–711).[7] But, even if long-established norms of political behaviour were alive enough to be meaningful, the place of the Carolingians within that political system was never again challenged after the civil war of 714–19. Whilst Martell himself respected established political forms, ruling in the name of the Merovingians, his status as a prince, and a warleader, is acknowledged by contemporaries and clearly generated new forms of loyalty and legitimacy. On the death of Theuderic IV in 737, no new Merovingian was raised to the throne, although there was no attempt to raise Charles' family to the kingship, and official documents were still dated with reference to the last Merovingian king.

The political importance of careful respect to the constitutional niceties is demonstrated by the events that followed Martell's death in 741. The realm was divided between two of Martell's son, with Carloman based in Austrasia and Pippin in Neustria, and a third brother, Grifo, excluded altogether and imprisoned. But Carloman and Pippin struggled to assert their authority beyond the Frankish heartlands, and were forced to campaign in Aquitaine, and east of the Rhine, right through the years 742–6. The sword was not the only response to this concerted challenge: in 743, a new Merovingian king was crowned, thus ending a six-year interregnum and injecting the regime with a healthy dose of traditional legitimacy. More novel was a concerted attempt to rally the church behind the new regime. A series of church councils were convoked, the first since the 670s, with the express aim of reforming Frankish society, but also, by assembling bishops, abbots, and an audience of prominent laymen, to mobilise the elite behind a programme of moral rectitude and Christian mission.

It was the renewed outbreak of internal crisis in 747–53 that was the immediate impetus for a further search for legitimacy that ultimately led to the raising of Pippin to the kingship in 751. But by the end of the 740s internal crisis took on different forms from those of the 710s. Malcontents did not contest the position of the Carolingian family itself, but aligned themselves with the different factions within the family. Whilst the continuation of Carolingian power was not challenged, individual Carolingians faced a more urgent threat from disgruntled relatives with backing from the peripheral principalities. The precise course of events is shadowy – later Carolingian propaganda had no interest in remembering six years of family conflict – but the tensions among Martell's sons broke into the open in 747, following Carloman's decision to visit Rome. Carloman's motives – was he visiting Rome as a pilgrim, or seeking to renounce the world and enter a monastery? – are unclear, but his mother and the pope were both important influences over his actions. His absence and the confusion over his future plans, however, created the opportunity for Grifo to canvass for support, winning over those unhappy with the current order: before he was killed in an ambush in 753, he sought the backing of, in turn, the Saxons, the Bavarians, and the Aquitainians. Carloman's absence and Grifo's politicking allowed Pippin to stage a takeover of Neustria, which had been handed over to Carloman's son Drogo prior to the journey to Rome. Faced with the possibility of Carloman or his sons making a comeback from Italy, or Grifo raising an army from one of the peripheral principalities, rule in the name of the Merovingian king no longer gave Pippin a distinctive authority which delegitimised his opponents: what he needed was a means of reshaping the Carolingian family itself so that he was its sole head. Hence Pippin's dramatic decision, taken in counsel with bishops and aristocrats, to send the Merovingian who sat on the throne to a monastery and have himself made king.

The precise mechanism by which Pippin deposed the last Merovingian and secured the agreement of the Franks to his being made king instead is unclear. A well-honed account, rehearsed time and again in sources from the last decades of the eighth century and the first of the ninth, tells of how at the request of the Franks a mission was sent to the pope, who was asked if it was right that Pippin had the power, but not the name, of king; the pope, of course, replied that it made no sense, and gave his blessing to the replacement of the Merovingians, and so the last Merovingian was tonsured and packed off to a monastery, and Pippin was made king. It was a powerful story, mobilising the spiritual authority of the bishop of Rome as heir of St Peter to bless political change, and one which by the ninth century was a founding myth of the Carolingian state. But it is possible that the resounding emphasis in places on papal involvement is to a very great extent myth: the sources that stress papal involvement are all intimately linked to Charlemagne's court in the last decades of the century, and have a clearly ideological purpose, whilst the fully developed story is only found in works which postdate Charlemagne's coronation as emperor by the pope in 800. Strictly contemporary sources, including the papal biographies, give no hint at high-profile papal involvement, and nor do Byzantine accounts.

If we need to be careful about overemphasising papal involvement in 751, we should not underestimate the novelty of Pippin's coronation. For Pippin of necessity adopted a new king-making ritual. Merovingian regality had been carried in the blood, and Merovingians therefore became kings thanks to the pledging of support by their subjects, but this clearly would not suffice for Pippin. So Pippin was anointed with holy oil by bishops in a ritual inspired by the Old Testament; later accounts, which as we have seen need to be treated with care, stress the involvement of the Anglo-Saxon holy man Boniface. There are potential precedents for the ritual, notably in the Visigothic and Irish kingdoms, but its potency came from the way in which it drew on ideas of Christian kingship which had been gaining currency through the seventh century, which presented kingship as a moral office granted by God.

By being crowned king Pippin decisively placed himself at the apex of his both his family and the political system as a whole, and asserted his superiority both to his brothers and his nephews, real and viable rivals for Frankish support. In this context, the events of 751 should not be viewed in isolation; the new family order was not firmly established until the killing of Grifo by rivals in Aquitaine in 753, and the subsequent tonsure of Carloman and his sons. Even then, there were precedents for those forcibly packed away to monasteries growing their hair and returning, so Carloman and his sons, not to mention the Merovingians, were not definitively removed from the scene. Hence in 754 Pope Stephen took an unprecedented step, and crossed the Alps. Meeting Pippin at Soissons, the site of the anointing of 751, Stephen repeated the ritual, anointing not only Pippin but also his wife and sons: here was a new royal family for the Franks, confirmed into their new status by the pope, and one which excluded Pippin's brothers, nephews and cousins.

If the writing out of Pippin's opponents still lay in the future, and reflected a later and more secure stage of Carolingian kingship, Pippin still spared no energy in seeking to legitimate his regime. His coins, his revision of *Lex Salica*, and the administrative documents issued in his name tell a remarkably coherent story, drawing on the ideals of Christian kingship to present Pippin ruling with God's backing, and carrying out a royal ministry which centred on promoting the Christian faith and caring for the poor. This emphasis on the divine backing for Pippin's bishop-like care for the kingdom was aimed not only at those aristocratic allies who were now his subjects, but also at explaining Pippin's supremacy within the Carolingian family, and restricting claims on the throne to his immediate line.[8]

The expansion of the Frankish realm: Aquitaine and Italy

These new forms of legitimacy need to be placed alongside the developing relationship between the Carolingians and the landowning elites of the Frankish realm. Under Pippin and his successors, we see a new regularity and intensity in warfare, consciously aimed not only at securing the submission of opponents and the use of the spoils of war to reward followers, but at the subjection of territories. Year-on-year concerted campaigning against specific targets, notably Aquitaine under Pippin and Saxony under Charlemagne, committed huge resources, but ended with the wholesale integration of regions into the Frankish political system in a manner unparalleled under the Merovingians since the days of Clovis and his sons.

The first target lay in the south, in Aquitaine. Here, an elite of sizeable landowners was developing a distinct identity as Romans, as opposed to the Franks north of the Loire. Key allies of those Neustrians opposed to the Carolingians, they had fought in the civil war of the 710s. The military muscle commanded by Eudo, the Aquitainian prince, was such that Charles Martell maintained an uneasy truce through the 720s. In fact, it may have been only the collapse of the Visigothic kingdom, and the resulting activity of Islamic warlords in southern Gaul, which shifted the balance of power in Martell's favour. Although Eudo had successfully defeated Muslim armies in the 720s – another indication of the political strength of the Aquitainian principality – documentary sources suggest that Muslim raiding may have had a significant short-term impact on the economic power of landlords right across southern Gaul by the 730s. Martell himself took advantage of the situation to undertake a raiding and plundering expedition of his own in 731.

It was this renewal of hostilities which culminated in Martell's famous defeat of 'Abd al-Rahmān at an engagement known as 'the battle of Poitiers' and normally dated to 734. In fact, nearly every statement about this conflict dissolves into a sea of uncertainty on close inspection of the sources. The date should probably be corrected to 733, and the location to the vicinity of Tours, whilst claims that the Muslims had been invited in by Eudo to help resist Martell are propagandist, coming in pro-Carolingian sources which sought to present their sponsors as the true protectors of the church. Whatever the realities, traditional claims that saw Martell's victory as a battle which changed the course of history, turning back a concerted Muslim assault on Gaul, do not stand up to close scrutiny. Muslim raiding over the Pyrenees continued after Martell's victory, and was motivated by the need of the Muslim leadership for plunder and tribute to cement the loyalty of warbands of mixed composition, in particular the rebellious Berber garrisons of the Pyrenees; it thus mirrored Martell's activities in Aquitaine. These conflicts took place in the context of uncertain political allegiances in southern Gaul and across the Pyrenees, following the collapse of the traditional authority of the Merovingian and Visigothic courts in the 710s, and the seizure of power by warrior aristocracies from their peripheries. Eudo could ally with local warlords, Muslim as well as Christian, and raiding by Martell and 'Abd al-Rahmān was a response to the possibility of an independent political system emerging in the region.

Even then, the Aquitainian principality proved remarkably durable. Martell made no attempt to rule it directly, or to replace Eudo and his dynasty. Instead, he sought to build horizontal bonds of alliances and friendship: in the aftermath of the defeat of 'Abd al-Rahmān, Martell pacified Burgundy, concluding written agreements with the leading landowners of the region. Documentary evidence from elsewhere in the south clearly shows the cultivation of regional elites through time-honoured mechanisms. In 739, Abbo, rector of Provence, drew up a will that shows those who had opposed Martell had been labelled rebels, their lands confiscated and passed on in the name of the Merovingian king to Martell's allies.[9] For a further three decades, Carolingian power in the south remained a matter of negotiation, small-scale raiding, and personal ties. In moments of weakness, the Aquitainians were quick to participate in activities which our pro-Carolingian sources characterise as 'revolt': thus in the power struggle which followed Martell's death, and again in the brief period of political division after Pippin's death, Aquitainian muscle-flexing led to Frankish expeditions.

The full integration of Aquitaine into the Frankish realm only took place after 759, when Pippin developed a new policy of full-out warfare designed not only for plundering, tribute-taking, and the cowing of opponents, but also for territorial control. This direct Frankish engagement in southern Gaul had other consequences: the landed elites of that part of the former Visigothic kingdom that spanned the Pyrenees switched from a nominal allegiance to the distant Muslim rulers to the Franks, in return for a promise to respect their Gothic laws. The Aquitainians themselves, however, received no such deal: for a decade from 759–69 each year the Franks campaigned in Aquitaine in a systematic programme; a small group of a dozen Frankish aristocrats were implanted as counts, controlling the region with their followers. Even then, the bloody and protracted nature of Pippin's campaigning underlines the strength of the Aquitainian elite with their military followings and fortified strongholds: taming Aquitaine took the full strength of the Frankish army for a decade. Indeed, even on Pippin's death in 768, Aquitaine remained a real worry, its restive state feeding into tension between Pippin's sons, the new kings Carloman and Charlemagne, as memories of Aquitainian attempts to exploit the political division which had followed Charles Martell's death remained live.

Just as that earlier political division had resulted in the deepening of Frankish involvement in Italy, with Pippin's brother's family fleeing over the Alps and impelling Pippin into ever closer contact with the Lombard king in Pavia and the pope in Rome, so the division of the Frankish realm between Pippin's two sons in 768 was to provide a further impetus for Carolingian involvement in Italian politics. Although Italy, unlike Aquitaine, was beyond even the nominal claims of the Merovingian overlordship, there were long traditions of Frankish involvement beyond the Alps. Just as Carolingian expansion into the south and over the Pyrenees was a direct result of the collapse of the Visigothic monarchy, so the waning of Byzantine power in Italy created a power vacuum into which the Franks were pulled.

It was the popes who did the pulling. With the emperor in Constantinople unable to provide meaningful protection for notionally imperial provinces in Italy, and the pope in secular terms a regional power who could not compete on the battlefield with the Lombard kings and dukes, Rome needed potent but preferably distant and pliant allies. As early as Martell's time, popes were bestowing honorifics on and acting as spiritual sponsors to the Carolingians. But despite these personal ties, the Franks proved difficult to pull into Italy as unambiguous allies of the papacy, for they also had long-standing ties to the Lombard court. Martell, for example, allowed the Lombard king Liudprand to act as sponsor for his son Pippin in 737, and failed to act on papal appeals for military help in 739. Further attempts to involve the Franks as papal allies against the Lombards took place in the 750s. In 751, as Pippin replaced the last Merovingian on the Frankish throne, the Lombards seized the remaining Byzantine possessions in northern Italy. Only after Pope Stephen's visit to Pippin in Francia, and his anointing of Pippin's family, was Frankish military aid forthcoming, in 756. Even then, although the Lombards promised to return formerly imperial territory in central Italy to the pope, no such restitution was forced and the Frankish aristocracy appeared restive at the potential involvement of Pippin in Italy. For the next decades, a delicate balance of power was maintained, with the Lombard king Desiderius marrying his daughters to the dukes of Bavaria and Benevento, and attempting to negotiate a further marriage with Charlemagne in 770.[10]

It was in fact a dramatic shift in the internal politics of the Frankish realm and the Carolingian family that transformed the situation: the end of the fragile internal balance between Charlemagne and his brother Carloman with the latter's death in 771 left Charlemagne no longer dependent on external alliances, and instead he married into the Almena aristocracy, previously strong supporters of Carloman, by taking Hildegard as his wife. As Carloman's wife and daughters fled to Desiderius' court, and given the close links between Desiderius and Bavaria, the temperature of Frankish–Lombard relations dropped dramatically. Thus in 774, in response to a further papal appeal for military help, Charlemagne wasted no time in marching into Italy.

The Frankish military, enriched and battle-hardened by a generation of warfare in Aquitaine, swept through northern Italy meeting little resistance: after a short siege of the Lombard capital, Pavia, Desiderius surrendered. Charlemagne became king of the Lombards, initially pursuing a policy of limited change, allowing the Lombard dukes and landowning class to continue to rule as before, but the new regime, unlike its predecessor, enjoyed the wholesale support of Rome. Change took place in the aftermath of a revolt in 776, when several of the north Italian dukes, doubtless mindful of the well-honoured pathway to the throne at Pavia, rebelled: as a result, Frankish aristocrats were introduced and Italy tied into the web of patronage centred on the Frankish court, although below this new aristocratic overclass little changed.

Italian sensitivities were further acknowledged in the aftermath of Charlemagne's visit to Rome in 780–1, when his infant son Pippin was made 'king of the Lombards', under his father's authority but with an Italian court; the Aquitainians were simultaneously granted their own king, Pippin's three-year-old brother Louis. By granting them infant Carolingian subkings, Charlemagne allowed Italian and Aquitainian elites to continue to function with their well-established regional political systems, and to maintain their own identities, whilst binding them to the Carolingian family.

The expansion of the Frankish realm: east of the Rhine

In Aquitaine and Italy, the Carolingians absorbed coherent Christian polities. In the other sphere of Carolingian conquest, east of the Rhine, matters were different. The sources, written with hindsight, equate conquest expansion with the promotion of Christianity and simplify a complex religious and political situation. The regions beyond the former Roman frontier had long been subject to Christian influence thanks to their subjection to the Merovingian kings, and the seventh century had seen an increasing impetus to missionary activity within the Merovingian church, through the agency of churchmen from the Romanised provinces of central and southern Gaul, and the development of a theology of mission by Frankish bishops such as St Amand. By the very end of the seventh century, this activity was given further impetus by missionaries from newly-converted England, men like the Anglo-Saxon Willibrord, drawing on the traditions of exile and pilgrimage inherited from the Irish church, operating with the spiritual blessing of the pope and the physical support of the Carolingians from 690 to 739.

The subsequent promotion of the cults of the leading Anglo-Saxon missionaries through the writing of hagiography in the late eighth and early ninth centuries tends to project the missions east of the Rhine as a matter of an alliance between Anglo-Saxon saints and Carolingian kings converting resolutely pagan peoples. But careful reading of the surviving material suggests a more ambiguous reality, that of a long history of mission by Franks as well as Anglo-Saxons, and of communities long exposed to Christianity but lacking a formal ecclesiastical structure. This was a world where indigenous cultural practices had melded with Christianity in a myriad local variations; a world where the inhabitants of

Frankfurt, 'the ford of the Franks', could commit an infant girl to the grave in a white silk tunic marked with a gold cross, accompanied by pots filled with the cooked flesh of bears and other wild animals.[11] Our perspective, however, is distorted by the emphasis in our sources on a handful of Anglo-Saxon missionaries whose cults were actively promoted by their disciples and encouraged by Carolingian rulers in the late eighth and ninth centuries: as a result, crucial individuals like Pirmin, an Aquitainian holy man active in southern Germany, constantly slip beneath our horizon and out of history.

The complexities of this situation, and the difficulties of our sources, are exemplified by the career of the Anglo-Saxon missionary Boniface. Boniface came to join the mission led by Willibrord in 716, and was active, again with papal blessing and Carolingian support, along the entire eastern frontier of the Frankish realm until his martyrdom in 754. Fostering an extended gaggle of disciples and founding a network of monastic houses, his mission produced a veritable hagiographical industry in the later eighth century. The authors in this tradition aimed to produce true 'missionary lives', founded on heroic deeds in a black-and-white clash with stubborn and recalcitrant pagans. As Boniface's biographer, Willibald, and his correspondents occasionally make clear, this was not an encounter with an alternative belief-system of red-blooded paganism. In searching for a vocabulary for their opponents, Boniface and his followers were frequently forced to use the language of heresy and sacrilege. In its classic definition heresy related to a theological position consciously and consistently held in opposition to the church's acknowledged teachings, whereas here it is a far more elastic concept, denoting a religious practice that Boniface's circle deemed aberrant. Where this self-styled holy man who actively sought a martyr's death saw 'pagan superstition' or 'obdurate error', others might see honest mistakes or even harmless custom. So when Boniface complained about a Bavarian priest who mangled his Latin pronunciation, the pope wrote, horrified, that a slip of language did not make a heretic. The kind of campaign in which Boniface and his followers were involved is best shown by the 'list of superstitions and errors' for suppression, drawn up and circulated at a church council in 743: it is a list of practices rooted in folklore and popular culture, ingrained rituals of agrarian life deemed unbecoming by bishops like Boniface, who wrote to the pope condemning the secular festivals marking the new year at Rome in similar terms.[12]

Boniface's hard line was far from universal: indeed, his major opponents were themselves bishops, such as the Irishman Clement, whom Boniface had deposed for his unorthodox views and practices, or the charismatic preacher and rival holy man Adalbert, likewise deposed on grounds of heresy. It is in the nitty-gritty of church foundation and ecclesiastical organisation that his legacy was most important, but also most controversial, for here his activities cut across the spheres of influence which had been built up in the late Merovingian period by Frankish churchmen. Bishops like Milo of Trier or Gewilib of Mainz were drawn from impeccably aristocratic circles closely allied to the Carolingians, and through their contacts their churches built up claims to property and power east of the Rhine, claims which Boniface's circle of disciples and church foundations, and his papally-authorised jurisdiction over missionary activity east of the Rhine, threatened. Boniface was to wage a campaign of complaint against 'Milo and his kind', complaining that these bishops behaved just the same as their aristocratic clients and kinsmen, drinking, hunting and fighting; but he had to tread carefully, and his successes, such as the deposition of Gewilib and his subsequent replacement by Boniface himself, were rarer than is sometimes realised. The subsequent writing up of Boniface and his circle probably misleads, in that it encourages us to make a wholesale and unqualified identification between their efforts and the expansion of the Frankish kingdom. In fact, the reality was more complex, as Boniface admitted in his letters: he had no alternative but to work through the Frankish court if he was to carry out his mission, but his relations with different rulers varied, and he could on occasion complain about the court as a den of corruption, doubtless frustrated by the political influence of the likes of Milo.[13] Ultimately, indeed, the success of Boniface, and still more of his shadowy and politically more ambiguous contemporaries like Pirmin, may have rested on the fact that they could not be seen as straightforward agents of Frankish imperialism taking their orders from the Carolingian court. It is probably no accident that the holy men responsible for the integration of the provinces east of the Rhine were outsiders not wholly associated with any one political faction – missionaries from southern Gaul and Ireland as well as England – who were able to act as intermediaries between the rough independence of these frontier communities and the Frankish court.

The focus of our narratives on the careers of missionaries means that the political processes that saw the integration of the eastern regions into the Frankish realm are murky. Frisia, although its rulers were pagan, had long-standing links with the Merovingian world: in the early decades of the eighth century the Frisians were firm allies of those Neustrian Franks opposed to Carolingian rule, and Martell's victory in the civil wars of the 710s seems to have brought them into the Carolingian sphere. Legal documents connected with the abbey of Echternach, founded thanks to Carolingian patronage by Willibrord in 698 show an evolving relationship between landowners in Toxandria and Willibrord, and eventually with Charles Martell himself, and archaeology suggests that hand-in-hand with this shift of political and religious allegiance went an intensification of landlord control over the peasantry. In Thuringia in central Germany, the local ruler, Hetan, although condemned by Boniface's biographer as a pagan, had likewise been a supporter of Willibrord, and as in Frisia the evidence for any real Frankish authority over landowning elites is scarce: a similar development to that suggested by the Frisian evidence, with local elites opting into the patronage of holy men like Willibrord, which ultimately connected them into the social circles associated with the Carolingian court, is likely. The hagiography associated with Boniface's circle, with its emphasis on conflict, thus distorts a subtle shifting of allegiances in which religious or political coercion played only a limited role.[14]

These cultural and social transformations were worked out far more violently in Saxony. Saxon society was very different from that in the other regions subject to Carolingian conquest. Although subject to nominal Merovingian overlordship, landowning elites were relatively diffuse and decentralised. This was a society of farmer-warriors, grouped together as a loose confederation: Carolingian texts describe local assemblies debating and making decisions.[15] We should resist the temptation to present Saxon society as some kind of primitive democracy, for this was still an unequal society dominated by male warriors whose position rested on the labour of the unfree and semi-free. Nonetheless, in a society without kings, courts, or an infrastructure of extensive political authority, even the top tier of landowners had limited horizons. In this decentralisation lay the strength of Saxon society: for the communities of warrior-farmers of much of northwestern Europe, becoming a part of the Saxon confederation was an attractive option precisely because it did not involve submission to a formal political hierarchy, with the demands for service and tribute that entailed. Indeed, by the eighth century communities across much of northern Germany were coalescing together in a shadowy process which rested as much on social and cultural affiliation as on military might: to Frankish eyes, the inhabitants of this region were Saxons. And from the early years of Charles Martell's reign on, Frankish kings engaged in a pattern of pre-emptive raiding, plundering and tribute-taking, designed to ensure quiescence, generate tribute, and deter Saxon activities of a similar order.

This pattern of border warfare changed dramatically under Charlemagne. Carolingian power rested on military success as the mechanism to mould the aristocracy together, and Pippin's reign had shown the possibilities offered by intensive annual campaigning. With the final pacification of Aquitaine, Saxony was an appealing target for continued expansive warfare, which offered apparently easy pickings. It also offered Charlemagne the opportunity of saving souls by fighting in the name of Christianity, for the Saxons had remained resolutely pagan. Saxon resistance to Christian conversion, in fact, once again points to the cultural coherence of Saxon society: without kings or extensive aristocracies to work through, missionaries had to preach directly to fighting and farming communities whose traditional religious practices were rooted in the landscape, and to whom the world of Christian rulers had limited appeal. From the outset of the Saxon campaigns, Charlemagne put the religious issue at the forefront, destroying the major cult site known as the Irminsul in 772. Warfare had not been previously espoused by the Christian church as a means of winning converts – although Christian rulers had often played on their credentials when encountered with non-Christians – and Charlemagne's initiative here marks a new self-assertiveness by the Franks, seeing themselves as God's chosen people whose destiny was coterminous with the spread of true Christianity. By 776, captives were undergoing forced mass baptism, and Charlemagne's personal identification with the programme of conquest and conversion was demonstrated by the foundation, in 777, of a new centre for Frankish rule and the Christian church in Saxony: Carlopolis at modern Paderborn. Although the initial complex was quickly destroyed in a Saxon counterattack, Paderborn was to remain the political and religious centre of Frankish power in Saxony.

In fact, Saxony proved remarkably difficult for the Franks to conquer: Charlemagne's biographer, Einhard, gave the Saxon wars pride of place, commenting that the forty years they spanned were a reflection of Saxon treachery.[16] In fact, not only is the forty-year span misleading, so is the notion of Saxon treachery. In a decentralised confederation such as this, individual groups of

Saxons might submit, and their leaders give hostages, but this was no guarantee of the behaviour of the Saxons as a whole: Carolingian perceptions, lumping together all these loosely linked groups as a single people, the Saxons, mislead. Control of the fortified centres around which Saxon resistance was organised – and around which military elites do seem to have been emerging in the eighth century – was vital, and even this did not guarantee control of the countryside. Moreover, the experience of concerted aggression by the Franks further stimulated the development of Saxon elites, with the warleader Widukind approaching the status of a 'national' leader by the 780s. By the 790s, Saxon resistance was isolated to the east and north, and the remaining campaigns until 804 were concerned with mopping up these regions, not with control of the Saxon heartlands.

The forceful imposition of Christianity further aroused Saxon resistance, heightening as it did the cultural differences between conquerors and conquered. Frankish puzzlement at the ease with which Saxons could undergo baptism and adopt a new faith, yet remain tied to traditional religious practices and resistant to the demands of the new institution of the church, led to hard-line legislation, imposing secular penalties, and ultimately death, to those who resisted Christianisation or failed to pay the tithe. Indeed, Frankish experience in Saxony led to a fascinating and more or less unprecedented debate on the methodology of mission, with Alcuin, one of Charlemagne's key advisors, urging a more gentle and gradual line seeking to educate rather than coerce, the latter only likely to breed resistance.[17] Christianity mattered not just because of the Franks' ideological investment in their identification as God's chosen people. It offered a way to transform the cultural conservatism of rural Saxony, through a network of priests and churches necessarily manned by Frankish churchmen. The interlocking processes of Christianisation and Carolingian conquest facilitated the development of a new social hierarchy. A new generation of Saxons, educated in Frankish churches and Frankish aristocratic households where they had been brought up as hostages or guests, formed a new elite of counts and churchmen, happy to enjoy the extensive rights of command and the concentration of landowning that conquest and Christianisation entailed. Where their forefathers had ensured the continued remembrance of the dead beyond the grave by the erection of the barrow burials so favoured by late Merovingian elites along the Rhine, this new generation of Saxon aristocrats avidly invested in monasticism, with its 'gold card' service of prayer for the souls of the dead.

Further south, the duchies of Alemannia and Bavaria were politically firmer and therefore posed a different challenge to the Carolingians. Alemannia, indeed, was politically coherent enough to remain securely outside Boniface's sphere of activity, and had both a structure of bishops on former Roman sites such as Strasbourg and Constance, and several wealthy monasteries. The Aleman ducal family had been consistently opposed to Martell and his father in the early eighth century, and Alemannia had been the object of successive Frankish campaigns, culminating in the Frankish victory at Cannstadt in 746, where according to later tradition the flower of the Aleman elite were slain. The documentary evidence supplied in the archives of the monastery of St-Gallen suggests a more nuanced picture, documenting as it does the continuing vitality of local networks of

Aleman landowners around the monastery through the eighth century; these ties led to the deposition of the abbot of the St-Gallen in 755 and the abbey's subjection to the pro-Frankish bishop of Constance. As was later the case in Aquitaine and Bavaria, the Carolingians took care to dismantle the ducal office and its resources: in the immediate aftermath of 746 Alemannia lay in the control of two favoured Frankish aristocrats, Warin and Ruthard, remembered with real hostility in the local sources. By the last quarter of the eighth century, however, a thicker network of counts begins to appear and spread through the province, recruiting local landowners and tying them into the Carolingian system.

The Frankish takeover of Bavaria, the most easterly of the peripheral principalities, was more complex, longer drawn out and, intriguingly, almost entirely peaceful. Precisely because of its distance from the Frankish heartlands, Bavaria had always enjoyed a great degree of independence, and by the eighth century this political system enjoyed real strength and coherence. The Agilolfing family which ruled Bavaria actively built up the church, recruiting missionaries from elsewhere in the Frankish realm such as St Rupert, founder of the bishopric of Salzburg, St Emmeram of Regensburg, and St Corbinian of Freising; their sponsorship of church reform actually predated that of the Carolingians, with Duke Theudo establishing a regular structure of bishoprics in 716. Theudo also fostered ties of alliance with the Carolingians, marrying a sister of Plectrude, Martell's stepmother. Carolingian connections were to play a central role in every subsequent ducal succession within Bavaria, but they were also manipulated by Bavarian rulers anxious to maintain their traditional freedom of manoeuvre. Martell intervened in the ducal succession after a long civil war between rival claimants in 717–25, and married into the Agilolfing family; in 736, when the direct Agilolfing line ended, he engineered the succession of Odilo. On Martell's death, Odilo married Chiltrude, one of Martell's daughters, without her brothers' permission, and revolted; on Odilo's death, it was one of Martell's sons, Grifo, who had himself made duke and went into revolt. Carolingian sons, daughters, and cousins, politically secure in the Bavarian duchy, were potent leaders capable of attracting a significant aristocratic following from across the eastern portions of the Frankish realm.

Bavaria posed an implicit threat to the efforts of first Pippin and then Charlemagne to construct a political order centred on their own person, as the career of the last Bavarian duke, Tassilo, demonstrates. Tassilo was Chiltrude and Odilo's son, and so Charles Martell's grandson, combining Agilolfing and Carolingian blood. In 748, at the age of eight, he was installed as duke of Bavaria in Grifo's place by Pippin, and placed under the guardianship of his mother – remember, Pippin's sister – who died in 755. Pippin vigorously asserted his claims over Bavaria: legal documents in the duchy were dated from the year of Pippin's reign, and the Bavarians in 748 swore not to rebel against him. But, although Tassilo was in no theoretical sense independent, Bavaria remained structurally separate from the Frankish kingdom. Indeed, as Tassilo reached maturity, his diplomatic and military activities and ecclesiastical policy made him a real force: marriage to Liutbirga, a daughter of the Lombard king Desiderius, cemented close political links with Italy and facilitated connections with the papacy, whilst reforming synods at Dingolfing and Neuching in 772, and lavish patronage of important monastic foundations like Mondsee, underlined his control of the duchy. The surviving records of ducal endowment of these new monasteries also hint at a complex system of land-gifts whereby dukes secured aristocratic support. And Bavaria enjoyed an open frontier with Slavic tribes in the east that offered real opportunities for lucrative and charisma-building campaigning against genuine pagans whom the Bavarian church was seeking to convert. In 772 a scholar attracted by the glittering lights of Tassilo's court was even able to laud his patron as a 'new Constantine' for his victories against the pagans.[18]

These internal developments within Bavaria were the backdrop for repeated attempts by Charlemagne to humiliate his cousin into submission. Tassilo was dangerous enough a potential rival for the sources consistently and insistently to blacken his name. According to the official version, written up after Tassilo's fall in the *Royal Frankish Annals*, the Bavarian duke was patently disloyal, a breaker of oaths and, worst of all in the macho aristocratic society of the eighth century, a deserter. For – so the official Carolingian historiography claims – in 757 shortly after coming of age, Tassilo had visited his uncle Pippin at Soissons and performed a ritual subordinating himself to Pippin as a his lord, and swearing oaths of loyalty; subsequently, in spite of the obligations created by this ritual, he had refused to fight on his lord's behalf, and in 763 he even left a campaign without his lord's permission. For generations, this account has been taken as an accurate description of Tassilo's entry into a relationship subordinate to Pippin, rooted in personal lordship, early in his reign, whilst the memory of Pippin's intervention in 748 was still fresh. The *Annals* underline the humiliating nature of Tassilo's subjection, and so heighten the heinous nature of his alleged breaches, by claiming that he became a vassal of Pippin's, a status which was at this date rare and normally restricted to those of relatively humble origins. However, by juxtaposing the account of the *Royal Frankish Annals* and subsequent pro-Carolingian sources with the fragmentary testimonies of regional chronicles, Matthias Becher has demonstrated that the official Carolingian account is a tissue of misrepresentations. To contemporaries, Tassilo had done nothing more than enter into a relationship of friendship and alliance with his uncle, and there was no question of his personal dependence.[19]

Tassilo's case was worth rewriting to this extent precisely because the 780s and 790s – the period immediately preceding the creation of the *Royal Frankish Annals* – had seen a concerted campaign to force his subjection to the Frankish king, and the full integration of Bavaria into the Frankish kingdom. The account in the *Annals* provided a historical justification for this new assertiveness on Charlemagne's part. In 781, following the intervention of the pope, at that point closely allied to Charlemagne, Tassilo had visited his cousin at Worms and sworn unspecified oaths (we do not know what they signified). This meeting signalled that the relationship between Bavarian duke and Frankish king was a live issue, for the first time in a quarter of a century. In a complex series of triangular negotiations that culminated in the visit of two Bavarian churchmen, Arn of Salzburg and Hunric of Mondsee, to Rome in 787, Charlemagne pushed the claim that Tassilo had failed to meet his obligations to Pippin, demanding a renewal of his oaths. Tassilo, for his part resisted – surely a sign that Charlemagne's claims were novelties, not the recapitulation of a submission which had previously taken place – and it is testimony to his political standing that the Pope was reluctant to intervene. Eventually, when in 788 Tassilo refused to swear the oaths or visit Charlemagne as requested, Frankish armies were assembled and marched on Bavaria: no combat broke out, however, as a significant body of Bavarian aristocrats – many of whom had ties of kinship and property beyond the duchy's frontiers – swapped sides and left Tassilo no choice but to surrender. He was then made to give up the regalia of the Bavarian duchy and tonsured in a monastery; his standing was such that six years later, in 794, he was again summoned from the monastery and made to recite the charges brought against him. Bavaria was subsequently ruled by a series of counts, overseen by Charlemagne's brother-in-law, Gerold, but tellingly not by a duke, who wielded too much independent power.

Beyond plunder and tribute

The eighth century saw a huge increase in the area ruled directly from the Frankish court. It is possible to overestimate the role of warfare in this success story: whilst Aquitaine and Saxony were subjected to year-on-year campaigning, elsewhere the threat of the sword alternated with more peaceful processes, as landowning elites were encouraged to plug into the patronage systems of the Frankish aristocracy and their kings. The wartrail was thus one central aspect in Carolingian success, primarily important for the loyalties it generated, based on the expectation of annual plundering and tribute taking. Charlemagne's biographer, Einhard, writing sometime between 817 and 827, looked back nostalgically on his hero doubling the size of the Frankish kingdom: there had been a saying, he claimed, that went 'if a Frank is your friend, he's certainly not your neighbour'! Although Einhard drew on classical models of Roman imperial biography, his commemoration of his former lord and master – he had been talent-spotted in youth for his intellect and served his career as a courtier at Charlemagne's court – privileged wars and conquests, and it has cast a long shadow down the centuries, obscuring the processes whereby landed elites realigned their interests and found a place within the Frankish kingdom.[20]

For expansion could not go on forever. Einhard wrote long, long, after the annual campaigns under royal leadership had ceased: his account is here tinged with his nostalgia for a golden age which was ending even as he began his courtly career in the last decades of the eighth century. By the 790s the pace of campaigning was slowing, and the king was leading armies in person less frequently. Charlemagne made a series of conscious and sensible strategic decisions about when and where to stop, and with the defeat of the Avars in 793, following a three-year campaign led by his sons and generals, planned large-scale expansive warfare was over. The end of expansion necessitated a new policy of frontier commands coupled with political and cultural influence over neighbouring rulers. And, now the mutual loyalties of the wartrail could no longer glue together the Carolingian system, the less visible processes of social and political integration becoming all the more important if the fruits of three generations of Frankish success were to be enjoyed. If we take enough care, and read outside of the bald accounts of Carolingian propagandists, it is possible to detect an echo of the voices, truculent and suspicious, of those who found themselves forced to adapt to the new political order. By listening for these grumbles, we begin to gain a clue of the scale of the challenge faced by the Carolingians in ruling their expanded realm.

Our first echo dates from 786, when a group of disaffected landowners from central Germany entered a sworn conspiracy against Charlemagne. Though the official sources, written with hindsight and propagandist intent, downplay the scale of the revolt and label the rebels as disaffected Franks, an account written by the abbot of Murbach on the upper Rhine, suggests that this was a serious threat.[21] It points to Charlemagne's direct interference in the affairs of regional society, in particular his meddling in the making of marriage alliances, as the flashpoint. The rebels swore to kill Charlemagne if he ever crossed the Rhine again, and voiced their opposition with respect to a resolutely Merovingian political geography, in which they were a distinct people, the Thuringians, left to do as they pleased in their region. A settlement was only reached thanks to the mediation of the abbot of Fulda; the rebels were taken to various shrines in Francia and made to swear their loyalty on relics. The message – that they were subjects of the Frankish king to whom they owed absolute loyalty – was reinforced by the punishments of blinding, execution and expropriation, reserved for traitors, meted out to the ring-leaders. In response to the revolt, not only were sworn associations like that formed by the rebels banned, but oaths of fidelity to the king were taken from all free adult males across the kingdom. That is, exclusive horizontal groupings were no longer allowed, but the obligations of all free men to the king were to be insisted upon. Charlemagne was no longer the leader of a loose aristocratic alliance, but the apex of a hierarchical political system that rested on vertical obligations of loyalty held together by a supernatural glue of solemn undertakings made on holy relics.

Our second story comes from the central Italian abbey of San Vincenzo al Volturno in 783.[22] The abbot, a Lombard named Poto, left Mass early, so as to avoid the prayers for the health of the king and his family on which the regime insisted; he was alleged to have said that were it not for his responsibility to secure the best for the monastery, he would treat Charlemagne no better than a dog and get rid of the Franks. A faction of monks of Frankish origin brought a series of accusations against Poto. The case was referred to the pope, who brokered a compromise whereby the abbot was found innocent – he denied slandering Charlemagne and claimed he had only left Mass early because of urgent business – and the competing factions of monks reconciled. Whereas in central Germany, Charlemagne had been able to negotiate a settlement which allowed physical retaliation against his opponents, in central Italy we have a more delicate situation. San Vincenzo stood on the borderlands of the realm, and enjoyed good relations with the Lombard dukes of Spoleto and Benevento, who acknowledged Charlemagne's overlordship but were effectively independent princes. Nonetheless, the San Vincenzo affair does have marked similarities with the Thuringian revolt. It again points to the role of monasteries as both focal points for regional elites, and key agencies through which the regime sought to assert itself. It again points to elites beyond the heartlands of Carolingian power reluctant to acknowledge any vertical relationship of subjection to the Frankish king, and instead talking up an independent, non-Frankish, identity. Finally, it points to the importance of a supernatural web of oath and prayer, invoking God in the support of the king of the Franks. Prayers for the king and kingdom, insisted upon again and again by the regime, tied the realm together, complementing and supplementing the oaths of fidelity sworn by free men across the realm. Rituals of this kind could not prevent inevitable political conflicts, but they could create a Carolingian-centred framework within which the landed elites of western Europe pursued their interests. After all, conspiracies and claims like those revealed in our two episodes, turning on the possibility that Carolingian kingship might be simply rejected, were replaced by new patterns of unrest by the 790s, as malcontents rallied around slighted Carolingians and rebelled in support of their alleged claims. This framework was to hold good for a century. To understand how the embrace of Carolingian kingship succeeded in holding together the landed elites of western Europe, we need to analyse the cultural and social system it sustained.

Bibliographical essay

General works

Pride of place must go to R. McKitterick, ed., *New Cambridge Medieval History* II (Cambridge, 1995), which is firmly focused on the Carolingian Empire and includes studies of all major issues, as well as an excellent bibliography: it is the first port of call for all topics in eighth- and ninth-century Frankish history. There are a number of textbook accounts of the Carolingian Empire, most of them giving pride of place to Charlemagne in particular, and looking dated in their reading of society and politics in particular. R. McKitterick, *The Frankish Kingdoms under the Carolingians, 751–987* (London, 1983) remains a really thorough introduction to the cultural and political history, and M. Costambeys, M. Innes and S. Maclean, *The Carolingian World* (Cambridge, 2007), which introduces newer themes in political, social and economic history; D. Bullough, *The Age of Charlemagne* (London, 1965) remains the most useful of older works, whilst P. Riché, *The Carolingians: A Family who Shaped Europe* (Philadelphia, 1993) offers a traditional narrative; there are a wealth of other textbook accounts, most outdated in their interpretation of social and political development.

Sources in translation

There is a wealth of source material available. P. Dutton, *Carolingian Civilisation: A Reader* (Peterborough Ont., 1993) is an excellent collection, the starting point for anyone wanting a flavour of the period. Various narrative, documentary and legislative sources for the reign of Charlemagne are available in H. Loyn and J. Perceval, *The Reign of Charlemagne* (London, 1975) and P. D. King, *Charlemagne: Translated Sources* (Kendal, 1986); these are, sadly, the only way to gain a flavour of the documentary and legislative riches, the volume of which can thus easily be underestimated. Pride of place in any study of Charlemagne must be given to Einhard's life, which is available in many translations, including in the collections listed above; the best way into Einhard is the collection of material tr. P. Dutton, *Charlemagne's Courtier* (Peterborough, Ont. 1997), which provides material on Einhard's career to contextualise the biography; the major annals are likewise translated in the various collections, and for the *Royal Frankish Annals* see B. Scholz, *Carolingian Chronicles* (Ann Arbor, 1972), whilst the continuations of the *Chronicle* of Fredegar, tr. J. M. Wallace-Hadrill (Oxford, 1960) give the official view of the early years of Carolingian kingship; for later rewritings of seventh- and eighth-century history see above all the *Prior Metz Annals*, tr. P. Fouracre and R. Gerberding, *Late Merovingian France* (Manchester, 1996). For Boniface and his circle see C. H. Talbot, *The Anglo-Saxon Missionaries on the Continent* (London, 1954), for the hagiography and a short selection of letters; T. Noble and T. Head, *Soldiers of Christ* (London, 1998) also has a good selection of hagiography, and all of Boniface's correspondence is tr. E. Emerton, *The Letters of St Boniface* (New York, 1940). A selection of Alcuin's letters, unfortunately selected from an English perspective, is available in S. Allott, *Alcuin of York* (York, 1974). P. Godman, *Poetry of the Carolingian Renaissance* (London, 1985) is an excellent way into the most vivid but also most difficult source on the Carolingian court. Insights into Charlemagne's court are also available from the biographies of his cousins Adalard and Wala, but these were shaped by the conflicts of Louis the Pious' reign in which their subjects were such central actors: for a translation see A. Cabannis, *Charlemagne's Cousins* (Syracuse, 1974). For the view from Rome and Ravenna, see R. Davis, *The Lives of the Eighth-Century Popes* (Liverpool, 1992) and *The Lives of the Ninth-Century Popes* (Liverpool, 1995), and D. Deliyannis, *Agnellus of Ravenna: The Book of the Pontiffs of Ravenna* (Washington, 2004); unfortunately most of the voluminous papal correspondence from this period remains untranslated.

Kings and kingship

Most new work continues to be structured around the reigns of individual rulers: most of the resulting conference proceedings include invaluable overviews of cultural and social developments as well as political studies, and are invaluable ways into the period. On Martell, see now P. Fouracre, *The Age of Charles Martell* (London, 2001); Pippin, an interesting and important figure, remains neglected, but a special issue of the journal *Francia* 9 (1976) contains a series of useful French and German studies, and see now M. Becher and J. Jarnut, eds, *Das Dynastiewechsel von 751* (Münster, 2005), with several papers in English; this recent interest is in part a reaction to R. McKitterick's questioning of traditional accounts of the centrality of papal involvement in 751, see e.g. 'The illusion of power in the Carolingian annals', *English Historical Review* 115 (2000), revised in her *History and Memory in the Carolingian World* (Cambridge, 2004).

On Charlemagne, the classic collection of studies, most in French or German, is W. Braunfels, ed., *Karl der Grosse. Lebenswerk und Nachleben* (Dusseldorf, 1965–7) 5 vols; for an overview of recent approaches, in English, see the essays collected in J. Storey, ed., *Charlemagne: Empire and Society* (Manchester, 2005), and the useful collection of essays, several in English, inspired by the anniversary of Charlemagne's meeting with Pope Leo at Paderborn in 799, P. Godman, J. Jarnut and P. Johanek, *Am Vorabend der Kaiserkrönung* (Berlin, 2002). These thematic treatments have more to offer than the recent flood of biographies, most of which retell the story told by Einhard and the *Royal Annals* at the expense of proper analysis: the pick of the crop that has appeared so far is M. Becher, *Charlemagne* (New Haven, 2003), whilst R. Collins, *Charlemagne* (London, 1998), offers a solid narrative. The forthcoming studies by R. McKitterick and J. Nelson promise to use the biographical form to offer more sustained rethinking of the man and his reign.

Sustained rethinking is timely because an exciting strand of recent work has interrogated the sources anew, in particular asking questions about their role as conscious constructions and manipulations of the past rather than simple reports of 'what really happened'. The essays collected in R. McKitterick, *History and Memory in the Carolingian World* (Cambridge, 2005) are of great importance here: see earlier 'Constructing the past in the early Middle Ages: the case of the Royal Frankish Annals', *Transactions of the Royal Historical Society* 7 (1997). Matthias Becher's careful reconstruction of the relationship between Charlemagne and Tassilo of Bavaria, their implications and their misrepresentation in the *Royal Frankish Annals* was important here for using local annals to get behind the façade of court historiography: *Eid und Herrschaft: Studien zum Herrscherethos Karls des Grossen* (Sigmaringen, 1993) and see now S. Airlie, 'Narratives of triumph and rituals of submission: Charlemagne's mastering of Bavaria', *Transactions of the Royal Historical Society* 9 (1999). Einhard and his biography of Charlemagne will be the subject of a major new study by David Ganz (for a taster see his chapter in Storey, ed., *Charlemagne*); recent work underlines how carefully his clever representation of his hero needs handling: e.g. M. Innes, 'The classical tradition in the Carolingian renaissance', *International Journal of the Classical Tradition* 3 (1997) and M. Kempshall, 'Some Ciceronian models for Einhard's life of Charlemagne', *Viator* 26 (1995). Several of the essays in Y. Hen and M. Innes, eds, *The Uses of the Past in the Early Middle Ages* (Cambridge, 2000) are useful on the links between historiography and ideology. Finally, a series of studies by J. Nelson have attempted to gain insight into Charlemagne's own personality: e.g. 'The voice of Charlemagne', in R. Gameson and H. Leyser, eds, *Belief and Culture in the Middle Ages* (Oxford, 2001).

Regional studies and landowning elites

Aristocratic networks have been one of the major subjects of study among Carolingianists for over half a century now: for a bibliography on aristocratic identity, kinship and lordship see chapter 10 below. The works that follow offer ways of understanding the Carolingian impact on the various regional landowning elites of the early medieval west. Regional studies have been a major growth area which in the process have transformed our understanding; drawing on a German tradition of studying the structure of elites and aristocratic families, more recently the example of French regional histories pioneered by the likes of Georges Duby for the post-Carolingian period, scholars have recreated the dynamics of local communities and their changing relationships to the political centre. All of this is possible, of course, thanks to the richness of the documentary material. R. Le Jan, ed., *La Royauté et les élites dans l'Europe carolingienne* (Lille, 1998), gives a good range of case-studies of relationships between kings and regional elites, mainly in French or German. One topic that is of central importance but has only just begun to receive attention is the role of ethnic identities – and particularly the interaction between regional identity and Frankish kinship – in these relationships. P. Geary, *The Myth of Nations: The Ethnic Origins of Europe* (Princeton, 2001) has some thought-provoking pages that ought to stimulate further debate, and see the important study by W. Pohl, 'Zur Bedeutung ethnischer Unterscheidungen in der frühen Karolingerzeit', *Studien zur Sachsenforschung* 12 (1999).

The areas east of the Rhine are best-studied. On Saxony, M. Becher, *Rex, dux und gens. Untersuchungen zur Entstehung des sachischen Herozogtums im 9 und 10 Jht* (Husum, 1996) draws on recent work about ethnicity; the Carolingian conquest itself is surprisingly little studied, but D. Green and F. Siegmund, eds, *The Continental Saxons* (Woodbridge, 2001) surveys a wide range of evidence, and there are useful insights in B. Effros, 'De partibus Saxoniae and the regulation of mortuary custom. A Carolingian campaign of Christianisation or the suppression of Saxon identity?', *Revue Belge de Philologie et d'Histoire* 75 (1995), C. Carroll, 'The bishops of Saxony in the first century after Christianisation', *Early Medieval Europe* 8 (1999), and E. Goldberg, 'Popular revolt, dynastic politics and aristocratic factionalism in the early Middle Ages: the Saxon Stellinga reconsidered', *Speculum* 70 (1995). For the Rhineland, M. Innes, *State and Society in the Early Middle Ages* (Cambridge, 2000), with full references to earlier German literature; on Alsace, H. Hummer, *Politics and Power in Early Medieval Europe: Alsace and the Frankish Realm, 600–1000* (Cambridge, 2006); on Alemannia, M. Borgolte, *Geschichte der Grafschaften Alemanniens im fränkischer Zeit* (Sigmaringen, 1983) is fundamental, with a companion prosopography of *Die Grafen Alemanniens* (Sigmaringen, 1984). W. Brown, *Unjust Seizure: Conflict, Interest and Authority in an Early Medieval Society* (Ithaca, 2001) gives insight into the transformation of Bavarian society; for all aspects of Agilolfing and Carolingian Bavaria there are a number of important German works, e.g. H. Wolfram, *Die Geburt Mitteleuropas* (Vienna, 1987) and H. Wolfram and A. Schwarcz, eds, *Die Bayern und ihre Nachbarn* (Vienna, 1985).

The Frankish heartlands, the key areas, urgently need proper study: prosopographical essays studying individual families or local histories of specific cities and churches predominate. For eighth-century Austrasia two books by M. Werner – *Adelsfamilien im Umkreis der frühen Karolinger* (Sigmaringen, 1982) and *Die Lütticher Raum im frühen Karolingerzeit* (Sigmaringen, 1984) – are indispensable, whilst for the west H. Atsma, ed., *La Neustrie* (Sigmaringen, 1989) is useful. On Burgundy, and indeed for much of the region south of the Loire, similarly there has been little in the way of synthesis since the first half of the twentieth century. On Aquitaine, M. Rouche, *L'Aquitaine des Wisigothes aux Arabes, 418–781*

(Paris, 1979), is good on the last days of 'independence', and on Carolingian rule there are a number of papers by J. Martindale collected in her *Status, Authority and Regional Power* (London, 1997), whilst C. Lauranson-Rosaz, *L'Auvergne et ses marges* (Le Puy, 1987) is rare among French regional studies in giving good coverage to the ninth century. P. Geary, *Aristocracy in Provence* (Stuttgart, 1985) is fundamental on the south in the first half of the eighth century.

Italy is much better studied, but mainly in French and German studies of social transformations from the ninth to the twelfth centuries. C. Wickham, 'Aristocratic power in eighth-century Lombard Italy', in A. C. Murray, ed., *After Rome's Fall* (Toronto, 1998) is fundamental on the Lombard kingdom on the eve of the Carolingian conquest, whilst E. Hlawitschka's prosopography of *Franken, Alemannien, Bayern und Burgunder im Oberitalien* (Freiburg, 1960) illuminates the Frankish takeover, and see A. Castagnetti, *Teotisci nella 'Langobardia' carolingia* (Verona, 1995) for issues of identity. Excellent local studies in English are C. Wickham, *The Mountains and the City* (Oxford, 1998) on Lucca, M. Costambeys, *Piety and Property in Early Medieval Europe* (Cambridge, 2007) on the Sabine, and R. Balzaretti, *The Lands of St Ambrose* (Turnhout, forthcoming) on Milan. The magisterial P. Toubert, *Les structures de Latium médiéval, IX–XII siècles* (2 vols, Paris, 1973) inspired a series of studies such as L. Feller, *Les Abruzzes médiévales, IX–XII siècles* (Rome, 1998) and J.-P. Delameau, *Arezzo: Espace et sociétés 715–1230* (Rome, 1996); H. Keller, *Adelsherrschaft and städtische Gesellschaft im Oberitalien, 9–12 Jht.* (Tübingen, 1979) represents a different, German, historiographical school.

Warfare and society

On the role of warfare in Carolingian society the fundamental treatment is T. Reuter, 'Plunder and tribute in the Carolingian Empire', *Transactions of the Royal Historical Society* 35 (1985), complemented by his article in R. Collins and P. Godman, eds, *Charlemagne's Heir* (Oxford, 1989). Military strategy, especially the role of heavy cavalry – long overstated – and its logistics have been dealt with in a series of specialist studies, best accessed via two recent surveys, B. Bachrach, *Early Carolingian Warfare: Prelude to Empire* (Philadelphia, 2001) and G. Halsall, *Warfare and Society in the Early Medieval West* (London, 2002). The relevant chapters of S. Reynolds, *Fiefs and Vassals* (London, 1994) constitute a final devastating blow to the gradually discredited view that military necessities inaugurated a social revolution in the Carolingian countryside thanks to the widespread adoption of 'feudal' systems of land tenure; for the older orthodoxy see F. L. Ganshof, *Feudalism* (London, 1953). The fact that formal systems of personal dependence did not accord to the neat totalising models developed by an older generation of historians should not, however, lead to us ignore them: compare M. Innes, 'Practices of property in the Carolingian Empire', in J. Davies and M. McCormick, eds, *Rethinking the Early Medieval West* (Aldershot, 2007).

On the ways in which Carolingian warfare was ritualised and legitimated see M. McCormick, 'The liturgy of war in the early Middle Ages: crisis, liturgies and the Carolingian monarchy', *Viator* 15 (1984), along with the relevant chapters of his

Eternal Victory (Cambridge, 1986); articles by Fouracre and Nelson in G. Halsall, ed., *Violence and Society in the Early Medieval West* (Woodbridge, 1998); for aspects of the aristocracy's martial identity see R. Le Jan in F. Theuws and J. Nelson, eds, *Rituals of Power from Late Antiquity to the Early Middle Ages* (Leiden, 1999), K. Leyser, 'Early medieval canon law and the origins of knighthood', in L. Fenske *et al.*, eds, *Institutionen, Gesellschaft und Kultur im frühen Mittelalter* (Sigmaringen, 1984), reprinted in his *Communications and Power in Medieval Europe I: The Carolingian and Ottonian Centuries* (London, 1994) and J. Nelson, 'Ninth-century knighthood', in C. Harper-Bill, ed., *Essays in Medieval History Presented to R. Allen Brown* (London, 1989), reprinted in her *The Frankish World* (London, 1995).

Notes

1. Ermold the Black, *Panegyric on Louis the Pious*, relevant section tr. P. Godman, *Poetry of the Carolingian Renaissance* (London, 1985), pp. 225–6.
2. Einhard, *Life of Charlemagne*, tr. P. Dutton, *Charlemagne's Courtier* (Peterborough, Ont., 1997), ch. 24.
3. Prologue to Salic Law: M. Garrison, 'The Franks as the new Israel', in Y. Hen and M. Innes, eds, *The Uses of the Past in the Early Middle Ages* (Cambridge, 2000); continuation of Fredegar: M. Wallace-Hadrill, ed., *The Fourth Book of the Chronicle of Fredegar with its continuations* (Oxford, 1960); *Prior Metz Annals*: P. Fouracre and R. Gerberding, *Late Merovingian France* (Manchester, 1996).
4. C. Wickham, 'Aristocratic power in eighth-century Lombard Italy', in A. C. Murray, ed., *After Rome's Fall* (London, 1998).
5. See T. J. Rivers, tr., *The Laws of the Alamans and Bavarians* (Philadelphia, 1977).
6. This took place in 742 under Martell's son Pippin, according to the ninth-century *Gesta episcoporum Autissiodorensium*, ed. G. Waitz, *Monumenta Germaniae Historica Scriptores* 13 (Berlin, 1881), pp. 393–400, esp. pp. 394–5.
7. *Liber Historiae Francorum* ch. 50, tr. Fouracre and Gerberding, *Late Merovingian France.*
8. See Garrison, 'The Franks as new Israel?' for the activities of the scribe Baddilo in both writing the new *Lex Salica* prologue and the remarkable charter for the refounded family monastery of Prüm advertising Pippin's royal ministry (ed. E. Muhlbacher, *Die Urkunden Pippins, Karlmanns und Karls des Grossen: Monumenta Germaniae Historica Diplomata* I (Berlin, 1906) no. 16; these sentiments are echoed in legislation and in a special issue of coins bearing the legend 'eleimosina' ('alms'), and fit with the family tradition reported a generation later by Paul the Deacon, *Gesta episcoporum Mettensium*, ed. G. Pertz, *Monumenta Germaniae Historica Scriptores* 2 (Berlin, 1829), on St Arnulf's prophecy that the descendents of his younger son, who had used his *facultates* for the good of the poor, would become kings. Pippin's royal representation through these media deserves sustained study.
9. P. Geary, *Aristocracy in Provence* (Stuttgart, 1985).

10. J. L. Nelson, 'Making a difference in the eighth century: the daughters of Desiderius', in Murray, ed., *After Rome's Fall.*
11. A. Hampel, *Der Kaiserdom zu Frankfurt am Main, Ausgrabungen 1991–3* (Nussloch, 1994).
12. Boniface, *Letters* 30 (Rome), 54 (Bavarian priest), tr. E. Emerton (New York, 1940). 'List of superstitions and errors', tr. P. Dutton, *Carolingian Civilisation* (Peterborough, Ont., 1994).
13. See Boniface, *Letters*, tr. Emerton, esp. nos 47 (Adalbert and Clement), 51 (distaste for court).
14. F. Theuws, 'Landed property and manorial organisation in northern Austrasia', in Theuws and N. Roymans, eds, *Images of the Past* (Amsterdam, 1991), and M. Costambeys, 'An aristocratic community on the northern Frankish frontier, 690–726', *Early Medieval Europe* 3 (1994).
15. *Life of Lebuin*, tr. C. H. Talbot, *The Anglo-Saxon Missionaries on the Continent* (London, 1954).
16. Einhard, *Life of Charlemagne*, ch. 7, tr. Dutton.
17. Alcuin, *Letters*, tr. S. Allott, *Alcuin of York* (York, 1974) nos 3, 56, 59, 133, 137.
18. M. Garrison, 'Letters to a king and Biblical exempla', *Early Medieval Europe* 7 (1998).
19. M. Becher, *Eid und Herrschaft: Untersuchungen zur Herrscherethos Karls des Grossen* (Sigmaringen, 1993).
20. Einhard, *Life of Charlemagne*, tr. Dutton: the first of the three sections of the biography – by far the longest – covers wars and conquests.
21. *'Annals of St Nazarius'* s.a. 786, tr. P. D King, *Charlemagne: Translated Sources* (Kendal, 1987), pp. 154–5.
22. *Codex Carolinus*, ed. W. Gundlach, *Monumenta Germaniae Historica Epistolae III* (Berlin, 1892), nos 66–7, pp. 593–7.

10

'Peace, unity and concord among the Christian people': Carolingian order and its architects

Contents

Summary

Assemblies, capitularies and counts

Essay: Carolingian palaces

Kinship, lordship and aristocratic society

Peasants and polyptychs

Towns and trade

Bishops, councils and correction

Essay: The Carolingian court and the diffusion of culture

Bibliographical essay

Summary

As the pace of military expansion slowed in the last decades of the eighth century, new techniques were developed to consolidate Carolingian rule of the vastly extended Frankish realm. The royal court, progressing between a series of monumental new palace complexes in the Frankish heartlands, became the central political stage, with the engagement of landed elites with the king institutionalised through regular assemblies at which decisions were made, patronage dispensed and friendships and alliances made and renewed. These practices – and the ideals of consensus that they informed – were further reinforced through the increased use of written instruments (capitularies) to communicate the decisions reached by kings in counsel with their advisors. Through the capitularies, and through the person of the count, the public meetings at which local landowners did business were directly tied to king and court.

These political strategies were successful because they provided a framework within which local landed elites could prosper. Carolingian kingship allowed the able and ambitious to wield influence on a scale and over distances unheard of since late Roman times, thanks to the hierarchies of office and the steady flow of patronage through grants of land in benefice. Systems of aristocratic kinship and lordship thus entwined themselves around the infrastructure of court politics and royal patronage, binding together networks of kin and supporters to patrons who enjoyed royal favour and could ensure continued goodwill and reward; they complemented and supported kingship. In the countryside, the careful management of ecclesiastical and royal land, and the opportunities it brought for landowners who might double as stewards or receive land-grants, led to an intensification of production so as to meet more ambitious demands on the part of courts, churchmen and aristocrats; one important by-product was the enlivening of networks of exchange.

Similar changes were effected to the structure of the church, with profound cultural effects. Carolingian rulers not only participated in the traditional cultivation of royal prestige through cultural patronage, but also fostered debate at their court over the correct ordering of Christian society. As a result, diverse local traditions on matters ranging from baptismal rites to monastic rules were replaced by new practices derived from texts promoted as authoritative, and approved as articulating correct practice. The councils and debates through which this process of 'correction' took place encouraged an *esprit de corps* among the ecclesiastical leadership, and one rooted in their partnership with Carolingian kings and their involvement in their court. Central to the process was thus the articulation of a clear infrastructure of hierarchical authority within the church. Status here was no longer rooted in the charismatic appeal of individual holy men, but in the legitimating traditions of the institutional church as recorded and interpreted by bishops.

Assemblies, capitularies and counts

By the 780s the wealth, status and contacts brought by half a century of military success had given rise to a change in political style. Charlemagne now led armies in person less frequently, and the church reforms and cultural revival begun in Pippin's time were increasingly central to his rule. Integral to this new politics were the annual assemblies at which king and aristocracy met to discuss the state of the realm. These assemblies had deep roots: since the sixth century Frankish kings had met the elites of their kingdoms at the Marchfield, the occasion for the issue of much of the surviving Merovingian legislation. But under the Carolingians the importance of the assemblies as occasions for the giving and receiving of counsel acquired a new profile, and were more closely linked to the Christian calendar of the great church festivals. The Marchfield was moved to May under Pippin, and transformed from an annual muster prior to the inevitable campaign to a more ritualised occasion focused on the giving of counsel and gifts to the king immediately following on from the solemn festivities of Easter. The narrative of the *Royal Frankish Annals*, for example, is structured by the royal itinerary and the church calendar, and insists on the role of counsel and consensus on these occasions in binding together king and people. What had been relatively spontaneous and unselfconscious rites of the wartrail were formalised as institutions for the governing of a Christian kingdom. Whereas kings had previously relied on a ready flow of plunder and tribute on the wartrail, they now insisted on 'annual gifts' being brought to the annual assembly, and presented in the full public view, by major aristocrats and churchmen. Long-standing practices of having promising young aristocrats raised at court were reinvigorated under Pippin and Charlemagne, but with a new insistence on the role of the court as the place for the moral instruction that was necessary for the future rulers of Christian society.

The most characteristic, and most important, of our sources for Carolingian government are the direct product of this new style of 'assembly politics' with its emphasis on consensus and counsel. These are a voluminous series of documents known as the capitularies. These written records take their title from the habit of writing up decisions chapter by chapter (Latin *capitula*). This convention was borrowed from the records of church councils, and it was the development of a programme of church reform pursued through conciliar legislation from the councils of 742 onwards that gave impetus to the capitularies. The very earliest documents often combined the ecclesiastical decrees with rulings on secular affairs reached at royal assemblies in which laymen as well as clerics participated. Under Pippin, legislation of this kind was issued at Ver in 755, and the first major capitulary of Charlemagne's reign recorded the deliberations of a similar council held at Herstal in 779. The form itself was not unprecedented: surviving Merovingian legislation such as the edict of Paris (614) had marked similarities. But from the last decade of the eighth century capitularies were produced with a new regularity. In the *Admonitio Generalis* ('General Admonition') of 789, Charlemagne made a series of injunctions, addressed to different classes ('to priests', 'to all our subjects' and so on), inspired by the desire to create 'peace, unity and concord among the Christian people'. Thereafter, we have a much thicker and more continuous run of capitularies, reaching its peak in the first

Essay

Carolingian palaces

In place of the annual campaign, royal palaces emerged as the central political stage. In a sense, this was a move back towards the seventh-century system of court-based politics, but in a different social context and, above all, on a far, far larger scale. The last decades of the eighth century saw the construction of a series of new purpose-built palace complexes in a novel, monumental idiom, most famously at Aachen, but also at other sites such as Ingelheim and Frankfurt. All were new palaces, not former haunts of Merovingian rulers, and all were situated in the Carolingians' political heartlands. Aachen, intensively developed in the years around 790, lay in the Ardennes, close by major complexes of family and royal property and rich hunting reserves. The choice of site was not influenced by modest previous occupation so much as by the hot springs: Einhard claimed that Charlemagne's attachment to Aachen was conditioned by his excellence at swimming. He painted a memorable picture of over a hundred courtiers bathing alongside their master, in a sociability designed to cement bonds amongst the political elite; but springs could also symbolise baptism and be the sites of rites of renewal.[1] Whilst the distance and pace of the royal itinerary decreased considerably from the 790s, the new palaces were not intended to function as sedentary capitals: they were to be the central places in the new system, where elites who had previously fought shoulder-to-shoulder with the king now came to meet their ruler. Charlemagne now seldom

Figure 10.1 Charlemagne's Palace Chapel at Aachen

Figure 10.2 Internal view of the Palace Chapel at Aachen

Figure 10.3 Charlemagne's sarcophagus showing the rape of Prosperina, from the Aachen Domkapitel

travelled south of the Loire, or east of the Rhine-Main valleys, but expected elites from the outlying provinces to visit him in the heart of the empire. Architecturally, the new forms adopted reflected the expanded ambit of Frankish rule. Imperial sites such as Ravenna exercised a considerable influence, notably over the Aachen palace chapel, and the throne room at Ingelheim was modelled on the audience chambers of Roman emperors. Such borrowings were a means of articulating the new claims and self-confidence that political success had brought: Charlemagne thus had a statue of Theodoric on horseback brought from Ravenna to stand by the entrance to Aachen. But palace complexes were also carefully designed so as to create hierarchies of space that were integral to the experience of power. Thus Charlemagne's personal quarters at Aachen were on the second floor from where, it was claimed, he could see what was going on throughout the palace complex and in the private dwellings of the courtiers and aristocrats that ringed the royal buildings. Favoured courtiers like Einhard might wait here and catch the royal ear as the king processed along walkways visible but not accessible to all. These led to the sacred space of the chapel with its throne, and beyond to the truly public space outdoors, where throngs of petitioners bustled around the lodgings of the great and good.[2]

decade of the ninth century, when on occasion we have several complementary capitularies issued in the same year, addressing different issues and addressed to different royal agents.

These royal instruments were fairly heterogeneous, varying from lists of amendments to be made to existing law-codes to specific instructions to named royal agents; from miscellaneous lists of behaviour fitting in a Christian society to specific measures meant to deal with particular problems. Their very existence points to an expectation that royal decisions would be recorded in an authoritative written form. Some capitularies from the ninth century even outline arrangements whereby copies were to be distributed to specific addressees, and master copies stored in the palace archives. Under Charlemagne's successor Louis the Pious one high-ranking royal official, Abbot Ansegisus of St-Wandrille, made a collection of capitulary legislation from those archives which was used by some subsequent legislators for reference.

This material is unprecedented both in its scale, and in its insistent force, in early medieval Europe, including Byzantium. Its interpretation is central to our understanding of Carolingian government. Here, the capitularies, and by implication Carolingian government, have been much criticised by historians. There has been an almost unavoidable temptation to judge the capitularies as if they were the legislative instrument of a modern state, and thus to judge them a failure. Some historians have thus pointed to the *ad hoc* nature of some capitulary injunctions, the repetition of some measures, and the mixed content of many capitularies, and asked if these were anything more than royal wishlists. But capitularies were not designed to be legislative instruments of a kind familiar to us, for Charlemagne did not have a recognised infrastructure of administrative competencies through which such instruments could be routinely enforced. Here, a comparison with the not dissimilar material that was issued by the Roman emperors of late antiquity and collected in the Theodosian Code is instructive. The late Roman material, like the Carolingian, is often reactive, responding to *ad hoc* and specific problems; because of this, like the Carolingian material it can be repetitive and inconsistent. But Roman emperors ruled through a hierarchy of officials through which petitions were passed and imperial responses enacted; and those who drafted their decrees did so in regular forms, informed by a series of well-established legal rules. Charlemagne's kingdom lacked this structure of formal rules of legal procedure and regular administrative processes through which his instructions could take effect. Capitularies, by replicating the discourse of counsel and collective decision-making that informed assemblies, were written reminders of, and replacements for, cajoling conversations with the ruler, tying the elites of the expanded kingdom to the increasingly sedentary court.

Those historians who have argued that capitularies were not 'true' royal legislation, merely written records of decisions that took their force from oral promulgation, and in any case rested on the consent of the people not the will of the ruler, thus miss the central point. Capitularies need to be understood as part of a process of political communication, not legislation in the sense we understand it. They were persuasive precisely in as much as they bound in the counts and bishops who were to put them into action. Hence their insistence that they articulated collective decisions implicated in a face-to-face relationship with the king. And what is striking here is the sheer volume of evidence that these written instruments did facilitate dialogue between kings and their agents. Here we can point to the number of surviving manuscripts, and the presence, among those manuscripts, of copies of capitularies definitely destined for named individuals. We can also point to the evidence of surviving records of local property disputes and transfers, preserved as charters – deeds to property – in the ecclesiastical archives of the Carolingian world. These records reveal the public meetings and negotiations through which conflict and claims were resolved, and the important role of royal agents and royal mandates in those meetings. Whilst the nature of this material makes it difficult to track down a specific injunction from a given capitulary being enacted in the localities, it does indicate a world in which counts and their like gained legitimacy and respect because they were royal agents carrying out royal orders.[3]

One of the main innovations outlined in the capitularies was the implementation of a universal oath of fidelity to the king. Kings had used oaths, as guarantees of loyalty, since Merovingian times. At the beginning of Charlemagne's reign they were expected from leading aristocrats, who became 'faithful men' of the king. At a lower social level, oaths of mutual obligation between allies – pacts of 'friendship' – and the swearing of loyalty by retainers to their masters to create retinues or *trustes* were likewise widespread practices with long precedents. In the world of the annual campaign, such groupings were tied to the king by common endeavour on the wartrail. But they also created potentially dangerous alternative sources of loyalty that could threaten the king when things turned sour. Already at Herstal in 779 Charlemagne outlawed sworn bands (*trustes*), and subsequently there was a concerted attempt to limit the ability of aristocrats to raise armed posses in the pursuit of legal rights through the institution of feud. Major incentives were offered for peaceful coming to terms and punishments meted out to those who sought violent redress. Capitularies also banned the swearing of oaths of mutual obligation because of the danger of 'conspiracy': associations or 'gilds' to ensure Christian burial, charitable giving to the indigent, or to fight fire, were allowed, but the oaths which cemented them were to be sworn in the name of the king. And, worried by the experience of revolt, in 789 Charlemagne required that all free men were to swear loyalty, on holy relics, to the king in the person of his local representative; a requirement repeated and further explained in subsequent legislation.[4]

This careful regulation enabled oath-taking to be used as a powerful supernatural glue holding together the kingdom. Obligations to kin and patrons which mediated, and potentially competed with, obligations to the king were thus to be avoided; if all had sworn loyalty to the king, none could claim that resistance to his wishes was legitimate. But the swearing of the oath was soon seen as encompassing much more than this. In 802 it was ordered 'that it should be publicly expounded to all, in such a way that every person can understand, how important and how many are the matters that this oath comprehends'. These matters included not only faithfulness to the king and respect for his property, orders and rights, but also care for the church, charity for widows, orphans and pilgrims, the avoidance of injustice and that 'everybody should personally strive ... to maintain himself fully in God's service'. The oath of fidelity was sworn in the public meetings at which local landowners met to do business; some documents suggest that the oath of loyalty to the king was comparable to the baptismal oath to God, as marking full membership of the community and constituting a binding agreement to conduct oneself so as to please God and king. Oaths thus defined the boundaries of a Christian society and the obligations incumbent on its members.[5]

Among the expectations of behaviour guaranteed by the swearing of the oath was 'the accomplishment of justice'. Concerns about justice pervade the capitularies: they centre on the conduct of counts, the main public officials in the localities. The 'justice' they were to deliver was rooted in the need to ensure that king and church got their due: royal and ecclesiastical property was to be safeguarded, public obligations jealously guarded. But it surpassed these self-interested specifics, as kings sought to create a universal expectation among the free that public justice was available to all. The charters reveal a world in which landowning communities kept order through public meetings, rooted in patterns of elite sociability, with business conducted in a world of feasting and hunting at the major settlements of their locality. The capitularies attempted, in a piecemeal accumulation of exhortations and injunctions, to draw a firmer boundary between this social intercourse among the great and good, and the hearing of legal cases. When Charlemagne forbad counts from cutting short hearings so as not to miss the hunt, he was trying to divide off legal hearings from the public sociability that articulated the solidarity of local elites. Among the earliest and longest-running concerns were the conduct and timing of legal hearings: instructions were given as to their regulation and location, and the cases of the poor were to be heard first, so as to ensure that they had access to justice without difficulty. The etiquette of dispute settlement was also subject to regulation. There was an expectation that the giving of judgement would be accompanied by the giving of gifts in recognition of the honour due to the judge, but the gifts themselves were to be appropriate, and care was to be taken to avoid any suspicion of bribery or undue influence.[6]

None of this was an attempt to move away from a system of public collective judgement in the context of face-to-face relationships. But these vigorous communities of landowners were to understand they were responsible to the king, and ultimately to God, for ensuring that their business was done according to Christian norms of justice. In the famous injunction of 802 – that counts were to judge justly according to the written law – they were not being chastised for their ignorance or incompetence, but reminded that they were upholding universal written rules rather than exercising their personal discretion to broker a compromise settlement.[7] Those local 'good men' who served as panels hearing and deciding on the truth of legal claims were likewise reminded of their responsibilities. Their role, deciding on the relative plausibility of competing claims in the light of their local knowledge, was formalised, particularly through the setting up of sworn inquests, in which panels gave testimony on oath. The capitularies use a new collective term for them: from the 780s they are called *scabini*. An older generation of historians saw here an index of full-scale administrative reform, with the creation of a new, more professional, class of legal experts, but it is clear that precisely the same men, respected local landowners, continued to serve on local judgement panels. The change in the terminology reflects not a change of personnel or function, but the reception of the message of the capitularies. Those engaged in the settlement of disputes were not simply attempting to keep the peace among their peers in their community, but they were also responsible to God and king for dispensing just judgement.

The nature of the surviving evidence makes it tricky to gauge how the exhortations of the capitularies were received in the localities. From surviving capitulary manuscripts, charters and letters, we get the occasional glimpse of local public meetings listening to the wishes of their king, as voiced by their count. Thus in 802 the Bavarian landowners giving testimony in a complex property suit were reminded how earlier that year, when they had sworn fidelity to the emperor, it had been explained to them that implicit in their oath was a promise to behave 'truthfully and without deceit' when in court; in 803, a group of Parisian landowners attended a meeting with their count at which a parchment outlining revisions to their Frankish law was read out, and to which they signed their names. In assessing the evidence, we should remember that the capitularies were not imposing changes in personnel or social structures, nor implanting a technique of surveillance over landowning communities. They aimed fundamentally at a programme of re-education, promulgating a new ethos in which landowning elites were encouraged to see their dominant role in terms of a hierarchy of office in which they were responsible to the king, as God's representative on earth, for the maintenance of 'peace, unity and concord among the Christian people'. As such, they could offer new ways of understanding status and legitimating local power, in particular for counts, whose role acquired a new moral seriousness: by the 820s, Louis the Pious was reminding counts, in his 'admonition to all the orders of the realm', that they shared with the king responsibility for performing the God-given 'ministry' of ruling Christian society.[8]

This new moral seriousness may have been useful for counts in the localities: certainly the new terminology of public power as 'ministry' (*ministerium*) was rapidly adopted in local charters. Quite how the capitulary programme changed the nature of government as experienced on the ground is difficult to unpick from the surviving evidence. The position of count, after all, was not new, but had long roots in the Merovingian and late Roman past. By late Merovingian times, however, with the decay of the municipal institutions that had previously underpinned local government, it is not really clear what counts actually did: they certainly enjoyed a local pre-eminence, reflected in their chairing the public meetings at which local business was done, and could dispense legitimate violence against those deemed wrongdoers as a result. The capitularies, with their creation of a set of expectations about the job of the count which, although made piecemeal, cumulatively approached something like a formal 'job description', can be read as a means of clarifying and sharpening the role of counts. By the ninth century we can trace complaints about counts who did not conduct themselves according to these norms of 'ministry' devolved from above, for example in the complaints about injustice made by Archbishop Agobard of Lyon to Count Matfrid of Orleans, then the most powerful figure at the royal court.[9]

Rhetorical injunction and instruction were not, of course, enough on their own. Thanks to the charter evidence, which shows us counts in their counties, dispensing justice and networking with local landowners, it is even possible to trace the outlines of the patronage politics through which kings sought to transform counts into royal agents. Countships were monopolised by powerful aristocrats with local roots, although there were occasions when respected and well-connected local landowners who were not descended from families of the first rank acted as counts. Counts might hope that their offspring would, in time, succeed them, as did Count Orendil, who in 815 left land to the church of Freising on condition that it be granted out to his son should he follow in his father's 'ministry'.[10] But a straightforward succession, of the kind that Orendil desired, was far from the rule. Even if they felt obliged to keep a countship within a given family, kings had room for manoeuvre: the breadth and fluidity of contemporary definitions of kinship gave them a range of related candidates rather than one pre-eminent heir. In any case, an ambitious count's son might have secured a vacant countship before his father's death, thus leaving the king free to choose a new candidate; or he might be made to wait.

Counties were in any case of varying size, and counts had access to varying resources. Whereas in the west, counties themselves rested, very loosely, on the Roman infrastructure of cities and their territories, and thus had a certain coherence, further north and west counties were looser and less defined, centred on important places or on settlement areas. Very careful analysis has shown that kings tended to focus their strategies of control of certain strategically important areas, whilst acknowledging *de facto* aristocratic control elsewhere. Thus Michael Borgolte has shown how in Alemannia, Pippin initially ruled through a small number of figures based on rich royal estates around Zurich; in less politically central areas looser indigenous systems of aristocratic lordship were allowed to continue until the reign of Louis the Pious. It is only very occasionally that outsiders, wholly dependent on royal will and needing at least the threat of coercive force to have their will done, were imposed: in Alemannia, this happened in the initial aftermath of conquest, and thereafter on a tiny handful of occasions for clear strategic reasons, for example in Rhaetia in the southern Alps in the 810s, where the result was a series of complaints about the depredations of these incomers. In the west, where countships had a firmer institutional identity, it may have been slightly easier to bring in new men, particularly in areas where royal estates predominated and allowed a newcomer real social and economic muscle. In the early ninth century, for example, the major countships of the Loire valley, those of Tours and Orleans, were granted to a succession of royal favourites, all of them aristocrats, but aristocrats from elsewhere: even here the result was negative publicity from local churches, and eventually civil strife owing to the rapid coming and going of counts as the prevailing political winds repeatedly changed.[11]

All of this begs the question of what counts actually did. After all, they had no administrative or institutional apparatus through which they operated: the land-tax with its complex systems of assessment and registration had long gone, and Carolingian attempts to record royal rights produced lists stating specific dues to be made from specific estates, not the generalised application of abstract rules. Given their required attendance at royal assemblies, and their despatch on royal business, whether campaigning, investigating reports of injustice, or acting as envoys and messengers, counts were busy men. Their patterns of movement were determined by the demands of kin and king, and patterns of landholding that were scattered over a wider area than their county. They were thus far from ever-present in their counties. The charter evidence shows local rhythms of collective action and public business continuing with counts only intermittent attendees, bringing news and orders from the palace and attempting to resolve the most explosive or important disputes (the capitularies, indeed, insisted that cases involving personal freedom or landed property had to be heard before the count), but otherwise represented by local deputies. Where we have enough evidence to trace the activities of these figures – some called viscounts, some hundredmen, some simply styled judges or agents of the count – the overwhelming impression is one of continuity, with the same trusted locals continuing to act as the leaders within their community even as counts came and went.

Even insistence on the universality of the most important 'public function' expected from the free, military service, did not rest on a process of registration or a series of rules that counts could use as an institutional apparatus of power. Here, eighth-century expansion had been fuelled by the eagerness of landowning elites to win royal favour through participation on the wartrail; changing military needs in the decades after 800 saw a series of royal attempts to set down the basis on which military service would be required. Whilst these were informed by the notion that all free men owed an obligation to serve their king, they also recognised that in practice an universal levy would be unsustainable and valueless, other than in defence against marauding invaders; the stress was on identifying individuals with the necessary training and insisting on their participation, whilst approving mechanisms by which they might be supported by their kin and neighbours who thus performed their service to the king through the supply of equipment, provisions or labour. The cumulative effect of these changes, indeed, was to reduce the ability of counts to exercise patronage in their interpretation of these public dues: lists of all free men expected to serve were kept, and mobilisation organised through special royal agents and instructions.[12]

In other words, whilst royal appointment gave counts the right to rule, the ability to rule was rooted in relationship with the landowning communities of the localities. Counts lacked an administrative infrastructure independent of their personal contacts and qualities, and coercion was only an intermittent possibility. Taking the local evidence for these processes of rule seriously is important, because it undercuts the deeply entrenched view that counts posed the main threat to royal power and the integrity of the Carolingian state. The often-repeated view that, in the course of the ninth century, counts were able to use their office to establish an unbudgeable local position independent of kings, and so to treat counties as family possessions to be passed on as if they were property, was in fact never more than an attempted explanation for political change. As a hypothesis is cannot be sustained, because the documentary evidence shows counts continuing to work through public meetings run by local landowners.

Counts may have been the basic agents of royal government, but in a vastly expanded empire they were a fairly heterogeneous group, several hundred individuals with diverse capabilities and competencies. They were too numerous to be an effective cadre, intimate with the ruler and able to transmit his will, hence the need for repeated exhortations in the capitularies. Rule of the Frankish kingdoms had long rested on the identification of reliable regional leaders, able to mediate between court and king on one hand, and landowning communities on the other: in late Merovingian times such figures were often styled 'duke' (*dux*), and under the early Carolingians whole provinces had similarly been ruled via trusted intermediaries. By the beginning of the ninth century these structures, which met the needs of both regional communities and the royal court in facilitating contact between the two, were being formalised in new terms. Crucial here was a group of royal officials known as the *missi dominici* – literally, 'the lord's sent ones'. *Missi* were originally royal agents sent on one-off missions or errands, to investigate a particular problem, and tended to be chosen from among the ambitious youngsters in the king's service at the palace. But their duties slowly expanded, until a capitulary of 802 outlined a system of pairs of *missi*, one churchman and one layman, covering the Frankish heartlands of the empire, and a 'job description' detailing the responsibilities of the *missi* on their annual tour of the region for which they were responsible; thereafter *missi* were systematically used to implement the royal will.[13]

The *missi* have often been depicted as a nascent professional administrative class of dedicated royal officials, designed to impose the royal will on often recalcitrant counts. Certainly, the creation of a regular system of paired *missi*, ecclesiastical and lay, was from the outset designed as a way of ensuring that counts lived up to the expectations of the capitularies: they were substitutes for the royal presence, and the prime recipients of much capitulary legislation. The two most important areas of activity – the taking of oaths of loyalty, and overseeing of military service – were increasingly reserved to them. However, *missi* were not outsiders, nor were they subject to different pressures and problems from counts. Just as the ecclesiastical *missi* were prominent local bishops or abbots – in fact where possible the local archbishop – so their lay partners were aristocratic landowners to a man, chosen from the ranks of local counts. This pattern of appointment ensured the necessary local purchase: *missi* needed to be able to impose themselves on the counts and communities they supervised. In fact, lay *missi*, by virtue of the appointment, stood at the apex of a regional social hierarchy, raised above their relatives and rivals by the royal will, and able to take complaints or requests direct to the royal ear, as well as exercising considerable patronage by virtue of their position. This new hierarchy was articulated in ideas of royal service and 'ministry'. It was only in times of political crisis – notably in the 830s, and then again in the 890s – that these leading aristocrats were referred to as the rulers of regional communities – *dux* of the eastern Franks, or the equivalent. Whilst Carolingian kingship was fully functioning, aristocratic hierarchies were articulated as pyramids of honourable service, rooted in a shared responsibility to God for right rule. The emergence, in the tenth century, of self-standing regional hierarchies culminating in a '*dux* by God's grace' thus marks a crucial break from Carolingian practice.

Kinship, lordship and aristocratic society

If aristocrats were the indispensable partners of Carolingian kings, this partnership allowed them to build up extensive networks of patronage and power on a scale unparalleled by their ancestors, but which were largely dependent on the continued enjoyment of public office and royal goodwill. The eighth century thus saw the creation of a far steeper hierarchy within the aristocracy. The late Merovingian world had been dominated by a series of regional aristocracies, each with their own identity – as Aleman, Aquitainian, Bavarian and so on – and their distinct political system, normally revolving around a ducal court. The will of Abbo of Provence illustrates the systems of landholding and patronage that such a framework could sustain, and Abbo, as the leading figure in Provence, was entered into a series of horizontal alliances beyond his region, notably with Charles Martell; but even Abbo had no personal interests beyond the Rhone valley and the Mediterranean coast of southeastern Gaul.[14] Those families which had prospered within the late Merovingian system in Neustria in particular were probably richer still than Abbo, for the landowning networks dependent on the court at Paris in the seventh century surpassed those elsewhere in the Frankish world; and the richest Austrasian families enjoyed complex webs of contacts and kin in the 'wild east', the frontier territory beyond the Rhine. But – with the exception of the Carolingians by 700 – it is difficult to see any one family with supra-regional interests. In the course of the eighth century, as successive generations of Carolingians shared the spoils of political expansion with their followers, this all changed: the top tiers of the Frankish aristocracy came to amass scattered webs of land, kin and clients which criss-crossed the entire Frankish world. By the ninth century, the extensive character of the interests of this new 'imperial aristocracy' is increasingly evident in the footloose activities of its leading members. Hugh, for example, a descendent of the old Aleman ducal family with extensive interests along the upper Rhine, was rewarded for his loyal service to Charlemagne with the plum Neustrian countship of Tours, but after a series of political falls and comebacks ended his career in Italy where he had acquired interests thanks to the patronage of his Carolingian son-in-law, Louis the Pious' son Lothar. The central point about the likes of Hugh is that, although they had acquired huge resources, in the form of land and offices, and put down roots in a number of different regions, they had done so within the Carolingian system; whilst Hugh could thus cope with a political setback by shifting the focus of his activity – for example retreating to his son-in-law's Italian court when stripped of his Neustrian offices – he could not work outside a Carolingian framework, or independently of Carolingian kings.[15] The greater opportunities for aristocratic enrichment implicit within the Carolingian system thus came with a price: a greater dependence on royal patronage and a necessary engagement with royal courts on the part of those who wished to prosper.

The emergence of this 'imperial aristocracy', moreover, did not sweep away the regional networks of kinship and landownership that had preceded it. Beneath the sweeping arcs cut by figures like Hugh as they rode from court to court in search of favour were figures with more local horizons, whose engagement in the public meetings through which counts worked underpinned the system as a whole. The aftermath of Carolingian takeover might see a fairly sharp division between a small group of Frankish conquerors and the community of landowners they ruled, particularly where conquest had been violent or contested. But within a generation, once control was established, policies could be reserved and a wider community of regional landowners embraced and enriched through the Carolingian system: in Alemannia, for example, Charlemagne disgraced the heirs to the hated first Frankish agents, restoring some confiscated lands and taking the local girl Hildegard as his wife.[16] Elsewhere – for example in Bavaria or Thuringia – the process of takeover was more seamless still.

For all the welcoming embrace of Frankish rulers once their control was assured, landowners maintained their own local identities: when they acted together, as contingents in royal armies or collectivities in times of political unrest, they were referred to as the Alemans, the Aquitainians, the Bavarians and so on. Royal policy, indeed, encouraged these regional identities, not only correcting existing law-codes for these various 'peoples', but even, in a series of initiatives in 802, having new ones drawn up where they were lacking. These regional identities were used to refer to the constituent segments of the Frankish Empire, the *regna*, or kingdoms, which were added onto sections of the Frankish heartlands when political divisions were made, and to which royal sons were sent as subkings in their youth; they were to re-emerge in the tenth century as the basic political units, ruled once again by aristocratic dukes. To see here the underground persistence of separatist traditions rooted in ethnic conflict between Frankish conquerors and their subject peoples is mistaken. There was no hard and fast division between the 'imperial aristocracy' and these regional elites, for members of the 'imperial aristocracy' could only operate through plugging into local networks of patronage and property, whilst ambitious regional families might hope to rise to the ranks of the 'imperial aristocracy' by winning royal favour. Royal policy used existing ethnic labels to identify territorial segments within the framework of the Carolingian system, and these ethnicities were badges worn by regional collectivities rallying to the side of particular Frankish kings; they were not used to divide Frankish conquerors from their ethnically differentiated subjects. True, Italian observers might identify newcomers from north of the Alps as 'Teutons' on account of their evident cultural and linguistic differences, whilst individuals might begin a court case by professing their legal identity, as a Frank, say, or a Burgundian. But even the emergence of this principle of 'the personality of the law' pointed to the fluidity of identity, not the existence of clearly defined ethnic divides: the scattering of interests and interpenetration of different levels within the elite simply meant that it could no longer be safely assumed that the entire community of regional landowners would share the same legal identity. Hence the need to make a formal profession. Hence too the complaints of some that the system was open to abuse by troublemakers, such as those thuggish landowners in Lyons who outraged Archbishop Agobard by seeking to escape punishment for their misdeeds by claiming that Burgundian law gave them the right to establish their innocence through trial by battle. It was quite possible to identify without reservation with Frankish kingship on the level of high politics, whilst maintaining a sense of the separate regional traditions of the landowning community, as the collection of stories about Charlemagne and his heirs made by the monk Notker of St-Gallen in the 880s eloquently shows.[17]

These processes of integration were facilitated by the relatively open and fluid nature of aristocratic kinship. Here, the thickening of the documentary evidence thanks to the survival in ecclesiastical archives of thousands of land-grants enables us to reach a detailed understanding of family structures for the first time in early medieval history. Kinship was bilateral, in that maternal kin as well as paternal might entertain claims to inherit property, particularly property which had come from their bloodline. Inheritance was partible, in that it rested on the equitable division of an individual's property between those who entertained claims on a share, not the passing on of an integral complex of property to a favoured heir. Hence we often find a series of kinsmen and women owning 'shares' or 'portions' of land at a given location, and passing them on in their turn. Although the range of kin acting together in some contexts could be quite wide – the groups commemorated in prayer at some favoured monasteries, and acting together in legal conflicts, could be extensive, bringing together uncles and cousins – in terms of the inheritance of property, partition tended to privilege a relatively restricted group: mother, father, children, perhaps grandparents or the odd aunt or uncle, but no more. In other words, bonds between the members of households consisting of a married couple and their immediate dependants constituted the most practical level of kinship, and informed the redistribution of property, but these restricted familial units were tied together into a wider web of kin who could be called upon in a crisis. Given the lack of pre-Carolingian evidence, the origins of these patterns must remain unclear. It may be that the relative informality and openess of early medieval kinship structures were particularly useful for elites enjoying few of the formal political privileges or economic prerogatives of their Roman predecessors, facilitating the brokering of alliances within a broad and open-ended landowning class. Certainly the Carolingian system, with its potential for the amassing of extensive interests but also its need for local support to maintain those interests, must have encouraged aristocrats to use their kinship networks in this way.

Kinship mattered because it gave an individual a wide range of potential patrons at court and allies in the localities. But the very practices which created priceless connections of this kind also discouraged the agglomeration of concentrated complexes of property and their transmission wholesale from generation to generation; partition might be manipulated through grants made to a favoured church which functioned as a family 'land-bank', but it could not be bypassed. Hence the importance of public office and royal favour, which gave their recipients a different kind of resource, not subject to the claims of kinsmen or liable to be dismantled through partible inheritance. This was not a case of partible inheritance failing to do what its owners needed, or acting as an irrational customary brake on family strategy. Partible inheritance maintained the extensive kinship networks necessary to gain favour at court or exercise office in the localities, but an individual's fortunes were dependent on receiving and hanging on to grants of *honores* – literally, honours – that is, offices and land-grants. Here, Carolingian practice marked an important new departure. Whereas the Merovingians, like the rulers of the other successor states of the post-Roman west, had exercised patronage through the making of outright grants of property, the Carolingians granted their followers life-interests alone in estates that remained ultimately royal property. In this, they were adapting the widespread practice of churches making precarial (life-tenure) grants to their favoured patrons. Indeed a significant proportion of royal grants was actually from church land placed at the king's disposal under the terms of the agreements made at church councils in the 740s and subsequently renegotiated and reaffirmed. The giving of 'benefices', as royal grants of this form were known, thus altered the rules of royal patronage.

Merovingian kings, for example, had been ready to strip aristocrats who were found guilty of disloyalty of property, presumably because much of that property was royal in origin. By the ninth century Carolingian expropriations of family land were rare, but revocations of *honores* and benefices far more common. This should not be seen as an index of Carolingian weakness, for the point was that without benefices and *honores* an ambitious aristocrat would quickly sink to the level of the local gentry, unable to maintain their involvement in the world of court politics. The anxiety of holders of benefices fearing redistributions in times of political unrest or following a royal succession was very real: in the 820s and 830s, for example, the influential courtier Einhard penned a series of pained letters on the part of friends and relatives who feared impoverishment and loss of status as a result of political disturbance.[18]

For much of the nineteenth and twentieth centuries, the granting of benefices by Carolingian kings was seen as a reflection of wider social changes. In a hypothesis which had a certain attractive simplicity, but unfortunately negligible support in the sources, it was argued that Charles Martell, in order to prevail over his opponents, and in particular to defeat 'Abd al-Rahmān, had to recruit a new style of army, based on heavy cavalry; this was only possible through the widespread gift of benefices to support this new class of warriors, who were thereby tied into the personal service of the Carolingian kings through special – and largely unprecedented – bonds of lordship. The attractiveness of this proposition lay in its ability to explain the rise and fall of political systems in sweeping terms of clashes of civilisations characterised by huge technological divides. However, Martell's defeat of 'Abd al-Rahmān, as we saw, cannot be seen in epoch-making terms as stemming a hitherto unstoppable tide of Islamic advance; it was part of a struggle for supremacy over a politically fragmented and increasing independent southern Gaul. No contemporary source links his victory to any change in tactics or recruitment, and whilst horses were as fundamental a part of Frankish aristocratic identity as weapons, this had been the case under the Merovingians and there is no evidence for their increased importance on the battlefield in the course of the eighth century. The granting out of benefices was a means for the Carolingians to rework the systems of patronage and property that structured aristocratic society so as to embed royal authority: its importance should not be underestimated. But there is no real support for the argument that the granting out of benefices was particularly linked to the obligations to perform military service, or that it rested on a new form of personal lordship – often referred to as 'feudalism'[19] – whereby the recipient of a land-grant reciprocated through tight obligations to serve their lord. Carolingian legislation insisted that holders of benefices, like counts and other recipients of royal favour, should perform military service when called, but capitularies and documents also show benefice-holders performing a range of other services, from taking messages to carrying out legal investigations, on behalf of kings. There is nothing here to suggest that the holding of benefices created a specific set of obligations, rather than general expectations of acting for the 'lord king' as and when requested.

Nor can the sources sustain the idea that grants of benefices and the rise of new forms of lordship were transforming the fabric of Carolingian society. By the last decades of the eighth century, those who held royal benefices were regularly referred to by a new term, as *vassi dominici*, literally 'vassals of the lord [king]'. The term 'vassal' had previously denoted relatively humble service within a master's household, and its spreading by the end of the eighth century to refer to well-to-do landowners is rooted in their service at the Carolingian court at a formative stage in their careers. These practices were rooted in the aristocratic life-cycles, with ambitious youths spending a period serving in the household of powerful patrons before contracting a marriage and acquiring the resources to form a household of their own; they had Merovingian precedents, for example in the ties between kings and their *leudes*, who had served at the palace, in the royal bodyguard. Carolingian patterns of patronage here differed primarily by more clearly and insistently articulating the continued obligations of former members of the royal household towards the king even once they had set up home in the countryside: here, the insistence on continuing royal rights over benefices meant that these relationships were a matter of formal obligation. By the first decades of the ninth century, as descendents of benefice-holders sought to maintain their position, grants might be made to individuals who promised to maintain their ancestors' tradition of loyal service, the position of *vassus dominicus* became a template for honourably rewarded usefulness among members of local landowning elites. *Vassi dominici* were thus landowners who held benefices, but not other offices; as such they were a specific subset of the wider community of 'faithful men', which at its widest included all free men, whose general obligations towards the king had been made concrete by swearing the oath of fidelity. Entering into a special relationship with the king involved taking a special oath in person, kneeling before the king and swearing to serve him faithfully: holders of *honores* of all kinds were expected to perform this ritual on receipt of such favours, and when a new king took the throne loyalty was to be demonstrated through the repetition of these rites, or else benefices and *honores* might be redistributed to new favourites.

The language and rites of 'vassalage' were used to describe the basic interpersonal bonds that held together high medieval society in the eleventh and twelfth centuries. As a result, historians reading Carolingian references to *vassi dominici* have read back later practices and see here a fully-fledged system of personal lordship, used by kings to tie aristocrats into the structures of royal power but increasingly defining relationships within landowning elites too. Such anachronisms need to be avoided. The language of 'fidelity', and the performance of fitting service to the 'lord king', was open-ended in its implications. 'Fidelity' was expected in a general sense from all free men within the kingdom, as the universal oath made clear, and the holders of benefices and *honores* simply swore to demonstrate these general qualities in a positive sense in recognition of the specific favour they had been shown. We therefore cannot see here coherent practices of 'vassalage', initially associated with the holding of benefices but eventually applied to *honores* or countships, whose control thus became rooted in personal lordship not public office. Carolingian sources refer repeatedly and unthinkingly to the obligations of the people to the 'lord king', not because specific ties of personal lordship were sweeping aside more general obligations – after all, the practice of referring to the ruler as 'lord' had been introduced by Diocletian at the end of the third century – but to articulate the personal ties owed by all the free to their ruler. It is impossible for us to make a distinction between relationships and rituals expressive of the king's personal lordship over specific individuals from those articulating divinely ordained rule over all, because in Carolingian eyes the king stood at the apex of an all-encompassing hierarchy of personal obligations. As such, he was lord of all, as the oath of fidelity made clear. As a result, Carolingian kings encouraged the exercise of lordship as underpinning the proper order of society. Capitularies granted all free men the right to choose their lord, and attempted to ensure that lordship was exercised to the benefit of all parties, by outlining the actions which could be seen as breaches of the mutual trust in which obligations were rooted: a man plotting against his lord could thus be subjected to physical discipline, but a lord who acted against the interests of his man, by attempting to reduce him to servitude, threatening force, or sleeping with his wife, could be abandoned for another.

Such systems of mutual dependence and patronage had long precedents reaching into the Roman past, and were central to the structuring of the early medieval countryside. Throughout the ninth century and beyond, they continued to work alongside – indeed to complement – patterns of landownership centred on the ownership and inheritance of family land. Given the open kinship structures and systems of partible inheritance favoured by the aristocracy, and the patterns of extensive and mobile power they supported, this is scarcely surprising. There was little scope for the formation of agglomerations of land immune from the claims of kin and the processes of inheritance, which would have been necessary for the widespread creation of benefices to reward followers. Aristocratic lordship remained rooted in the household: aristocrats had entourages of youngsters, recruited from their clients, friends, and relatives, and when these youngsters could contract a marriage and secure the property to support a household of their own, they remained implicated in the patronage of their lord. The vocabulary for these relationships remained relatively imprecise and varied, not least because within these entourages bonds of kinship, friendship and locality interacted with and reinforced one another: we read of individual aristocrats having 'followers' (*satellites*), 'associates' (*socii*), categories which might overlap with those 'close in blood' (*propinqui*) or 'of the household' (*domestici*). Although royal legislation could on occasion use the terminology of 'vassals' as a catch-all for such relationships, it generally preferred to talk simply of 'lords' and their 'men', underlining that we are dealing with reciprocal obligations of a general form, not a new legal template. If benefices featured in these relationships, they were most usually royal benefices, for which an influential lord might lobby on behalf of his men. Here, then, systems of aristocratic lordship and the granting of benefices by kings were practices that complemented and reinforced one another.

The ties of lordship encouraged by Carolingian kings, and the benefices they granted, underpinned a sharpening internal hierarchy within the aristocracy. The top tier of aristocrats, with scattered family interests around the empire, could use their access to royal courts to solicit favours for their followers, but their ability to function as successful patrons and desirable kinsmen was dependent on their ability to ensure a continued flow of rewards. Such men needed kings just as much as kings needed them: aristocratic factions competed for access to the flow of royal favour. In the course of the ninth century, a series of expectations was increasingly invoked as constituting the grand rules of political behaviour: that royal favour should be available to all, and access to royal courts not monopolised by any one faction, and that decision-making ought to rest on open collective discussion in royal assemblies. As a result, the contours of political conflict were determined by accusations that kings had acted wilfully, without proper consultation, or were in the pockets of over-mighty advisors. These charges, although resting on a shared ideological template, were made strategically, by individuals wishing to discredit their opponents and argue their way back into favour; they were inevitable, because a system centred on competition for patronage inevitably generated 'ins' and 'outs', and even the most carefully orchestrated assembly was likely to leave some aristocrats grumbling about the talents going unappreciated. But they point to aristocratic competition for access to royal courts and royal favour, not a clash between weak kings and an aggressive aristocracy secure in the localities.

Peasants and polyptychs

The emergence of this clearer hierarchy within aristocratic society had significant implications in the countryside, as the archaeological evidence for a series of changes in the structure of rural settlements suggests. In the eighth and ninth centuries settlements tended to find fixed focal points, most often in new cemeteries and the associated churches, around which habitation clustered. These new, stable and nucleated, settlements point to a tightening of the bonds of community among the peasantry, but their emergence goes hand-in-hand with the gradual distancing of landed elites from village society, as we begin to find clear evidence for aristocratic residences in the countryside. Pre-Carolinigan elites had stayed in wooden 'hall' structures as they toured their estates; excavated sites show a similar repertoire of buildings, with elite households distinguished simply by their respective sizes, levels of material culture, and the area of the surrounding enclosure. Sharper internal hierarchies can be seen developing within villages in the Carolingian period. At Laucheim in Bavaria, for example, the largest compound was extensively redeveloped in the course of the eighth century, with its 'hall' dwarfing its nearest rival, its door served by a metalled path crossing a large fenced-off compound with a number of barn-like structures used for food storage. Elsewhere, for example at Pettegem in Flanders, halls were rebuilt in stone. Aristocratic households were soon seeking to differentiate themselves from their neighbours, marking themselves off in space: Pettegem, for example, was an isolated enclosure of a hall, church and associated structures, presumably founded as a dedicated aristocratic centre distant from the hustle and bustle of village life, whilst at Laucheim the largest compound was gradually set apart from the heart of the settlement. Family monasteries, from the seventh century onwards, were perhaps an important precedent here, similarly separate and increasingly built in stone; certainly the new, isolated, aristocratic compounds of the ninth century normally centred on a paired church and hall. Sites like Pettegem show the elite, for the first time since the collapse of the Roman *villa* economy in the fifth century, leaving its physical imprint on the countryside through constructing dedicated country residences clearly differentiated from peasant households and separated from village life. As the documentary evidence confirms, they were the nodes of aristocratic kinship and patronage networks. In the post-Carolingian period, a significant proportion continued in use, eventually being redeveloped as castles, but the extent to which they had defensive functions in Carolinigan times remains unclear. Like royal palaces, they had ditches and palisades which served as boundary markers as much as military emplacements, and like royal centres they were increasingly built two storeys high as the ninth century wore on, but this does not make them purpose-built strongholds articulating the military control of a local lord over the locality.[20]

Parallels to these structures can be seen on royal estates, whose centres were taking the form of two-storey stone buildings from Charlemagne's time onwards; archaeologically, indeed, aristocratic residences and royal estate centres are indistinguishable. This once again points to the wholesale implication of aristocratic networks within the structures of royal patronage: after all, aristocrats anxiously sought grants of royal estates as benefices, and where they were not granted out as benefices such centres still needed trustworthy stewards to run them, recruited from local landed elites. The organisation of royal estates is particularly well documented from the late eighth century onwards thanks to the emergence of a new class of documents known as 'polyptychs'. Polyptychs were lists of the various dues and obligations owed by the peasantry on royal and ecclesiastical lands: the fullest ninth-century examples, from major monasteries such as St-Germain-des-Près, give a household-by-household breakdown allowing insight into the demography and family structures of peasant society. There were distant precedents for this form of documentation in the tax registers of the late Roman and early Merovingian past; some major Merovingian churches, such as the bishoprics of Tours and Le Mans, had adapted such lists to record the collection of dues from peasants on their lands in the late Merovingian period. The major aim of Carolingian polyptychs, however, was the documentation of the dues – whether paid in cash or in kind – and the labour and services owed by each peasant household. Their compilation was a response to royal instructions – Charlemagne, for example, provided a series of templates in the 'brief examples', model surveys of real royal and ecclesiastical estates. These were closely linked to his capitulary 'concerning estates' (*de Villis*), which laid out the responsibility of the stewards running royal estates, ensuring that their resources were used as the king saw fit, rather than finding their way into the stomachs of royal officials or onto the tables of local men. Here, then, Carolinigan list-making and legislation aimed at keeping tabs on the managers of royal estates, just as capitularies laid down the parameters within which counts were meant to operate; similar practices inevitably spilled over onto ecclesiastical estates, given the role of kings as 'protectors' of church land, and the granting of benefices 'on the royal word'.[21]

The polyptychs were designed to ensure that ecclesiastical and royal resources were intensively exploited, so as to meet the sizeable demands made by the expanded economies of cloister and court. They not only attempted to ensure that the activities of stewards were aligned with their master's needs, but also detailed the full range of obligations on peasants, whether free or unfree, and could be produced as legal evidence of those dues. These demands were imposed through a particular form of estate organisation, originating in the seventh-century royal heartlands of the Paris basin but exported under Carolingian auspices in the eighth century and rapidly spreading, particularly east of the Rhine, in the ninth: the manor. Manors, as we have seen, were formed through the setting aside of a part of the land to be worked directly for the landlord, by peasant families, some free, some unfree, each of which also had a small plot of their own on which rent – paid in kind or increasingly in the ninth century in cash – was due. Modern economic historians have tended to accentuate the efficiency of this structure, in encouraging larger-scale activity and investment that scattered peasant plots owing rent alone; primarily, though, its attractiveness to landlords lay in its responsiveness to their needs, for the 'reserve' was exploited according to their wishes. The polyptychs encourage us to see a countryside divided up into great estates, but their evidence needs placing in a wider context: manors were most dominant where they were longest established, in the Paris basin, but their distribution was uneven. They remained rare, for example, south of the Loire, where older structures of extensive rent-collection and personal dues remained common; in northern Italy, they were spreading rapidly in the last decades of the eighth century, but lordly 'reserves' remained small-scale or scattered, and so manorial structures were in decline by the tenth century; even in the eastern parts of the Frankish heartland, where manors had spread in the aftermath of the dual processes of political consolidation and Christianisation, they might interleave with other patterns of property-holding rather than forming self-contained blocks made up of entire villages. And manors were first and foremost means of organising ecclesiastical and royal land, resting on the ownership of a tract of the countryside; such control normally rested on royal rights, and manors east of the Rhine were typically formed where churches had received extensive territorial grants from kings. If we wish to understand patterns of aristocratic and peasant landholding, we need to turn to the thickening stream of documentary evidence: here aristocratic manors remain rare, if not wholly invisible, precisely because structures of kinship and inheritance did not favour the form of extensive control on which they rested. No wonder grants of ecclesiastical and royal land, where manorial structures were more widespread, were so eagerly sought, for they provided a different kind of resource from the scattered and subdivided holdings and residences that remained the primary form of landholding.

The mixed nature of landholding had important implications for the social structure. It meant that in spite of the steepening social hierarchy, peasants were able to maintain their access to public meetings, and local power thus remained rooted in the community politics of rough and ready negotiation among free landowners. There were, of course, important regional variations here, but even in the regions where manors were most dominant, there is good documentary evidence for peasants continuing to assert their freedom, and the rights and obligations that went with it, through public courts. Public meetings were, inevitably, hierarchical and subject to the informal influence of aristocratic patrons, but nowhere in the Carolingian evidence can we see them swept aside, or find lords exercising formal rights over the peasantry. Unfree peasants were subject to lordly discipline, as they always had been, and the status of unfree tenants of manorial estates must have been made all the more apparent by the collective obligations they had to perform, which symbolised unfreedom. Free peasants who cultivated ecclesiastical or royal land performed their distinctive dues, but the polyptychs enshrined the demand that they perform public obligations for the king, notably military service and its equivalents, alongside kin and neighbours. They thus participated in the traditions of collective public action that defined membership of the village community. Manors were thus not closed systems: after all, peasants implicated in the manorial economy had kin, interests, perhaps even neighbours who were free proprietors. Indeed, the spread of the manor widened the range of strategies open to peasant families. The large-scale planned clearances made by manorialising lords brought new land under the plough, for example, thus making it possible to support more mouths by supplementing inherited land parcels with manorial plots; the evidence for demographic growth, and indeed overcrowding on some estates, is suggestive. Some peasants, of course, found themselves under pressure. Kings, in response, repeated exhortation after exhortation designed to protect the poor but free from oppression, and to prevent them from slipping into servitude or starvation when the recurrent crises of a countryside at the mercy of climatic fluctuations hit. These were the cyclical problems of pre-modern agrarian economies, and whilst we can see Carolingian kings acknowledging their currency and attempting to deal with them, from the legislation alone we can say little about the changing face of rural society. Ultimately, it makes most sense of the full range of sources if we think of an unsteady, seesaw-like, balancing of contradictory forces: the increasing distance between aristocrats and peasants versus the vitality of public collective action, the problems posed by failed harvests versus the opportunities opened up by the manorial economy.

These contradictions are rooted in dynamism. The world of the polyptychs augured a new level of economic management, in which extensive estates were more intensively exploited to meet heightening elite demands. This made for potentially greater surpluses as the rural economy became more specialised, but this was a world of both more opportunities and greater risks. The archaeology suggests that Merovingian rural settlements were characterised by a mixed economy with a variety of crops and livestock, which minimised the need for routine exchange; even pottery-making and metalwork seem to have been performed on a relatively local level within rural communities. Carolingian settlements, however, show a more intensive cereal agriculture geared to the generation of surpluses, and a higher degree of specialisation; craft production was organised through monastic and royal estates, and perhaps aristocratic households, and mass-produced fine pottery such as Badorf and Tating ware began to be distributed on a regional level. The manorial economy played an important role in bringing about these changes, with lordly investment allowing better tools or water- and windmills, and manorial organisation demonstrating the efficiency of new three-year systems of crop rotation. But these changes transformed the rural economy as a whole, as peasant proprietors were able to specialise themselves, maybe trying some cash-cropping, and draw on the example and resources of the manorial sector. This dynamism was not rooted in any technological breakthrough: the rural economy still rested on animal and human labour, and harvests were at the mercy of climatic disasters which were recorded assiduously by contemporary historians, and even debated anxiously as manifestations of God's will at court. So the efficiency gains that went with the economies of scale allowed by manorialisation, and the greater specialisation it encouraged, were matched by higher risks of wholesale disaster if the harvest failed: the regimes of the Merovingian period had been less exposed to such setbacks precisely because of their small-scale and mixed nature. It is thus no surprise that the surpluses suggested by the capitulary 'concerning estates' (*de Villis*), although difficult to interpret – do the figures represent the total harvest or make allowances for seedcorn or other forms of consumption? was this a poor year or the norm? – point to a rural economy on the perennial verge of crisis. These dangers should not encourage wholesale pessimism; they rather point to a year-by-year struggle to reach a higher level of activity.

Towns and trade

For much of the twentieth century, it was believed that the Carolingian economy was essentially land-locked and self-sufficient, a verdict espoused by Henri Pirenne, who saw the Carolingian Empire, inward-looking and cut off from the Mediterranean world, as marking the definitive shift from ancient to medieval society. But the archaeological discoveries of the last third of the twentieth century have fundamentally undermined Pirenne's views. The most spectacular finds have been those indicating a flourishing network of long-distance exchange around the North Sea coast in the eighth century, connecting the great rivers of northwestern continental Europe to England and Scandinavia through 'gateway communities' or 'emporia' at Dorestad, near the mouth of the Rhine in the modern Netherlands, and Quentovic at the mouth of the Canche in modern France. Excavations of parts of the site of Dorestad, complemented by the recent discovery of Quentovic, have been combined with the finds from closely linked sites in England and Scandinavia in an effort to understand the origins and development of this network. The primary objects of exchange were luxury goods, notably the jewellery and prestige-laden adornments through which elites demonstrated their status. Documentary evidence for royal officials levying tolls at Dorestad and Quentovic has been combined with some archaeological suggestions of planning – notably at the major English site of Hamwic near modern Southampton – to suggest that the emporia were the results of rulers in England, Francia and Scandinavia seeking to encourage luxury exchange. Kings might thus profit through the levying of dues on trade and also control the flow of the high-status goods which were of such importance to landed elites. Aspects of this model may need qualifying, particularly the emphasis on royal initiative. The early development of Dorestad, for example, is difficult to see in terms of royal control, for it coincided with a period in the late seventh and early eighth centuries when the Rhine delta was on the political and religious frontier between Francia and Frisia; Dorestad itself changed hands several times in this period. It may make more sense to think of a relatively informal network of high-status exchange, meeting the demands of increasingly assured landed elites with a shared taste in material culture, operating through seasonal beach markets on good natural sites; as this network gradually thickened in the course of the seventh century, trading settlements near the mouths of great rivers like the Rhine and the Thames emerged; and by around 700 rulers were institutionalising and regulating such trade, through establishing control over sites such as Dorestad, clearly important to both Franks and Frisians, or through investment in purpose-built new sites such as Hamwic, or Ribe in Denmark. This model might be supported by changes in the coin evidence. The seventh century saw the widespread use of an apparently non-royal silver currency of *sceattas* around the North Sea, but in the 670s the Frankish court began to mint a royal silver coinage of a similar nature, in a development which marked a fundamental shift away from the remnants of the essentially fiscal coinages of late Roman and post-Roman times, to a coinage designed to be a medium of high-level exchange. Under Pippin and Charlemagne royal control of the coinage was re-established, and royal issues, their weight and silver content carefully controlled, were the only legitimate coin within the frontiers of the Frankish kingdom: the high volume of coin generally, and in particular the quantity and range of coins minted at sites such as Dorestad and Quentovic, suggests successful royal regulation of long-distance trade.

Whilst the exchange of goods such as amber and furs from Scandinavia, fine cloaks from England and quernstones and wine from the Rhine was the primary reason for this network of sites, once established they quickly acquired other functions. From the outset, sites such as Dorestad, Hamwic or Ribe seem to have been centres for the production of luxury goods, not just their exchange. At Dorestad, for example, the earliest clear phases of activity in the excavated area, beginning *c.* 675, show the creation of a series of large wooden buildings along the river front, each with its own jetty to aid the loading and unloading of beached ships: these were not simply 'warehouses', for there is considerable evidence for the processing and manufacture of raw materials assembled here, for example in finds of 'waste' raw amber and of detritus associated with metalwork. Several hundred kilometres down the Rhine, at Mainz in central Germany, similar if smaller-scale developments can be detected around a generation later, *c.* 700: here the warehouses and workshops erected on a strip of land along the riverbank housed metalworkers responsible for the distinctive 'Tassilo-chalice'-style decoration which was so fashionable among eighth-century elites, producing brooches and belt-buckles which were not only prized by the aristocracies of the city's hinterland but were also exported along the Rhine and found at sites as distant as York in England and Birka in Sweden.[22]

Initiatives of this kind may have been encouraged by the wide-ranging connections institutionalised through the North Sea emporia, but they ultimately also had important effects on regional patterns of production and exchange. Dorestad, after all, was 200 hectares in size, and beyond the jetties and workshops along the river front was a series of plots, three or four rows deep, each with a wooden 'house' similar to the 'halls' found on rural sites and various appendages. Whilst its population must have fluctuated season by season, it was home to several thousand permanent residents. The demand for food – particularly for the large numbers of seasonal visitors – as well as for raw materials – not only amber and metal but wood for boats and houses and leather for tools – could only be met through regional networks, and it is possible to trace the emergence of a series of secondary centres geared to such needs in Dorestad's hinterland. This process, at Dorestad and elsewhere, was a powerful force encouraging specialisation for the market in the surrounding countryside.[23] It also meant that, when Dorestad, like its constellation of trading partners, declined in the course of the ninth century, the regional networks of exchange and specialisation it had encouraged remained, and were able to find new outlets in more local markets. One obvious outlet for such activities were the sites of Roman cities, natural central places thanks not only to the presence of bishops in cities, but also the physical survival of walls and the network of Roman roads. Even at their nadir, in the seventh and eighth centuries, when cities were primarily marked by the concentration of churches in and around them, they remained places where landed elites had interests and met for secular business; populations of several thousand would be a fair estimate for such cities. Carolinigan legislation, in stressing the responsibility of bishops for preventing profiteering and ensuring fair weights and measures, strongly suggests that this made them the natural primary markets in a region. But in the course of the ninth century, economic activity reached a level where a more localised tier of markets sprang up in the countryside, primarily around aristocratic and ecclesiastical centres in the ninth and tenth centuries; some of these became the nuclei for medieval towns, others remained simply local markets.[24]

What underlay the ninth-century decline of the North Sea emporia? Viking raiding, especially after the 830s, is highly visible in the sources – Dorestad was raided four years running from 834–7 – and so has inevitably been favoured as an explanation. It must have affected the dynamics of trade, but the archaeology and coins suggest that it was a complicating factor in a longer-term pattern that it did not cause. A trading settlement like Dorestad worked according to an annual cycle, and the seizure rather than sale of its wares for those four years in the 830s whilst hardly helpful was not necessarily fatal. None of the excavated areas has shown any 'destruction layer', and the coins suggest that, although its economic peak had been reached in the 820s, extensive activity continued through the middle decades of the ninth century. This pattern of gradual decline rather than calamitous collapse is paralleled at Quentovic, where great abbeys and aristocrats sought to maintain their interests right through the middle decades of the ninth century.[25] Archaeologically, there are clear signs that changes within the exchange networks served by the emporia might explain their decreasing profile. At Dorestad, the jetties onto which wares were unloaded were repeatedly lengthened, until the longest were almost 200 metres long, a development which can partially be explained by the silting of the river and changing sea-levels, but also probably points to the increased importance of deeper draught vessels able to carry larger cargoes, which could not be dragged through shallow water and 'beached' for unloading but needed deeper anchorages; the changing focus of activity in London may reflect a similar development. In other words, once the initial boom of long-distance luxury exchange started to encourage more regional trade of higher-volume and lower-value material, the rationale of the emporia – characteristically low-lying undefended sites with no previous settlement history, where shallow vessels with low-volume luxury cargoes could easily be grounded – passed, and new markets suited to an economy of regional production eclipsed them. Whilst most of the major emporia – Dorestad and Quentovic in Francia, Hamwic in England – were abandoned in the end, it was possible for other sites to evolve. Rouen and Mainz, initially prominent in serving the North Sea network in the eighth century, had become nodal points of regional exchange by 900. The volume of coin production, and royal grants of market rights, suggest the rapid growth of these new networks in west Francia in the ninth century, and in east Francia in the tenth. International contacts did not, of course, end entirely – Rouen, thanks to its political connections with Scandinavia, was a major international port in the tenth century – but they no longer defined exchange networks, which were now rooted in their regions.

In this transition, the Viking factor should not be dismissed: after all, it was in the nature of emporia sites that they were undefended and difficult to fortify, and the new centres emerging by 900 were characteristically more compact and defensible, with the Roman walls being repaired at many cities in the last decades of the ninth century. But the Viking factor is complicated by the fact that these raiders hailed from areas that were also major trading partners, and the onset of raiding, as we shall see, is best explained in terms of the involvement of Scandinavian warlords in Frankish politics. In other words, one-time customers, as they were pulled into political conflicts within the Frankish world, might seize goods from areas controlled by their enemies, with plunder replacing trade as the mechanism of exchange; on several occasions in the ninth century we indeed hear of Viking warbands, on reaching peace with the Frankish 'hosts', engaging in trade, that is selling on the spoils of their plundering.[26] Activity of this kind can scarcely have been beneficial to the traders of Dorestad or Quentovic, but paradoxically it may have actually stimulated the patterns of regional exchange which were increasingly the engines of economic change: after all, Viking activity was a potent solvent dissolving land or treasure into liquid wealth through plunder, tribute-payment and ransom, and the archaeology suggests that this new wealth was largely spent in Anglo-Saxon and Frankish markets rather than returned to Scandinavia. Viking raiding was destructive for its victims, but it should not be seen as a catastrophic external factor sweeping aside existing economic systems; rather, it was an agency accentuating and accelerating the existing dynamics of change.

We can thus see the steeper social hierarchy and more intensive systems of agrarian exploitation encouraged by the Carolingian political system creating a new series of economic connections across northwestern Europe. These developments were paralleled by the intensification of economic linkages between northwestern Europe and the Mediterranean world. Through their interests in Italy in particular Frankish elites were able to acquire exotic luxury goods, which rapidly gained prominence as status symbols in the course of the ninth century. Some attempts have been made to see these changes as the result of royal initiatives comparable to those underpinning the development of the North Sea emporia. Excavations at the central Italian abbey of San Vincenzo al Volturno, founded in 703 but extensively patronised by the Carolingians, have shown a huge programme of rebuilding, and the creation of a series of workshops devoted to craft production under Abbot Joshua (792–817), making the monastery a powerful economic actor until its sack by Muslim raiders in 881.[27] But to see San Vincenzo as playing a role akin to the northern emporia – a 'monastic city' playing a central role in a consciously articulated economic policy – is probably misleading. Carolingian patronage here was essentially an attempt to win over a powerful regional ally, and the ninth-century activity is closely paralleled in major monasteries north of the Alps, where investment in craft production went hand-in-hand with the more intensive management of monastic lands documented by the polyptychs, and had important knock-on effects for the rural economy as a whole.

In fact, the rhythms of economic change in the eighth- and ninth-century Mediterranean differed significantly from better-studied developments around the North Sea. The North Sea economy took off against a background of very little exchange even on the most local of levels, in a thoroughly ruralised society; hence it initially needed a new network of specialised trading settlements. In Italy, and indeed around the shores of the Mediterranean more generally, even though city populations had collapsed and the cityscapes been transformed, a still-living matrix of city life remained as the basis of social organisation. Landowners of all shapes and sizes, not only bishops but also aristocrats and more modest figures, were thoroughly implicated in city life. Rural estates thus remained intimately tied to urban centres, and a certain level of city-based redistribution, and with it some economic specialisation, was inevitable. As a result, even the collapse of the economic connections that had bound the ancient Mediterranean together in the course of the seventh century did not lead to the end of local exchanges: relatively modest but deeply embedded networks survived even at the nadir of long-distance trade, in the first decades of the eighth century, as an agreement concerning trade along the Po in 715 demonstrates.[28] Once long-distance economic connections were reactivated, the matrix of city settlements provided a ready-made series of local markets, tied into existing social networks and well-served by road and river communications: in the ninth century these were pulsing not only with increasing quantities of local produce – cash crops of chestnuts, vines and olives – but also with oriental luxuries, such as silks and spice.

Pioneering new work by Michael McCormick, resting on the accumulation of a series of different datasets for communication and exchange – not only the distribution maps of archaeological data, but also the methodologically groundbreaking compilation of databases for the documented movements of people – has placed our understanding of the chronology of these developments on a new footing. In the first half of the eighth century, Mediterranean contacts were limited: intermittent contacts between Constantinople and its southern Italian provinces, and a slightly higher level of Islamic shipping along the North African coast to southern Spain. From the later eighth century, and particularly in the period *c.* 775–825, however, an increased volume of activity becomes visible; most importantly, the major axes of communication and exchange shifted as new networks linking the North African coast to the western Mediterranean, and connecting the Adriatic to major Mediterranean routes, emerge.[29] The origins of this reorientation remain obscure, but political change within the Islamic world probably played an important role: the disruptive effects of the Islamic conquests of Byzantine Africa and the Visigothic kingdom had been exacerbated by a series of revolts, fuelled by the demands of the now Islamised Berber communities of these provinces and tied into the internal conflicts which eventually led to the 'Abbasids *da'wla* or revolution. The establishment of the 'Abbasid Caliphate in the decades after 750 re-established political stability within the Islamic world under rulers such as Harun al-Rashīd (786–809). Within this framework the Islamic elites which were increasingly putting down roots in the caliphate's western provinces could begin to develop connections implicit in the geography of the Mediterranean: shipping along the North African coastline, after all, naturally passed close by Sicily, and economic linkages were an inevitable result. As well as Islamic traders operating from the cities of the North African coast, and from Cairo, the major Islamic city of the Near East and a crucial valve into the long-distance networks of the Indian Ocean, Italian shipping became increasingly visible in this region in the decades around 800: the trading networks of cities such as Naples have their origins in this period. The parallel thickening of contacts around the Adriatic may in part have been a response to the possibilities of plugging into this north–south exchange across the Mediterranean, but here the major agents were shippers operating from Venice, which first appears in the sources in the eighth century and which in the first half of the ninth century stood alongside Dorestad as the major entrepôt of the Carolingian economy, as the coin evidence confirms.

None of this was a wholly organic process. The forging of connections around the Mediterranean rested on the activities of intermediaries of a new kind. Now that the political framework of the Byzantine state barely extended beyond the Aegean, the state-led movements of goods and personnel which had already slowed to a trickle in the seventh century were little more than an irregular drip. The pioneers forging these new connections were not the holders of state-franchises whose position was underpinned by the imperial administration, but merchants operating across cultural and political divides. Indeed, the effective independence of many of the major Italian players is one striking feature of these networks. Naples, for example, although acknowledging the authority of the emperor in Constantinople had slipped beyond direct imperial control in the course of the eighth century and by the ninth century its rulers were pursuing an increasingly independent 'foreign policy', making alliances with Islamic rulers and other Italian cities for strategic ends. Venice, perched between the land and the sea at the top of the Adriatic, was a 'gateway community' that stood on the edge the Carolingian political system, its rulers making treaties with the Frankish kings but acting independently, and acknowledging the nominal authority of Constantinople; its emergence followed the loss of the remaining imperial possessions in northern Italy by the Lombards, culminating in the fall of Ravenna, the seat of the governor and the inevitable destination of shipping from Constantinople, in 750.

What was exchanged for the silks, spices and other oriental luxuries so avidly sought by western elites in Italian markets? One suggestion is that slaves were the primary European export: human captives, it has been argued, were a crucial component of the plunder and tribute which fed Carolinigan expansion, exported to meet the needs of Islamic societies in which slavery was an economically central institution. Whilst slaving clearly did play a role – the modern term 'slave' originates in the export of Slavs from the frontiers of east Francia, a movement well-documented in the tenth century but originating in the ninth – it is difficult to see it as the main motor of economic change. Slaves, of course, leave little in the way of archaeological traces, but although there is a scattering of anecdotal and circumstantial evidence for ninth-century slave-trading, particularly by Viking and Muslim raiders, it is difficult to see Charlemagne's Saxon wars as primarily aimed at slave-taking – the sources talk of Saxon warriors taken hostage, not forced into slavery, and peasants resettled within Francia – and harder still to see a mechanism for large-scale slaving after the end of concerted Frankish expansion. It therefore makes more sense to stress the increased productivity of the European countryside, such a central feature of the Carolingian system; oriental imports thus found their way from Italian markets north of the Alps in exchange for the goods produced on the manors and in the monastic workshops of western Europe.

Bishops, councils and correction

Part and parcel of the Carolingian achievement was a reshaping of the church. Carolingian kings from Pippin's time onwards had been enthusiastic sponsors of programmes of church 'reform'. 'Reform' with its modern overtones of positive adjustment can be a misleading term. Contemporaries talked of 'correction' or 'renewal', that is a return to what were seen as timeless norms of proper practice. In fact, however, time after time 'correction' involved turning to texts that were read as authoritative statements of universal standards. In that the texts most frequently promoted by the Carolingians' ecclesiastical advisors had not previously been invested with formal authority, 'correction' thus often involved establishing norms where practice had been various and localised, if necessary by legislative force. Whilst the rhetoric of correction thus allowed the Carolingians and their ecclesiastical allies to reshape the church, and portray their opponents as enemies of proper Christian order, it should not be seen as a cynical ploy of legitimation. After all, it was not called into being at the royal whim, but was developed in the first half of the eighth century by churchmen of diverse origin as they encountered the Christian cultures on the peripheries of the Frankish kingdom. At root, what was at issue was the integration of a series of regional communities that had developed their own cultural and religious traditions, memorably characterised by Peter Brown as 'microchristendoms'.[30] The political consolidation of the Frankish world in the eighth century made these regional differences all the more apparent, and the imposition of prescribed uniform standards was the almost inevitable response. After all, it was difficult for kings and their advisors to see the Franks as a chosen people, united before God, if religious practice within the kingdom was marked by diversity. The religious and political dimensions of this drive for 'correct Christianity' cannot, therefore, be meaningfully separated. But the norms that were created came to define the western European, Latin, Christian tradition.

The royal court drove these processes. Here, learned or renowned scholars were actively headhunted as potential advisors, and under Charlemagne in particular the cultural patronage dispensed by the king led to competition amongst courtiers anxious to demonstrate their virtuosity. Prestige culture of this slightly precious if not precocious kind had been associated with courts since late antiquity, and the changing scale of Carolingian patronage in part mirrors the expanding political scope of Carolingian kingship. Whilst Pippin emulated the more successful of his sixth- and seventh-century Merovingian predecessors by attracting Frankish churchmen renowned for their learning to his entourage, under Charlemagne increased political involvement in the Mediterranean world led to a conscious recruitment campaign. This was in part a response to the Roman heritage of recently imperial cities such as Ravenna, but more importantly it was an acknowledgement of the fact that in Italy cultural patronage was an important aspect of political authority, as at the Lombard courts at Pavia and Benevento and the papal court at Rome. Some aspects of Carolingian court culture can be seen as reactions to the expectations now invested in the Frankish kings by their new subjects: the architecture and decor of new royal palaces north of the Alps, for example, owed much to Italian idioms of power and prestige, whilst on a more modest scale the monograms which served as royal symbols on coins and documents drew on Mediterranean traditions.[31] It is thus no surprise to find Italian scholars, now enmeshed with the Carolingian court, colouring its cultural milieu: Paul the Deacon, who knew both Pavian and Beneventan courts first hand, crossed the Alps to plead for the release of his brother, held hostage, but Charlemagne's patronage kept him at court for several years. A succession of southern Gallic and Hispanic figures, no longer able to plug into the patronage networks radiating from Visigothic kings, found fame and fortune in Francia, most notably the Goth Theodulf, who was eventually rewarded with the bishopric of Orleans. Add to the mix the continuing involvement with the Frankish kings of Anglo-Saxon and Irish churchmen, and the cosmopolitan range of scholarship that animated the Carolingian court becomes clear.

The intensity of Carolingian involvement with this wider initiative of 'correction' owed much to the fact that they were newcomers to the throne, suffering from what might be called a 'legitimacy deficit'. Carolingian kings presented themselves as fulfilling a resolutely Christian office, rooted in care for the church, and for the powerless and weak: kings were thus expected to be committed to the hard work of 'correction'. The court was important as a clearing house for individuals, ideas and texts, and as a locus for learned debate through which the proper shape of 'correct' Christianity emerged. In part, this

Essay

The Carolingian court and the diffusion of culture

The poems of court scholars, read in conjunction with the brief comments in Einhard's *Life of Charlemagne*, can suggest a static picture, evoking a fixed circle of 'professional' resident scholars. This is misleading. Individual coming and going as the court itself was constantly reformed was the order of the day. Einhard wrote with hindsight, successfully setting a template which informed expectations about royal patronage through the ninth century, whilst many of the most vivid poetic evocations of court life were similarly exercises in nostalgia, where individuals now burdened with the pressing cares of office as abbot or bishop imagined past golden days of scholarly debate. The court was thus as much an imaginative as a physical space. There was no formal court 'school' with defined membership, but instead preferment through a royal household which prized learning, but whose institutional foundations were the royal chapel, and the writing-office or chancery manned by palace chaplains. Even Charlemagne's famous 'court library' was actually a shifting collection of manuscripts stored in the treasury and seen as a part of the palace chapel.[32] In and of itself, the expanded range and scale of cultural patronage explains the scholarly tone of the Carolingian court, which led to important developments in 'intellectual' culture. Latin poetry was established as the preferred medium in which the likes of Theodulf or his great rival, the Anglo-Saxon scholar Alcuin, sought contact with 'those golden hands that take away poverty' or celebrated the magnificence of a king who 'loved poets'.[33] But, crucially, Carolingian court culture was ultimately more than a narrow and self-consciously emulative idiom of conspicuous display, and individuals like Alcuin or Theodulf were not simply providers of flattering panegyric and intellectual curiosities. Both were central figures in the programme of 'correction' that aimed at nothing less than the wholesale Christianisation of society. Once they left permanent residence at court to take up important abbacies or bishoprics, they brought with them not only books, ideas and resources, but also a sense of urgent common endeavour and a network of contacts who could be cultivated through systems of gift-exchange which included letters, poems and manuscripts. As a result, the court served as much as a cultural framework for discourse over the correct ordering of church and society as a physical reality. This nexus of ideas and individuals is the key to understanding the most striking cultural developments of the period – the rapid adoption of a new script, Caroline miniscule, and of new liturgical rites and texts across the empire. It shaped a cultural unity rooted in shared ambitions and common endeavour: this, not bureaucratic uniformity of practice, was the crucial achievement of Carolingian 'correction'.

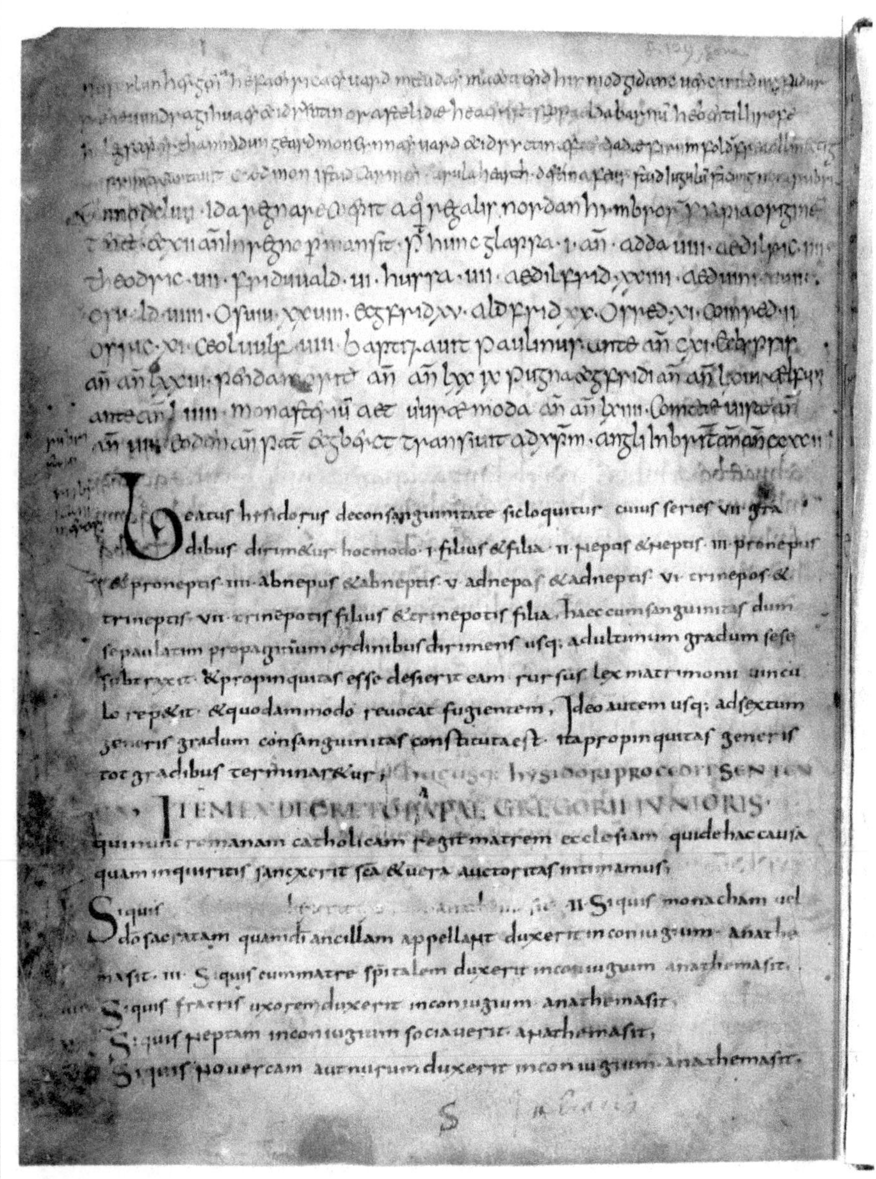

Figure 10.4 'Moore Bede' folio. A note in this manuscript of Bede's *Ecclesiastical History*, produced by the monks of the author's own abbey of Wearmouth-Jarrow, records its acquisition for the collection at Charlemagne's court

Figure 10.5 Lorsch Gospels cover. The magnificent ivory cover which adorned one of a series of magnificent illuminated Gospel Books produced at Charlemagne's court; this one was acquired by the abbey of Lorsch, whose abbot was one of the signatories of Charlemagne's will, after the emperor's death

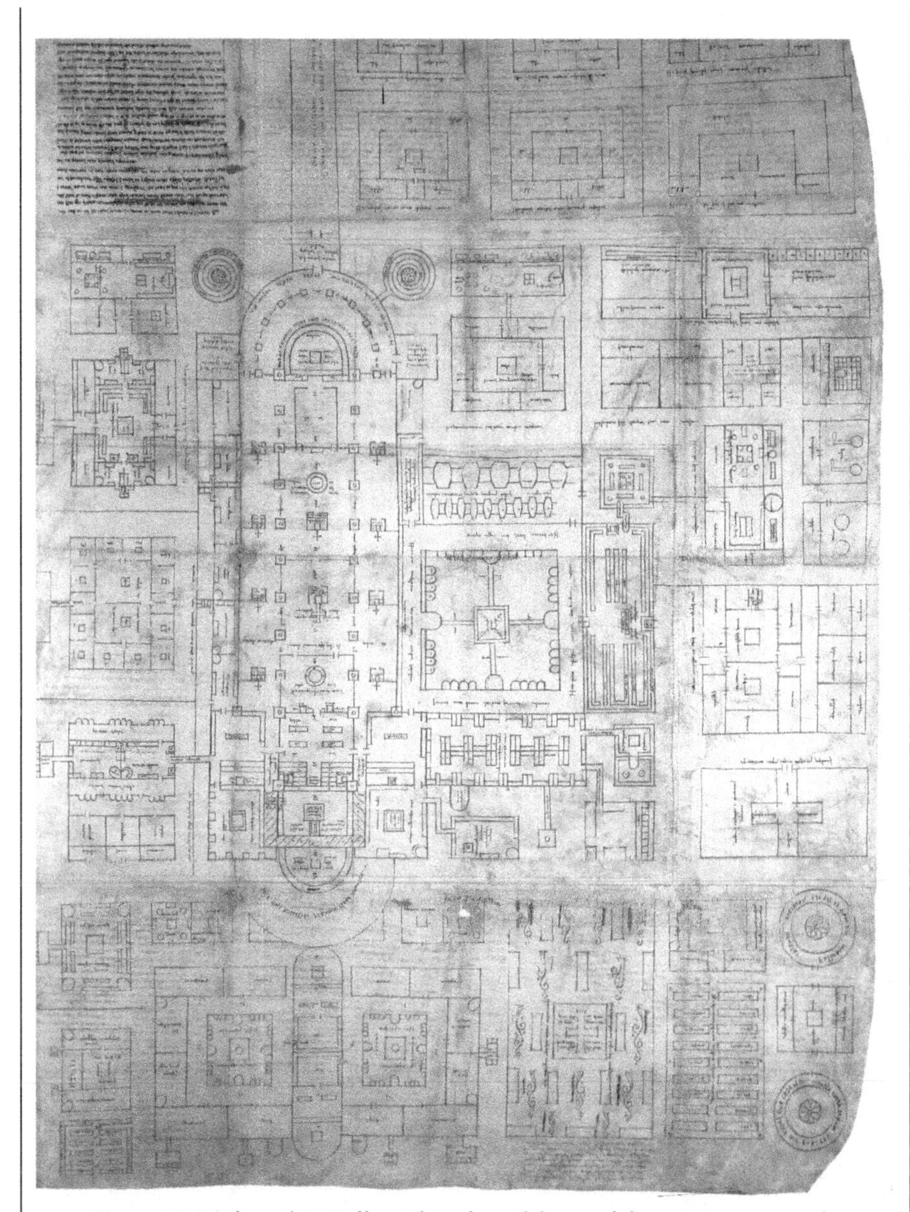

Figure 10.6 Plan of St-Gallen: This plan of the model monastery, strongly influenced by the 'corrected' monastic rule and observance agreed at the Council of Aachen in 817, was sent by the Bishop of Constance to the abbot at St-Gallen; it demonstrates the continuing involvement of abbots and bishops in court-centred debates over 'correction'

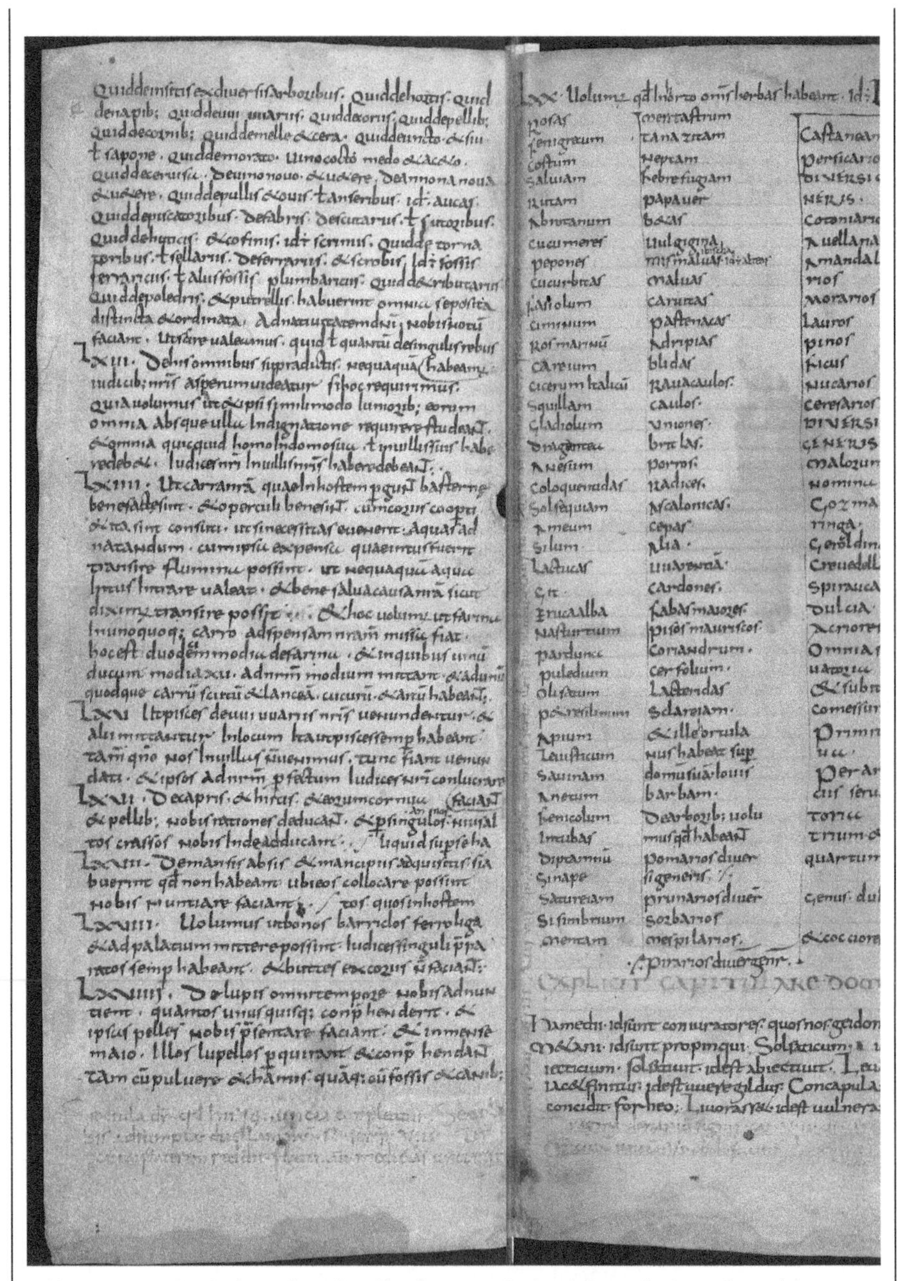

Figure 10.7 Capitulary *de Villis*. Charlemagne's careful regulation of royal estates, evidenced in the capitulary *de Villis*, was to serve as a template for the efforts of ninth-century abbots and bishops to maximise the income for their estates

was defined by contact with Christian traditions that the Frankish court came to see as aberrant, in the process more clearly shaping a distinct Latin Christianity, which of course it saw as 'correct'. In the last decades of the eighth century, debate at the court over controversies raging in both the Byzantine and Hispanic churches played an important role in sharpening ideological and theological boundaries. Byzantine attempts to end the internal dissensions which had been caused by the imperial policy of iconoclasm – the banning of the use of images in worship – led to the summoning, at Nicaea in 787, of a church council in the great tradition of universal councils: here the eastern bishops formally abandoned iconoclasm, and the conciliar acts, eagerly received by the popes who saw the possibility of rapprochement with Constantinople on matters doctrinal, were forwarded to the Frankish court. The Frankish reaction was unexpectedly hostile, given that imperial policy was moving towards western opinion, which was unperturbed by the whole issue of images. The circle of scholars around Charlemagne saw the Byzantine position as theologically incorrect, and a response – the so-called *Libri Carolini* (literally, 'books of Charles' or 'Caroline books') – was drafted by Theodulf condemning Greek 'error' and challenging the universal credentials of Nicaea.

Whilst much in the Frankish response was a result of cultural mistranslation – both literally, in that the decline of Greek learning in the west meant that Charlemagne worked from a poor Latin translation of the conciliar acts, but also more fundamentally in that the cultural issues at stake in eastern controversies over images had no resonance in the west – it also marked a new level of self-confidence. In 794, a council of western bishops under Charlemagne's leadership held at Frankfurt confirmed these condemnations, presenting the Latin church under Carolingian leadership as a bastion of universal orthodoxy against the 'church of the Greeks'. The self-appointed role of Charlemagne and his advisors in ensuring orthodoxy had implications for the western, Latin, church, too. The bishops at Frankfurt also confirmed Alcuin's condemnation of an important strand of theological opinion within the Hispanic church, labelled by its opponents as 'Adoptionism' and seen as a revival of ancient disputes about the relation of Christ to God. The spokesman for this 'heresy', Felix, was deposed from his position as bishop of Urgell.

There were striking similarities between the attack on 'Adoptionism' and the response to Greek 'error'. Alcuin intruded into a local dispute whose terms he failed to fully grasp, and condemned his opponents for maintaining a theological position which had deep roots in the cultural heritage of the Visigothic church, but was wholly alien to the Anglo-Saxon and Frankish traditions. 'Adoptionism', however, was not simply a matter of external error, but a threat to the integrity of the Frankish church, for Felix and many of his followers were the dominant party in those areas of the Pyrenees which had recently passed under Carolingian rule; one of the features of the whole dispute was the inability of Elipandus, archbishop of Toledo and architect of a policy of co-existence with the Muslim conquerors, to impose his definition of orthodoxy on those Christian communities beyond the frontiers of al-Andalus. Felix's deposition began a generation of pastoral work by the agents of the Frankish king aimed at correcting distinctive local observances, for example different modes of baptism from the Frankish 'norm'; these aspects of the whole affair bore unmistakable echoes of the campaigns led by Boniface east of the Rhine a generation earlier.

The cultivation of scholarship at court thus enabled the Frankish church to define itself as coterminous with 'correct' Christianity: debates condemning various Byzantine ecclesiastical initiatives continued to be an important mechanism for articulating Frankish orthodoxy through to the end of the 820s. But perceptions of Frankish 'correctness' were not only, nor even primarily, rooted in differences between Frankish and Byzantine practice; they were a direct result of the urgent moral energy put into the business of 'correcting' the Frankish church on the most basic of levels. The cosmopolitan cultural mix of the Frankish court, and the diverse intellectual traditions and textual resources available there, encouraged genuine reflection on 'correction' in its most literal sense: the correct reading and understanding of holy texts. The court, at the heart of Frankish society, was also a mechanism for the dissemination of texts and ideas. This milieu explains the development of Frankish interest in collections of canons of church councils, which defined the law of the church as an institution; in the texts and traditions of the liturgy, the ritual of the church; and in the chant in which crucial parts of the liturgy were performed. Time and again, 'correction' here involved an attempt to return to 'Roman' tradition, meaning the 'true' traditions of the early church, whose authoritative status was enshrined by the prestige of the church of Rome itself. Roman texts, for example, played an important role in the development of canon law, whilst liturgists promoted what they believed was the Roman liturgy and Roman chant, cutting across centuries of organic development from late antique exemplars in the churches of Latin Europe.

The paradoxical nature of this sense of a return to 'correct' practice is exemplified by arguably the most important aspect: the 'correction' of the Latin language itself. Across much of the Frankish world, spoken language had slowly evolved from Latin through the post-Roman period; Merovingian written Latin thus stood in an organic relationship with a living spoken language which had long since departed from the norms of the classical 'golden age'. Anglo-Saxon scholars, particularly Alcuin, brought a new cultural resource, in the insular tradition of teaching Latin as a foreign language to native Germanic speakers through the work of grammarians; the increased cultural and political profile of the Germanic-speaking regions and its elites meant that these traditions found fertile ground. But those schooled in this tradition of scholarship found their learned Latin to be distant from the spoken language of the population of Gaul, Italy or Spain. And in a religious culture in which the correct performance of liturgical ritual played a central role, matters of language and pronunciation were taken seriously. In a circular 'on the cultivation of letters' from *c.* 780, for example, Charlemagne urged upon the abbots and bishops of his realm the importance of ensuring the correct use of language in worship, for 'uncouth expression' might not only obscure the sense of what was being said, but also – and far worse – inadvertently introduce error.[34] The imposition of 'correct' standards of Latin orthography and pronunciation ultimately derived from grammatical texts which were seen as authoritative guides was thus necessary to ensure that prayers were successful and error was avoided. But it also opened up a gulf between the formal language of the church and its rites, and the vernacular of the people even in those formerly Roman areas where a Latin Christian culture had enjoyed a continuous history since late antiquity.

Concerns about slips obscuring meaning or introducing doctrinal error were also a fundamental drive behind the correction and circulation of texts, even the text of the Bible itself, to which Theodulf and others devoted considerable scholarship. One crucial development here was the transformation of the systems of writing, so as to facilitate the production and circulation of manuscripts bearing 'correct' knowledge. Here, the development and rapid diffusion of a new script, called 'Caroline miniscule' by specialists, ties in closely with efforts to correct Latin and promote learning by the court. 'Caroline miniscule' can appear more legible than the range of scripts – most of them variations on the cursive official handwriting of the late Roman period, but with considerable variations, notably in those areas where insular missionaries had introduced a wholly different script system – used in the Merovingian period, but that is largely a result of the fact that it provides the model for modern typescript. Although there were considerable regional variations, betraying the schooling of different scribes, within 'Caroline miniscule' – hence specialist palaeographers can venture dates and places of origin for surviving manuscripts – it did provide a common model, comprehensible to all readers regardless of its place of origin. It was also a faster script, better suited to the systematic production of manuscripts undertaken by many Carolingian monasteries in particular. Although the court played an important role in its dissemination, it was not simply imposed from above. The new script itself seems to have originated in experiments at monasteries close to the court, before gaining an official imprimatur, and being exported from the court to the great churches of the kingdom thanks to the circulation of books, scholars and above all scribes, and so quickly becoming the accepted norm. This pattern of diffusion – not uniformity imposed by legislative instrument, but unity through the export and adaptation of personnel and resources – laid the foundations of Carolingian 'correction'.

Just as the reshaping of aristocratic hierarchies took place through decisions debated in assemblies and transmitted through capitularies, so 'correction' of the church was rooted in the deliberations of regular councils of churchmen, their decisions preserved in written form in canons which were collected and circulated: the processes were parallel and overlapping, with royal assemblies attended by the major bishops and abbots of the realm, and capitularies often covering ecclesiastical as well as secular matters. The convocation of church councils or synods had its own special formal protocols, invoking the great tradition of collective decision-making by bishops, which marked it off from the routine process of deliberation at assemblies and the production of capitularies. But the revival of church councils was a royal initiative, and their timing and location, particularly in the eighth century, was determined by the royal itinerary; Carolingian conciliar activity was thus intimately related to the processes of royal government. The holding of councils began in 742, immediately after Charles Martell's death, partly as an attempt by Pippin and his brother Carloman to rally ecclesiastical support; Boniface, whose expectation of regular 'national' meetings of bishops was shaped by the experience of the Anglo-Saxon church, claimed that these were the first such meetings for 70 years, and it certainly is the case that the political and social changes of the decades around 700 had seen traditions of collective episcopal action atrophy.[35] Thereafter, councils became regular events, initially dominated by identifiable cadres and groupings within the Frankish church but soon, as agencies for binding collective decision-making, attended by the bishops and leading abbots of the kingdom *en masse*. Through them, influential churchmen who enjoyed the ears of kings were able to shape the views of their fellow abbots and bishops, and develop a programme of reform.

One vital, and too easily overlooked, result, was the development of an identifiable *esprit de corps* rooted in a sense of collective religious leadership. This soon found ritual expression through collective prayer: at Attigny in 762 the attendees entered an agreement of confraternity, offering regular prayer for one another and undertaking to perform Masses and other pious acts of commemoration for the soul of any deceased member. These bonds of prayer should not be dismissed as an incidental extra: these were rites which mattered to contemporaries, creating everlasting associations and obligations, and through them the myriad churches of the kingdom, each embedded in its local landscape of patronage and piety, were bound together into a corporate entity with wider horizons. From the latter part of the eighth century confraternities involved not just personal obligations between abbots and bishops, but institutional ones which tied together the priests and monks of individual foundations with their peers and brethren elsewhere in the kingdom: the scale of these networks of prayer, crisscrossing the Frankish world and binding its great churches, and particularly its monasteries, is vividly demonstrated by the confraternity book created by the monks of Reichenau in 824, which documents confraternities with hundreds of other churches expressed by the listing of tens of thousands of names for whom prayers were said. Confraternity in prayer articulated a sense of a Frankish church with a mission to ensure the salvation of its people. And because the agency for this mission was the Frankish kingdom, prayer for the souls of kings and their family, and for the health and stability of the kingdom, likewise came to be expected of all abbeys and bishoprics in the last decades of the ninth century. These bonds, as a spiritual glue which defined the Frankish kingdom as God's chosen vehicle, paralleled and reinforced the oaths of fidelity taken on holy relics from all free men, developed in precisely the same period. Just as oath-taking defined membership of society, so liturgical rites of prayer defined cultural boundaries.

Participation in conciliar activity thus shifted the horizons of religious practice: churchmen no longer served a 'microchristendom' rooted in local landscapes and face-to-face relationships, but were part of a spiritual cadre responsible for an imagined community of Christians which was coterminous with the Frankish kingdom. These changes had their practical elements, notably the creation of a formal internal hierarchy of church organisation. Central to this system were archbishops. The jurisdiction of the archbishops over the other bishops within their provinces originated in the late Roman administrative geography on which the structures of late antique church government were based, but social and political change in the course of the Merovingian period had undermined these provincial structures. The renewal of the office of archbishop arose from the special status granted by the pope to specific individuals in the course of eighth-century mission: Boniface, for example, was granted oversight over missionary activity east of the Rhine. Soon the favoured churchmen of the Frankish rulers, men like Chrodegang of Metz, were receiving similar personal recognition. In the last decades of the eighth century, however, the acknowledgement of the leading role of specific individuals within the church in this manner gave way to the recreation of an institutional structure of church provinces whose bishops were subject to their archbishop. Across much of Gaul, this simply involved reinvigorating ancient provincial geographies, although east of the Rhine it involved creating new hierarchies, with Boniface's former see of Mainz granted supremacy over a vast province from Saxony down to the Swiss Alps, but Bavaria allowed its own provincial organisation under Salzburg. This new hierarchy crystallised in the 780s, although in southern Gaul, where there was a mosaic of often tiny bishoprics, and many archiepiscopal provinces were smaller than northern dioceses, there was some reorganisation, completed by the end of Charlemagne's reign.

At the apex of the archiepiscopal hierarchy stood the royal court, where a favoured royal advisor might enjoy the position of head of the royal chapel, or archchaplain: under Charlemagne, Hildebold combined the role with that of archbishop of Cologne from 784–819. Royal leadership of the church could not have been more clearly articulated, for although the pope enjoyed a privileged position as a source of authoritative rulings, and a guarantor of procedural correctness, he was essentially outside a hierarchy focused on the court. Papal judgement was sought when necessary but the internal structures of the Frankish church did not articulate hierarchical papal government. The development of learning in canon law in the ninth century further upgraded the role of the pope, particularly as a source of appeal for Frankish bishops where they felt that their rights had not been properly respected. But although papal judgement was sought in many of the *causes célèbres* of ninth-century ecclesiastical politics – particularly under an energetic pope such as Nicholas I (858–69) – it was invoked strategically, as a matter of final appeal not routine jurisdiction. The pope, although a recipient of Carolingian protection, was never fully a part of the Carolinigan church, not least as his role also involved being the point of contact between eastern and western empires.

It was bishops, however, who remained the central figures in Frankish church organisation. In the ninth century, there were attempts to upgrade understandings of archiepiscopal jurisdiction, justified by collections of conciliar canons into which forged material was inserted, notably in the collections of 'pseudo-Isidore' and 'Benedict the Levite'. But when archbishops like Hincmar of Rheims sought to act on such claims, moving beyond oversight of episcopal appointments and the exercise of judgement when necessary to instigate a more bureaucratic discipline, they were eventually defeated by the collective judgement of their peers: witness Hincmar's frustrated attempts to deal with his namesake, nephew and suffragan, Bishop Hincmar of Laon. Carolingian 'correction' insisted on the jurisdiction of bishops over all churches, and all aspects of ecclesiastical life, within their dioceses. Although notionally resting on the boundaries of former Roman provinces, it is difficult to see late Merovingian bishoprics as strongly territorial entities: the seventh-century wave of monastic foundations, in particular, was accompanied by a series of grants of immunity from episcopal interference, and episcopal authority was increasingly articulated through ownership of monasteries and churches: hence the planned foundation of episcopal monasteries at strategic sites within their dioceses by some late Merovinigan bishops. By the middle decades of the eighth century, the activities of Anglo-Saxon and Frankish holy men, missionaries and bishops had created a mesh of crisscrossing ecclesiastical constellations, with the scattered group of monastic foundations associated with an individual like Boniface or Chrodegang linked to their episcopal seats, but also connected to the foundations of their followers and associates. Whilst this was most marked in Austrasia and the regions east of the Rhine, even in Neustria the patterns of ecclesiastical patronage through which Carolingian control had been established encouraged a similar web. Carolingian 'correction' inevitably altered the rules here. Councils insisted on episcopal jurisdiction over the monasteries of their dioceses, and by the last third of the eighth century the constellations of churches like those that had formed around Boniface and Chrodegang were slowly dismembered: Mainz and Metz lost control of the network of monastic foundations inherited from their former bishops. Dismemberment was not total: the network of small monastic foundations built up by Abbot Fulrad of St-Denis remained the property of his abbey after his death, but they did not constitute a separate and independent entity articulating a non-territorial alternative to episcopal government. Chrodegang's major foundations near Metz, for example, were allowed to remain in the bishopric's hands as buttresses for newly territorialised episcopal power, but his outlying foundations east of the Rhine were dissociated, some subjected to regular episcopal jurisdiction, whilst Lorsch – like Fulrad's St-Denis and Boniface's Fulda – acquired a privileged status which maintained its independence of the episcopal hierarchy.

The precedent for the privileged status acquired by these and 50 or so other major monasteries of the Frankish kingdom lay in the Merovingian past. Seventh-century kings had cultivated close relationships of mutual dependence with the major monasteries of Neustria, and under Pippin these relationships, particularly with St-Denis, were reactivated and reaffirmed, and a handful of other houses, notably the family foundation at Prüm, were similarly favoured. Charlemagne extended the scope of his 'protection' to a more extensive network of major monasteries, using them as points of entry into the local aristocratic networks of patronage and property in which they were so central: through the 780s in particular he can be seen consciously bringing a series of aristocratic foundations in the regions east of the Rhine and south of the Loire under his control as a means of entrenching his rule. Once they came under royal 'protection', monasteries entered into a direct relationship with the king, who ultimately exercised control over abbatial appointments. Boniface's foundation at Fulda, for example, was by the 780s ruled by Baugolf, an aristocratic convert who had served as a count in Pippin's entourage in his youth, and it was through Baugolf, loyal to his

Carolingian masters but responsive to the networks of local landowners whose patronage sustained his monks, that the major regional revolt of 786 was resolved.

Royal 'protection' brought with it other obligations too, to supply the king with the appropriate support, whether in the form of hospitality or troops. But it also brought privilege, and it was increasingly combined with grants of immunity to create a special class of 'royal monasteries' directly answerable to the king and so independent of the jurisdiction of local bishops in ecclesiastical matters, and indeed counts in secular affairs. Under Louis the Pious, the dovetailing of protection with immunity reached its logical conclusion, as all earlier privileges were called in and reissued in a standard form at the beginning of his reign. In a closely related process, royal monasteries were divided into three classes according to their resources, the poorest to support the king through prayer alone, but others to provide produce also, and some soldiers as well. Through the ninth century, abbots eagerly sought a renewal of these 'liberties' each time a new king ascended to the throne, not because such grants were seen as revocable, but as a reminder of the special links between kings and monks: this was not a system of wilful royal control so much as a personal relationship in which loyal service was the honourable return for the confirmation of a privileged status. The precise terms of this service might be a matter for negotiation: west Frankish kings in the second half of the ninth century, for example, occasionally found themselves criticised when they found it necessary to grant out abbeys to favoured aristocrats who served as 'lay-abbots'. But that service was the accepted and honourable return for the privileges that assured proper monastic life was not doubted. Indeed, every effort was made to preserve the purity of the monastic life through the creation of internal boundaries between the cloister, still a place of secluded monastic life exempt from outside demands, and other structures – guesthouses and gatehouses – where monks interacted with their secular patrons and protectors. Even lay-abbots were far from disastrous for their charges, for frequently they would be earmarked specific estates for their exclusive use, and a long-serving and respected monk given oversight over the communal life of the community, arrangements which were also adopted when kings built up favoured bishops like Archbishop Hatto of Mainz by granting them the abbacy of far-flung constellations of monasteries.

This close relationship between monks and kings rested on more than a cynical recognition of mutual self-interest. Carolingian kings were deeply interested and involved in monasticism, which, after all, had begun as a movement allowing laymen to seek spiritual perfection through communal life governed by a rule. Charlemagne and Louis the Pious were both rumoured in old age to have considered retiring to a monastery; Louis' son, Lothar, in fact did so. This interest in monastic life informed royal sponsorship of monastic 'reform', with the regimes and rules developed by favoured churchmen actively championed. The Rule of St Benedict, developed in sixth-century Italy as a 'rule for beginners', but soon acquiring a high status thanks to the posthumous reputation of its author, was increasingly privileged by Carolingian churchmen. The consistent promotion of the Rule of Benedict marked a move away from the characteristic monastic culture of the early medieval period, where monastic founders created their own regimes based on a range of illustrious models and adjusted according to practice, towards a new world where there was a single authoritative text on which all monastic observance was to be based. Modern historians, for whom Benedictinism and monasticism are often synonymous, fail to realise that this was a Carolingian equation. Any attempt to characterise Merovingian monasticism in terms of disorder or indiscipline takes the rhetoric of reformers at face value: the creative adaptation of specific rules for individual communities lay at the heart of pre-Carolingian monasticism, and the Carolingian insistence of the Rule of Benedict thus was not a response to corruption or decay, but an attempt to impose a new universal blueprint for monastic life. Uniformity of practice across the empire as a whole, so as to weld the monastic communities of the Frankish kingdoms together as a single engine of prayer, was the goal here. The crucial developments went hand-in-hand with the reworking of monastic liberties, in the first years of Louis the Pious' reign. Louis' court in Aquitaine had promoted the monastic observances developed by Benedict of Aniane, particularly in those leading monasteries that were new recipients of royal 'protection'. When Louis succeeded his father, Benedict of Aniane's interpretation of the Rule of Benedict of Nursia was enforced as the norm for monastic discipline across the empire as a whole. An approved version of the Rule and a closely regulated set of observances agreed at the Synod of Aachen in 817, a 'model monastery' created for Benedict at Inde close by the royal palace at Aachen, and Louis' archchaplain, Benedict's disciple Helischar, began an active programme of inspection designed to encourage the monasteries of the empire to bring their existing practices into line with the Aachen decrees. These developments were to define the parameters of monastic life through the ninth century; tenth-century reformers promoted further refinements to this existing template, rather than setting it aside or responding to its failure.

These changes accentuated the role of monasteries as 'powerhouses of prayer', their intercession with God particularly potent thanks to the disciplined perfection and collective liturgical virtuosity of their inmates. This intercession was exercised for the good of king, kingdom and people, that is in support of a state which understood itself as fulfilling a divinely appointed mission for the salvation of its subjects. Royal protection and uniformity of observance thus pulled together what had been individual islands of perfection, 'holy households' working for immediate associates and patrons, and welded them into an agency of professional prayer whose role was part of the wider project of Carolingian kings and bishops. This had several important implications for the nature of monastic life itself. The relatively small foundations, dominated by a single aristocratic family and differing little in size or shape from an estate centre, which were typical of the seventh and eighth centuries, are far less visible by the ninth. These tiny centres of family memory were swallowed up by the major monasteries, which offered commemoration of a different character on a different scale: witness those acquired for St-Denis by Fulrad, or the foundations given up by their owners to Fulda and Lorsch under Boniface's and Chrodegang's successors, after which they became cells or churches owned by the major monastery, and perhaps run by a handful of monks, but tied into a far larger economy of prayer. The growing popularity of special Masses, commissioned specifically to be said for the souls of the dead, as the most potent form of intercession, was one important factor in encouraging investment in the new, larger-scale, monasticism. The largest foundations, like Fulda by the ninth century, boasted several hundred inmates, and complexes of churches dedicated to Masses and prayer. This needed resources, and the scale of patronage and range of patrons acquired by the major Carolingian monasteries is clear both from the documentary records of land-donations, and the liturgical records of thousands of names for whom commemorative prayer and Masses were to be said: aristocrats bought into these services rather than founding their own familial centres of piety. These changes marginalised the role of women: the daughters, widows and aunts who had often run small family foundations were now excluded from the preferred form of intercessory activity, seeking individual solace as vowesses, but marginal to the principal networks of prayer and power.

This emphasis on the liturgy in general, and the Mass in particular, meant that most monks were now expected to be full priests. As a result, monastic recruitment increasingly rested on the training of child oblates – young boys given up by their families to the monks to be trained from youth so as to acquire the necessary standing to become a monk-priest. The increased scale of monastic communities, and the expanded resources and protection this involved, made them the main educational institutions of the Carolingian kingdoms: some boys might undergo a part of their education there without undergoing the full-blooded monastic training expected of oblates, a fact recognised by reformers' attempts to differentiate 'internal' from 'external' schools. These patterns, whereby aristocratic families plugged into the currents of holy power pulsating through the monasteries of the empire by giving up sons to be educated by the monks, also led to fundamental changes in the formation of the ecclesiastical leadership. Prior to Carolingian reform, the boundaries between clerical and lay office were relatively permeable, at least for laymen wishing to enter the parallel hierarchy of the church. The definition of the priestly caste as something identifiably distinct from the secular elite in dress and deportment, and the expectations of a long training rooted in monastic discipline which guaranteed that the holy texts of Bible and liturgy had been wholly internalised, created firmer boundaries which could no longer be crossed with ease. The seventh century had seen a succession of powerful bishops who had served in a secular capacity at royal courts in their youth before undergoing a rapid change of status and receiving high ecclesiastical office. There were still echoes of this pattern in the second half of the eighth century. The future Benedict of Aniane, for example, was son of the count of Toulouse and a high-ranking official at Pippin's court before his 'conversion' to the monastic life on which he took on the name of his exemplar, casting aside his secular name Wittiza. Charlemagne's cousins Adalard and Wala of Corbie were both forced to 'retire' from the secular office and court life into monastic life, whence they made political comebacks as well-connected abbots. But by 800, such high-status 'conversions' were rare and remarkable: the best-documented comparison to the cases of Adalard or Benedict is that of Einhard, who from the late 820s was increasingly devoted to the service of the

Roman relics housed in the monastery at Seligenstadt, but he was a different kind of figure, a career courtier who never formally held high office in either the secular or the ecclesiastical hierarchy.[36] The monastic formation of the bishops of the ninth-century empire is remarkably consistent, and its implications remain to be worked out, for it meant that monastic discipline and monastic education shaped the leadership of the church almost to a man: it was fundamental to the world view of the likes of Hincmar, archbishop of Rheims from 845–82, or Hraban Maur of Mainz (847–56).

The architects of Carolingian 'correction' thus effected important changes to the nature and function of monasticism, transforming earlier small-scale attempts to pursue a perfect life in a holy household through promoting an authoritative text that was revised and reinterpreted to create a hierarchical institution providing intercession with God. This shift – from charismatic contact with the holy rooted in local initiatives to a new world of carefully regulated, routinised and professionalised hierarchies leading ultimately to Heaven – can be seen as central to Carolingian Christianity as a whole. The eighth century had seen charismatic leaders in areas new to Carolingian control – notably the provinces east of the Rhine and south of the Pyrenees – condemned and deposed as heretics on account of their threat to the church's new-found integrity. By the ninth century, however, accusations of heresy were primarily reserved for theological debates on 'the errors of the Greeks'. The major exception was the second-generation Saxon convert Gottschalk, educated as an oblate under Hraban Maur at Fulda. Gottschalk's intellectual virtuosity allowed him to revisit fundamental teachings about God's omniscience and whether it was compatible with human free will, issues last properly discussed in the west by Augustine and his contemporaries. His teaching, although it found many supporters, was ultimately condemned as heretical thanks to the implacable opposition of the two major churchmen of the time, Hincmar and Hraban. The complexity of the theological issues was such that even when 'safe' intellectuals such as John Scottus Eriugena and Ratramnus of Corbie were commissioned to refute Gottschalk's teachings they were unable to agree on a common line, and were not exempt from the suspicion of heresy themselves. But Hincmar and Hraban both saw Gottschalk as ultimately a troublemaker working outside the regular structures of the church – Hraban because Gottschalk had contested his oblation and talked his way out of Fulda, Hincmar because of Gottschalk's association with his predecessor and *bête noire*, Ebbo – and feared that his discussion of predestination to Heaven and Hell could only prevent the laity from performing good works. Those whose class and gender meant that they could simply be silenced were dealt with less respectfully: when a lay woman began preaching scandalous doctrines in 847, Hraban had her whipped and locked up.[37] By and large Hraban, Hincmar and their contemporaries steered rapidly away from accusations of heresy in even the most heated of debates, instead condemning their opponents as schismatic, breaking with the universal tradition of the church encapsulated in its canons.

This move from charismatic personal authority to hierarchical routine is also apparent in perhaps the central aspect of Carolingian religious life: the cult of the saints. The late Merovingian period was an age of contemporary and politicised sancitity. Leading churchmen were quickly promoted as saints, their cults informing the continued collective activity of their followers; inevitably, given the interpenetration of aristocratic politics, monastic foundation and episcopal office, these figures were politically involved and politically controversial. Even with the consolidation of Carolingian power in the middle decades of the eighth century, leading churchmen – not only Anglo-Saxon missionaries like Boniface, but aristocratic bishops like Chrodegang – were seen by their followers as living holy men who attracted gifts of churches and land, hence the wide-ranging constellations of interest they were able to build up. They were, however, the last of their type. Once we move into the ninth century, contemporary sanctity only existed beyond the frontiers of the Frankish Empire. Major bishops – the likes of Hraban of Mainz or Hincmar of Rheims – were no longer holy men invested with a personal charisma, but managers of an institutionalised church hierarchy. The change of sensibility that accompanied the institutionalisation of the holy is underlined by the changing profile of relics. The veneration of relics had been a central aspect of Frankish religious practice through the Merovingian period, and followers of the holy men of the seventh and eighth centuries had struggled to control their relics. Carolingian 'correction' confirmed this centrality, insisting that all churches must have relics under their altars, whilst subjecting relic-cults to episcopal regulation, as bishops would need to be convinced of the bona fides of relics before consecrating the altars that housed them, and were required to approve all relic-translations. Relics, of course, once they were housed in altars and subjected to episcopal regulation, were wholly institutionalised sources of contact with the holy. And rather than preserving the memory of a recently dead figure who had attracted a personal following embedded in aristocratic networks, relic-cults were increasingly tied up with a potent but distant past that did not directly animate allegiances and alliances in the present. This could be a means of avoiding or eliding a recent past which was problematic in the new world of Carolingian kingship: the churches of Saxony, for example, rapidly acquired a string of Roman relics in the ninth century, precisely because their conversion at swordpoint had not supplied usable histories or heroes. But it also reflected a wider change in the meaning of sanctity, and in elite piety. Already in the 760s, Chrodegang acquired a series of relics of early martyrs from Italy for his monastic foundations, and the Frankish elite quickly developed a taste for exotic tokens of an almost timeless and legendary vintage; by the 820s and 830s leading courtiers like Charlemagne's biographer Einhard and the archchaplain Abbot Hilduin of St-Denis were competing to acquire genuine Roman relics for their churches.[38]

Although Einhard and Hilduin's Roman relics toured the countryside and finally resided at their monastic foundations, they were first unveiled at Aachen as part of a competition for standing at the imperial court. This is no accident, for at the apex of the newly institutionalised hierarchies created by Carolingian 'correction' stood the court. Clerical careers might now be based on monastic education, but preferment followed from spending time at court, most probably as one of the gaggle of ambitious young clerics attached to the royal chapel, under the archchaplain, a parallel but now separate hierarchy from the aristocratic youths serving in the royal household and awaiting advancement to secular office.

This career path formed the horizons of all the great figures of the Carolingian church: Hincmar of Rheims, for example, was 'talent-spotted' by the archchaplain Hilduin, and spent the latter part of Louis the Pious' reign in the royal chapel, before being granted the vacant archbishopric of Rheims by the young Charles the Bald, whose knowledge of Hincmar's talents was rooted in their shared time at his father's court. The development of a programme of ecclesiastical and monastic reform, and the implementation of regular synods and assemblies, transformed the position of abbots and bishops from that of leaders of their own institutions to that of officials in an empire-wide church whose job was the implementation of an empire-wide programme of reform and of agreed standards. These measures not only allowed kings to tap the church's wealth and power, but also transformed abbots and bishops into royal officials, who were used in secular as well as ecclesiastical matters. The church as an institution cannot thus be separated from Carolingian kingship, and to see in Carolingian church reform an attempt to buttress the 'state' through appropriation of the 'church', misses the inseparable interpenetration of royal and divine power in contemporary eyes. This interpenetration worked both ways: whilst kings could draw on the institutional support of the church and the service of individual churchmen, they were expected to reciprocate by protecting the church's liberties and listening to the advice of churchmen, particularly of bishops in council. Where kings overstepped the mark – as a host of ninth-century rulers from Louis the Pious on did – they were the recipients of episcopal admonition, which needed treating with respect. This was not a premonition of later conflicts between 'church' and 'state' as separate and separable institutions, but a necessary correlate of the mutual dependence of bishops and kings.

What effect had all this episcopal admonition and legislation on religious practice in the countryside? Carolingian reform meant that the priests staffing the churches that dotted the countryside were to be made answerable to their bishops, and expected to fulfil their role according to certain basic requirements. An insistence on fitting priestly behaviour and adequate instruction to allow the provision of pastoral care – above all baptism and burial – and preaching to the rural population were the central concerns of conciliar legislation. To a very large degree, then, an insistence on episcopal authority here was a mechanism for the integration of hundreds of priests, embedded in the rural communities they served and tied into local networks of obligation and status, into a wider ecclesiastical hierarchy. Recurrent legislation regarding the powers of lay patrons or founding families over 'their' churches, for example, was aimed not at stamping out what were seen as their proper and reasonable claims, but at ensuring that the churches they supported were fit for purpose, able to provide proper pastoral care and carry out the wishes of Carolingian reformers: thus the unfree were not fitting persons to serve as priests in their master's churches. Legislation did not just concern itself with the legal status of priests: far more, it was concerned with the personal behaviour that articulated their public position. Central to the concerns of reformers was the requirement that priests be immediately identifiable as different from their lay kin and lords: they were to follow separate codes of conduct and dress which marked them off as a sacred caste responsible to God for the souls of their flocks. Thus priests were forbidden from too close an involvement in the rites of secular solidarity which underwrote social networks: they were not to carry weapons, nor to hunt, nor even to follow hunts as spectators, and their participation in the lewd festivities of feasting, and the hustle and bustle of secular business in public meetings or involving buying, selling or lending were severely delimited. These injunctions, of course, were constantly reiterated, doubtless in part because of the recurrent temptations and pressures on priests of all kinds to engage in the rites of secular community, but also because activities such as hunting, and dress-codes linked to weapon-carrying, had become the markers whereby priests defined themselves as a separate social group with their own special status and role: repeating bans on hunting was a way of reinforcing these boundaries and so reasserting the special role of the priesthood.[39]

'Correction', then, was not so much a campaign against slackening standards or corrupt practices, as an attempt to tie together a mosaic of Christian communities of varying shapes and sizes through the person of their priests. The problem for modern historians is assessing the extent to which the wishes of reformers were actually carried out in the countryside. Here, rather than begin an endless cycle of assertion and counter-assertion as to the effectiveness or otherwise of conciliar decrees, it makes more sense to look at the significant tranches of evidence which show a concerted and continued effort to transmit new norms. Perhaps most impressive is the body of bishop's legislation, modelled on royal decrees and so termed 'episcopal capitularies'. Beginning in the last decades of the eighth century, we have over 50 examples of this genre, in which bishops listed rulings, reflecting the injunctions of church councils adapted to local circumstances, in a concise chapter-by-chapter form so as to establish rules for the priests within their dioceses. The chance survival of a number of inventories, including booklists, and the apparently practical nature of many Carolingian manuscripts containing compendia on ecclesiastical matters suggest that bishops took their mission to correct and educate seriously.[40]

Whether priests were able and willing to stick to the absolute letter of all this episcopal injunction is ultimately, of course, unknowable; what is far more interesting is the fact that Carolingian 'correction' led to significant changes in the culture and society of the countryside. On a practical level, this is clear in two ways. First, if priests were to constitute a separate caste charged with heavy responsibilities for the moral wellbeing of their flocks, they needed an economic basis that allowed them to maintain their distance from the muddy and murky day-to-day realities of making a living. Crucial here was the insistence that all Christians were not only morally expected to pay the tithe – that is, to give up a tenth of their wealth as an offering to God – but also that this was an obligation which kings and their representatives would enforce through full legal process. As a result, the tithe became a fixed part of the agrarian economy, soon rooted in custom but essentially consisting of a tenth part of the harvest or its equivalent; norms about the use of the tithe, which was to be divided into parts to support the priest, to maintain the church, and to give alms, were refined and repeated through the whole range of legislative genres available to reformers. The regularisation of the tithe was a vital and often overlooked aspect of the proliferation of rural churches in the eighth and ninth centuries which is so visible in both archaeology and the documentary sources. A part of the tithe could, of course, end up in the pockets of church 'owners', and indeed many major monasteries acquired significant rights to collect tithe in the parishes of churches they founded or were given, but tithe became a basic aspect of the rural economy and one which was ultimately inseparable from the new ubiquity of priests and their churches in the countryside. Tithing, moreover, involved the setting of firm territorial boundaries for the congregation of each church: it thus played an important role in formalising the bonds of community in the countryside, and creating a regular network of rural churches.

This network transformed the contours of rural culture and society in a second way, by allowing the Carolingian church to insist on its control over the crucial rites of passage through which individuals entered into and departed from the earthly life, through baptism and Christian burial. Baptism – through which an individual became a member of the community of Christians and was cleansed of sin – had originally been a rite whereby adults made their commitment to Christ. But as Christianity became a matter of social fact rather than individual choice, infant baptism became the norm, and it was insisted on by Carolingian legislation, and often performed once a year for all infants, at Easter, in a ritual of communal renewal. The proper performance of baptismal rites, in forms which were uniform across the Carolingian world, were matters of real concern, and controversies over the integration of areas with divergent Christian traditions, whether east of the Rhine or south of the Pyrenees, turned on the importance of the correct performance of baptismal rites. Baptism was understood as an oath taken to God, in which biological and spiritual kin, parents and godparents, played a central role. A significant number of tracts explaining the significance of baptism, and the moral and theological basis of the undertakings it involved, survive, again showing a concerted effort to use this rite of passage as a point of instruction. In other words, oaths taken at baptism held together Christian society, articulating the obligations incumbent on its members and defining its boundaries, just as oaths of fidelity to the king defined participation in the public sphere.

Just as baptism marked entry into Christian society, so rites of burial marked departure from it. Here, thanks to the archaeological visibility of changing patterns of burial, there can be no doubting the scale of actual change taking place in the Carolingian period. For central to the changes in settlement patterns that marked the Carolingian countryside – the physical concentration of habitation around fixed anchorage points in the landscape – were churches with their churchyard cemeteries. The Merovingian church had concerned itself relatively little with rites of burial, seeing no problem with essentially familial and secular rites of feasting and gift-exchange around graves reflected in both written sources and the cemetery archaeology. Most Merovingian cemeteries, particularly in northern Gaul and Germany, were not associated with church buildings or structures, but by the seventh century even here burial in and around churches was a way for the powerful to express their social status and associate their ancestors with the relics of the saints. The relocation of community cemeteries into the consecrated space of churchyards, or the building of churches on existing cemetery sites which now became holy ground, however, was largely a phenomenon of the eighth and ninth centuries. It placed the community of dead ancestors at the heart of the community of the living, for the new churchyard cemeteries at the physical centre of villages doubled as public spaces for meeting, buying and selling, and collective action of all forms. Not all of these changes can be seen as a straightforward response to the wishes of bishops, imposed from above. The stabilisation of settlement structure around newly-founded churches was a longer-term process of social change, as was the foundation of new cemeteries more intimately connected with the everyday abodes of the living. But Carolingian 'correction' animated these new cemeteries and settlements, placing the church and the Christian dead at the heart of the community. Carolingian legislation sought to anonymise individual ancestors, merging them into the community of the Christian dead. Above-ground markers of all kinds, barrows and the like, were banned, as burial was to take standard Christian form, and social status in the grave was now expressed through lavish patronage to fund commemorative Masses and prayer which purged sin, or for members of the elite through privileged burial, perhaps in a monastery. Carolingian churchmen also Christianised death, adopting liturgical rites of purification designed to ensure the dead were cleansed of sin and eased into the otherworld which had originally been developed for a privileged few in monastic settings as the basis for the funerary process, and insisting on clerical control over funeral rites. It is precisely as Carolingian bishops began insisting on clerical control over death-ritual that worries about secular rites at the graveside – the drinking, feasting, singing and dancing in cemeteries that accompanied wakes for the dead – first surfaced, precisely because they threatened new-fangled priestly claims.

Insistence on the appropriate education of priests – above all on their basic Latinity – was thus not an idle whim. It was necessary if priests were to fulfil their ministry of providing pastoral care through performing the liturgy, administering penance and preaching. Priests, of course, now performed the services of the church in a 'corrected' Latin which emphasised their distance from their flocks even in those areas where the spoken vernaculars had evolved organically from Latin, and Carolingian church ritual likewise accentuated the hierarchical authority of the priest over his congregation. There was, nonetheless, room for other forms of communication, which might take place in a different register: the 'correction' of Latin and the Christianisation of the Germanic-speaking areas east of the Rhine meant that preaching, in contrast to the holy rites, might take place in the 'tongue of the people'. The moral oversight of the church theoretically extended to all areas of life, and the range of issues covered in the many surviving manuscripts of sermon collections is vast. Integral to this moral oversight was penance, the mechanism whereby Christians confessed their sins to their priests and made amends in order to receive God's forgiveness. Once a deathbed drama which washed away all sins, by the Carolingian period the practice of recurrent penances through the lifetime for specific sins was well established, and whilst the formal framework of annual confession that was required of all Christians by the high medieval church lay well in the future, penance was a central element of Carolingian culture. Carolingian reformers, moreover, through their reading of ancient texts, encouraged the initiation by churchmen of major penitential rites as public punishments for moral crimes threatening the social order: practical evidence for the imposition of these potentially humiliating rites, which involved laymen laying aside their weapons and other badges of status and humbling themselves, on those deemed guilty of wanton bloodshed, incest or sexual misdemeanours is not difficult to find.

Historians have long labelled the cultural developments associated with the court of Charlemagne and his successors the 'Carolingian renaissance', drawing a comparison with the Italian Renaissance of the fourteenth and fifteenth centuries and the conscious attempts to revive the Roman world of classical antiquity it involved. In fact, as we have seen, concerns about 'correct Christianity', not the revival of an alien and ancient culture, lay at the heart of Carolingian efforts. It is a startling statistic that only around 2,000 manuscripts written prior to 800 survive, as opposed to 7,000 for the ninth century alone: no matter how much allowance is made for differential survival rates, these figures suggest a vast upsurge in cultural activity.[41] The explosion of book production, and the comparable increase of new works being compiled, was a response to the overwhelming need for books in a hierarchical church founded on authoritative texts: thus over 95 per cent of our surviving manuscripts contain material concerned with the nitty-gritty of Christian observance. Even lay book ownership, for which there is considerable evidence – particularly among those aristocrats intimately involved with the court, where cultural virtuosity was a necessary accomplishment – were similarly Christian in orientation: Dhuoda, for example, wrote a tract of maternal advice for her son William, serving at the court of Charles the Bald, which was deeply imbued with the fashionable pieties of the time.[42] The 'renaissance' label, then, misleads us as to the thrust of Carolingian efforts, but it does serve as an important reminder that the promotion of scholars and texts by the Carolingians did give some individuals the intellectual resources to explore the literary heritage of the ancient world, engaging with timeless issues of philosophy or appreciating the literary classics of the Latin tradition. Thanks to their interests and efforts, much of classical literature that would otherwise have been lost was salvaged. Crucial historical texts like Ammianus' *Histories* or Tacitus' *Germania*, for example, survived only via single manuscripts copied by the monks of ninth-century Fulda.[43] In the intellectual circles that revolved around the court but also encompassed former courtiers dotted across the abbeys and bishoprics of the empire, clever classical allusions might be appreciated as demonstrations of virtuosity. For a career courtier like Einhard, the classical tradition could even be used to cause a stir, for by signalling that his biography of Charlemagne was aiming to emulate Cicero's eloquence, and by making extensive use of Suetonius' biographies of the Roman emperors in it, Einhard was marking out a new literary agenda distinct from existing traditions of hagiography and panegyric. But even for Einhard, the classicising was no more than a clever literary gloss: when he came to debate the serious political matters of the day, he used the genres of admonition and counsel that were the inseparable correlate of contemporary theories of Christian kingship, telling tales of saintly apparitions dictating booklets of advice and demons confessing Satan's plans.[44]

Historians have been interested in these traces of 'renaissance' not only because the traditions of scholarship on which they rested are easy for them to identify with, but also because they seem to provide a context for the revival of the imperial title under Charlemagne. After all, the notion of empire, and the ghost of the Roman past, reverberated down the centuries to the age of Napoleon at least: Charlemagne's own imperial coronation, on Christmas Day 800, was thus a potent source of precedent for a millennium, and was naturally debated in terms of Roman revival. These accretions and associations, however, relate to the needs of later European statesmen and their advisors, not to the Carolingian period itself. Even for Einhard, using his classical learning to compare his former master to the Roman emperors of antiquity, the imperial title was ultimately linked to Charlemagne's care for the 'Christian religion', and particularly his personal relationship with the popes, not to any political programme rooted in Roman precedent. The events of Christmas Day 800 ultimately rested on the tightening of links between the Frankish court and the papacy over the preceding three generations. When Pope Leo III feel victim to a plot and fled Rome, it was natural for him to travel to the palace at Paderborn in Saxony to seek Charlemagne's help. Charlemagne's return to Rome in 800, where Leo was allowed to clear himself of the accusations against him, confirmed his close links with the city and his special role as secular protector of the papacy. In terms of its legal and political implications, Leo's coronation of Charlemagne was simply an acknowledgement and regularisation of the fact that he was fulfilling this imperial role, and right through the ninth century and beyond the specific implications of the imperial title were limited to particular obligations towards the city and church of Rome. The gradual distancing of the papacy from Byzantium, both politically and theologically, had prepared the way here: perceptions of a distinct western Christian world which could no longer be seen as an adjunct of a Roman Empire based on Constantinople were most clearly voiced in the 'donation of Constantine', a forged document prepared by someone in the papal administration at some point in the second half of the eighth century, which claimed that Constantine had passed over all imperial rights in the west to the popes on his deathbed, and thus legitimated the creation of a separate western imperial tradition. Although the 'donation' was known to some, such as Einhard, the empire it suggested was scarcely acceptable to the Frankish court, and in any case in a world where Rome was a vague cultural memory detached from the basic institutions of power it had limited value to the Franks, although it did serve as a foundation charter for papal control of Rome and its immediate hinterland.[45] What the 'donation' does show is a more general tendency to use the vocabulary of empire to describe political authority in Italy, a tendency rooted in the continuing allegiance of much of the peninsula to Constantinople well into the eighth century. It is no accident that in Constantinople it was feared that Charlemagne's imperial coronation was the prologue to his seizure of the remaining Byzantine possessions in the south, notably Sicily, and it is striking that the imperial title did not replace Charlemagne's existing self-representation as 'king of the Franks and Lombards' but augmented it with 'governing the Roman Empire'.[46] Against this background of Charlemagne's investment in symbols of authority familiar to an Italian audience, claiming the imperial title was natural, and probably inevitable. But for Charlemagne's advisors north of the Alps, empire was inextricably linked to the claims of the Frankish kingdom to be a bastion of orthodoxy coterminous with 'correct' Christianity, claims already clearly made at Frankfurt in 794. To the extent that empire was translated north of the Alps, it was rooted in the ritual uniformity and correct observance of the Frankish church. Thus Charlemagne's son and successor, Louis the Pious, could style himself as a 'Christian Emperor' whose office was based on 'the unity of the church and the Christian people' and exercised through the 'sacred palace and church'.[47] It is to the fate of this Christian empire that we finally turn.

Bibliographical essay

The bibliography for chapter 9 above gives details of the major general works, and most important translated sources, which are the starting-point for studying the issues discussed in this chapter.

Structures of power and the Carolingian 'state'

The fundamental study of royal government is K.F. Werner, 'Missus-marchio-comes: Entre l'administration centrale et l'administration locale de l'empire carolingien', in W. Paravicini and K. F. Werner, eds, *Histoire comparée de l'administration IVe–XVIIIe siècle, Beihefte der Francia* 9 (Munich, 1980). Werner's articles, which use a thorough understanding of the centrality of aristocratic networks to study the interface between court and localities, are essential for understanding the working of Carolingian government; they are collected in *Structures politiques du monde francque* (London, 1979). Because Werner's work is published in French and German it has influenced only the work of specialists in the Anglophone world, meaning that the older perspective adopted by F. L. Ganshof – who tended to read capitularies as straightforward descriptions of centralised bureaucratic institutions and remained uninterested in the social networks through which kings ruled – dominates in many accounts. Ganshof's studies, collected in *Frankish Institutions under Charlemagne* (Providence, RI, 1968) and *The Carolingians and the Frankish Monarchy* (Providence, RI, 1971), must thus be read in the light of more recent work.

Controversy continues to rage over the nature of Carolingian government, partly because differing verdicts turn on fundamental differences of approach and method, partly also because they are intimately related to positive and negative assessments of the period as a whole. The most recent synthesis is M. Innes, 'Charlemagne's government', in J. Storey, ed., *Charlemagne: Empire and Society* (Manchester, 2005). On the suitability of the term 'state', S. Airlie, J. Jarnut and W. Pohl, eds, *Staat und Staatlichkeit im frühen Mittelalter* (Vienna, 2006) is invaluable, with important papers in English by Airlie and de Jong; see also M. de Jong, 'Sacrum palatium et ecclesia: l'autorité royale sous les carolingiens', *Annales HSS* 58 (2005).

The capitularies and the role of writing in government have been the focus of much debate. Important works here are R. McKitterick, *The Carolingians and the Written Word* (Cambridge, 1989) and J. L. Nelson, 'Literacy in Carolingian government', in R. McKitterick, ed., *The Uses of Literacy in the Early Middle Ages* (Cambridge, 1989), and the discussion in chapter 2 of P. Wormald, *The*

Making of English Law I (Oxford, 1999), and new approaches developed by C. Possel, 'Audience and recipients of Carolingian capitularies', in C. Possel, H. Reimitz, P. Shaw, eds, *Texts and Identities in the Early Middle Ages* (Vienna, 2007); the footnotes of these contributions give references to the large volume of fundamental work in German, esp. the monumental study by H. Mordek, *Bibliotheca capitularium regum Francorum manuscripta* (Munich, 1995).

Now that historians are aware of the pitfalls of an over-institutional reading of the capitularies, they are beginning to investigate the role of royal courts and public assemblies in priming the networks through which kings ruled. D. Bullough, 'Aula renovata: the Carolingian court before the Aachen palace', *Proceedings of the British Academy* 71 (1985), reprinted in his *Carolingian Renewal* (Manchester, 1991), is fundamental on Charlemagne's court; more recently see S. Airlie, 'The palace of memory: the Carolingian court as a political centre', in S. Rees Jones and A. Minnis, eds, *Courts and Regions in Medieval Europe* (Turnhout, 2000), and M. Innes and J. Nelson in C. Cubitt, ed., *Court Culture in the Early Middle Ages* (Turnhout, 2004), which also includes an invaluable discussion of the archaeology and architecture of palaces by U. Lobbedey; also R. Samson, 'Carolingian royal palaces and the poverty of ideology' in M. Lowcock, ed., *Meaningful Architecture* (London, 1994), and M. de Jong's paper in J. Davies and M. McCormick, eds, *Rethinking the Early Medieval West* (Aldershot, 2007). Various of the papers in M. de Jong and F. Theuws, *Topographies of Power in Late Antiquity and the Early Middle Ages* (Leiden, 2001) are also relevant, e.g. M. Innes' attempt to look at the ways in which royal and aristocratic power were embedded in the political landscape. The move away from institutions towards networks has allowed royal women and queens to move into the spotlight: see S. Maclean, 'Queenship, nunneries and royal widows in Carolingian Europe', *Past & Present* 178 (2003), and a series of articles by J. Nelson, collected in her *The Frankish World 750–900* (London, 1996) and *Rulers and Ruling Families in Early Medieval Europe* (London, 1999).

Another area of new interest is political ritual, now seen not only as a statement of royal ideology, but also as a vital arena where the relations between kings and their subjects were negotiated through public performance. The best introduction is J. Nelson, 'The Lord's annointed and the people's choice: Carolingian royal ritual', in D. Cannadine and S. Price, eds, *Rituals of Royalty* (London, 1988); see also her collected essays *Politics and Ritual in Early Medieval Europe* (London, 1986); also several of the essays in J. Nelson and F. Theuws, eds, *Rituals of Power from Late Antiquity to the Early Middle Ages* (Leiden, 1999). A series of articles by P. Buc have attracted controversy: see his *The Dangers of Ritual* (Princeton, 2001) and the review article by G. Koziol, 'The dangers of polemic', *Early Medieval Europe* 11 (2002).

Aristocracies

The fundamental work was done by German scholars using the techniques of historical prosopography in the second half of the twentieth century, and developing a new understanding of the social changes of the ninth to twelfth centuries:

T. Reuter, ed., *The Mediaeval Nobility* (Amsterdam, 1979) translates a series of the most significant articles, including K.-F. Werner's fundamental 'Important noble families in the realm of Charlemagne', outlining the contours of the 'imperial aristocracy'. The main issues in these debates were the continuity of aristocratic power, the structures of aristocratic kinship and the extent to which the aristocracy was a distinct social class: these are now comprehensively re-examined in R. Le Jan, *Famille et Pouvoir dans le monde Franc* (Paris, 1998). The work of S. Airlie brilliantly builds on this scholarship to elucidate the political role of the Carolingian aristocracy: see e.g. his contribution to R. McKitterick, ed., *New Cambridge Medieval History* II (Cambridge, 1995). See also the papers in A. Duggan, ed., *Nobles and Nobility in Medieval Europe* (Woodbridge, 2000).

Current work is stressing the complex relationships between different strata of aristocratic society, and examining the ways in which aristocratic power was exercised in the localities. Crucial here has been a series of studies of the resolution of conflict, and the creation of social networks. W. Davies and P. Fouracre, eds, *The Settlement of Disputes in Early Medieval Europe* (Cambridge, 1986), esp. the essays by Davies, Nelson, Wickham, was the starting-point here, whilst a group of North American scholars asked similar questions of the post-Carolingian evidence: W. Brown and P. Gorecki, eds, *Conflict in Medieval Europe* (Aldershot, 2004) has an excellent introduction tracing the implications of this burgeoning tradition. This new emphasis on the complementary relationship between aristocratic power and royal authority has resulted in a series of focused local studies – e.g. books by Brown, Costambeys, Hummer and Innes listed in the bibliography on regional societies in chapter 9 – which are vital for our understanding of the Carolingian world. G. Althoff, *Family, Friends and Followers* (Cambridge, 2003) studies networks from a different perspective, whilst several recent conferences collect useful essays, some in English: *Settimane di Studi del centro italiano sull alto medieovo Spoletò* 42 (1995) and 44 (1997), both on justice, and *Mélanges de l'École français de Rome* 111 (1998), on property transfers.

Society and economy

Carolingian social history is best approached through local studies of landowning and kinship such as those suggested in the bibliography for chapter 9 above; C. Wickham has interpreted this material, e.g. in his contributions to R. McKitterick, ed., *New Cambridge Medieval History* II (Cambridge, 1995), R. McKitterick, ed., *Short Oxford History of Early Medieval Europe* (Oxford, 2001) and C. La Rocca, ed., *Short Oxford History of Early Medieval Italy* (Oxford, 2002), and at more length in several of the articles collected in his *Land and Power* (Rome, 1994) and in the relevant sections of *Framing the Early Middle Ages* (Oxford, 2005). For another recent attempt at synthesis see the relevant chapters of M. Costambeys, M. Innes and S. Maclean, *The Carolingian World* (Cambridge, 2007). New research has rendered older textbook accounts such as G. Duby, *The Early Growth of the European Economy* (London, 1974) outdated, but G. Duby, *Rural Economy and the Country Life in the Medieval West* (London, 1968) remains invaluable to the student for the collection of translated documents, particularly polyptychs, it contains.

On peasant society and the Carolingian countryside, the pioneering case-study, and a thought-provoking place to start, is W. Davies, *Small Worlds: The Village Community in Early Medieval Brittany* (London, 1988). Archaeological material on rural settlement is now best approached via H. Hamerow, *Early Medieval Settlements* (Oxford, 2002), and see also C. Loveluck's chapter in J. Storey, ed., *Charlemagne* (Manchester, 2005), and for Italy the controversial R. Francovich and R. Hodges, *Villa to Village* (London, 2005). On manors, most of the major advances have been made in French studies, such as those collected in A. Verhulst, *Rural and Urban Aspects of Early Medieval Northwest Europe* (London, 1992) and J. P. Devroey, *Études sur la grande domaine carolingienne* (London, 1993); happily this strand of research is now accessible to the Anglophone through A. Verhulst, *The Carolingian Economy* (Cambridge, 2002), with a good bibliography. On a different tack, two recent studies look at estate structures in the context of wider changes: F. Theuws, 'Landed property and manorial organisation in northern Austrasia', in Theuws and N. Roymans, eds, *Images of the Past* (Amsterdam, 1991) and M. Costambeys, 'An aristocratic community on the northern Frankish frontier, 690–726', *Early Medieval Europe* 3 (1994). On the closely related issue of peasant freedom and serfdom, there is a series of good recent syntheses: W. Davies, 'On servile status in the early middle ages', in M. Bush, ed., *Slavery and Serfdom* (Manchester, 1996); H.-W. Goetz, 'Serfdom and the beginnings of a "seigneurial system" in Carolingian Europe', *Early Medieval Europe* 2 (1993); J.-P. Devroey, 'Men and women in early medieval serfdom', *Past & Present* 166 (2000). Also, on peasant voices as recovered through legal pleadings, R. Balzaretti, 'The monastery of San Ambrogio and dispute settlement in early medieval Milan', *Early Medieval Europe* 3 (1994).

On towns and trade, there has been a plethora of recent books, most inspired by archaeological advances in our understanding of the North Sea economy. R. Hodges, *Dark Age Economics* (London, 1982) set the ball rolling here; see most recently his *Towns and Trade in the Age of Charlemagne* (London, 2001), and compare A. Verhulst, *The Rise of Cities in Northwest Europe* (Cambridge, 1999). R. Hodges and B. Hobley, *The Rebirth of Towns in the West 700–1050* (London, 1986) has an invaluable range of case-studies. On the coin evidence see now S. Coupland, 'Trading places: Quentovic and Dorestad reassessed', *Early Medieval Europe* 11 (2002). Studies of Carolingian towns have arguably suffered, however, from being framed by debates about trade and a search for precedents for high medieval urban life: as a result of this focus the kind of rich and three-dimensional picture of towns as places with manifold and changing social functions which has begun to characterise the best work on late Roman and post-Roman urbanism is lacking. On trade, recently attention has shifted back to the Mediterranean, thanks in part to Hodges' excavations at San Vincenzo al Volturno, on which see his *Light on the Dark Ages: The Rise and Fall of San Vincenzo al Volturno* (London, 1997), and R. Balzaretti's review article in *Early Medieval Europe* 8 (1999), but primarily due to the monumental work of M. McCormick, *Origins of the European Economy: Communications and Commerce 400–900* (Cambridge, 2001) – and see his 'New light on the Dark Ages: how the slave trade fuelled the Carolingian economy', *Past & Present* 177 (2002). More recently still, C. Wickham, *Framing the Early Middle Ages* (Oxford, 2005) offers a different interpretation, situating the growth of markets in a wider context of increasing aristocratic demand. See also the excellent collection of essays in I. Hansen and C. Wickham, eds, *The Long Eighth Century* (Leiden, 2001), and a series of case-studies of cities in their regional context by R. Balzaretti, 'Cities and markets in early medieval Europe', in G. Ausenda, *After Empire* (Woodbridge, 1996), and 'Cities, emporia and monasteries: regional economics in the Po valley, 700–875', in N. Christie and S. Loseby, eds, *Towns in Transition* (Aldershot, 1996); see also W. van Es, 'Dorestad centred', in J. Besteman, H. Bos and H. Heidinga, eds, *Medieval Archaaeology in the Netherlands* (Assen, 1990).

Church and culture

The Frankish church and the 'Carolingian renaissance' are probably the best-covered areas, with several excellent recent syntheses – given the huge volume of specialist research, this is just as well! R. McKitterick, ed., *Carolingian Culture: Emulation and Innovation* (Cambridge, 1994) covers all aspects, whilst the relevant essays in McKitterick, ed., *New Cambridge Medieval History* II (Cambridge, 1995) are also excellent. The relevant chapters in P. Brown, *The Rise of Western Christendom* (2nd edn, London, 2001) are a particularly stunning synthesis on the eighth century.

On conversion and Christianisation in the eighth century, W. Levison, *England and the Continent in the Eighth Century* (Oxford, 1946) remains a classic, but it needs to be read alongside more recent reassessments of the major primary sources – the lives of Anglo-Saxon missionaries – such as those undertaken by I. Wood, *The Missionary Life* (London, 2001). On Boniface, see also T. Reuter, ed., *The Greatest Englishman* (Exeter, 1980), esp. Reuter's chapter, and M. Wallace-Hadrill, 'A background to Boniface's mission', in his *Early Medieval History* (London, 1975); Chrodegang is rescued from the historiographical shadows by M. Claussen, *Chrodegang of Metz and the Reform of the Frankish Church* (Cambridge, 2005). J. Cavadini, *The Last Christology of the West: Adoptionism in Spain and Gaul, 785–820* (Philadelphia, 1993) is a challenging reinterpretation of the theology of those Hispanic thinkers condemned by the Carolingians, which has important implications for our understanding of the 'Adoptionist' controversy.

On ecclesiastical institutions and church reform, see R. McKitterick, *The Frankish Church and the Carolingian Reforms, 789–895* (London, 1977), whilst M. Wallace-Hadrill, *The Frankish Church* (Oxford, 1983) has some valuable chapters, and a series of recent essays by M. de Jong provides much food for thought (see e.g. her contribution to Storey, ed., *Charlemagne,* and her magisterial survey 'Carolingian monasticism' in McKitterick, ed., *New Cambridge Medieval History* II). B. Rosenwein, *Negotiating Space: Privileges of Immunity in Early Medieval Europe* (Ithaca, 1998) is important on the relations between kings, bishops and monasteries, although it omits the crucial period of institutionalisation in the century after 780. M. de Jong, *In Samuel's Image: Child Oblation in the Early Middle Ages* (Leiden, 1996) is fundamental on Carolingian monasticism, studying the recruitment of child oblates as a means of understanding the social role on monasticism; this complements recent studies of regional societies which are based on the documentary records of property transfers between aristocrats and monks. Bishops would repay further study, but see now M. Moore, *A Sacred Kingdom: Bishops and Frankish Royal Power* (Philadelphia, forthcoming). There are a number of German studies on the relationship between royal needs and ecclesiastical institutions e.g. F. Felten, *Abte und Laienabte im Karolingerreich* (Munich, 1980) and F. Prinz, *Klerus und Krieg im frühen Mittelalter* (Munich, 1974), whilst F. Prinz, *Frühes Mönchtum im Frankenreich* (Munich, 1965) is the basic study of monastic foundations, and W. Hartmann, *Die Synoden der Karolingerzeit im Frankenreich und Italien* (Munich, 1989) is basic on church councils.

The literature on Frankish relations with the papacy is voluminous, particularly on the momentous events of the eighth century: T. Noble, *The Republic of St Peter* (Philadelphia, 1984) is the best study, and see also J. Hallenbeck, *Pavia and Rome: The Lombard Monarchy and the Papacy in the Eighth Century* (Philadelphia, 1982), D. Miller, 'The Roman revolution of the eighth century: a study of the ideological background of the papal separation from Byzantium and the alliance with the Franks', *Mediaeval Studies* 36 (1974) and R. Schieffer, 'Charlemagne and Rome' in J. Smith, ed., *Early Medieval Rome and the Christian West* (Leiden, 2000). P. Classen, *Karl der Grosse, das Papsttum und Byzanz* (Sigmaringen, 1988) is the fundamental study of political relations between Charlemagne, Rome and Constantinople, and see J. Herrin, *The Formation of Christendom* (London, 1987). These issues remain neglected for the ninth century.

On high culture, see the essays collected in B. Bischoff, *Manuscripts and Libraries in the Age of Charlemagne* (Cambridge, 1994), D. Bullough, *Carolingian Renewal: Sources and Heritage* (Manchester, 1991), R. McKitterick, *Books, Scribes and Libraries in the Frankish Kingdoms, 6th to 9th Century* (London, 1994) and *The Frankish Kings and Culture in the Early Middle Ages* (London, 1995), R. Sullivan, ed., *The Gentle Voice of Teachers: Aspects of Learning in the Carolingian Age* (Columbus, OH, 1995). On language, R. Wright, *Late Latin and Early Romance in Spain and Carolingian France* (Liverpool, 1982) and R. Wright, ed., *Latin and the Vernacular Languages in the Early Middle Ages* (Leicester, 1991). On poetry, P. Godman, *Poets and Emperors* (Oxford, 1987). On art history, C. Chazelle, *The Crucified God in the Carolingian Era* (Cambridge, 2001) and L. Nees, *A Tainted Mantle* (Philadelphia, 1991) provoke thought. Finally, P. Dutton, *The Politics of Dreaming in the Carolingian Empire* (Lincoln, NE, 1994) combines cultural, literary and political analysis.

Carolingian 'popular culture' remains strangely understudied, given the historiographical high profile of studies of 'the religion of the people' in medieval studies. In part, this is because most Carolingianists have been wary of received depictions of a barely Christian countryside animated by 'pagan survivals'; much effort has been devoted, importantly, to demonstrating that the 'superstitions' castigated by post-Carolingian bishops were not in fact remnants of living pre-Christian religions so much as customary accretions which had in origin been perfectly compatible with a Christian identity. It is thus no accident that the major study of 'popular belief', V. Flint, *The Rise of Magic in Early Medieval Europe*

(Oxford, 1991), is written by an outsider to the period and largely bypasses these important issues about the definition of religious identity; compare J. Smith's discussion of 'Religion and lay society' in McKitterick, ed., *New Cambridge Medieval History* II. There has been significant research on a variety of points of contact between the church hierarchy and popular practice. On penance, for example, see M. de Jong, 'Transformations of penance', in F. Theuws and J. Nelson, eds, *Rituals of Power* (Leiden, 1999) and R. Meens, 'The nature and frequency of early medieval penance', in P. Biller, ed., *Handling Sin* (York, 1998); on death and burial, F. Paxton, *Christianising Death: The Creation of a Ritual Process in Early Medieval Europe* (Ithaca, 1989) and C. Treffort, *L'église carolingienne et la mort* (Lyons, 1996), whose discussions of the liturgical and normative sources could be usefully combined with the archaeological and architectural material; on baptism, S. Keefe, *Water and the Word: Baptism and the Education of the Clergy in the Carolingian Empire* (Notre Dame, 2002). Priests – the crucial intermediaries – and indeed the infrastructure of the local church remain little studied: see, however, J. Nelson, 'Making ends meet', *Studies in Church History* 24 (1987), reprinted in *The Frankish World* (1996). On one aspect of religious culture where 'elite' and 'popular' piety met – relic-cults – little has been done to unpick class and gender differences in practice, but the implementation of institutionalised control over relics remains clear: see P. Fouracre, 'The origins of the Carolingian attempt to regulate the cult of the saints', in J. Howard-Johnston and P. Hayward eds, *The Cult of Saints in Late Antiquity and the Early Middle Ages* (Oxford, 1999), J. Smith, 'Old saints, new cults: Roman relics in Carolingian Francia', in Smith, ed., *Early Medieval Rome and the Christian West* (Leiden, 2000), and P. Geary, *Furta Sacra: Thefts of Relics in the Central Middle Ages* (Princeton, 1977). On women's piety and the implications of Carolingian 'reform', see J. Smith, 'The problem of female sanctity in Carolingian Europe,' *Past & Present* 146 (1995).

One area of exciting new work has been gender relations and ecclesiastical attempts to advise the laity on Christian lifestyles: see J. Smith, 'Gender and ideology in the early Middle Ages', *Studies in Church History* 34 (1998), J. Nelson, 'Monks, secular men and masculinity', in D. M. Hadley, *Masculinity in Medieval Europe* (London, 1999) and S. Airlie, 'The anxiety of sanctity', *Journal of Ecclesiastical History* 43 (1992).

Surprisingly few of the many important churchmen and scholars of the period have received biographical treatment. On Alcuin, there is now D. Bullough, *Alcuin: Achievement and Reputation* (Leiden, 2004), whilst M. Garrison's forthcoming book will shed important light on Alcuin's self-fashioning. On Hincmar, there is a three-volume study by J. Devisse, *Hincmar, archevêque de Reims* (Paris, 1975), but the best way into his thought is J. Nelson, 'Kingship, liturgy and law in the political thought of Hincmar of Rheims', *English Historical Review* 92 (1977), reprinted in her *Politics and Ritual in Early Medieval Europe* (London, 1986), and M. Wallace-Hadrill, 'History in the mind of Archbishop Hincmar', in R. Davis and M. Wallace-Hadrill, eds, *The Writing of History in the Middle Ages* (Oxford, 1980); on Hraban, M. de Jong, 'The empire as ecclesia: Hraban Maur and Biblical exegesis for rulers', in Y. Hen and M. Innes, eds, *The Uses of the Past in the Early*

Middle Ages (Cambridge, 2000). Most exciting of all is the possibility of getting close to the subjectivity of a highly educated layman and laywoman through their writings: J. Smith, 'Einhard: the sinner and the saints', *Transactions of the Royal Historical Society* 13 (2003), (for Dhuoda) P. Dronke, *Women Writers of the Middle Ages* (Cambridge, 1984), chapter 2, and M. Claussen, 'God and man in Dhuoda', *Studies in Church History* 27 (1990), and 'Fathers of power and mothers of authority', *French Historical Studies* 19 (1996).

Notes

1. See J. Nelson, 'Aachen as a place of power' in M. de Jong and F. Theuws, eds, *Topographies of Power from Late Antiquity to the Early Middle Ages* (Leiden, 2001).
2. See M. de Jong, 'Charlemagne's *solarium*', in J. Davies and M. McCormick, eds, *Rethinking the Early Medieval West* (Aldershot, 2007).
3. This argument is developed in M. Innes, 'Charlemagne's government', in J. Storey, ed., *Charlemagne: Empire and Society* (Manchester, 2005).
4. The capitulary legislation is discussed by F. L. Ganshof, 'Charlemagne's use of the oath', in his *The Carolingians and the Frankish Monarchy* (Providence, RI, 1971) and R. Le Jan, *Famille et Pouvoir dans le monde franc* (Paris, 1995), pp. 122–30; see e.g. capitulary of Herstall (779) and 802 capitulary for the *missi*, both tr. P. D. King, *Charlemagne: Translated Sources* (Kendal, 1987) pp. 200–5, 233–42.
5. 802 capitulary for the *missi*, tr. P. D. King, *Charlemagne: Translated Sources* (Kendal, 1987), pp. 234–5; T. Bitterauf, ed., *Die Traditionen des Hochstifts Freisings* (Munich, 1905), no. 186; H. Wartmann, ed., *Urkundenbuch der Kloster St-Gallen* (St-Gallen, 1863), no. 187.
6. See the discussions of P. Fouracre, 'Carolingian justice: the rhetoric of improvement and the contexts of abuse' and R. Le Jan, 'Justice royale et practiques socials dans le royaume franque', in *Settimane di Studi di centro italiano sull' alto medieovo Spoleto* 42 (1995).
7. Capitulary of 802, tr. King, *Charlemagne*, p. 239, where just judgement takes place according to *lex scripta* not *suum* [i.e. the judge's] *arbitrium*. For wider context, P. Geary, 'Extra-judicial means of dispute resolution', *Settimane* 42 (1995).
8. Bitterauf, ed., *Die Traditionen des Hochstifts Freisings* no. 186; *Monumenta Germaniae Historica Capitularia Regum Francorum* I, ed. A. Boretius (Hannover, 1883), nos 39, 150.
9. L. van Acker, ed., *Agobard of Lyons: Opera Omnia*, Corpus Christianorum Series Medievalis 52 (Turnhout, 1981), pp. 225–7; tr. W. L. North for the Internet Medieval Sourcebook, www.fordham.edu/halsall/source/agobard2.html.
10. Bitterauf, ed., *Die Traditionen des Hochstifts Freisings* no. 225.
11. M. Borgolte, *Geschichte der Grafschaften Alemanniens im fränkischer Zeit* (Sigmaringen, 1983); compare, for the Loire valley countships, Adrevald of Fleury, *Miracula S. Benedicti*, excerpts ed. G. Waitz, *Monumenta Germaniae Historica Scriptores* 13.1 (Hannover, 1887), pp. 373–97.

12. On military service see T. Reuter, 'The end of Carolingian military expansion', in P. Godman and R. Collins, eds, *Charlemagne's Heir* (Oxford, 1989); M. Innes, *State and Society in the Early Middle Ages* (Cambridge, 2000), pp. 143–53.
13. The capitulary of 802 is tr. King, *Charlemagne*, pp. 233–42; fundamental on them are J. Hannig, 'Zur Entstehung des karolingische Königsbotenorganisation', *Mitteilungen des Instituts für Osterreichische Geschichtsforschung* 91 (1983) and 'Zentralle Kontrolle und regionale Machtbalanz', *Archiv für Kulturgeschichte* 66 (1984).
14. P. Geary, *Aristocracy in Provence: The Rhone Basin at the Dawn of the Carolingian Era* (Stuttgart, 1985).
15. On his career see P. Depreux, *Prosopographie de l'entourage de Louis le Pieux* (Sigmaringen, 1997), no. 164.
16. See Borgolte, *Grafschaften Alemanniens.*
17. Agobard of Lyon, 'Against the laws of Gundobad', ed. van Acker; Notker, *Deeds of Charlemagne*, tr. L. Thorpe, *Two Lives of Charlemagne* (London, 1971).
18. See Einhard's letters, tr. P. Dutton, *Charlemagne's Courtier* (Peterborough Ont., 1997).
19. Though of course 'feudalism' has a wider sense, that of a social system resting on the dominance of a militarised aristocratic elite over the peasantry; this social-scientific, typological, sense actually evolved out of the tighter, legal-tenurial, definition, because of the important role 'feudalism' in this sense had enjoyed in ideological debates in early modern Europe; hence the tangled historiographical knots the terminology has caused.
20. Laucheim: I. Stork, 'Zum Fortgang der Untersuchungen im frühmittelalterlichen Gräberfeld, Adelshof und Hofgrablege bei Laucheim', *Archäologische Ausgrabungen im Baden-Württemburg 1992* (Stuttgart, 1993); Pettegem: D. Callebaut, 'Résidences fortifiées et centres administratifs dans la vallée de l'Escaut, IX–XI siècles', in P. Demolon, H. Galinié and F. Verhaege, eds, *Archaeologie de villes dans le nord-ouest de l'Europe, VII–XII siècles* (Douai, 1994).
21. See the excellent selection of material tr. G. Duby, *Rural Economy and the Country Life in the Medieval West* (London, 1968), pp. 361–86.
22. E. Wamers, *Die frühmittelalterliche Lesefunde aus der Löhrstrasse im Mainz* (Mainz, 1994).
23. W. van Es and W. Verwers, *Excavations at Dorestad I: The Harbour, Hoogstraat 1* (Amersfoort, 1980), and for the supply chain see W. van Es, 'Dorestad centred', in J. Besteman, J. Bos and H. Heidinga, eds, *Medieval Archaeology in the Netherlands* (Assen, 1990).
24. A. Verhulst, 'The origins and development of medieval towns in northern Europe', *Past & Present* 122 (1989), on a region where new sites predominated.
25. S. Coupland, 'Trading places: Dorestad and Quentovic reassessed', *Early Medieval Europe* 11 (2002) with reservations.
26. See e.g. T. Reuter, tr., *The Annals of Fulda* (Manchester, 1992), s.a. 882.
27. R. Hodges, *Light on the Dark Ages: The Rise and Fall of San Vincenzo al Volturno* (London, 1997).

28. See p. 263 n.45.
29. M. McCormick, *Origins of the European Economy: Communications and Commerce, 300–900* (Cambridge, 2001).
30. P. Brown, *The Rise of Western Christendom* (2nd edn, Oxford, 2001), chapter 16.
31. J. Mitchell, 'L'arte nell'Italia longobarda e nell'Europa carolingia', in C. Bertelli and G. P. Brogiolo, eds, *Il futuro dei Longobardi* (Milan, 2000); I. Garipzanov's discussion in *Early Medieval Europe* 14 (2006).
32. D. Bullough, 'Charlemagne's court library revisited', *Early Medieval Europe* 12 (2003).
33. See the poems of Alcuin and Theodulf tr., P. Godman, *Poetry of the Carolingian Renaissance* (London, 1985), pp. 119–80.
34. 'On the cultivation of letters' (*De Litteris Collendis*), tr. King, *Charlemagne*, pp. 232–3.
35. Boniface, *Letters*, tr. E. Emerton (New York, 1940).
36. See Ardo's *Life of Benedict of Aniane*, tr. P. Dutton, *Carolingian Civilisation: A Reader* (Peterborough Ont., 1994); the life of Adalard, tr. A. Cabannis, *Charlemagne's Cousins* (Syracuse, 1974), and for Einhard, P. Dutton, tr., *Charlemagne's Courtier: The Complete Einhard* (Peterborough Ont., 1997) with J. Smith, 'Einhard: the sinner and the saints', *Transactions of the Royal Historical Society* 13 (2003).
37. Reuter, tr., *Annals of Fulda*, s.a. 847.
38. See Einhard's *Translation of Marcellinus and Peter*, tr. Dutton, *Charlemagne's Courtier*, with P. Geary, *Furta Sacra: Thefts of Sacred Relics in the Central Middle Ages* (Princeton, 1977).
39. See e.g. F. Prinz, *Klerus und Kreig im frühen Mittelalter* (Munich, 1974).
40. E.g. C. Hammer, 'Country churches, clerical inventories and the Carolingian renaissance in Bavaria', *Church History* 49 (1980); Y. Hen, 'Knowledge of canon law among rural priests: the evidence of two manuscripts of around 800', *Journal of Theological Studies* 50 (1999); the episcopal capitularies urgently need sustained study.
41. These figures are based on the contents of the series *Codices Latines Antiquiores*, cataloguing every manuscript before 800, and on the late Bernhard Bischoff's catalogue of ninth-century manuscripts; if allowance is made for the fact that a very high proportion of the pre-800 material actually dates from the later eighth century the upsurge is more marked still.
42. Dhuoda, *Manual*, tr. C. Neel (Lincoln, NE, 1991) or M. Thiebaux *Manual for her Warrior Son* (Cambridge, 1998).
43. See L. G. Reynolds, *Texts and Transmission: A Survey of the Latin Classics* (Oxford, 1983).
44. See Dutton, tr., *Charlemagne's Courtier* for Einhard's complete oeuvre.
45. 'Donation of Constantine', tr. Dutton, *Carolingian Civilisation*, pp. 13–19.
46. Theophanes, *Chronicle*, tr. C. Mango and R. Scott, *Byzantine and Near Eastern History, 284–813* (Oxford, 1997), a.m. 6293, for reports of a 'secret plan' on Charlemagne's part to assemble a fleet and seize Sicily; in this connection, note the Sicilian envoy received at Aachen in 799, *Royal Frankish*

Annals, tr. B. W. Scholz, *Carolingian Chronicles* (Ann Arbor, 1974), s.a. 799, and the defection of the official Leo, 'a Sicilian by birth', to Charlemagne at Rome in 800, reported in *Royal Frankish Annals* s.a. 811.

47. See in particular the *Ordinatio Imperii* of 817, tr. Dutton, *Carolingian Civilisation*, pp. 176–9.

11

Paradoxes of empire: western Europe in the ninth century

Contents

Summary

Chronology

Map 9: The Carolingian world in the ninth century

Interpreting the ninth century

The imperial title and the problem of political unity

Carolingian kingship at its zenith

Frontiers, raiders and traders: the frontiers of the Christian empire

The end of the Carolingian Empire

Bibliographical essay

Summary

Carolingian rule of the vastly expanded Frankish realms relied on a hierarchy of kings, with kings' sons granted royal status and setting up courts in outlying areas. Perceptions of unity thus always rested on a sense of proper hierarchical order within the Carolingian family itself; hence Charlemagne managed his family with the greatest care. However, all his legitimate sons predeceased their father except Louis the Pious, who thus succeeded to imperial authority. Louis' family management, however, broke down in the first half of the 830s, when his efforts to 'hire and fire' aristocrats from high office at will created a faction of influential former advisors who were able to egg his sons into revolt. Louis' own death in 840 thus saw not an ordered succession but a brief civil war following which his three surviving sons, Lothar, Louis the German and Charles the Bald, received equal kingdoms. This did not inaugurate cultural, social or political fragmentation, or weaken Carolingian kingship. Intensive links across the internal boundaries of the empire meant that the system became more complex, but within their kingdoms kings were more independent and intrusive. The end of empire only came following a crisis within the Carolingian family which left just one adult legitimate male, Charles the Fat, alive by 884. Because a distant emperor could not meet the urgent needs of regional elites for a Carolingian based in their kingdom, able to exert authority and dispense patronage, Charles' regime soon ran into problems. In 888, after his deposition, the constituent kingdoms of the empire thus chose kings from their own leading men.

The ninth century also saw the transformation of Frankish relations with their neighbours in Scandinavia, central Europe and the Mediterranean, as the process of military expansion that had been characteristic of the eighth century ended. Cultural influence, economic interaction and political alliance across the new frontiers were the inevitable result, but one which sucked the emerging elites of Scandinavian and central European kingdoms into Frankish politics, and resulted in the direct involvement of Carolingian kings in Italy in the politics of a Mediterranean world in which Islamic fleets threatened Byzantium's remaining western possessions. These processes meant that Vikings – not to mention Slavic and Muslim raiders – were an ever-present factor within Frankish politics in the ninth century, but one which did not threaten to bring down the system as a whole.

Chronology

781	Charlemagne sets up sons Pippin and Louis as kings of Italy and Aquitaine
793	Conspiracy against Charlemagne led by son Pippin 'the Hunchback'
806	'Division of the kingdoms' succession agreement
808	Danish king Godofrid raids at Reric and exacts tribute from Frisia
813	Death of Pippin of Italy; Louis crowned emperor by Charlemagne
814	Charlemagne's death; Louis the Pious seizes Aachen and accepted as successor
817	*Ordinatio Imperii* includes only Louis' sons; Bernard of Italy rebels
822	Louis the Pious performs public penance for Bernard's death
823	Charles the Bald born to Louis' second wife, Judith
826	Harald Klak 'king of Danes' baptised at Ingelheim
827	Beginnings of Islamic conquest of Sicily
828	Counts Hugh and Matfrid removed from office
830	'Loyal rebellion' led by Pippin of Aquitaine; Louis briefly loses control
833	Renewed rebellion; Louis the Pious performs public penance and is deposed
834	Louis stages comeback
840	Death of Louis the Pious; renewed civil war breaks out between sons
841	Battle of Fontenoy: first open warfare between Franks since 717
843	Treaty of Verdun creates equal kingdoms for Lothar, Louis the German and Charles the Bald
845–82	Hincmar archbishop of Rheims
846–70	Rastislav king of Moravians
847–56	Hraban Maur archbishop of Mainz
848	Louis II campaigns against Muslims in southern Italy
855	Death of Lothar I
863	Khan Boris of Bulgaria converts to Christianity
866	Islamic campaigns in southern Italy create emirates of Bari and Otranto
866–85	Mission of Cyril (died 869) and Methodius (died 885) in central Europe
869	Death of Lothar II
869–85	Zwentibald king of Moravians
875	Death of Louis II 'Emperor of Italy'
876	Louis the German takes control of Italy, crowned emperor, dies
877	Charles the Bald invades Italy, crowned emperor, dies
878	Fall of Syracuse, last Byzantine stronghold in Sicily, to Muslims
879	Boso of Vienne, son-in-law of Charles the Bald, made king of Provence
888	Charles the Fat deposed; kingdoms raise kings from their own aristocracies

Interpreting the ninth century

It is usual to see the ninth century in terms of decline and fall. This rests on a comparison with the reign of Charlemagne, as presented for posterity by Einhard. In this view, whereas Charlemagne's rule was typified by internal stability underpinned by wars of conquest, the end of expansion inevitably led to internal problems in the shape of civil war and political division, internal problems which were exacerbated by the raiding of Scandinavians along the coastline and rivers of northern Francia, Slavs and Magyars along the Franks' eastern frontier, and Muslims from Africa and Spain along the coasts of Italy and southern Gaul. Political decline is normally traced in two stages. The second half of the reign of Charlemagne's son, Louis the Pious, and its aftermath, in the 830s and 840s, saw the end of the Frankish Empire as a single political unit; renewed internal crisis sparked by the absence of able Carolingian males in the 880s ended with members of regional aristocracies being made kings in their own segments of the empire in 888. Explanations for these events place differing weights on internal rivalries within the Carolingian family, and the problems created by raiders from outside as causes; but all are agreed that the fundamental point at issue was the relationship between king and aristocracy.

After 888 leading aristocrats were raised to kingship across the empire, although the Carolingian line itself did not disappear. As aristocrats-turned-kings, these families were effectively following a path trod a century and a half earlier by the Carolingians themselves. This simple fact has tempted successive generations of modern historians to see the ninth century in terms of the 'rise of the aristocracy' at the expense of kingship. It is only more recently that researchers, looking more closely at the ninth century in terms of the problems and possibilities faced by contemporary rulers, have begun to redress the balance. In particular, the role of the aristocracy, who are normally cast as arch-villains by declinologists, has undergone fundamental reassessment as half a century of detailed research has transformed our understanding of aristocratic activities and interests. It is now clear that, whilst aristocrats keenly guarded the interests and status of their family, friends and followers, we cannot see them as an antagonistic counterforce to kings, motivated simply by the desire to entrench their local position and resist the initiatives of royal government. In fact, as we have seen, Carolingian kingship had from the outset rested on partnership with the aristocracy; ninth-century aristocrats wanted stable royal government which, by offering patronage, position and protection, provided a framework which entrenched and legitimated their local interests. And the Carolingian system offered the greatest families the chance of exercising far-flung authority, and acquiring far-flung interests, right across the empire. Those at the apex of the 'imperial aristocracy', who had risen to power alongside the Carolingians in the eighth century, actually built up their position through Carolingian courts. When, after 888, some of their number found themselves raised to kingship, this was a move designed to prop up the system and provide able Carolingian-style rule in the absence of adult Carolingian candidates.

The tendency to paint the ninth century in shades of doom and gloom is in fact testimony to the quality and quantity of source material. Whereas the historian of

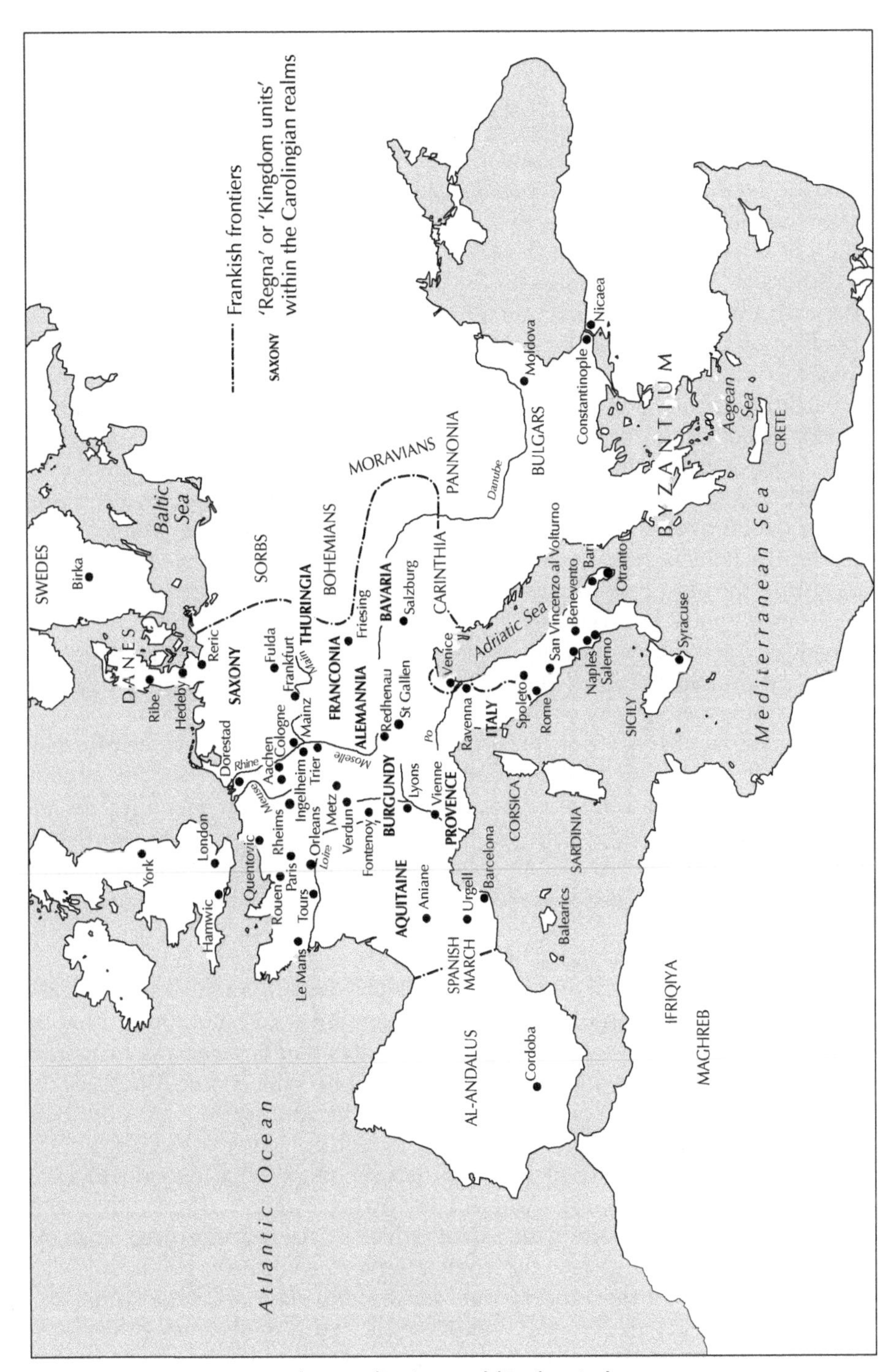

Map 9 The Carolingian world in the ninth century

Charlemagne is dependent on a handful of bare, annalistic, accounts, to be filled out with Einhard's classicising but also discreet portrait of the man, and the documentary riches of capitularies and charters, the historian of Charlemagne's ninth-century successors has a wealth of material unrivalled across early medieval Europe. For Charlemagne's successor, Louis the Pious, for example, in addition to a body of legal and documentary evidence which surpasses his father, we have no fewer than three biographies – two, one written in verse, one in prose, written whilst he was still alive and the third immediately after his death – a haul unparalleled by any other early medieval ruler, whilst his reign and its immediate aftermath are also given vivid coverage in the histories of Nithard, an illegitimate grandson of Charlemagne, writing on the commission of one of Louis' sons. These historical narratives are supplemented by the continuations of the tradition of annalistic writing sponsored by Charlemagne's court, but ninth-century annals do not reflect court commissions so much as the thoughts and prejudices of political participants: the two crucial, but by no means isolated, texts are the so-called *Annals of St-Bertin*, based on the accounts of two bishops, Prudentius of Troyes and Hincmar of Rheims, with close connections to the west Frankish king Charles the Bald, and the *Annals of Fulda*, which in fact reflect the views and interests of the most powerful east Frankish church, the archbishopric of Mainz. And contemporary historical narrative such as this is only the tip of an iceberg: alongside it can be placed a wealth of shorter pieces, reflecting the particularities of a specific time and place, whether in the form of accounts of dreams or visions, poems or letters, biography or Biblical commentary.[1]

This material shares a polemical quality: individuals wrote to justify their position, offer coded advice about future action, and to denigrate and on occasion ridicule their opponents. Reading it takes us inside contemporary political debate, and impresses us with the sense of moral urgency that meant that this debate mattered. If the Franks were God's chosen people, then their fate rested on taking the right course so as to please God, whilst problems and misfortunes must reflect wrong decisions and God's displeasure. Because of this, debate centred on the person of the king and the moral life of the royal court. Kings from the past could be used as models, so that already by the 880s Charlemagne had acquired the status of an almost legendary figure who exemplified kingship, being used by Notker of St-Gallen as a source of pointed and often humorous stories to instruct his Carolingian, Charles the Fat, in kingship, and by Hincmar of Rheims as the exemplar of good political practice to be imitated by another young Carolingian, Carloman.[2] Centred on the person of the king, such polemic worked through the portrayal of the moral life of the royal household, the palace, which was a microcosm of the kingdom as a whole: Hincmar's advice to Carloman thus took the form of a tract on 'ordering the palace', which he claimed was based on an old account by Adalard, a cousin and contemporary of Charlemagne's. In such a discourse, improper behaviour at court was a sinful stain on the kingdom as a whole, and those key figures who dominated the court, so dispensing the practicalities of political patronage and controlling access to the king, were objects of an intensely personalised debate. Royal women, and above all royal wives, responsible for the smooth running of the royal household which was simultaneously a 'sacred palace', thus had a role which combined the familial and the public: it is no accident that the ninth century saw crucial developments in the notion of queenship as a public office. But just as queens were expected to safeguard the morality and order of the palace and so the realm, they were vulnerable to attack from those discontented with the current balance of power in the palace: from Louis the Pious' second wife, Judith, onwards, we find accusation after accusation spanning the whole range of sexual misdemeanors as well as illicit magic. Royal advisors were likewise recurrent targets for authors who often wished to bring down the power-brokers in the current regime and replace them with their own patrons: criticising the good king's bad advisors was a relatively safe way of commenting critically on royal policy. Thus an author like Thegan, writing a biography of Louis the Pious in 836, could seek to promote the interests of his network of east Frankish friends and patrons by tracing Louis' misfortunes to the self-interested advice of two fallen advisors, Archbishop Ebbo of Rheims, attacked as a social upstart, and Count Hugh of Tours, ridiculed as a coward. Those wishing to push their own claims as wise counsellors could present themselves as mouthpieces for advice which came, ultimately, from God. Thus Einhard presented Louis the Pious with a pamphlet recording the advice given to one of his dependants by the Archangel Gabriel in a vision.[3]

This wealth of material gives a real feel of contemporary debate for the first time since the fourth century. Indeed, it is arguably fuller and more vivid than the late Roman material. Whilst court politics of the early medieval variety clearly always and everywhere produced intense and often vituperative political debate, the sudden production of written polemic in this volume, where previously we have only distant echoes of vigorous argument reflected through chronicles and hagiographies, marks an important shift. This was a new form of political conflict, one in which the sword may have been a traumatic last resort, but the pen played a central role in urging, persuading and justifying. And these pamphlet wars make for plentiful sources, but ones which need careful handling because of their partial nature. Given that these texts were written at each other, for small, knowledgeable and passionate audiences, they need reading as part of a debate, and relating to the shadowy interest groups that shaped them. The real strength of so much recent research which has reshaped our understanding of the ninth century is that it has shown how different factions formed around the accusations and counter-accusations recorded in our texts, rather than debating whether a particular queen really was an adulteress.

And, finally, we must be aware of the danger of this rich material showing argument in action, injuries being nursed and rivalries fostered. They encourage us to write of political conflict, to make argument the focus of our narrative. This creates a very different perspective from that we acquire from the very different source material on the eighth century. But to some extent at least, the contrast is illusory, a product of the ability of Charlemagne's court to produce and promulgate an interpretation of the past into which all groups were tied, and so to elide the recurrent crises, revolts and unrest which characterised his reign. As we saw, to recreate the unease and discontent of regional elites, or the viewpoints of the likes of Tassilo, we have to tread carefully and work from fragments: we simply do not have the equivalent of our ninth-century source material. In other words, we have a very different perspective on the ninth century than we do on the eighth, because political debate had come to take on a written dimension hitherto lacking: this should not lead us to see debate, dissent and opposition as new phenomena. Ninth century political debate centred to an unprecedented degree on the written word, perhaps reflecting in this the insistence of the regime on recording the practical outcomes of debate in written form in the capitularies and associated material. Indeed, much of the political polemic that characterised the period from the 820s to the 880s attempted to influence royal action and justify often agonisingly difficult actions in recurrent crises which arose when the normal mechanisms of debate and agreement through the annual assembly and the community of the palace had broken down. In other words, by writing about the good kings of the past who encouraged wide and open debate, or condemning bad advisors who prevented current kings from hearing the views of their subjects, these authors were drawing on a series of experiences and expectations about 'consensus politics' encouraged by rulers themselves.

The imperial title and the problem of political unity

The tendency to view the ninth century in terms of decline does not only rest on the changed quality and quantity of source material. Above all, historians have interpreted the ninth century in terms of failure because of the fact of political division. However, contemporaries understood the issue of political unity differently from modern historians. The Frankish realms had enjoyed unity, in the sense of political power being wielded from one court in the name of a single ruling figure, since the late seventh century, and since the accession of Charles Martell this unity had been maintained without open military conflict between rival groups of Franks, as opposed to ruthless political manoeuvre. The maintenance of unity was not the result of any programmatic statement, imposing a new pattern of succession or guaranteeing the unity of the realm. But nor was it an accident. In fact, there had been recurrent but always short-lived attempts to respect the standing of all of a ruler's sons by implementing political divisions, notably after Martell's death in 741 and Pippin's in 768. That these attempts had failed, after tense periods where civil war and family strife had been bubbling close to the surface, reflects the preference of Frankish elites, both secular and ecclesiastical, for maintaining a system where there was a single location of legitimate ruling authority. This was a habit rooted in long and successful experience, not an ideological programme or political fad.

By the 780s the new scale of a vastly expanded empire necessitated a change in political structure, as Charlemagne dispatched his younger sons Louis and Pippin as kings of Aquitaine and Italy respectively. Subkingship of this type did not mark a formal political secession from the empire, as familial and moral ties bound the sons to their father, and there were severe limitations on the freedom of action enjoyed by subkings.[4] But by providing a local Carolingian king complete with court Charlemagne was able to tie the political ambitions of Aquitainian and Italian elites to the Carolingian family: they could work through their own king and within the Carolingian system. Subkingship was thus a means of accommodating regional difference within the Frankish polity. In both Aquitaine and Italy, distant from the Frankish heartlands and with strong traditions of self-government, this was a means of strengthening Frankish rule, not least as both kings were young boys and so ended up being brought up alongside and socialised with the flower of their kingdom's nobility. Italy, after all, had a long tradition of political independence and a sophisticated system of royal palaces and estates dotted through the cities and countryside of the north; Pippin was able to plug these traditions into the Carolingian system, and also lead Italian armies in central and eastern Europe against Avars and Slavs, as well as asserting Frankish claims over the independent princes of southern Italy. Aquitaine not only had a tradition of political independence, but following the collapse of the Visigothic kingdom was also potentially a source of influence and authority for the inhabitants of the formerly Visigothic provinces either side of the Pyrenees, imperfectly integrated into the Islamic political system centred on Cordoba. Indeed, it was the presence of a Carolingian court in Aquitaine that cemented the allegiance of the still-Christian elites of formerly Visigothic Septimania, and the activities of Aquitainian armies with a Carolingian king at their head that brought Catalonia into the Frankish Empire. Thanks to Louis' third, posthumous, biographer, we have an intriguing account of the creation of a system of palaces in Aquitaine, mimicking the royal centres of Francia, and Pippin likewise created a topography of Carolingian royal authority across north Italy, adapting Lombard traditions; Pippin's court, judging from the manuscript and literary evidence, was an important cultural centre, whilst Louis' nurtured a religious movement centred on the monastic practices of Benedict of Aniane. The Aquitainian and Italian courts thus played vital roles in the development of Carolingian kingship in miniature, and in the slow extension of Frankish overlordship to areas where concerted campaigning on the model of Charlemagne's Saxon adventures was impossible.[5]

This multiplicity of kingship within the Carolingian family underpinned Charlemagne's plans for his own succession. Here Charlemagne had to balance the claims of all his legitimate sons to kingship with a reluctance to effect a division of the Frankish heartlands born out of a century's political experience. Restricting the succession to one son alone was not only risky, in that in the event of an early or unexpected death it could leave the whole succession issue open, but would also undoubtedly provoke political unrest, as factions would inevitably form around those excluded. The dangers were illustrated by the serious revolt which broke out in 793 in support of Pippin 'the Hunchback', gradually pushed out of the court and finally excluded from the succession after his mother's death and father's remarriage, his status undercut by misleading claims about his illegitimacy and physical disability. So maintaining Carolingian kings in Italy and Aquitaine, whilst passing the Frankish heartlands on to the eldest surviving son, the young Charles, made sense as a means of maintaining the unity of the polity whilst ensuring the continuity of the family line and the loyalty of the peripheral provinces. This arrangement, clearly envisaged from the moment at which Louis and Pippin were elevated in 781, was formally enacted in 806, in a succession agreement known as the *Divisio Regnorum* – literally, the 'division of the kingdoms' – drawn up with the consent of the Frankish elite and carried to Rome for papal approval by Einhard. It laid down rules of conduct for relations between royal brothers – rules that had hardly been necessary whilst Charlemagne, as father, ruled from Aachen and expected obedience from his sons in Italy and Aquitaine, but that in the envisaged new order were vital. For part and parcel of the political system under Charlemagne was a careful management of the Carolingian family itself. Charlemagne himself practised serial monogamy, that is only entering one long-term union at a time, but was careful to avoid producing a surfeit of legitimate heirs: marriage was not at this date a sacrament of the church, and the exact definition of fully legitimate marriage was in the process of definition, a fuzziness Charlemagne exploited so as to effectively restrict legitimate status to the sons of Hildegard. His illegitimate sons, as well as his daughters, were kept at Aachen: these were potential sources of Carolingian blood, and so not to be married into the aristocracy where they might produce rival claimants to the throne. Both Louis and Pippin were allowed to marry and so produce legitimate heirs, in marked contrast to their elder brother, 'young Charles' (so called to differentiate him from his father), who was brought up at Aachen alongside his sisters, illegitimate brothers and other key advisors such as Charlemagne's cousins Wala and Adalhard. Young Charles was clearly being groomed to be the eventual heir to the Frankish heartlands, but the absence of any marriage on his part, or that of his sisters and relatives, left the longer-term pattern of succession an open question, as part of a policy of 'family management' which left Charlemagne's centrality to the system as a whole unchallenged.[6]

In the event the division of 806 was never effected, as both young Charles and Pippin of Italy predeceased their father, leaving Louis of Aquitaine the only surviving son, but the basic principles of multiple kingships within the family was maintained. Charlemagne confirmed Pippin's son, Bernhard, as king of Italy, thus seeking to create an Italian Carolingian line within the framework of the family and the empire, and moved slowly to confirm Louis as his heir, making him swear to respect the positions of his relatives. Thus even Louis' succession on Charlemagne's death in 814 was hardly the passing on of a united empire under one ruler, but the passing on of seniority within the family, and so control of Aachen and the Frankish heartland, to Louis, with the expectation that provincial desires for an accessible Carolingian and the royal dreams of Louis' cousins and son would lead to the continuation of a complex hierarchy of kingships. Indeed, such were the vested interests in the maintenance of multiple kingships that Louis' seizure of Aachen and so power in 814 was far from assured: he marched rapidly north from Aquitaine but there were still drawn swords and scuffles between Louis' supporters and those close to Wala, the key figure in the old regime and a Carolingian himself. Louis' succession, indeed, is the first example of a recurrent feature of ninth-century politics: the role of Carolingian kingships in the outlying provinces of the empire in providing political stability in times of division and dissent at the centre. For Louis brought with him a court elite fashioned by their common roots in Aquitaine.

Louis himself has sometimes been seen as attempting to implement a more rigid system based on an ideal of imperial unity that precluded subordinate kingships.

Certainly his propagandists wasted no time in presenting him as the prodigal son, whose succession reflected God's will. But, although the ideology of Christian empire was insistently developed through his reign, there is no hint that the unity of the Christian empire was seen as incompatible with the continuation of a hierarchy of Carolingian kingships with the emperor at the apex. Immediately on his accession, Louis had moved to reshape the Carolingian family in his own image, removing his father's daughters, granddaughters and illegitimate sons from Aachen. This was motivated by political insecurity: the possibility of a bid for the throne on the part these indirect branches of the Carolingian family had been very much alive in 814, and Louis condemned the loose sexual practices at his father's court as a means of blackening the reputation and delegitimising the claims of these potential rivals. The issue of succession was addressed directly in 817, when, after some intense debate and three days of alms-giving, fasting and prayer, an agreement was reached and published in a document known as the 'Ordering of the Empire' (*Ordinatio Imperii*). This played on the need to ensure the 'unity of the church and the Christian people' and provided for the succession of Louis' eldest son, Lothar, as emperor, with sole responsibility for dealing with the papacy; his brothers Pippin and Louis were, nonetheless, still kings in their own right, their realms centred on Aquitaine and Bavaria respectively. The tension surrounding its negotiation should not be seen as a result of ideological conflict between an 'imperial unity' party and those supporting the rights of younger sons, but rather as the result of the problematical position of Louis' cousin, Bernard, who had been made king of Italy in succession to his father, Pippin, by his grandfather Charlemagne in 811. The final document is wholly silent on Bernard's position, which Louis had sworn to respect before being crowned emperor by his father, but which was clearly threatened by Lothar's special responsibilities towards the pope, and the clause granting Lothar the kingdom of Italy on Louis' death. In the event, Bernard rapidly proclaimed his discontent, and attracted significant support not only from Italy, but from across the empire as a whole. Rather than negotiating a settlement, though, Louis had his nephew tried for rebellion and sentenced to blinding. Bernard clearly presented a real threat to Louis: after all, as an able Carolingian with young sons and a secure base in his subkingdom, his position was no different from Louis' prior to 814, and he made an attractive proposition for discontents across the empire as a whole. In the event his blinding led, unintentionally, to his death, an event which shook confidence in the regime, with public criticism of Louis' 'bad advisors': but Louis' main potential opponent was removed, and his sons never subsequently entertained royal claims. In 822, on the death of Benedict of Aniane, he was secure enough to do penance for Bernard's death, in the model of the Roman emperor Theodosius, and bring back some of his father's advisors, notably his illegitimate sons, and so establish a regime which could claim to be inclusive. In the following year, as Louis' second wife, Judith, gave birth to a fourth son, Charles (later known as 'the Bald'), Lothar, the eldest of Louis' sons by his first wife, was crowned co-emperor with his father, thus confirming the pre-eminent status granted by the *Ordinatio Imperii* of 817.[7]

In the decade after 817, Lothar in Italy, Pippin in Aquitaine and Louis in Bavaria were able to build up strong networks of regional support, demonstrating abilities which made them appealing sources of patronage for elites right across the empire. As a result, when political crisis at the centre undermined confidence in the rule of their father, their support was eagerly courted. When, after 828, Louis lost the support of significant members of the Frankish elite in an increasingly frantic political atmosphere, the result was not merely tense mutterings: discontents sought out the support of Louis' sons to stage what could be portrayed as 'loyal rebellions', designed to restore 'right order' at the court and so 'correct' Louis' regime. The first revolt, which broke into the open in 830, is in many ways the most shadowy. Following the straight refusal of a royal assembly to do Louis' bidding and campaign against the Bretons, in the summer of 830 Louis temporarily lost effective control to a faction headed by Pippin of Aquitaine, and tacitly backed by his brothers, particularly Lothar. Although Louis was able to win back support and re-establish his control, chastising his sons, their grip on their kingdoms remained secure. Attempts to move against Pippin in Aquitaine and the younger Louis in his sphere of influence east of the Rhine in 833 led to the formation of an alliance between Louis' sons. As father faced sons at a site known as the 'Field of Lies' in the upper Rhine valley, Louis' supporters deserted him, apparently moved by the accusations made by his sons, and the presence of the pope in Lothar's entourage, and Lothar's status as co-emperor. Louis was imprisoned and subsequently, in a fascinating and unprecedented move, formally deposed: Louis was tried by a tribunal of bishops for a list of crimes (such as compelling his subjects to break oaths and to fight in Lent), and sentenced to public penance. As public penance involved setting aside all insignia of worldly office, this effectively stripped him of his imperial and royal titles, leaving Lothar, long ago crowned co-emperor, in official control; Louis was then pressured to take up a monastic vow to complete his penance. The procedure is striking: it shows just how deeply the political ideology of Christian kingship had put down roots, in that the list of accusations against Louis centred on his failing to live up to the ministry (*ministerium*) of kingship, as defined in a series of political tracts, capitularies and church councils in the first part of his reign. So too the use of penance as a means of doing atonement for these crimes picked up on Louis' own earlier actions, notably his voluntary penance in 822 for Bernard of Italy's death. Louis' deposition, although this time carried out through a formal process, once again proved short-lived: there were enough members of the Frankish elite who felt uneasy at the enormity of their actions for a campaign to restore Louis to gain momentum, possibly aided by the misgivings of Louis of Bavaria. In 834 Louis was to undergo a richly ceremonial recoronation as emperor, and those behind his deposition were tried. Even then, however, the secure position of Louis' sons within their subkingdoms on the periphery made the wholesale re-establishment of paternal control impossible.

Louis could take the high ground on the allegiance owed by sons to fathers, and use his renewed control of the Frankish heartlands to back up moral with political capital, forming alliances with one son against his brother and attempting to impose his will, but ultimately their provincial powerbases were secure, and Frankish elites were drawn into the webs of patronage leading back to the Aquitainian, Bavarian and Italian courts. Pippin of Aquitaine's death in 838 removed one source of resistance, and allowed Louis to attempt to move against the growing power of Louis of Bavaria east of the Rhine, whilst building up political support for Charles the Bald in the west now Pippin was gone. When Louis the Pious died, in 840, it looked, briefly, as if Lothar, as eldest son and emperor, might succeed in recreating a dominant position reminiscent of that envisaged in 817. But conflict had now become a matter of habit: complaints of arrogance against Lothar probably reflect the fact that aristocrats were growing used to having their support rewarded, not expected. Lothar's brothers, Louis of Bavaria and Charles the Bald, were able to rally sufficient support to join together and resist their brother, Louis' eastern supporters defeating Lothar's backers in 841, and then Louis and Charles themselves defeating Lothar at Fontenoy in 841. This escalation of conflict into open battle, Frank against Frank, was deeply traumatic; it proved short-lived. Lothar, his ambitions checked, agreed a truce and negotiated a settlement with his brothers whereby the empire was split into three, with trusted agents of each of the brothers agreeing a final division in 843 in the Treaty of Verdun.

If the convoluted politics of the 830s amply demonstrate the importance of Carolingian kingships in the provinces, what is rather less clear are the reasons for the outbreak of this internal conflict. Most modern historians have emphasised the birth of Charles the Bald and the inevitability of rivalry between Charles and his half-brothers. Certainly Louis' determination to provide a kingdom for Charles is one factor that runs right through the unrest of the latter part of Louis' reign. These efforts were said by some of Louis' opponents to have upset the settlement reached with such sacred ceremony in 817, although the very first attempt to carve out a kingdom for Charles, in 829, had taken scrupulous care to remain within the letter of existing succession agreements, and accusations of breaking them did not make it into the list of crimes with which Louis was charged in 833. More important than any latent respect for the precise content of the 817 succession agreement was the delicate balance of power between father and sons that the attempts to provide for Charles rocked, and even here Charles' status was a complicating factor but hardly the root cause of instability. Tension was inherent in a system in which royal fathers and sons enjoyed overlapping claims to both material resources and to political support: the imperial aristocracy nurtured interests which transcended the various regions of the empire and thus had connections and obligations to both fathers and sons. Lothar, for example, spent most of his time in Italy after 823, partly because the running of two fully-fledged imperial heartlands would have placed too great a stress on the palace system, but through his marriage he maintained close links with the aristocracy of the imperial heartlands. Similarly, Louis of Bavaria married Emma, the sister of his stepmother, Judith, and a member of the most powerful family in Alemannia: throughout the 830s Alemannia was thus the object of competition between Louis and Emma on the one hand, and Judith and her son Charles the Bald on the other.

Changing balances within the family as sons married, set up courts of their own, and developed networks of kinship and patronage around them, were a recurrent feature of Frankish politics, and could be negotiated, with care and time: Louis' regime had already done precisely that twice, once in 814–17 with the dispersal of Charlemagne's advisors, and once again in 822–3 with the death of Benedict of Aniane and the birth of Charles the Bald. What broke down in the lead-up to the revolts of the 830s was trust between Louis and an important faction within the imperial aristocracy, which then saw in Louis' sons a way to hold on to their position and status. Hand-in-hand with the ideology of Christian kingship went the perception that in this new Christian empire, all were responsible to God for their position. Hence Louis could admonish 'all the orders' in his kingdom on their duties, and present all those exercising power, counts as well as bishops, as sharing in a collective Christian ministry delegated from God through the emperor.[8] These ideological changes chimed with political imperatives: in the new system, a generation after the end of annual expansive campaigning, it opened up the possibility of treating their local dominance as an office, a position which not only needed confirming by the king through the grant of countships, but also could be removed if it had not been properly discharged. The official account of the first period of Louis' reign, in the continuations of the *Royal Frankish Annals*, emphasises precisely this possibility: complaints against individuals for bad conduct were heard at the imperial court, and debated by those present, and ultimately those found to be incompetent or immoral were removed from their offices. This marked a sea change in the operation of royal patronage, and one badly in need of more research. In 828 these new practices, and the new understanding of public office which underpinned them, were applied to the leading lights of the imperial elite. A campaign had been dispatched to the Spanish march, and met with failure, perhaps because of inadequate preparation. Louis, however, held an inquest which found the army's two leaders, Count Hugh of Tours and Count Matfrid of Orleans, culpable and deprived them of their offices; all those with grievances or complaints against Hugh and Matfrid's conduct when their position had been unchallenged were encouraged to come forward. Hugh and Matfrid had been the key players at court, Louis' closest advisors, for a decade. This purge was thus an attempt to reshape the court elite, making space to bring in new faces, but it also demonstrated that the ideology of office applied to all, and that all were answerable to the political community as a whole for their actions. It may also have been an attempt to manage the heated debate about right order and fitting conduct in political life that the flowering of the Carolingian renaissance, and Louis' earlier public espousal of the ideology of a shared royal ministry, had encouraged. Contemporary sources point to a sense of impending crisis the roots of which are difficult to pin down, but which led to church councils and royal counsellors compiling lengthy tracts of advice on right order within the empire, and by identifying Hugh and Matfrid as failing in their responsibilities Louis may have been attempting to deal with this implied criticism and signal a new start.

A stable empire no longer expanding definitely needed new mechanisms for rulers to manage their aristocracy, but the ideology of office intersected with a different way of thinking about aristocratic status, in terms of honour. In contemporary language, offices were *honores*, literally 'honours', a terminology which demonstrated the centrality of the exercise of public office to an individual's and family's name and standing – their 'honour' in a more abstract, social sense. And we know that Hugh and Matfrid's fate did constitute a public humiliation, for which they were mocked by their opponents: stories pointing to their cowardice as a reason for the failure of the Spanish campaign circulated. The ripples caused by their fall spread wide. Hugh and Matfrid had strong family roots in the Rhine and Moselle valleys respectively, and through their countships clients and supporters in the Loire region, whilst as the emperor's favoured counsellors they had built up contacts across the empire as a whole. These networks not only now had to find new ways of protecting their interests at court and having their cases brought to the imperial ear; they also faced potential ruin, as the grants of royal and ecclesiastical land and office with which they had been primed were now brought into question, and thus stood implacably opposed to the new men brought in by Louis in Hugh and Matfrid's place.

This kind of disruption to well-oiled networks of influence and patronage was hardly unique: it was part and parcel of the political landscape in a court-centred polity like the Carolingian Empire, and there are plenty of other examples before and after of aristocratic families and ecclesiastical institutions dealing with parallel changes without the far-reaching political disruption that followed on from the fall of Hugh and Matfrid. But in this specific context, it was the spark that started a conflagration, flaring as it did in a uniquely combustible situation. For one thing, the ideology of ministry provided a language in which the actions of kings could be debated and criticised, and so could be mobilised by aristocrats and churchmen to legitimate their actions, as well as by kings to exalt their own status. For another, Louis was now in his fifties, with adult sons who were both able and ambitious and a second wife no older than her stepsons. In such a context, Louis' actions inevitably had effects at the courts of his sons. Lothar was, after all, married to a daughter of Hugh of Tours, whilst the disastrous campaign of 828 had taken place within Pippin's kingdom, and Louis' new chief advisor, Bernard of Septimania, was also the most powerful landowner in the borderlands between Pippin's kingdom and Islamic al-Andalus. Able to shelter and garner support through the agencies of able Carolingian rulers, those stripped of office would emphatically not disappear, but instead could prosecute campaigns of accusation, claim and threat against the new men who had been raised in their place. In an expanded but no longer expanding empire imposing a new understanding of public office as something which could be removed may have been a political necessity, but it inevitably also created a situation in which political divisions within the imperial aristocracy interacted with tensions within the Carolingian family, the one reinforcing the other. Thus through the 830s we find recurrent conflict around the key honours of which Hugh and Matfrid had been stripped in 828, and around those held by the family of Bernard of Septimania: even the deaths of Hugh and Matfrid, in Italy in 837, did not end what had now become an endemic conflict over local position, in which rival parties nursed competing claims and looked for Carolingian patrons. The outcome was a situation in which the loose inclusive hierarchy of Carolingian courts around which were spun complex webs of patronage gave way to a system predicated on conflict between independent rival Carolingian courts competing for aristocratic loyalty: an outcome confirmed by the civil war which followed Louis' death.

Carolingian kingship at its zenith

The troubles of the 830s and the civil war of 840–3 were thus important not so much because they brought about the division of the empire – there had always been an acknowledgement of multiple Carolingian kingships – but because the end result was that real imperial power exercised by one Carolingian over his relatives was no longer a possibility. Lothar tried his hardest to make the imperial title meaningful, for example having his uncle and ally Archbishop Drogo of Metz made papal vicar north of the Alps, and so potentially attempting to control the Frankish church as a whole. But the imperial title quickly became tied to political control of the kingdom of Italy and the close relationship and special responsibilities towards the pope that this created. On Lothar's death in 855, the imperial title passed without comment to his son Louis II, king of Italy (called 'emperor of Italy' by some sources north of the Alps – the imperial title was now coterminous with rule of Italy). Although Louis the German and Charles the Bald were both briefly crowned emperor before their deaths in 876 and 877 respectively, they gained the imperial title through seizure of Italy. The imperial title carried some wisp of moral superiority, a link with the now legendary Charlemagne and a recognition of 'good kingship', but in practical terms of territorial authority it meant nothing concrete beyond Italy, and in particular the city of Rome. Indeed, the extent to which the imperial title did continue to matter to ninth-century rulers north of the Alps is perhaps the most eloquent testimony to the fact that even after 843 kings continued to think of their ambitions and their status within the framework of the Carolingian Empire as a whole, not simply in terms of the segments created out of civil war in the 830s and 840s.

In fact, the truly radical feature about the settlement of 843 was the equality of the Carolingian kingships it created. Whereas in the political practice of Charlemagne and Louis the Pious, and in the succession plans of 806 and 817, the unity of the Frankish heartlands under the rule of the senior Carolingian had underpinned their dominance of the political system as a whole, the crisis of the 830s and Lothar's failure to build on his imperial title in 840–3 made for a very different kind of system. The division enshrined in the Treaty of Verdun in 843 were designed to create a system in which all three brothers enjoyed equal resources and so political parity: the aristocrats ordered to negotiate the division were given detailed inventories of royal property across the empire to help them in this goal. They also, of course, had to respect the political realities made apparent in the civil war: Lothar's control of Italy and support from the court establishment in the heartlands of the empire, Louis' dominance in much of the eastern part of the empire, where he had styled himself as 'king in eastern Francia' since 833, and Charles' footholds in Aquitaine and parts of west Francia, thanks to the strenuous efforts of his mother and late father. The result was a division which split up the old heartlands and the concentrations of royal wealth and royal palaces there: Carolingian kingship on the periphery, which had emerged as the basis for stability in the struggle for control of the empire, now determined the political division of Francia proper. Louis thus gained Bavaria, Alemannia, Saxony and eastern Francia as far as the cities and palaces of the Rhine valley; Charles

Aquitaine and western Francia as far as the Meuse; and Lothar a long and thin middle kingdom, stretching from the Frisian coast in the north, down a long corridor between the Meuse and the Rhine, including Aachen, to Alsace, Burgundy, Provence and Italy.

Modern historians have often been tempted to see the partition of 843 as marking the birth of the nation-states of modern Europe, and to trace the origins of modern France and Germany from the kingdoms of Charles and Louis in particular. This is a mistake. The kingdoms it created were cobbled together by the contingencies of political compromise: they were far from being homogenous entities on any level, and the division of 843 actually cut across administrative boundaries within the church, and across patterns of aristocratic, ecclesiastical, and royal landowning. Nor did it lay down boundaries that were to prove long-lasting: through the ninth century we see recurrent divisions reflecting changing balances of power within the Carolingian family. Nor can the kingdoms created in 843 be seen as enjoying any cultural unity. Much is sometimes made of the oaths of mutual loyalty sworn between Charles' and Louis' followings at Strasbourg in the midst of the civil war in 842, and recorded in careful detail by the contemporary historian and follower of Charles, Nithard. The Strasbourg oaths were sworn not in the usual correct Latin of the Carolingian renaissance, but in the romance and Germanic vernaculars which were the normal spoken language of western and eastern Francia respectively: Nithard's account is thus a key piece of early evidence for the development of the vernacular languages. But a close look at Nithard's account underlines that the use of the vernacular here was not the cultural expression of homogenous and closed regional aristocracies. It was Louis' following which swore in the romance vernacular of western Francia, and Charles' in the Germanic vernacular of the regions east of the Rhine. In other words, this was a ritual gesture of political solidarity, not a reflection of ingrained cultural difference: in it, the two rulers and their entourages of ambitious and mobile young aristocrats were addressing the concerns of those regional communities of landowners on whose support they depended.[9]

A look at the horizons of the aristocrats in Charles' and Louis' entourages at Strasbourg confirms that division cannot be seen as a simple acknowledgement of the regional roots and growing strength of aristocratic power. Charles enjoyed close links with Alemannia through his mother, and had married into the Rhineland aristocracy in the course of the civil war. He thus attracted ambitious young aristocrats from these areas to his standard, whose careers in the west Frankish kingdom created in the division of 843 can be traced: indeed, Robert the Strong, the dominant figure in ninth-century west Frankish politics and forefather of the Capetian royal dynasty of medieval France, was a Rhinelander who followed Charles west. Thanks to generations of careful research into the prosopography of the Carolingian aristocracy – that is, the use of legal and other documentation to reconstruct the networks of the men who fleetingly appear in our chronicles as political movers and shakers – the continued international horizons of the imperial aristocracy even after 843 are becoming clear. Robert and his family, for example, did not forget their eastern roots and eastern lands, and it was they and their like who, disenchanted with Charles the Bald in the 850s, were able to use their links with their homeland to invite various east Frankish rulers to invade and relieve them of Charles' 'tyranny'; as late as the 890s, when Robert's son Odo was struggling for the west Frankish throne, his cousin Megingoz was the dominant figure in the old heartland of Lothar's kingdom, the region between the Meuse and the Rhine, and a crucial link between Odo and the court of the east Frankish Carolingians. This 'imperial aristocracy', that is, continued to be active on an European stage, and thus interacted with multiple Carolingian courts, rather than having their horizons confined to just one kingdom.

The implications of this continued aristocratic interconnectedness in a divided empire need taking seriously. The succession agreements of 806 and 817 and their successors had been concerned with working out the ground rules of aristocratic loyalty in an increasingly multi-centred political system, seeking to regulate marriages and property deals which crossed the boundaries between different kingdoms and might therefore cause political discord. From the 830s, these fears became a reality. Many vivid examples come through in the surviving collection of letters written to various kings and courtiers by Einhard on behalf of his friends and relatives, which shows just how traumatic political division could be for those whose interests crossed political frontiers: here, the concern is not inherited family land, but the fact that kings would expect oaths of loyalty, and political support, from all those who held public office, or grants of royal or church land, in their kingdom.[10] With formal political division after 843, these issues did not go away: family ties inevitably continued across frontiers. For any individual, holding office, or royal land, in more than one kingdom was a political impossibility, but families might maintain agglomerations of influence and office, by maintaining connections with more than one court. Inherited family land, too, inevitably continued to crisscross political boundaries. Throughout the ninth century Carolingian rulers felt no qualms about removing office and royal and ecclesiastical estates from aristocrats who had fallen from favour, but inheritances were far harder to touch, and although we read of periodic purges, families normally seem to have been able to maintain a grasp on inherited land. The regular summit meetings between Carolingian kings which are such a marked feature of Carolingian politics after 843 need to be understood against this background. Although modern historians have been unimpressed by the ideology of fraternal concord promulgated on these occasions, to aristocratic families whose interests spanned the Frankish kingdoms, the notion of a collectivity of kingdoms held together by familial affections would have made vivid sense.

Indeed, the emergence of a new multi-centred political system, in which the most powerful aristocrats could access competing sources of royal patronage in the courts of rival Carolingian kings, created a more complex and more unstable politics. Conflicts within the Carolingian family could interact with rivalries within and between aristocratic families with alarming ease. Able and ambitious aristocrats lived in fear of falling from favour with their chosen Carolingian, and the loss of status and position that this entailed, but there was always the possibility of recovering face, and building up a new powerbase, with a different Carolingian. Kings likewise had to manage their aristocracies carefully, so as not to create a muttering of malcontents ready to search for alternative sources of patronage. The inherent instability of a game whose actors had far-flung interests and multiple sources of patronage is best illustrated by an example. In 861, the east Frankish king Louis the German found three brothers Odo, Berengar and Abbot Waldo guilty of 'infidelity': they had been plotting with one of Louis' sons, Louis the Younger. Stripped of their offices, but holding onto their family land (doubtless because Louis still needed the support of their kinsman, notably their father), they approached a kinsman, Count Adalard, the key figure at the court of Charles the Bald where he was seneschal, and one of the major landowners in the heartlands of the middle kingdom; Adalard was able to get his ambitious young relations Odo and Berengar appointed as counts by Charles the Bald in the west, and Lothar II in the middle kingdom, respectively. Four years later, Louis the German made all his sons subkings; Louis the Younger, acting without his father's consent, contracted a marriage with a kinswoman of Adalard's, in the hope of winning over support and fomenting rebellion against his father; but the marriage alliance disrupted the status quo in the western and middle kingdoms too, where Adalard and his kin were immediately suspect; Odo and Berengar were again stripped of office and returned to the east seeking rehabilitation.[11] Beneath the hardening and softening relationships between Carolingian men, and the recurrent crises of royal succession, which appear to dominate ninth-century politics, we should not forget these complex webs of aristocratic ambition, based on kinship, property and office.

As Odo and Berengar's comings and goings eloquently illustrate, for all the differences in political style between rival Carolingian courts, the fundamentals of politics revolved around the same issues right across the empire: royal distribution of *honores* and so of aristocratic honour. And a distinctive feature of politics in the generation after 843 was that this process encompassed not only the granting out of countships and royal lands, but also 'dishonouring' those who had proved themselves unworthy through their removal: hence the travails of Odo and Berengar. Since the seventh century, Frankish aristocrats, when they were granted public office, expected to hold it for life. Although kings had always had the ability to remove real troublemakers, this was exercised carefully and rarely, in full-blown political crises, normally after outright rebellion. The more frequent – if not yet regular – cycles of 'hiring and firing' that are visible in the middle decades of the ninth century thus mark an important new departure. Although the whole technology of government through capitularies and *missi dominici* rested on a notion that counts had a definable job for which they were to be held to account, when Louis experimented with using it to remove individuals from office in the 820s and 830s, the result, as we have seen, was political upheaval. Civil war and then political division, however, created a world where kings could and did remove aristocrats from office in their kingdom, and aristocrats could respond by seeking alternative sources of honour and honours. These processes were not necessarily smooth. Even where a countship became vacant through the natural death of its holder, that individual's kin and heirs might resist a royal appointee, and on several occasions we read of local civil wars. But such cases do not indicate that countships were becoming something akin to heritable positions: kin and heirs had always exercised such hopes, and the fact that in the middle decades of the ninth century these hopes were increasingly pursued through violent resistance point to the determination of a new generation of Carolingian kings to assert their control over countships. When, as he left to campaign in Italy in 877, Charles the Bald left instructions that if any counts died whilst he was away, they were to be replaced with their sons, he was acknowledging that in the normal run of things, such a succession would have been far from automatic, but subject to royal whims; in the exceptional situation of an absent king, family succession would be tolerated as a means of avoiding destabilising conflict.[12] It would be a mistake, therefore, to see Carolingian kingship as weakened by the upheavals of the 830s. Political division meant more Carolingian courts, better able to intervene in the distribution of power in the localities, but also more potential sources of patronage for ambitious landowners. This was a politics in which the stakes were higher for both kings and aristocrats, as kings were able to exercise patronage with greater abandon, but as a result were subjected to greater risks, and aristocrats could rise higher faster, but fall vertiginously and without warning.

Of the rival courts emerging after 843, most is known about that of Charles the Bald in the west. This is no accident. In 845 Charles appointed Hincmar to the key archbishopric of Rheims, which he held until his death in 882. One of the most prolific authors among Carolingian churchmen, he has left us a rich seam of letters, tracts spanning fields as diverse as church discipline, theology and political thought, and conciliar and capitulary legislation, as well as offering a detailed and opinionated piece of contemporary history in his sections of the *Annals of St Bertin*. Hincmar, although loyal to the king and dynasty, was free with his criticism of contemporaries, and even kings when they disappointed him, giving us a rich insight into Charles' regime. But his career needs placing in the context of the wider cultural vibrancy of the ninth-century church, and the flamboyant patronage of culture by Charles, rightly styled by one historian a 'Carolingian renaissance prince'. The intellectual and social networks created by king and court informed ninth-century political culture to the core: this was a world in which clerics could cull examples from Roman history and send them to kings and courtiers in the expectation of an eager response, in a court culture which avidly consumed ornate illuminated manuscripts representing the ruler and his court in the full traditions of classical and early Christian art.[13]

This cultural milieu, and the web of patronage and wealth expanding from the court, does much to explain the innovative aspects of Charles' kingship. Arguably the greatest law-giver of all Carolingian kings, Charles revived the practice of issuing regular capitularies, which had been in abeyance since the mid-820s. And Charles' legislation, peaking with the great edict of Pitres of 864, is marked for its sophistication, with regular cross-references back to the capitularies of Charlemagne and Louis the Pious, and also systematic borrowing from the Roman law of the Theodosian Code. Unthinkable as such legislation would have been without informed counsellors and a receptive courtly public, such borrowings were not simply matters of intellectual curiosity. To give one striking example, among the aspects of late Roman public law so self-consciously revived was the notion of treason ('lèse-majesté'), which coloured earlier Frankish notions of personal and political disloyalty ('infidelity') with a sense of public crime against the political community as a whole. This was not merely a legal gloss: Frankish rulers since the seventh century had generally avoided physical punishment of their opponents, favouring exile, monastic imprisonment or disgrace reached by the 'judgement of the Franks', but under Charles on a handful of occasions execution was seen as fitting punishment for those guilty of what was now seen as a crime against the body politic as a whole, here building on his father's use of the punishment of blinding. Similarly, in the ritual of his court Charles drew eagerly on late Roman, early Christian and Byzantine precedents designed to exalt the status of the ruler: where his father had introduced the ritual of supplicants grovelling by kissing the emperor's feet, in court ritual under Charles the earthly king was increasingly identified with Christ, the king of Heaven. No wonder Charles's opponents could make accusations of 'tyranny' – again, unheard of for centuries – and even Hincmar could balk at Charles' adoption of increasingly hierarchical court rituals, designed to elevate and differentiate the king from his advisors, in his last years.

The intellectual sophistication, and the ideological developments, of Charles' court grew from developments already apparent in Louis the Pious' reign. The consistent application of these notions is most clear in the development of liturgical rituals of king-making, which reached what was to become their 'standard' form under Charles, and also in the emergence of the first rituals of queen-making. These rituals were developed as ways of legitimating Charles' power at crucial junctures in his reign, for example the conquest of the kingdom of his nephew, Lothar II, after the latter's death in 869. But the ideology of kingship as ministry could also be used to make criticism of rulers who were seen as failing in that ministry; and Hincmar, the most persistent essayist on the theme, could use the discourse to suggest areas where kings could do better. So whilst the ideology of Christian kingship was, on one level, driven by the need to legitimate, it ultimately shaped a discourse that could cut both ways. And Christian kings needed helpers to share in their duty to correct their subjects and so please God, helpers who shared in their ministry: not only bishops, like Hincmar, whose role as advisors, and if necessary critical friends, was so legitimated, indeed encouraged, but also aristocrats holding public office. One necessary correlate of this was the sense that the legislation of capitularies was an expression of not just the ruler's will, but of the 'consensus of the faithful', resting on the agreement of all those sharing in the government of the kingdom and so pleasing God. Under Charles, this notion of consensus, already given a high profile in Louis' legislation, reached centre stage. Indeed, the first major act of Charles' reign, the agreement reached between the new king and his ruling elite in 843 and recorded in the capitulary of Coulaines, essays at length this notion of a royal ministry ruling through the consensus of the faithful. But whilst kings and their favoured courtiers presented their actions as arising from a legitimating consensus, those who were out of favour or who felt their views had been ignored might see things differently: it is no accident that the most developed and most famous essay in consensus politics, Hincmar's tract *On the Governance of the Palace*, was penned precisely when the elderly archbishop had been pushed out of the inner circles of a new king, Carloman, whose chief counsellors were Hincmar's rivals.[14]

So Charles' court saw an exaltation of royal power and an insistence on royal prerogatives derived from Christian thought and the Roman past, but within a discourse of Christian kingship which also gave a voice to counts, bishops and abbots as participants in a hierarchy of divinely ordained power. In terms of political practice, Charles' kingship likewise was driven by an urgent and practical need to engage with landowning elites. His kingship immediately stands out for its itinerancy. Charles' brothers, like their father and grandfather, moved their court in the course of the year, their itinerancy having the nature of a slow and stately progress, from a favoured winter residence with a small retinue of immediate advisors, to a carefully chosen destination to pray in Lent and then celebrate Easter in high fashion, before holding the major public occasion of the year, the annual assembly in May; the summer and autumn might then see further movements to favoured residences for hunting, feasting, meeting the aristocracy and taking counsel at a relatively informal level. Whilst Charles' itinerary revolved around the same underlying calendar with its ecclesiastical and political imperatives, the pace of his movement was greater than that of any earlier Carolingian ruler, or indeed his brothers: in a reign spanning four decades, it was rare for him to stay in one place for a month.[15] The reasons for this changed pattern are difficult to discern. Although Charles' father and grandfather had tended to stay longest at the great palace complexes of the Rhine and Moselle valleys, beyond the frontiers of Charles' western kingdom, there was no shortage of royal land and palace sites in a region which had been the site of important royal centres since Merovingian times: Charles, indeed, cultivated a personal relationship with the great abbey of St-Denis, laying the ground for its later emergence as the favoured abbey of French kings, and towards the end of his reign developed Compiègne as his 'Carlopolis', echoing and rivalling his grandfather's palace at Aachen. It may, instead, have been political imperative that determined Charles' near constant movement. Unlike his brothers, Charles did not have long-standing links with the regions he won in the civil war of 840–3, and a core area of his kingdom, the Loire valley, had been the cradle of political conflict right through the troubles of the 830s. In the south, Charles' nephew Pippin enjoyed considerable support in Aquitaine, being recognised by many there as king in succession to his father Pippin of Aquitaine until his defeat in 848. Moreover, Charles' western kingdom allowed few possibilities for military expansion or the type of campaigning activity which could bond king to aristocrats: the Spanish March, the one area where there were non-Carolingian, indeed non-Christian, opponents, was distant from royal interests and left to the native aristocracy. But if Charles' itinerancy had its roots in the need to win over the elites of a strange and unstable kingdom, however, it eventually became a matter of policy, a policy that did have important implications for royal resources. For itinerancy of the kind practised by Charles institutionalised a tight relationship between the king and his abbots and bishops, ideally placed to act as hosts for the royal court as it perambulated the kingdom on a far more regular basis than was the case for less itinerant kings elsewhere. It is no accident that in the great crises of his reign it was the support of the church that Charles could ultimately rally, as in 858, when western bishops remained loyal even as aristocratic support evaporated, assembling in council at Quierzy and rebuking Charles' invading brother in a tract penned, inevitably, by Hincmar.[16]

Viewed against the spectacular ideological developments of Charles' reign, the kingship of Louis the German in east Francia can appear disappointing. In part, this reflects genuine cultural differences between eastern and western kingdoms. The east Frankish church, after all, was in an institutional sense less than a century old, created in the course of the eighth century. So, whilst it is clear that Louis' court, like his brothers', was a magnet of cultural patronage, its output looks slightly conservative, even old-fashioned. The eastern equivalent of Hincmar was, initially at least, Hraban Maur. Hraban, a pupil of Alcuin's, had established himself as the leading Biblical commentator of his day in the time of Louis the Pious, and had initially backed Lothar, losing his abbacy of Fulda as a result. In 847, however, Louis appointed him archbishop of Mainz, a position which gave him effective control of the east Frankish church until his death in 856. Hraban's Biblical commentary used the Old Testament to reflect on contemporary issues and right order in this world and as archbishop of Mainz he began a tradition of regional councils which continued to the end of the ninth century, concerned with the nitty-gritty of church discipline, the administration of tithe and baptism, the eradication of false prophets, and the disciplining of violent or immoral laity. Through the Fulda connection – the intellectual powerhouse of eastern Francia – the court also became connected with the development of vernacular Old High German as a literary language, for at Fulda, through its involvement in mission, pragmatic attempts at writing in the vernacular had already begun. At Louis' court experiments in using the vernacular as a medium for fully-fledged literary composition produced works such as the vivid vernacular version of the Gospels produced by Hraban's pupil, Otfrid of Weissembourg.[17]

Louis' court was not, then, a backwater, and the development of the vernacular was itself an innovation that made eminent sense in view of the linguistic makeup of the kingdom. Although we know that Louis issued decrees, we have no tradition of capitulary legislation of the kind so visible in the west; indeed, even *missi dominici*, assiduously kept up by Charles the Bald precisely because of the need to make capitulary legislation effective, are difficult to trace in Louis' kingdom. This should not be seen as an index of political failure: on the contrary, the structure of Louis' kingdom meant that he had less need for this apparatus of rule than his brother. Louis' kingdom enjoyed a long 'open frontier' with various Slavic tribes to the east, and there is good evidence for the importance of this frontier in allowing Louis' aristocracy the opportunity to take plunder and tribute and form solidarities based on common military endeavour, particularly in the far southeast where there was significant piecemeal territorial expansion along the Danube, in the region formerly dominated by the Avars. Louis' kingship, indeed, had a markedly military public image, drawing on this experience of frontier warfare. The political stability ingrained by frontier warfare was further embedded by the political geography of the east Frankish kingdom, made up as it was of four segments which had strong identities: Saxony in the north, Alemannia and Bavaria in the south and southeast, with east Francia or Franconia along the Rhine and Main in the middle. Although the most powerful aristocrats had interests which crisscrossed these internal boundaries, Louis was able to deal with these regions as blocks: east Frankish armies and assemblies were summoned in terms of these provincial units, and there were clear conventions as to where kings met with each. The appointment of Hraban to the archbishopric of Mainz in 847 opened the door into the rich royal estates of Franconia, where the palace of Frankfurt was developed in conscious imitation of Aachen to the extent that it became 'principal seat of the kingdom', with a network of smaller lodgings, royal abbeys and forests full of game around it: this became the political stage on which eastern elites met with their king.[18] These practices, by facilitating communication between the king and regional elites, bypassed the need for the issuing of capitularies and dispatch of *missi dominici* on the lines of the west. After 865, when Louis made his three sons subkings, based in Bavaria, Alemannia and Franconia respectively and married into regional elites, these processes of communication between regions and court were eased still further. The shallower social hierarchy which characterised east Francia – where great estates were fewer than in the west, and small and middling landowners more common – further embedded direct communication between the court and regional communities of landowners at the heart of eastern political practice.

Last but far from least we come to the kingdom of Lothar. This is all too easily relegated to a bit part in a story focusing on western or eastern Francia, but it remained in a very real sense the heart of the Carolingian Empire. The lack of attention is largely due to the lack of a year-by-year account written with the kind of access that underlies the *Annals of St-Bertin* for the west, or the *Annals of Fulda* for the east, and a lack of secondary research because, unlike the kingdoms of his brothers, Lothar's realm was not the lineal ancestor of any modern European nation-state. In fact, the written sources that do survive give the impression of a stable and successful regime: Lothar received fulsome panegyrics and tracts on Christian kingship from the likes of the Irish scholar Sedulius Scottus, and his court is associated with a number of lavish illuminated manuscripts, pointing to its importance as a centre of cultural patronage comparable to his grandfather's.[19] The documentary evidence, too, shows Lothar enjoying the rich royal resources of the Carolingian heartlands between the Meuse and Moselle, and the prestige which went with the imperial associations of Aachen. Indeed, even the most cursory look counters the impression given by studies of western and eastern Francia of kingdoms whose politics and aristocracies were relatively self-contained after 843. With a careful and largely successful management of political patronage, Lothar was able to court the support of the 'imperial aristocracy', so many of whom had substantial inherited lands in this region; these interests brought the great families of the empire into Lothar's ambit even when individual members held office in eastern or western Francia.

Whilst these extensive links continued through to the end of the ninth century at the very latest, the politics of these imperial connections changed dramatically after Lothar's death in 855. Lothar's kingdom, of the three created in 843, was the one with the most difficult political geography, cobbled together as it was from a number of distinct regions: a fact perhaps reflected in the lack of any court historiography reflecting the interests of the kingdom as a whole. Lothar had responded to this by adopting a strategy also used by his brothers, and adapting the institution of subkingship to give these relatively discrete regions an accessible Carolingian court. In the case of Italy, ruled successfully by Lothar's son Louis II since the civil war, this was no more than an acknowledgement of existing practice since the Carolingian conquest; Provence, the middle section of the middle kingdom, had been given another of Lothar's sons, Charles, after revolting in 845. Politically crucial for the empire as a whole, however, were the heartlands in the north. Here Lothar was succeeded by his son Lothar II, both of whose uncles were inextricably pulled into the politics of his kingdom because of its prestige, but also its political centrality to the family strategies of those aristocratic families which really mattered. Explicit intervention in Lothar's kingdom – which gradually came to have an identity of its own, derived from its ruler, and be referred to as 'Lotharingia' – took two forms. The first was attempts to negotiate agreements over the fate of Lothar's kingdom. The second, intimately related, came in a long-running conflict over Lothar's marital affairs. Lothar had formed a relationship with Waltrada in youth, but sought to repudiate her as his partner and contract a marriage with Theutberga to win over a rival political grouping, and in the hope of producing an heir. Lothar's projected remarriage not only threatened the position of his partners' kin and their contacts at court, but also, more importantly, undercut the ambitions of both of Lothar's uncles, who hoped to establish control over the heartlands of the empire, with their rich symbolic and material resources. Given the lack of a firm and widely agreed definition of what constituted a legitimate marriage, the moral and legal status of Lothar's projected 'divorce' was also a minefield. Here, the fact that political boundaries crisscrossed ecclesiastical provinces and episcopal solidarities meant that bishops from the eastern and western kingdoms soon became involved in passing judgement, as inevitably did the pope on such an issue of canon law. The outcome of a long-running and often scandalous series of accusations and counter-accusations over divorce, punctuated by synods of bishops loyal to Lothar and their eastern and western brothers, was to thwart Lothar's plans.

Neighbours, raiders and traders: the frontiers of the Christian empire

If military expansion had fuelled eighth-century Frankish politics, then the stabilisation of frontiers posed new problems for the rulers of the ninth-century Christian empire. We have already examined the internal political response, in terms of the creation of new hierarchies designed to tie landed elites into the Carolingian system. But the shift also necessitated a change in the mechanisms for maintaining frontiers and managing neighbours. Although frontiers could be understood in linear terms, they were not guarded by dedicated garrisons. Frontier counts, termed *marchiones* (singular: *marchio*) were given extensive powers to maintain friendly relations with immediate neighbours and levy the military services from landowners necessary to safeguard Frankish interests. The result was close cultural, economic and political contact between the landowning communities on either side of the empire's frontiers, particularly in the long land frontier in the east. Low-level raiding was something practised both by Franks and by their neighbours, but co-existed with other forms of activity. Long-term contact also meant that leaders from beyond the frontier were inevitably pulled into disputes between rival groups of Franks with whom they were allied. These patterns of acculturation had similarities with those frontier interactions which had played such a central role in the transformation of the late Roman Empire, but their mechanics differed, for this was a political system based on militarised landowners, not professional armies paid through taxation. Scandinavians and Slavs could not therefore serve in a professional Frankish army or rise through a military establishment to power at the heart of the Carolingian system; the patterns of their activity in the Frankish world were primarily those of intermittent raiders, and this stands in marked contrast to the role of barbarians in the later Roman period. The ninth century, moreover, was a period of expanding international trade finding new routes whose control was an object of intense political competition, and these economic concerns were vital in determining the patterns of interaction between Franks and their neighbours.

The effects of such interaction are best known in the case of Scandinavia, for here the direct contacts between Frankish and Danish rulers that followed from the conquest of Frisia and Saxony coincided with the beginnings of the so-called 'Viking age'. 'Viking' is a modern label for Scandinavians of diverse origins whose activities had their distinct logics: we should hesitate before unthinkingly lumping together men from modern Norway colonising parts of the British Isles and the North Atlantic, Swedes active in continental Russia, and Danes around the Anglo-Saxon and Frankish coasts of the North Sea. The problem for us in seeking to understand the rationale for the activities of Scandinavian warbands in ninth-century Europe lies in the opaque nature of our sources: our earliest Scandinavian sources come in the form of sagas first written centuries later, whilst Frankish accounts need handling with care. Peaceful contact with Scandinavian traders, or with warbands seeking the employment of Frankish kings, tended to attract no comment, but the Scandinavian raiding which was such a recurrent feature of ninth-century Frankish life is repeatedly cast as God's punishment meted out to the Franks. Here, churchmen were eager to accentuate religious difference, writing of 'gentiles' or 'heathens', but to imagine some kind of pagan crusade against the Frankish church is mistaken. Religious difference was important because it allowed writers to engage in a heightened rhetoric, identifying the raiders from the north with the rods of God's wrath, and calling on rulers to redouble their efforts to create a truly Christian society so as to please God. This rhetoric often reads in fairly apocalyptic terms, but it was deployed carefully, with very specific goals, and we should hesitate before seeing it as reflecting a widespread moral panic. When the bishops assembled at the council of Meaux-Paris in 845 presented Viking raids as a fulfilment of Biblical prophecies seeing the agents of God's ire descending from the north, they sought the return of church property and used the rhetoric of divine punishment as a means of admonishing kings and forcing them to act.[20] Authors of contemporary history could similarly organise their accounts carefully so that raids appeared as divine comment on the actions of a particular individual, and we need to be aware of this conscious manipulation of narrative for polemical purposes. Two different continuations of the *Annals of Fulda*, for example, give contrasting accounts of Charles the Fat's handling of a large Viking army besieged at Asselt in 882, one clearly designed to present the peace reached there as a sham and finger the blame at Charles' principal advisor, the other stressing the advantageous nature of the agreement reached.[21] In fact, where it is possible careful tracking of the activities and leadership of individual Viking warbands suggests patterns more comprehensible than the apparently anonymous and random raiding suggested by a cursory read of our sources. Viking leaders sought the fame and fortune necessary to ensure the current loyalty and future expansion of their warbands; success as a warlord brought the renown that attracted new followers, and could be vital in bids for power within Scandinavia.

This intimate engagement of Scandinavian elites with the Frankish world had its roots in the changes wrought to the political map of northern Europe by the Frankish conquests of the eighth century. Owing to our lack of written sources, we are dependent on archaeology for an understanding of the development of early medieval Scandinavian society. Here, changing patterns of the deposition of grave-goods in burials, and in the internal structure of rural settlements, suggest that a warrior-elite was slowly able to establish itself in the sixth, seventh and eighth centuries. Although this is often analysed in terms of a process of 'state-formation', the archaeology does not demonstrate the emergence of a stable, unitary, kingdom in Denmark or elsewhere, as opposed to the creation of a more settled social hierarchy. Carolingian written sources tend to identify individuals of royal status as 'king of the Danes' but this reflects imprecise Frankish perceptions, not Danish realities, which may have been more a matter of a number of broadly defined dynasties that claimed royal status competing for a shifting overlordship. Scandinavian geography, however, made lasting or extensive overlordships difficult to weld together: the Jutland peninsula was the main area suited to the kind of intensive agrarian exploitation common in the Frankish world, but elsewhere strategies combining agriculture with fishing and hunting made more sense. In that waterborne travel was likewise the natural means of travel in a world of fertile coastal strips and islands ringing mountainous interiors, the result was that emerging elites invested in boats as well as weapons, and were involved in waterborne exchange. As a result, competition for royal power partially rested on control of exchange through the trading settlements which had been growing through the eighth century: the account of the activities of the Frankish missionary Anskar suggests that major trading centres such as Hedeby in Denmark and Birka in Sweden were the objects of bitter struggles between rival claimants to royal status.[22]

The political importance of trade and trading centres meant that Scandinavian rulers were inevitably pulled into increasing contact with their Frankish neighbours in the course of the eighth century. The Frankish conquest of Frisia had brought with it direct control of a long stretch of the North Sea coast which was ecologically and geographically intimately linked to southern Scandinavia, and Denmark in particular, whilst the integration of Saxony into the Carolingian realm meant that Franks and Danes were now neighbours. The results were clear already by the first decade of the ninth century, when attempts to exercise control over trade led to political conflict. The trading post at Reric, near modern Lübeck, in the territory of the Franks' Slavic allies, the Abrodites, effectively bypassed the major Danish centre at Hedeby as an outlet to the Baltic. The Danish king Godofrid responded by raiding Reric and forcibly removing the craftsmen settled there to Hedeby, simultaneously reinforcing the fortified dyke which marked the Danes' southern border, and despatching a fleet of over a hundred ships to ravage the Frisian coast; although nominally Frankish subjects, the Frisians agreed to pay a large annual tribute in silver to Godofrid, much to Charlemagne's ire.[23]

Godofrid, however, died in 810, leading to a series of complex conflicts between various kindreds claiming the throne, and the next two decades witnessed determined attempts by the Carolingians to offer their political backing to friendly claimants to royal status within Denmark. This Frankish diplomacy involved offering both material and ideological support. A bloody conflict for Godofrid's throne saw the death of the two leading contenders: Sigifrid, who claimed kinship with Godofrid, and Anulo, kinsman of Godofrid's short-lived successor Hemming. Anulo's brothers Harald Klak and Reginfrid were accepted as joint kings in 812. They were soon defeated and driven out by the sons of Godofrid, but by 819 Harald was able to return thanks to the political support of the Frankish emperor and the assistance of his Abrodite allies, driving out two of the sons of Godofrid and sharing royal status with the remaining pair. An uneasy stand-off followed, with both parties seeking alliances with rival Abrodite leaders and attempting to win Frankish backing, before Harald was formally converted to Christianity, with the emperor standing godfather to him, at Ingelheim in 826. This process brought with it Frankish delegations led by bishops who as well as founding churches at the major trading centres such as Hedeby were also effectively Frankish political agents. The activities and interests of these missionaries crossed the political frontier: their bishopric was founded at Hamburg, although after this proved vulnerable to coastal raiding it was moved to Bremen, still within the Frankish realm. The royals favoured by the Franks were similarly given interests along that part of the North Sea coast under Frankish control, with Harald Klak granted the county of Rüstringen in Frisia 'so that he would be able to find refuge there if his possessions were ever in danger', the first of a succession of Danish leaders to hold territory in the region.[24] These grants both acknowledged the economic and geographic ties between this region and Denmark, and attempted to safeguard the busy trade along this coast by building up a local strongman dependent on Frankish support as its protector; it was also a potent mechanism to give royals like Harald the economic muscle and political resources to make good their claims within Scandinavia.

The period from *c.* 790 to 830 saw a number of small-scale raids, particularly on coastal monastic sites, a phenomenon common to Britain and Francia which is probably ultimately explained in terms of the buccaneering and piracy inevitably attracted by a context of increasing exchange between societies whose cultural norms and economic organisation differed in important ways. But it saw no repeat of the kind of activity augured by Godofrid. Whilst we cannot know how Frankish cultural and political influence was received within Scandinavia, it does seem clear that the strategy exemplified by Harald Klak's career was an effective mechanism for managing the complex connections tying Frankish and Scandinavian elites. It was only from the 830s, with the onset of civil war in Francia, that large-scale Viking raids, numbering tens or even hundreds of ships, began. This was not simply the result of Scandinavian opportunists aiming to exploit the internal divisions of the Frankish world. In 828 the conflict between Harald Klak and the sons of Godofrid already threatened to pull in the Franks: negotiations over Harald's standing and the confirmation of peace between the Franks and the Danes had stalled when Harald – perhaps anxious at being sold out by his erstwhile allies – ravaged and pillaged several villages in Danish territory, and the sons of Godofrid retaliated by driving out the Frankish force assembled on the border.[25] In 828, there was still just one source of political authority within Francia, and the sons of Godofrid had sent envoys to the imperial court explaining the necessity of their actions given Harald's provocation. But by the 830s, when Louis the Pious stood at loggerheads with his sons, conflict of this kind was more likely to escalate as tensions within the Carolingian family interacted with struggles for dominance in Scandinavia, and competing Danish factions sought the patronage of rival Carolingians and so were sucked into the internal conflicts of the Frankish world. The series of raids on Dorestad between 834 and 837, for example, should be understood as the spilling over of rivalries, like those apparent in 828, into an economically crucial area where favoured Danish royals like Harald had been granted interests by their Frankish allies. In the civil war of 840–3, we find Harald fighting alongside Lothar and receiving more Frisian territory for his trouble, in an alliance that was condemned as scandalous by Lothar's rivals, who claimed that it involved supporting pagans against fellow Christians, although they likewise had their own Scandinavian allies. The escalating raids on the Frankish coast in this period were an extension of the civil war by proxy, as Viking warlords sought to profit at the expense of the enemies of their Frankish masters: Lothar's allies, for example, seem to have been responsible for raiding Quentovic, the leading trading centre in the area under Charles the Bald's control in 842, moving onto its major partners in England before returning home.[26]

Even once the Frankish political scene had stabilised, this remained a world of many Carolingian kings offering rival sources of patronage to ambitious Viking warlords. The period from the 830s to the end of the ninth century saw a proliferation of Viking leaders entering into the service of Frankish kings, an arrangement which also involved their baptism and public profession of the Christian faith, a fact which did not prevent the writers of polemic from attempting to blacken the names of their enemies by making accusations of ungodly alliances with pagans. It would be mistaken to dismiss this widespread practice as foolish and inevitably leading to disaster. In the 880s, Notker of St-Gallen could present the active recruitment of Scandinavian followers as a practice to be imitated, indicative of strong kingship, although he also mocked the commitment of those who received royal favour to the Christianity they professed: so sought after were the gifts received in return for swearing fidelity and undergoing baptism that, Notker jokingly claimed, one year so many Vikings turned up at Easter that supplies ran low, and one wizened warlord who had been returning year after year solely to get an annual gift complained about their declining quality![27] The potential of such arrangements is shown by the fate of Dorestad in the middle decades of the ninth century, when it was held along with much of Frisia by the Viking leader Horic, and enjoyed relative peace as a result: Horic's protection meant that this vulnerable region suffered just two raids between 847 and 863, one defeated before it could cause any damage, the other the direct result of Frankish attempts to repudiate Horic and replace him with a rival Viking leader. As Horic's case illustrates, an arrangement of this kind pulled Scandinavian leaders into the complex and convoluted internal politics of the Frankish world, and Viking warlords were just as vulnerable to changing royal priorities as their Frankish counterparts. For the likes of Horic, however, raiding rather than rebellion was the standard response to fluctuating political fortunes. Raiding needs to be seen as a strategic activity, a means of seizing directly the liquid wealth so vital to the coherence of a warband when less violent mechanisms for acquiring this necessary fuel, through gift-exchange, tribute-taking or payment from Frankish rulers, were not forthcoming; it was also a potent way of forcing Frankish hands, and soliciting an offer of honourable and lucrative service, or of signalling discontent when a Frankish master appeared likely to renege on solemnly-made undertakings. Careful work is needed on the connections of individual Viking leaders, so far as they can be unpicked from our evidence, and on the interrelationship between patterns of Viking activity and factional conflict within the Frankish world if we are to understand fully the impact of Viking raiding on Carolingian politics. What is clear, however, is that in spite of their frequent presentation as agents of divine wrath in polemically charged sources, Vikings were anything but outsiders, striking unpredictably and at random like forks of lightning suddenly descending from the sky. They were part of the political system and their raiding needs to be understood in that context.

This is not to whitewash Viking raiders and see their activities as analogous to those of Frankish aristocrats. Viking leaders were motivated by the strategic necessities of amassing wealth and acquiring renown, aims which could be pursued by a range of overlapping strategies. Entering into the service of a Frankish king, after all, involved the receipt of status-enhancing gifts: Notker commented on the magnetic pull of high-quality Frankish weaponry for Vikings leaders, and the archaeology suggests that Frankish swords, as well as the belts and buckles which were badges of royal favour granted out by Frankish rulers, were prized in Scandinavia. But such goods could be sold or seized too, and Viking warbands could switch between plundering, tribute-taking and buying with what can seem like bewildering ease. Peacemaking with Vikings typically involved the ransom of noble hostages and special treasures, and it was the concentration of well-born monks with landed kin and gold and silver adornments which could be either sold back or melted down that made monasteries particularly attractive targets for plundering. These practices naturally spilled over into the buying of peace, paying off Vikings to leave without plundering, hostage-taking or seizing tribute. Arrangements for the raising of ransom payments thus shaded into the levying of Danegeld to buy peace. The buying-off of Viking raiders by Carolingian kings, notably Charles the Bald, has attracted a bad press from historians, but buying peace with Danegeld was only ever one amongst a range of strategies, never a general or widespread response, as a careful reading of the annals of the reign make clear. In a political situation where multiple bands of Vikings were a complicating factor that interacted with aristocratic discontent and inter-Carolingian rivalry, it could be a sensible option. Viking leaders swore to leave their erstwhile victims unmolested and leave their territories, or even on occasion to enter their service, in return for entering into peaceful relations and receiving agreed payments, and where their subsequent paths can be traced they seem to have kept their word: our sources, which tend to encourage the lumping together of all Vikings as an undifferentiated mass, can obscure this. Carefully used, Vikings whose loyalties or goodwill had been bought could be a useful political resource: at various stages in his reign Charles the Bald seems to have encouraged Viking leaders with whom he had concluded peace to plunder the territories controlled by rebellious aristocrats and sons, as well as to drive out other Viking warbands. Such strategies were potentially controversial, as the criticisms made by Hincmar make clear, but even here we should remember that the complex arrangements for the collection of Danegeld payments took the form of an embryonic system of taxation, and one which hit hardest at the church along with merchants – these were the two groups who had easiest access to liquid wealth and, not coincidentally, were also the prime targets for Vikings plundering.

The charged accounts of pagan hordes bringing chaos and destruction from the north, taken at face value, might encourage us to imagine Viking raiding as calamitous in its effects, leading to social meltdown. Certainly, for much of the nineteenth and twentieth centuries Vikings in the ninth and tenth centuries were cast in a role analogous to that of barbarians in the fourth and fifth, an outside agency of almost random violence. For some scholars, the activities of this 'second wave' of invaders constituted a veritable 'assault against Christian Europe' which fatally weakened the Frankish church and undermined Carolingian kingship, ushering in a new world of local strong men offering military protection in return for personal loyalty.[28] Seductive in its sweeping simplicity, such an argument simply cannot be sustained in the light of the evidence: not only does it rest on a misreading of the rhetoric of the narrative sources, but the archaeological and documentary evidence is utterly incompatible with such a picture of dramatic collapse. The effects of Viking activity – whether experienced directly, through plundering, or indirectly, through the paying of ransom, tribute or geld – were to put extreme pressure on the major repositories of wealth. Churches of course suffered, but – as in Britain – it was primarily for vulnerable coastal sites that this had significant implications, with the monks of St Philibert, for example, abandoning the island of Noirmoutier and taking the relics of their patron with them. The integrity of the institutional church as a whole, however, was unimpaired. For kings, Viking activity was a potential irritant and a constant complication. But the royal response to the Viking threat involved initiatives that augured the more intensive government of their realms. The Danegeld was the closest thing to a land-tax seen in Francia for over two hundred years. The obligations of all free men to serve their king received their strongest emphasis in legislation designed to counter the Viking threat: as well as stressing the universality of the obligation to fight in defence of the fatherland, kings like Charles the Bald insisted on the public services that enabled him to create a network of fortified bridges and strongholds which impaired Viking mobility along the riverways of the west Frankish kingdom.

The political threat posed by the Vikings should not be overestimated: when Franks met Vikings in pitched battles, the Franks invariably won, hence the emphasis in Viking strategy on the waterborne mobility and movement that enabled them to avoid direct confrontation. When and where Viking leaders were able to attract and absorb a series of smaller warbands into their own followings, and recruit an army of several thousand – or, in the preferred reckoning of chroniclers, maybe approaching a hundred ships – Frankish elites tended to put their internal quarrels to one side and deal with the threat. It is noticeable, for example, that in spite of well over half a century of Viking warlords holding public office on behalf of their Carolingian masters in Frisia, no lasting Viking principality was to develop in the area: when in the early 880s the Viking leader Godofrid built on the traditional position enjoyed by his predecessors and, after an unprecedented marriage into the Carolingian family, asserted his control not only over Frisia but also its hinterland in the Frankish heartlands down the Rhine and Moselle, he was rapidly and definitively driven out. Smaller Viking forces, which did not threaten the integrity of the Frankish system, were more easily bought off, re-employed or diverted against opponents. Indeed, the lasting presence of Scandinavians in Normandy, an area periphery to the politics of the west Frankish kingdom, rested on just such an initiative in the early tenth century, with the settlement of a pliable Scandinavian leader a means for Charles 'the Straightforward' to create a military force independent of the noble factions of the region.

The effects of Viking raiding on the countryside are more elusive. The increased demand for liquid wealth may have been a potent factor in encouraging a more intensive estate management by major landowners, many in west Francia insisting on rent payments in cash. But peasants could also seize the initiative when landlords fled Viking raiders. In 859 when peasants in the Loire valley bound together to resist the Vikings, they were massacred by their Frankish lords who feared the implications of such self-determination, but peasant initiative could take other forms: legislation suggests that peasants might make a quick profit by equipping or provisioning Vikings, and complaints about runaway tenants might even imply that some were becoming Vikings themselves. It is certainly difficult to see self-standing aristocratic lordship emerging in the place of traditional public obligations as the basis for the protection of the rural population. Whilst there is evidence for fortified refuges being used in times of extreme danger, the documentary evidence suggests that these were often traditional defensible centres – walled Roman sites or prehistoric hill forts whose upkeep was a public obligation for the good of the community – rather than proto-castles auguring a world of aristocratic lordship. When, in 864, Charles the Bald ordered that all fortifications which did not have a royal licence be torn down he was ensuring that new refuges fitted into these traditional patterns of public activity, not ordering the destruction of aristocratic households.[29] The Vikings were complicating agents working within the Frankish political system, whose activities thus exerted pressure that might accelerate change, but did not alter the basic dynamics of Frankish society.

Viking activity along the North Sea coasts and major riverways of Francia was a remarkable phenomenon. Similar processes of influence, interaction and intermittent conflict across political boundaries can be detected at work both in Brittany and in central Europe. In Brittany, there was a long tradition of native rulers acknowledging Frankish overlordship when forced to do so, whilst patronising their own churches and maintaining political independence. In central Europe, Frankish territory bordered on various Slavic groupings little touched by Christianity down a long and relatively open land frontier. Here, raiding only reached deep into the Frankish interior in the first decades of the tenth century, following the arrival of a new nomadic grouping, the Magyars, but the Franks did face an increasingly confident and coherent kingship – that of the Moravians – which was consistently able to mobilise dangerous armies for much of the ninth century. These neighbours – rulers of coherent polities able to command considerable manpower – were active on the Franks' southeastern frontier, along and beyond the middle Danube. Further north, little is known of the dealings of commanders of the Saxon and Thuringian marches with their Slavic neighbours – Abrodites, Sorbs, Bohemians and others – but the sources suggest that Frankish patronage of client-rulers was punctuated by occasional low-level raiding. These patterns could also include Frankish cultural influence, notably through the export of Christianity to friendly elites: Louis the German, for example, presided over the baptism of fourteen Bohemian leaders in 845.[30] The archaeology makes it clear that the basic social dynamic was the emergence of an increasingly confident militarised elite, evident in the creation of aristocratic strongholds marked off by wooden palisades and often located on hilltops. As in Scandinavia, these processes led to intense internal competition for overlordship, in which Frankish interventions could play a crucial role, in the ninth century, but was to result in the creation of a lasting political geography of Christian kingships. But central Europe was a very different landscape from Scandinavia. It was this landscape which determined that the focus of Frankish attention, and the location of the most impressive Slavic polities, was in the middle Danube and its hinterland: in the course of the ninth century this region was to become an increasingly important channel of commerce and communication eastwards.

In central Europe, the major opponents of the Franks from the middle decades of the ninth century were the Moravians. Under Rastislav (846–70) and his kinsman Zwentibald (869–85) the Moravians were a serious and independent force that commanded a significant deal of attention from the Frankish rulers. Unfortunately, our understanding of the dynamics of the relationship has been obscured by one of those strange but frustrating historical controversies which has arisen over the location of the Moravians. A variety of ingenious arguments have been advanced for alternative locations without it ever being established that the traditional identification of the early medieval Moravians with modern Moravia, north of the middle Danube in the Czech Republic, is false. Here there is archaeological evidence for large-scale and carefully organised urban settlements at Mikulčice and Staré Mešto which square well with the assessment of our sources. The Moravian kingdom – it is sometimes termed 'the great Moravian Empire', but this label rests on a mistranslation of a tenth-century Byzantine source – emerged in the aftermath of the Carolingian conquest of the Avar khaganate. The fall of the Avars simply removed a system of overlordship and tributary dominion across much of central Europe, but the destruction of the khaganate caused larger-scale change in its former heartlands, home to the Avar elite and the khagan's court. Here, although the archaeology does not indicate large-scale shifts of population or social structure, in the early ninth century we meet a bewildering array of ethnic labels – the Avars themselves appear for the final time in 822 – which presumably reflected an unstable kaleidoscope of small-scale groupings. In the second quarter of the ninth century, the label 'Moravian' begins to be used consistently of the Slavic leaders in this area, presumably reflecting the creation of a more stable system of overlordship. The debate over the location of Moravia is thus particularly unhelpful given that such a system was most likely extensive and segmentary.

Beneath the political narrative of oscillating alliance and conflict, there are hints at the interconnection of Frankish and Slavic elites based on shared martial values. The illegitimate son of the illegitimate Carolingian Arnulf had a Slavic mother, hence his name, Zwentibald. Another Zwentibald, king of the Moravians, for example, began his career as a subking but was able to overthrow his kinsman Rastislav by entering into an mutually advantageous alliance with a Carolingian subking, Carloman of Bavaria. Claimants to royal status like Zwentibald were thus not simply clients seeking backing against their rivals, but warlords whose assistance was invaluable for feuding frontiersmen and ambitious Carolingians; and they were far from wholly dependent on their Frankish allies. Witness Zwentibald's resistance to Carloman's subsequent claims of overlordship, which even led to the staging of a mock trial at a royal assembly at which Zwentibald was declared guilty of infidelity and stripped of his office just as if he were a Frankish count. Frankish claims did led to piecemeal political expansion, notably down the Danube valley itself, whilst some Slavic leaders were happy to function as something like client-rulers, for example in Pannonia where the Slavic prince Pribina could also be represented as a count answerable to the Carolingian kings, dominating the region from a fortress at Moosburg near Lake Balaton which later served as a key Frankish outpost. Christianisation, in a slow process of cultural osmosis, was another result. The church of Salzburg had long been involved in providing priests, churches and books for the Slavs of Caranthia and Pannonia since the eighth century, and was the natural place for the likes of Pribina to look.

Moravian relations with the Franks were characterised by an oscillation between an acknowledgement of the necessity of this type of creeping Francisation, an inevitable correlate of the processes whereby Slavic elites consolidated more stable systems of domination, and a reaction against it fuelled by the fear that accepting alliance and assistance was to submit to Frankish influence and ultimately overlordship. The Moravian rulers, for example, inevitably adopted Christianity, but the political implications of accepting missionaries from Frankish bishops who might thus exercise jurisdiction over the nascent Slavic church made the institutional mechanics a matter of tense wrangling. Nor were the Moravians the only ambitious central European rulers facing such choices.

Further east, in the fertile agricultural lands around the mouth of the Danube, a nomadic elite that had splintered from the Avar federation in the seventh century, and styled themselves Bulgars, had established a powerful political system of its own. Although the Bulgar khans had first emerged as allies of the Byzantine emperors, a useful counterweight to the Avars and potential source of military manpower, in the course of the eighth century they were able to establish themselves as a potent independent force. The adoption of Christianity was the logical next step for rulers who had been aligning themselves with the traditional gods and claiming to function as representatives of a transcendental order; it was also probably a vital mechanism of social integration, as the Bulgar elite, initially a separate tribute-consuming class united by the culture of the steppe – witness the stunning rock carvings at Madara, unparalleled in Europe – merged into the ranks of local landowners. Constantinople, which had a long tradition of using mission as a diplomatic and political tool, responded to Khan Boris' conversion in 863 by supplying Slavic-speaking missionaries, the brothers Cyril and Methodius. But Boris – who took on the baptismal name of Michael – was uneasy about the apparent acceptance of Byzantine influence and claims to overlordship, and looked east, to the Latin church, for an independent brand of Christianity, writing both to Rome and east Francia requesting missionaries. Pope Nicholas was to seize the opportunity to expand papal influence into central Europe, despatching a missionary team equipped with detailed written advice of what aspects of traditional Bulgar culture were to be tolerated and which outlawed. Cyril and Methodius, although exiled by Boris, received a warm welcome at the Moravian court: after all, their mission offered an opportunity to become Christian whilst avoiding Frankish influence. Thereafter, ecclesiastical affairs in central Europe were to be dominated by a long-running and frequently obscure struggle for jurisdiction, with Cyril and Methodius seized and tried first by Frankish bishops and then by the pope. In spite of Cyril's death in 869, Methodius was eventually able to return to Moravia until his death in 885, where he was closely watched by Frankish bishops. Controversy over jurisdiction was complicated by one remarkable innovation undertaken by Cyril and Methodius. Their Slavic background had meant that, in keeping with long-standing Byzantine policy, they were able to preach in the tongue of their flock, but they went a step beyond both precedent and imperial policy, and introduced a Slavic liturgy, performing the holy offices in their entirety in the vernacular, and developing a written version of the Slavic language, Old Church Slavonic, with its distinctive Cyrillic script. This initiative was condemned as heretical by their Frankish enemies, although it may actually have been inspired in part by Frankish interest in the written vernacular. More importantly, though, it had an obvious appeal to Slavic rulers like Zwentibald, anxious to weld together his subjects through their new religion, as well as underwriting the separation of the Slavic and Frankish churches.

These complex but fascinating cultural and political interactions had their economic context too. More secure elites meant more consumption of high-status goods, and the remarkable careers of Cyril and Methodius, and the cultural policies of Boris-Michael and Zwentibald, rested on the growing importance of the Danube as a hub within central Europe: it is no accident that the 860s also saw the resumption of regular land contacts between Constantinople and western Europe. The importance of this nexus should not be underestimated: the land route east had been a staple of Roman emperors, memorably used by Julian in his seizure of power, but since the seventh century it had been severed and Europe's cultural, economic and political geography had been reorientated by a sharp east–west division. This reconnection was not fundamentally challenged even by the destruction of the cultural and political constellation wrought by Moravian rulers and Byzantine missionaries in the last decade of the ninth century. The agents of change here were a steppe nomad confederation, the Magyars, once again classically seen as uncontrollable destructive forces wreaking havoc to established social systems. Their arrival in the middle Danube can on one level be seen as rooted in the geophysical fact that the Carpathians marked the westernmost extension of the Eurasian steppe and so attracted such confederations in a cyclical process. But on another level the irruption of the Magyars at this particular juncture was anything but a random variable: they had long contacts with Constantinople and first raided Francia as allies of the Moravians as long ago as 862. Their pulling into central European politics in the 890s was in part a reflection of imperial worries: both Byzantine and Frankish rulers had good reason to encourage Magyar intervention, as a means of diverting the attention of increasingly ambitious and assertive Bulgar and Moravian rulers. Once the Magyars had arrived on the scene, they inevitably found reward in the politically fragmented Frankish world: in 899 Arnulf paid them to raid his rival Berengar in Italy, but after Arnulf's death Berengar was able to buy peace in return for tribute payments, which were also forthcoming from Constantinople. As a result, the first decades of the tenth century saw raiding focused on the east Frankish kingdom until a combination of military force and tribute was able to buy peace there too: in the meantime, however, the Magyars had not only established themselves in the former Moravian realm, but also asserted control over the lucrative trade routes along the Danube.

The complex patterns of acculturation and interaction along the Franks' eastern frontier thus had important consequences, setting in train processes that were to result in the cultural, economic and political realignment of central Europe, notwithstanding the generation or so of disruption caused by the Magyar irruption. In the western Mediterranean, whilst the underlying dynamics of economic and political expansion remained the same, the patterns of change that resulted differed. After all, here the Franks did not face relatively small-scale warrior-elites across a land frontier, but connected with a series of maritime routes that led, ultimately, to an ideologically and politically coherent system in the caliphate. Contact between Franks and Muslims not only took place largely across the sea, it was also mediated through a mosaic of small political units, most of them effectively if not formally independent actors, in southern Italy. Here, the crisis of Byzantine power in Italy in the first half of the eighth century had seen the Lombard duchies of Benevento and Spoleto joined as effectively independent actors by the rulers of those parts of the mainland which remained nominally subject to the emperor, such as Naples. Rome too was now detached from the imperial infrastructure: Constantinople's decision to end the regular grain shippings from Sicily to Rome in the 730s, in an effort to pressure the popes over their anti-imperial line on iconoclasm, encouraged eighth-century popes to undertake a more intensive management of their rights in central Italy, which was to become the foundation of a regional political system centred on Rome. Whilst Charlemagne's conquest of the Lombard kingdom in northern Italy had led to some competition over the symbolic acknowledgement of authority further south – with both Charlemagne and his Byzantine counterparts, for example, despatching forces to encourage the submission of the Lombard dukes of the south – it did not alter this fragmented political geography. Similarly, further west the submission of the Christian elites of modern Catalonia to Frankish rule did not alter the fact that Islamic emirs and Christian warlords either side of the religious 'frontier' worked effectively independently in their regional context, not as direct agents of Aachen or Cordoba.

In this fragmented western Mediterranean world, the eighth century had seen not only the nadir of long-distance trade, but also a turning inward by the major imperial powers. Byzantine involvement in Italy, as we saw, amounted to little more than the very occasional despatch of fleets as a means of exerting diplomatic pressure. In the Islamic world, the conquest of North Africa and then the Visigothic kingdom was quickly followed by internal struggles, with competition for power between rival groups within the newly conquered provinces tying into wider political conflicts of tribal and religious allegiance that ultimately were arguments about the proper structure of an Islamic state. After the 720s, we thus find only intermittent evidence for small-scale raiding on the islands of the western Mediterranean. When, in the second half of the eighth century, the 'Abbasids rebuilt a stable political system within the Islamic world, it was one in which the provinces of the western Mediterranean were peripheral, with the capital moved east from Damascus in Syria to Baghdad, newly founded in 761 and closer to the heartlands of 'Abbasid support. As a result, the Mediterranean was far less important to the systems of exchange and redistribution that sustained the caliphate under the 'Abbasids than it had been in the first generations of Islamic expansion. This was also the case politically. The disparate warbands active in eighth-century al-Andalus were welded together by rulers claiming descent from the Umayyad dynasty which had preceded the 'Abbasids, and so this westernmost province of the Islamic world was not even nominally under Baghdad's control, whilst the 'Abbasids allowed the Aghlabids, an Arab dynasty which had acquired local roots, to act as provincial governors in Ifrīqiya in return for an annual tribute in recognition of Baghdad's entitlement to a cut of provincial tax income. That these western Mediterranean provinces, distant and distinct from the major networks for the circulation of tax revenue and manpower which sustained the caliphate, were minimally involved in the convoluted politics of the 'Abbasid court through the later eighth and ninth centuries is striking. The 'Abbasids at no point felt the need to move against the Umayyad emirs in al-Andalus, whilst when, at the very end of the ninth century, the Fatimid dynasty sought to create its own political system it made little use of its native North Africa, quickly going native after seizing Egypt and allowing its original powerbase further west to drift away.

One result of these political changes was that the revival of trade in the late eighth and ninth centuries took place in a politically fragmented Mediterranean, on the fringes of imperial systems whose focus lay elsewhere. This meant that the establishment of new economic connections around the shores of the western Mediterranean was quickly followed by frequent reports of piracy and seaborne raiding here, in a process with clear parallels with the outbreak of Viking activity in the North Sea. As with the Vikings, our sources are frustratingly opaque, and our ignorance of the identity and interests of most of the pirates and raiders they mention may obscure more complex patterns of political alliance and competition; unlike the Vikings, however, they were actors in a complex and extensive political system immune from and independent of Frankish cultural or political influence. The importance of understanding the Islamic context for episodes of raiding is demonstrated by Frankish reports of the submission of the Balearic Islands off the eastern Spanish coast to Charlemagne in 799 in return for protection against the raids of Muslim pirates. These raids, however, were in reality the attacks of forces loyal to the Umayyad regime against the provinces of a number of emirs who had rebelled, and the despatch of a Frankish fleet to offer protection in reality an opportunistic intervention.[31] Frankish aggression of this type was a marked feature of the first two decades of the ninth century, with campaigns against 'pirates' and 'raiders' allegedly menacing Sardinia and Corsica, and even an expedition to North Africa. What was at stake here was control of the islands of the western Mediterranean, increasingly important in new patterns of trade and, in the case of Sardinia and Corsica, also crucial resources for the realigned papacy. The Frankish fleets active in these years – presumably recruited from the coastal cities of Gaul and northern Italy – were in fact asserting Frankish protection against the activities of Muslim rulers in both al-Andalus and Ifrīqiya. Their activities could encompass plundering and tribute-taking, but ultimately threatened to force the submission of the islands of the western Mediterranean and so enable domination of the thriving sealanes which joined them. But – as the example of the Balaerics suggests – Islamic rulers did not act as one, and the activities recorded as 'raiding' in our western sources in fact related not only to internal struggles within Islamic regimes such as those evident in 799, but also to competition between the Umayyads in al-Andalus and the Aghlabids in Ifrīqiya for regional dominance which also led to conflict over modern Morocco.

This is clearest in the case of Sicily, an obvious target for plundering, where raiding slowly escalated. After 827, the Aghlabids attempted to conquer the island, maintaining permanent garrisons to exercise territorial control over the fruits of annual raids; here they were in part inspired by the success of attacks on Crete by their rivals from 824. In fact, conquest took over half a century to complete, with Islamic control of Sicily as a whole only assured with the fall of Syracuse, the capital and principal garrison of the Byzantine province, in 878. Conquest took so long in part because of the geography of an island divided by its mountainous interior: the rapid initial Islamic successes were in the low-lying hinterlands of the southern coast, with obvious natural connections south across the sea and – so the archaeology would suggest – rapidly integrated into an economic system centred on North Africa, whilst the eastern coast, facing the toe of Italy and along a crucial route for trade north up the Italian coast, remained stubbornly in Byzantine hands. But the long-drawn-out conquest was also a result of the fissiparous nature of Islamic politics in the western Mediterranean: Arab and Berber groups from Umayyad al-Andalus and the fringes of Aghlabid territory in North Africa were soon also involved as semi-independent marauding forces, as Sicily became a magnet for adventurers and exiles, and its Islamic garrisons soon acquired their own political voice, on occasion rebelling against their distant masters in support of the claims of their own leaders and the expectations of the rank-and-file for a proper share of the lucrative spoils of their activities. Indeed, once their foothold in Sicily was secure, the territorial conquest of the entire island was not necessarily the prime objective of Islamic leaders: their activities were also focused on generating further plunder through raiding in the western Mediterranean – in the 830s and 840s we hear reports of raids along the Italian coast, even up the Rhone in Gaul – and on exercising control over the sea. By the 860s, such activities were expanding into the Adriatic: in 866 Muslim forces conquered the Byzantine cities of Bari and Otranto on the heel of Italy, thus controlling a crucial point of entry into the Adriatic and the main route for shipping travelling from Venice to Constantinople. The threat posed to the Adriatic and Aegean, where Byzantine and Venetian dominance had been previously little threatened, was such that the emirate of Bari proved short-lived, destroyed by a coalition of Byzantines, Franks and Lombards in a series of campaigns completed by 876. But it does underline the extent to which Muslim 'piracy' and 'raiding' aimed at controlling communication and exchange, and as such was a direct threat to Byzantine authority in southern Italy.

These activities were to transform the politics of the western Mediterranean. Sicily, after all, had long been the wealthiest and most important Byzantine possession in the west, and Byzantine control of the island and the route through the Straights of Messina up the Italian coast had been a crucial element in the continued allegiance of south Italian cities such as Naples to Constantinople. The Muslim irruption meant that the dukes of Naples were able to conduct a more independent politics, designed to further the economic interests of their city, and therefore on occasion involving alliance with Islamic rulers and a refusal to aid Byzantine campaigns. The splintering of the framework of imperial authority meant that trading cities – Amalfi or Gaeta, for example – emerged as self-standing economic and military powers. The political fragmentation of central and southern Italy into a series of regional units focused on major cities did not only affect these Byzantine possessions, and it provided opportunities for regional dukes and their equivalents to cement their position as powerful military protectors. In Rome, for example, the popes were responsible for the organisation of the city's defences; the building of a new extended circuit of walls by Leo IV (847–55), and the construction of a fleet under John VIII (872–82), accentuated the papacy's independent political power. These developments did not signal the undermining of the position of either Carolingian kings in the north or Byzantine emperors in the south: they rather confirmed the status of much of central and southern Italy as a world of small polities nestling in the gaps between a series of extensive political systems, somewhere where local leaders enjoyed a substantial degree of independence and shifted allegiances between distant rulers. Muslim raids and conquests here, indeed, augured a period of intensive political competition over this region. The activities of sizeable military forces despatched from Africa, Constantinople, and the north competing for control harked back to the days of Justinian's 'reconquest', albeit on a far smaller scale. Although Byzantine fleets had been despatched very occasionally to deal with local problems in the eighth century, such activity was exceptional; the response to the Muslim assault on Sicily, and in particular the campaign to retake Bari and Otranto, resulted in the regular military and political intervention of Constantinople in southern Italy for the first time for the best part of two centuries, reanimating the circuits of imperial power in the region. Similarly, for an able Carolingian king secure in the north of Italy like Louis II, the response to the Muslims was an opportunity to demonstrate effective kingship and provide military protection not only for Rome – and here Louis worked successfully in co-operation with successive popes – but also further south, leading to a series of campaigns against Muslims in the southern Lombard duchies, and against the emirate of Bari. These activities in the south involved drawing on the resources of the Lombard duchies – Louis' campaigns in 848 led to the creation of a duchy of Salerno out of part of the duchy of Benevento – and intervening in their politics, not without opposition. The aim here was not conquest: the practical limitations of Louis' position were made clear in 871 when following the 'liberation' of Bari he was taken captives by Adelchis of Benevento and forced to negotiate his release. But Louis' activities were a powerful means of asserting his authority over southern Italian rulers. The sharp exchanges between Louis and his Byzantine counterparts over the imperial title – best documented in a famous letter of 871 rehearsing Frankish claims to inherit the Roman legacy – belong in this context of expanding ambitions in central and southern Italy.

The episodes of Scandinavian, Slavic and Muslim raiding which pepper our ninth century sources contrast with the triumphant narrative of conquest that dominated Frankish accounts of the eighth century. It is no surprise that this contrast has influenced many modern historians, particularly those writing in the first half of the twentieth century, and encouraged them to see in these ninth-century developments a process comparable to the wanton destruction wrought by barbarian hordes on the Roman world, a 'second wave' of barbarian 'enemies of Christendom'. But the contrast in our sources needs handling carefully. Eighth-century Frankish expansion was not seamless or unchecked. It was violent, and its representation in our sources carefully constructed. Conquest meant that the complex politics of these formerly peripheral regions – the oscillating alliances and enmities of Scandinavian and Slavic leaders with their neighbours, now firmly part of the Frankish world, and the activities of southern Italian potentates and Muslim fleets – thus became matters of far more direct concern to Frankish courts, and get far better reported in our sources. Our evidence might thus suggest that raiding and plundering were new, when we have good reason to believe that they had been one aspect of local interactions between Danes and Saxons, Bavarians and Slavs, and indeed Muslims and Mediterranean islanders, in the eighth century. Of course, the interest of Frankish rulers, and the increasing volume of communication and exchange between the Franks and their neighbours, encouraged more intensive interaction: raiding on the scale we see along the Frankish and Italian coasts, for example, clearly was a new development. Here, internal divisions created by changes within the Carolingian system could suck in outsiders. But what is most striking is the extent to which Frankish kings were able to manage these threats, co-ordinating political responses based on effective royal protection: these were tensions born of the dynamics of acculturation and exchange around the fringes of the Frankish Empire, not threats to its basic fabric.

The end of the Carolingian Empire

Through the first half of the ninth century it was natural to think of the Carolingian world as a series of interconnected influence that nonetheless still had a recognisable core in heartlands of Lothar's realm. In the second half of the ninth century and the first decades of the tenth the balance slowly and subtly altered, as politics increasingly turned on eastern and western rulers squabbling and scrabbling for control of Lotharingia. After Lothar II's death in 869, his kingdom became the bone of contention between his uncles, and then their sons. As a result, for a generation, Lotharingia was a kingdom without a king or court: the region's aristocracy became used to negotiating with Carolingian kings from the outside, based in the eastern and western kingdoms. The inevitable result was a slow polarisation of the Lotharingian aristocracy. Rather than organising itself into loose groupings aiming to control the court of their own king, the efforts of rival Carolingians to gain a toehold in Lotharingia created firmer rival factions, one focused on the Moselle, the other on the Meuse.

The fate of Lotharingia was in many ways paralleled by that of Italy, at the other end of the long, thin, middle kingdom created in 843. Louis II had plugged into the traditions of kingship rooted in the north Italian plain, with its rich network of estates and palaces. Pavia, the traditional seat of the kings of Italy, was his principal residence, and a tight network of patronage led from the court to the cities, abbeys and bishoprics of the Po valley and its surrounds, with Louis' wife, Engilberga, at its heart. Louis' rule in Italy was marked by a regular tradition of law-giving in capitulary form, surpassed only by Charles the Bald. His close involvement with the papacy, particularly following his crowning as emperor in 850, included military campaigns to protect Rome from Islamic raiders. But, in the absence of any male heirs, his kingdom fell prey to his uncles and cousins after his death in 875. Later Italian chroniclers, writing with hindsight, saw this as marking the end of political order; by the tenth century, indeed, the kingdom of Italy enjoyed a reputation for political instability due to its division into rival factions, each of which tended to back rival claimants to the kingship and so prevent firm rule.[32]

The ending of Lothar's line thus left rich prizes in Lotharingia and Italy at the mercy of Charles the Bald in the west, and Louis the German in the east. This was a real watershed: even for the generation that had known political division, these areas had been the heartlands of the empire. Lotharingia, in addition to the symbolic capital and royal resources associated with Aachen and the other great palace complexes, was also where the 'imperial aristocracy' had inherited lands; Italy brought with it the imperial title and the rich resources of the Po plain. The scramble for Lotharingia and Italy inevitably led to intensified conflict within the Carolingian family, as eastern and western Frankish kings raised invading armies. It also coincided with a crisis within the Carolingian family. Louis the German and Charles the Bald died, in quick succession and in turn, after they had seized Italy and been crowned emperor in 876 and 877 respectively. This left a gaggle of young, unproven Carolingians, of roughly equal standing, none with real experience of politics on a big stage. In the event, however, a series of misfortunes meant that, by 884, there was only one legitimate adult male Carolingian left: Charles the Fat.

Charles, one of Louis the German's three sons, was in many ways well placed to be the ruler who ruled, once again, over a united empire on the model of his great-grandfather and namesake, Charlemagne. As subking of Alemannia, he had built up a secure powerbase in an area that was geographically central, and also important for controlling the Alpine passes and thus access to Italy: hence already in 879 it was Charles, from his Alemannian base, who had been accepted as king of Italy and crowned emperor by the pope in 881. That Charles was able to secure Italy and the imperial crown before the deaths of his remaining brother and Charles the Bald's surviving son, Louis the Stammerer, in 882, reminds us that Charles' rise to prominence did not rely solely on chance. With Charles' control of east Francia and Italy secure, in 884 he was able to gain the west Frankish crown, as only a child, Charles (later known as 'the Straightforward'), remained living of Charles the Bald's grandchildren. For all that Charles the Fat's partisans played on Charlemagne as an imperial model, this Charles' empire differed radically in structure from that of his great-grandfather. Even after 884, for example, the constituent parts of the empire maintained their own, regnal, identities: official documents were dated not with reference to Charles' imperial rule, but in terms of the years that Charles had been king in west Francia, or Italy. Moreover, the ruling elites of these constituent kingdoms were by now used to dealing with their own Carolingian, locally resident and readily accessible. Whilst Charles struggled skilfully to build up trusted agents as intermediaries between his court and the various regions of the empire, the shift in political scale was traumatic. Charles' closest advisors, friends and kinsman from Alemannia, soon began to attract criticism: the key figure Liutward, bishop of Vercelli, was targeted by Archbishop Liutbert of Mainz, whose office traditionally brought dominance at the east Frankish court. Nor was it clear that Charles' rule offered a solution to the chronic lack of male heirs that had been so evident in the 870s and 880s: whilst Charles' tutor, Notker of St-Gallen, could talk up hopes for Charles' two young sons, the future was far from clear.

These tensions began to affect confidence in the regime, which was hardly helped when Charles himself suffered an epileptic fit at a crucial public assembly. As a result, in 888 Charles was confined to a villa, and deposed, before dying in 889. The agency for Charles' deposition was a royal assembly, primarily attended by eastern Franks: they raised Arnulf, an illegitimate grandson of Louis the German grizzled with experience of frontier warfare in Bavaria, as their king. Ruling elites elsewhere in the empire, cut off from legitimate Carolingian rule, set about choosing new kings for themselves, again through the agency of regnal assemblies and subsequently episcopally co-ordinated inauguration rituals. In the absence of adult male Carolingians, they opted for aristocrats of proven political experience. In west Francia, troubled by Viking invasions, Odo, count of Paris, was chosen in preference to the surviving infant Carolingian, Charles 'the Straightforward', although Odo's opponents subsequently crowned Charles as a rival. In Italy, Count Berengar of Friuli, a leading aristocrat whose grandmother was Louis the Pious' daughter, was proclaimed king; Berengar's position, however, was quickly contested by Wido of Spoleto, who had made an abortive bid for the west Frankish throne. In Burgundy, Count Rudolf acceded to the throne, and in 890 Louis, son of Boso of Vienne, was made king in Provence. Sensibilities about the legitimating power of Carolingian blood were tempered by Arnulf's coronation as emperor, and the visits paid to Arnulf by the likes of Odo. But this was a legitimating ritual gloss to what was essentially a new political system. Arnulf's attempts to reassert the centrality of the Carolingian family in the political system, by setting his son Zwentibald up as king of Lotharingia, failed abjectly: the Lotharingian aristocracy, used to dominating their kingdom on their own, in the name of a distant king, failed to accept Zwentibald, who was eventually murdered in 899 as a result of his involvement in a violent aristocratic feud.

Carolingian political problems in the ninth century are often linked to the practice of partible inheritance, which gave all legitimate sons a claim to the throne. In fact, a close look at patterns of partition and succession makes it clear that this is not the case. Succession of sons was closely controlled by fathers, so as to keep control of their kingdoms: Charles the Bald, for example, had carefully manipulated his succession, using the position of subking of Aquitaine as a means of testing his son's mettle, but keeping tight control and sending those he deemed unsuited for kingship into ecclesiastical careers. Louis the German and Lothar had likewise used the institution of subkingship to tie regional elites to the Carolingian family and give their sons political experience, and had also likewise kept their sons under tight reins so as to keep the ultimate political destiny of their kingdoms under control. Indeed, careful Carolingian management of succession is one reason why, in the 870s and 880s, the movement was not towards political partition but reintegration. In the meantime, however, the constituent parts of the empire had grown used to their own, local, Carolingian kingships: even a province like Alemannia had its own Carolingian, with his Aachen-style palace, distributing patronage, holding assemblies, and offering an accessible kingship to regional elites. The level of support for political leadership on the level of these constituent kingdoms of the Carolingian Empire had already been seen in Provence, where Count Boso of Vienne had been made king in 879, in a regime which was short-lived due to united Carolingian opposition: Provence had enjoyed its own Carolingian kingship under Lothar I's son Charles, but this had fallen into abeyance, and Boso owed his position in the south not to inherited local family power, but to his role as Charles the Bald's brother-in-law and chief advisor. In the political crisis of the 880s, when accessible Carolingian kingship that met regional needs was not forthcoming, there was nothing else for regnal elites but to raise kings from their own innards, as the chronicler Regino of Prüm memorably put it. But if the aim was to recreate a working Carolingian-style system, it failed, for without the Carolingian blood that differentiated kings from aristocrats, the new kingships created in 888 suffered from a legitimacy deficit. The legitimating apparatus of anointing and coronation rang hollow when it was used to raise one aristocrat over his fellows: as Regino again noted, precisely because of the ability and equality of leading aristocrats, conflict within each kingdom inevitably followed.[33]

In the decades after 888, the forms of Carolingian consensus politics continued to be observed – indeed, in a world of aristocrats-turned-kings expectations about taking proper counsel from all parties were more important than ever – but they were increasingly hollow. Within the Carolingian system, those who felt that their views were not being fully heard or their interests neglected had been able to seek new sources of patronage within the ruling family, or to urge the king to abandon his current bad counsellors, and kings had worked hard to maintain a delicate balance. In the new political world, those excluded from the centre had fewer options, and were increasingly driven to challenge the political dispensation with drawn swords. After 888 court politics within each kingdom were increasingly hijacked by a single aristocratic grouping, their rivals cut off from patronage, left out in the cold and eventually forced to turn to force of arms to have their voices heard. In the end, the powers inherent in Carolingian kingship were too great to be exercised by one aristocrat over his neighbours: attempts to intervene in the disposition of local honours were increasingly abandoned. But violent though this process may have been, politics still remained a matter of influencing public authorities exercised through royal courts who claimed their power was derived from God. Discontented aristocrats fought to get themselves heard at court, to have a stake in the public life of their kingdom, not to secede into local lordships. Carolingian kingship, even as it was transformed, thus provided the template for the politics of medieval Europe.

Bibliographical essay

Once again, the bibliography for chapter 9 gives details of the major general works and most of the primary sources available in translation.

Primary sources in translation

In addition to the major source collection in Dutton, *Carolingian Civilisation*, most of the major narrative sources are available in translation. See e.g. B. W. Scholz, *Carolingian Chronicles* (Ann Arbor, 1972) for Nithard's *Histories*, which is also in Dutton, who also has a translation of Thegan's *Deeds of Louis the Pious*. A. Cabannis, *Son of Charlemagne* (Syracuse, 1971) has the Astronomer's life of Louis the Pious, and his *Charlemagne's Cousins* (Syracuse, 1974) the biographies of Adalard and Wala; L. Thorpe, *Two Lives of Charlemagne* (London, 1969) has Notker's *Deeds of Charlemagne* as well as Einhard's *Life*; on the latter, Dutton, *Charlemagne's Courtier* has not only a far superior translation, but also Einhard's *Letters* and his *Translation of Saints Marcellinus and Peter*, both of vital importance for the upheavals caused by the revolts against Louis the Pious as well as priceless sources for social and cultural history. J. Nelson, *The Annals of St Bertin* (Manchester, 1991) and T. Reuter, *The Annals of Fulda* (Manchester, 1992) are the two major historical works of the period after Louis the Pious; forthcoming in the same series is S. Maclean's translation of the chronicle of Regino of Prüm, the last major work of Carolingian historiography. Hincmar of Rheims' *On the Governance of the Palace* is an idealised and highly polemical description of consensus politics, designed to influence a malleable young ruler: it is tr. D. Herlihy, *The History of Feudalism* (New York, 1970) or in Dutton. Dhuoda's *Manual* of advice for her son William gives an insight into aristocratic piety and family relationships: it is tr. M. Thiebaux (Cambridge, 1998) or C. Neel (Lincoln, NE, 1991). Two tasters of ninth-century political thought are E. G. Doyle, *Sedulius Scottus: On Christian Rulers and Poems* (Binghampton, NY, 1983) and R. W. Dyson, *A Ninth Century Political Tract: The De Institutione Regia of Jonas of Orleans* (Smithtown, 1983), whilst the life of a politically involved intellectual is evoked by G. Regenos, ed., *The Letters of Lupus of Ferrieres* (The Hague, 1966). Finally, C. H. Robinson, *Anskar, Apostle of the North* (London, 1921) and M. Kantor, *The Vita of Constantine and the Vita of Methodius* (Ann Arbor, 1976) or *Medieval Slavic Lives of Saints and Princes* (Ann Arbor, 1983) give insight into Scandinavia and central Europe respectively.

Kings and kingship

Louis the Pious' reign is best approached through the essays in P. Godman and R. Collins, eds, *Charlemagne's Heir: New Perspectives on the Reign of Louis the Pious (814–40)* (Oxford, 1990); E. Boshof, *Ludwig der Fromme* (Darmstadt, 1996), offers a rather traditional political narrative. M. Innes, '"He never even bared his white teeth in laughter": the politics of humour in the Carolingian renaissance', in G. Halsall, ed., *Humour, Politics and History in Late Antiquity* (Cambridge, 2002), shows how images of Louis created in contemporary history were shaped by political necessities and need careful handling; see also E. Ward, 'Agobard of Lyons and Paschasius Radbertus as critics of the Empress Judith', *Studies in Church History* 26 (1990), for Louis' wife Judith. Mayke de Jong's forthcoming book on 'the penitential state' will fundamentally reshape our understanding of Louis' reign through a careful reconstruction of the debates about the proper exercise of kingship evident in our rich source material. The civil wars of the 830s remain surprisingly little studied, given their central importance. The best way in, of seminal importance for understanding Louis' temporary deposition in 833–4, is M. de Jong, 'Power and humility in Carolingian society: the public penance of Louis the Pious', *Early Medieval Europe* 1 (1992). The renewed conflict following Louis' death is better served: here the seminal piece is J. L. Nelson, 'Public histories and private history in the work of Nithard', *Speculum* 60 (1985), reprinted in her *Politics and Ritual in Early Medieval Europe* (London, 1986); see also F. L. Ganshof, 'The genesis and significance of the Treaty of Verdun (843)', in his *The Carolingians and the Frankish Monarchy* (Providence, RI, 1971).

Of various kingdoms after 840, western Francia is the best studied. J. L. Nelson, *Charles the Bald* (London, 1992), is a good political biography; try also the various contributions in M. Gibson and J. Nelson, eds, *Charles the Bald: Court and Kingdom* (2nd edn, Aldershot, 1990). Nelson's many articles illuminate ninth-century kingship, particularly in the west Frankish kingdom: the three volumes of her collected essays are indispensable guides to the ninth-century Carolingian world: *Politics and Ritual in Early Medieval Europe* (Woodbridge, 1985); *The Frankish World 750–900* (London, 1996); and *Rulers and Ruling Families in the Early Middle Ages* (London, 1999). G. Koziol's forthcoming book will open an important new perspective on the period from Charles the Bald to Charles the Simple. On eastern Francia, there is now an excellent study of Louis the German, E. Goldberg, *Struggle for Empire: Kingship and Empire under Louis the German, 817–876* (Ithaca and London, 2006), which is preferable to the rather traditional German biography, W. Hartmann, *Ludwig der Deutsche* (Darmstadt, 2001); there are also good thematic articles in German in W. Hartmann, ed., *Ludwig der Deutsche und seine Zeit* (Darmstadt 2004), whilst for the political flavour of Louis' court see Goldberg's 'Frontier kingship, martial ritual and early knighthood at the court of Louis the German', *Viator* 30 (1999). T. Reuter, *Germany in the Early Middle Ages 800–1056* (London, 1992) is also excellent. The middle kingdom is sadly neglected, although S. Airlie, 'Private bodies and the body politic in the divorce case of Lothar II', *Past & Present* 161 (1998), provides brilliant illumination of a central episode; see also E. Screen, 'The importance of being emperor: Lothar I and the Frankish civil war 840–43', *Early Medieval Europe* 12 (2003). Material on Carolingian Italy remains difficult to access, particularly in English, though there is much of value in C. La Rocca, *Short History of Italy in the Early Middle Ages* (Oxford, 2002) and C. Wickham, *Early Medieval Italy* (London, 1981). F. Bougard, *La justice dans la royaume d'Italie* (Rome, 1995) is fundamental, and the articles by Bougard, Gasparri and La Rocca in R. Le Jan, ed., *La royaute et les élites dans l'Europe carolingienne* (Lille, 1998) valuable, whilst B. Rosenwein, 'The family politics of Berengar I, king of Italy (888–924)', *Speculum* 71 (1996) is the fundamental study of late Carolingian kingship, and S. Maclean's forthcoming work elucidates conflict.

On the Carolingian crisis of the 880s, the fundamental study is that of Simon Maclean, *Kingship and Politics in the Late Ninth Century: Charles the Fat and the End of the Carolingian Empire* (Cambridge, 2003). See also, for aristocratic ambitions, S. Maclean, 'The Carolingian response to the revolt of Boso 879–887', *Early Medieval Europe* 10 (2001), S. Airlie, 'The nearly men: Boso of Vienne and Arnulf of Bavaria', in A. Duggan, ed., *Nobles and Nobility in Medieval Europe* (Woodbridge, 2000), and for the emergence of new kingdoms after 888, S. Airlie, 'After empire: recent work on the emergence of post-Carolingian kingdoms', *Early Medieval Europe* 2 (1993).

Frontiers, raiders and traders

On Carolingian frontiers, J. Smith's essay in McKitterick, ed., *New Cambridge Medieval History* 2, and T. Noble's in Godman and Collins, eds, *Charlemagne's Heir*, are the best starting-points. J. Smith, *Province and Empire: Brittany and the Carolingians* (Cambridge, 1992) is an excellent case-study, whilst the Carolingian essays in W. Pohl and H. Reimitz, *The Transformation of Frontiers from Late Antiquity to the Carolingians* (Leiden, 1997) and M. Diesenberger and W. Pohl, eds, *Grenze und Differenz im frühen Mittelalter* (Vienna, 2000) are important.

Scandinavia and the North Sea in the 'first Viking age' are the subject of a voluminous bibliography. The best introductions are via the relevant chapters of P. Sawyer, ed., *Oxford Illustrated History of the Vikings* (Oxford, 1998). P. Sawyer, *The Age of the Vikings* (2nd edn, London, 1971) was a controversial reinterpretation, and his later *Kings and Vikings* (London, 1982) an excellent introduction to Scandinavia and Europe in the Viking age. These are preferable to any of the numerous books entitled 'the Vikings' or something similar. On Scandinavian society, see L. Hedeager, *Iron Age Societies: From Tribe to State in Northern Europe* (Oxford, 1992), E. Roesdahl, *Viking Age Denmark* (London, 1982) and K. Randsborg, *The Viking Age in Denmark: The Formation of a State* (London, 1980); also M. Axboe, 'Danish kings and dendrochronology', in G. Ausenda, ed., *After Empire* (Woodbridge, 1996) and B. Nasman in I. Hansen and C. Wickham, eds, *The Long Eighth Century* (Leiden, 2001). B Sawyer, *Custom and Commemoration in Early Medieval Scandinavia* (Oxford, 2001) is an important study of the rune-stone evidence, used to reconstruct Scandinavian society at a slightly later date. For trade networks, see H. Clarke and B. Ambrosiani, *Towns in the Viking Age* (Leicester, 1991). For Viking political relationships with the Franks, K. Maund, '"A turmoil of warring princes": political leadership in ninth-century Denmark', *Haskins Society Journal* 6 (1994), N. Lund, 'Allies of God or Man? The Viking expansion in European perspective', *Viator* 20 (1989); I. Wood, 'Christians and pagans in ninth-century Scandinavia', in P. Sawyer, ed., *The Christianisation of Scandinavia* (Alingsas, 1987) is crucial on the life of Anskar, whilst S. Coupland, 'From poachers to gamekeepers: Scandinavian warlords and Carolingian kings', *Early Medieval Europe* 7 (1998) reconstructs the careers of some Vikings in Frankish service. See also J. Nelson, 'Vikings and others', *Transactions of the Royal Historical Society* 13 (2003) and S. Coupland, 'The Vikings on the continent in history and myth', *History* 88 (2003). For the (mis)representation of Viking activity in Frankish sources, S. Coupland, 'The rod of God's wrath or the people of God's wrath', *Journal of Ecclesiastical History* 42 (1991), in part a response to M. Wallace-Hadrill, 'The Vikings in Francia', in his *Early Medieval History* (London, 1975); for a study of their political impact, S. Maclean, 'Charles the Fat and the Viking great army: the military explanation for the fall of the Carolingian Empire', *War Studies Journal* 3 (1998); on the foundation of Normandy, E. Searle, 'Frankish rivalries and Norse warriors', *Anglo-Norman Studies* 8 (1995).

On Frankish relationships with the various Slavic groups in central and eastern Europe, there are two suggestive syntheses by P. Heather: 'Frankish imperialism and Slavic society', in P. Urbancyck, ed., *Origins of Central Europe* (Warsaw, 1997) – an important volume – also his 'State formation in Europe in the first millennium', in B. Crawford, ed., *Scotland in Dark-Age Europe* (St Andrews, 1994). P. Barford, *The Early Slavs* (Ithaca, 2001) is excellent on the archaeology for the development of Slavic society, and see now F. Curta, ed., *East Central and Eastern Europe in the Middle Ages* (Ann Arbor, 2005). On Slavic state-formation the best study is

F. Graus, *Die Nationenbildung der Westslaven im Mittelalter* (Sigmaringen, 1980) and for an overview in English, F. Dvornik, *The Making of Central and Eastern Europe* (London, 1984). On Frankish frontier policy, there is much of value in C. Bowlus, *Franks, Moravians and Magyars: The Struggle for the Middle Danube 788–907* (Philadelphia, 1995), but it is sadly subordinated to an unhelpful argument about the precise geographical location of Moravia: see also M. Innes, 'Franks and Slavs, 700–1000', *Early Medieval Europe* 6 (1997) and, on the arrival of the Magyars, P. Stephenson, 'Early medieval Hungary in English', *Early Medieval Europe* 10 (2001). On mission, see F. Dvornik, *Byzantine Missions among the Slavs: Saints Constantine-Cyrill and Methodius* (New Brunswick, NJ, 1970) and A. Vlasto, *The Entry of the Slavs into Christendom* (Cambridge, 1970). Thanks to Pope Nicholas' interest, there is good work on the conversion of the Bulgarians: R. Sullivan, 'Khan Boris and the conversion of Bulgaria: a case study of the impact of Christianity on a barbarian society', *Studies in Medieval and Renaissance History* 3 (1966), pp. 55–139, reprinted in his collected papers *Christian Missionary Activity in the Early Middle Ages* (London, 1994). On Bulgaria, see F. Curta, 'Qagan, khan, or king? Power in early medieval Bulgaria', *Viator* 37 (2006) and T. Stepanov, 'Reconstructing notions of divine kingship in Bulgaria 822–36', *Early Medieval Europe* 10 (2001).

There is sadly little new work on the interactions between Carolingians, Byzantines and Muslims in central and southern Italy and the western Mediterranean, largely owing to linguistic and disciplinary boundaries. The literature on Mediterranean trade is helpful, and B. Kreutz, *Before the Normans: Southern Italy in the Ninth and Tenth Centuries* (Philadelphia, 1991) a good treatment of the politics of the region.

Notes

1. For full details of the primary source material, see bibliographical essay below.
2. Notker, *Deeds of Charlemagne*, tr. L. Thorpe, *Two Lives of Charlemagne* (London, 1971); Hincmar, *On the Governance of the Palace*, tr. P. Dutton, *Carolingian Civilisation: A Reader* (Peterborough Ont., 1997), no. 77.
3. Thegan, *Deeds of Louis*, tr. Dutton, *Carolingian Civilisation*, no. 26, esp. chs 20, 44, 55; Einhard, *Translation of Marcellinus and Peter*, tr. Dutton, *Charlemagne's Courtier: The Complete Einhard* (Peterborough Ont., 1997), III.15.
4. See B. Kasten, *Königssohne und Königsherrschaft im Frankenreich* (Hannover, 1997).
5. On Louis in Aquitaine, see the discussion of his anonymous biographer, the 'Astronomer', tr. A. Cabannis, *Son of Charlemagne* (Syracuse, 1971); Pippin's rule in Italy deserves proper study.
6. The *Divisio Regnorum* is tr. Dutton, *Carolingian Civilisation*, no. 23; on 'family management' and the 'Aachen establishment' see now J. Nelson, 'La famille de Charlemagne', *Byzantion* 61 (1991), reprinted in her *Rulers and Ruling Families in Early Medieval Europe* (London, 1999) and her 'Women at the court of Charlemagne', in J. C. Parsons, ed., *Medieval Queenship* (Stroud, 1993), reprinted in her *The Frankish World* (London, 1996).

7. The *Ordinatio Imperii* is tr. Dutton, *Carolingian Civilisation*, no. 28; for a taste of the criticism occasioned on Bernard's death see the *Vision of the Poor Woman of Laon*, in Dutton, no. 29.
8. *Monumenta Germaniae Historica Capitularia Regum Francorum* I, ed. A. Boretius (Hannover, 1883), no. 150.
9. Nithard, *Histories*, tr. B. Scholz, *Carolingian Chronicles* (Ann Arbor, 1974) or Dutton, *Carolingian Civilisation* no. 45, III.5.
10. See Einhard, *Letters*, tr. Dutton, *Charlemagne's Courtier*.
11. T. Reuter, tr., *The Annals of Fulda* (Manchester, 1992), s.a. 861, 865, 866, and J. Nelson, tr., *The Annals of St Bertin* (Manchester, 1991), s.a. 865; the politics fully worked out by M. Innes, *State and Society in the Early Middle Ages* (Cambridge, 2000), pp. 217–18.
12. *Monumenta Germaniae Historica Capitularia Regum Francorum* II, ed. A. Boretius (Hannover, 1885), no. 281, c.9.
13. M. Wallace-Hadrill, 'Charles the Bald: a Carolingian renaissance prince', *Proceedings of the British Academy* 64 (1978); J. Nelson, 'Translating images of authority: the Christian Roman emperors in the Carolingian world', in M. Mackenzie and C. Roueché, eds, *Images of Authority* (Cambridge, 1989), reprinted in Nelson's *The Frankish World.*
14. On the notion of consensus see J. Hannig, *Consensus Fidelium* (Munich, 1984) and J. Nelson, 'Legislation and consensus in the Reign of charles the Bald', in P. Wormald *et al.*, eds, *Ideal and Reality in Frankish and Anglo-Saxon Society* (Oxford, 1983), reprinted in her *Politics and Ritual in Early Medieval Europe* (London, 1986).
15. The data are assembled by C.-R. Brühl, *Fodrum, Gistum, Servitium Regis* (Cologne, 1968), with invaluable maps.
16. See J. Nelson, 'Charles the Bald and the church in town and country', *Studies in Church History* 16 (1979), reprinted in *Politics and Ritual.*
17. See M. de Jong, 'The empire as ecclesia: Hraban Maur and Biblical exegesis for kings', in Y. Hen and M. Innes, eds, *The Uses of the Past in the Early Middle Ages* (Cambridge, 2000) and D. Geuenich, 'Die volkssprachige Überlieferung der Karolingerzeit im Sicht des Historikers', *Deutsches Archiv* 39 (1983).
18. Frankfurt is called 'principal seat' by Regino of Prüm, *Chronicle*, ed. F. Kurze, Monumenta Germaniae Historica Scriptores rerum Germanicarum (Hannover, 1890), s.a. 876; on the complex, M. Schalles-Fischer, *Pfalz und Fiskus Frankfurt* (Göttingen, 1969).
19. See E. G. Doyle, *Sedulius Scottus: On Christian Rulers and Poems* (Binghampton, NY, 1983).
20. S. Coupland, 'The rod of God's wrath or the people of God's wrath', *Journal of Ecclesiastical History*, 42 (1991).
21. Reuter, tr., *Annals of Fulda*, s.a. 882, on which see S. Maclean, 'Charles the Fat and the Viking great army: the military explanation for the fall of the Carolingian Empire', *War Studies Journal* 3 (1998).
22. C. H. Robinson, *Anskar, Apostle of the North* (London, 1922).
23. On Godofrid see *Royal Frankish Annals*, tr. Scholz, *Carolingian Chronicles*, s.a. 808, 809, 810.

24. For the comings and goings between Harald and the sons of Godofrid see *Royal Frankish Annals* s.a. 812, 814, 819, 821, 826, 827, 828; on mission, Robinson, tr., *Anskar*.
25. *Royal Frankish Annals*, tr. Scholz, *Carolingian Chronicles*, s.a. 828
26. See Nelson, tr., *Annals of St Bertin*, s.a. 841, Nithard, *Histories*, tr. Scholz, *Carolingian Chronicles* 4: 2, clearly linked to the raids reported in 4.3.
27. Notker, *Deeds of Charlemagne*, tr. Thorpe, II: 19, and see also II: 17–18.
28. L. Musset, *Les invasions II: le second assault contre l'Europe chrétienne, VIIe–Xe siècles* (Paris, 1965), part I was subtitled *Les vagues germaniques.*
29. Nelson, tr., *Annals of St Bertin*, s.a. 859.
30. Reuter, tr., *Annals of Fulda*, s.a. 845.
31. *Royal Frankish Annals*, tr. Scholz, *Carolingian Chronicles*, s.a. 799.
32. See Simon Maclean's important forthcoming analysis.
33. See Regino of Prüm, *Chronicle,* ed. Kurze, s.a. 888.

Epilogue: the sword, the plough and the book

We began this book with Orosius debating the possibility that barbarian arms might come to prolong the Roman Empire; we end it with the crisis of the Carolingian Empire, and the fragmentation of the single political framework in western Europe that it represented. On one level, we might see in the Carolingian Empire the distant and indirect achievement of the possible future discussed by Orosius. After all, on Christmas Day 800 the title of Roman Emperor had been revived, and some at Charlemagne's court could present his realm in Gaul, Germany and Italy as equivalent to the western Roman Empire.[1] Yet, as we have seen, for Charlemagne and his successors the imperial title was a matter of prestige: it did not bring with it any formal jurisdiction or carry any substantive claims. Indeed, far more important than Roman precedent in Carolingian political self-consciousness was a sense that the Frankish realm was coterminous with a new cultural, distinct, unit: the Latin Christendom of the west. In this sense, it was possible to describe Carolingian rulers as leaders of 'Europe', an ancient geographical entity given a new ideological twist thanks to its identification with the Latin Christian church.[2] Whilst the Carolingians might thus identify theirs as the 'true' religion of Christians, they did so to define themselves against Constantinople's claim to represent a continuing Christian Roman Empire charged with universal rule. In other words, the Carolingians were not direct successors to the Roman emperors in the west, and their kingship could not build on any functioning Roman template, administrative or ideological. The emergence of a consciously and increasingly assertively distinct cultural and social system in the west was the result of half a millennium of development that had seen western Europe slowly disengaging from the ancient ties that had held together the Roman world. Crucial here was the shrinking of the gravitational field sustained by the cultural and economic forces that had pulled together the diverse communities of the ancient Mediterranean from the third century onwards, with the unity of the Mediterranean basin itself in crisis by 700, and the series of regional systems which had long been emerging in its hinterland now dominant.

Nonetheless, the route from the western Roman Empire of the fourth century to the Carolingian world of the ninth was anything but direct. This circuitous and convoluted passage owed much to the attempts of the imperial court in Constantinople to define a new Christian Roman world order. The new kingdoms of the west that arose in the fifth and sixth centuries did so against this backdrop. Although they built on the administrative and ideological foundations of Roman provincial government, none was able to provide the kind of new political framework for the west, resting on a fusion of Roman structures and barbarian armies and briefly suggested in Theodoric's dominance, which might have evolved into a direct successor state to the western Empire. The expanding ambitions of a new Christian imperial order led from the 'new Rome' give the lie to the usual characterisation of the fifth and sixth centuries as witnessing the decline of the Roman Empire. Constantinople's imperial claims were crucial in determining the shape of western development, for not only did they lead to military intervention which prevented Theodoric's legacy being built upon, but they also engaged a sizeable portion of Italian elites through the seventh century and beyond. This prevented the emergence of a strong Italian ruler able to remould the west into a new post-imperial order. Charlemagne was to translate the statue erected in Theodoric's honour from Ravenna to his new palace complex at Aachen, and his reign saw the casting of Theodoric, presented in his own time as the protector of Roman society in Italy, as the first Germanic master of the post-Roman west.[3]

But, precisely because it was not a direct successor of Rome, Charlemagne's realm rested on very different foundations from that of his Gothic hero. Carolingian kings ruled through processes wholly different from Byzantine emperors and Islamic caliphs, both direct successors to ancient empires whose structures they inherited and transformed. The disasters of the seventh century, for example, left Constantinople wholly dominant within the Byzantine world, and here a new ruling elite crystallised around the imperial court. Its personnel were of diverse origin – the decimation of eastern landed elites left ambitious provincials of modest background and able barbarians dominant – but united in the service of a state on whose structures they relied for their own position. In the Islamic world, the seventh-century conquests had created a far-flung elite united by its Islamic religious identity, and the extended ties of kinship and patronage inherited from the Arab past. Identities of clan and tribe interacted with religious controversies to provide ties holding together factions which spanned the Islamic world. The basis of this extensive ruling elite remained the special status of Islamic conquerors as recipients of provincial taxation, and even though new converts to Islam were challenging these privileges in the eighth and ninth centuries as Islamicised landowning classes emerged in the provinces, the fiscal demands of the state continued to structure patterns of power. In the west, in contrast, by the seventh century at the latest the processes by which the Roman state had redistributed the fruits of the countryside through the tax system had collapsed, and with them had gone the extensive connections that had tied together the provinces of the west. In a parallel process, the senatorial aristocracy – in the fourth century proportionately probably the wealthiest ruling class witnessed in pre-modern history – had gone too, fragmenting and merging with barbarian incomers and middling landowners to create a series of militarised regional elites. Unable to maintain the formal legal privileges that had informed senatorial status in the Roman world, they appropriated the language of ethnicity to articulate their new position, leaders of a wider but shallower landowning class which claimed a freedom rooted in service of their king. The political momentum of the eighth-century Carolingians was to tie these regional landowning communities into an extensive social system, defined not only by the Carolingian family itself but also by the 'imperial aristocracy' that coalesced around the Frankish court; ideologies of Christian kingship meant that the church foundations which had defined the fabric of post-Roman society could be bound together to give the new order an institutional backbone. The ruling elite of the Christian empire identified themselves with Frankish kings as leaders of God's chosen people. This political identity was rooted in the shared experience of the royal court and the powerful allure of royal patronage. It remained relatively loose and open-ended, something that could be embraced by regional communities with their own heritages and identities: the factional arguments over formal privilege which animated the caliphate were wholly absent, precisely because the administrative structures that underwrote sharp status divisions did not exist in the west. Carolingian kingship offered the churches and landowners of western Europe a legitimating and stabilising embrace, providing the aura and patronage that allowed them to confirm their local leadership. In a society where the collapse of the formal hierarchies of the ancient world had left patterns of power relatively diffuse, rooted in collective action and community leadership, engagement with the clearly articulated framework of public authority provided by Carolingian kingship was vital for elites to prosper. After all, even after the crisis of Carolingian kingship in the last decades of the ninth century, western society was governed by bishops in council and counts in courts: it was only in the course of the tenth and eleventh centuries, as they increasingly had to work without the royal embrace, that new structures of power, now presented in terms of formal rights of jurisdiction rooted in property law, emerged in a process that remains a matter of intense controversy. But this still lay in the future as our period drew to a close. The lasting significance of western Europe's early medieval path lay in the development of relatively open and fluid patterns of power rooted in land, and quite distinct from the formal structures of the ancient state and its successors elsewhere in Eurasia.

The peculiar position of the Carolingian Empire in this process is clear from the attempts of Carolingian thinkers to define the social hierarchies of earthly rule as a divinely instituted order sanctioned by the Bible. Jonas, bishop of Orleans from 817–40, had been educated at Charlemagne's court, and under Louis the Pious acted as something like a spokesperson for the Frankish episcopate, not least in its opposition to what were seen as suspect eastern teachings. Seeking to explain the basis of proper order in this world, he argued that God had divided mankind into three orders, priests, monks and laymen, each of which had its specific responsibilities that contributed to the harmonious functioning of earthly society as a whole. Jonas drew on the teachings of late antique church fathers, and particularly the writings of Augustine and Gregory the Great, whose Biblical commentaries had presented Noah, Daniel and Job as exemplars for different kinds of men serving God in different ways: priests charged with fulfilling a holy ministry, the continent whose abstinence from sexual intercourse signified a quest for individual perfection, and the married who worked for God through the trials and tribulations of this world. Jonas adapted this threefold scheme so as to give each segment of the Carolingian elite its distinct role: the traditional married order of laymen offered a template for the aristocracy, charged with ensuring that the church enjoyed justice, and entrusted with protecting the peace through arms; the order of the continent and chaste was identified with the monks, seeking to follow a perfect life, ensured peace through their prayers; whilst the order of clerics or priests was exemplified by the role of bishops, using their wisdom to oversee the other two orders, offering counsel and preventing sin. Jonas' scheme was not an isolated intellectual curiosity: not only is it paralleled in the writings of a series of other authors, but it responded to current concerns about the responsibilities of the Carolingian ruling elite. In 802, for example, Charlemagne had divided those attending the annual royal assembly into three – priests, monks and laymen – and asked each to consider its role and report back with recommendations for royal legislation. In a council held in 813 at Mainz a similar threefold division had taken place, with bishops instructed to study the canons of the church, monks the rule of Benedict and counts the secular laws. Jonas' own theology of the three orders of society had its origins in a similar process. In 818–19, Louis the Pious had issued a series of capitularies reforming secular laws and church governance and regulating monastic observance whose general preface presented these as measures designed to instruct members on the 'canonical and monastic institutions'. Afterwards Jonas himself was to write a handbook *On the Institution of the Laity*, outlining how they could fulfil the heavy obligations that their role as sharers in the divinely ordained mission to rule Christian society brought.[4]

Jonas' activities bear eloquent witness to the ambitions of the Carolingian court. His were not attempts at social analysis or description, but admonitions designed to help perfect social order by instructing a ruling elite in which abbots, bishops and counts all had their distinct but complementary roles, sharing a moral responsibility to assist kings in governing the Christian people. In that it was an instrumental programme designed to shape political action, Jonas' schema differed from the more famous tripartite division between those who prayed, those who fought and those who farmed, which was to become a stock description of social order in post-Carolingian Europe. First made by Haimo of Auxerre in the 860s, this functional division was winning popularity by 900; it described and legitimated a social order rooted in control over labour and land, where those with a monopoly on military force or on access to the supernatural ultimately controlled agrarian surpluses. As a controlling stereotype of social analysis, the very simplicity and force of this division gave it a status analogous to categories of class in modern industrialised societies: it identifies the very direct manner in which a militarised landowning class and the Christian church were able to control the fruits of land and labour in medieval Europe.[5] This very direct relationship, expressed in terms of property rights, between the plough, the sword and the book was the basis of medieval European society. This was the lasting legacy of the interconnecting processes of cultural, economic, political and social change which prevented the emergence of a direct successor state to the western empire. Instead, western social development was given a crucial defining twist by the efforts of Carolingian kings and their advisors to shape a new Christian order built on resolutely post-Roman foundations.

Notes

1. See the account of the Annals of Lorsch, tr. P. D. King, *Charlemagne: Translated Sources* (Kendal, 1987), pp. 137–45.
2. On Carolingian ideas of Europe, voiced in works such as Modoin of Autun's Eclogue and the Paderborn Epic, see K. Leyser, 'Concepts of Europe in the early and high middle ages', *Past & Present* 137 (1992), reprinted in his *Communications and Power in Medieval Europe I: The Carolingian and Ottonian Centuries* (London, 1994).
3. M. Innes, 'Teutons or Trojans? The Carolingians and the Germanic Past', in Y. Hen and M. Innes, eds, *The Uses of the Past in the Early Middle Ages* (Cambridge, 2000).
4. On Jonas' career, and his theory of the three orders, as laid down in his *Life of Hucbert of Liège*, *De Insitutione Laicali* and subsequently *De Institutione Regia*, see A. Dubreucq, ed., *Jonas d'Orléans: Le Métier de Roi* (Paris, 1995), esp. pp. 68–73. The crucial Biblical passage is Ezekiel 14: 13–20, interpreted since Augustine in the light of Luke 17: 34–6 and Matthew 20: 40–4, on the Last Judgement; in general see O. G. Oexle, 'Tria genera hominem', in L. Fenske *et al.*, eds, *Institutionen, Kultur und Gesellschaft im früheren Mittelalter: Festschrift Josef Fleckenstein* (Sigmaringen, 1984). For the assembly of 802 – which produced important legislation on both monastic and ecclesiastical observance and on the activities of *missi dominici* – see Annals of Lorsch, tr. King, s.a. 802; for 813, A. Werminghoff, ed., Monumenta Germaniae Historica Concilia aevi Karolini I (Hannover, 1906), no. 136; for 818–19, see Monumenta Germaniae Historica Capitularia regum Francorum I, ed. A. Boretius (Hanover, 1885), no. 137, which is echoed in Jonas' writing.
5. On the ninth-century transformation of the 'three orders of society' see the seminal study by D. Iogna Prat, 'Le "baptême" du schéma des trois ordres fonctionnels: l'apport de l'École d'Auxerre dans la seconde moitié du IXe siècle', *Annales: E, S, C* 31 (1986). On the 'three orders' as a central social theory of the post-Carolingian period, G. Duby, *The Three Orders: Feudal Society Imagined* (London, 1980).

Index

Abd al-Rahman, amir in al-Andalus, 234–5
Abinnaeus, Roman military officer, 26–32, 39
Adrianople, battle of, 80–2, consequences of, 87
Aetius, Roman general, 106–10, 321
Al-Andalus (Islamic Spain), 230–8
Alemans, 24, emergence of 71, in fourth-century Gaul 73, 77–9, in Frankish kingdom, 272–3, 289, 414–15, 437
Alcuin, Anglo-Saxon scholar, 365–6, 414, 458, 463–4
Alfred, king of Anglo-Saxons, 332, 366, 371–7
Ambrose, bishop of Milan, 45, 46, 47, 50, 52
Ammianus Marcellinus, and his history, 22–3, 36, 39, 52, on Constantius II, 27–8
  on barbarians, 68, 73, 74, 127, on battle of Adrianople, 81, and Carolingians, 479
Anglo-Saxons, raids on fifth century Britain, 321, 323–4, settlement in Britain, 331–7, Anglo-Saxon kingship and kingdoms, 346–54, conversion of Anglo-Saxons, 354–64, Anglo-Saxons and Vikings, 365–80
Anglo-Saxon Chronicle, 332, 347–8, 365, 366, 369, 374, 377
Anthemius, Roman Emperor, 116–7, 121
Arabs, and rise of Islam, 185–8
Arianism, and Arius, 47, in Vandal Africa, 116–20, 159–60, in Theodoric's Italy, 150, in Visigothic Spain, 219–22, in Lombard Italy, 240; in MerovingianGaul, 271–4
Army, armies: Byzantine: in Gothic wars, 164–6, in conflict with Persians, 184–5, in conflict with Arabs, 186–8; in Balkans, 194–6; in post-reconquest Italy, 199–200
  Roman: 23–4, 26–31, 33, barbarian recruitment into, 30, 79–80, 82, 83–6, 99–104, and frontiers of the Roman Empire, 74–80, disappearance of in fifth-century west 80–9, 103–4
  Arab in Islamic conquests, 186–8, in al-Andalus, 235
  in Visigothic kingdom, 225–6, in Lombard kingdom, 254, in Merovingian kingdom, 284, 292, in Carolingian world, 402–4, 438, 443
  Viking, 367–8, 522
Asturias, kingdom of, 235–6
Attila, Hunnic ruler, 72, 108–10
Augustine, bishop of Hippo, 20, 45, 48–9, 86, 400
Avars, settlement in middle Danube, 198–9, Carolingian conquest of, 417, aftermath of, 523–4

Bacaudae, 104–5, 107, 110–1, 320
Balthild, Merovingian queen, 294, 296, 298,
Barbarians, and Roman Empire, 23–4, 66–89, *see* also names of individual 'peoples'
Bede, Anglo-Saxon monk, theologian and historian, 325, 331–3, 345–64, 370

Belisarius, Byzantine general, 160–5
Benedict, Saint, abbot of Monte Cassino, 171, and Benedict of Aniane and Carolingian reforms, 469–70
Berbers, 118, and Islam, 192–3, settlement in Islamic Spain, 231, 234
Bishops, in later Roman Empire, 35–6, 44–6, in Visigothic kingdom, 223–9, and Lombard settlement, 243–4, in Lombard kingdom, 249–50, 254–5, in Frankish kingdom, 271–3, 278–81, 294, 404, 410–11, 438–9, 466–8, 472, 474–8, in early medieval Ireland, 342–4, in early medieval Wales, 345, in Anglo-Saxon England, 362–3
Boethius, Roman senator, 149–50
Boniface, Saint, Anglo-Saxon missionary, 406, 410–12, 464, 466–8, 470, 477
Bulgars, emergence of, 198–9, conversion of, 525–6

Caliphate, in comparison to west, 8, 187–8, emergence of, 186–8, relations with al-Andalus, 231–4, economic and political links with eighth and ninth century west, 455–6, 527–31
Carolingians, ancestors of, 295, and denigration of Merovingian church, 296–7, and denigration of Merovingians, 297, 400–2, and denigration of opponents, 410–11, 416–17, 'Grimoald coup', 299, rise of, 301–3, realms in eighth and ninth centuries, 400–534
Carthage, economic role of, 33, 191–3, bishop of, 45, and Vandal kingdom, 108, 116–20, 160, political role in Byzantine world, 168, 189, 191–3
Cassiodorus, Gothic History, 70, Variae, 145–9, 151, 166, 'retirement' to Vivarium, 171
'Celtic' culture, 'Celtic church', 'Celtic Christianity', 324–30, 337–46, 353–5
Charlemagne, 400–2, 409–10, 412–19, 429–80, 498–500, 517–18
Charles Martell 302–3, 400–5, 412, 415, 443
Childeric, Frankish king, 128–9, 269–71
Christianity: in Roman Empire, 20–2, 3506 39–50, in Visigothic kingdom, 220–1, 223–9, in Islamic al-Andalus, 230, 233, 237–8, in Lombard kingdom, 238–40, 250–1, 254–5, in Frankish kingdom, 271–3, 280–2, 286, 293–7, in post-Roman Britain, 327–30, in early medieval Ireland, 338, in Anglo-Saxon England, 354–64, and Carolingian expansion east of Rhine, 410–15, and Carolingian kingdoms, 400, 456–80, and Carolingian relationships with Scandinavia and eastern Europe, 517–26
Classical culture, 43–4, in Theodoric's kingdom, 149, in sixth-century Italy, 171, in Merovingian Gaul, 280–1, in Carolingian world, 478–9, 510–11
Charles the Bald, Frankish king, 501–13, 519–22, 531–2
Charles the Fat, Frankish king, 532–3
Chrodegang, bishop of Metz, 467–8, 470, 473
Cities, in later Roman Empire, 30–6, in post-Roman Spain, 219–20, in Islamic al-Andalus, 235, in Lombard Italy, 244–6, 248–50, in Merovingian kingdom, 277–82, 292, in post-Roman Britain, 323, and North Sea trade of eighth and ninth centuries, 350–3, 450–3, 517–19, in Carolingian world, 450–6.
Clovis, Frankish king, 271–7
Constans II, Emperor, 184, 201–2
Constantine, Roman Emperor, 24–8, 30, 32, 34, 35, 41–5, 47–8
Constantius II, Roman Emperor, 25–8, 52
Constantius III, Roman general then Emperor, 87, 103, 106
Constantinople, city of, and Imperial court in, 26, 33, 39, 42, 45, 50–1, 156–7, 159–60, 172, 182–4, 202, 204; purge of barbarians in 399–400, 84, 89, 129; in Mediterranean economy, 188–94
Councils, church, universal, 47, 157, 164, 163–4, 202–3, and western opposition to monothelitism, 201, in Visigothic kingdom, 220, 223–4, lack of in Lombard kingdom, 239–40, 254–5, in Merovingian kingdom, 281, 294, in Anglo-Saxon England, 363, and Carolingians, 429, 463–6

Counts, in Merovingian Gaul, 279, 282, 292, in Carolingian Empire, 434–9, 503–5, 508–10

Dagobert I, Frankish king, 287–90, 294–9
Dalriata, Scottish kingdom, 328–9, 378–80
Demography, in later Roman Empire, barbarian, 72–4; in fifth to seventh century Italy, 166–7, and sixth-century plague, 190–1, in Carolingian countryside, 449–50
Diocletian, Roman Emperor, 24–9, 31, 33–4, 37, 40–1, 48, 50–1, 53
Dukes (sing. *dux*, pl. *duces*), in Visigothic kingdom, 226–8, in Lombard kingdom, 244–6, in Merovingian Gaul, 282, 287–90, in eighth-century Frankish world, 403, 407–9, 438–40

Economics: *see* trade
Einhard, 375, 413–14, 417, 430–2, 443, 458, 471–3, 478–9, 494, 500, 508
Empire, Emperors, ideology of, Roman, 23–8, Byzantine, 156–9. 199–200, 204–7, Theodoric as Emperor, 144, Belisarius and Empire, 163–5, Empire in Carolingian world, 478–80, 500–1, 506, 530–2.
Ethnicity, ethnogenesis, ethonography, 6–7, 67–71, 73, 101–2, in Theodoric's Italy, 146–9, in Visigothic kingdom, 220, 222–3, Slavic, 197–9, in Islamic world, 187–8, in al-Andalus, 233–4, of Lombards, 240–5, in Merovingian world, 283–90, 292, in Carolingian Empire, 439–41, in Anglo-Saxon settlements in Britain, 331–7, 346–54, in ninth-century Britain, 374–80
Emporia, *see* cities, trade
Exchange, *see* trade

'fall of Rome', in historiography, 122–30, 159
Feddersen Wierde, 72, 73, 333
'feudalism', 6, and Carolingians, 442–6
Franks, in Roman world, 71, 78–9, 82, 99, 107, for subsequent history *see* Merovingians, Carolingians
Fredegar, Chronicle of, 285, 295, its continuations, 400
Frontiers: Byzantine in near East, 184–8, Byzantine in Balkans, 125–6, 194–9, 241–2
  Carolingian, 417–19, 513–14, 515–16
  Christian-Islamic in eighth and ninth century Spain, 236–7
  Roman, 23–4, 30–1, 66–7, 74–80, 98–103, 268–9

Gaiseric, Vandal king, 116–20
Germanic heritage, concept of, 6, 68
Germanus, bishop of Auxerre, 107, 320
Gibbon, Edward, 3, 39
Gildas, on the ruin of Britain, 321–5, 331–3
Goffart, Walter, 101
Goths, invasions and first settlements, 1–2, 24, 70–1, 79, 80–2, 84–6, 99, 107, 110, 113–14, Ostrogothic kingdom in Italy, 142–68; Visigothic kingdom in southern Gaul and Spain, 217–29
Gregory the Great, Pope 168–72, 189, 191, 199, 247, 250, 354
Gregory II, Pope, 205–7
Gregory III, Pope, 205–7
Gregory, bishop of Tours, historian and hagiographer, 268, 271–7, 292

Heraclius, Emperor 184, 185, 186–7, 189, 200–1
Heretics, heresy, 22, in Roman Empire, 47–9, in Vandal Africa, 118, in Byzantium 156–7, 163–4, and Carolingians, 411, 463–4, 472
Hincmar, archbishop of Rheims, 467, 472–4, 490, 510–11, 513, 521
History, history-writing, historiography: Ancient and medieval, techniques of, 2
  Carolingian 400–2, 494–8
  Development of modern, 1–15
  Islamic, 230–1
Hraban Maur, abbot of Fulda, archbishop of Mainz, 472–3, 513–14
Huns, 72, 80, 87, 106–11, 129–31

Iconoclasm, Italian response to 203–5, Carolingian reponse to, 462–3
Identity, *see* ethnicity, ethnogenesis
Islam: in historiography of late antiquity 5–6, Islamic historiography, 230–1, emergence of, 185–8, economic effects

of early Islamic conquests, 188–9, psychological effects of, 203–4; Islamic Spain, 230–8, campaigns in southern Gaul in 720s and 730s, 407–8, 443, economic relations with Carolingian world, 455–6, 527–31, *see* also Caliphate
Ireland, Irish, 321–4, 337–44, 365–7, 377–8
Isidore, bishop of Seville, 223–4

Jerome, 46–7, 53, on barbarians 68
Jews, Judaism, 39, 50, in Visigothic kingdom, 228–9
Jordanes, Gothic History, 70, 146–7
Julian, Roman Emperor, 22, 25–7, 31, 42, 45, 52, campaigns in Gaul 77–8, 79–80
Justinian, Byzantine Emperor, 157–67, implications of his reconquests, 182–4, and defence of Balkans, 194–5

Kingship, barbarian, 73–4, 101–2, of Alaric 85, of Theodoric, 142–55, Slavic, 196–7, 198–9, Visigothic, 219–29, Lombard, 241–8; Merovingian, 269, 273–7, 283–90, 297–303, 400–5, in post-Roman Britain, 321–3, 329, Anglo-Saxon, 337–8, 'Celtic', 337–8, in early medieval Ireland, 337–44, 367, 377–8, in early medieval Wales, 344–5, 377, Pictish, 345–6, Anglo-Saxon, 346–54, 361–2, 369–76, Carolingian, 400–2, 405–7, 417–19, 429–39, 456–80, 494–515, 531–4, in Viking age Scandinavia, 517–20

Law, in Roman culture, 38, issued by barbarian rulers, 128, Justinian's legislation, 158, Visigothic, 222, Lombard, 251–2, Merovingian, 276, 283–4, 290, in early medieval Ireland, 338–9, in Anglo-Saxon England, 362, and Carolingians, 429–36, 510–11
Leo III, Byzantine Emperor, 203–7
Leovigild, Visigothic king, 220–3
Liber Historiae Francorum, 285, 301, 404–5
Lombards, conquest and settlement of Italy, 168, 196, 238–48, Lombard kingdom, 248–55, and Papacy, 206, Carolingian conquest of, 409–10
Lothar, Frankish Emperor, 500–10, 514–15, 519
Louis the German, Frankish king, 500–10, 513–14, 531–2
Louis the Pious, Frankish Emperor, 400, 410, 469–70, 494–505, 518–19

Magnus Maximus, Roman usurper, 50, 82–3, 103, 318, 321
Marcellinus, chronicler, 123–4, 159
Martin, Pope, 201–2
Master of soldiers, *see* Aetius, Constantius III, Odoacer, Ricimer, Stilicho
Maximus the Confessor, 201–2
Mayor of palace, in Merovingian kingdoms, 286–7, 297–303
Merida, and Mediterranean economy, 190, in Visigothic kingdom, 219–20
Merovingians, 269–303
Migrations, barbarian, 3, 66–7, 72–3, *see* also barbarians, ethnogenesis
Mohammed, Prophet, 185–6
Monks, monasticism, 49, 171, in Visigothic kingdom, 229, in Lombard kingdom, 251–2, in Merovingian world, 294–7, under Charles Martell, 404, in Carolingian Empire, 468–72, in early medieval Ireland, 342–4, in early medieval Wales, 345, in Anglo-Saxon England, 363–4
Monophysitism, 156–7, 163–4, 200–3
Moravians, 523–6
Moors, *see* Berbers

Nations, national identity: and appropriation of early medieval history, 3, 6–7, 69–70
See also ethnicity, ethnogenesis
Ninian, Saint, missionary to Picts, 328–30
Nomads, nomadism, 71–2, 108–10

Odoacer, Roman general, 121–2, 128, 142–4
Orosius, author of Histories c.418, 1–2, 8, 20–2, 39, 86, 400

'Paganism': Anglo-Saxon, 356–62
in Frankish world, 282–3, 410–15
Roman, 39–42, 49–50, *see* also Julian, Senate, Victory, Altar of

Patrick, Saint, 321–4, 339, 343
Paul the Deacon, Lombard monk, poet and historian, 240–1, 245–7, 252, 457
Peasants, in Roman world, 32, and 'Slavicisation', 196–8, in Gothic wars, 165–7, in Visigothic kingdom, 226, in Lombard kingdom, 253, in Merovingian kingdom, 293–4, in Carolingian world, 446–50
Pelagius, 'heretical' teacher in late fourth century, and 'Pelagianism', 22, 48–9, 320
Petronius Maximus, Roman general then Emperor, 107, 111–12
Picts, 71, 321, 323–4, 330, 345–6, 378–80
Pippin, Frankish king, 400–2, 405–9, 415, 429, 437, 456–7
Pirenne, Henri, Belgian historian, 5–6, 188
Priscillian, Christian holy man, 42, 46, 49, 50
Popes, Papacy, in Roman Empire 42, 45, in Theodoric's Italy, 150, and Byzantine Emperors, 163–4, 168, representatives of western opinion in theological debates of seventh century, 200–3, and Byzantine iconoclasm, 203–7, and Lombard kingdom, 250–1, 254–5 and Carolingian rise to kingship, 406–7, and Carolingian conquest of Italy, 409–10, support for Anglo-Saxon and Frankish mission east of Rhine, 410–11, role in Carolingian church, 467, and Imperial coronation of Charlemagne, 478–80, and defence of ninth century Rome, 529–30
Population, *see* demography
Priscus, bishop of Panium 111
Procopius, Byzantine author, 117–18, 127, 149–51, 158–61, 163–4, 194, 196, 241, 250, 324

Ravenna, as seat of western Imperial court, 84–7, as seat of Theodoric's court, 152–5, as seat of Byzantine governor (exarch), 168, 192, 199, 203–4, as source of Carolingian court culture, 432, 456–7, 542
Recarred, Visigothic king, 220–3,
Ricimer, master of soldiers, 112–3, 115–16, 121–2
Rome, city: *see* also Senate, Popes
in Roman Empire, 20, 27–8, 33, sack of (410), 1–2, 86, anti-barbarian sentiment in, 88, in Byzantine Italy, 168–70, 191, 202, as source of Carolingian relics, 472–3; as source of 'correct Christianity' for Carolingians, 464
Royal Frankish Annals, 416–17, 429
Rusticiana, granddaughter of Boethius, 182
Rutilius Namantianus, 98

Salvian, priest of Marseilles, 110
Saints, cult of, in Roman Empire, 46, in Visigothic kingdom, 229, in Merovingian kingdom, 280–1, in Carolingian Empire, 472–3
San Vincenzo al Volturno, Italian monastery, 418–19, 454
Scots, 321, 323–4, *see* also Dalriata
Senate, of Rome, political role of, 23–4, 26, 51–3, 103–6, and sack of Rome, 86, approves Theodosian Code, 38, decline in Gothic wars, 166–7, disappearance of, 168, 171–2, contacts with Constantinople, 182.
Settlement, of barbarians in Roman provinces, 80–3, 98–103, of Vandals in Africa, 115–20, 159–61, of Goths in Theodoric's Italy, 147–9, of Goths and other barbarians in southern Gaul and Spain, 217, Islamic settlement in al-Andalus, 233–4, of Lombards in Italy, 241–5, of Anglo-Saxons in Britain, 331–7, of Vikings in Britain, 366–7
Settlements, in barbarian homelands, 72–4, in sixth and seventh century Italy, 167, in Merovingian world, 283, 293, in Anglo-Saxon England, 334–6, in Carolingian world, 446–50
Severinus, holy man, 125–6
Sidonius Apollinaris, Roman senator and bishop of Clermont, 101, 102, 114–5, 125, 268, 324
Slaves, slavery, in later Roman Empire, 32, in Visigothic kingdom, 226, slave soldiers in al-Andalus, 235, and Carolingian economy, 456

Slavs, emergence of and settlement in Balkans, 196–8, and Carolingian Empire, 523–6
Stilicho, master of soldiers, 83–6, 88–9, 103
Social structure, in later Roman Empire, 26–39, 50–53, barbarian 71–4, and 'Slavicisation', 196–9, in sixth century Italy, 165–7, in seventh century Italy, 199–200, in Visigothic kingdom, 226, in al-Andalus, 233–4, 235, 237–8, in Lombard kingdom, 252–4, in Merovingian kingdom, 278–83, 292–5, in early medieval Ireland, 338–44, Pictish, 330, Anglo-Saxon 334–5, 349–53, in Carolingian world, 439–50

Tacitus, Germania, 67–8, on kingship 74, and Carolingians, 479
Tassilo, duke of Bavaria, 415–17
Tax, links with Roman citizenship 20, links with Roman army, 26–9, administration of in Roman Empire, 31–4, and barbarian settlement, 101, in Theodoric's Italy, 146–7, in Vandal Africa, 160–1, in 'reconquered' Italy, 163, 199–200, 204–5, in Caliphate, 187–8, economic implications in Byzantine world, 189–90, in Visigothic kingdom, 222, 226, in Islamic al-Andalus, 233, in Lombard settlement and kingdom, 243–4, 249, in Merovingian kingdom, 279–80, 284, 291–2, in post-Roman Britain, 322, in Carolingian Empire, 437, 520–1.
Theodosian Code, 22, 23, 34, 37, 38, use by barbarian kings, 128, by Carolingians, 510
Theodosius I, Roman Emperor, 23, 30, 36, 38, 49–50, 81
Theodoric, Gothic king, 70, 128, 142–55, and Visigothic kingdom, 219
Theudelinda, Lombard queen, 246–8, 250
Toledo, role in Visigothic kingdom, 219–29
Towns, *see* cities, trade
Trade, in later Roman Empire, 33, beyond Roman frontiers 74–5, 77–8, Africa's role in late Roman trade, 108, 118–20, in post-Roman Mediterranean, 188–94, in Lombard Italy, 253, in post-Roman Britain, 325–6, Anglo-Saxon England and North Sea economy, 350–3, and Vikings, 365–6, 368, 450–3, in Carolingian world, 450–6, in Carolingian and Viking North Sea, 450–3, 517–22, along Carolingian Danube, 525–6, in Carolingian Mediterranean, 453–6, 526–30
Tribes, *see* ethnicity, ethnogenesis

Usurpers, in Roman empire, 23–4, 82–3, 85–6, 87–8, 103, in Roman Britain, 318

Vandals, invasions, 85, 86, 99, 108, in Africa 111–12, 115–20, 129–30, 159–61
Venice, emergence of, 455–6
Victor, bishop of Vita, 117, 127
Victory, Altar of, 22, 27–8, 50, 52
Vikings, in Britain, 365–80, and North Sea economy, 450–3, and Carolingian world, 517–22
Villas, in later Roman Empire, 36, in Vandal Africa, 119

Wales, 344–5, 377

Zosimus, Byzantine chronicler, on end of Roman rule in Britain, 318–20